THE MODERN CONSTRUCTION OF MYTH

The MODERN CONSTRUCTION *of* MYTH

Andrew Von Hendy

INDIANA
University Press

Bloomington & Indianapolis

This book is a publication of

Indiana University Press
601 North Morton Street
Bloomington, IN 47404-3797 USA
http://iupress.indiana.edu

Telephone orders	800-842-6796
Fax orders	812-855-7931
Orders by e-mail	iuporder@indiana.edu

The paper used in this publication meets the minimum
requirements of American National Standard for Information
Sciences—Permanence of Paper for Printed Library
Materials, ANSI Z39.48-1984.

MANUFACTURED IN THE UNITED STATES OF AMERICA

Library of Congress Cataloging-in-Publication Data

Von Hendy, Andrew, date
    The modern construction of myth / Andrew Von Hendy.
        p. cm
Includes bibliographical references and index.
    ISBN 0-253-33996-0 (alk. paper)
    1. Myth—History. I. Title.
    BL311 .V66 2002
    398.2'09'03—dc21
                                                    2001002075

1 2 3 4 5 07 06 05 04 03 02

For Ti

CONTENTS

ACKNOWLEDGMENTS   IX
INTRODUCTION   XI

1   From Fable to Myth   I

2   The Invention of Myth   25

3   The Struggle between Myth and "Suspicion"   49

4   Myth as an Aspect of "Primitive" Religion   77

5   The Role of Depth-Psychology in the Construction of Myth   112

6   The Modernist Contribution to the Construction of Myth   134

7   Neo-Romantic Theories of the Midcentury I: 154
     Myth as Mode of Thought and Language

8   Neo-Romantic Theories of the Midcentury II: 178
     Myth and Ritual in Quotidian Western Life

9   Folkloristic Myth in Social Anthropology I: 202
     Malinowski, Boas, and Their Spheres of Influence

10   Folkloristic Myth in Social Anthropology II: 230
     From Lévi-Strauss to Withdrawal from Grand Theory

11   No Two-Headed Greeks: 262
     The Folkloristic Consensus in Classical Studies

12   Myth and Ideology   278

13   Myth as Necessary Fiction   304

NOTES   341
WORKS CITED   363
INDEX   379

ACKNOWLEDGMENTS

Thanks to Editions Rodopi B. V. for permission to reprint as chapter 6 of the present work a (somewhat shortened) version of "The Modernist Contribution to the Construction of Myth," first published in *Modern Myths,* edited by David Bevan (Amsterdam: Rodopi, 1993), 149–188.

As with all such enterprises, many friends, colleagues, and family members have helped this one reach the light of day. Robert Chibka, Marjorie De Vault, Susan Diekman, Dayton Haskin, John Limon, John Mahoney, Frances Restuccia, Harriet Ritvo, and Margaret Thomas have been great moral supporters, as have Anne and David Ferry and Robin Lydenberg, who have also read and commented with their usual acuity on parts of the manuscript. Paul Doherty, Margaret Ferrari, and Jack McCarthy made crucial recommendations and then loaned the books. Steven Chapman shared with me some of his thinking about Romantic myth particularly congenial with my own; Robert Kern shared, in numerous conversations, his rich acquaintance with Romantic and Transcendentalist conceptions of language and the related scholarship; Alan Richardson pursued a query about Byron's "Heaven and Hell" with true scholarly zeal. Marc Manganaro and Barton Friedman both read a portion of the manuscript and supported fellowship applications. Robert Segal provided a scrupulous, constructive, and informed critique of the entire manuscript, a model of professional reading. In the beginning stage of the project Dennis Taylor was my enterprising co-teacher of a yearlong seminar supported, thanks largely to him, by a Boston College Mellon Grant. Judith Wilt, as department chairperson, provided a lightened teaching load at a psychologically crucial point. Mary Crane, the ideal office neighbor, has helped me over the years in such a variety of ways, from literal soup (chicken) to figurative nuts (computer rescues), that they can certainly not be catalogued in this space. My sons, James, Andrew, and Matthew, have spurred me on with their ominous, affectionately teasing allusions to "The Key to All Mythologies." Finally, my colleague and wife, Rosemarie Bodenheimer, my primary reader, has gone over every draft of every chapter and given me the benefit of her elegant sense of style and her editorial skill. My larger debt to her lurks behind the two small words of the Dedication.

INTRODUCTION

The essay that follows is an attempt to write a critical and interdisciplinary history of the concept of "myth" since its invention, or, perhaps more properly, reinvention, in the eighteenth century. My assumption that the modern construction of "myth" arises only in the eighteenth and early nineteenth centuries itself demands an explanation, which is forthcoming in the first three chapters. Some comparably fundamental assumptions can perhaps be got at by comment on my title. Anyone familiar with the multiplicity of definitions of "myth" may wonder why I speak of "construction" in the singular rather than employing the plural "constructions." I do so because this expresses my ambition to show that the broadest distinguishable significations of "myth," the types of theories that I call the ideological, the folkloristic, and the constitutive, all stem from and stand in relation to a fourth, a romantic or transcendental original.

"Construction" signifies both the process of building and the product. It also plies between the senses of "something built" and "interpretation" or "construal," as in "How can you put that construction on her words?" The ambiguities seem both rich and relevant. Myth as a concept has been subject to endless idiosyncratic definition, but the broadest categories of such constructions cluster in sets of family resemblances in the Wittgensteinian sense, of relationships that can be illuminated by being brought within the compass of a genealogical sketch. I have tried to derive these broadest of categories as inductively as possible, observing the Occam's razor of evolutionary taxonomy, the rule that to be considered a separate species, a plant or animal must be both a sufficiently radical departure from its ancestor and sufficiently differentiated from its congeners. Of course the results are anything but scientific. In the conclusion I express my reservations about whether the most valid number of primary categories is really four; it may be as few as three or as many as five or six. But my discrimination of four major conceptions of what myth is and does will have served its heuristic purpose if it contributes to clarifying the principal lines of development in the construction of the concept.

This taxonomic interest does not reign alone as an organizing principle of the essay; it shares this role with two others—diachronic and axiological. The shape of the work is actually a series of compromises among the three. To take the diachronic first, genealogy entails by definition a diachronic dimension as well as a taxonomical method. I have struggled to observe throughout my account a generally chronological framework. This proved to be at least a relatively manageable matter through the first four chapters, which carry the story to the end of the nineteenth century. The first chapter, "From Fable to Myth," focuses on some crucial moments in the development of the concept during the eighteenth century, while the second, "The Invention of Myth," examines its defining formulations in the work of two generations of German and English poets and philosophers. I regard this insistence on the romantic origins of myth (and their persistent presence to this day) as one of the principal features of my essay. To some readers this emphasis may seem to be beating on an open door, especially since the publication a generation ago of *The Rise of Modern Mythology* (Feldman and Richardson 1972). But I have found awareness of the concept's romantic roots to be very uneven across the scholarly generations and various disciplines. The pioneering historical study of myth in English, for instance, *The Quest for Myth* (Chase 1949), conspicuously leaps in its account of the origins of the concept from the mid-eighteenth century to the mid-nineteenth, ignoring the romantic movement altogether. Yet it argues at the same time for the identification of myth with literature, which is, of course, one of the key assumptions popularized by myth's romantic inventors. Chase is far from alone in exemplifying Santayana's dictum that those who do not know the past are condemned to repeat it. Two of the most popular mythographers of the twentieth century, Mircea Eliade and Joseph Campbell, similarly ignore romanticism altogether in their historical accounts of myth, yet both of them revert, utterly without self-consciousness as far as one can see, to versions of the central romantic claim that myth is the vehicle of insight into a timeless realm of transcendental values. While the masters of depth psychology, Freud and Jung, are themselves too well founded in German romanticism to be quite so innocent of the principal sources of their ideas about myth, their relative lack of emphasis upon these sources has ensured that their followers and students have largely neglected or underestimated their romantic provenance. In the newly ascendant human sciences in general, consideration of the historical sources of myth has tended, for understandable reasons, to be slighted in favor of current "scientific" theories. And there are academic disciplines even in the humanities—classics and religious studies come readily to mind—in which the radical impact of the romantic movement upon the conception of myth seems to an outsider curiously muted, as if the central tenets of romanticism have been for complicated reasons obscured or marginalized in those fields.

The third chapter, "The Struggle between Myth and 'Suspicion,'" takes up in part the entrenchment of romantic myth in nineteenth-century literary culture, but it also introduces the first appearances of all three of the major departures from the romantic base. The first of these is the ideological, the obviously antithetical, negative response articulated by Marx and Engels, in which "myth" signifies a widely propagated lie. The third, chronologically, is the constitutive sense of the concept, initially registered by Nietzsche, which defines myth as any foundational belief within a given culture, a construct understood to be at once necessary and fictive. This version of myth derives from one of the principal corollaries of the romantic definition—that myth is a belief around which a culture coheres—but it dispenses radically with the transcendental sanction. The innovations of both Marx and Nietzsche can be understood as "suspicious," contrarian responses to the very ensconcement of romantic myth in bourgeois culture, but the chronologically second of the three new departures cannot. This is Jakob Grimm's influential establishment of myth as a genre of story told in traditional oral societies and distinguished by its reference to matters of collective, usually sacred, importance. Even this version derives indirectly from romantic assumptions; ethnographic respect for "primitive" story would never have arisen without the previous romantic valorizing of the imaginative products of all humanity. But this anthropological or folkloristic notion of myth differs most conspicuously from the romantic, ideological, and constitutive versions in focusing upon small-scale societies remote in time or space; it says little or nothing about the possibility of myth's presence in the modern West. My fourth chapter, "Myth as an Aspect of 'Primitive' Religion," transplants the reader from the primarily literary culture that nourishes romantic myth into the empirical zone of the emergent social sciences. Here the pioneers of social anthropology and the "armchair" theorists interested in their studies of exotic populations parlay Grimm's conception of myth as a genre of sacred story in oral cultures into the key to unlocking the origin and nature of early religion.

Up to this point, roughly the end of the nineteenth century, tensions between my taxonomic and diachronic interests could be negotiated with what I hope is reasonable clarity. I was surprised in the course of this project, however, to discover how overwhelmingly the true century of myth is the twentieth. Beginning early in the century important elaborations of the concept, which then play off one another, seem to explode simultaneously in numerous fields. Primary adherence to chronology no longer appeared feasible; instead, I turned to an organization based most prominently on taxonomic considerations and only secondarily on chronology. As a result, chapters 5 through 8 pursue the major consequences of the new outbreak of romantic or transcendentalist thinking licensed by the great turn-of-the-century shift from theories of origin to theories of structure and from intellectualist and cognitive theories to emotive and expressive ones. These changes in intellectual fashion are already mirrored in the sequence of theories about "primitive" religion in chapter 4, but they come into their own in the theorizing about myth discussed in chapters 5 through 8. Chapter 5, "The Role of Depth-Psychology in the Construction of Myth," investigates the neo-romanticism inherent in Freud and Jung's connection of myth with the unconscious, while chapter 6, "The Modernist Contribution to the Construction of Myth," focuses on some representative literary artists of the early twentieth century—W. B. Yeats, T. S. Eliot, D. H. Lawrence, and James Joyce—whose imaginations were stirred by the new matrix of affective theory in anthropology and depth psychology. While these writers are not primarily innovators on the theoretical level, they register the new excitement about myth of their cultural moment, and they inspire the outbreak of literary theorizing that follows. The next two chapters, 7 and 8, deal with this literary activity as well as with comparably romantic theories stimulated by "ritualist" anthropology, Jungian psychology, and religious phenomenology. Chapter 7, "Neo-Romantic Theories of the Midcentury I: Myth as Mode of Thought and Language," takes up a number of savants who regard myth primarily as an archaic phenomenon, though with important residual consequences for the structure of modern experience. Chapter 8, in comparison, "Neo-Romantic Theories of the Midcentury II: Myth and Ritual in Quotidian Western Life," is reserved for thinkers who maintain that myth, however archaic in origin, continues to be an active force in everyday modern life. Chapters 7 and 8, as their titles suggest, carry consideration of these neo-romantic formulations roughly from the twenties through the sixties. By that point I might seem to be suggesting that the neo-romanticism unleashed at the turn of the old century spreads for seventy years in the environment of the new like a species with no natural enemies. The next four chapters, however, introduce two very effective rivals, the twentieth-century versions of folkloristic and ideological myth. Chapters 9 through 11 are devoted to the folkloristic theories that come to dominate the disciplines of social anthropology and, eventually, classical studies. The fact that folkloristic theories are clustered within these particular disciplines induces me to foreground for the first time theoretical developments restricted to specific academic fields, but my primary focus remains taxonomic rather than disciplinary. The goal is to produce an adequate account of twentieth-century folkloristic theories, not self-contained histories of theorizing within the disciplines.

In chapter 9, "Folkloristic Myth in Social Anthropology I: Malinowski, Boas, and Their Spheres of Influence," I revert to the early years of the twentieth century to pick up the continuity of modern anthropological fieldwork with the older, "armchair" speculation. The chapter is centered in the theories of myth of the two doyens of modern fieldwork and in each case pursues the reverberations of these in British and then in American anthropology, roughly through the midcentury. Chapter 10, "Folkloristic Myth in Social Anthropology II: From Lévi-Strauss to Withdrawal from Grand Theory," examines at considerable length the highly visible and idiosyncratic theory of the one major anthropologist to devote the greater part of his mature career to the study of myth. The latter third of the chapter traces the decline of grand theories of myth within anthropology and several related fields during the last quarter of a century. This withdrawal has been largely concurrent with Lévi-Strauss's late career, and I have cast my account of it as far as possible in terms of responses to him, specifically responses in the area of his specialty—traditional societies of the Americas.

There has been for the last forty years or so an ongoing revolution in the study of Greek and related classical myth, which has achieved something of a consensus in the field today. This is the subject of chapter 11, "No Two-Headed Greeks: The Folkloristic Consensus in Classical Studies." Some features of the current orthodoxy range well beyond the folkloristic theory, but, given the prominence of myth as a source of historical evidence about ancient cultures, acceptance of this theory has been fundamental to most of the further speculation. The phenomenon of this acceptance affords a remarkable instance of the power of the folkloristic conception of myth to undo romantic or transcendentalist assumptions in the very academic discipline that inspired these initially and profited most from their success.

The last two chapters stand in a noticeable dialectical relation to each other.

Chapter 12, "Myth and Ideology," returns yet again to the beginning of the twentieth century, this time to pick up the history of the ideological conception of myth, left fallow since Marx and Engels. Organized as a survey of the domains of each of Paul Ricoeur's three "masters of suspicion," Marx, Nietzsche, and (to a much lesser extent) Freud, it takes up especially the complex dialectic, and gradual rapprochement, of concepts of myth with concepts of ideology in a series of thinkers ranging chronologically from Sorel to Derrida. This chapter is related to the three preceding ones insofar as it describes an explicit critique of the pretensions of transcendentalist myth that complements the critique of it implicit in modern folkloristic formulations. But chapter 12 also stands in especially close relation to chapter 13, "Myth as Necessary Fiction." Twelve's topic, the ideological conception of myth, is the sibling rival of Thirteen's, the constitutive conception. Ideologists and constitutive theorists inherit alike the engendering romantic premise of the power and ubiquity of the mythologizing imagination, but where ideologists view this labile faculty with "suspicion," constitutive advocates regard it neutrally, if not positively, as, willy-nilly, the source of all values. Chapter 13 examines the work of five theorists who seem to have come to terms with the lessons of the ideological critique and yet discovered in myth possibilities that are "constructive" in both senses of the word. The chapter ends with a brief analysis of the antithetical terms employed by the theorists discussed in the last two chapters to designate myth and a specified contrary, where one is regarded as positive and the other as negative. These diacritical pairings suggest how structurally embedded in our thinking the concept of myth has become as an expression of our deep cultural ambivalence about issues of communal belief.

I suggested initially that my essay is shaped by a series of compromises among *three* competing interests—taxonomic, diachronic, and axiological—but I have yet to speak about this last. I mean by it that I have proceeded throughout principally by examining and assessing the claims of the individual thinkers who have seemed to me especially significant contributors to the construction of myth. I have tried to provide close and, if possible, fresh readings of these major theorists, even if that meant (as it has) being selective rather than all-inclusive. Sketches of the principal theories and theorists of myth are available in anthologies, encyclopedia articles, and handbooks (such as William Doty's recently revised *Mythography: The Study of Myths and Rituals*). My aspiration has been to restore the sense of traditions of discourse and intensity of argument that brief epitomes necessarily wring out. I have also conceived of detailed reading as some small check on the dangers attendant upon work in disciplines in which I have not been professionally trained. Understanding an utterance must depend ultimately upon how well its context is understood, but my explicit analysis of key passages ought at least to afford more expert interpreters in a given tradition of discourse a concrete basis for understanding where I may have gone astray. I have tried in each case, to be sure, to orient myself in that larger intellectual context, but my second procedural defense against ignorance has been to confine my axiological pronouncements to the topic of myth. In no instance of a seminal thinker—E. B. Tylor, say, or Émile Durkheim or Sigmund Freud—do I presume to offer a comprehensive assessment of the *oeuvre*.

If in some cases (the three mentioned are not random) my comments sound too brisk about the thinking or unappreciative of the true stature of the savant in question, I hope the reader will bear in mind the restricted scope of my judgments.

I would like to acknowledge, too, some directions consciously not taken. First, the construction of myth has been an international phenomenon as well as an interdisciplinary one, and when I first conceived of this project I hoped to do justice to that aspect of it. I have indeed attended to the indispensable theorists regardless of language, but I have focused in the end on work in English wherever it seemed possible to do so without distorting the history of the concept. This decision has depended partly on ease of reading for both the author and his likely audience, but principally on manageability of scope. A comparable linguistic chauvinism is quite noticeable in work in the field in other languages, and I now feel a sympathetic rapport with this limitation that wasn't part of my mindset when I started out.

Second, my "genealogical" compromise among taxonomic, diachronic, and axiological interests precludes for the most part doing justice to the strong traditions of discourse about myth within certain academic disciplines. I have been able by fortunate coincidence to manage it for modern social anthropology and to some degree for contemporary classical studies. But the stream of discourse in certain disciplines—notably religious studies, folklore, and nineteenth-century classical studies—appears only in discontinuous sections. Each field, to change the metaphor, has its moments in the spotlight, when strong theorists rise to prominence, but the reader will not get an adequate sense of what is going on in the wings. One handy way to suggest what might be lost is to note how frequently from the time of its invention onward "myth" is consistently linked in different disciplinary approaches with a second concept, in the verbal formula "myth and x." Literature presents us with "myth and symbol," folklore with "myth and tale," theology with "myth and religion," anthropology with "myth and ritual," philosophy (in the twentieth century) with "myth and fiction." The persistence of such yokings suggests that protean "myth" has often been felt to be best pinned in place by differentiation from a diacritical partner. Anyone working with myth has to come to terms with these partners, and familiarity with the tradition of discourse within the relevant field is certainly of great help. Nevertheless, consideration of myth by discipline has its serious drawbacks. Robert Segal, who has thought particularly long and hard about the classification of theories of myth, points out in some rare pages on methods of theorizing about theories, that comparison by discipline is "tenuous" because "differences among disciplines are often blurry, and similarities of theories within disciplines are often hazy" (Segal 1999, 1). My transdisciplinary categories should help to disperse at least these particular kinds of mists.

I would like to conclude on an autobiographical note that might offer some sense of where this approach to myth fits in the history of my own imagination. An attentive reader of the chapters that follow will notice that traffic in theories of myth peaked roughly in the 1960s. As a student of literature I was fascinated at the time by the celebration of myth in the work of the great modernist writers and had discovered that even the New Criticism kept a soft spot for myth in its ironic heart. Meanwhile, Northrop Frye's *Anatomy of Criticism* reigned supreme, offering the promise of an "archetypal" or "myth" criticism that constituted the first systematic critical challenge to the hegemony of the New Criticism. But the vogue was by no means confined to literary circles. Intellectual respect for Freud and Jung was at its height, as it was for Ernest Cassirer's *Philosophy of Symbolic Forms* with its presentation of mythic thought as one of the major modes of cultural symbolism. Mircea Eliade, Joseph Campbell, and Philip Wheelwright were in mid-career, spicing the air with their racier versions of myth, respectively religious, psychological, and semantic. Campbell was in the midst of publishing his tetralogy on comparative world mythology, while that remarkable phenomenon Claude Lévi-Strauss, whom all of us read whether or not we knew anything else about anthropology, was in the midst of *his* quite different quartet, *Mythologiques*. Even Rudolph Bultmann's theological "demythologizing," which rivaled Lévi-Strauss for notice in the popular press, contributed to an ambience in which the concept seemed significant. Particularly after the publication of Albert Lord's *Singer of Tales* in 1961, the Parry-Lord discoveries about the composition and recitation of oral narratives were becoming widely influential among students both of early literatures and of societies with strong oral traditions. The late '6os and early '7os brought the rise of new groups of folklorists interested in oral performance, especially of Amerindian societies, and the beginnings of that complex revolution in the understanding of Greek myth that is something of a consensus in the field today. Perhaps one might be forgiven for making the mistake of supposing in a vague way that we were closing in on this thing called "myth," that a unified field theory might not be far ahead.

By the time I began work on this project during the 1980s, the hot winds of the structuralist and poststructuralist critiques had blown steadily across those misty boglands and mysterious pools and dried the whole thing up. I thought I was going to write an account for my younger self of a historical phenomenon with a shape that included closure. This was my second big mistake about myth. As I've discovered in the course of the project, its disappearance from the fashionable critical scene says very little about its viability either in scholarly circles or in popular culture. It is alive and well in all four of the fundamental senses that I try to distinguish, or, if not quite so well as it used to be, at least adhering to life with a resilience that doesn't suggest imminent disappearance. My genealogical investigations and critical assessments have been deprived of a properly melodramatic conclusion. I hope they may serve instead as a useful status report on a concept whose two and a half centuries under construction constitutes one of the significant attempts at what the German philosopher of culture Hans Blumenberg calls the legitimation of modernity.

THE MODERN CONSTRUCTION OF MYTH

[1]

From Fable to Myth

A claim that "myth" is a modern invention had better begin with explanation. It's widely known, after all, that the modern world inherits the word and, in some sense therefore, the concept from ancient Greece. The Greeks had come out of the Mycenaean Age with a very rich tradition of oral story, a tradition upon which, some four hundred years later, Homer and Hesiod built their great hexameter poems. These poems themselves appear to have been composed orally sometime, in Homer's case perhaps a long time, before they were frozen in writing. This is the repertoire from which the Athenian tragedians of the fifth century drew most of the stories that Aristotle, writing after the great line had ended, still called in his *Poetics* "*mythoi.*" It makes sense to translate *mythos* as "plot" in this particular Aristotelian context, but in general the word appears to signify merely "traditional story." There are signs, however, from at least the sixth century B.C.E. that some writers had reservations about the reliability, nature, and uses of such tales.[1] These reservations culminate famously in Plato's contradictory attention to *mythoi* in certain of his Dialogues, attention so conspicuous that Plato himself appears singlehandedly to lift the concept into theoretical consideration. On one hand, Socrates attacks as ignorant liars the poets, rhapsodes, and other purveyors of the traditional stories. On the other, Socrates is a great inventor of comparable stories for his own purposes. In *The Republic,* for example, Socrates not only recommends the exclusion of poets from the commonwealth, but considers just as notoriously the positive advantages to the state of fostering deliberately in its citizens certain foundational *mythoi* of a sort we would call ideological. It appears, then, that Plato objects not to the deliberate, "wise" construction of apologues for educational purposes, but only to the scandalous content and unwarranted authority of old wives' tales. These attitudes suggest that by Plato's day certain intellectuals, at least, were thoroughly out of rapport with the oral basis of their culture. This trend accelerated rapidly during the Hellenistic period; commentators on the traditional stories learned to accommodate them to the dominant Platonic and Neoplatonic philosophies by reading them allegorically, as the moral teaching of ancient sages, merely concealed under a bait of fantasy.

Even when knowledge of Greek was virtually lost to the West during the decline of Rome and the early Middle Ages, both the *mythoi* and the tradition of allegorizing them survived, transmitted through the Roman culture that so enthusiastically adopted them. Renewed interest in this body of story was itself of course one of the defining features of the Western "Revival of Learning," but this renewal brought with it a curious split in terminology. While words such as "mythologist" and "mythology" appear early in the vernaculars (they are recorded even in English by 1425, and by the early seventeenth century most of the forms of this word in use now, including "mythic," "mythographer," and "mythologize" have been launched on their careers), we discover one striking exception: the word "myth," common enough in Latin, is nowhere to be found. In its stead, to signify the relevant kind of tale, the vernaculars resort to the Latin word for "story," *fabula,* and thus develop analogues of the English "fable." The key to this puzzling split in linguistic behavior lies in observing the meaning attached to "mythology" and its grammatical variants. They always refer to the hermeneutical activity of reading the stories allegorically. "Mythology" is not a body of stories, but the scholarly science of allegorical reading; "to mythologize" means, not to invent or relay a *mythos,* but to engage in that kind of interpretative practice. In comparison, the more vulgar word "fable," employed to signify the kind of story that was the object of this exalted reading, suggests a frail and humble thing. "Fable" generally carries a range of meanings; it *can* signify a story that has been demonstrated by the science of mythology to be full of the pith of ancient wisdom, but it also signifies the kind of foolish, idle, and often scabrous tale that demands face-saving by the mythologist if it is to avoid giving offense. It may well be precisely this ambiguous range of meanings that conferred on the word "fable" throughout the medieval and early modern centuries an ecological niche that might be expected from the rest of the etymological evidence to have been occupied by "myth."

After the word "myth" finally does make its belated and still tentative appearance in the decade of the 1760s, this ecological rivalry appears to be confirmed by the fact that the new term conspicuously comes to displace "fable."[2] But linguistic displacements of this sort indicate a felt need to discriminate something fresh in experience; new "myth" is not a mere synonym for old "fable." It displaces the older term for at least three basic reasons, the first two of which are complementary, the opposite sides of a coin. On one side, the seriousness of allegorized "fable" becomes increasingly discredited in the course of the late seventeenth and early eighteenth centuries, while, on the other side, the seriousness of unmediated, unallegorized "fable," that is, archaic and even "savage" story taken on its own terms, becomes increasingly recognized and accepted. "Myth" triumphs both negatively as an honorable name for the kind of story now discredited as "fable" and positively as a term that connotes the dignity of traditions of story previously regarded as below the threshold of canonical notice. If these first two reasons can be said to be literary, the third is religious. The era that followed a century of wars over religion in Europe produced epidemic defections from institutional Christianity and remarkable intellectual turmoil about the nature both of religion and of belief. It would be difficult to determine whether the rise of what we would call "comparative mythology" is more a cause or an effect of this turmoil. But there is nothing uncertain about the fact that studies of exotic story, obviously taken elsewhere as religious truth and loaded in any case with analogues to Christian belief and practice, became in the overwhelming majority of instances privileged sites for the working out of contemporary religious anxieties. The word "myth" comes into use perhaps above all to connote a religious dimension to story, a dimension allegorized "fable" had forfeited and to which unallegorized "fable" had never aspired. The linguistic shift from "fable" to "myth" in the 1760s marks, then, the outbreak of a revolution in Western conceptions of fantasy and storytelling in some ways comparable, as the poets were quick to note, to the contemporary political revolutions in America and France. The concept of "myth" that emerges by the end of the subsequent fifty-year process generally known as the romantic movement is so radical a departure from the two-thousand-year tradition of Neoplatonizing allegory, and so plainly a major move in the self-legitimation of modernity, that it seems appropriate to speak of the modern construction of myth as a fresh invention.

This first chapter follows myth's displacement of fable to the brink of its romantic transformation. The chapter commences by locating the beginnings of the shift, for practical purposes at least, "between Bacon and Fontenelle." Moving out from Fontenelle, it takes up briefly some possible explanations for the dwindling of allegorized fable, and then some defensive and hostile religious responses to the rise of the *un*allegorized version, before proceeding, first by way of Vico's *New Science,* to the positive amelioration in the status of this unmediated fable that leads to the appearance of "myth."

BETWEEN BACON AND FONTENELLE

Trying to pinpoint a shift in intellectual history is about as satisfying as attempting to determine the edges of the colors in a rainbow or sunset. But it does seem feasible, in searching for the first major crack in the two-millennia tradition of allegorized fable, to consider as crucial the two generations between the 1620s and the 1680s or '90s. On the more remote bank of this divide—which includes, significantly, the decades of the great rationalist system-builders—Francis Bacon presents an especially revealing case. He is not only one of the last advocates of the old allegorizing, but he also anticipates its demise without realizing it. When he discusses the fabling of classical antiquity in his late essay "On the Wisdom of the Ancients," he takes for granted, as his very title indicates, the basic assumption of the Alexandrian commentators. He offers in his brief preface four reasons for continuing to allegorize the ancient stories. First, in some the allegory is so obvious it's unavoidable. "Metis, Jupiter's wife is plainly counsel. . . . Pan the universe" (Bacon 1963, 696) (but it's significant that Bacon selects concepts here rather than narratives). Second, "some of them are so absurd and stupid upon the face of the narrative taken by itself, that they may be said to give notice from afar and cry out that there is a parable below" (697) (this is the traditional rationalization for allegory). Third, they are not mere inventions of the likes of Homer and Hesiod, but much older, already, when the poets repeat them, "relics of better times" (698) (they stem from some glorious first age). Fourth, parables serve paradoxically not only "to disguise and veil the meaning" but "also to throw light upon it." The wisdom of the first age "was either great or lucky" (*aut magna aut felix* in the original) (628). If we do not attribute intention to the original framers, we have to assume a kind of intuitive wisdom that enabled them to fall upon "matter which gives occasion to such worthy contemplation" (699). (In other words, an alternative kind of greatness.) In the twist he gives this last argument, Bacon might be said to adumbrate very dimly developments to come, specifically Vico, but this list of reasons displays his fundamental rapport with the long history of hermeneutical face-saving. His practice in the sequence of allegorized *mythoi* that follows reveals this allegiance even more starkly. First he summarizes the story, then proposes his allegorical interpretation, then embarks upon his detailed reflections. Thus, to take his first instance, he epitomizes the story of Cassandra and Apollo and then remarks that "this fable seems to have been devised in reproof of unreasonable and unprofitable liberty in giving advice and admonition" (701). His elaborations of this proposition, as in the other instances that follow, are a lively display of his practical intelligence, very much in the manner of his *Essays*. Bacon presents these apologues, however, not as original inventions, but as hermeneutical renderings inspired by an immanent "wisdom of the ancients."

It is not surprising, then, that when he identifies in another late work, his *New Organon* (1620), the four genera of mental error that interfere with clear thinking—the idols of the cave, the tribe, the marketplace and the theater, or, as we might say, errors in perception, personal biases, imprecise language, and illusory world views—he perceives no connection unless it be a negative one between these types of error and the reasons why the apparent absurdity of ancient story cries out for allegorizing (Bacon 2000, 40–56). For him the "wisdom of the ancients" stands entirely outside and prior to the modes in which a fallen humanity baffles its empiricism with fantastic mental barriers. Yet some composite of Bacon's *idola* is what most people in our day have in mind when they employ the term "myth" pejoratively in everyday speech or writing. What lies between Bacon and us is a movement of thought that joins together the two phenomena he perceives as irreconcilable, a movement that *unites* the invention of fables with the universal illusion-spinning of our kind.

The first relevant text we encounter on the near bank of the seventeenth-century divide is the *philosophe,* Bernard Fontenelle's "On the Origin of Fables," which probably dates from the 1690s, although it was not published until 1724. We find ourselves already in quite another intellectual environment. In this witty chat of an essay, Fontenelle takes easily for granted a developmental concept of history characteristic of the Enlightenment—humanity ascends from a condition of savagery to its present polish. Though Fontenelle does thus assume a "primitive mentality," he perceives no impediment to understanding how it works because human nature is universal. Fables are the first histories of all peoples, and they arise from the depths of human nature through the activity of psychological laws we recognize from our own experience—a combination of curiosity, speculation that is wide of the mark in proportion to our ignorance, and love of what is imaginatively striking. As the logical fruit of such premises, we find already in Fontenelle both the negative and the positive assumptions that will lead to the construction of "myth." First, he rejects the fundamental axiom of allegorical reading with the same surprisingly easy authority with which he lays down his novel premises. The topic is the last taken up in the essay and culminates in this dismissal, which could hardly apply more pointedly to Bacon's essay if it had been designed for the purpose. "No new Fables appear nowadays; we're content merely to preserve the old. But what can minds foolishly enamoured of Antiquity not manage to accomplish? They are bound to imagine that beneath the Fables are hidden the secrets of the Physical and the Moral. . . . The name of the Ancients is always imposing: but those who made the Fables were certainly not the men to be informed about moral and physical nature, nor to discover the art of disguising such knowledge under borrowed images. Let us not seek for anything in the Fables except the story of the errors of the human mind" (Fontenelle 1989, 201–202). Fontenelle's rejection applies a criterion of psychological realism that follows from his developmental philosophy of history. But his disdain of fable is not based solely on incredulity about its alleged origin. As Jean Starobinski points out (in a brilliant sketch of the subject of this chapter), "fable" signified increasingly in the latter half of the seventeenth century, not merely learned allegorizing, but the entire cultural syndrome of mediated allusions to these stories that passed current in polite conversation, in "poetry, theater, ballet, painting, sculpture, decorative arts," and even in handbooks of behavior where it was recommended as a valuable social acquisition (Starobinski, 725). This network of standard allusion had had of course a brilliant cultural career, but even by Fontenelle's day its conventions were frequently felt to be shallow and insincere, and this uneasy distaste only increased during the next century. Readers of English literature are familiar with Samuel Johnson's severities in his *Lives of the Poets* upon offenders such as Milton in his pastoral elegy *Lycidas,* and with Coleridge's recollection of his schoolmaster in *Biographia Literaria:* "Harp? Harp? Lyre? Pen and ink, boy, you mean! Muse, boy, Muse? Your Nurse's daughter, you mean!! Pierian spring? Oh aye! the cloisterpump, I suppose" (Coleridge 1907, I, 5).[3] Fontenelle objects to the existence of allegory among primal peoples on grounds of developmental improbability, and Coleridge's master objects to highfalutin' diction. These are symptomatic stands at opposite ends of a century of the deterioration of "fable," but they are recognizably akin in their demand for psychological realism and common sense in lieu of the conventional pieties toward classical learning.

But Fontenelle also turns the coin to its obverse side when he introduces the leveling "comparative method" that will eventually explode the canon. He finds, for example, "a stunning conformity between the Fables of the Americans and those of the Greeks" (197) and even argues that since they were "quite a recent people when they were discovered by the Spaniards, there are grounds for believing that the Americans would have come in the end to think as rationally as the Greeks" (198). The kind of comparative evidence that Fontenelle brings to bear here had been known in Europe at least since Cortez's soldiers reported their horrified recognition of the resemblances between the Catholic Eucharist and the cannibalistic rite of the Aztec priests. This evidence was just as objectively available to Bacon as to Fontenelle, but its true availability in the psychological sense depended upon an immense change in mindset about "the origin of the fables" in universal folly rather than in an exempt wisdom.

THE RELIGIOUS AMBIGUITIES OF ANTI-FABLE

Fontenelle must not be mistaken, however, for a "man of sensibility," a John the Baptist–like precursor to Herder. When he insists on the equality of humankind in the production of fable, he is not exalting fable but disparaging humanity. His essay concludes: "All men resemble one another so strongly that there is no People whatever whose follies should not make us tremble" (202). The Greek story of Orpheus is no less a record of the "errors of the human mind" than the Peruvian legend of Manco Capac to which he compares it. In Fontenelle's memorably dismissive epigram, Bacon's two separate phenomena are joined to devastating effect; Fontenelle's rejection of the ahistorical assumption behind the allegorizing of fable extends to any other theory that might pretend to rationalize its folly. In this respect, too, he is a harbinger of a large class of subsequent reactions. The history of eighteenth-century mythography is by no means an unbroken, triumphal march "from 'fable' to 'myth.'" On the contrary, that march is constantly disrupted by thinkers who treat fable as a threat to rationality or to revealed religion or to both. Embryonic instances of a third fundamental disposition toward fable—neutral scientific curiosity—do emerge later in the century, but a number of hostile and/or defensive responses dominate the first two-thirds. These are especially interesting here because in certain respects they play into the very aggrandizement of fable that they are out to prevent.

Under this focus, four major groups of anti-fabulists stand out.[4] These are the Enlightenment skeptics, the "two-religion" advocates, the proponents of an original monotheism, and the euhemerists. These categories refer to types of theories variously susceptible to combination with one another and often found so in particular cases. Upon one matter and only one matter are they all necessarily agreed—that the existence of cycles of heathen fable is scandalous. The principal issue that divides them is whether the "one true religion" is irretrievably implicated in this disgrace or whether its apparent guilt by association can be explained away.

Fontenelle is a pioneering member of the first group, the party of Enlightenment skeptics. Fontenelle unmistakably intends his ironic depiction of the absurdity of religion's heathen origins to tar Christianity with the same brush. We already find in him what becomes the favorite *praeteritio* of conspicuously exempting biblical revelation from one's generalizations. He declares that there are no peoples "whose History does not begin in Fables, except the Chosen People, among whom a particular concern of Providence preserved the truth" (Fontenelle 1989, 198). Thinkers of this sort, modeling themselves upon the deductive systems of the great seventeenth-century rationalists, base their fundamental assumptions upon intuitions of "common sense" and take for granted as Fontenelle does the operation of psychological covering-laws. One eventual result, however, is a sentimental deism of the sort made famous by Rousseau. Even as it mocks all forms of belief in fable, it encourages a religious adherence to "the light of Nature" that contributes in the long run to romantic pantheism.

The second anti-fabular position, which Frank Manuel christened "the two-religion theory," appears particularly popular among deists and others inclined to believe that a pure "natural religion" must always have been available to right-thinking humanity. According to this theory, Bacon's "wisdom of the ancients" included those sages' recognition that they could preserve and transmit to privileged insiders their esoteric, rational monotheism only by encasing the truth in the vulgar, entertaining tales of an exoteric polytheism. This fiction of origins is instantly recognizable as a theological version of the ancient justification for the allegorizing of traditional story. Bacon's subscription to this view is what blinds him to any connection between these traditional tales and the endemic mental errors of the race. The theory also accommodates contrary attitudes toward institutional religion and particularly "priestcraft." Some view the concealment of esoteric wisdom as the prudent policy of wise men, while some (Hume, for example) condemn it as cynical imposture, the work of a priestly caste that preserves its own power by encouraging what it knows to be superstition.

The "two-religion theory" is adaptable, too, to the third position, whose adherents believe that fable arises by degeneration from a primordial monotheism. This is also an ancient speculation, found convenient by the early church fathers for accommodating Judaeo-Christian monotheism to the obvious existence of plural religions. It is the obverse or serious side of Fontenelle's *praeteritio*, which could itself be taken as a declaration of genuine belief if it were read without irony. An impressive variety of thinkers shelters under this umbrella, particularly in England. As with skeptical anti-fabulism, certain aspects of the theory of degeneration actually play into the positive transformation of fable. Theories of degeneration offer undreamed-of possibilities for the writing of imaginative history. Thus, two of the most fanciful and ingenious English degenerationists, Stukeley and Bryant are remembered today principally as minor sources for the private mythology of William Blake's visionary narratives.

The fourth and last type of anti-fabular theory is euhemerism, the ancient theory that religion begins in the worship of deified mortals. It, too, combines easily with other hypotheses; it is typically constellated with degeneration from original monotheism and/or with the "two-religion" conspiracy. The special popularity of euhemerizing in the eighteenth century is related to certain literary phenomena of the age—the Baroque taste for supplying *realpolitik* subplots for plays on mythological subjects, for example, and the disparagement of classical allusions not sincerely felt. Some of this euhemerizing is openly anti-religious—intended to include the founder of Christianity in its reductions—and some is on its surface indifferent with respect to religion. Yet all of it suggests, as the literary phenomena do, too, a profound religious subtext. Some of Johnson's remarks in *Lives of the Poets,* for example, suggest that the intensity of his objection to mythological allusion arises not so much out of annoyance with outworn convention as out of scandal that the poet would feign participation in a conceptualizing of the sacred that he does not sincerely feel. Acceptable allusion would carry the stamp of internal imaginative assent; when the poet toys with what was once a living form of belief he mocks the font of religion within himself. So, too, modern euhemerism conceals an unexamined assumption that humanity bears within itself a theogonic principle. This is an implication that reaches overt expression in Blake's "All deities reside in the human breast" (Blake 1965, 37).

In fact, it isn't merely euhemerist thinking that carries this particular religious subtext. Even the imaginative zest of the degenerationists covertly glamorizes alternative sacred traditions. Of the three types of theories that purport to defend revelation against the encroachments of relativizing fable, only the "two-religion" variety, which is, after all, the theological complement to allegorized fable itself, fails to display some degree of religious ambiguity. Most revealingly of all, perhaps, even theories of the first group—Enlightenment skepticism like Fontenelle's—tend as if in spite of themselves toward the affirmation expressed in Blake's epigram. This double movement in much of the anti-fabular resistance, as of a countercurrent under the surface one, is finely epitomized in Jean Starobinski's observation that "in the intellectual history of this century, the sacralization of myth is closely associated with the humanization of the sacred" (Starobinski, 732). From this point on, in any case, we leave the resistance for the direct and positive shift from "fable" to "myth."

GIAMBATTISTA VICO: "POETIC WISDOM" AS THE MASTER KEY

In relation to the movement "from 'fable' to 'myth,'" the appearance of *The New Science of Giambattista Vico* in 1725, months after the publication of Fontenelle's essay, is like a lightning flash that illuminates a huge landscape far in front of a traveler before she is enclosed again in darkness. The work was not a territory immediately possessed; it remained very little read outside Italy during the eighteenth century; its rediscovery and effective impact dates from the 1820s and 1830s.[5] But it is at the same time too brilliant a glimpse into the mountain ranges ahead to be ignored. The "New Science" of Vico's title is simultaneously a tribute to his heroes among the great rationalists of the seventeenth century who shaped his intellectual life, and an expression of his astonished conviction that he had rather paradoxically discovered, by following their models, a realm of experience in which the inductions of experimental science applied even more validly than to the physical world.[6] In what is probably the most celebrated passage in *The New Science,* he asserts that only God can comprehend completely the physical world since He alone made it, but "the world of civil society was certainly made by men and . . . its principles are to be found within the modification of our own human mind" (Vico 1984, 331).[7] The word "modifications" (rather, say, than "productions") is particularly significant in this formulation because it recognizes that if civil institutions are entirely human constructions and civil institutions have changed, then the mind of humanity has changed. In more current diction, consciousness itself turns out to be historically conditioned; assumptions about a universal human nature must be reconsidered. This contemporary commonplace is to Vico a source of endless astonishment, as well it might be since he still sees himself as engaged in a search for scientific "covering laws." The relativistic implications of his propositions would not, could not, be appreciated fully until after Hegel and after Michelet's celebration of Vico as a harbinger of historicism.

As sharply as Vico discriminates all three of the evidential tools recognized by modern historiography as valid sources of information about the ancient world—language, antiquities, and mythology—his most original contribution here is his remarkable promotion of mythology. "It follows," he says in his opening section on method, "that the first science to be learned should be mythology or the interpretations of fables . . . the first histories of the gentile nations" (51).[8] His contemporaries would have agreed that mythology is the science of interpreting fables and perhaps (as Fontenelle does) that fables were the first histories of the gentile nations, but to appreciate the novelty of Vico's conclusion from these premises one need only recall Fontenelle's dismissal of fable as "the history of the errors of the human mind." From whence does Vico derive his contrary confidence that mythology is the "first science" of a history of civil society?

Vico's conception of fable departs utterly from his contemporaries. It anticipates Schelling in the nineteenth century in finding this sort of traditional story "tautegorical" and Cassirer in the twentieth in finding it a "symbolic form" of cultural construction. We can perhaps best grasp this conception by starting with Vico's most melodramatic insight into the creative process of archaic humankind: "The first gentile peoples, by a demonstrated necessity of nature, were poets, who spoke in poetical characters. This discovery, which is the master key of this Science, has cost us the persistent research of almost all our literary life, because with our civilized natures we cannot at all imagine and can understand only by great toil the poetic nature of the first men" (34). Vico does not differ from Fontenelle in his Hobbesian view of what these men of the First Age were like; they were asocial, cyclopean giants, scattered over the Earth after the Flood, in many respects "stupid, insensate and horrible beasts" (374). Nor does he differ from Fontenelle in viewing them as imaginative but irrational speculators about natural phenomena and divinities. But he differs utterly from the *philosophe* in the *value* he places on the imaginative acts of these *giganti.* When he says that they were "poets, who spoke in poetical characters," he anticipates the romantic valorizing of imagination as surely as Fontenelle's disparagement of it typifies Enlightenment rationalism. The creatures of the First Age, who "were all robust sense and vigorous imagination," must have begun the construction of culture "with a metaphysics not rational and abstract like that of learned men now, but felt and imagined" (375). "In that human indigence, the peoples must have been all vivid sensation in perceiving particulars, strong imagination in apprehending and enlarging them, sharp wit in referring them to their imaginative genera, and robust memory in retaining them." On one hand, his *giganti* dwell in a "human indigence," poor in the cultural acquisitions that have since polished the race; on the other, they are sublime poets because no weight of convention, particularly of ratiocination, inhibits their creativity. The fables created by such giants of the archaic imagination may appear uncouth, but they embody in compressed form the stupendous rudiments of the human world.

In order to grasp in more detail Vico's conception of these accomplishments, we have to investigate certain topics in book 2. This book, "Poetic Wisdom," is the heart of *The New Science,* Vico's actual demonstration of his "master key."[9] "Poetic Wisdom" is Vico's most general label for what he variously terms in other contexts "poetical characters" (*carrateri poetici*), "imaginative genera" (*generi fantastici*), or "imaginative universals" (*universale fantastaci*).[10] Book 2 consists of Vico's attempt to catalogue and explain, under such headings as "Poetic Metaphysics," "Poetic Logic," "Poetic Morals," and so forth, the major categories of the "imaginative universals" that have come down to us. All of the categories in book 2, therefore, are articulations of the "master key," lessons in how to read the fables as what Cassirer will call "mythical thought." For our purposes, the long section "Poetic Logic" is the heart of the heart. Here Vico focuses specifically upon the linguistic and tropological basis of the distinction between the "imaginative universals" that characterize the fabular activity of the First Age and the mere "intelligible universals," the conventionalized abstractions that characterize modern thought and speech.

This crucial distinction is pegged to Vico's stadial metahistorical theory. He discovers in the history of antiquity three distinct "ages," which he labels, following Herodotus's report of ancient Egyptian tradition, the Ages of Gods, Heroes, and Men. He claims for each age distinctive conceptions of human nature, customs, natural law, government, systems of jurisprudence, and so forth. Most important for us, the ages exhibit fundamental *linguistic* differences. It is hard to disagree with Hayden White when he declares that this employment of a linguistic and tropological model for defining stages in the evolution of consciousness constitutes the most original aspect of Vico's entire metahistorical scheme (White 1978, 208–209). We can get quickly to the core of his linguistic schema by meditating on the single, concise dictum that in the Age of the Gods "the first nations thought in poetical characters, spoke in fables and wrote in hieroglyphs" (429). Each of the three parts of this declaration rewards exploration.

"Poetical characters" are the same as "imaginative universals" or "imaginative class concepts." The word "character" does evidently carry some of the sense of "fictional personage," since, in most of the concrete examples that Vico offers, his *giganti* invent personifications to signify a set of particulars—"Jove" for awesome natural phenomena, "Thrice Great Hermes" for "civil wisdom," and the like. Yet these personifications are not mere instances of the trope of prosopoeia. When the Romantic historians discovered Vico, they were particularly impressed by two specific feats. First, Vico anticipates by two generations Wolf's hypothesis (1795) that "Homer" is the eponymous name of the Greek people as creators of their epics during the Heroic Age. Second, he anticipates Niebuhr's demonstration (1806) of how Roman historians (most obviously Livy) misrepresented the city's early history by failing to understand how it had been distorted in oral tradition. Vico demolishes, in particular, the fiction that Rome had derived its jurisprudential principles, the legendary law of the Twelve Tables, from Greece. These two anticipations are both results of Vico's conception of the "imaginative universal," which enables him to conceive even of Roman law as a slowly evolved "serious poem."[11] This last example shows why, if "poetical characters" are not simply instances of prosopoeia, they are not products of euhemerizing either. Vico has sometimes been called a euhemerist, but the designation is inaccurate for two reasons: "imaginative universals" are not fabular deifications of particular historical individuals and they are not imposed subsequent to events; they are *constitutive* of those events.

As these examples suggest, an "imaginative class concept" is not simply an Aristotelian universal, a mental abstraction from concrete sensuous particulars, that signifies a class only analogically. The "imaginative class concept" communicates *univocally* the nature of what it represents because it still participates in the concrete and affectively perceived particularities of the signified. It does not merely represent its particulars; it remains at the same time identified with them. Judged by the standards of Western rationalism from Aristotle to Austin, claims of this sort are mere wishful thinking. But Vico's "imaginative universal" is no freak in modern intellectual history. It is a forerunner of the Romantic concept of "symbol," very close, for example, to the spirit of Blake's assertion that "every Class is an Individual" (Blake 1965, 63). In fact, in its ambition to unite cognitive generalities with affective particularities it is the initial registration of what will become a familiar problematic of late nineteenth- and twentieth-century human sciences, and one that will come to seem endemic to modern theories of myth.[12] Donald Verene points out that Vico's foremost twentieth-century advocate, Benedetto Croce, "regards the imaginative universal as the great error of Vico's thought" because it "contains an unmediated contradiction in which the imaginatively intuited particular and the rationally universalizing concept are not brought together" (Verene 1981, 68). We will be obliged on numerous occasions in subsequent chapters to consider whether this profound and accurate criticism of Vico is not equally applicable to all modern attempts to close the epistemological gap between general and particular by versions of Romantic "symbol" or "myth."

In fact, at this point in his "Poetic Logic" Vico plunges with the boldness of a pioneer into a tangle of related linguistic and metahistorical antinomies characteristic of later Romantic thinking. Only detailed analysis for which there is no room here could convey the consecutiveness and subtlety with which Vico works them out to his satisfaction, but the most important ones must be sketched briefly even at the risk of slighting these qualities. Each of the linguistic antinomies is related to the ultimate metahistorical one—the *aporia* between a synchronous, "ideal eternal history" (*storia ideale eterna*) and the diachronous sequence of ages. The more general of the linguistic antinomies is the contradiction between Vico's claims for the univocal nature of language in the Age of the Gods and certain indications in his text, both implicit and explicit, that this language is already fallen and merely analogical, as he affirms language to be in the succeeding ages. Even his dictum that "the first nations thought in poetic characters, spoke in fables and wrote in hieroglyphics" betrays the strain. At first its transition from thinking to speaking may seem unproblematical, but Vico describes the thought of the First Age as "mute," or "almost entirely mute" (446), which appears to signify a privileging of the silence of perfect comprehension over any utterance. It follows that speech is by definition inadequate to the full apprehension of "poetical characters." His assertion that "the first nations . . . wrote in hieroglyphs" extends these same assumptions. He follows the fashion of his day in considering the then-undeciphered glyphs of the ancient Egyptians (and to a somewhat lesser degree the ideograms of the Chinese) as the best examples of how the earliest scripts of the race embody a language of the gods. The very etymology of "hieroglyph" expresses the concept of a sign that conveys access to the sacred without further mediation. This notion adds to the issue of whether, in the apprehension of truth, silence is not superior to speech, a second issue: whether a visual image that communicates in a flash of intuition is not superior to discourse. These indications of a falling away between thought and speech in the First Age itself are counterbalanced by passages in which Vico not only sets in apposition the three terms "fable," "*mythos*," and "*vera narratio*" (401), but also identifies them with the mute language of the gods and insists that they "contain meanings not analogical but univocal" (34). But the paragraph (401) in which Vico, for the first time (so far as I know), both introduces the singular "*mythos*" and equates it with "fable," is followed quickly by another (403) in which he declares that "the fables being imaginative class concepts . . . the mythologies must have been the allegories corresponding to them." This distinction, which suggests that Vico has not quite shaken off the Baconian notion of allegory or the "two-religion" theory, appears to reopen a gap, this time between the fable itself and its *explication,* that threatens another rent in the fabric of the univocal. The problematic with which Vico wrestles in this unprecedented manner seems inherent in all claims that language attains the full presence of the signified. Vico's struggles with it may perhaps be best understood in terms of Derridean supplementarity. Indeed, a deconstructive undoing might turn on Vico's remark that the language of the First Age is *"almost* entirely mute" (my italics).

Vico's second and narrower linguistic antinomy is a specialized version of the first. It can be stated thus: figurative language is as close as we can come to participating in the power of the original "poetical characters," but figurative language is the very mark of our fall. It is characteristic of Vico that in his attempt to understand the transition from the crude sublimities of the *giganti* to our imaginatively impoverished selves, he should link his general conception of imaginative devolution to a corresponding, but more specific, theory about the major tropes of classical rhetoric. Vico agrees with the central epistemological tradition in Western philosophy that univocal language is not figurative; figures are of the essence of analogical thinking. Yet he is obliged to suppose that his passionate and imaginative giants were the originators of what little imaginative power we still possess. He finesses this difficulty by distinguishing between "trope" and "figure." Tropes, he says, "were necessary modes of expression of all the first poetic nations. . . . But these expressions . . . later became figurative when, with the further development of the human mind, words were invented which signified abstract forms or genera" (409). As the proportion and strength of these merely "intelligible characters" wax over the course of time, the strength and proportion of the original tropes wane into dwindling figures. Figurative language, the language of "symbol," is characteristic of the Age of Heroes. Their poetry must have been magnificent by the standards of a later age; splendid as "Homer" seems to us, he is merely a belated collective voice on the edge of the Age of Men, a faint echo of the residual sublimity still accessible to the heroes.

The major tropes themselves echo their origins in the gigantic sublime. In fact, their internal hierarchical status is a function of their approximation to these origins. Metaphor is "the most luminous and therefore the most necessary and frequent" (404); "luminous," presumably, in permitting some part of the original radiance of truth to shine through. As we might say, it is the privileged trope because it is closest to a transcendental signified. Vico values especially the type of metaphor that "gives sense and passion to insensate things . . . every metaphor so formed is a fable in brief" (404). To the extent that prosopoeia is abbreviated fable and fable is "poetical character," metaphor still participates in the primal univocity. But metaphor displays a history of degeneration into lesser figures. "As these vast imaginations shrank and the power of abstraction grew, the personifications were reduced to diminutive signs. Metonymy drew a cloak of learning over the prevailing ignorance of these origins" (402). We encounter again here a form of the central antinomy. Metonymy and synecdoche originate like metaphor in the primal matrix and presumably still inherit what power they have from their source, yet being only the names for things derived from "sensible ideas," they were also inferior from the start to personifying metaphor and have degenerated farther and faster. The metonymy that draws a cloak of learning over ignorance of origins is thoroughly fallen; it sounds startlingly like Derridean displacement of metonymic meaning along a chain of signifiers.

But Vico's comments on his fourth trope, irony, reveal his tropological antinomy at its most acute. "Irony" still enjoyed in the eighteenth century a long-standing and quite limited signification, concisely rendered in Johnson's *Dictionary* as "a mode of speech in which the meaning is contrary to the words." No term, however, not even "myth" itself, was more radically transvalued by the Romantics and promoted to a position of central significance. Irony becomes not so much a trope of rhetoric as a world-view, the essence of which might be described as a self-conscious awareness of living in a divided or "fallen" state of experience. As between these views, Vico's treatment of the trope is amphibious. On one hand,

he assumes the traditional definition, but, on the other, he so situates the origin
of irony in his diachronic schema that he anticipates, even invites, the romantic
transvaluation. He proposes that irony, unlike the other figures, "could not have
begun until the period of reflection . . . because it is fashioned of falsehood . . .
which wears the mask of truth" (408). Irony indicates by its very presence the state
of experience; it cannot have been invented in the Age of the Gods: "Since the first
men of the gentile world had the simplicity of children, who are truthful by nature,
the first fables could not feign anything false" (408). Like the Houyhnhnms of
Vico's contemporary, Swift, the violent, sensuous giants could not knowingly utter
"the thing that is not." Granted his grand hypothesis about the nature of the *giganti,*
Vico's logic is impeccable here, but his deduction that a major trope could not have
been derived from the cyclopean founders drives a formidable wedge between the
imaginations of the "first nations" and our present condition.

Vico's displacement of irony confronts us sharply with two features of his
metahistorical theory that constitute between them the broadest of his paradoxes.
The first of these is that his theory, erected on the cusp of the great changeover
from traditional ideas of human decline to modern evolutionary ones of "progress,"
presents us with contrary movements. Insofar as history is a record of the loss of
imaginative and linguistic power, Vico's pattern is still a degenerative one. But
his treatment of that loss is strikingly free of nostalgia. He does not mourn the
decline of a faculty for which the race has been compensated by gains in rationality,
civility, manners, morals, linguistic precision—in short, civilization. He subscribes,
on balance, to an Enlightenment persuasion and must, in principle, be relieved
that the tumultuous imaginative conceptions of the *giganti* belong safely to an
irretrievable past. And yet, as Blake was to say of Milton, Vico is "of the Devil's
party without knowing it." One of the most general ways of conceptualizing the
huge shift in thinking, feeling, and judgment that comes to be labeled romanticism,
is to regard it as the replacement of mimetic and pragmatic aesthetics by expressive
ones (Abrams 1953). Vico's conception of imagination is expressive through and
through: "Since these genera . . . were formed by most vigorous imaginations . . .
we discover in them true poetic sentences, which must be sentiments clothed in
the greatest passions and therefore full of sublimity and arousing wonder" (34). We
owe especially to Locke the standard equations made in the next two and a half
centuries between the minds of "primitives," children, and illiterates, on one hand,
and language, on the other, that is simple, vivid, and concrete (Manuel 1959, 132,
142). But his admirer, Vico, is the first to integrate these ideas into a vision of
primal mythopoeia so persuasive it is capable of counterpoising the whole weight
of his Enlightenment confidence in the progress of civilization.

Vico's Janus-like ambiguity about the course of history is enabled, or at least
sheltered, by the broader antinomy of his metahistorical scheme that raises the
question of whether history is genuinely contingent at all. On one hand, history
unfolds in a diachronic sequence of ages, but, on the other, these ages are recycled
in a pattern that suggests behind it a timeless Platonic archetype or what Vico
called an "ideal, eternal history."[13] This *ricorso* of the pattern has been read through
the spectacles of Nietzsche by certain influential modernist artists, such as Yeats

and Joyce, and is still widely taken in literary circles to signify the eternal return of the same. If it did so signify, Vico's "barbarian nations" would have had to be *giganti* who recreated from scratch their own "poetical characters," reconstituted the original tropes, and so forth. But Vico's *schema* is much closer to Hegel than to Nietzsche—history proceeds in a spiral; repetitions are analogical, not identical. Even thus understood, however, the concept of *ricorso* tends to spatialize the flow of time and hypostatize the categories of recurrence. The problem can be highlighted by focusing upon one remarkable, admittedly anomalous, passage in which for once it breaks into the open. "As gods, heroes and men began at the same time (for they were, after all, men who imagined the gods and believed their own heroic nature to be a mixture of the divine and human natures), so these three languages began at the same time, each having its letters which developed along with it" (446). Vico appears to confess here that the very distinctions upon which he bases his diachronous *schema* were the arbitrary constructions of humankind at a single point in the past. On that day when we invented the concept of the three ages, together with their appropriate qualia, the fallen trope of irony must have been operating in full force and humankind always already imagining itself dwelling in permanent exile from the univocal creativity of its giant founders. *The New Science* is not itself nostalgic, but in this passage we glimpse the seeds both of the early romantic yearning for an irretrievable paradise of univocal expression and a crucial part of the high romantic response. This unique voicing of the philosophical idealism implicit in Vico's "ideal, eternal history" foreshadows those romantic metahistorical theories in which the contingencies of diachronic history are enclosed within the timeless pattern of a circle-without-sequence held to be characteristic of myth.

THE VINE OF FABLE DISCOVERED

Vico's *New Science* lays out a brilliant vision of the majesty of human fabling, only to deny modern access to the power.[14] But suppose we take advantage of his lightning flash to focus for a moment on that distant mountain range. Almost exactly a century later, in 1829, Cambridge undergraduate Alfred Tennyson won in his senior year the prestigious Newdigate Prize for poetry, with a Keatsian dream-vision called "Timbuctoo." The dreamer stands on Gibraltar, looking toward Africa and brooding on the rumors of lost civilizations, especially that of ancient Timbuctoo. He is visited by an angelic spirit who shows him a vision of the city in its medieval glory. The spirit tells him that it was raised there and mourns because Timbuctoo will soon appear to European rediscovery merely as a mud-walled town of huts. This guide eventually identifies itself: "I am the Spirit, / The permeating life which courseth through / All th'intricate and labyrinthine veins / Of the great vine of Fable" (Tennyson 1975, 835). The talented undergraduate was probably quite unaware that the conception that comes to him so naturally via his romantic models, and with which he feels so much at home—the storytelling of the entire race as an organic unity—was a construction fewer than three generations old. This conception of "the great vine of Fable" builds up in the middle decades of the eighteenth century out of a traffic among at least three interrelated trends. The first of these is the free circulation throughout England, France, and Germany of the same expressive assumptions about fable that are doubly locked away in Vico's unread book. The second is the relativizing of literary history, though this should perhaps simply be called the *rise* of literary history, since the very act of historicizing literary production creates the perception of its relativity.[15] The third is the concomitant expansion of the literary canon. We could follow the reciprocal working of these three trends by focusing on virtually any part of the vast shift in critical thinking "from Classic to Romantic," but the relatively minor subset of the transition from "fable" to "myth" must remain our target.

We might start with the century's reassessment of its twin cynosures of secular and sacred writing, Homer and the Bible. Alexander Pope captures with his usual wit the ahistorical Homer when he describes Virgil's decision to imitate the Homeric epics in his *Aeneid:* "But when t'examine ev'ry Part he came, / *Nature* and *Homer* were, he found, the *same* (Pope 1963, 148). Vico, however, strikes the keynote of the new with his claim in book 3 of *The New Science,* "Discovery of the True Homer," that "Homer" is the eponymous "poetical character" for the epic-composing Greek people at the edge of the Heroic Age. By the turn of the century, Vico's historicizing view culminates in F. A. Wolf's philological disintegration of "Homer." In his *Prolegomena* of 1795, Wolf identifies Homer with the oral traditions of *Das Volk,* into which Homer must have been born, and suggests an embryonic theory of metaphor that resembles Vico's "poetic character." What happened to Homer during the century began also to happen to the Bible. As theologians and other scholars came gradually to think of the Scriptures as a collection of historical documents, they arrived at the collateral recognition of them as forms of literary expression. The large tracts of poetry in the Hebrew Bible, for example, now accepted as the historical creations of a people, began to be understood in remarkably Viconian terms as simultaneously the violent utterance of an unpolished race and verse of unparalleled grandeur and loftiness. How does uncouth vehemence produce exalted refinement? In the wake of Boileau's translation and interpretation of Longinus (1674), this concept swells in importance through the following century.[16] It tends to engross all of the irrational, mysterious aspects of aesthetic experience unaccounted for in neoclassic theories of "the beautiful." With respect to poetic utterance it has traditionally included the claim that the strongest of emotions eventuate in diction and figures on one hand simple and direct, and on the other noble and pure. To include ancient Hebrew poetry under this rubric, then, is to locate it as an instance of the claim of the early poetry of every nation to the same exalted origin in religious emotion and expression in the mode of "the sublime."

Concurrent with the historicizing of Homer and the Bible, there is an immense expansion in the range of mythologies that European *literati* are learning to take seriously. And this new comparativism is doubled by the rise of ethnology. Though even the rudiments of professional fieldwork were more than a century and a half away, speculators about the nature of fable understood by the beginning of the eighteenth century, for example, the profound cultural significance of the fabling of the Americans. Many of the theorizers of fable, Fontenelle and Vico among them, refer explicitly to the empirical evidence of American storytelling practices and mythologies, and unmistakably do so because *they accept the continuity* between their own fabling and that of these "savages" under whatever laws govern the fabular productions of humanity.

Finally, the expansion of fable turns downward, and inward as well. First it turns "downward," in the sense that Europeans begin to attend to the marginalized storytelling of their indigenous traditions. The early landmark of this movement is Paul Henri Mallet's *Monuments* (1756), which reintroduces the Norse mythology preserved in the *Eddas*. To appreciate the impact of this publication upon the literary nationalism of the next hundred years, one need only reflect that at this date *Beowulf,* the *Nibelungenlied,* the *Chanson de Roland,* the Welsh *Mabinogion,* the Finnish *Kalevala,* and the Irish *Tain Bo Culaigne* were all still unrecovered, to say nothing of the great mass of European folktale and folklore. As this list suggests, the expansion of the canon moves downward in two senses scarcely distinguished by midcentury antiquarians. The first depends upon recognizing and then appreciating the aesthetic presuppositions in earlier phases of high culture. This leads most immediately to the recovery of the great medieval narratives mentioned above. But the second, more radical downward recovery depends upon recognition of popular culture and its matrix in an oral tradition at least partly independent of letters. This second sweep of the net, even more important in the long run for the folkloristic conceptualizing of "myth," manifests itself in the initiation of the folklore movement and of the slow discovery of the nature of "oral literature."

The expressive aesthetics that enables this historicizing and relativizing of the canon not only encourages the "outward" geographical and "downward" historical movements that result in the discovery of "the great vine of Fable"; it also produces a whole other dimension of response, referred to above as the "inward." "Inwardness" is a figure here for an internalizing movement of mind that manifests at least two distinct phases. The first phase is the desire of the eighteenth-century rehearser of fable to enter so intensely into its spirit that he makes it live again for a contemporary audience. And this desire trembles on the brink of a far more radical and ambitious one. Surely a contemporary fabulist can recapture the spirit of ancient story only to the extent that he or she somehow reclaims at least part of the imaginative power that inspired its original makers. And why, if this is a power that has been always and everywhere manifest in the fabling of humankind, should the modern author not be able *to originate from within* this kind of storytelling?

At this point in thinking about the impact of the discovered "vine of fable," it may help to consider briefly the exemplary liminal case of James Macpherson, whose *Poems of Ossian* was so wildly popular, and controverted, throughout Europe during the sixty years or so after its publication that his career can be regarded as a highly symptomatic cultural episode. Although Percy's *Reliques* was not published until 1765 (and his translation of Mallet as *Northern Antiquities* only in 1770), the older poets of his generation—the two Wartons, Collins, and Gray, all of whom shared his antiquarian enthusiasm—had already been urging for twenty years a programmatic recuperation of indigenous oral tale.[17] The publication in 1760 of *Fragments of Ancient Poetry Collected in the Highlands of Scotland and Translated from the Gaelic or Erse Language* by James Macpherson, a young schoolmaster, met their anticipatory prescriptions. He was swept off to Edinburgh and taken up enthusiastically by various *illuminati* of the "Scottish Renaissance." In accord with the post-Mallet fervor for surviving national traditions, Macpherson held that behind his discovered lyrics lay, as he put it in his introduction to *Fragments,* "episodes of a greater work which relate to the wars of Fingal" (Macpherson 1966, 5). He there proposes that "one work of considerable length, which deserves to be styled an heroic poem, might be recovered and translated, if encouragement were given for such an undertaking" (7). Encouragement certainly was given, and Macpherson, staked to the ancestor of a successful grant application, set off on his grand collecting tour of the Highlands. The results were *Fingal, An Ancient Epic* (1762) and *Temora, An Epic Poem* (1763), both *written,* according to Macpherson, by the ancient bard "Ossian." Macpherson's prose poems, collected as *The Poems of Ossian,* swept the Continent on a scale that rendered tepid even their reception in the British Isles.

Charges of fraud arose early. They fall into two broad categories, one relatively unsound but effectively damaging, the other sound but ineffectual, and both very revealing of contemporary attitudes. The unsound but damaging basis for doubting Macpherson's "discovery" is that, although he claimed to work from a combination of manuscripts and oral sources, he was never able, when challenged, to produce a single manuscript. The unsoundness of this criticism lies in its ignorance of an independent tradition of *oral* storytelling. Macpherson reveals himself as sharing this misunderstanding when he concedes to his critics that he *ought* to be able to back his oral sources with written ones. In fact, the most serious element of imposture in his work is that, believing this, he pretended that he had seen such manuscripts. The more sound reason for doubting Macpherson stems from internal rather than external evidence; its basis is stylistic and historical. As Macpherson's most persistent critic, Malcolm Laing, eventually demonstrated, *The Poems of Ossian* is a virtual cento of the King James Bible, Dryden's *Aeneid,* Waller, Prior, Pope's versions of Homer, and so forth. If echoing famous predecessors were a crime, few novice writers would escape prison, but the heavily conventional and derivative nature of Macpherson's diction and figures might well have exposed more effectively than it did how remote he was from the translation or even the paraphrase of specific originals. On the contrary, Macpherson was believed partly because of the perceived *rightness* of his style, a mixture of genteel sentiment and lofty diction that appealed to the new taste of the so-called "age of sensibility." More importantly here, *Ossian* triumphs because of the contemporaneous enthusiasm for the discovery of cultural connections with an indigenous past. Northern Europe had got itself an epic poet of its own. That he is a noble savage of irreproachable Rousseauian sentiment, and therefore, as some good judges maintained, a greater master than Homer, is merely further matter for self-congratulation.

Macpherson's career is particularly significant here because his aspiration trembles on the verge of the invention of an original mythology. Harold Bloom suggested a generation ago that we think of eighteenth-century "forgeries" of medieval work like Chatterton's and Macpherson's as analogous to biblical pseudepigrapha, that is, belated, anonymous writings attributed to an earlier authority. Pseudepigrapha appear to result from an overwhelming urge to extend and "improve" the earlier font of vision, to make it say what one feels it ought to have said. In the act of turning scraps of folktale and song into two literary epics, Macpherson projects his own shadowy sublime. But to achieve any more direct a breakthrough he would have had to act upon a conviction that the modern poet possesses the power of a Homer or an Ossian. Thomas Gray, probably the best poet of the day, and the person in the British Isles widely recognized to be the best qualified by talent and interests to judge Macpherson's claim, was consulted early on, before the publication of *Fragments.* Gray tells his friend Dr. Wharton about his quandary in a letter of June 1760: "The whole external evidence would make one believe these fragments . . . counterfeit, but the internal is so strong on the other side, that I am resolved to believe them genuine. . . . In short, this man is the very daemon of poetry, or he has lighted on a treasure hid for ages" (Gray 1935, II, 680). In spite of his suspicions, Gray is taken in, like others, partly by Macpherson's style, partly by his own long-held desire that just such indigenous matter be discovered. But the deepest reason for his dilemma, granted his impression that the poetry is brilliant, is that this brilliance must stem either from genuine Ossian or from Macpherson himself and, if the latter is the case, establish the obscure Scot as "the very daemon of poetry." The phrase expresses Gray's intuition that the modern poet who could invent such a work would be possessed by the myth-making power of the primitive sublime. But in his Pindaric ode, "The Bard," published just three years before, Gray had constructed, like Macpherson, his own medieval, Celtic personification of this aspiration, only to stop short of accepting the possibility of an incursion of this power into the modern world.[18] He is ultimately persuaded to accept the genuineness of Macpherson's "Ossian" by the brinksmanship he shares with the Scot,

NOSTALGIA FOR RELIGIOUS BELIEF: THREE POETS

In focusing thus far on expressive aesthetics and comparative mythology, I have largely left out of account the third major component in the transition from fable to myth—nostalgia for uncomplicated, unselfconscious religious belief. This strategy does have a certain justification; religious nostalgia, or at least its voicing, is, on the whole, the slowest of the three components to develop. The preceding sections are centered upon the outburst of the new expressivity and comparativism in the 1760s, whereas the writers whose poems will be considered here—Schiller, Wordsworth, and Hölderlin—are of the next generation. With the debatable exception of Schiller, these are writers normally and deservedly thought of as high romantics. But romanticism develops in a series of phases that, though roughly chronological, are partly psychological too, overlapping one another in the half-century between 1780–1830 to an extent that depends upon the shape of individual careers. With respect to the specific development of the concept of myth, I distinguish four such phases, designated here in shorthand as nostalgia, vision, doubt, and despair. The first, nostalgia, is closely akin to the state during the 1760s of the other components of the shift from fable to myth; it expresses an analogous yearning and frustration, connected in this case explicitly with the sense of being abandoned in a mechanistic world. That this nostalgia peaks so belatedly, almost concurrently with the stage of visionary breakthrough in the construction of "myth" out of "fable," probably indicates how deeply vision is a reaction to the sense of religious crisis that pervades the stage of nostalgia.

The poets considered here share two specific ways of conceiving of their abandonment, the first being "dissociation of sensibility" and the second a sense of what Schiller calls *"entgötterte Naturr,"* a natural environment emptied of divinity. The phrase "dissociation of sensibility" was invented by T. S. Eliot as a name for the condition of modern poets that prevents them from achieving the unity of thought and feeling still available in Western culture (according to Eliot) as late as the early seventeenth century. Eliot invented the phrase, but the distinction of inventing the concept, or at least formulating it decisively, belongs to Friedrich Schiller in his essay "On Naive and Sentimental Poetry" (1795).[19] The essence of the *topos* of "dissociation" consists in the claim that once upon a time humans were not the creatures of divided consciousness they are now. Precisely where in time a given writer locates the catastrophic division is strictly secondary and depends upon his or her ideological assumptions. Schiller, who inherits both the century's metahistorical speculations and the peculiarly German obsession with classical Greece that arose also in the 1760s, pitches the break in the conveniently large gap between the Greeks and us. To appreciate Schiller's rationale for this choice we must turn to the second specific feature of this religious nostalgia, the sense of a natural frame void of deities. That *this* issue should define for many romantics the crisis of the age may reflect both the triumph of the worldview of Newtonian physics and the growing emphasis upon natural religion, evident, for example, in the deists, the Encyclopédistes, Rousseau, Hume, and d'Holbach. The key to the crucial connection between natural religion and the emptied frame of things perceived by the speakers in these poems may lie in Herder's dictum (probably inspired by Heyne) that "the mythology of every people is an expression of the particular mode in which they viewed nature" (Herder 1966, 199) It is as if Schiller, Wordsworth, and Hölderlin, having taken this judgment profoundly to heart, *therefore* look out upon desolation.

Schiller combines these two topics in his essay; the criterion for locating the divide between unified and dissociated sensibilities is the relation of the poets to their natural environment. The central thesis of the essay is that the "naive" poets of antiquity enjoyed perfect rapport with nature while taking it for granted, whereas the "sentimental" poets of modernity are highly aware of the desirability of this rapport but hopelessly cut off from it by the very self-consciousness that engenders their yearning. Schiller's nostalgia is obviously a complicated matter; modernity's self-consciousness renders it, in a sense, superior to antiquity, even in the quality of its response to nature. But the price it pays is endless longing for the state of simple unity it may not reclaim. This view of the condition of "sentimental" modernity broadly resembles Vico's, but, unlike Vico, Schiller casts the loss in terms of natural religion and openly mourns the result.

This is the state of affairs dramatized in *"Die Götter Grieschenlands,"* which was first published in 1788, seven years before the essay, and became the celebrated manifesto of the new nostalgia. The speaker sets the tone immediately: when the gods ruled, those *"Schöne Wesen aus dem Fabelland . . . / wie ganz anders, anders war es da!"* (Schiller 1962b, 169).[20] This characterization of the gods as beautiful beings from the land of fable creates an immediate ambiguity about their ontological status. Do they still exist in some permanent land of fable? Did they ever exist in any other? At the end of the poem, and more conspicuously in the original version, the gods recede down the stream of time, but toward a permanent place. The tone of this conclusion comes near to suggesting that the presence of the gods in this *Fabelland* is some consolation for their departure down the stream, or, to put it more abstractly, that aesthetic beauty is the modern compensation for loss of religious faith. But it is important to notice on the way to this conclusion the movement of the speaker's mind into a completely unironic celebration of "the wholly other" condition of life over which the gods presided. *There* the relation of signifier to signified was also unproblematic. The second stanza begins: *"Da der Dichtung zauberische Hülle / Sich noch lieblich um die Wahrheit wand— / Durch die Schöpfung floss der Lebensfülle / Und was nie empfinden wird, empfand."* *There* there was no gap between subject and object; truth and poetry were one. Poetry wrapped only a magical transparence about the thing signified, and the signified poured the fullness of life through the verbal construction. *There* what will never again be felt, the unity of consciousness with its intended object, *was* felt. Vico might be envious of so concrete an account of the "poetical character" as experienced by his giants of the First Age.

The speaker grieves most centrally the loss of what we have come to call since Buber "I-Thou" relations with the objects of consciousness in nature: *"Wo jetzt nur, wie under Weisen sagen, / Seelenlos ein Feuerball sich dreht / Lenkte damals seinen goldnen Wagen / Helios im stiller Majestöt"* (170). In the next phase of romantic mythopoeia, the visionary poet will be able to assert as Blake does that when the sun rises he sees not "a round Disk of fire somewhat like a Guinea," but "an innumerable company of the Heavenly host crying Holy Holy Holy is the Lord God Almighty" (Blake 1965, 555). This is precisely what the poet of the phase of nostaliga insists he cannot do. His frightened visual recognition of the absence of the gods tears from him a cry whose echo confirms that nature is now an abandoned place, incapable of what Robert Frost, much further along in the same tradition, will call "counterresponse": *"Durch die Walder ruf ich, durch die Wogen, / Ach, sie widerhallen leer"* (172). In the following stanza, perhaps the most famous in the poem, the speaker approaches yet more explicitly the central paradox of "On Naive and Sentimental Poetry," that it is our very love of nature that torments us most, because we are debarred from experiencing it as "thou." Nature is said to be unknowing of the joy she nevertheless imparts, majestic, but unaware of her majesty. She gives her creature bliss though she cannot share it, moves him to a praise she cannot feel. Above all, her inmate knows she is guided by Spirit, but she herself does not. The lines express astonished outrage that the source of such refreshment cannot feel the moral life it inspires. They personify nature, of course, in the gesture of asserting that this may not be done, but this fallacy only underlines the pathos of our aloneness. Newtonian physics requires that we experience the theater of our imaginations as the *"entseelte Wort"* of the law of gravity. This nature is, finally, *"entgötterte,"* an epithet it is tempting to translate outright as "demystified" (172). Compared to this, the "sentimental" *Fabelland* of modern art is a bitter consolation prize.

In spite of its considerable differences in style and sensibility, Wordsworth's sonnet "The World Is Too Much with Us" is a recognizable reworking of Schiller's theme and quite possibly of his poem.[21] Where Schiller's speaker makes a scapegoat of scientism, however, and speaks as a victim of historical necessity, Wordsworth's commences by denouncing our "sordid" hearts that attract us to "the world" where we "lay waste" in "getting or spending" certain intrinsic "powers" that ought, apparently, to have been reserved for rapport with "nature": "This Sea that bares her bosom to the moon; / The winds that will be howling at all hours, / And are up-gathered now like sleeping flowers; / For this, for everything, we are out of tune; / It moves us not" (Wordsworth 1933, 259). This moment of stillness and witness to the intimacy of sea and moon is itself so moving that it appears at first to contradict the speaker's assertion that we're *not* moved. The outburst that concludes the sonnet, however, puts in perspective the moment that has suddenly wrung from him his rage at modern inadequacy: "Great God! I'd rather be / A pagan suckled in a creed outworn / So might I standing on this pleasant lea / Have glimpses that would make me less forlorn; / Have sight of Proteus rising from the sea, / Or hear old Triton blow his wreathed horn." These last two images are related to the earlier pair of wind and sea, but only as Schiller's "naive" (or unified) is to his "sentimental" (or divided). The sea alone with the moon may be "sublime," but a sea broken by the rising of Proteus is a *setting,* a field of force that literally comes to a head in the manifestation of the god. In similar fashion, the sound of Triton's horn, as compared to howling wind, is expressive of agency, of intention. The imagined child of paganism effortlessly projects numinous presence where the modern observer at his best can manage only pathetic fallacy. Wordsworth's speaker is particularly close to Schiller's in his compressed figure of this child as "suckled in a creed outworn." Suckling expresses here, as elsewhere in Wordsworth, the closest possible oneness with nature; yet this belated speaker understands simultaneously that the "creed" is "outworn." The contradiction acknowledges historical necessity just as surely as Schiller's image of the gods borne down the *Zeitfluss;* "outworn" rhymes with Triton's "horn" and the inevitable "forlorn." Wordsworth's poem is grounded like Schiller's in Herder's assumption that a people's mythology expresses its conception of nature. But it responds to the conclusion that follows with self-loathing and angry despair rather than witty sarcasm and wistful consolation.

The great poet of this crisis, however, is Hölderlin. Schiller's and Wordsworth's poems are expressions of a mood relatively rare among their *oeuvres,* but Hölderlin's work *is* the poetry of religious nostalgia. Far from mourning a historically inevitable loss as Schiller and Wordsworth do in their nostalgic poems, Hölderlin is constantly tormented by the possibility of an imminent *parousia.* He idealizes and yearns for "the gods of Greece" with an intensity unimaginable in Schiller and is persuaded that "the gods of the future," whatever else they may be, must somehow be the Greek deities revived. This advent of the old-new gods could occur at any moment, but whenever it does it will be mediated through nature. For Hölderlin, as for Schiller and Wordsworth, mythology follows conception of nature, and for him nature is simply what we call the elements out of which divinity appears. In "Am Quell der Donau" he imagines the divinely born emerging out of nature as out of a bath. This conception of nature as matrix of *parousia* explains why his landscapes are so characteristically heavy with significance.

For a glimpse of these themes in motion, we might focus for a moment on the structure of what is perhaps Hölderlin's finest expression of his desire for a viable religious mythopoeia, the hymn "Germania." It commences abruptly with the speaker's recognition that he may no longer invoke *"Die Götterbilder in dem alten Lande"* (Hölderlin 1980, 400). He feels checked in his desire to retreat to these gods he loves by a sense of dread *"Gestorbene zu weken."* This fear strains against his tense awareness that the landscape is in a state of expectation: *"Dem voll Erwartung liegt / Das Land."* In the second stanza he enters more intensively into the baffling status of these *"Entflohene Götter"* whom he should no longer invoke, but who yet seem to linger and *"so die Erde neubesuchen"* (402). Yet it's not they who will come, or at least not as they were: *"Dann die da kommen sollen, drängen uns / Und länger säumt von Göttermenschen / Die heilige Schaar nicht mehr im blauen Himmel."* These new gods who press us are apparently less in our image; they drive the pictures of the old gods from the sky (in a figure remembered in the Magi poems of Heine and Yeats); they are the gods of a rougher age. At this point, the hinge of the entire poem, the speaker realizes in a burst of confident trust, that the elements themselves will rain down the appropriate deities together with their names: *"Vom Aether aber fällt / Das treue Bild und Göttersprüche reegnen."* Out of nowhere the eagle appears, the eagle of Hölderlin's poem of that name, his symbol of divine inspiration, flying from the Indus, following the course of history and of sacred poetry.

We discover just as suddenly, at the beginning of the fourth stanza that the eagle is seeking, among the lands over which he flies, *"Die priesterin, die stillste Tochter Gottes."* The priestess is of course the personification of Hölderlin's yearning land, the figure eventually identified by the speaker as "Germania." We are told that in a recent death-threatening storm (both personal and historical crisis of disbelief) *"Es Ahnete das Kind ein Besseres"* and in amazed response to her great faith *"die Macht der Höhe"* sent *"den Boten"* (who may or may not be the eagle but is now called *"der Jugendliche"*). This angelic messenger delivers to Germania a speech of Annunciation that constitutes the remainder of the poem. He tells her that she has been elected to bear *"ein schweres Glük"* (404) that has apparently been growing in her ever since the messenger and she met secretly in the woods and flowers at some unspecified time in the past. (Her good fortune is "heavy" because it is the sort of responsibility for theophany that Hölderlin himself both desired and dreaded.) Not only has she already been chosen, but the messenger says that ever since he left her originally she has been uttering prophecies, particularly through her rivers. The temporal vagueness of these remarks indicates that the moment of *parousia* is somehow both always already present and yet still imminent. All Germania has to do, the messenger tells her in the wonderful opening verses of the sixth stanza, is to drink the winds of morning until she is opened up and names what is before her eyes.

If the hymn ended here it would belong with the visionary poetry of Blake and Novalis in the next phase of the construction of "myth." Instead it coils and recoils for another stanza and a half through an obsessive recapitulation of Hölderlin's major tensions. The voice of the messenger, while it continues to the end, seems to become again the voice of the original narrator, and this ambiguous double voice manages simultaneously to envision Germania *in the future* keeping her feast-days amid her rejoicing people and yet to re-create the situation between observer and landscape at the beginning of the poem, where nothing has yet happened. The action of the poem appears to transpire in an instant in which the *parousia* stalls in place. In this, the poem's conclusion is true to the emotional dynamics of its author. Hölderlin is himself suspended between rejection of the necessity of belatedness to which Schiller and Wordsworth submit and honest inability to sustain faith in the power of the imagination to transcend its historical circumstances. His is the poetry of a terrible, anxious *waiting,* the most powerful of all romantic yearning for the mythopoeia of a vital religion.

[2]

The Invention of Myth

Belief in myth as a solution to the crisis expressed in the poetry of religious nostalgia presumes the presence within modern persons of some inalienable faculty for producing it. The confidence that tips the balance from longing for this power to affirmation of its presence arises in the larger context of what we know as the romantic movement, that profound revision of a network of related concepts such as "ego," "author," "artist," "art," and "literature." This movement appears as an effort, in certain respects reactionary, in others radical, to legitimate modernity by asserting, in defiance of certain Enlightenment thought and of Kant, that humankind can indeed attain transcendental knowledge of things as they really are. This claim is based upon exaltation of the autonomous ego and its "original genius." It is also based upon the allegedly authoritative witness of the *products* of this genius, such as "Literature." Until the end of the eighteenth century, "literature," like "learning," was a quality a *person* was said to possess. The romantic hypostatizing of "Literature" as an objective entity, a super-genre, in the sense still familiar today, indicates a felt need to establish a special category of writing distinguished from ordinary rhetorical performance by features that confer upon it a cachet of authority. The specific sub-genre that eventually comes to be designated as "myth" is the very template of "Literature," a type of narrative that conveys insight so inexhaustible in its significance that it transcends its mere local occasion and historical situation.

ALLEGORIES OF FABLE: BLAKE AND NOVALIS

Even as Schiller, Wordsworth, and Hölderlin mourn what they feel as irretrievable loss, artists and thinkers around them in what I have called the phase of "vision," are beginning not only to affirm the mythopoeic power of the race as its permanent possession, but also to construct narratives that are both instances of that power and allegorical accounts of how it overcomes the orphaning "dissociation of sensibility." Narratives of this sort I call "allegories of fable."[1] All three of Blake's "epics," the unengraved *The Four Zoas* (1795) and *Milton* and *Jerusalem,* whose engravings were launched by 1804, are instances of this genre; each represents in plot and characters the psychological dynamics by which a creative artist overcomes his divided self and inaugurates an apocalyptic moment of renewal.[2] Of these three, *The Four Zoas* expresses this allegory most directly.

Blake's Zoas are both the "four living creatures" of the biblical visions of Ezekiel and John and "[t]he Antediluvians who are our Energies . . . the Giants who formed this world into its sensual existence and now seem to live in it in chains" (Blake 1965, 39). It is as if the *giganti* of Vico (whose work Blake did not know), lived on, trapped in the diminished minds of the descendants for whom they framed the phenomenal world. The Zoas represent specific "Energies": Tharmas, our "common" or unifying sense of taste and touch; Luvah, our passion and sexuality; Urizen, our rational intellect; and Urthona, our imaginative power. As long as these powers are integrated in the corporate human, Albion, he dwells in a state of unified sensibility, but as the poem opens, these Energies have already begun to fall into disorganization and discord: first Tharmas, then Luvah, then Urizen. Just as it is unclear when this ruin commences (it may be, as among some Gnostics, identical with Creation), it is unclear whether the collapse of the Zoas causes the fall of Albion, or vice versa; both are the same condition considered under different aspects.

As the Zoas disintegrate, their Vehicular Forms, Emanations, and Spectres split off. "Vehicular Forms" are the contracted avatars of the Zoas in the fallen world, the two important ones in Blake's major prophetic poems being Urthona's appearance as Los, the spirit of poetry and prophecy, and Luvah's as Orc, the spirit of passion in rebellion, rather analogous to Freudian libido. The "Emanations," somewhat analogous to the Jungian concept of the "anima," are the female halves of the Zoas with whom the Zoas must be reunited in order not to be merely raging masculine abstractions, missing half their "humanity." The Spectres are analogous to the Jungian archetype of the Shadow, projections of the worst or most feared aspects of the self. In fact, these Spectres are sometimes called Shadows. The poem is subtitled "The Torments of Love & Jealousy in the Death and Judgment of Albion the Ancient Man," a fair epitome of the usurpations, struggles, and alliances among these displaced and disorganized fragments of a psyche. As Albion lies dying on the Rock of Ages in the Sea of Time and Space, his Energies disintegrate until, in an abrupt reversal, Los breaks out of his selfhood in an act of forgiveness that enables him to reintegrate both his Shadow and his Emanation, Enitharmon. This crucial act enables in turn the reintegration of Los in Urthona, of all the Zoas in Albion, and the triumphant vision of the Last Judgment as Eden restored in which the poem ends.

To appreciate this plot as "allegory of fable," it's worth looking more closely at the significance of Los and his interaction with his Shadow and Emanation. Near the beginning of the poem we are told of Urthona, the principle of imagination, that "in the Auricular nerves of human life / Which is the Earth of Eden, he his Emanations propagated / Fairies of Albion afterwards Gods of the Heathen" (Blake 1965, 297). Urthona propagates in the "Auricular nerves" because poetry and prophecy, especially before writing, lived by the ear. Urthona's special element in Eden, among the four traditional ones, is "Earth," which Blake wonderfully identifies with the ear as the site of poetic imagination. Here Urthona creates the "Gods of the heathen," alias all the non-Judaeo-Christian mythologies of the world.[3] Urthona's fall, unlike those of the other Zoas, is not narrated; he never wanders or struggles in his own person, only in that of his Vehicular Form, Los. In the topographical survey of the ruined world of Albion toward the end of Night the Sixth, we are told about Urthona only that his realm has become "a World of Solid darkness / . . . rooted in dumb despair" (344). The imagination, unlike the other "dissociated" faculties, does not desert its post out of mad ambition to usurp the powers of others; it is more passively to blame, becoming dark with benightedness and tongue-tied with despair. This is the Blakean version of Vico's decline of the imagination between the Ages of Gods and Men.

Because the imagination does not altogether lose its calling to "Vision," it becomes the ground of resistance to the fallen condition and ultimately the agent of its overcoming. In *Jerusalem* even the Spectre of Urthona, Los's Shadow, is twice praised "because he kept the Divine Vision in time of trouble" (191, 252). And Los himself, though often confused, rash, jealous, selfish, never forgets who he is. He tells Blake himself in *Milton,* "I am that Shadowy Prophet who Six Thousand Years ago / Fell from my station in the Eternal Bosom. / I the Fourth Zoa am also set / The Watchman of Eternity, the Three are not" (116, 118). Los is continually building Golgonooza, the city of art, beating out the spaces and times within which organized life is possible, creating, in short, human culture. "For every Space larger than a Globule of Mans blood / Is visionary; and is created by the hammer of Los" (126).

Toiling endlessly to shape and repair the fallen world is one thing; transforming it is another. According to Blake the latter requires continual forgiveness of the sins of "the Reprobate," an unselfish act of love possible to envision only through the medium of imagination, which is why, in *The Four Zoas,* it originates in Los. Apart from his Emanation and his Shadow, Los is a mad artist, obsessed by private fantasies in which he can't persuade others to believe. Apart from Los, Enitharmon, like all the detached Emanations, falls into idolatrous construction of the natural world and into corrupt sexual behavior, while the Spectre of Urthona lusts after Enitharmon and prostitutes his art as a drudge in the service of the same natural world. In the crucial confrontation in Night the Seventh, after Enitharmon tells "the tale / Of Urthona" (353), that is, recalls Los to his ideal self, Los embraces the Spectre "first as a brother / Then as another Self," and only then is the Spectre able to make Los understand that he *is* "thy real Self," through union with whom alone lies the way to reconciliation with Enitharmon. *By hearing its own tale,* told by its "soul" or "anima," Imagination recognizes its apocalyptic nature. It realizes that, if integrated with the exigencies of its exercise in the fallen world (its suppressed female and shadow sides), it can work concretely in living humanity and so transform the fallen world from within. Besides allegorizing the psychological dynamics necessary for a visionary renewal of humanity, Blake thus affirms the power of the contemporary artist to create it. Where the poets of the nostalgic phase feel cut off from original mythopoeia by the scientific worldview, Blake denies their enthymeme, that a living religion must come out of nature: "THERE is NO Natural Religion" (Blake 1965, 2). Los never seems more a personification of Blake's own best visionary aspirations than when he asserts in *Jerusalem,* "I must Create a System, or be enslav'd by another Mans / I will not Reason & Compare: my business is to Create" (151).

Our second allegory of Fable is the *märchen* narrated in the middle of Novalis's *Heinrich von Ofterdingen* by the magician-poet, Klingsohr. Like the internalized quest-romances of the English writers, the literary fairytale developed by their German contemporaries often asks to be read as a representation of the power of mythopoeia to renovate consciousness. The first phase of the plot commences with a *Faust*-like Prologue in Heaven. The city of Arcturus lies frozen in a night, which is obviously another version of the night of consciousness after a fall from unified sensibility. The ancient hero, Perseus, who is Iron as well as a constellation, stirs up Arcturus and his daughter, Freya, Peace, the enchanted princess who languishes on her couch until the awakening kiss of the true hero. Roused temporarily from his nightmare, Arcturus commands Perseus to hurl his sword into the cosmos. When Perseus obeys, his sword bursts against the mountains of Earth. This etiological myth of the origin of polar magnetism seems to signify something like the promise of transcendent truth embodied in physical nature. But, for Novalis as for Blake, the initiative for change does not lie in nature; it must come from humankind, which is, in Novalis's famous phrase, "the Messias of Nature."

The setting shifts to the analogue of this scene on middle-earth, a busy household presided over by a Father named Sinn, who has by Herz, usually just called The Mother, a son, Eros, and by Eros's nurse, Ginnistan, a daughter named Fable. Two other adults (tutor and governess?) live in the household, a pedant called The Scribe and a rather superior young woman named Sophia, Wisdom. With the exception of Sophia, this conceptualizing of the primary components of humankind is very close to Blake's. The Father compares approximately to Tharmas, Herz and Eros to Luvah and Orc, The Scribe to Urizen, and Ginnistan and Fable (roughly, irresponsible fantasizing and visionary narrative) to the fallen avatars of Urthona—that is, to Los's Emanation, Enitharmon, his Spectre, and Los himself. We promptly witness the disintegration of this harmonious hierarchy. The Father enters carrying a small iron rod. The Scribe recognizes its magnetic properties, but loses interest in the rod once he's "explained" it. But when Ginnistan, playing with it, touches the sleeping Eros, he leaps from his cradle full-grown, "dressed only in his long golden hair," the figure of the virile young hero (Novalis 1964, 125). For him the iron ring of fate (into which Ginnistan has twisted the rod) is the sign of the shattered sword; it calls forth his destiny as the new Perseus who will rescue the new Andromeda, Princess Freya. But he sets off on his mission accompanied by the irresponsible fantasizer, Ginnistan, who seduces and confuses him; as he embraces Ginnistan he's filled with longing for Freya. In psychological terms this is adolescent eroticism dominating an uncertain sense of identity; in historical terms, the diversion of libidinal energy from its revolutionary potential. Meanwhile, back at the ranch, with Eros gone, The Scribe, Rationality, seizes control of the household very much as Urizen usurps power in the *Zoas* after Luvah's departure from his proper station. At this point, however, the young child, Fable, comes into her own.

Fable escapes by finding a concealed door behind Sophia's altar and a stairway leading down into a dark cavern. The visionary projection of human desire cannot be utterly repressed by any tyranny. Or, as Blake puts it, "There is a moment in each Day that Satan cannot find" (135). Fable's dove-like innocence turns out to be the wisdom of the serpent. When she encounters the Sphinx guarding a crucial door, she outdoes it at its own riddling game. Fable, after all, personifies for Novalis (and his narrator, Klingsohr) a figurative, riddling mode of speech. To the question of what she's seeking, Fable replies, "My possessions" (132). By the end of the tale we discover that these are nothing less than the properties of that same "Golden Age" that Blake declares it is the endeavor of his work to restore (545). When the Sphinx asks, "Where do you come from?" Fable replies, "From ancient times." And when the Sphinx objects, "You are still a child," she responds, "And shall remain a child forever." Whereas Eros grows up under the touch of iron, Fable, *märchen,* remains a toddler of the proper age for enjoying fairytales even in the act of mastering the physical and moral cosmos. For Novalis the canonical form of fable *is* fairytale, as a number of his aphorisms profess. Though Fable appears helpless and vulnerable, she is the toughest of the household characters. When the Sphinx asks contemptuously, "Who will stand by you?" she replies, "I stand alone." Fable is as elusive of official sponsorship as of official repression. At this point she turns the tables, demanding, "Where are my sisters?" a question that demonstrates she is not truly lost but grasps intuitively the structure of the world and her place in it. The Sphinx, whose job it is to block the door to the Fates, equivocates, but cannot reply effectively to Fable's own riddles, and the little girl marches triumphantly through the door.

She improvises a mastery over the Fates analogous to her baffling of the Sphinx. She asks her "pretty cousin" to give her "a little something to spin." Storytelling is related to the Fates in its spinning of the threads of human destiny. Novalis's fresh metonymical version of this trite metaphor for literary creation affirms, however, that fabling has the power not merely to imitate Fate but to rival and even supplant it. Fable describes herself in her spinning-song as weaving the single strands of individual destinies into one unified and therefore apocalyptic web. The Fates are temporarily saved from destruction by the unexpected arrival of the Scribe in hot pursuit of Fable. His appearance indicates the close alliance of rationality with fatalism. Fable tells him in her whimsical, *faux-naive* style that if he only had an hourglass and scythe he would look like the Fates' brother. If, that is, he added the inexorability of temporal passage to his mechanistic *ratio* of space, he would be that vision of historical necessity that crushes the poets of the preceding phase.

Fable once again escapes captivity by finding a hidden exit, this time a ladder going up through a trap-door into "Arcturus' room" (135). Fable has suddenly completed a journey of discovery that connects the three realms of the tale. Beneath the household of the disunified sensibility lies the dark realm of Necessity, while above rises the chamber of the King whom Novalis designated in a well-known letter to Friedrich Schlegel as "Chance, the spirit of life." While Necessity underlies the two higher levels, its rule of them is a perverse usurpation; when Fable successfully threads all three and binds them together again, the millennium is underway. The working out of the stages of the millennium and the resolution of the several plights of the household members occupies a considerable portion of the fairytale. Suffice it to say here that near the end, Perseus presents to Fable the spindle of the Fates, predicting, "In your hands this spindle will delight us forever, and out of *yourself* you will spin for us an unbreakable golden thread" (147 [my italics]). In the fallen world there can be only an analogy between existential fate and fictional narrative, but in the renewed Golden Age, for Novalis as for Blake, the two are one. Since the imagination contains the universe, it constructs its history according to the heart's desire. The *märchen* concludes with Fable—presiding over a masque-like scene of the sacred unions of properly sorted-out couples—spinning and singing "the kingdom of eternity." Yet even this final tableau insists on what is radically elusive and subversive about storytelling. Fable spins an eternity of sexual bliss for the united couples, but she herself remains always an asexual child. Though she has instigated and directed the millennium, she does not reign on any throne. She remains apart, rejoicing (like Dante's Fortuna) in her own blessedness, responsible to and for no one. She knows the world of experience, but she does not suffer it. Here Novalis parts company even with Blake. Blake's Eden is a creative fire in which the contraries of the dialectic are constantly consumed. Novalis's Eden is only what Blake calls "Beulah," "a pleasant lovely Shadow / Where no dispute can come" (1965, 128). Whereas for Blake, "the Human Imagination Divine" has defined its desire by experiencing the hell of the fallen state, Novalis's Fable remains untouched, fey and daemonic, a faculty of ourselves more radical than our experience. But allegories of Fable like these, whatever their distinctive differences, bespeak the climax of romantic confidence in the autonomy of the ego, the power of the imagination to transcend its historical circumstances, the authority of the aesthetic. They proclaim the arrival of modern mythopoeia.

THEORIZING MYTHIC CONSCIOUSNESS I: FRIEDRICH SCHLEGEL'S "TALK ON MYTHOLOGY"

In Germany, where "myth" first explicitly displaces "fable, the classicist C. G. Heyne, and the younger J. G. Herder, partly inspired by Heyne, were familiarizing their audiences with the new concept as early as the 1760s. Thus, while practicing poets were scarcely any more quick than in England to claim for themselves the

power of mythopoeic invention, there was a slowly enlarging theoretical discourse
on the topic that finally breaks the barrier in two works that belong to the
annus mirabilis of 1800, when Blake is working on *The Four Zoas* and Novalis
begins *Heinrich von Ofterdingen*. These are Friedrich Schlegel's *Dialogue on Poetry* and
Friedrich Schelling's *System of Transcendental Idealism*.

Loosely modeled on Plato's *Symposium*, the *Dialogue on Poetry* is the fictionalized,
first-person account of a discussion on the preassigned topic of "poetry" among
pseudonymous members of the Jena *Atheneum* circle. Four of the participants present
set-pieces, the second of which is "Talk on Mythology," a short lecture delivered
by "Ludovico," the pseudonym for Friedrich Schelling himself.[4] The very fact that
Ludovico chooses to address the topic of poetry by giving a talk on mythology
reveals how thoroughly he takes for granted the virtual identification of the two
concepts. At first he appears to make a very discouraging distinction—a mythology
is a set of traditional sacred narratives, whereas poetry is the aesthetic product of
individual modern artists. But this distinction becomes increasingly, and deliberately, blurred in the course of the "Talk." "Our poetry," Ludovico declares in his
keynote, "lacks a focal point such as mythology was for the ancients; and one could
summarize all the essentials in which modern poetry is inferior to the ancients in
these words: 'We have no mythology'" (Schlegel 1968, 81). This assumption, that
modern individual performances are inferior because not grounded in communal
belief, echoes Herder and Schiller, but takes on a harder edge because of its bold
circularity: belief enables poetry, poetry belief; moderns *could* match antiquity
if they could reestablish that magical reciprocity—and they can: "We have no
mythology. But, I add, we are close to obtaining one, or, rather, it is time that
we earnestly work together to create one" (81). Ludovico affirms the revolutionary
assumption of Blake and Novalis; the answer to not being born into a coherent
mythology is to pull yourself up by your own bootstraps, to participate in the
creation of the one you desire. In the next paragraph Ludovico confronts, only to
co-opt, Schiller's doctrine of "dissociation." Mythology, he says, will come to us
by an entirely opposite way from that of previous ages, which was everywhere the
first flower of youthful imagination, directly joining and imitating what was most
immediate and vital in the sensuous world. Ludovico accepts Schiller's distinction
between the "naive" and the "sentimental," but gives it an optimistic twist. "The
new mythology, in contrast, must be forged from the deepest depths of the spirit;
it must be the most artful of all works of art, for it must encompass all the others;
a new bed and vessel for the ancient, eternal fountainhead of poetry, and even
the infinite poem concealing the seeds of all other poems" (81–82). Modernity's
belatedness is also its opportunity. We are challenged by virtue of our historical
position to create "the most artful of all works of art," ones that will "encompass all
the others," that will, first of all, then, triumph over the "dissociation of sensibility"
by a dialectical synthesis that sublates even the Greeks. The speaker breathes utter
confidence that modernity can attain to and work in "the deepest depths of the
spirit" where this "new mythology . . . must be forged." This confidence is based on
his conviction that the *ancient* fountainhead is also *eternal*. Schlegel's figure of the
mythology to come as "a new bed and vessel for the ancient eternal fountainhead"

is akin to Blake's epigram "The Cistern contains; the Fountain overflows"; Schlegel applies it, however, not merely to individual creativity but also, in Schiller's manner, to the historical rise of a brand-new supergenre that will recontain the *source* (in the original etymological sense), of the "eternal fountainhead."

Just as Ludovico accepts, but transvalues, Schiller's metahistorical fiction of "dissociation," he concurs with Schiller in the Herderian assumption that a culture's mythology will reflect its view of nature. But instead of reaching Schiller's conclusion that the domination of a scientific materialism guarantees, therefore, that modernity is permanently exiled from mythology, he concludes that this worldview can itself be transformed by the power of imagination. "What else is any wonderful mythology," Ludovico asks, "but hieroglyphic expression of surrounding nature in this transfigured form of imagination and love" (85)? The issue is not what nature as Kantian *noumena* actually is, but how our projections transfigure it to our understandings. Following Heyne, Ludovico urges upon his fellow poets "the study of physics, from whose dynamic paradoxes the most sacred revelations of nature are now bursting forth in all directions" (88). But he also suggests that the new physics requires the assistance of poetry: "especially in physics . . . nothing is more needed than a mythological view of nature" (84). Science and poetry must unite in the creation of a physics that is also a living, lived mythology.

This dream forces Schlegel back upon the emerging problematic we have already encountered in Herder and in the "Talk" itself, the question of how the individual modern poet can possibly create what has been notoriously held to be the product of ages of communal belief. Schlegel's solution is that the individual poet who surrenders to this living frame of things will not go far wrong in contributing his mite toward the construction of a mythology. For, once the individual's good-faith effort is made, the result is up to universal process.[5] "Mythology is . . . a work of art created by nature. In its texture the sublime is really formed; everything is relation and metamorphosis, conformed and transformed" (86). Schlegel's conviction that individual fabulizing contributes unwittingly to the evolution of a unified sublime explains his ease before the apparent paradox that "ancient poetry" is both "a chaos" and "a single, indivisible and perfect poem" (82). The judgment is a matter of temporal perspective; "poetry" is "a chaos" insofar as it consists, from close up, of the fragmentary productions of disparate individuals, but "a perfect poem" insofar as it manifests a unity of spirit comprehensible in historical perspective.

At this point in the "Talk" Ludovico introduces a direct comparison between the cultural situation of contemporary artists and the role of the individual in the formation of a mythology. This is a passage famous in the literary history of romanticism for its introduction of the terms "romantic" and "arabesque" and its descriptive definition of what we now call "romantic irony," but it is also important in the romantic construction of "myth." "Here I find a great similarity with the marvellous wit of romantic poetry which does not manifest itself in individual conceptions but in the structure of the whole. . . . This artfully ordered symmetry of contradictions, this wonderfully perennial alternation of enthusiasm and irony . . . seem to me an indirect mythology in themselves" (86). Any given romantic poem can contribute only indirectly to a "new mythology" because its "enthusiasm" (or belief) alternates with subversive "irony," but that same self-conscious (Schiller's "sentimental") alternation is what guarantees that the poem does in fact contribute indirectly because it restores us to that matrix out of which the gods themselves proceed. It serves to "transport us again into that beautiful confusion of imagination, into the original chaos of human nature, for which I know as yet no more beautiful symbol than the motley throng of the ancient gods" (86). These gods have *become* a unified "beautiful symbol" but they too originated out of the "chaos" of imaginative invention as a "motley throng." When Schlegel makes Ludovico say that the new mythology must conceal "the seeds of all other poems," he includes those of the past. He joins Herder in asserting the propaedeutic value of fertilizing the new with the old. "To accelerate the genesis of the new mythology, the other mythologies must also be reawakened" (86–87), not out of nostalgia but because this return to the matrix of mythopoeia will stimulate the fresh growth. This new romantic mythology aspires to incorporate organically past and future. It must be *"the* infinite poem" (my italics) because it is the single coadunation of all story, the "Vine of Fable" itself.

This last proposition—that our self-conscious dividedness will actually be the means by which we achieve the mythology that encompasses the rest—is perhaps more expressive of Schlegel's own central concerns than it is of the actual Schelling's, but the "Talk" is on the whole a very insightful and sympathetic sketch of the young Schelling's thinking about myth. Nevertheless, we need to turn to Schelling's own work to consider a number of significant features of this thinking that are registered only inadequately, if at all, in the "Talk." These include the concept of the artwork as symbolic expression, the relation of this romantic concept of "symbol" to the narrative genre of "myth," the development of a circular metahistorical pattern expressive of the problematic relation of myth to historical contingency, and (the one major development unforeseeable at the time of the "Talk") the evolution of world mythology as a theogonic process.

THEORIZING MYTHIC CONSCIOUSNESS II: SCHELLING AS PHILOSOPHER OF MYTH

Judged by commitment over a lifetime, no artist of the period was more enthusiastic about the new concept of "myth" than the philosopher Friedrich Schelling. Whether or not he actually authored the so-called "Oldest System-Program of German Idealism" (1796), the fragment is riddled with ideas and phrases that turn up in Ludovico's "Talk," and its declaration that "mythology must become philosophical . . . and philosophy must turn mythological" might stand as epigraph in the front of Schelling's career.[6] The first three of his four as yet undiscussed contributions to the construction of "myth" make their appearance in the concluding pages of his youthful masterpiece, *System of Transcendental Idealism,* as the crowning speculations of a long deduction.

Schelling is, of course, one of the most important of those thinkers who struggle in the immediate aftermath of Kant's "critical philosophy" to reclaim for knowledge the foreclosed realm of what Kant stamped as "transcendental." Unable to escape the terms of debate Kant so powerfully established, these thinkers seize upon certain soft spots in the second and third *Critiques* from which to rebuild cases for valid modes of knowing that evade the categories of logical "understanding." The two such prior attempts most meaningful to Schelling are Fichte's and Schiller's. Fichte, the great philosopher of the transcendental, or (as it is more currently fashionable to say in a pejorative sense) "autonomous" ego, deduces the existence of the objective world from the existence and nature of this ego. Fichte's system is a two-term one; the ego realizes itself by a process of definition against what is not itself, the objective world. Schelling's major innovation upon Fichte is to reconceive this dialectic process as triadic. The ego does objectify itself as in Fichte, but this combination transcends itself in a third and higher stage of mind or spirit that recognizes itself in human self-consciousness and in this act recovers its own evolutionary history. We have already experienced in Ludovico's "Talk" some intimation of what the existence of such an unconscious teleological process might mean in relation to the work of the individual poet. But in order to appreciate the epistemological issue raised by this metaphysics—*how* self-consciousness obtains its insight into the union of the consciousness with unconsciousness, the subjective with the objective—we have to turn to the second of the influential mediators between Schelling and Kant, Friedrich Schiller.

In the *Critique of Judgment,* published only in 1790, Kant appears to conceive of aesthetic judgment as affording a middle way between the mind's pragmatic "practical" judgments and the logical categories of the understanding. In his "Analytic of the Beautiful," for example, he claims that our judgments of beauty both in nature and art "reconcile" opposites: they are pleasurable, yet disinterested; seemingly purposive, yet without stateable purpose; presented as universal propositions, yet not logically compelling; general, yet based solely on particulars. Schiller, in his *Letters on the Aesthetic Education of Man* (1795), seizes on this *via media* and promotes the amphibious, paradoxical status of the aesthetic "play-drive" as a faculty of mind capable of mediating between the subjective and the objective, the ideal and the real.

Deeply influenced by *Letters* as well as by the *Critique of Judgment* itself, Schelling goes further in his *System* than any literary theorist of that heady age in his exaltation of art as the reconciler of subject and object, conscious and unconscious. Kant's "aesthetic judgment" and Schiller's "play-drive" produce in Schelling a double response. They persuade him of the existence of an independent realm of aesthetic values that cannot be reduced to terms other than its own, but they also point him toward a genuine "autotelic" or "autonomous" aesthetic, that is, one focused upon the product, the artwork itself. Kant's and Schiller's own aesthetics do not cross this line; they remain "expressive" and "pragmatic" in orientation, focused upon mental faculties in artist or audience. Schelling, however, condenses from their insights, from Goethe's practice, from whatever hints of the new orientation are in the air, an aesthetic that transfers the site of the mental reconciliations of Kant and Schiller to the things that artists make. In the conclusion of *System* he characterizes impressionistically this mode of communication for which he does not yet have a name:

> Art is paramount to the philosopher, precisely because it opens to him, as it
> were, the holy of holies, where burns in eternal and original unity, as if in a
> single flame, that which in nature and history is rent asunder, and in life and
> action, no less than in thought, must forever fly apart. The view of nature,
> which the philosopher frames artificially, is for art the original and natural
> one. What we speak of as nature is a poem lying pent in a mysterious and
> wonderful script. Yet the riddle could reveal itself, were we to recognize in
> it the odyssey of the spirit, which, marvellously deluded, seeks itself, and in
> seeking flies from itself. (Schelling 1978, 232)

Art is the philosopher's "true . . . organ" because the work of art is a synthesis of the
artist's subjective consciousness with whatever degree of the unconscious objectivity
of "nature" he or she has succeeded in wresting into form. Art discloses some of
the "dark ground," as Schelling calls it earlier, that mere discursive analysis always
skates over. But it follows that art achieves this feat in media that by definition
exclude adequate translation and Schelling's figures dramatize this elusiveness. Art
permits us to penetrate the *shekinah* of the Temple of nature for a glimpse within
the holy of holies of ground and consciousness, object and subject, burning in the
flame of "eternal and original unity." It affords us an intuition that the poem "lying
pent" in the undeciphered hieroglyphics of nature will turn out to be the epic of
consciousness itself, the "odyssey of the spirit" still far from its homecoming.

By the time of his Jena lectures of 1801, Schelling had accepted August
Schlegel's recommendation that this "infinite represented in finite fashion" should
be called "symbol."[7] It is no exaggeration to say, as Tsvetan Todorov does, that "if
we had to condense the romantic aesthetic into a single word, it would certainly
be the word 'symbol.'" Encouraged by Leibniz's relatively narrow semiotic usage,
the word had come to signify in the course of the century a type of sign, as in the
phrase "mathematical symbol," a usage that still prevails in the sciences. In the
humanities, however, quite another tradition obtains ever since Kant's definitive
intervention in the *Critique of Judgment*: "Notwithstanding the adoption of the
word *symbolic* by modern logicians in a sense opposed to an intuitive mode of
representation, it is a wrong use of the word . . . for the symbolic is only a *mode* of
the intuitive" (Kant 1986, 222).[8] Schiller, so alert a Kantian in general, recognized
the close connection between this definition of "symbol" in section 59 and Kant's
definition in section 49 of what he calls the "aesthetic idea" as "that representation
of the imagination which induces much thought, yet without the possibility of
any definite thought whatever, i.e., *concept,* being adequate to it" (175–176). Schiller
began using "symbol" in the sense of Kant's "aesthetic idea" in his correspondence
with Goethe, who promptly took it up. It isn't surprising that Schlegel, a welcome
visitor at Weimar, should recommend it in print to Schelling, or that Schelling,
with his close connections to both Weimar and Jena, should quickly seize the
point.

In his Jena lectures Schelling is already valorizing and sharpening the sense of
his new term, "symbol," by contrasting it with "allegory." This distinction becomes
so important a feature of the problematic of "symbol" that it requires a bit of further
attention here. Goethe and Schiller began employing the contrast in conversation

and correspondence, and by 1797 it appears in print (Todorov 1982, 212). After he first formulates it for himself in that same year, Goethe remains its most famous sponsor; influential versions of it appear in several texts across the rest of his career. Todorov's excellent synopsis of Goethe's various versions can serve to characterize the normative romantic understanding of the distinction: "Symbol . . . is productive, intransitive, motivated; it achieves the fusion of contraries; it is and signifies at the same time; its content eludes reason; it expresses the inexpressible. In contrast, allegory . . . is . . . transitive, pure signification, an expression of reason." As Todorov goes on to point out, the two concepts can't be distinguished formally since both "designate the general through the intermediary of a particular." Instead, they are distinguished psychologically "through the process of production and reception; . . . the symbol is produced unconsciously, and it provokes an unending task of interpretation; the allegory is intentional, and can be understood without 'remainder'" (206–207). "Allegory" as thus defined has reached the nadir of its modern discrediting. Its deployment in romantic contexts is essentially diacritical; it is the linguistically unmarked term, signifying that which fails to be "symbol." The distinction, as Hazard Adams remarks in the preface to a particularly elaborate analysis of it, is "not fundamentally one between types of poetic tropes, or between a metaphysical and a rhetorical term, but between what was regarded as the poetic and the non-poetic" (Adams 1983, 12). "Symbol" is "poetry," and art that does not succeed in making itself thus intuitively felt is mere "allegory." The conflation of the first two terms and the scapegoating of the third are moves in the ideological construction of an authoritative mode of access to transcendental truth.

The final step in securing this glorification of aesthetic intuition is the transformation of the romantic symbol from a mode of communication primarily "tautegorical" into one primarily "miraculous." "Tautegorical" is K. P. Moritz's term in his influential *Götterlehre* (1792), (a term later reappropriated by Schelling via Coleridge) to designate mythology as a self-referential category that eludes exhaustive allegorical explanation.[9] I employ it here by logical extension to designate the "intransitive" nature of the post-Kantian "symbol" itself. In the usage of Kant and Goethe and the young Schelling, "symbol" is manifestly "tautegorical." Even though it appears to verge upon "the sublime," there is nothing specifically theological about it. By the eighteen-teens, however, "symbol" has become for various key theorists—Schelling himself, Friedrich Creuzer, Coleridge—"miraculous." This is Hazard Adams's useful label for symbol conceived as participating in some transcendent religious reality.[10] Coleridge's descriptive definition in *The Statesman's Manual* (1816) is a textbook example. As distinguished from "allegory," "a symbol . . . is characterized by the translucence of the Special in the Individual or of the General in the Especial or of the Universal in the General. Above all by the translucence of the Eternal in and through the Temporal. It always partakes of the Reality which it renders intelligible; and while it enunciates the whole, abides itself as a living part of that Unity of which it is the representative" (Coleridge 1972, 30). It's true that this definition refers in context to the revealed word of God ("the statesman's manual" is the Bible) and it might be argued, therefore, that Coleridge does not authorize any assumption that "symbol" in this "miraculous" sense appears in secular productions.

But he declares in the preceding paragraph that it is "Imagination, that reconciling and mediatory power, which . . . gives birth to a system of symbols . . . consubstantial with the truths of which they are the conductors" (29), and immediately after his descriptive definition, in spite of his strategic placement of the words "eternal" and "reality," he characterizes "symbol" (in Greek) as "tautegorical." By the time of Carlyle's *Sartor Resartus,* in any case, the reservations of the pioneers are ignored in that general hardening of the arteries of romanticism characteristic of the later nineteenth century. The "miraculous" conception of "symbol" becomes the norm, and various versions of it survive intact to take on new life in the twentieth century—in literary modernism, in depth psychology, in religious phenomenology. This part of Schelling's legacy is still richly invested.

The second of Schelling's principal contributions in *System* to the romantic construction of "myth" is establishing the relation of "symbol" to the narrative genre of "myth." In the process he blurs the distinctions between them. Schlegel represents Ludovico as doing the same in the "Talk on Mythology" when he presses the paradox that "ancient poetry" is both a "chaos" and "a single, indivisible and perfect poem." The actual Schelling virtually glosses this rather cryptic passage in *System* when he proclaims that "the basic character of a work of art is that of an unconscious infinity. . . . The mythology of the Greeks . . . arose among a people, and in a fashion, which both make it impossible to suppose any comprehensive forethought in devising it, or in the great harmony whereby everything is united into one great whole" (225). Greek mythology *en bloc* is taken as a *single* symbol. More precisely, since Schelling holds like Coleridge that in symbol the particular and the general signify each other, each separate story may be symbolic, *but the whole is also symbolic.* This is the only direct allusion to Greek mythology in *System.* But in his Jena lectures Schelling expands this kernel into an extended fifty-page demonstration that "mythology is the necessary condition and first content of all art" by presenting Greek mythology, taken both as a whole and in representative parts, as the ideal instance (Schelling 1989, 45).[11] Perhaps the most positive construction that can be put upon this evasion of the central theoretical problem is that Schelling's tendency to identify "symbol" and "myth" displays very clearly how the romantics' replacement of "fable" by "myth" is closely analogous to their valorizing of "symbol" over "allegory." Schelling's conflation of "myth" with "symbol" confuses an act of intuitive perception with a discursive genre of narrative. It comprises another part of his legacy that will be all too apparent in twentieth-century theorists of myth who aspire like him to melt discursivity into a flash of intuition.

This eagerness to spatialize discourse in the name of instantaneous perception connects with Schelling's third special contribution in *System,* his metahistorical conception of mythology as unfolding temporally in a spiral pattern. This idea, too, is adumbrated in the vision of a return to a Golden Age that concludes Ludovico's "Talk," but its boldest expression follows in the conclusion of *System* hard upon the celebration of art as a revelation of unity:

> Philosophy was born and nourished by poetry in the infancy of knowledge, and with it all those sciences it has guided toward perfection: we may thus

> expect them, on completion, to flow back like so many individual streams into the universal ocean of poetry from which they took their source. Nor is it in general difficult to say what the medium for this return of science to poetry will be; for in mythology such a medium existed, before the occurrence of a breach seemingly beyond repair. But how a new mythology is itself to arise, which shall be the creation, not of some individual author, but of a new race, personifying, as it were, one single poet—that is a problem whose solution can be looked for only in the future destinies of the world, and in the course of history to come. (233)

Schelling accepts the standard Enlightenment view of an ameliorative evolution of consciousness from a state of wild imagination into the cultivated hegemony of "science." He even conceives of it in a triad of stages analogous to Vico's. But instead of swallowing like Schiller the depressing corollary that science's gain is poetry's loss, he joins Blake and Novalis in a visionary escape from history. Where the two poets insist that historical contingency can be overcome by an apocalyptic act of consciousness, Schelling bends the tragic line of irreversible historical time into a cosmic and comic circle. He extrapolates two future stages that repeat the first two in reverse order, thus presenting a symmetically stadial metahistory of five phases: the "universal ocean of poetry," the intermediate stage of "mythology," the present reign of intellect, the intermediate stage in the return, and "the ocean of poetry." We can label the stages still more schematically as (1) poetry, (2) mythology, (3) science, (4) mythology, and (5) poetry.

"Poetry" is obviously conceived of here in its widest romantic sense as the faculty that, in Shelley's phrase, "marks the before unapprehended relations of things." Schelling's figure of it as a "universal ocean" suggests Ludovico's "beautiful confusion of imagination . . . the original chaos of human nature," an undifferentiated matrix where all conception is potentially present, but in solution. The most original aspect of Schelling's schema, however, is his positing of an intermediate stage of mythology not only behind but ahead, between us and our return to the "ocean" of reintegrated imagination. Schelling probably derives from Herder the idea of mythologizing as a historical phrase in the evolution of culture, but he realizes with more historical concreteness that ancient "science" did indeed grow out of mythological conceptualizing, as in the instance of the pre-Socratics. And this idea produces the further one that mythology must possess an intrinsic mediating quality, which guarantees its historically symmetrical destiny as the mode of thinking that will conduct the scientism of the modern world toward the millennium of the restored oceanic imagination. This conception of the relation of mythology to science is probably the source of Ludovico's utopian counsel in the "Talk" that the way to establish a contemporary mythology is to recast physics in the mythopoeia of totalizing philosophical systems like those of Spinoza and certain unnamed Idealist thinkers. When Schelling speaks of a "*seemingly* irresolvable breach" (my italics) between science and poetry, he acknowledges Schiller's "dissociation" only to deny its permanence. His fourth stage, the return through mythology, is "visionary" in the sense that Blake's and Novalis's allegories of fable are; it imagines a repair of the "fallen" divisions between thought and emotions, subject and object, consciousness and unconsciousness.

The fifth stage, vaguely specified indeed, sounds less like a historical phase than it does a kind of limit-concept. It shares this quality with the first age, which requires us to imagine something like the condition of Vico's giants just before they began to shape their "poetical ideas." But Schelling does not envisage the fifth stage as a simple return to the first. I have implied as much above by referring to the first stage as "undifferentiated" and "in solution" and to the fifth as "restored" and "reintegrated." Evolution, for Schelling, as later for Herbert Spencer in a contrary materialist mode, is articulation and differentiation. It follows that the mythologizing of the fourth stage cannot repeat exactly that of the second. The once historically "naive" or unified sensibility has passed through the furnaces of the "sentimental" or "dissociated" sensibility, and only its redemption by the "progressive universal poetry" of romanticism can constitute the "new mythology" of the fourth stage. A *fortiori*, the fifth stage must be, not some condition of pastoral rest like Blake's "Beulah," but, rather, like his state of "Eden," a condition of "Mental Warfare," a constantly evolving dialectic interchange in the flames of creation. In short, we are contemplating here, as might be expected from the inventor of the triadic dialectic and the first systematic process philosophy, not a mere cyclical but a spiral metahistorical vision of the race's redemption from the contingency of its historical situatedness by its own power of mythogenesis. This is Schelling's equivalent of the visionary poems of his contemporaries. It is a highly influential contribution, as they are, to two major tenets of the romantic construction of myth that are potentially in conflict and in fact ground in the twentieth century two very different conceptions of myth. The first tenet is that mythology belongs to an unconscious, teleological process that is ultimately outside of human time and history, though humans experience its effects from inside. The second tenet, however, is that, as Vico discovered, humans make their social world, and mythopeia, broadly understood, is constitutive of culture.

Schelling's first three contributions are all clearly registered in *System,* published when he was twenty-five. His fourth and last, however, the conception of the unfolding of world mythology as a theogonic process, is the much slower product of the latter part of his career and its ultimate version was published only posthumously in 1856 in *The Philosophy of Mythology*. Like a number of his set, Schelling experienced, in his case around 1803–1804, a renewal of religious belief. Most of his subsequent work can be seen as an effort, extending over a half-century, to reconcile the themes of traditional Christian theodicy with a process philosophy. As part of this effort he transmutes his earlier conception of mythology as stages of a circular metahistorical pattern into the idea of mythmaking as an evolving theogonic process.

The basic elements of this transmutation show up almost immediately, as one can handily see by comparing the version of Schelling's favorite "epic" trope that appears in his *Philosophy and Religion* lectures of 1804 with the version of it in *System* that we have already examined. "History is an epic composed in the mind of God; its major parts are: that which represents the going forth of mankind from its center to its greatest distance from Him and the other which represents its return. The former is the *Iliad,* the latter the *Odyssey,* of history. In the former, the direction was centrifugal, in the latter it is centripetal. . . . The ideas, the spirits, had to fall from their center and enter into nature, the general sphere of the Fall, into particularity, in order that afterwards they might, as particulars, return into the indifference, be reconciled to it, and be in it without disturbing it."[12] In the earlier version there is no author, no "Homer" who composes "the great design." Schelling has now transferred responsibility for the direction of history from a purely immanent creative process to "the mind of God." The terms of the stadial metahistory are recast accordingly. Union with God in "the center" replaces the original "ocean of poetry." Our current state of divided sensibility and mechanistic *wissenschaft* is "the greatest distance from Him." Schelling's assertion that "the ideas . . . *had* to fall" (my italics) in order to return into the "indifference" (God as Absolute) displays the impact upon his thinking at this time of the theosophy of Jacob Boehme.[13] Boehme advances the hypothesis of two "centers" in God: a dark principle of Will that is the source of His being, its "Unground," and a contrary principle of light and love that continually struggles with and masters the dark. Schelling defines a person as an individuating consciousness, and even a personal God must therefore evolve, unlike the former impersonal Absolute. God is indeed Alpha and Omega, "but as Alpha he is not what he is as Omega" (Lovejoy 1936, 323).[14] Out of His internal contestation a cosmic fall occurs, probably identical with the Creation represented in *Genesis.* Schelling's bold trope of history as God's double epic suggests that the "ideas" implicit in the eternal event of God's self-overcoming are concretized in external creation and experienced by humankind in the temporal discursive mode of evolving mythological narrative, as part of a divine process by which they are to be fully reintegrated within the triumphant Deity.

Schelling's theological reconstruction of his circular metahistorical theory still preserves the characteristic ambiguity of the "visionary" phase of romanticism about the relation of the transcendent to linear history. In fact, Schelling resorts, in order to conceptualize this relation, to the same pseudo-Gnostic theosophical tradition that inspires Blake and Novalis. Schelling's reconceiving of God in terms of organicism and dialectical sublation does qualify him as a genuine precursor of modern process theologies, but he does not identify God wholly with becoming as, say, Whitehead will do. Instead, he adopts a Boehme-like compromise; God's moment of self-realization "takes place" simultaneously as an internal event in the *nunc stans* of eternity and as the unfolding of history in the fallen world. When Schelling eventually reframes this providential pattern specifically in terms of the development of world mythology, he will continue to preserve this ambiguity so crucial to romantic transcendence.

In the ten years or so after *Philosophy and Religion,* Schelling concentrated more directly upon the classical issues of theodicy. But he was much impressed and stirred into renewed involvement in mythology by Friedrich Creuzer's *Symbolik und Mythologie der Alter Völker* (1821). Schelling's refutation in his treatise on *The Deities of Samothrace* of Creuzer's thesis about these gods, the Cabiri, and his objections to Creuzer's conceptions of "symbol" and "myth" during the disputes over Creuzer's *Symbolism* stimulate the work on mythology that occupies him through the 1820s, is the subject of his Berlin lectures in the early 1840s, and is published posthumously as *The Philosophy of Mythology.*

Schelling finally fuses in this work his theological speculations, his metahistorical schema, and his convictions about the evolution of world mythology. What happens between the Alpha and the Omega of God's sublation of his dark principle is reflected in the fallen world of time in the parabolic voyage of mankind's sacred storytelling. A passage like the following from the theoretically significant introduction testifies to this fusion of concerns: "As long as man remains in the center, he sees things . . . as they exist in God. . . . But even though fallen, man may still wish to reclaim his central position. . . . Then, man's struggles and gropings to cling fast to this disordered and fragmented but still primarily divine moment will produce a mediating world. . . . This world of the gods is produced in an involuntary manner as a consequence of the necessity imposed on man through his primal condition" (Schelling 1957, 206).[15] Humanity utters through its mythological constructions fragmented but valid intuitions of its former "central position." Each human group engaged in such corporate efforts produces "a mediating world," a given culture's unique version of the universal intuition. Furthermore, humanity produces this mediating world "in an involuntary manner" imposed by its "primal condition." Schelling makes here the stunning Platonic assertion that thanks to inherent recollection of our original unity with God, *we have no choice but to produce mythology.* He may even be claiming that we have no choice about *how* we produce it; the *anamnesis* of the archetypes may follow invariant laws of the evolution of consciousness. "Mythology arises . . . as a consequence of a process, especially of a theogonic character, in which human consciousness finds itself engaged by its own nature" (204). This is the apotheosis of Schelling's early faith that an evolutionary process beyond human ken will ultimately transform individual efforts into a genuine mythology. He now envisions the evolution of religious consciousness itself as clearly teleological, a "theogonic process" of which, as he later remarks, "the true religion will be the last mythology which reunites all previous Moments" (212).

Schelling intended that the principles enunciated in his introduction should be validated by his subsequent exposition of the dialectical history of world mythology. He carries this history up to the point where it yields to Christianity, the further dialectical evolution of which is reserved for his complementary late study, *Philosophie der Offenbarung* (1856). Schelling's insistence that Christianity is not simply "mythology" but "revelation" implies that it must be destined to be somehow "the last mythology" spoken of in the "Introduction." This ultimate role does not necessarily preclude further "theogonic" evolution within Christianity itself; by definition, after all, the process must in some sense continue as long as human imagination exists. But Schelling attends only to his retrospective history, and what he produces is of no further theoretical value. His dialectical treatment of mythology resembles nothing so much, in its Eurocentric exclusions and inclusions and its remorselessly forced triads, as Hegel's lectures written at almost exactly the same time and published, also posthumously, as *The Philosophy of History.* The former schoolmates are parochial, arbitrary, and implausible in similar ways. Whatever may be the case with respect to theology, Schelling's theoretical contributions to the construction of "myth" end with his introduction to *The Philosophy of Mythology.* But these contributions—his insistence on the power of the modern artist to create myth anew, his conception of it as "tautegorical," his endowing of it with "miraculous" access to the transcendent, his envisioning of its salvific role in the evolution of consciousness, and his thematizing of its ambiguous relation to an eternal paradigm— are so definitive of the romantic construction of "myth" that Schelling's thought lives on wherever it does.

THE ROMANTIC IDEOLOGY OF MYTH RECONSIDERED

Up to this point, I have presented the crucial formative assumptions in Blake, Novalis, Schlegel, and Schelling, with a minimum of reservation. But the romantic foundations of the construction of "myth" determine so much of the concept's subsequent history—often in ways that have been ignored or misunderstood—that a more critical look at these assumptions here should repay the investment many times over. Within the last generation the entire romantic ideology has been reexamined in terms that certainly apply to that essential product of autonomous authority, the "new mythology." In *The Literary Absolute* Philippe Lacoue-Labarthe and Jean-Luc Nancy make the case that "Literature" is specifically the invention of the Jena *Atheneum* group. "Literature" signifies for these critics not merely the self-contained realm of the aesthetic, but also writing concerned to produce its own theoretical basis and therefore dismissive of the traditional distinction between "poetry" or "fabulation" on one hand and "criticism" or "theory" on the other. They demonstrate that this conceptual bootstrapping of "Literature" not only elicits the supplement, in the Derridean sense, of endless critical explanation, but that the writers, particularly Friedrich Schlegel in his "fragments" and Novalis in his "aphorisms," were well aware of this ironic supplementarity and built it into their work in an effort at sublation.

Schelling states the unadorned major aporia with exemplary honesty when, as we've seen, he permits himself to confess at the end of his vision of spiral return in *System,* "But how a new mythology (which cannot be the invention of an individual poet but of a new generation that represents things as if it were a single poet) can itself arise, is a problem for whose solution we must look to the future destiny of the world and to the course of history alone." Schelling understands that endless acts of isolated and socially powerless modern mythopoeia may not add up to the thing he imagines the Greeks had. But he also refuses to surrender his faith in the teleology of a beneficent universal Process. He simply sets cheek by jowl, without even a gesture toward resolution, his "enthusiasm" and his "irony." Schlegel puts into the mouth of his fictive Schelling an apparently optimistic exhortation. But, if we look closely at the argument supporting Ludovico's "enthusiasm," we see it offers only the coldest of comforts—indefinite, if not endless, deferral. Romantic poetry itself does not produce any new mythology except the "reflexive" sort that consists of celebrating the power of the imagination *to* produce a new mythology. Contemporary writers ambitious to come up with the actual goods are advised to reawaken the old in order to "accelerate the genesis of the new." A viable mythology, then, is both behind them and ahead of them, but it is not *for* them. In fact, they are for *it,* in the same sense in which a dedicated revolutionary sacrifices his or her happiness for the benefit of future generations. Even Ludovico's inspirational example, the way the "chaos" of ancient Greek story became "a single, indivisible and perfect poem," is double-edged; it acknowledges that the construction looked like "chaos" at the time and exists as "indivisible" artifact only at the other end of a Hegelian telescope. The message to the modern artist is to sustain his or her "wonderfully perennial alternation of enthusiasm and irony," actually the record of painful personal struggle, in the hope that in the deferred millennium the self-conscious irony will be transformed into the very thing that it is not.[16]

A comparable aporia dogs the central epistemological mechanism of authoritative romantic insight, the "symbol." Its advocates gloss over a serious conceptual difficulty. As we've considered briefly in the case of Schelling, they generally induce us to think of "symbol" as apprehended in the flick of an eye, even while they apply the concept to entire narratives, or collections of narratives, as in the instances of Greek mythology as a whole and the Bible. This usage raises, but evades, the question of how the *parousia* of the eternal in time can possibly be distributed over a plot. The difficulty was exposed in a manner that caused a considerable stir among German theorists by the appearance of Friedrich Creuzer's *Symbolik und Mythologie der Alten Völker.* As Creuzer's very title indicates, he makes a crucial distinction between symbol and myth, and he does this by facing up to the contrast between symbol's immediate presentability and myth's narrative dimension. The results are epitomized in this direct comparison: "In symbol a universal concept takes on earthly garb and steps as a meaningful image before the eye of the soul. In myth the full soul manifests its premonitions or knowledge in a living word. It is also an image, but of a sort that reaches its inner meaning by another route, through the ear" (Creuzer 1821, vol. 1, 90). Symbol retains its transcendental qualia; it is visual, instantaneous, and involuntary. But myth is auditory, discursive, and intentional. It isn't surprising that this distinction precipitated a scholarly row. Up to this point contemporary romantic speculation about the relation between the two terms was conveniently hazy and undertheorized. Creuzer's formulation of it becomes the classic registration of a major aporia in the transcendental conception of myth that persists to this day. Even Creuzer, and even in this epigrammatic moment, blurs the clarity of his contrast by resorting to the third term, *"bild,"* "image," of which myth as well as symbol is said to be a mode. This backsliding notion of narrative as, after all, just a kind of "image" was to have a large impact in twentieth-century literary criticism after its valorizing in *symboliste* and modernist aesthetics. "Image" becomes perhaps the single most abused word in midcentury aesthetics. Creuzer's introduction of it in this context did not, however, fool his critics about his conception of the relative status of symbol and myth. Schelling, for example, objects in his introduction to *The Philosophy of Mythology,* as Burton Feldman points out (Feldman and Richardson, 388), that Creuzer's distinction relegates "myth" to the secondary, inferior status of "allegory."

But what if myth, by virtue of its nature as narrative, is indeed more appropriately thought of as allegory? This possibility, so inimical to the romantic conception of myth, was revived a generation ago, and as a direct result of Creuzer's influence. When Walter Benjamin was writing his dissertation, *On the Origins of German*

Tragic Drama (1924–1925), he consulted Creuzer in connection with his chapter on allegory in the Baroque *trauerspielen* and recognized the value of his distinction if applied negatively. That is, he takes Creuzer as having exposed a contradiction that discredits the "miraculous" symbol and establishes all mere secular meaning as "allegory." Since all interpretation is hopelessly after the fact, "allegories are, in the realm of thoughts, what ruins are in the realm of things" (Benjamin 1971, 178).[17] Benjamin's brief and gnomic hints become the nucleus of Paul de Man's revaluation of the romantic distinction in his influential essay "The Rhetoric of Temporality." De Man attacks the "symbol" as self-mystification, in "bad faith," and promotes "allegory" as the honest recognition of the ineradicable gap between experience and meaning. He remind us, too, of the extent to which the romantics linked "allegory" with "irony" on the very grounds of temporality that underlie Creuzer's distinction. "The art of irony," he says, "reveals the existence of a temporality that is definitely not organic, in that it relates to its source only in terms of distance and difference and allows for no end, for no totality. . . . Allegory and irony are thus linked in their common discovery of a truly temporal predicament [and] in their common demystification of an organic world postulated in a symbolic mode" (De Man 1983, 222). De Man takes a darkly existentialist view of a condition that thinkers like Schlegel and Schelling fondly hope will be sublated in an evolving process, but he is right about their frequent association of "allegory" with the "ironic" side of the alternation between "enthusiasm" and "irony."[18] On this view, even the hard-core inventors of "Literature" concede implicitly that unless or until redeemed in the course of time, "myth" is not the "enthusiastic" breakthrough of symbolic poetry into transcendent truth, but the "ironic" discourse of allegorical narrative struggling to make sense.

When we examine the practice of poets who shared the assumptions of the theorists (and were much more instrumental in effecting their wide dissemination in literary culture during the later nineteenth century), we encounter increasingly paradoxical versions of this same gap between aspiration and achievement. If even Blake and Novalis produce allegories of fable rather than the transformative mythologies whose possibility they affirm, it isn't surprising that later romantics express darker reservations. On one hand, these poets accept and celebrate their alleged roles as visionaries and, following Goethe's early success, develop the mythological poem as an outward and visible sign of an inward grace. On the other, the celebrated poems do not so much enact moments of unqualified visionary triumph as thematize their failure to do so. These efforts are increasingly paradoxical; as the poets become ever more successful in persuading themselves and their public that they are, in Shelley's phrase, "the unacknowledged legislators of the world," they express increasingly severe discouragement about their failures to become such lawmakers. However modern students of romanticism categorize and explain it, they are quite well agreed about the gradual darkening of tone in German and English writing between 1790 and 1830. I have distinguished with respect to myth two stages after the visionary optimism of Blake and Novalis: one of "doubt," in which celebrations of visionary access alternate with self-critical analysis of inability to sustain them, and one of "despair," in which the poet dramatizes compulsively, perhaps morbidly, the gap between yearning for such vision and his existential plight.[19] Among English poets, Wordsworth's practice may illustrate "doubt" as it earlier did "nostalgia," while certain poems of the most important younger writers affected by him, Shelley and Keats, should probably fall under the rubric "despair."

Wordsworth explicitly juxtaposes and struggles to reconcile his phases of "nostalgia" and "doubt" in the discussion of Greek myth in book 4 of *The Excursion* (1814). According to a standard literary-historical view, this well-known passage contributed significantly to the popularity of Greek mythology in England and America in the later century.[20] No doubt it did, but only by virtue of some quite willful reading. In trying to cheer up "the Solitary" (Wordsworth "nostalgic"), whose rapport with the world has been alienated by Enlightenment rationalism, "the Wanderer" (Wordsworth "doubting") argues that the "all-pervading Spirit upon whom / Our dark foundations rest" has never left mankind without spiritual resource (Wordsworth 1933, 969–970). After men no longer experienced divine revelation directly, Providence arranged, among the Persians, the Babylonians, the Chaldeans, that they should come to know divinity through personifications of nature. "The Wanderer" echoes German thought when he maintains that this mode of conceiving deity culminates in the polytheism of the Greeks. The passages describing how the Greeks transformed their landscapes (218–762, 848–887) are particularly glowing verse, reminiscent of "The World Is Too Much with Us." But, just as the sonnet risks a sentimental reading that is distracted by the beauty of the images from the starkness of what is being said, so do these passages in *The Excursion*. In the actual argument, the "Solitary" responds to the "Wanderer's" eloquence with an anguished objection that such faith is no longer possible, and the Wanderer implicitly concedes this when he replies that, fortunately, belief in personified deities is only one of the possible modes by which the "all-pervading Spirit" can sustain our imaginations. We can still find the divine through nature. As a child hears a seashell express "mysterious union with its native sea," so the shell of the cosmos imparts to the ear of Faith "authentic tidings of . . . central peace, subsisting at the heart / Of endless agitation" (1140–1146). As in the case of the figures of sea, moon and wind in the "nostalgic" sonnet, the beauty of the figure here may tempt the reader to sublimate the honest implication of the analogy— that an adult would have to recover the wishful naiveté of a very young child in order to mistake the "endless agitation" of his or her own circulatory system for "authentic tidings" from the cosmos.

Wordsworth enacts in this passage a struggle, out of the mere celebration of the Greek mode of mythopoeia, "sentimental" in both Schiller's sense and his own, toward a positive assertion of the visionary power that must still lie in that matrix out of which all mythologies emerge, the interactions between the creative mind and its natural environment. But he achieves his most direct and important statement of this effort only with his "Prospectus" in the preface to the poem. There the poet, feeling the onset of power to write his long-meditated "philosophical poem," affirms that his theme is greater even than Milton's in *Paradise Lost* since he will investigate a place more sublime and terrific than the one Satan explored—"the

Mind of Man" (40). This is a realm "to which the heaven of heavens is but a veil" (30). Behind the *shekinah* of any natural mythopoeia, then, lies "Beauty—a living presence of the earth" (42). Attended by her the speaker avers that this world can be transformed. "Paradise and groves / Elysian, Fortunate Fields—like those of old / Sought in the Atlantic Main—why should they be / A history only of departed things, / Or a mere fiction of what never was? / For the discerning intellect of Man / When wedded to this goodly universe / In love and holy passion, shall find these / A simple produce of the common day" (46–55).

The passage presents in itself an unshadowed assertion of the power, even the political power, of vision; Novalis himself could ask no more. In fact, the speaker's wedding appears to be the same event as the triple marriage that concludes Klingsohr's *märchen*. But the speaker is describing what *would* be the case if the wedding *were* consummated. What he says next admits how hypothetical, how deferred that event must be: "I, long before the blissful hour arrives, / Would chant, in lonely peace, the spousal verse / of this great consummation—and by words / Which speak of nothing more than what we are, / Would I arouse the sensual from their sleep / Of death" (56–61). The exalted tone, continuous with the preceding passage, partly masks the enormity of what is here conceded. Wordsworth struggles with the problem identified so bluntly by Schelling—the gulf between private and public vision. The speaker contradicts himself in a manner that deconstructs his aspiration. If he could really command words so unequivocal that they "speak of nothing more than what we are," so apocalyptic that they "arouse the sensual from their sleep / Of death," then the "blissful hour" would be at hand; it would arrive instantly, as in the epic wish-fulfillments of Blake and Novalis and the Shelley of *Prometheus Unbound*. But the speaker's yearning to be indulged in the consolation of chanting this spousal verse "in lonely peace" and "long before" the hour arrives confesses an awareness that no matter *how* eloquently he speaks out, he must content himself with private withdrawal and endless deferral.

Shelley's "Ode to the West Wind" is a darker version of this same transaction. He follows the older poet in two essential matters. First he withdraws his emotional investment from the construction of an actual revolutionary mythology to the mere contemplation of the visionary power to do so. Then he beseeches the "Spirit" of the organic cosmos to make him "the trumpet of a prophecy" that would both precede, and yet somehow also inaugurate, the millennium of the new mythology (Shelley 1966, 215). But where Wordsworth's speaker expresses a dignified wish for private consolation, Shelley's utters a desperate, near-hysterical prayer. After celebrating for three stanzas the power of the autumnal wind to alter the earth, the sky, and the sea, he acknowledges in the fourth the gulf between his self-consciousness and these natural elements. In the terrible cry "O lift me as a wave, a leaf, a cloud," as again in the tropes for his "dead thoughts" in the fifth stanza (a heap of "withered leaves," "ashes and sparks" from a not-quite-extinguished hearth), he expresses his wish to *be* such involuntary organic matter if only he might be swept like it before the Spirit. Shelley locates the power of prophecy itself, not in the wedding of mind and universe, but in the impersonal rape of the one by the other. As in the case of "Prospectus," the exalted tone and diction of the "Ode's" conclusion has swept many a reader before it.[21] Yet the imperatives of this last stanza—"Make me thy lyre," "Be thou me," and the rest—are still part of the speaker's striving with the wind in "sore need" of identification with it (215). Meanwhile, the fourth stanza stands uncorrected as a mercilessly clear recognition that this demand will not, cannot, be met.

For our purposes, Keats's most significant probings of what he recognized as "dark passages" first explored by Wordsworth are his mythological narratives, "Hyperion" and "The Fall of Hyperion." "Hyperion" is the fragment of an epic about the supersession of the Titanic deities by the Olympians, and especially of the sun god, Hyperion, by Apollo. Keats plainly identifies the Titans with his own early pastoral poetry, the Olympians with his "gradually darkened" consciousness, and Apollo's apotheosis with own his visionary ambitions. When the narrative reaches the point where the author must dramatize this necessary apotheosis, Apollo, apparently overwhelmed by the access of visionary knowledge, utters a shriek, loses consciousness, and the poem breaks off, unfinished.

When Keats made a second attempt on this subject during the following summer, he produced a second fragment, "The Fall of Hyperion," a strikingly different poem as far as it goes. The nature of Keats's changes in the story demonstrate his rapidly maturing awareness of the questionability of visionary aspirations. This growth is expressed most profoundly in his change of generic model from "objective" classical epic to "subjective" medieval dream-vision. The essence of the medieval genre is that its narrator recounts a dream framed in the circumstances of his waking life and constituting a commentary on something with which he needs to come to terms. This radical shift of genre expresses Keats's recognition that the stages of consciousness represented in the earlier version were in fact autobiographical, and the change enables him to commence this time with a prologue that dramatizes directly an anguished and intricately plotted interrogation of the dreamer-poet's claim to visionary authority. Although Keats does manage to reach briefly again in this version the actual story of Hyperion's fall, even this story, because it is now mediated for the dreamer through the consciousness of Moneta (the Admonisher, his principal interrogator), becomes part of the testing that will determine whether he is a mere "dreamer" or a genuine poet, a visionary capable of pouring out "a balm upon the world" (Keats 1966, 201). It appears that the subsequent reenactment of the entire epic action would have been part of this purgatorial inquisition. And we know from the narrator's opening remarks that in spite of Keats's representation of a process of deepening vision, the dreamer's doubts about his status are never resolved within the poem. Whereas the true "poet," according to Moneta, employs his prophetic power for social good, the "dreamer" can be granted even by her only the backward contemplation of the cost of evolving consciousness. Moneta merely leads him further on his exploration of the "dark passages." "The Fall of Hyperion" follows some of them further into the shadows than even Wordsworth had permitted himself to go. It finds a way to explore, in more detail than Wordsworth's or Shelley's comparable testimony, the burden of responsibility that belief in the romantic ideology of myth loads upon the individual artist. Even the chief German theorists of this ideology, like the line of English poets who struggle to live by it, testify incisively to its *aporiae* as well as its aspirations. They pass along to their successors in the nineteenth and twentieth centuries their conflicts between self-doubt and persuasion that authoritative vision is theirs to create. The self-doubt is subsequently often ignored by later readers while the visionary power is accepted as fact. This is an irony of reception-history that will crop up recurrently in later chapters.

[3]

The Struggle between Myth and "Suspicion"

The romantic inventors of "myth," theorists and poets alike, consciously construct it as a privileged site in the modern agon between belief and disbelief. And the history of the new concept remains during the nineteenth century largely the record of an intensifying struggle between what Schlegel called "enthusiasm" and "irony." On one hand, the notion of "myth" as vehicle of access to transcendence becomes increasingly reified in middle-class culture, particularly in literary circles. On the other, this success generates the first major counterattacks, the critiques that culminate in Marx and Nietzsche. These latter introduce into the construction of the concept two of the three major kinds of theories that depart from its romantic glorification. The line of thought that proceeds from Hegel to Marx introduces the conception of myth as false consciousness, that is, as ideological, while Nietzsche registers, somewhat proleptically, that view of myth as pragmatically necessary fiction that I've termed on the strength of some of its later manifestations as constitutive. The third major departure from the romantic matrix, subsequently referred to as the folkloristic or anthropological also makes its definitive appearance at this time, most conspicuously in the work of the Brothers Grimm. This third strain does not, at first, fit the pattern of arising out of a dialectical quarrel with its romantic origins. In the longer run, however, this strain's novel tack of taking "myth" seriously as an actual genre of storytelling combines with ethnological fieldwork to produce another, and perhaps the most thorough, of departures from transcendental pretensions. The chapter that follows juxtaposes accounts of the rise of these three new views of myth against evidence of the entrenchment, especially in literary and artistic circles, of the originary romantic premises.

HEGEL'S "STRUGGLE OF ENLIGHTENMENT WITH SUPERSTITION"

It's worth recalling that G. W. F. Hegel began his career in intense association with Schelling and Hölderlin, even collaborating with them on a small treatise on myth. Though his mature philosophy is ultimately a severe rationalism, he knew romanticism from the inside. In the section of *Phenomenology of the Spirit* (1807) titled "The Struggle of Enlightenment with Superstition," he offers a remarkable account of the contestation, an account that could serve not merely as prolegomenon to his own contribution to the first major critique of romantic myth, the one that leads to Marx, but also to the pattern to be described in this chapter as a whole. As usual in the *Phenomenology,* the account manages to suggest simultaneously an epitome of the intellectual history of the preceding decades, an oblique confession of Hegel's own mental growth, and the prophetic discovery of a spiral developmental pattern that promises repeated versions of the same struggle throughout the course of modernity. Basing himself upon Kant's famous definition of Enlightenment, Hegel declares the essence of that historical phenomenon to be the universalizing of "pure insight," which he defines as "the spirit that calls to every consciousness: be *for* yourselves what you are *in* yourselves—rational" (Hegel 1967, 588).[1] "Insight" first finds "belief" to be a "tissue of superstitious prejudices and errors," and then "sees the consciousness embracing this content organized into a realm of error, in which false insight is the general sphere of consciousness" (561). This characterization of "insight's" discovery is a momentous one; it not only identifies for the first time what will commonly come to be called "false consciousness," but it also equates that consciousness with a sum of social practices, thus opening the way for the Marxian conception of "ideology."

It's very tempting to examine in detail the subsequent brilliant analysis of the struggle between the two contrary forms of "pure consciousness" (561), but we must skip to the conclusion where Hegel insists that belief has been reduced to "the same thing as enlightenment; . . . the difference is merely that one is enlightenment satisfied, while belief is enlightenment dissatisfied" (589). If this characterization of modern religious belief and/or of romanticism appears like neutrality forgone in favor of "enlightenment," the reader has only to take in the stunning concession in Hegel's continuation: "It will yet be seen whether enlightenment can continue in its state of satisfaction; that longing of the troubled, beshadowed Spirit, mourning over the loss of its spiritual world, lies in the background. Enlightenment has on it this stain of unsatisfied longing" (589). Both states are now utterly contaminated with one another and ripe to become a third thing, as yet unknown.

For reasons that begin to be apparent, the question of where Hegel stands in relation to this struggle is famously susceptible to contrary answers. On the side of "belief," he can be said to accept the romantic view that, while an alienated consciousness is of the essence of modernity, an interiorizing dialectic sublates the contraries of "enthusiasm" and "irony."[2] In Hegel's history of consciousness, in fact, romantic art phases directly into religion in ways that will remind readers of English poetry of Blake's conception of Jesus as the Divine Imagination. Hegel would thus appear to sanction the most idealized readings of productions like the poems of Goethe or Wordsworth and hence to underwrite, with his widespread influence in the later century, the romantic claim to authoritative vision.[3]

On the side of "enlightenment," however, Hegel's account of the stages in the return of Absolute Spirit to itself presents a view of mythopoeia that is, by romantic standards, belittling. The three modes of knowing Absolute Spirit—art, religion, and philosophy—may appear equal in the sense that each is a valid way to grasp the same object. But they constitute a privileged hierarchy in two respects, one conceptual and one narrative. "Conceptual" is an almost unavoidable play on words here. The operative distinction that creates the hierarchy of value among the three modes of knowing Spirit depends upon Hegel's concept of "concept" (*der Begriff*). This assumes that conceptualizing is perfected in proportion as it approaches complete abstraction and sheds the figurative representations (*die Vorstellungen*) that cling to sensuous apprehension.[4] Art is therefore inferior to religion because it must embody its intuitions of the Absolute in sensuous forms, whereas religion, denying antithetically that any particulars are adequate, is a direct *feeling* of relation to the Absolute. But religion is in turn inferior to philosophy since it must still express its feeling in figurative representations, whereas philosophy, sublating the contraries, apprehends the Absolute in purely rational concepts. The pejorative potential in these relations becomes even more apparent when they are studied in conjunction with the narrative or diachronic aspect of the system. Since Hegel identifies his logic with his metaphysics, and both with his history of consciousness, he takes it for granted that the process of world history will unfold this set of conceptual relations. Art and religion, however honorable their historical roles, are veils between humanity and its ultimate mental clarity. What emerges, therefore, is a more wily metahistorical theory of Enlightenment, and it is this side of Hegel's thought that inspires the first major critique of romantic "myth."[5]

STRAUSS AND FEUERBACH: MYTH AS FALSE CONSCIOUSNESS

In his letter of defense addressed to the Director of Studies at Tübingen after the publication of his *Life of Jesus* (1835), D. F. Strauss presents himself as an unworldly, idealistic young scholar quite surprised that the pursuit of current developments in his field should give offense.[6] He points out how natural it is that one who combines "two designated directions in present day theology, the philosophical and the critical," should come out where he does (60). To grasp Strauss's role in the critique of myth, it will be useful to pry apart these two "directions" whose combination, he insists, is the sum of his originality.

First, the "critical" direction. The radical questioning of the authenticity of various aspects of both Testaments was the work of the skeptics, deists, and rationalists of the preceding century. The "critical" trend to which Strauss refers is not so much hostile debunking as an attempt by believing theologians to subsume this critique. In his introduction to *The Life of Jesus,* Strauss locates himself in the history of this latter movement in a section called "Development of the Mythical Point of View." Obviously modeling himself on Hegel, the young scholar presents *his* method as the discovery toward which the movement has been struggling. The method is this: first, he presents what he calls the "supernatural" elements in the narrative, as literally asserted and traditionally understood; then he presents the antithesis, the rationalistic objections of modern unbelievers; finally, he sublates both in his "mythical point of view." He focuses, for example, on the "Annunciation and Birth of John the Baptist" in *Luke,* briefly summarizing the story, presenting at length the "offense against our modern notions" and then the rationalistic theologians' clumsy and even silly attempts to explain them away (perhaps, for example, John's father, Zacharias, mistook a flash of lightning for an angel). Strauss then swoops to the rescue with his "mythic" explanation that John's ministry and his relation to Jesus were so strongly associated with the latter's messiahship that the circumstances of John's birth too were patterned after miraculous elements in the births of Ishmael, Isaac, Samson, and Samuel. The great bulk of *The Life of Jesus* applies this same procedure to constellations of improbability in the birth and early life of Jesus, the history of his public ministry, his teachings, miracles, and, above all his passion, death, resurrection, and ascension.

The *Life of Jesus* resembles Frazer's *Golden Bough* in owing some of its widespread impact outside of its field of specialization to being an ingeniously organized and strikingly well-written presentation of matter that had been accumulating piecemeal for several generations in more recondite sources. But the work's impact is also more negative than Strauss (perhaps disingenuously) is willing to allow. In his seminary letter he says he felt free, "supported by the philosophical conviction of the intrinsically true content of *New Testament* history [compare Hegel], to allow its historical form to be ruthlessly investigated by criticism" (60). The investigation is ruthless indeed. In the first place, Strauss's summaries of the "supernatural" are *de facto* reductions to absurdity. In the second, his long, painstaking assemblages of just what readers might find questionable are particularly compendious massings of objections; they owe much of their power to their overwhelming accumulation. But the crucial factor in the work's negative impact is that its attempts to sublate these troubling cruces by the "mythical method" are much less convincing than their deadpan initial presentations. This is largely the result of Strauss's fundamentally negative conception of "myth." He writes as if there had been no romantic movement in Germany. He has the word "myth," by now fashionable, and he has absorbed the eighteenth-century idea that it signifies the spontaneous product of a whole people, but he combines this conviction with his Hegelian notion that the representations thus produced comprise a tissue of false consciousness, veiling the concepts of pure religion. As one consequence of this combination of ideas (even constructive contemporary critics like his teacher, Baur, pointed this out), Strauss underestimates the degree to which "myth" in the New Testament may be conscious. Luke may have *intended* to associate the births of John and Jesus with those of Samson and Samuel. This is a line of thought that supersedes Strauss by the turn of the century under the guise of "Form Criticism."[7] But Strauss seems never to have grasped his critics' point clearly. In order to do so, he would have had to be able to take in the romantic conception of mythopoeia as a positive faculty of mind.

Instead, Strauss's "myth" is Hegel's *vorstellung* writ large, everything that gets between us and pure *begriff*. Strauss passes on to Feuerbach and Marx, however, two elements of the theory not conspicuous in Hegel. The first might be called, in Comtean phrase, "the religion of humanity," and the second the explicit historicizing of myth. The first marks the most important difference between Hegel's philosophy of religion and Strauss's. Hegel makes it quite clear, in his *Philosophy of History* lectures, for example, that he believes the concrete universal was once historically realized in the person of Jesus Christ. Strauss, who maintains even in his seminary *apologia* that the goal of Hegel's philosophy of religion is "to spiritualize the positive, factual element in Christianity . . . to sublimate it," is scandalized by this ultimate backsliding (Horton Harris 1973, 59). "Is not the unity of the divine and human natures," he asks in his "Concluding Dissertation," "much more a real one in an infinitely higher sense, when I conceive the whole of humanity as its realization than when I single out an individual? . . . Is not an incarnation of God from eternity, a truer one than an incarnation limited to a particular point in time" (Strauss 1970, vol. 2, 779–780)?[8] This version of the Incarnation not only epitomizes Strauss's "religion of humanity"; it is also the climax of his general policy of saving Christianity for modern belief by rescuing its timeless significance from the gross limitations of material history. Since Strauss aspires to shed historical concreteness here, it may seem perverse to say that he teaches Feuerbach and Marx the lesson of myth's historical situatedness. But he does so by negative example. The romantics and Hegel conceive much more profoundly than Strauss the problematics of the relation of eternity to time, synchrony to diachrony. Where Hegel's "concrete universal," for example, permits belief in a historical though interiorized Jesus (like Blake's), Strauss creates a theological version of one of the great *aporiae* of historicism. On one hand, he envisions myth as the product of a historically outmoded *weltanschauung;* on the other, he assumes that *he* transcends his moment to apprehend a timeless essence of Christianity.[9] Feuerbach and Marx accept the historical contextualizing of myth, but, having done so, insist that this insight must therefore be applied with methodological rigor to contemporary consciousness.

Feuerbach still makes an immense effort to save religious belief for the modern world by interpreting Strauss as demonstrating that humanity owes it to its *own* divinity to purify itself of all forms of false consciousness. It's Feuerbach, rather than Strauss, who expresses in *The Essence of Christianity* the marked shift in cultural taste more or less concurrent with the deaths of Hegel and Goethe (in 1831 and 1832). Where Strauss still advocates a Hegelianized theology, Feuerbach rejects all systematic idealism in the name of what he calls "materialism." His use of the term is very loose but obviously makes the sort of gruff appeal to pragmatic empiricism still current in ordinary language. "I found my ideas," he growls in diction Marx remembered, "on materials which can be appropriated only through the activity of the senses. I do not generate the object from the thought, but the thought from the object" (Feuerbach 1957, xxxiv). Based on this reversal of relation between the Hegelian subject and predicate (to use Feuerbach's own formulation of his achievement), he declares that all religion is the hypostatizing of subjective feelings. "Religion is human nature reflected; mirrored in itself" (63). When objectified outside humankind as a realm of supernature, however, these representations are repressive, idolatrous delusions, "projections" in the modern psychological sense.[10] Feuerbach therefore builds his exposition of "The True or Anthropological Essence of Religion" by contrasting it with "The False or Theological Essence." In the anthropological sense, "to think is to be God" (40). Every prayer "discloses the secret of the Incarnation, every prayer is in fact an incarnation of God" (54). "In prayer man adores his own heart, regards his own feelings as absolute" (125). Feuerbach's Christology presents this epigrammatically elegant revision of Strauss's: "Christ . . . is the consciousness of the species. . . . He therefore who loves man for the sake of man, who rises to the love of the species, he is a Christian, is Christ himself" (269). But whenever morality "is based on theology, whenever the right is made dependent on divine authority, the most immoral, unjust, infamous things can be justified and established . . . To derive anything from God is nothing more than to withdraw it from the test of reason, to institute it as indubitable, unassailable, sacred, without rendering an account of *why*" (274). Passages like this last expose the political gravamen of Feuerbach's assault, which is why Left Hegelians like Marx conceived of him as their spokesman until disabused by his cynicism about practical politics.

Feuerbach conveys a distrust deeper even than Hegel's or Strauss's of the cultural role of mythopoeia. His ambivalence is particularly apparent in his scattered approaches to a phenomenology of imagination. On one hand, he declares that "only the imagination . . . is the preservative from atheism" (203), that "God exists in heaven . . . for this heaven is the imagination." But, on the other, he consigns this familiar romantic idealism, Blake's "Jesus the Human Imagination Divine," to a distinctly secondary status à la Hegel. Humanity is Christ, but when human beings imagine Christ, even in abstract Trinitarian terms, they are already projecting: "Man as an emotional and sensuous being is governed and made happy only by images, by sensible representations. . . . The second Person in God . . . is the nature of the imagination made objective. . . . the satisfaction of the need for mental images. . . . a declension, a falling off from the metaphysical idea of the Godhead" (75–76). This passage is most remarkable, not because Feuerbach joins the long procession of heretics from Trinitarian orthodoxy, nor even for its theological application of the Hegelian valorizing of *begriff* over *vorstellung,* but because it introduces a tragic paradox. "Religion," as Feuerbach says elsewhere, "sacrifices the thing itself to the image" (182). Our power of mythopoeia is at once what makes us happy and breaks our hearts, what frees and what oppresses. This deep ambivalence Feuerbach communicates to Marx together with his aspiration toward a "material" critique of consciousness.[11]

MARX AND ENGELS: "MYTH" AS IDEOLOGY

Marx absorbs the thinking of Hegel, Strauss, and Feuerbach in the process of growing through what look amusingly like the perfect Hegelian *bildung;* before he settles on his politically committed economics and journalism, he aspires to be, in turn, poet, theologian, and philosopher. These abortive careers figure scarcely at all in most accounts of Marx's thought, but they are significant with respect to his role in the construction of "myth."[12] They mark the stages of a dialectic by which he evolved out of the dominant romantic concept the first, and arguably the most directly oppositional, of its basic modifications.

Even Marx's youthful doctoral dissertation reveals that, unlike Strauss and even Feuerbach, he recognizes consciously and explicitly the deep connections between Hegel and the romantics. Under the guise of commenting on why Plato employs myth, he identifies with surprising accuracy, and attacks in a style already distinguished by mauling irony and swift allusion, what "myth" had come to signify in his own day:

> Plato is not satisfied with his negative interpretation of the Absolute. It is not enough to plunge everything into the depths of a night where, as Hegel says, all cows are black. Here Plato avails himself of a positive interpretation of the Absolute. And its essential, self-grounded form is myth and allegory. Where the Absolute stands on one side and limited positive actuality on the other, and the positive is still to be maintained, it becomes the medium of absolute light which bursts into a fabulous display of color. The finite and positive signifies something other than itself. . . . The entire world has become a world of myths. Every form is an enigma. . . . This positive representation of the Absolute with its mythico-allegorical garb is the fountainhead and heartbeat of the philosophy of transcendence. (Marx 1967, 59)

Here Hegel's famous (and friendship-destroying) sneer in the preface to the *Phenomenology* about Schelling's concept of "indifference" as "the night in which all cows are black" is turned by implication upon Hegel's own "night" of "the Absolute." This figure is then troped again, sardonically, in describing how the "night" becomes, by some magical property of "the positive," "absolute light" that reconstitutes the empirical world as a rainbow spectrum of "myth and allegory." This dissertation was written during the same year in which *The Essence of Christianity* was published, but the twenty-three-year-old Marx seems to have assimilated Feuerbach's critique already. In one respect, in fact, he seems to have gone beyond it; he identifies the enemy much more precisely, in the naming of the new doctrines of "symbol" and "myth" and in his parodic introduction of Schlegel's figures ("the fountainhead and heartbeat of transcendence").

But Marx does learn from Feuerbach over the next few years a method of critical analysis that he attempts to extrapolate from religion onto social structure. We can see him at this in an essay of 1844: "The basis of irreligious criticism is this: *man makes religion. . . . But man . . . is the human world,* the state, society. This state, this society produce religion which is an *inverted world consciousness* because they are an *inverted world*" (Marx 1978, 53). Behind the inversions of Feuerbachian religious projection, according to Marx, lurk its true causes, the larger inversion of social relations of which religion is only one symbolic coding. "The immediate task of philosophy," Marx announces, "is to unmask human self-alienation in its *secular* form now that it has been unmasked in its *sacred* form" (54). Here is both a surprisingly sound kernel of the concept of "ideology" and a dismissal of Feuerbach as one whose work is essentially done. The frequent quotation of the eleventh and last of Marx's "Theses on Feuerbach" (1845), ("The philosophers have only *interpreted* the world . . . the point, however, is to *change* it") makes it appear that Marx objected to Feuerbach principally because of his lack of commitment to political action. In terms of the development of Marx's ideas, however, his strictures in Thesis VI are much more significant: "Feuerbach resolves the religious essence into the human essence. But the human essence is no abstraction inherent in each single individual. In its reality it is the ensemble of social relations" (145). The idea that the "human essence" is inherent in each single individual is also, of course, the basis of Comte's "religion of humanity" and of the subsequent "liberal humanism" of the nineteenth and twentieth centuries. We find it concretely expressed in innumerable forms—in the novels of Feuerbach's English translator, George Eliot, for example. Marx's recognition of "humanism" itself as an idealized mask of social relations removes the last block to his vision of a human consciousness pervaded completely by a falsifying mythopoeia of these relations.

Marx set down his "Theses" in the spring of 1845, just as he was beginning the particular collaboration with Engels the title of which supplies the definitive name for the condition of consciousness that is their target. They called their manuscript *The German Ideology,* a phrase heavy with Marx's characteristic irony.[13] The word "ideology" carried no pejorative connotations when it first became current among the savants to whom the Convention of 1795 had entrusted the management of the newly founded *Institut de France.* On the contrary; when the term was popularized (if not coined) by Antoine Destutt de Tracy in his *Éléments d'Idéologie* (1801–1815), it conjured up the optimistic hopes of the combined Enlightenment and Revolution for a new science of human thinking. But the idealistic French intellectuals came to be despised and derided by Napoleon, who attacked them, in a style of demagoguery paradigmatic for modern dictators, both for their powerlessness to effect events and their responsibility for everything that went wrong in the Empire, including his Russian campaign. Marx, a great admirer of Napoleon, also identifies the *Idéologues* with their disorganized condition after the July Revolution, in the course of which they had got the parliamentary government for which they had long battled. Marx and Engels intend their title, then, to be doubly offensive. The German Idealists and romantics are both assimilated with the French intellectuals as naive fools and contrasted with them as religious reactionaries rather than republican social scientists. *German* ideology is damned twice over as both chimerical and sinister.

What is perhaps most apparent about the authors' descriptive definitions of "ideology" in the introductory section of the work is their determination to extirpate from their critical thinking every last trace of romantic idealism, to articulate a method that will be systematically antithetical to it. "In direct contrast to German philosophy which descends from heaven to earth, here we ascend from earth to heaven. . . . Morality, religion, metaphysics, all the rest of ideology and their corresponding forms of consciousness, thus no longer retain the semblance of independence. They have no history, no development; but men, developing their material production and their material intercourse, alter, along with their real existence, their thinking and the products of their thinking. Life is not determined by consciousness, but consciousness by life" (154–155). Formulations like this score much higher for wit than for accuracy. They are thick with undefined terms and express a naively positivistic "reflection theory" of the relation of thought to "the real" that will cost later Marxist thinkers endless pains to refashion. But the very young authors are focused primarily upon establishing their broad antithesis. As Hegel finds whole continents without history because they fall outside his conception of the evolution of consciousness, so here it is the highest modes of Absolute Spirit, deprived of independent development, that "have no history." They are products of a condition of reflexive consciousness in which "men and their circumstances appear upside-down as in a *camera obscura*" (154). Marx and Engels are thus enabled to reach the point of seeing Idealism as "upside-down," by elements in their thinking—materialism and political radicalism—that do not derive principally from their Hegelian heritage. But their conception of "ideology" is nevertheless the culmination of a critique that originates within romanticism itself and evolves gradually into its antithesis. Even though Marx's and Engels's practice of ideological critique in their mature work concentrates upon political and economic formations, the concept always retains, if only on the level of figurative language, something of its origins in criticism of literature, philosophy, and religion.

The concept of ideology that Marx and Engels worked out in their long-unpublished tract appears in a number of contexts in their published writings, most conspicuously in the *Manifesto of the Communist Party* (1848) and most significantly for Marxist theory in the passage from the preface to *A Contribution to the Critique of Political Economy* (1859) that is the *locus classicus* of the relation of base to superstructure. But the most effective disseminations of the concept by far are Marx's practical examples of how to analyze it. *The Eighteenth Brumaire of Louis Bonaparte* (1852), for example, is a brilliant model of the demystifying of current political propaganda. "Hegel," it begins, "remarks somewhere that all great world-historical facts and personages occur, as it were, twice. He has forgotten to add; the first time as tragedy, the second as farce" (594).[14] Marx had been hinting for some time that he saw the history of the nineteenth century as the comic re-run of a tragic plot, and Bonaparte's coup gave him the perfect opening to read in these events a parody of the Revolution and the First Empire. History is a nightmare from which the Stephen Dedaluses of bourgeois culture cannot awake because they do not know how to do anything but travesty the past. Ideology prevents us from seeing the present moment as it is. Marx says of the French, "They have not only a caricature of the old Napoleon, they have got the old Napoleon himself, caricatured as he would inevitably appear in the middle of the nineteenth century" (597). They have got their tragic hero, but, since he is playing in the farce of industrial capitalism, he is not tragic and not a hero. In Borges's story, Pierre Menard cannot rewrite *Don Quixote* in the present; even when he succeeds in re-creating a paragraph of it word for word, the paragraph doesn't mean what it did in Cervantes's day. Marx's detailed exposure of the ideology of revolution is a foil for his vision of the real thing. "The social revolution of the nineteenth century cannot draw its poetry from the past, but only from the future. It cannot begin with itself before it has stripped off all superstition in regard to the past" (597). In his powerful conclusion, Marx attributes such a stripping, unintended to be sure, to Bonaparte himself: "He divests the whole state machine of its halo, profanes it and makes it at once loathsome and ridiculous" (617). The hapless Bonaparte supplies an inadvertent model of how to dismantle an ideology, a practice here defined in so many words.

The whole of *Das Kapital* can be viewed as a similar exercise. Marx attempts to do for nothing less than the nineteenth-century capitalist mode of production what he does in *The Eighteenth Brumaire* for a paradigm of its politics. This struggle to get out from under the nightmarish weight of the economic base requires so massive an effort of research, documentation, and exposure—of "genealogy" in Nietzsche's sense—that a reader can lose sight of the method. But there is a famous moment, comparable to the conclusion of *The Eighteenth Brumaire,* when Marx's diction and figures take on a doubly ironic religious cast that allegorizes demystification itself. This is the section on "The Fetishism of Commodities and the Secret Thereof." "A commodity," it begins, "appears at first sight a very trivial thing, and easily understood. Its analysis shows that it is, in reality, a very queer thing, abounding in metaphysical subtleties and theological niceties" (319). After a brief demonstration that "the mystical character of commodities does not originate . . . in their use value," Marx goes on to suggest where this character does originate. "To find an analogy, we must have recourse to the mist-enveloped regions of the religious world. In that world the productions of the human brain appear as independent beings endowed with life. . . . So it is in the world of commodities with the products of men's hands. This I call the Fetishism which attaches itself to the products of labor, so soon as they are produced as commodities" (321). The concept of the "fetish," introduced into the study of religions by de Brosses in 1760, had become quite popular in the mid-nineteenth century. Comte adopts it as the lowest and earliest substage of the first, "theological," age of humankind, and even the novelists pick it up. Melville's Ishmael describes with consistent wryness Queequeg's relations with his "little god," Yojo, and the narrator of *The Mill on the Floss* is tender about Maggie Tulliver's "fetish," the long-suffering doll in the attic. Marx introduces his own wooden fetish, the standard philosopher's example of the kitchen table: "So soon as it steps forth as a commodity, it is changed into something transcendent. It not only stands with its feet on the ground, but, in relation to all other commodities, it stands on its head, and evolves out of its wooden brain grotesque ideas" (320). It stands upside down like Hegel, and its wooden brain makes it a blockhead. Behind the fooling, Marx's intent is deadly. Here alone in *Das Kapital* the oldest Western archetype of idolatry appears, because we are in the shrine of capitalism. The commodity, an entity whose value beyond labor and use is created out of nothing, is worshiped as the true god. As the symbolic declaration of intent to demystify, "The Fetishism of Commodities" is the key signature for the whole of the work.

Marx's reversion at this point to religious metaphor regrounds his new technique in its philosophical and theological origins. His conception of "ideology" clearly appears here as just the sort of antithetical development predicted in general terms by Hegel's extrapolation of the historical "struggle of enlightenment and superstition" into a dialectic intrinsic to the modern age. Though Marx himself offered no models outside of politics and economics, it is no accident that when versions of romantic myth break out afresh in the twentieth century, new versions of ideological critique appear as their most intimate and effective enemy.

CARLYLE AND GRIMM: "MYTH" AS CULTURE-INFORMING STORY

While the romantic construction of "myth" is thus generating its contrary, it is actually triumphing in bourgeois literary and artistic circles and hardening into an orthodoxy of sorts. One of the most important theoretical manifestations of this entrenchment is the hypostatizing of "myth" as a distinct *genre* of story. The earlier romantics, though they invent the concept, still lack the word, still make do with "fable," or "vision," or speak of creating a new "mythology," meaning a collection of separate stories that ought somehow cohere to create a unified system of belief. Although these writers distinguish "symbolic" narrative from mere "allegory," they neglect the theoretical question of whether there is a distinct *kind* of story that functions "symbolically." Creuzer's *Symbolik,* however, does confront the question head-on, and the ensuing controversy launches singular "myth" on its modern career. The blossoming of this usage, first in Germany in the teens and twenties of the nineteenth century, testifies to the growing persuasion that there is indeed an encounterable, and creatable, type of narrative charged with power to "inform" a culture as the soul, had been held, since Aristotle, to inform the body.

The prime English representative of this focus, Thomas Carlyle, is an important mediator not only between the literary periods traditionally labeled "Romantic" and "Victorian" but between German thought and English. In the former role he promotes in discursive prose assumptions that were largely inspiration for verse among the earlier romantics, while in the latter he functions rather as de Staël, Cousin, Michelet, and Quinet do in France, popularizing the new German ideas. He also presents a telling contrast to Marx, since his similar social concerns, especially during the "Hungry Forties," carry him to contrary conclusions about the value of mythopoeia. While he reacts as indignantly as Marx to the horrors of unchecked free enterprise, he finds his ideal solution in the renewal of a culture made coherent by myth and celebrates the role of "the hero" as myth-bringer.

Though not a systematic thinker, Carlyle does hold consistently that the material world is everywhere emblematic embodiment of "Spirit."[15] His philosophy, for which he popularized the labels "Transcendentalism" and "Natural Supernaturalism," is another Idealist attempt to reassert humanity's ability to exceed the limits of "pure reason." "'Rightly viewed,'" preaches Professor Teufelsdröckh in Carlyle's principal vehicle, *Sartor Resartus,* "'no meanest object is insignificant: all objects are as windows, through which the philosophic eye looks into infinitude itself. . . . All visible things are emblems. . . . Matter exists only spiritually, and to represent some Idea and body it forth'" (Carlyle 1937, 72–73). Carlyle's central figure for these material transparencies is derived from Goethe's *Faust,* but elevated into the principle of a literary "anatomy" in the "Clothes Philosophy" of *Sartor Resartus:* "'All emblematic things are properly Clothes. . . . Must not the Imagination weave garments, visible Bodies, wherein the invisible creations and inspirations of our Reason are, like Spirits, revealed?'" (73).[16]

Carlyle's most usual non-metaphorical name for these "emblems" is "Symbol," a term that his own practice did even more than Coleridge's to naturalize in English. Carlyle's distinctive variation, however, reflects the new "Victorian" socializing of the vatic imagination. The descriptive definition of "symbol" in *Sartor* is set in the context of a passage exalting the workings of unconscious process over conscious verbalizing: "'Speech is of Time, Silence is of Eternity'" (219). But "Symbol" mediates between the two: "'In a Symbol there is concealment and yet revelation . . . by Silence and by Speech acting together comes a double significance. . . . There is ever some embodiment and revelation of the Infinite; the Infinite is made to blend itself with the Finite, to stand visible, as it were, attainable there'" (219–220). Compared to Schelling or Coleridge, Carlyle emphasizes "Symbol's" concrete manifestation and attainability. Man "'everywhere finds himself encompassed with Symbols, recognized or not recognized. . . . Not a Hut he builds but is the visible embodiment of a Thought'" (220). This "Hut" is itself a good "emblem" of "Symbol" since the latter includes everything humankind has ever constructed for its mental shelter. For a comparable conception we have to turn to Blake's Los and Enitharmon weaving time and space for human habitation. "Symbol" is the the tool with which humanity fabricates its cultural world out of the eternal silence.

The success of *Sartor Resartus* is particularly responsible, too, for popularizing the word "myth" in English. Its first appearance attested in the OED is in 1830. Carlyle, writing concurrently (*Sartor* was completed in 1831), still deploys the unfamiliar word in its alternative German form, *mythus.* He introduces it just at that point in *Sartor* where Teufelsdröckh acknowledges that what he wants is the "'authentic *Church-Catechism* of our present century'" (189). He apostrophizes Voltaire as having demonstrated sufficiently that "'the Mythus of the Christian Religion looks not in the eighteenth century as it did in the eighth.'" "'But what next?'" he cries out, "'Wilt thou help us to embody the divine Spirit of that Religion in a new Mythus, in a new vehicle and vesture that our Souls . . . may live?'" (194). As the figures of "vehicle" and "vesture" of "Soul" indicate, Carlyle thinks of *mythus* as a particular species of "Symbol," namely, the class of "'religious Symbols . . . what we call Religions: as men stood in this stage of culture or the other and could worse or better body-forth the Godlike'" (224). Religion itself refers very broadly here, not primarily to cult, but to whatever notions of the sacred actually enable communities in a particular *"stage of culture"* (my italics) to "body-forth" a permanent spiritual principle in a particular, local mythology. Carlyle's insistence on "symbol" as concrete manifestation leads him, in spite of his transcendentalism, away from the earlier emphasis upon mythopoeia as expression of individual genius and toward the consideration of it as communal construction. In this respect, too, his take on myth chimes with the contemporaneous rise of systematic ethnology.

Implicit in Teufelsdröckh's demand for "a new Mythus," is a further assumption we now take so much for granted that it would be easy to miss its novelty in *Sartor.* This is the recognition that because the cultures that create and are created by their symbols grow old and die, their symbols perish with them and new ones are born in their place. Prior romantic thinkers stress the permanence of the Spirit to which the transcendental ego gains momentary access, but Carlyle's historicist perspectivism prompts him to right the balance by contemplating the temporality of that access. When Teufelsdröckh labels his own central belief as "*natural* supernaturalism'" (my italics), his creator expresses his rather paradoxical view of cultures and of the myths that inform them as spiritual *organisms.* Cultures behave like the rest of nature; this recognition pervades Carlyle's writings. In *Heroes, Hero-Worship and the Heroic in History* (1841), for example, he asserts that ancient Norse mythology acknowledges this truth in the symbol of the World-tree, Igdrasil, whose "boughs are Histories of Nations" (Carlyle 1968, 27).

It might be imagined that a thinker who stresses the communal properties of both "symbol" and "myth," and their consequent material perishability, would find little room for the activity of the individual visionary as mythmaker. But Carlyle is a synthesizer. Rather than rejecting or ignoring the role of the solitary creator, he transforms it, too, into his collectivist key. Just as he anticipates ethnological research by viewing myth as a concrete source of cultural adhesion, he rewrites the romantic poet as the visionary genius at the root of every successful culture. In *Sartor,* Teufelsdröckh's personal conversion to "natural supernaturalism" results from a brief glimpse, like that represented as obtained by various other romantics, into the heart of the symbol-generating, universal process of nature. But when he confesses that "'the authentic Church-Catechism of our present century has not fallen into my hands,'" his creator is aligning him with the consciousness of inadequacy that plagues Wordsworth and Shelley and Keats. Nevertheless, Carlyle permits his Teufelsdröckh the utter confidence that every past culture was shaped by a seer who *did* discover its authentic catechism, and that this necessary discovery must prevail in any future case. The conviction that behind every great mythology lurks a great man impels Carlyle in *Heroes, Hero-Worship and the Heroic in History* to invent his own brand of euhemerism. He maintains that Norse mythology "came from the thoughts of Norse men—from the thought, above all, of the first Norse man who had an original power of thinking" (27). This locution fudges the issue of whether the primal genius originated the mythology or merely put his stamp upon it, but, in either case, his people, recognizing "a present God," elevated him to divinity as "Odin." If we could penetrate the silence shrouding the origins of the world's mythologies, we would presumably encounter a similar apotheosis at the heart of each.

Carlyle's version of "the Hero" constellates succinctly the ambiguities of his contributions to the construction of "myth." On one hand, it, too, manifests a new concreteness of attention to the communal aspects of myth that preludes the rise of "anthropological" theories. Romanticized euhemerism aside, Carlyle's Odin is not all that far removed from the deific role of the culture-bringer that ethnologists were soon to find widespread in world mythologies. On the other hand, Carlyle's Odin euhemerized, although thrust safely backward (like Vico's giants) to the origins of culture, is still clearly the romantic "unacknowledged legislator." In *Heroes and Hero-Worship* Odin is the archetype whose avatars reappear in the successive lectures in increasingly constrained, diminished social roles. The sequence—divinity, prophet, poet, priest, man of letters, king—matches significantly (with the exception of its last term) Northrop Frye's sequence of "displaced" heroic agency in his theory of historical modes in *Anatomy of Criticism.* Both repeat the Hegelian model of ambivalence about modernity. As the owl of Minerva takes flight only at dusk, both "myth" and "hero" are only now, in their sadly degenerate condition, truly appreciable. And the "man of letters," however diminished, is nevertheless the surviving vessel of divinity, prophecy, poetry, and priesthood. This transposition of the problematic that so tormented the earlier romantics into the related problematic of the role of "the Hero" in the modern world reverberates with increasing loudness during the next hundred years. Theorists who continue to see transcendental possibilities in myth discover, particularly through the medium of insights garnered from ethnology and psychology, new profundities in Carlyle's conjunction of the concepts of "myth" and "hero."

It could be said by way of summary, then, that Carlyle has his brushes with the two other kinds of theories of myth that appear contemporaneously with his: the ideological and the folkloristic. As a prophet against the times, protesting "cash payment" as "the sole nexus of man with man," he anticipates Marx's recognition that the dominant religion of his day has become the fetishism of commodities (Carlyle 1918, 215). But Carlyle's understanding of the concept of "ideology" marks the ultimate gulf between the two full-bearded fulminators. Carlyle takes it to signify, not a web of false consciousness, but, in the Idealist vein of its originators, any theory by which one's life is dominated.[17] So, too, he touches, somewhat vaguely, upon Jacob Grimm's folkloristic conception of myth as a distinct, culture-informing genre of narrative that lives and dies in specific environments. But in this case also, by insisting on the abiding supernature behind these local and relative manifestations, he remains fundamentally committed to his romantic patrimony, an important transmitter of its transcendentalism.

In 1835, the year before the actual publication of *Sartor Resartus,* Jacob Grimm published his *Deutsche Mythologie.* This work is the fourth and last in a sequence of productions by the Brothers Grimm that are of unrivalled importance in concretizing the European conception of "myth" as a distinct narrative genre. In this series—*Kinder-und Hausmärchen* (1812–1815), *Deutsche Sagen* (1816–1818), Wilhelm's *Die Deutsche Heldensagen* (1829), and Jacob's *Deutsche Mythologie*—the pair establish between them a set of generic distinctions among three terms—"myth," "legend," and "fairytale"—that remains to this day a standard tool of folklorists, ethnologists, and others in classifying oral narratives. The Grimms themselves seem to have clarified their triple distinction slowly over a generation. The brief sketch of the generic differences that becomes the basis for refinements among subsequent folklorists appears only with Jacob Grimm's preface to the 1844 edition of *Deutsche*

Mythologie: "Looser, less fettered than legend, the Fairy-tale lacks that local habitation, which hampers legend, but makes it more home-like. The Fairy-tale flies, the legend walks; the one can draw freely out of the fulness of poetry, the other has almost the authority of history. . . . The ancient mythus, however, combines to some extent the qualities of fairy-tale and legend; untrammelled in its flight, it can yet settle down to a local home" (Grimm 1883, vol. 3, xv).[18] Grimm works here with two criteria—cross-cultural motility and epistemological status. "Fairy-tale" is "unfettered" in terms of both; it travels far, wide, and quickly even across cultural borders, and it is free to employ "the fulness of poetry," that is, fictional invention. "Legend," in contrast, is local, rooted in particular cultural settings, and received "almost" as history. "Myth" exhibits what may look in this context like paradoxical features of the two criteria; it is said to be "untrammelled in its flight," yet localizable. These properties are not actually contradictory, however, because "myth" is "untrammelled" for Grimm only in the second sense of being highly imaginative, whereas it is either anchored like legend to familiar landscapes or at least loses its sway, virtually by definition, at cultural borders. Furthermore, its imaginatively "untrammelled" nature does not result in its being regarded like "fairy-tale" as fiction; instead, though Grimm does not see fit make the point explicitly here, /to "myth," is normally the narrative of sacred events, hence commanding even more emphatically than "legend" belief in its truth.

Twentieth-century folklorists and anthropologists eventually find ways to apply these distinctions with a fair degree of neutrality, but such is not the Brothers' immediate legacy. The folklorists and ethnologists of the nineteenth century receive from them instead a panoply of attached romantic assumptions. As Burton Feldman points out, the Grimms were associates of the rather mystically inclined and intensely chauvinistic Heidelberg group that included Creuzer, Görres, Brentano, and Arnim (Feldman and Richardson 1972, 408). Creuzer and Görres both held that the "Germanic" or "Teutonic" nations originated in an Indian homeland before spreading across the north of Western Europe, and that they had there been vouchsafed an original revelation by "the One" (as Jacob Grimm also denominates this shadowy deity in his preface (li). "Teutonic" mythology originally emanated from this source but gradually decayed, leaving behind only disordered fragments and faint echoes. Legends and fairytales are therefore the shards of "myth." These devolutionary hypotheses are fueled by the ongoing discoveries of law-like continuities in the evolution of the Indo-Germanic family of languages. Even so distinguished a participant in this philological revolution as Jacob Grimm is hence confirmed by false analogy in his persuasion that contemporary "Germanic" society must be the remote degenerate descendant of what was once an organically unified "Teutonic" culture. From this point of view, the sequence of the Grimms' works, devoted respectively to fairytale, legend, and myth, constitutes a series of increasingly deeper incursions into the buried "Teutonic" past in quest of the original revelation. The Grimms thus bequeath to subsequent folklorists and ethnologists the potentially glittering tool of their generic distinctions clotted with the mud and rust of a degenerationism that often blunts its cutting edge well into the 1960s. But even this influential piece of romantic obscurantism is a small price to pay for the introduction into the discursive construction of myth of its folkloristic strain.

NATIONAL STORY AS "PARABLE OF MYTH": TENNYSON'S *IDYLLS* AND WAGNER'S *RING*

If Blake and Novalis can be said to write "allegories of fable" that represent the romantic moment of full confidence in the mythopoeic power of the individual, perhaps it's suitable to say that midcentury artists like Tennyson and Wagner produce "parables of myth" that represent the later romantic moment of quest for the indigenous roots of viable communal myth. In *The Idylls of the King,* Tennyson transforms Malory's *Le Morte D'Arthur,* a quite straightforward fifteenth-century recension of earlier Arthurian romances, into a symbolic Carlylean parable about myth as a manifestation of the eternal in historical time. Tennyson immediately establishes his parabolic bent in "The Coming of Arthur." Malory tells the story as if he had no more reason to doubt the historicity of Arthur than of Henry the Fifth, whereas Tennyson not only clearly doubts it but makes his doubt his theme. The hero comes out of eternity; his claim on allegiance cannot be established by fact, but only by the operation of a hermeneutical circle; belief creates him, and he creates belief. Arthur puts others to the test by his deeds, and each has to choose without conclusive empirical proof.

This perspectival view of truth as a subjective, "lived" intuition appears everywhere in the midcentury, but Tennyson's version is special in its application to the workings of culturally constitutive "myth." Camelot is the monument to belief in Arthur, the chief externalization of the state of inward grace. Tennyson makes out of the very lack of archaeological evidence for its existence a Carlylean symbol for the evanescence of all culture. When Gareth, the first recruit we witness joining Arthur, encounters the great Gate of the city, he and his followers experience its illusionary quality: "For barefoot on the keystone, which was lined / And rippled like an ever-fleeting wave, / The Lady of the Lake stood; all her dress / Wept from her sides as water flowing away" (Tennyson 1975, 299). This "ever-fleeting wave" is connected especially with the coming and passing of Arthur. It suggests here the fluidity of the very stone of Camelot. "A blast of music" peals out of the city, and as the youngsters jump back in surprise, an ancient, bearded man stands before them asking who they are. The "blast" might be as natural as the carvings, but it comes with an abruptness that makes it seem like an expression of the city itself. This association of architecture with both moving water and music is sustained throughout the poem, as if to say that the entire phenomenal world is an "ever-fleeting wave" whose deep ground-tone we can sometimes hear. When Gareth tries to lie to the old man (Merlin) to preserve his incognito, but nevertheless demands with no sense of irony that the elder tell them "the truth" about the city, Merlin delivers one of his riddling bardic replies: "a fairy king / And fairy queens have built the city, son; / They came from out a sacred mountain-cleft / Toward the sunrise, each with harp in hand / And built it to the music of their harps . . . / For an ye heard a music, like enow / They are building still, seeing the city is built / To music, therefore never built at all, / And therefore built forever" (299, 300). Camelot is "built to music" in the same sense as Teufelsdröckh insists that his hometown of Weissnichtwo and the walls of ancient Thebes have been. But as an expression of the permanent longing of humanity, always in process, always in part unrealized, it is "built forever."

If Camelot represents the first principle that Tennyson learned from Carlyle, that "myth" informs a culture, Merlin personifies the second, that "myths" die. The story of Merlin's seduction and permanent imprisonment by Vivien nestles poisonously at the heart of the *Idylls;* an organism's decline commences with a mysterious shift of balance at the peak of its powers. "Then fell on Merlin a great melancholy; / He walk'd with dreams and darkness, and he found / A doom that ever poised itself to fall" (356). This morbidity is the contrary of the complex gaiety of the active Merlin who playfully warns Gareth. Merlin shifts from enchanter to enchanted, just as Carlyle claims in *Past and Present* (1843) that England itself has done. He passes from committed sage, whose knowledge is power while it shines in use, to paralyzed intellectual, whose despair is a self-fulfilling prophecy. We feel his absence increasingly through the social collapse represented in the remainder of the *Idylls.* The mythmaker fails the myth, and the myth follows him down.

Tennyson concludes *The Idylls of the King* by returning Arthur to the remoteness of legend in a manner that dramatizes simultaneously both the transience of his reign and the permanence of the principle that inspires it. The story is told by Bedivere, the sole survivor of the last battle, when, like Conrad's Kurtz, he is "no more than a voice" and is situated like T. S. Eliot's old magus in "The Coming of the Magi" among "new faces, other minds" (434). At the end of "Guinevere" we watch from her point of view as Arthur, riding off to the final battle, disappears in the mist that will also shroud the battlefield, an obvious figure for the return of his story into legend. As Bedivere tells it, this battle is fought in "a land of old . . . / Where fragments of forgotten peoples dwelt" (435). And Bedivere carries the dying Arthur to "a place of tombs / Where lay the mighty bones of ancient men" (436–437). The surprising profusion of homely natural images in this idyll also insists on the stubborn survival of life; for example, "the many-knotted water-flags / That whistled dry and stiff about the marge." To the dismayed Arthur the north wind that clears the mist, "and beats upon the faces of the dead" (436), seems to deny all meaning, but to the survivor, Bedivere, it is "the voice of days of old and days to be." When the barge bearing the King's body disappears at the horizon, he returns irretrievably into the condition of legend in which his very existence cannot be proven. But when Tennyson revised his youthful "Morte d'Arthur" for his new conclusion of 1869, he added a final line: "And the sun rose, bringing the new year." Arthur melts into the natural phenomenon, the matrix of all mythopoeia. This new ending suggests much the same point as the conclusion of Wallace Stevens's "World as Meditation," where Penelope cannot distinguish for certain between the renewal of dawn and her belief in the approach of Ulysses. As long as humanity witnesses "sunrise," the mythopoeia that informs culture will be renewed.

The most spectacular of the numerous nineteenth-century "parables of myth" is probably Richard Wagner's *Der Ring des Nibelungs.* Merlin claims that Camelot is built to an endless music of which humanity sometimes catches a throb; Wagner produces a version of this music of process as the continuous accompaniment to his story. We hear it at its most pure in the mysterious hum of the E-flat major triad that opens the overture to *Das Rhinegold*. Wagner claims in his autobiography that this music suddenly possessed him during a mental crisis brought on by his inability to begin writing the score for the verse *libretti* he had already prepared. Falling into a doze, he felt he was sinking in rushing water, the sound of which turned into the E-flat major chord. This chord, he says, continued to resound unchanged even while it also broke up in melodic passages of increasing speed that suggested the flowing element in which he was immersed. Just as the reiterated chord, in the opera itself, is Wagner's version of the "ground-tone" of Camelot, the mounting arpeggios in the oboes and strings indicate the rise toward narrative; they swim upward into myth, the moment when the parting curtain discloses the Rhinemaidens in their grotto celebrating the beauty of their gold.

This opening thus confronts us immediately with Wagner's conception of the relation of the story to the music. Schopenhauer, whose philosophy Wagner was so taken with during these years, divides existence between the universal energy he calls "Will" and the human constructions of it that he termed "Representations" (*Vorstellungen*). He also valorizes music as the greatest of the arts because it alone is a direct representation of Will. In Schopenhauer's terms, the relation of any other mode of representation to music is that of primary to secondary. But in the essays Wagner wrote during his musically quiescent years (roughly between 1848 and 1852), he makes it clear that his artistic ideal is Greek drama, which he celebrates for its combination of all the arts, it religious significance, its communal nature, and above all its basis in traditional *mythoi*. Hence, it is not surprising that the Wagnerian *Gesamtkunstwerke* exalts myth as the form of secondary representation closest to the primary music of the will, or, to put it more concretely, that the timeless flow of the Rhine projects out of its depths the event that inaugurates a cycle of history.

Wagner's plot fuses the Norse mythology of the Icelandic *Eddas* with what William Morris, who forged his own "parable of myth" out of this same material, called "the great story of the North," the tale of Sigurd or Siegfried, the dragon-killer, as told in the Icelandic *Volsungasaga* and the German *Nibelungenlied*.[19] By the mid-nineteenth century the chauvinistic constraints upon Wagner to choose this particular story make Tennyson's choice of the Arthurian romances seem almost arbitrary. For Wagner, as for Tennyson, however, this medieval material could be regarded as of communal cultural significance—as proper *myth*—only if recast in the mode of what Matthew Arnold called "high seriousness." Where Tennyson portrays the Carlylean life-cycle of a legendary kingdom, Wagner rationalizes the loss of the so-called "Teutonic" mythology by an account of why and how the Age of the Gods must cede to the Age of Humanity. The theodicy is Feuerbachian. The gods must pass because their rule is based solely upon their willful assertion of power. This is epitomized in Wotan's tearing off of a branch of the World-ash, Ygdrasil, to fashion his Spear of Law. In the course of the tetralogy, he learns from his own mortal children—first through the mutual devotion of Siegmund and Sieglinde and then through the revolt of Brünnhilde—a version of Schopenhauer's doctrine of loving renunciation as the chief refuge from Will. This moral revolution brings Wotan to peaceful resignation, but nothing can save Valhalla from "the twilight of the gods," or, in Feuerbachian terms, from the evolution of consciousness that conducts humanity from worship of inferior theological projections to love of its own best self.[20] Unlike Tennyson's, Wagner's "parable of myth" is double-edged; it can be taken as celebrating either the supersession of an outmoded mythology by a fresh one or humanity's promethean rejection of all externalized deities. Either way, however, the two artists are in rapport with Carlyle and Grimm in conceiving of myth primarily as a principle of cultural cohesion.

"MYTH" AS PERSONAL SALVATION: RUSKIN AND ELIOT

While nostalgic artists with patriotic and epic ambitions like Tennyson and Wagner dramatize myth as culturally cohesive belief, many of their contemporaries entertain a view of it built upon the negative corollary that in the actual absence of such cohesion in the post-Christian West, myth offers private access to religious inspiration. The more that secular values prevail in the marketplace and religion is accorded its own sphere of sensibility, inaccessible to reason but also irrefutable by it, the more "myth" appears to be a genre capable of conveying permanent truth to the sensitive bourgeois seeker. This is an assumption with a large future in the twentieth century, but it is in fairly wide circulation by the latter half of the nineteenth. It can be found expressed, for example, in conventional, backward-looking terms in the writings of John Ruskin and in a set of anticipatory forward-looking variations in the late fictions of George Eliot.

Ruskin's voluminous writings include a number of essays and parts of essays devoted to mythology, but the most revealing of his fundamental assumptions about myth is "The Queen of the Air."[21] This piece grew out of a public lecture at University College, London, in 1869, and it condescends annoyingly toward an audience that the speaker seems to assume (perhaps correctly) is made up of young ladies at school and working men bent on self-improvement. The condescension is useful here because it prompts Ruskin to lay out explicitly a good deal of current truism. He tells his audience that "in nearly every myth of importance . . . you have to discern three structural parts—the root and the two branches—the root is physical existence, sun or sky or cloud or sea; then the personal incarnation of that; becoming a trusted or companionable deity with whom you could walk hand in hand, as a child with its brother or sister; and, lastly, the moral significance of the image, which is in all the great myths eternally beneficent and true" (Ruskin 1905, 300). In each of the three subordinate sections that comprise the work, Ruskin proceeds from the "root" to the "branches," from the physical phenomena to the moral implications of how these are personified. His treatment of the "root" is a sentimentalized and dogmatic version of the passages on Greek mythology in Wordsworth's *Excursion*. It is sentimentalized in glossing over all that is troubled in those passages, and dogmatic in repeating unreflectively what is by this time the near-universal assumption, first given currency by Herder a century before, that a people's mythology is "rooted" in its conception of nature. As for the two branches protruding from this root, Ruskin is not much interested in the first, personification, except as it displays the second, ethical significance. This neglect of personification will probably seem just as well to anyone who considers for a moment the chasm between the deities represented by Homer or the tragic dramatists and Ruskin's recommendation to his audience to imagine that the Greeks perceived them as hand-holding siblings out of some photograph by Charles Dodgson. This sentimentalizing of the first "branch" is matched by that of the second; "all the great myths" are "eternally beneficent and true," a qualification that leaves the definition of "great" to be determined by some right-thinking gentleman of impeccable taste. "So the great question in reading a story is always, not what wild hunter dreamed, or what childish race first dreaded it, but what wise man first perfectly told, and what strong people first perfectly lived by it. And the real meaning of any myth is that which it has at the noblest age of that nation among whom it is current" (301). These remarks obviously exclude from "greatness" and from the realm of "the eternally beneficent and true" any storytelling that cannot be sufficiently bowdlerized or reduced to moral uplift. They illuminate, unfortunately, the potential for namby-pambyness that lurks even in the "high seriousness" of Tennyson's and Wagner's medievalism.

Ruskin subscribes explicitly to the by now conventional romantic repudiation of "allegory" in favor of "symbol," but the reductiveness of his practice raises in acute form the question of whether or not this is for him a distinction without a difference. He turns romantic transcendence against the new historical relativism; "modern historical inquiry" does not understand "true imaginative vision." "You may obtain a more truthful idea of the nature of Greek religion and legend from the poems of Keats and the nearly as beautiful . . . recent work of Morris, than from frigid scholarship" (309). Historical situation matters not; all true poets are at one in being able to decipher the universal moral maxims hidden in "the dark sayings of nature." The peculiar intensity of Ruskin's rejection of historical relativism in the realm of myth may help to explain why his own readings are no less moralistic than, or even different in kind from, those of the Neoplatonic tradition of allegorized fable. The principal basis of the romantic distinction, the alleged inexhaustible suggestiveness of "symbol," is virtually eliminated in the mythographer's utter confidence that permanent moral significance is as obvious as it is timeless. This new allegorizing is characteristic of popular mythography both in Victorian England and in the America of Bulfinch's *Mythology* and Hawthorne's *Thrice-Told Tales*. The next step is the production of school texts with versions suitable for improving the morals of the young.

There *is* a passage in George Eliot's *Daniel Deronda* in which the stuffy hero, discussing the meaning of the now fashionable term "myth" with the ladies of the Meyrick household, sounds like he's paraphrasing "The Queen of the Air" (George Eliot 1967, 523). But Eliot's last two novels, *Middlemarch* and *Daniel Deronda,* present significant versions of the active operations of myth in everyday life that do not come into their own until celebrated by the modernist poets and novelists of the early twentieth century. In *Middlemarch* we encounter a suggestion that people may actually embody mythological archetypes, and in *Daniel Deronda* that "myth" operates within us at an unconscious level.

Eliot thematizes myth in *Middlemarch* in two related ways. First, she represents her heroine, Dorothea Brooke, both as yearning in the midst of her upper-middle-class idleness for myth in the Carlylean social sense, and as embodying in her person modern versions of Antigone, Ariadne, and Psyche. But Eliot introduces a further layer of irony. She depicts Dorothea's husband, Edward Casaubon, as a scholarly mythographer, pathetically unable to perceive, not only who his wife is or what she longs for, but also the very movement in the construction of myth, namely German romanticism, that could transform his scholarship and, if truly internalized, his and Dorothea's marriage as well. These counterpointed themes mingle richly in the brilliant chapters (19–23) that represent the Casaubons' honeymoon in the Rome of 1829 and their encounters there with Casaubon's cousin, Will Ladislaw, and his friend, the Nazarene painter, Adolph Naumann.

Eliot's representation of Casaubon as mythographer would be interesting here quite apart from novelistic talent. Eliot was probably one of the best-informed persons in England on the topic of mythography; she had no need to research the state of knowledge in the field during the 1820s as her *Notebooks* show that she did, for example, in the case of Tertius Lydgate's biomedical ambitions. In fact, twenty years before writing *Middlemarch,* she identified, in a review of Mackay's *Progress of the Intellect,* the broad historical pattern that governs her representation of Casaubon's *Key to All Mythologies* and Will Ladislaw's criticism of it: "The introduction of a truly philosophic spirit into the study of mythology—an introduction to which we are chiefly indebted to the Germans—is a great step forward from . . . the orthodox prepossessions of writers such as Bryant, who saw in the Greek legends simply misrepresentations of the authentic history given in the book of *Genesis*" (George Eliot 1963, 37–38). Will characterizes Casaubon as an epigone of Bryant and his work as outmoded by that of "the Germans."

Rich as the portrait of Casaubon is, historically as well as psychologically, Eliot's most original contribution to the construction of myth in these chapters is her treatment of Dorothea and, to a lesser extent, Casaubon himself as archetypal embodiments. As she stands musing in front of the statue of Ariadne in the Vatican, watched herself by Ladislaw and Naumann, the narrator compares her to the Ariadne, and Naumann enthusiastically sums her up to Will as "a sort of Christian Antigone—sensuous force controlled by spiritual passion" (141). In the next chapter Eliot makes Casaubon recommend to his wife Raphael's frescoes of Cupid and Psyche in the Faresina, a move introduced principally, it seems, so that the narrator can establish throughout the rest of the section a running comparison between their marriage and the story of Cupid and Psyche. If Casaubon had a spirit capable of being moved by the pictures he coldly and pedantically recommends, he would also be able to see his own Psyche yearning for her Eros. Casaubon is also Minotaur to Dorothea's Ariadne, Dis to her Persephone. But these are only some conspicuous strands in a rich web of accumulating allusion and imagery that presents the newlyweds as actors in archetypal relations whose key eludes their consciousnesses.[22] In thus teetering on the edge, at least, of the idea that human beings embody mythical archetypes, Eliot anticipates by a generation the remarkable claims of certain modernist writers that we are indeed inhabited by such entities.

Eliot also experiments in the latter third of her final novel, *Daniel Deronda,* with a notion of myth closely connected in the twentieth century with belief in embodied archetypes, namely, that myth is rooted in a racial unconscious. In connection with the account of Daniel's discovery of his Jewish heritage and his commitment to Zionism, the narrator tells us that the mental life of the visionary Mordecai-Ezra, Daniel's *alter ego,* "wrought so constantly in images that his coherent trains of thought often resembled the significant dreams attributed to sleepers by waking persons in their most inventive moments; nay, they often resembled genuine dreams in their way of breaking off the passage from the known to the unknown" (George Eliot 1967, 523). The narrator subsequently represents these hypnogogic images in archaeological figures. We're told, for example, that in a youthful poem Ezra describes thus a vision of a tomb hidden on Mt. Nebo: "'There the buried ark and golden cherubim / Make hidden light: / There the solemn faces gaze unchanged, / The wings are spread unbroken: / Shut beneath in silent awful speech / The Law lies graven.'" At this point, the poet introjects the location of the tomb: "'Solitude and darkness are my covering, / And my heart a tomb; / Smite and shatter it, O Gabriel! / Shatter it as the clay of the founder / Around the golden image'" (534). The Law graven in the poet's heart speaks there in silence (like the Law that speaks in the heavens in Psalm 19), but if the tomb were "excavated" by some act of angelic intervention, it would communicate its golden truth to the world. The angels, both the golden ones in the tomb on Nebo and the archangel invoked as the shatterer of the heart, are themselves figures for archetypal images that communicate the true correspondence between unconscious knowledge within and the world outside. Hence, Ezra isn't surprised to perceive Daniel from the bridge at sunset as the latter rows downstream as the "Being answering to his need . . . approaching . . . or turning his back towards him, darkly painted against a golden sky" (530). Daniel is a literal fulfillment of the angelic visitant who will untomb the Law in Ezra's heart.

The narrator presents Daniel's need for Ezra as not only the existential but also the imagistic complement of Ezra's need for Daniel. Deronda's desire for social and religious commitment "lay in his own thought like sculptured fragments certifying some beauty yearned after but not traceable by divination" (571). Daniel's "sculptured fragments" are analogous to Dorothea's perception of Rome as "a vast wreck." Both searchers seek rescue from what the narrator of *Deronda* calls "the dead anatomy of culture" (413). But, whereas Dorothea suffers the common, unrescued fate of the modern Western *bourgeoisie,* Daniel is saved by an encounter with a prophet who *can* divine the integral temple of which these "sculptured fragments" were once parts. In his excited speech at the workmen's club, Ezra casts this imagery in terms of one of the important subtexts of the novel, the relation of isolated individuals to the mass social and political movements of the century: "'The heritage of Israel is beating in the pulses of millions; it lives in their veins as a power without understanding, like the morning exultation of herds; it is the inborn half of memory, moving as in a dream among writings on the walls, which it sees dimly but cannot divide into speech'" (596). We are invited to believe that Daniel's attraction to Judaism, insofar as it exceeds rational explanation, stems from this "inborn half of memory" to which Ezra's vision can fit the other half, can divide the glyphs on the walls into articulate communication. Ezra's comparison of this "power without understanding" to "the morning exultation of herds" is an evocative figure for the emotional pull of the unconscious. It reflects Eliot's Lamarckian belief, acquired from her friend, Herbert Spencer, in the racial inheritance of acquired mental characteristics. At a time when Freud was still a young research associate in biology (and several years before he read *Daniel Deronda* at the urging of his fiancée), Eliot thus anticipates a large role for the unconscious in the salvific access of "myth" to the modern mind.[23] But her intuition, that myth rides upon darker forces than transcendentalists acknowledge, seems a casual one, ungrounded in the sort of conceptual system that Freud, for one, would supply. The next significant round of *literary* contributions to the construction of myth will break out only subsequent to developments in other fields—the vitalist philosophies of Nietzsche, Bergson, and James and related activity in the newly fashionable social sciences of ethnology and depth psychology.

NIETZSCHE: RITUAL TRAGEDY, LIFE-ENHANCING ILLUSION, AND THE HAMMER OF ICONOCLASM

Few would deny, I imagine, that Nietzsche's writings are entangled in the construction of myth. But specifying his contributions can be confusing, principally for the reason hinted at in the heading; he is involved at different moments of his relatively brief career in at least three, if not all four, of the main kind of theories. With respect to his mature philosophy and its ultimate impact on the construction of myth in the twentieth century, the last two alluded to in the heading—the constitutive and the ideological—are the more important. But we must not ignore Nietzsche's dealings with romantic or transcendental and folkloristic theory in his early *The Birth of Tragedy Out of the Spirit of Music*. That Nietzsche later disparaged the book as philosophy does not repeal the facts of its reception history in the field of mythography.

His brush with folkloristic theory is brief but intense; it amounts to focusing the attention of classical scholarship upon the ritual origins of Greek tragedy. This refocusing itself is probably of more consequence in the construction of myth than is Nietzsche's specific hypothesis about these origins. By opening a temporal perspective far deeper and more anthropologically sound than the preceding century-long glorification of Greek rationality, Nietzsche inspires directly the first-generation leaders of the so-called "myth and ritual" school, Robertson Smith, James Frazer, and especially Jane Harrison and the other "Cambridge Ritualists." As for Nietzsche himself, this venture into an anthropological or folkloristic theory of myth ends with *The Birth of Tragedy*. His dip into an investigation of ritual is somewhat comparable to Carlyle's into myth as a concrete genre of foundational story; in each case a thinker whose orientation is primarily literary and philosophical glimpses intuitively the beginnings of a whole other kind of approach, which he then pursues no further.

The Birth of Tragedy grapples in somewhat more sustained fashion with Nietzsche's romantic heritage, if only because his central hypothesis is a plainly visible (though profoundly critical) reworking of Schopenhauer. Nietzsche adopts wholeheartedly Schopenhauer's basic metaphysical claim about "the world as will and representation." Even the mind with which we construct our representations is an aspect of Will, part of the universal dynamism turned back upon itself in the weaving of endless illusion. According to Schopenhauer, however, humanity has devised three temporary modes of escape from the indignity of such relentless pain: selfless pity for the suffering of others, religious ascesis and aesthetic contemplation. In these three modes of experience, moments occur in which "all at once the peace which we were always seeking . . . comes to us of its own accord, and it is well with us . . . for we are for the moment set free from the miserable striving of the will; we keep the Sabbath of the penal servitude of willing; the wheel of Ixion stands still" (Schopenhauer 1966, 174). If these three modes of "Sabbath" are not themselves illusion, then what is their ontological status? By introducing this condition of "willlessness" Schopenhauer seems to subvert his monism of dynamic process and confirm a central tenet of romantic ideology, the ability of the beleaguered ego in such paradoxical moments to recoup its autonomy and thus transcend itself.

In *The Birth of Tragedy*, Nietzsche restores by a deliberate and creative misreading of Schopenhauer both the dynamic monism and the conception of the ego as the site of ceaseless illusion. We can watch this sleight of hand at work in the very first section, where he substitutes for Schopenhauer's three conditions of willlessness the two conditions of the Apollonian and the Dionysian:

> We might apply to Apollo the words of Schopenhauer when he speaks of the man wrapped in the veil of *maya*. . . . "Just as in a stormy sea . . . a sailor sits in a boat and trusts in his frail bark: so in the midst of a world of torments the individual human being sits quietly, supported by and trusting in the *principium individuationis*." In fact we might say of Apollo that in him the unshaken faith in this *principium* and the calm repose of the man wrapped up in it receive their most sublime expression.
>
> In this same work Schopenhauer has depicted for us the tremendous *terror* which seizes a man when he is suddenly dumbfounded by the cognitive form of phenomena. . . . If we add to this terror the blissful ecstasy that wells from the innermost depths . . . at this collapse of the *principium individuationis,* we steal a glimpse into the nature of the *Dionysian.* (Nietzsche 1967a, 35–36)

Nietzsche's prime gesture of misreading is to transform the significance of Schopenhauer's metaphor. Schopenhauer's sailor on the stormy sea of Will sits "quietly" amid torments, trusting himself to his "frail" bark of consciousness because he can do nothing else and constantly terrified when any "making strange" of his ordinary numbness reminds him of just how frail his craft really is. But Nietzsche's sailor is either an Apollo, contemplating the situation with an "unshaken faith" in his autonomous ego that permits "calm repose," or, if his sailor's consciousness *is* threatened with extinction, he is a Dionysus who feels, right along with terror, "the blissful ecstasy that wells from the innermost depths." Nietzsche's restoration of an inescapable monism of naturalistic process is more ferocious than Schopenhauer's transcendental exceptionalism. The Apollonian and the Dionysian conditions offer no transcendence in the romantic sense—both are assertions of the will-as-ego against itself. The first is the disposition to enjoy the beauty and order of the ego's constructions *knowing they are illusions,* and the second is the disposition to embrace the source of suffering by fusing with it, merging the suffering fragment with the dynamism of the whole. The most salient feature of this rewriting of Schopenhauer is Nietzsche's almost violent reversal of his predecessor's mood. The Apollonian and Dionysiac conditions are an exaltation of consciousness and of life, contrary to Schopenhauer's bitter distaste for both.

Hence it's not surprising that, although Nietzsche also inherits from Schopenhauer his aesthetics of music and tragedy, these are reconceived along the lines predictable from his revision of the latter's metaphysics. Nietzsche sacks their transcendental empires and divides the spoils between Apollo and Dionysus. Music is the greatest of the arts for him, not because it succeeds in the paradoxical enterprise of directly representing the Will itself for our *contemplation,* as Schopenhauer claims, but because it flows most successfully between the two poles of Dionysiac transport out of selfhood and Apollonian will-to-representation, excluding any moment of transcendental not-willing. From Nietzsche's assumption that the other arts are similar in nature, it follows that the differences between them and music are ones of degree rather than kind. This is why he can entertain the hypothesis, inconceivable to Schopenhauer, that tragedy, which is for both of them, as for Wagner, the second greatest art, is born "out of the spirit of music." Basing his theory on Aristotle's brief hint in the *Poetics* that tragedy arose from the satyr-play, Nietzsche speculates that the participants in the ecstatic chorus gradually produced from this experience of "primordial unity" (37) a mediated world of visual and especially narrative art. The result is inevitably tragic because what the creators express is "the contradiction at the heart of the world" (71), the paradoxical relation between their Apollonian illusions and the underlying Dionysiac process. Nietzsche is unsatisfactorily cryptic both about how humans can inhabit this romantic, Schillerian condition of "primordial unity" and about how, exactly, it gives rise to its Apollonian contrary. But in tragedy, he insists by way of summary, "Dionysus speaks the language of Apollo; and Apollo, finally the language of Dionysus" (130). This, too, is a recognizably romantic claim, but it hearkens back beyond the conventional pieties of the romanticism of Nietzsche's day to something like Blake's fierce conviction that the denizens of humanity's highest state, "Eden," burn in the mental warfare of infinite contraries.[24]

This warfare produces "myth," which is inevitably religious. The plots (*mythoi*) of the drama are all variant expressions of what Nietzsche calls "the mystery doctrine of tragedy: the fundamental knowledge of the oneness of everything existent" (74). In ritual drama "the one truly real Dionysus appears in a variety of forms . . . entangled, as it were, in the net of the individual will. . . . In truth, however, the hero is the suffering Dionysus of the Mysteries" (73). Compared to this genuinely religious insight into the "contradiction at the heart of the world" the very claim of any religion to have a historical foundation reveals a vulgar loss of grip on the authentically sacred. Nietzsche declares that this usurpation by "historical" religions occurs only as "the feeling for myth perishes" (75). These historical pretenders may still offer their worshipers glimpses of the sacred, but only in proportion as they preserve something of the "feeling" for the one, timeless Mystery that preceded them. By the standards of twentieth-century anthropological and classical studies this is dubious speculation, but Nietzsche's youthful affirmation makes a glittering career for itself in its twentieth-century avatars, first among myth-and-ritual theorists, then among modernist novelists and poets, then Jungian depth psychologists, and finally popular midcentury mythographers like Robert Graves and Joseph Campbell.

In spite of his later dissatisfaction with *The Birth of Tragedy,* Nietzsche never repudiates either his early hypothesis about the ritual origins of myth and tragedy or the revision of Schopenhauer's metaphysics on which that hypothesis is based. Instead, he drops in his mature work the special case of the ritual origins of Greek tragedy in order to embrace a much wider, constitutive sense of "myth" already implicit in the early essay. "Myth" now appears, not merely as a series of masks of the perennial Mystery religion, but as socially constructed illusion. Even when focused upon "myth" as social illusion, however, Nietzsche exhibits a thorough ambivalence about its workings that appears related to his early distinction between the Apollonian and the Dionysiac responses to life. On the affirmative, Apollonian side, myth may be a "vital lie." Once the concept is understood to include all our cultural constructs, it falls under the Darwinian rule that it must be an evolutionary adaptation essential to our survival. As Nietzsche phrases it in a famous passage, "The falseness of an opinion is not for us any objection to it. . . . The question is, how far an opinion is life-furthering, life-preserving, species-preserving, perhaps species-rearing; and we are fundamentally inclined to maintain that the falsest opinions (to which the synthetic judgments *a priori* belong) are the most indispensible to us; that without a recognition of logical fictions . . . man could not live" (Nietzsche 1954, 384). Nietzsche's deliberate embrace of Kantian "synthetic *a priori* judgments" in spite of his conviction that these are "the falsest opinions," underscores his determination *"to recognize untruth as a condition of life"* and thus to locate his pragmatic, biologistic contestation of truth and lie "beyond good and evil" (384).

Nietzsche's affirmative, constitutive view of myth as "vital lie" has had a large impact upon constitutive theories in the twentieth century. But the weight of his negative, "Dionysian" testimony on the other side of the issue has proved equally potent, especially within the last generation. Indeed, this negative analysis of myth becomes the most far-reaching of our major "hermeneutics of suspicion" precisely in proportion as it takes for granted, but dreads, myth's universal potential as socially constructed lie. Particularly as mediated through Heidegger, this suspicion looms behind poststructural and deconstructionist projects, combining so readily there with the less comprehensive Marxian form of suspicion as to form distinctive and powerful new versions of the kind of theories I've labeled ideological.

In an early fragment that dates from only the year after *The Birth of Tragedy,* Nietzsche declares "truth" "a mobile army of metaphors, metonymns and anthropomorphisms . . . which have been enhanced . . . poetically and rhetorically, and which after long use seem firm, canonical and obligatory to people: truths are illusions about which one has forgotten that this is what they are; metaphors which are worn out and without sensuous power, coins which have lost their pictures and now matter only as metal" (Nietzsche 1976a, 46–47). This fragment, a favorite with Foucault and a source of Derrida's conceit of "white mythology," appears only posthumously, but we can trace its sentiment everywhere in earlier publications. In *The Twilight of the Idols,* for example, Nietzsche applies the notion of truth as hypostatized trope to his Humean analysis of causes. "In its origin language belongs in the age of the most rudimentary form of psychology. We enter a realm of crude fetishism. . . . Everywhere it sees a doer and doing; it believes in will as *the* cause; it believes in the ego . . . as substance, and it projects this faith . . . upon all things" (Nietzsche 1976b, 482–483). Marx's fetishism of commodities is broad enough, but according to Nietzsche the structure of language itself, originating in what he takes to be a historical age of fetishism, idolatrously endows with life abstractions from the universal dynamism of will. His concomitant attack upon the substantiality of the ego is directed not only against post-Cartesian philosophy in general, but against romantic and Idealist claims for its autonomy in particular. This distinctive concatenation of disparagement—of the construction of concepts together with the substantiality of the entity doing the constructing—constitutes perhaps Nietzsche's principal lesson for twentieth-century poststructuralism.

In *Beyond Good and Evil,* Nietzsche finally discovers his definitive label for the activity traditionally glorified in Western philosophy as thinking: "it is we alone who have devised cause, sequence, reciprocity, relativity . . . motive and purpose; and when we interpret and intermix this symbol-world . . with things, we act once more as we have always acted—*mythologically*" (404). The practice described in this definitive word is obviously not just that of professional philosophers; it is entrenched in the nature of language as a social institution; our entire "symbol-world" is invented and disseminated myth. "I am afraid we are not yet rid of God because we still have faith in grammar" (Nietzsche 1976b, 483). Both the past and the physical world, the objects of history and science, are matters of mythopoeic perspective. The French Revolution is a "terrible farce," made significant only because "the noble and visionary spectators of Europe have interpreted from a distance their own indignation and enthusiasm . . . *until the text has disappeared under the interpretation*" (Nietzsche 1954, 423). As for the physical sciences, "Against postivism, which halts at phenomena—'There are only *facts*'—I would say: 'No, facts is precisely what there is not, only interpretations'" (Nietzsche 1967b, 267). Under the pressure of so radical a nominalism and perspectivism, myth as life-enhancing untruth can transmute in the blink of an eye into the idol to which one must take the hammer of iconoclasm.

In the construction of "myth," then, Nietzsche gathers and disseminates elements of all four major types of theories. There's an irony of the sort usually called poetic justice in the career of a thinker who celebrates the extra-rational wholeness of life in *The Birth of Tragedy* by setting up Plato's Socrates as his primary straw man, but then proceeds to remind us, in his later clarity about the contrary functions of myth, of no one so much as Plato. He is no Platonist, of course; his rejection of metaphysical dualism is consistent across his career. He is no Hegelian, either, because of his rejection of any sublation of contraries, but he certainly epitomizes dramatically in his later thinking about myth Hegel's recognition of the modern struggle between "superstition and enlightenment."

[4]

Myth as an Aspect of "Primitive" Religion

Although the romantic or transcendentalist conception of myth dominates the first half of the nineteenth century and endures in belletristic and religious circles to this day, it loses its cultural hegemony in the latter part of the century to its anthropological or folkloristic counterpart. This may be described provisionally as the conception of myth as a kind of narrative that *others,* ancient or "primitive," remote in time or in space, have regarded as sacred. Where practitioners of the transcendental version exalt the power of the *contemporary* imaginist to create or re-create myth, folkloristic theorists assume either that Western modernity has outgrown myth or else that what myth may have become in the modern world is no proper concern of theirs.

This conception of myth bears some obvious marks of its descent from eighteenth-century attitudes toward "fable" before the term's romantic transformation. Where the romantic construction is primarily the work of philosophers and poets in rebellion against Enlightenment rationalism, the folkloristic version is primarily that of students of archaeology, law, history, sociology, psychology, and anthropology proper—thinkers who accept in principle the Enlightenment aspiration toward the empirical investigation of civil institutions. But even though the new theorists descend in certain respects from Enlightenment traditions of social thought, their speculations about "myth" are also characterized by a striking *dis*continuity from it. This discontinuity is, in the first place, quite literally chronological. With the exceptions of Comte (discussed briefly below) and the anti-romantic line from Hegel to Marx traced in the preceding chapter, no important non-romantic theory appears between Dupuis's *Origin of All Cults* in 1795 and Tylor's *Primitive Culture* in 1871. And this temporal hiatus harbors a congeries of intellectual and cultural shifts quite sufficient to guarantee that any return to Enlightenment values in mythography will be return with a difference. One of these shifts stems from the romantic movement itself. Even while nineteenth-century practitioners of the human sciences remain indifferent to the transcendental claims of romantic individualism, they adopt virtually without remark the earlier view of myth as Vichian key, that is, as the repository of a culture's social values. When this successful romantic transvaluation of story combines with historical relativism and with the new expansion of the temporal scale of human development, the result is the launching of intensive ethnological investigations of the sacred stories of "primitive" societies.[1]

In recent years a number of valuable studies have foregrounded the ideological bent of this new ethnology.[2] Most of its ideological aspects are not the direct business of this study, but there is one large exception; namely, the outbreak among "armchair" anthropologists of theorizing about "primitive" religion. The extent of this obsession gives rise to the suspicion that, behind the shift to empirical modes of argumentation, the appeal of "primitive" religion is motivated by the same anxieties that produced the romantic invention of myth. In any case, to conceive of myth as *sacred* story is inevitably to link it closely to religion. Hence it isn't surprising that beginning with Comte, myth in its anthropological sense is widely perceived as a subordinate feature of the religion of exotic societies. Why and how myth is regarded as a *subset* of religion remains to be specified in particular cases, but the fact of their close connections requires a certain amount of attention in the chapter that follows to theories of "primitive" religion as well as myth.

My roughly chronological account of these theories also turns up a curious small-scale repetition of Enlightenment thinking followed by romantic reaction. The initial cognitive theories of Auguste Comte, E. B. Tylor, and Herbert Spencer gradually reveal their dark undersides and give way to the emotive theories of Robertson Smith and Lucien Lévy-Bruhl that stimulate, if they do not express, a second wave of romanticism. Even the ideas of two of the most influential thinkers in this sequence, J. G. Frazer and Émile Durkheim, both self-professed paladins of Enlightenment, are so bent by the force field of the emotive theories fashionable by the turn of the century that they are turned, in specific instances, against their originators' rationalism. The chapter concludes with an account of the rise of the first so-called "myth and ritual" school out of Nietzsche, Frazer, and (surprisingly perhaps) Durkheim. It begins, however, with the anomalous and amphibious theory of F. Max Müller. Some of Müller's premises are so blatantly transcendentalist that the theory might have come up in the previous chapter. But Müller does advance a linguistic explanation of "myth" as cognitive failure, and his work is primarily related in terms of influence and scholarly dialogue to the more positivistic cognitive theories that follow it.

MAX MÜLLER:
MYTH AS A DISEASE OF LANGUAGE

When Friedrich Max Müller's *Comparative Mythology* was published in 1856, Müller was a quite young Sanskrit scholar who had moved to England from Germany ten years earlier to supervise the publication by Oxford of his four-volume edition of the *Rig Veda* (the cost to be borne, interestingly, by the East India Company).[3] The popularity of *Comparative Mythology,* which made Müller's reputation, stands in revealing contrast to the fate of another significant work on myth published in the same year, Schelling's posthumous *Philosophy of Mythology.* In another of the endless ironies of history, Schelling's work is ignored and Müller's hailed on all sides, even though the theological implications of Müller's theories are as regressive as Schelling's are progressive. Where Schelling anticipates twentieth-century process philosophies, Müller hearkens back to the likes of Bryant and Warburton in the eighteenth. His anachronistic goal—to show that world mythologies are degenerations from an original monotheism—is a real-life version of (and possible inspiration for) that of George Eliot's fictional Edward Casaubon in *Middlemarch.* Nevertheless, his new "comparative mythology," because it adopts an aggressively "scientific" posture, jostles off-stage the now outmoded masterpiece of Idealist dialectic. The following passage from Müller's *Science of Language* (1873) is simultaneously an eloquent celebration of the new prestige of "induction," and an almost comic example of its cooption by a thinker strikingly backward-looking in every respect *except* in his occupation of a fashionable field of research and an ear for modish patter:

> The great schools of philosophy in the 18th century were satisfied with build-
> ing up theories about how language might have sprung into life, how religion
> might have been revealed or invented, how mythology might have been put
> together by priests, or poets, or statesmen, for the purposes of instruction, of
> amusement, or of fraud. Such systems, though ingenious and plausible . . .
> will have to give way to the spirit of what may be called the *Historical School*
> of the 19th century. The principles of these two schools are diametrically
> opposed; the one begins with theories without facts, the other with facts
> without theories. The systems of *Locke, Voltaire* and *Rousseau,* and in later
> times *Comte,* are plain, intelligible, and perfectly rational: the facts collected
> by men like *Wolf, Herder, Niebuhr, F. Schlegel, W. von Humboldt, Bopp, Bournouf,*
> *Grimm, Bunsen,* and others, are fragmentary, the inductions to which they
> point incomplete and obscure, and opposed to many of our received ideas.
> Nevertheless, the study of the antiquity of man, the Paleontology of the
> human mind, can never again be allowed to become the playground of mere
> theorizers, however bold and brilliant, but must henceforth be cultivated in
> accordance with those principles that have produced such rich harvests in
> other fields of inductive research. (Müller 1899, vol. 2, 433–444)

Müller's epigrammatic "theories without facts . . . facts without theories" chimes with Marx in *The German Ideology,* but by the time Müller proclaims his defiance of "received ideas" he is riding upon them rather than opposing them. He reveals the deeply romantic cast of his intellectual inheritance when he ranges Enlightenment thinkers so simplistically as foes of empiricism and romantics as its friends. His inclusion of Comte as an epigone of Enlightenment foreshadows his response to the positivistic theories of Tylor and Spencer. To the end of his long career in English anthropology (his own definition of his field), he remains an arch-opponent of Darwinism, insisting, like our contemporary "creationists," that his evolutionary antagonists are mere spinners of unverifiable theory, whereas he himself builds always upon induction from fact. Hence the confidence with which he views himself as engaged in a "Paleontology of the human mind."

As Müller's list of romantic savants indicates, his "science" consists in the employment of philology in historical research. The tradition in which he proudly situates himself had indeed achieved by midcentury the status of a paradigm for the human sciences. Within twenty-some years of William Jones's pioneering work, and a decade before the voyage of *The Beagle,* the new philologists, preeminently Bopp, Rask, and Jacob Grimm, had succeeded in establishing two stunning propositions: that a vast network of Indo-European languages had evolved from a common "Aryan" original, and that this evolution had proceeded, and was still proceeding according to patterns of phonemic change so regular as to deserve to be called "laws." For the next half-century, would-be innovators in the social sciences and humanities appealed constantly to this model science of human behavior to lend color to their own projects. Much of the success of *Comparative Mythology* can be attributed to Müller's colonizing extension of this philological rule of law over the unmapped, disorderly territories of mythology.

The opening pages of *Comparative Mythology* are sufficient to indicate how far Müller is from pure induction, how beset by traditional religious presuppositions. "As far as we can trace back the footsteps of man, even on the lowest strata of history, we see that the divine gift of a sound and sober intellect belonged to him from the very first; and the idea of a humanity emerging slowly from the depths of an animal brutality can never be maintained again. . . . *Human language* forms an uninterrupted chain from the first dawn of history down to our own times . . . and this language, with its wonderful structure, bears witness against such unhallowed imputations" (Müller 1909, 9–10). Müller's insistence on the linguistic gulf between humans and other species is still borne out by twentieth-century ethnology, ethology, and linguistics; no human groups have ever been found without a language of remarkable grammatical sophistication and no non-human species (though some can be taught certain rudiments) has yet been discovered to possess one. But the existence of this gulf does not, of course, disprove Darwinian developmentalism; it demonstrates only that we are ignorant of all but the past few minutes in the linguistic evolution of our species. Müller's regressiveness is underwritten by his convictions that human history is scarcely older than the *Vedas,* that humanity was specially created a few thousand years ago with its "divine gift" of reason intact and that evolution from lower species is therefore an impossibility. In his later journalistic debates with the evolutionists, Müller avoids the issue of biblical creationism by representing himself as a Kantian, unwilling to pass beyond the empirical limits of a linguistic phenomenology. This stance, which enables him to be more clear-sighted than the evolutionists about the enormousness of the linguistic gap between humans and other animals, also permits him to preserve his uncritical *a priori* assumptions about the origins of humanity.

Müller's new science of comparative mythology turns out to be the employment of philology to recover the pristine religious concepts of "Aryan" origin as these are embodied in the mythology of the *Vedas*.[4] This project aspires to recover the original divine revelation from which mythology is a falling-away. The "fact" of this degeneration motivates Müller's development of his theory of mythology as a "disease of language." Like other nineteenth-century mythographers (most ironically, like his principal antagonist, Andrew Lang), Müller is scandalized by the violence and sexual frankness still so evident behind the heavily rationalized mythology of Greece. His response is a philologist's version of the bowdlerizing impulse current among popular retailers of this mythology such as Kingsley, Bulfinch, and Hawthorne. Müller devotes roughly the first two-fifths of *Comparative Mythology* to a series of etymological restorations whose subtext seems to be that the family life and political and religious sentiments of the ancient "Aryans" were of Biedermeier respectability. He concludes, therefore, that something must have gone disastrously awry between the *Vedas* and the nastiness of Homer and Hesiod. This something is linguistic usage. After the initial period of perspicuous relations between words and things, humans proved themselves inept philologists. The original "Aryans" naturally expressed their religious concepts in figurative language. During the "Mythological or Mythopoeic Age" (12) that followed, however, people forgot the etymologies of their ancestors, took literally radical metaphor, prosopoeia, and the gender of nouns, and confused homonyms, synonyms, and "polynyms" (different epithets for the same thing.) They were thus beguiled into conjuring up nonexistent personages and elaborating stories, often disgusting, about their behavior. In contrast, then, to the *Urdummheit* postulated by the evolutionists, Müüller portrays a kind of *nachträglich dummheit*, a period during which humanity took leave of its original "sound and sober intellect" in favor of a state of linguistic naiveté entirely unknown to observation.

Müller's exposition of this theory displays at least two sets of conceptual inconsistencies already well established in the problematics of romantic theory and repeated across the entire history of the modern construction of "myth." The first of these is the confusion first isolated by Creuzer, by whom Müller is much influenced, between myth as concept and myth as narrative (in Creuzer's terms, between "symbol" and "allegory"). When Müller speaks of "Aryan" myth or mythology, he generally signifies the pure concepts intuitively available to humanity in the dawn of time, whereas myth in the "Mythopoeic Age," though it begins in conceptual error, has somehow, by definition, degenerated into story. The second set of inconsistencies is closely related. On one hand "mythopoeia" is the special product of a historical era, the "Mythopoeic Age," but, on the other, it is the permanent, structurally guaranteed result of mistaking the literal for the figurative and vice versa. In the last chapter of *The Science of Language*, Müller adopts for the nonce a compromise between his synchronic and diachronic versions: "There is a time in the early history of all nations in which the mythological character predominates to such an extent that we may as well speak of it as the mythological period. . . . But the tendencies which characterize the mythological period . . . continue to work under different disguises in all ages, even in our own. . . . Whenever any word that was at first used metaphorically, is used without a clear conception of its metaphorical meaning, there is danger of mythology . . . or, if I may say so, diseased language" (455–456).

If Müller had been able to pursue rigorously the consequences of this latter line of thinking, he might have developed a critique of transcendentalist claims to mythopoeic authority as strong as those of Marx and Nietzsche. But this achievement would have required a Saussurean revolution in linguistics and a systematic anti-metaphysical bias that we don't find in combination before the linguistic theories of myth produced by Roland Barthes and Claude Lévi-Strauss in the 1950s. Müller does resemble Lévi-Strauss in presuming that the ideal unit of "myth"—what Lévi-Strauss calls a "mytheme"—is conceptual rather than narrative, and he resembles Barthes in treating "myth" as "diseased language," to be cured by exposing the illogicality of its semiotic manipulations. Lévi-Strauss has in fact praised Müller as a precursor in the discovery of conceptual coding as the basis of mythology, while criticizing him for attempting to decipher all myth "by means of a single and exclusive code"—the astronomical.[5]

What Lévi-Strauss calls the "astronomical code" is Müller's remorseless etymological tracking of the blunders that constitute ancient mythology back to their origins in responses to celestial phenomena, mainly solar. But Müller is not a nature mythologist; he does not claim that his Ur-"Aryans" *worshiped* natural phenomena. Rather, like Creuzer and Jacob Grimm, he holds that his "Aryans" understood intuitively that the natural world emanates from a Neoplatonic One who is alone to be worshiped. From Heyne and Herder onward, however, through the romantics and well into the early twentieth century in the case of German philology and anthropology, the assumption that mythology is inspired by natural phenomena dominates the field. It is hardly surprising, therefore, that Müller should attempt to integrate this "received idea" into his own theory. What is surprising is that he treats the mythopoeia of natural phenomena as error, thus radically undermining this most popular of theories. But neither he nor his large audience seems to notice. Müller, like Tylor after him, occasionally refers to Wordsworth (with revealingly inconsistent approval) as an example of the survival of this sort of mythopoeia in the modern world, but he does so without the slightest glimmer of suspicion that Wordsworth and his German and English compeers, including Müller's own poet father, might have *invented* the genre, that explanations of myth as personifications of natural phenomena might be little older than Herder and Schiller. In this respect, too, his devotion to non-inductive transcendentalist and religious presuppositions thwarts his gropings toward the radical linguistic critique of which he trembles on the brink.

Müller's theory of myth was eventually subsumed in a more ambitious design. Throughout his career he promoted the serious study of Eastern religions, and in 1873 launched, as general editor, the great Oxford series of *Sacred Books of the East,* which first made many of the classics of India and China accessible to Western readers. His eventual aspiration, as Eric Sharpe sums it up, "was to elaborate a complete science of human thought . . . in four stages, beginning with the science of language, and passing through the science of mythology and the science of religion, to the final goal of the science of thought" (Sharpe 1975, 40). This project, with its situating of myth as one of four interrelated modes of human symbolizing, albeit an erroneous one, suggests the plan carried out a generation after Müller's death by Ernst Cassirer in his *Philosophy of Symbolic Forms* (1923–1929). The combination of Müller's neo-Kantian phenomenology and his philological bent leads him to anticipate not only the general "linguistic turn" of Cassirer, Langer, and others, but even Cassirer's specific set of the major categories of cultural symbolizing. Here, as in the very different cases of Barthes and Lévi-Strauss, we see Müller apprehending, without quite being able to grasp clearly what he was after, a major theory of myth of the century ahead.

COMTE, TYLOR, AND SPENCER: MYTH AS THE RECORD OF ERROR

No work brings the new human sciences into focus on our topic like *Primitive Culture* (1871). Tylor's gift for synthesis enables him to fit together under his visionary conception of the holistic scope of "culture" a great deal of the accumulating evidence from archaeology, philology, folklore, ethnology, and other comparative studies. He organizes so striking a conspectus of "primitive culture" that anthropology in England becomes for a generation, as Max Müller himself put it, "Mr. Tylor's science" (Stocking 1987, 195). Mythology bulks large in this science; Tylor presents it as a fundamental category of "primitive" culture, on the same taxonomical level as language, arithmetic, religion, and ritual. Since Tylor seems generally to follow Comte in his conception of "primitive" religion, his treatment of "myth" as an independent category and his devotion of three chapters to it comes as something of a surprise. This major emphasis upon mythology is probably a tribute to Max Müller, by whose theory Tylor was so struck that he permitted it to come, at least in this one respect, between him and his normally Comtean orientation.

Comte's schema of a stadial metahistory, reminiscent of those of his country-men, Turgot, Condorcet, and Saint-Simon, as well as of Hegel and Schelling and the newly visible Vico, is another tripartite one. Humanity passes through three "states" of development—the theological, the metaphysical, and the scientific.[6] The broad outline of these states persists throughout Comte's career, though his exposition of them in his *Cours de philosophie positive* (1830–1842) is his most detailed and definitive account.[7] After outlining there his three general states, he devotes individual "les-sons" to each of the three major subdivisions of the "theological" state—fetish-ism, polytheism, and monotheism. Fetishism corresponds to "primitive" religion, within which it is possible to distinguish an earlier "spontaneous" phase and a later "systematic" one. Comte's fetishism resembles De Brosses's eighteenth-century account of it, and Comte's adoption of the term undoubtedly has much to do with its broad dissemination in the nineteenth century. Fetishism, according to him, begins among nomadic tribes, spreads only gradually to sedentary peoples, and is eventually systematized, first as organized religion and then as an aspect of the community's military might. At this point it is transmogrified into polytheism, of which the historical religions of antiquity are examples. Polytheism itself may be divided into three moments: the "conservative," "intellectual," and "social." In the first the gods are taken seriously by the standards of local piety, in the second the mythology of the religion is interpreted by philosophers and poets, and in the third it is co-opted as state religion. Polytheism gives way in turn to a sequential development of monotheism that need not concern us further here, since mythology is strictly an affair of the outmoded polytheistic phase.

For our purposes, the most striking feature of Comte's developmental history is the lateness of mythology. Comte writes on the verge of the great reconception of the evolutionary time scale, and hence entertains a notion of the "primitive" that is shallow in both the literal and figurative senses of the word. As one result, he conceives of the phase of fetishism as entirely *pre*-mythological. Furthermore, his conception of mythology, like that of his romantic predecessors and contemporaries, is so fixated upon the Greek model that he ties its appearance to the second, "intellectual" moment even within polytheism itself. This is why he waxes eloquent in lesson 53, along conventionally romantic lines, about how favorable the polytheistic phase was, in its last two moments, to the genius of poet and artist. Thanks to the eventual triumph of the folkloristic conception of myth that was coming into its own even at the time Comte was writing, it's hard for us to believe that he did not at least envision the rise of mythology in the first, "conservative" moment of polytheism when the gods were the objects of local piety. Just what material, after all, did the poets and artists work with? But Comte is silent on this point; mythology appears only in connection with the second moment, as if its self-conscious interpreters were also its originators, as indeed he may have believed.

This view of mythology as a late and sophisticated product in the evolution of religion is very influential in the positivistic tradition; we will find it again in Tylor, Spencer, Frazer, and Durkheim. Mythology is thus doubly denigrated. First, like all religion, it is outmoded superstition; the "theological" stage of humanity properly belongs to the past. Second, even as religion, myth is "intellectual," rationalized, and sentimentalized by art. This second assumption also appears, *a fortiori,* among theorists like Robertson Smith and Jane Harrison, who conceive of religion in the first place as affect rather than cognition.

But the claim that Comte considers religion and myth as outmoded requires, before we leave *him* behind, one important qualification. It follows from his belief in the recapitulation of phylogeny by ontogeny that the "theological" state belongs not only to the childhood of the race but also to that of the individual. Religion (and therefore mythmaking) thus arises instinctively in childhood and has to be outgrown or displaced just as the race has done. Conversely, surviving human groups dominated by religion and myth, namely the "savage" or "primitive," are stuck in childhood. Their analogue in the modern West is the one class of adults not only permitted but even encouraged not to grow up—that is, artists. It's no accident that, in Comte's associative thinking, poetry and the other arts exhibit a special affinity for mythology. The modern poet is a natural mythologist because arrested developmentally, like the "savage," in childhood. This set of analogies becomes the standard positivistic way of accounting for the existence of the arts; they will reemerge repeatedly in this chapter and the three following ones, particularly as an *explanation* for the romantic belief in the modern survival of mythopoeia, now an *idée reçue*.

Tylor subscribes in *Primitive Culture* to a recognizably Comtean conception of the evolution of religion, but only with significant alterations. He tells us that he means by "animism" pretty much what Comte means by "fetishism," "a general theory of primitive religion, in which external objects are regarded as animated by a life analogous to man's" (Tylor 1974, 132). He departs from Comte, however, by relegating "fetishism" to what he calls "a subordinate department, the 'worship of stocks and stones,'" and by extending animism to cover Comte's second phase, polytheism, as well. Thus, where Comte presents the sequence fetishism, polytheism, monotheism, Tylor gives us animism A, animism B, and monotheism. Furthermore, A and B are not distinctly separated moments, so that for all practical purposes we simply have animism (subsuming fetishism) gradually becoming more elaborate and giving way to a monotheism itself so far from rigorous or uniform that it allows plenty of room for the incursion of animism even here. These are serious departures; they eliminate Comte's dubious stadial schema in favor of a more fluid development, and they reflect, in their deeper sense of "the primitive," Tylor's assimilation of both the expanded time scale and the folkloristic sense of the evolutionary continuum between popular and "artistic" storytelling. For Tylor, Greek mythology, too, is a product of animism.

These changes evidence in two respects the impact of Max Müller upon Tylor's conception of myth. First, Tylor follows Müller in taking myth to be a species of mental error. This general judgment is obvious in his list of the mechanisms of what he calls "the mythic faculty": "the processes of animating and personifying nature, the formation of legend by exaggeration and perversion of fact, the stiffening of metaphor by mistaken realizations of words, the conversion of speculative theories and still less substantial fictions into pretended traditional events, the passage of myth into miracle-legend, the definition by name and place given to any floating imagination, the adaptation of mythic incident as moral example, and the incessant crystallization of story into history" (Tylor 1958, 415). This "mythic faculty" produces by these operations results so uniform that "it becomes possible to treat myths as an organic product of mankind at large, in which individual, national and even racial distinctions stand subordinate to universal qualities of the human mind" (415–416). Myth thus demonstrates the "psychic unity" of the race, even if it does so negatively. In a sense more rigorous than Fontenelle's, myth is for Tylor a "history of the errors of the human mind." But in spite of Tylor's *empressement* with Müller (which remained a difficulty for Tylor's followers in the ensuing quarter-century of battle between Müller and the evolutionists), Tylor's conception of the mechanisms of error is considerably broader than Müller's "disease of language."[8] Only the third item above in his list of eight, "the stiffening of metaphor by mistaken realization of words," corresponds to Müller's linguistic criteria. Most of the other items are wider modes, several of them generic, of processing fancy as fact. Tylor perhaps comes closest to a comprehensive definition of "myth" when he speaks of "the incessant crystallization of [fictive] story into [believed] history." In keeping with this broader view of what constitutes myth, he remarks, "I am disposed to think (differing here in some measure from Professor Max Müller's view of the subject) that the mythology of the lower races rests especially on a basis of real and sensible analogy, and that the great expansion of verbal metaphor into myth belongs to more advanced periods of civilization. In a word, I take material myth to be the primary, and verbal myth to be the secondary formation" (298–299). Between Tylor's courtliness and his penchant for synthesis, it is difficult to tell if he recognizes here how radically his linguistic philosophy actually differs from Müller's. It is the difference between an idealist conception and a positivist one, language as intuitive correspondence between mind and thing, initially implanted by a Creator, and language as evolutionary development from a natural prelinguistic condition. Tylor's own assumptions here—about an analogical form of reasoning and a "material myth" that precede language—glide lightly over profound issues in linguistic philosophy. But it seems clear enough from our distance that his grounds for extending the reach of myth backward into the "primitive" and forward into the "civilized" are fundamentally irreconcilable with Müller's. One can't simultaneously understand "myth" as wholly the result of a degenerative disease of language and as primarily a "material" construction that develops synthetically with the evolution of thought.[9]

The second important respect in which Tylor's orbit around Comte is affected by the pull of Müller is in his conception of "animism," although in this case Müller and Comte are pulling in the same direction. Tylor's difference from Müller here is only a matter of degree. Müller foregrounds linguistic distortion as the major cause of mythology and treats personification of nature as a minor and ancillary one, whereas Tylor, adhering more closely to Comte, reverses the emphasis: "First and foremost among the causes which transfigure into myths the facts of daily experience, is the belief in the animation of all nature, rising at its highest pitch to personification" (Tylor 1958, 285). Tylor devotes about two-thirds of his entire discussion of myth to this category. As a rather ironic consequence of his reversal of Müller's emphasis, Tylor pumps conspicuously into his discipline one first-rate piece of transcendentalist thinking that Müller downplays—the notion celebrated among the German and English romantics that myth is created by personifying the natural world. It is a tribute to the strength of the acceptance of this idea that even so determined a rationalist as Tylor shows no sign of recognizing either its recentness or its sources. His promotion of it helps to explain why we find the godfathers of modern social anthropology, Franz Boas and Bronislaw Malinowski, in the 1910s and 1920s respectively, still considering it necessary, when reviewing current theories of myth, to identify nature-myth as their number one enemy.

This advocacy of animism is perhaps made easier for Tylor because he generally assumes as Müller and Comte do, that it is a mode of projection safely confined to the Western past. Under pressure, however, from the increasingly received romantic assumption that a faculty for mythopoeia survives in humanity, Tylor makes, occasionally, a pair of inconsistent and potentially subversive concessions. The first is that the "mythic faculty" is still available to us, albeit in fossilized form. "Savages have been for untold ages, and still are, living in the myth-making stage of the human mind" (Tylor 1958, 283). This admission at least envisions a social and geographic barrier between "them" and "us," but the second class of exceptions does not. Passages in *Primitive Culture* locating animism firmly in archaic times alternate with others that repeat the analogy popularized by Locke and ratified by Lamarck's biology between the states of "savagery" and childhood. "In our childhood we dwelt at the very gates of the realm of myth. In mythology, the child is, in a deeper sense than we are apt to use the phrase, father to the man. . . . We may here again claim the savage as a representative of the childhood of the human race" (283). In this passage, rife with diction and figures taken directly from the romantic poets, mythopoeia is still a liminal faculty confined to childhood. But it is elsewhere extended to adults, beginning with those childlike adults, the poets: "A poet of our own day has still much in common with the minds of uncultured tribes in the mythologic stage of thought" (315). "Wordsworth, that 'modern ancient,' as Max Müller has so well called him, could write of Storm and Winter, or of the naked Sun climbing the sky, as though he were some Vedic poet at the head-spring of his race" (305). In one well-known passage, Tylor even asserts that all sympathetic modern students of myth "live near this frontier-line and can go in and out" (317). Perhaps Tylor merely means here that adult enthusiasts are capable of reassuming momentarily their childish credulity, but even so, the concession opens a theoretical possibility at odds with the gravamen of his rationalist argument. It communicates a suggestion, officially unauthorized as it were, that the mind of the contemporary Westerner conceals a tract dominated by animistic thinking.

In pointing out these minor incoherences in Tylor's rationalism, I do not want to be mistaken as arguing that he is a closet transcendentalist. Such lapses are significant especially *because* they are aberrations in a generally strong and consistent rationalism. They indicate points of strain that link Tylor to the transcendentalist theories that precede him and the affective theories that follow (just as his rationalism disjoins him from these). As a final instance of such significant moments of incoherence in Tylor's personal struggle with the grand problematic of "myth," I will call attention to his remarkable (and very influential) promotion of the status of myth within the discipline of anthropology. The only major theorist comparable to him in this respect is Claude Lévi-Strauss. A glance backward at Tylor's list of the causes of mythmaking will show that not all myth is animism, just as all animism is not necessarily myth. Myth and religion, whatever their degree of overlap, are not the same thing. By locating myth, as he does in *Primitive Culture,* on the same conceptual level as language, mathematics, and religion, Tylor presents it as an independent cultural product with its own intrinsic laws of development. The fact that he views it thus may account for his peculiar deployment of the phrase "mythic faculty." His perhaps unwary use of the word "faculty" inevitably connotes a distinct power of mind, as in "faculty psychology," and thus suggests something like the conception of "the mythic" as a major mode of symbolic thought as subsequently developed by Ernst Cassirer in his *Philosophy of Symbolic Forms.* Cassirer's, of course, is fundamentally an *affective* theory, entirely incompatible with Tylor's view of myth as a species of logical error, nor does Tylor's conception of it as mistaken scientific speculation permit any truck with it as an independent mode of thought. But significant inconsistencies like the exalted location of myth as a cultural phenomenon, and the phrase "mythic faculty" that slips out in connection with this high estimate, should not be blinked away; they are valuable indications of certain fault lines in Tylor's rationalist treatment of the problematic.

Herbert Spencer's once highly modish views of "primitive" religion and myth for the most part complement Tylor's. The first volume of his *Principles of Sociology* (1876) is devoted to the study of "primitive man," and over half the tome is about religion. What Spencer most broadly finds is a foregone conclusion, another instance of his master-idea of "superorganic evolution": "A system of superstitions evolves after the same manner as all other things. By continuous integration and differentiation, it is formed into an aggregate which, while increasing, passes from an indefinite incoherent homogeneity to a definite coherent hetereogeneity" (Spencer 1985, 423).[10] The actual "system of superstitions" that Spencer discerns is a "ghost theory" of the origin of religion, which plays for him the part that "fetishism" does for Comte and "animism" for Tylor.[11] All "primitive" religion evolves by way of the projected conception of the human "soul through various differentiating versions of ancestor-worship until each mythology has its major and minor presiding agents" (442). Like Comte and unlike Tylor, Spencer confines mythology entirely within religion. Mythology is said to be "primitive" religion's most heterogeneous (that is, most highly developed) elaboration. It is the flower of "primitive" religion, but it has no independent status as a mode of thought. Spencer's more systematic positivist rigor thus avoids any inconsistent concessions to transcendentalist conceptions of myth.

Spencer's systematic commitment to a rise from undifferentiated homogeneity to "definite coherent heterogeneity" also ensures that, unlike Tylor, he plainly declares the impossibility of any compromise with Max Müller's notion of original linguistic revelation. He goes straight for the absurdity of Müller's asking us to believe that the species that began with the power to think abstractly subsequently found itself unable to express abstraction except in terms of the concrete. In the controversy that follows, Spencer articulates very clearly the gulf between the conceptions of "primitive" religions and myth characteristic of the new positivism, and the various strains of neo-Kantian idealism against which positivism continues to struggle.[12]

ROBERTSON SMITH:
MYTH AS THE RATIONALIZATION OF DEED

The sort of Whiggish confidence in "progress" so apparent in Tylor and Spencer seems to lose way gradually during the '70s, and during the '80s less intellectualist views of human nature and of social behavior come into their own. This discounting of rationality is noticeable over the next generation in many fields. In philosophy, for instance, we encounter the irrationalist theories of Schopenhauer, Nietzsche,

James, and Bergson; in social theory the work of Tönnies, Pareto, Sorel, and Weber; in psychology the emphasis on instinct in Tardes and Ribot, Le Bon's work on the behavior of crowds, and Freud and Janet on the influence of the unconscious. This sea change also affects the theorizing of the "armchair" thinkers, fascinated with human origins, who continue to construct "primitive" religion and myth out of the data of ethnology. We find in the newer theorists a shift toward explanation of myth in terms of affect, whether this affect be thought of primarily as individual emotion or as the expressive behavior of groups.

William Robertson Smith's *Lectures on the Religion of the Semites: The Fundamental Institutions* (1889) presents an important transitional case in the turn toward affective theory. It is transitional in the sense that Smith makes a powerful case for ancient *religion* as affective, while maintaining the status of *myth* as cognitive. Smith wastes little time in laying down in "Lecture I" a manifesto of the new perspective. He points out that the modern Westerner's experience of religion naturally inclines him, in investigating "some strange or antique religion" first to "search for a creed and find in it the key to ritual and practice" (Smith 1969, 16). Smith does not name but plainly has in mind the cognitive approaches of Tylor and Spencer: "But the antique religions had for the most part no creed; they consisted entirely of institutions and practices." Here, in a single sentence, is the heart of the manifesto. It follows that students of ancient religion must attend primarily not to what its practitioners said but to what they did. "No doubt men will not habitually follows certain practices without attaching a meaning to them; but as a rule we find that while the practice was rigorously fixed, the meaning attached to it was extremely vague, and the same rite was explained by different people in different ways, without any question of orthodoxy or heterodoxy arising in consequence. . . . The rite, in short, was connected not with a dogma but with a myth" (16–17). Smith has internalized perfectly here Tylor's doctrine of "survivals." "Practices" are better evidence of "primitive" religion than "meanings" because the former, being traditional, habitual, and unreflective are more conservative. "Myth" obviously means here an *ex post facto* rationalization, even though of a sort that must evade dogmatic precision if it is to accommodate the range of practitioners' interpretations of why they do what they do. Smith lays this out in his next paragraph with an elegance and clarity that make it the *locus classicus* of what later comes to be called rather helplessly the "myth and ritual school" or "the ritual theory of mythology":

> In all antique religions, mythology takes the place of dogma; that is, the sacred lore of priests and people, so far as it does not consist of mere rules for the performance of religious acts, assumes the form of stories about the gods; and these stories afford the only explanation that is offered of the precepts of religion and the prescribed rules of ritual. But, strictly speaking, this mythology was no essential part of ancient religion. . . . Belief in a certain series of myths was neither obligatory as a part of true religion, nor was it supposed that, by believing, a man acquired religious merit and conciliated the favor of the gods. What was obligatory and meritorious was the exact performance of certain sacred acts prescribed by religious tradition. This being

> so, it follows that mythology ought not to take the prominent place too often assigned to it in the scientific study of ancient faiths. So far as myths consist of explanation of ritual, their value is altogether secondary, and it may be affirmed with confidence that in almost every case the myth derived from the ritual and not the ritual from the myth. (19–20)

Thus Smith launches a new part of the problematic of "myth," the complex debate about its relation to the almost equally contested concept of "ritual." If the characteristic romantic or transcendentalist stamp upon the construction of "myth" is its linking with "symbol," the corresponding anthropological mark is this conjunction of myth with "ritual." Smith does allow that not every myth explains a rite, but he argues that "in this case the secondary character of the myths is still more clearly marked. They are either products of early philosophy . . . or they are political in scope." These remarks appear to reflect implicit acceptance of Tylor's notion that "myth," is always intellectual hypothesis. Even though it is informal, non-binding explanation, myth cannot be the unreflective, conventional act that ritual can. Myth, therefore, may be of supplemental use in the study of ancient religions, but we must be very careful how we employ this tool, since "the myth apart from the ritual affords only a doubtful and slippery kind of evidence" (19).

In its distrust of the psychological speculation involved in *both* cognitive and affective theories, Smith's preference for behavior over self-explanation in the analysis of religion plainly anticipates the "sociological" approach of Durkheim and later social anthropology. We thus encounter for the first time in *The Religion of the Semites* the profound methodological issue we will confront again in more self-conscious form in the case of Durkheim—the question of whether or not it is possible to supply satisfactory accounts of human behavior that prescind entirely, or attempt to prescind, from all attribution of motive. We know from introspection that we do not ourselves seem to perform most conscious acts without motive, and we infer on compelling evidence that the same is true of other humans, and sometimes, indeed, of certain other species. It is consequently very difficult to avoid psychological attribution even when our theory calls for a completely "objective" account of social behavior. In his incisive *Theories of Primitive Religion,* E. E. Evans-Pritchard classifies both Smith and Durkheim as "sociological" thinkers for whom religion is "a social, that is an objective, fact" (Evans-Pritchard 1965, 53). Insofar as both writers attempt to confine themselves, out of methodological principle, to accounts of religion as group behavior, this classification is entirely unexceptionable. But what if these accounts, quite apart from authorial intention, also invite psychological speculation along certain lines about the motives behind this group behavior?

If we compare the representations of archaic and primitive religion in Smith and Durkheim with those in Tylor and Spencer, we can see why so many of their contemporaries and successors felt encouraged to read the "sociologists'" versions as calling for psychological supplement. A list of affective implications in Smith's theory might start with his very valorizing of "practice" over "belief," ritual over myth. This anti-intellectualism is a sibling of the voluntarism that begins to gain adherents in various fields throughout the century. It is akin to the philosophies of Schopenhauer and Nietzsche, for example, and had already found perhaps its most famous romantic formulation when Goethe's Faust corrected the opening of the Gospel of John by substituting the deed for the word: *"Im der Anfang war die Tat."* Second, Smith's insistence on the *identification* of religious with social institutions in archaic societies, which he shares with thinkers as diverse as Fustel de Coulanges in France and Tönnies in Germany, expresses a fantasy comparable to the those of Schiller and Wordsworth about a condition of unified sensibility in which the tormented and isolated consciousness of the modern individual does not exist. (This fantasy, as we've seen repeatedly, cohabits easily, as it does again in Smith, with a Whiggish persuasion of the superiority of modern individualism, and may indeed be provoked in the first place by disappointment with the fruits of that putative superiority.) Third, Smith's accounts of the ritual practices of the ancient Semites suggest situations of highly charged emotional investment. These matrilineal clans identify themselves on one hand with their gods and on the other with their totemic animals: "The sanctity of a kinsman's life and the sanctity of the godhead are not two things, but one, for ultimately the only thing that is sacred is the common tribal life, or the common blood which is identified with the life. Whatever partakes in this life is holy, and its holiness may be described indifferently, as participation in the divine life and nature, or as participation in the kindred blood" (289).

Passages like this are crucial in the establishing of totemism as a major institution of "primitive" religion. As editor of the ninth edition of the *Encyclopedia Britannica,* Smith persuaded the young James Frazer to write (in 1885) a new entry on "totemism," which he subsequently expanded and published as a monograph in 1887. It was this essay, together with *The Religion of the Semites,* that drew the attention of the scholarly world to McLennon's rather languishing concept and persuaded Durkheim a few years later to erect it into *the* universal institution of early religion. A second concept transformed in this passage and others like it is "sacrifice." The prevailing theory at the time Smith wrote was Tylor's, which happens, rather ironically, to be consistent with the traditional view of Christian theology that sacrifice is a "gift" to the deity.[13] Arguing that it was the totemic animal that was sacrificed, Smith interprets sacrifice as the first step in an act of communion. "Throughout the Semitic field, the fundamental idea of sacrifice is not that of a sacred tribute, but of communion between the god and his worshippers, by joint participation in the living flesh and blood of a sacred victim" (345). Smith represents this bloody rite of totemic communion as the society's celebration of its own unity in the ecstatic celebration of its oneness with the rest of life. This account of "primitive" religion may be less lurid than Nietzsche's of the communal roots of Greek tragedy, which it generically resembles, but it surely invites the sort of reading Freud was to give it in *Totem and Taboo.* For reasons like these it makes sense to speak of Smith's conception of "primitive" *religion* as implicitly affective even though his method of analysis is "sociological" and his conscious conception of myth is cognitive.

J. G. FRAZER: THE "COVENT GARDEN SCHOOL" AND "THE COMPARATIVE METHOD" UNBOUND

In 1890, the year after Smith's *Lectures,* the young classicist whom he had recruited to write some key anthropological articles for the *Britannica* published a two-volume work with the catchy title *The Golden Bough.* If James Frazer had abandoned his book to its fate at this point, would it have become the best-known anthropological work of the next hundred years? Instead, in a series of expansionary revisions rather resembling those of his younger contemporary, Marcel Proust, Frazer first altered his argument significantly for the three-volume second edition of 1900 and then continued to transform the work while issuing as separate book-length studies a number of parts eventually incorporated into the twelve-volume third edition of 1911–1915.[14] But even granted this quarter-century of elaboration and the wide-spread readership achieved by Frazer's popular one-volume abridgment of 1922, the real puzzle is why this work, whose faults were so tellingly identified from the start by its professional reviewers, a work that never established its authority within mainstream anthropology, should have had so significant a cultural impact. An appropriately broad answer would make a substantial chapter in a cultural history of the earlier twentieth century.[15] But even consideration of a much narrower matter, the contribution of the *Bough* to the construction of "myth," calls for some preliminary examination of those intrinsic qualities that account for its widespread appeal.[16] Frazer is not, in *The Golden Bough,* an original or even consistent thinker about myth (as distinguished from ritual). Why, then, is *The Golden Bough* so conspicuous a feature in the topography of the subject?

We might begin by considering Frazer's basic argument in relation to two of the most important structural features of his mode of argumentation—his "compara-tive method" and his heavy reliance on analogy. Both of these are represented conveniently in Frazer's initial presentation of his argument to his publisher, Macmillan:

> The book is an explanation of the legend of the Golden Bough, as that legend is given by Servius in his commentary on Virgil. According to Servius the Golden Bough grew on a certain tree in a sacred grove of Diana in Aricia, and the priesthood of the grove was held by the man who succeeded in breaking off the Golden Bough and then slaying the priest in single combat. By an application of the comparative method I believe I can make it probable that the priest represented in his person the god of the grove—Virbius, and that his slaughter was regarded as the death of the god. This raises the question of the meaning of a widespread custom of killing men and animals regarded as divine. I have collected many examples of this custom and propose a new explanation of it. The Golden Bough, I believe I can show, was the mistletoe, and the whole legend can, I think, be brought into connexion, on the one hand with the Druidical reverence of the mistletoe and the human sacrifices which accompanied their worship and, on the other hand, with the Norse legend of the death of Balder. . . . This is a bare outline of the book which, whatever may be thought of its theories, will be found, I believe to contain a large

store of very curious customs, many of which may be new even to professed anthropologists. (Robert Frazer 1990b, 52–53)

The first ominous phrase is "the comparative method." Frazer invokes its fashionable resonance just as Müller did, but he has in mind a specific mode of argument far more radical than Müller (or Macmillan) could well have conceived. It requires combining Smith's faith in the significance of ritual "survivals," Tylor's rationalist confidence in "covering laws" of human development, and German folklorist Wilhelm Mannhardt's "law of similarity," (to the effect that similar customs, however different the societies in which they are contextualized, bespeak similar motives in their practitioners).[17] This "law" is an obvious forerunner of the ethnologist Adolph Bastian's concept of *Elementardenken,* fundamental ideas common to humankind. Mannhardt started as a Müllerian, but, disillusioned by conflicting historical speculation about "primitive Aryans," he turned to fieldwork among those whom he regarded as their living mental contemporaries, the peasants of Central Europe. During the '60s and '70s he produced a series of works loaded with examples of folk-beliefs and agricultural rituals purporting to demonstrate the survival of a perennial, perhaps neolithic, religion centered in celebration of the cycles of nature. The entire project of *The Golden Bough* is built in turn upon acceptance of this proposition, an essence memorably captured in Andrew Lang's characterization of Frazer and his followers as "the vegetable school, the Covent Garden school of mythology" (Lang 1969, 206). Frazer owes to Mannhardt both his fundamental hypothesis and his conception of method—the accumulation of instances, huge in proportion to the tentative and malleable generalizations to be induced from them. But he also owes to Mannhardt (and partly to Tylor) the heart of his "comparative method," the juxtaposing on a continuum of the researches of the folklorist and the ethnologist. Willingness to do this depends upon assuming that the mental processes of living "folk" and "primitives" are *semper et ubique* identical with one another and with a past stage of the entire human race. The result is an ahistorical *purée,* not only of social and historical contexts but of literary and dramatic genres and of the talents, motives, and degree of reliability of informants. Frazer's "comparative method" has come in for such general obloquy that it is easy to forget how much it is logical outcome and deliberate synthesis of much that was in the air. By the 1920s Frazer himself addressed the criticism of his method that is still current, but could never grasp its force, so deeply did he take for granted the assumptions of Tylor, Smith, and Mannhardt that ground his procedure.

The second point at which Frazer's synopsis for Macmillan is apt to strike us with proleptic force is when he follows up his assertion about the ritual at Nemi by saying, "This raises the question of the meaning of a widespread custom of killing men and animals regarded as divine." Actually, the particular ritual behavior at Nemi does *not* logically raise the general topic, except in the mind of the scholar who has "collected many examples of this custom" and now proposes to unload them in the hope of bludgeoning the reader into accepting any specific instance of analogous behavior as a manifestation of Mannhardt's "law of similarity." The last part of the letter sketches the skeletal outlines of a large argument articulated on just such a principle. Virgil's "golden bough" is related to mistletoe, which is associated with Druids, who conjure up human sacrifice, while both mistletoe and sacrifice connect with Balder, and so round the circle to the priest of Nemi. So much of the *Bough* is strung together in this fashion that Stanley Edgar Hyman, a most sympathetic witness, calls it "a vast argument from analogy" (Hyman 1959, 237).

Before glancing briefly at the ultimate results of these two principles—the "comparative method" and the amassing of juxtaposed analogies—in the shape of the last edition of the work, we should consider a third, thus far undiscussed, structural ingredient. Between the two-volume edition of 1890 and the three-volume one of 1900, Frazer changed his mind about the focus of his argument. The text of 1890, as the letter to Macmillan suggests, is designed to prove, by way of the stalking-horse of the rite at Nemi, the existence of the perennial fertility religion with its slain gods. The text of 1900, however, introduces a new emphasis upon magic, including the famous attempt to distinguish the kinds of magic along the lines of Hume's "laws of association."[18] Frazer now joins the line of thinkers who construct the development of consciousness according to a tripartite metahistorical scheme. Thought evolves from "magic" through "religion" into "science." Frazer's sequence strongly resembles Tylor's amendment of Comte in its insistence that a phase of magic preceded religion, which is thus displaced to the middle stage, occupied, according to Comte, by theology and metaphysics. Frazer calls attention to the importance of his new schema by altering his subtitle from "A Study in Comparative Religion" to "A Study in Magic and Religion." This metahistorical scheme has been scarcely less severely treated than his "comparative method." The first of the two major objections to it is that, since Frazer treats magic as proto-science, his intrusion of religion between it and science as a higher evolutionary stage is inconsistent. This criticism, however, neglects to take into account Frazer's conception of religion as primarily a system of *belief,* far more sophisticated than "fetishism" or "animism" and only secondarily a pragmatic affair of propitiation. While religion may be regarded on its practical side to be superstitious regression from the proto-science of magic, on its theoretical side it must be considered to be based upon superior reasoning; it is a hypothesis that arises only when magic is perceived to fail. Frazer's conception of religion is so thoroughly intellectualist that he probably regarded as nugatory the differences between it and Comte's second stage. The second major objection to his tri-stadial scheme is more seriously damaging, however. Since the general discrediting of metahistorical attempts to explain cultural development, there has been broad agreement that "magic," "religion," and "science," far from marking successive stages in mental development, appear to coexist across the known history of cultures. Frazer fails to adduce convincing evidence for any stadial progression. In fact, this feature of the *Bough,* somewhat old-fashioned even at the time in its Whiggish rationalism, raises with special acuteness the question of how such a late intellectualist comes to be drafted into the new army of emotionalists.

An answer to this question must focus on the two contrary effects produced by the combination of Frazer's "comparative method," "vast argument from analogy" and dubious metahistorical scheme in the twelve-volume, forty-five-hundred-page third edition. The reader is invited, on one hand, to regard the work as a compendium of information. Its conceptual lattice, after its metahistorical reinforcement as before it, is overwhelmed by the anthemia of brilliantly presented "facts" sprawling everywhere. In commenting about his ambitions for *The Golden Bough* Frazer frequently adopts the classic attitude of the positivistically inclined scholar—that his real contribution to his infant science lies in his assemblage of evidence, whereas his theories are highly provisional. Many of the work's non-professional readers in particular seem to have taken Frazer at his word, regarding it primarily as a rich and vivid trove of "primitive" and "folk" behavior that ethnologists and folklorists were understood to have been accumulating for several generations in obscure learned journals. At the same time, however, some large portion of *The Golden Bough's* fascination certainly lay in its claim to *unify* a huge range of hitherto disjunct "facts." Beneath the welter of apparent differences in the behavior of human communities over huge tracts of time and space lies the perennial fertility religion, and Frazer is its prophet. If, for some readers, the attraction of the work has seemed to reside in the parts—in its function as a thesaurus of exotic beliefs and practices—for others it has resided in the whole, its vision of a "timeless" *ur*-religion of which the historical religions of the Mediterranean and Near East, including Christianity, are merely mythologized elaborations.[19]

Indeed, Frazer's remarkable rhetorical stance in the *Bough* would persuade readers to take it simultaneously as thesaurus of "facts" *and* as unified-field theory. While his employment of the humble-scientist *topos* encourages the reader to regard him as the mere assembler of evidence that some future genius might know what to do with, the verve of his magisterial style communicates a sense that he *is* this genius, in command of an ideal vision building through the slow accumulation of the stubborn details. In an incisive analysis of Frazer's "voice of authority" and related rhetorical strategies, Marc Manganaro demonstrates how cunningly these two apparently contrary stances prop one another. Apparent humility before the "facts" helps Frazer to rationalize and protect the manifold ambiguities of his theorizing, which is thus freed to inform uncritically a "timeless" artifact capable of being all things to all readers (Manganaro 1992, 18–67). As Manganaro makes evident, Frazer constructs his central dichotomies in a manner that creates the need for himself as essential integrator. His "humble" insistence on the distinction between fieldwork and theory in fact "reifies the quite historically and ideologically contingent constructs of fieldwork and theory in the interests of the comparativist" (33). In similar fashion, his frequent insistence on the literal and nonliterary at the expense of the literary and figurative in fact mystifies the analogical and hence figural basis of his own comparative method.

This eminently literary artfulness marks above all Frazer's construction of the mental continuities and discontinuities between "primitive" humankind and the modern European. Frazer is more skilled than his predecessors in representing both sides of the historicist paradox—the other as almost unimaginably different yet intimately knowable in its ultimate sameness. On one side, it's his eye for the striking instance of strangeness that led so many of his early readers to find the exoticism of the work a compelling introduction to "primitive" belief and practice. On the other, the work makes its most dramatic impression in its insistence on the kinship of universal human experience; the real thrust of Frazer's moral passion consists in the imagination of continuities. He does not seem to have intended consciously to stress the more regressive aspects of this kinship with quite the illocutionary force they took on for many of his readers. His rationalist confidence in cultural progress may have helped insulate him from full recognition of the effect of his argument. But there is in the *Bough* a dark undertow, flowing (as it does in a surprising proportion of Victorian literary expression) not so much in what is asserted in propositional form as in a contrary current of tone and imagery. Once, at least, it breaks the surface with remarkable directness: "It is not our business here to consider what bearing the permanent existence of such a solid layer of savagery beneath the surface of society, and unaffected by the superficial changes of religion and culture, has upon the future of humanity. The dispassionate observer, whose studies have led him to plumb the depths, can hardly regard it otherwise than as a standing menace to civilization. We seem to move on a thin crust which may at any moment be rent by the subterranean forces slumbering below" (Frazer 1966, vol. 1, 236). This outburst could be explained in social terms as one of the innumerable, surprisingly widespread intuitions of those years about the approaching war. But it sounds more like Freud than Frazer, and for very good reason. Frazer gives over here his customary concern with the origins and evolution of the human mind and views it instead in terms of structure. Seen thus, "savagery" is no longer an abandoned cultural zone, safely confined to the past; we carry it within us, a "solid layer" repressed and "slumbering" volcanically beneath a "thin crust" of civilization.

For the most part the clash between Frazer's Whiggish rationalism and his sense of the "savagery" within results in the formation of an affective compromise. He veils his fear, perhaps even from himself, in that mood of elegy so common in nineteenth-century writing and so palpably related to the century's "disappearance of God."[20] In spite of his stance as dispassionate investigator of outmoded superstition, he communicates to many of his younger readers a powerful attraction for the natural mystery religion he reconstructs. At the same time, he inculcates in them precisely the message about the structure of mind that breaks out explicitly in the passage we have just considered. As a result, the relation of this younger generation to Frazer resembles the transformation noted in chapters 1 and 2 between romantic generations; where the (mentally) older generation, Schiller and Wordsworth, mourn elegiacally for the irretrievable era of unified sensibility, the younger, Novalis and Blake, assert the power of the transcendental ego to recover that unity. In comparable fashion, a depth psychologist like Jung and modernist poets and novelists like Yeats, Lawrence, Eliot, and Pound transform the combination of Frazer's (mostly covert) message about the structural survival of "savagery" into the very basis of an escape via myth from the oppression of history into the timelessness of a perennial religion. This mediation constitutes Frazer's most historically important contribution to the construction of "myth."

Compared to this, it hardly matters that Frazer is inconsistent and uncritical about the precise nature of myth. His relative carelessness arises partly, no doubt, because he assumes with Comte, Spencer, and Smith that myth is a secondary and "literary" aspect of "primitive" religion. He employs the term freely, but in shifting contexts. Robert Ackerman, a particularly close student of this subject, observes that the *Bough* presents "at least three different and incompatible theories concerning myth: euhemerism, intellectualism, and ritualism."[21] I would add only that it sometimes appears to endorse also the theory of myth as personification of natural phenomena, which may be compatible with intellectualism, but certainly not with the other two. Frazer thus manages to occupy each of the popular positions of the preceding two centuries. Of these four his apparent wholehearted acceptance of ritualism in his first edition is by far the most important, not least because it inspired the other Cambridge Ritualists. Yet Frazer later repudiated them and also declared his conviction that Robertson Smith, like himself, considered even primary ritual behavior to be fully rational.[22] If we trust these late assertions, we may have to conclude both that Frazer ultimately perceived the emotivist implications of ritualism and that he never imagined the extent to which the central argument of *The Golden Bough* appears to others to support them.

ACTING OUT DURKHEIM: LÉVY-BRUHL'S "PARTICIPATION MYSTIQUE"

One of the most remarkable tributes to the turn-of-the-century vogue of "primitive" religion is Émile Durkheim's surprising mid-career abandonment of his brilliant studies of sociological method and current social behavior for what was to become a twenty-year trek into the thickets of speculation about the origins of religion. Durkheim himself, in an often-cited letter, attributed his conversion to the "revelation" of "Robertson Smith and his school." What he found in Smith would have been, first, the crucial identification in traditional societies of religion with the total social life of the community and, second, the suggestion that in the relatively simple laboratories of such groups the basic elements of this identification could be isolated for study to a degree impossible in the heterocosm of the modern West. His turn to the ethnographies of Australian (and secondarily Amerindian) societies is an especially frank instance of the degree to which the obsession with "primitive" religion was driven by contemporary anxieties. In his masterwork of 1912, *The Elementary Forms of the Religious Life: The Totemic System in Australia,* Durkheim exposes at least three overarching ambitions—epistemological, sociological, and political. First, as conscious as Dilthey or Husserl of the epistemological crisis confronting the human sciences at the turn of the century, he claims to have discovered nothing less than a new solution to it. In his introduction he represents the century-old clash between idealism and positivism, Kant and Spencer, in terms of the debate about whether the categories of thought derive strictly from experience or from the inborn constitution of the mind. After a critique of both extremes, he proposes his resolution: "If the social origin of the [Kantian] categories is admitted," then it is possible to preserve both the priority of experience and the apriorist conviction that "man is double" (Durkheim 1965, 27). Individual experience is indeed constrained by preexisting categories, but these categories are not the work of God or Nature; they are "essentially collective representations" (28–29). "A special intellectual activity is therefore concentrated in them which is infinitely richer and complexer that that of the individual. . . . In so far as he belongs to society, the individual transcends himself, both when he thinks and when he acts" (29). The anatomy of the "elementary forms of the religious life" that follows is a massive exemplary instance of such collective thought and action in the sphere of what Durkheim had learned from his teacher, Fustel de Coulanges, to think of as the dominant institution of traditional societies. But this massive instance, though it might seem at first remote from contemporary concerns, also serves Durkheim's sociological ambition—to demonstrate the interrelatedness of social phenomena—and his political ambition—to rationalize the transfer of religious sentiment from institutional religion to the secular state, Durkheim's "sacred" Third Republic.

In *"De la définition des phénomenes religieux,"* the programmatic essay that leads off the second volume of his new journal, Durkheim insists that the study of religion must be conducted by special application of "the rules of sociological method," as these were laid out in 1895 in his crucial theoretical essay of that name (Durkheim 1899, 22). The student must consider the topic, without preconceptions, as a set of "social facts." The method excludes teleological arguments, individual intention, and, as far as possible, all psychologistic explanation. Not surprisingly, the view of religion that results is, in theory at least and, for the most part, in practice, severely intellectualist, as is the concept of "collective representations." In Durkheim's most theoretical elaboration of this latter concept—the essay he coauthored in 1903 with his young nephew and eventual successor, Marcel Mauss, *"De quelques formes primitives de classification: contribution à l'étude des représentations collectives"*—the authors conclude from their examination of several central Australian and Native American societies that "primitive" peoples extrapolate their systems of classification from what they know best, their social structures (Durkheim 1963). To understand the social structure is to understand the fundamental taxonomies is to understand the system of collective representations is to understand the religion, and so around the loop.

Durkheim's subsequent analysis of the "elementary forms" of religion as they are manifested in Australian totemism leaves myth out in the cold. This exclusion is in keeping with his acceptance of the general post-Comtean consensus that myth is a late phenomenon in the evolution of religion. "Even the most elementary mythological constructions," he remarks in a typical notice, "are secondary products which cover over a system of beliefs, at once simpler and more obscure, vaguer and more essential" (232). It is possible to extract a synthetic Durkheimian view of myth from similar remarks scattered through the text. Myth is a specifically religious but late mode of collective representation, usually associated with ritual, generally in an etiological role.[23] Only one passage in the text, however, rises to the level of methodological explanation. "We shall make use of myths when they enable us to understand these fundamental ideas better, but we shall not make mythology itself the subject of our studies" (122). The two reasons offered for this rule are that "in so far as it is a work of art, [myth] does not fall within the jurisdiction of the simple science of religions" and that "the intellectual evolution from which it results is of too great a complexity to be studied indirectly and from a foreign point of view. It constitutes a very difficult problem which must be treated by itself, for itself and with a method peculiar to itself." The fear of myth as art is a direct echo of Comte's rather shallow and parochial view of it as primarily a literary product of classical Greece and Rome. But distrust of myth because of the complexity of its "intellectual evolution" is far more cogent. This concern foreshadows Lévi-Strauss's reluctance, in his structural theory of myth, to deal with complex narratives because it is so difficult to parse them into their underlying grid of mythemes.

But even though Durkheim is not an original contributor to the direct construction of myth, his indirect contributions, backed by his distinction as a student of "primitive" religion, are very significant. Apart from the concept of "collective representations" itself, his advocacy of totemism—the designation of human groups by supposedly related natural phenomena—as the elementary form of religion elevates him to the company of Frazer (*Totemism and Exogamy,* 1910) and Freud (*Totem und Tabu,* 1912–1913), as one of the three great popularizers of the concept. The troika achieved this feat, it's true, just at the point when the unity of the phenomena covered by "totemism" was beginning to lose credibility among professional anthropologists.[24] But they cast a long shadow; Radcliffe-Brown and Malinowski, for example, continue to take totemism seriously well after the damaging critiques of the nineteen-teens because of its advocacy by Durkheim.[25]

Durkheim's most important indirect contribution to the construction of myth, however, is a thoroughly unintended one. By stressing the corporate unity of religious thought and behavior in "primitive" societies, he stimulated the growing neo-romantic vision of a closed community that, as R. R. Marett put it in a well-known phrase, "dances its religion" (Marett 1910, 12).[26] His fate, in this respect, is quite like Frazer's; he is a self-identified rationalist whose intentions, in a climate of opinion in which emotivist explanations of thought and behavior were rapidly superseding intellectualist ones, are "misread" by certain contemporaries of emotivist persuasion. The list is large and impressive; it includes some of Durkheim's closest associates and followers, and it may be useful, before we turn to significant instances among early folkloristic theorists of myth, to consider briefly three features of Durkheim's argument that have stimulated such "reading against the grain."

The first of these is that in urging his Comtean view of "primitive" religion as uniting its believers "into one moral community" (Durkheim 1965, 62), Durkheim does not always escape emotive language and psychologistic attributions in the manner of Bergson or William James. "Every religion," he says, "is a means of enabling men to face the world with greater confidence" (219). Participants in a rite "feel that the ceremony is good for them" (402). "The real function of a cult is to awaken within the worshippers a certain state of soul composed of moral force and confidence" (431). Second, when Durkheim attempts a climactic pinpointing of the origin of Australian religion in the social occasions known as *corroborees,* this kind of motive and psychologistic talk is especially thick on the page. This controversial section of the text provokes the English anthropologist E. E. Evans-Pritchard, in general a strong subscriber to the usual social scientist's view of Durkheim's achievement, to complain that "it contravenes his own rules of sociological method, for fundamentally it offers a psychological explanation of social facts . . . No amount of juggling with words like 'intensity' and 'effervescence' can hide the fact that he derives the totemic religion of the Blackfellows from the emotional excitement of individuals brought together in a small crowd, from what is a sort of crowd hysteria" (Evans-Pritchard 1965, 67–68).[27] Whether this judgment is correct or not, it is symptomatic. In fact, Durkheim's representation of such closed societies' morale-building self-worship is sometimes considered to have contributed, unwittingly of course, to the rise of fascism. No less a prime witness than Marcel Mauss confessed to this possibility in the 1930s: "We never foresaw . . . how many large societies . . . could be hypnotized like Australians are by their dances. . . . This return to the primitive [is] too powerful a verification of things that we had indicated."[28]

The third and most seriously vulnerable aspect of Durkheim's argument is his attempt in the last sections of *The Elementary Forms* to confront the nature of what his theory necessarily implies, the evolution of "primitive" religious thought into modern scientific reasoning. This is not a new theme in Durkheim's work. In *Primitive Classification* (as that essay is titled in translation) he and Mauss added to their four chapters on "primitive" societies a final one on China because that country exemplifies, in their judgment, a culture that lingers midway between the "primitive" and the modern in the degree of its reliance on an undemythologized taxonomy of symbolic correspondences. Far from being merely tacked on, this chapter illustrates the authors' important corollary that "the history of scientific classification is . . . the history of the stages by which the element of social affectivity has weakened progressively." But this corollary obviously entails in turn that the "collective representations" of primordial societies are initially loaded with affective elements. The authors assert that "every mythology is fundamentally a classification" (77), but they also demonstrate that the converse holds true in "primitive" thought; every classification is fundamentally a mythology, destined to be demythologized *à la Comte* in the progress of the "scientific" worldview.[29] Where along the way and how, if at all, did humanity shed affective, mythological thought? The problematic that Durkheim confronts again in *The Elementary Forms* with such mixed results for his intellectualist theory of religion is thus rendered salient for a number of major contributors to the folkloristic construction of "myth." The "Cambridge Ritualists," especially Gilbert Murray and Francis Cornford in their studies of the evolution of religion and philosophy in ancient Greece, recognized it early and sought its resolution in emotive theory, as did Lucien Lévy-Bruhl in his pioneering work on cognitive differences between "primitive" and modern thought. It is now time to turn to actual instances of theorists of myth who "misread" or rewrite Durkheim along emotive lines.

This trend commences with his closest collaborators. In a brief two-part article on myth, framing a review of the year's work in *L'année sociologique* itself, Henri Hubert (probably with Mauss's concurrence) compromises with the Durkheimian position by allowing that myth, although a collective thing, "is imposed on the individual like a category of his thought" (Hubert 1903, 269). This mental condition is later qualified as "a state of thought quite confused and almost subconscious," and he concludes by remarking that "as soon as one aspires to give it a rational explanation, it dies, or, rather, it metamorphoses. We don't follow it in its transformations" (271). The bent of both Hubert and Mauss toward emotive explanation becomes more marked in subsequent writings, but it was left to Lucien Lévy-Bruhl to produce a full-scale undermining of Durkheim from within. He was not a member of the *équipe,* but a slightly younger contemporary and friend of Durkheim's, who had followed his fellow Sorbonnais in abandoning a distinguished career in another field, in his case the history of philosophy, for the armchair study of ethnology and speculation about the mental experience of "primitives." Lévy-Bruhl perceived himself, and was widely perceived by others, as an adherent of Durkheim's or at least a fellow traveler. Hence, when his first and most influential work in the field, *Les fonctions mentales dans les sociétés inférieures* appeared in 1910, Durkheim was trebly embarrassed. He had been anticipated, by a well-intentioned friend, presenting a theory of "primitive" thought that was, although Lévy-Bruhl seemed not to understand this, radically at odds with his own intellectualist one.

We can see the "misreading" at work even in Lévy-Bruhl's enthusiastic embrace of what he rightly grasps as the key concept of "collective representations." He tells us he learned from Comte that "the higher mental functions should be studied by the comparative, that is, sociological method" (Lévy-Bruhl 1985, 15). But Comte "found the way barred . . . by a sociology . . . which actually was a philosophy of history" (15). The true, empirical route was opened by "the anthropologists and ethnologists of the English school" (16), who nevertheless made the serious mistake of attempting to explain the mental life of "primitives" by consulting their own as a standard. Lévy-Bruhl prescribes as the antidote to their ethnocentric intellectualism, "the study of collective representations" (14). On closer inspection we discover that Lévy-Bruhl can imagine "collective representations" as refuting "the English school" only because he conceives of them as both emotive in content and culturally relative. Lévy-Bruhl had in fact decided in his previous book, *La morale et la science des moeurs* (1903), that *moral* standards are relative because people living in different social conditions actually reason differently. In *La morale,* too, he considered himself to be following Durkheim, without seeming to recognize that the latter, quite as much as the intellectualists of "the English school," explains the mental life of "primitives" by consulting his own as the standard. This blindness explains why, in his introduction to *Les fonctions mentales,* Lévy-Bruhl identifies his fourth major intellectual debt—after those to Comte, "the English school," and Durkheim—as being to "the fairly large number of psychologists who, following Ribot, aim to show the importance of the emotional and motor elements of mental life" (1985, 14–15). Théodule Ribot's psychology is another highly influential manifestation of the turn-of-the-century awakening to the impact of instinct, habit, and emotion on so-called "rational" thought. Durkheim himself apparently appropriated from Ribot the concept of "collective representation," and he could scarcely have done so without realizing that his readers would be likely to associate the phrase with Ribot's affectivity. Ironically, then, it's Durkheim, not Lévy-Bruhl, who wrenches the concept to his own purposes. When Durkheim confronts the problem of the evolution of thought, he concedes at most, as we've seen, that collective representations must have begun in emotive states. But he so privileges their development away from "motor excitement" and toward higher cognition that he is scarcely willing to entertain the historical reality of such moments, even when he apparently describes the religious representations of his Australians as generated in them. Confronting the same evolutionary problematic, Lévy-Bruhl emphasizes the contrary explanation. True to Ribot (and, he supposes, to Durkheim), he assumes that all human cognition originates in and must carry some degree of emotive charge, albeit this emotional element is more prominent in the collective representations of "primitive" societies than in modern scientific reasoning.

These are the principal assumptions behind his notoriously controversial determination in the first, theoretical part of *Les fonctions mentales,* that "the most general laws governing collective representations" (15) are the "mystical" and the "prelogical." He means by "mystical" merely that primordial collective representations are not "purely or almost purely intellectual or cognitive, but . . . blended with other elements of an emotional or motor character . . . It would be difficult to exaggerate [their] intense emotional force" (36–37). Whereas Durkheim assumes that a collective representation transcends by definition the private affect of individuals, Lévy-Bruhl considers any such abstraction a gross impoverishment of what a "representation" actually represents. For him, strong emotion is integral to the meaning. Nearly every commentator has bemoaned his unfortunate decision to designate this state as "mystical." Lévy-Bruhl himself is not unaware of the danger; he attempts to prevent it by precise stipulation (38), but he fails miserably, as usual in such cases, to deflect the current of modern usage, according to which the word characterizes a religious transport that defies accountability. It is partly as a consequence of this bad choice of label that Lévy-Bruhl has suffered an amount of misconstrual, exceeded, perhaps, only by that provoked by his second key term "prelogical."

The distinction between the "mystical" and the "prelogical" is between content and form. To borrow for a decent purpose the inaccurate and racist title assigned to the English translation of *Les fonctions mentales,* Lévy-Bruhl is interested not only in what but in "how natives think." "Their representations," he claims, "are not connected with each other as ours would be" (69), but are linked instead by what he calls "the law of participation." According to this "law," "objects, beings, phenomena can be . . . both themselves and something other than themselves" (76). Lévy-Bruhl invokes here the much-handled example of the Bororo of Brazil, assuring the astonished anthropologist, von den Steinen, that "they are araras [red parakeets] *at the present time,* just as if a caterpillar declared itself to be a butterfly" (77). As Lévy-Bruhl coolly observes, "All communities which are totemic in form admit of collective representations of this kind." According to him, such representations defy that cornerstone of Western logic, known since Aristotle as the "law of non-contradiction," which declares that a thing cannot be simultaneously both what it is and something else as well. This defiance, and no more, is what he means by tagging such representation as "prelogical." Again his choice of epithet is unfortunate, but in this case he would seem to have qualified his usage quite carefully. First, he denies that "primitives" exercise a logic utterly different from ours; he intends to indicate merely that "primitive" thought "does not *exclusively* [my italics] obey our logic" (71). Second, he reminds us that he speaks only of collective representations; in much of the pragmatic business of quotidian life the "primitive" individual reasons just as anyone else would. Third, and most importantly, he denies that he is identifying a historical stage in the evolution of thought. "By *prelogical* we do not mean to assert that such a mentality constitutes a kind of antecedent state, in point of time, to the birth of logical thought. Have there ever existed groups . . . whose collective representations have not yet been subject to the laws of logic? We do not know, and in any case, it seems to be very improbable" (78). Regardless of these qualifications, however, the term "prelogical" has been frequently found even more offensive than "mystical" and has drawn down upon its author sweeping accusations of the very racism and Eurocentrism he meant to oppose.

Having thus introduced in *Les fonctions mentales* his dominant theoretical concepts, Lévy-Bruhl proceeds to examine over the course of his subsequent career a number of the principal categories of such "mystical" and "prelogical" representations. He commences in *Les fonctions mentales* itself with languages, number systems, and "institutions in which collective representations governed by the law of participation are involved," (that is, beliefs and rituals). He then studies philosophical representations in *La mentalité primitive* (1922), religious ones in *L'homme primitive* (1927), and *Le surnaturel et la nature dans la mentalité primitive* (1931) and mythological and symbolic ones in *La mythologie primitive* (1935) and *L'expérience mystique et les symboles chez les primitives* (1938). In the course of his expansive fulfillment of his long project, Lévy-Bruhl did modify his methods (to avoid the increasingly discredited Frazerian "comparative method") and withdraw his claim for the "prelogical," but he never recanted, as has sometimes been claimed, the heart of his emotive theory. What does happen is that "the mystical character prevails over prelogic" (Cazeneuve 1972, 12). In the last three works, that is, Lévy-Bruhl drops his focus on the logical form of collective representations in favor of their content as expressive conceptualizations of the sacred. Much has been made of Lévy-Bruhl's alleged recantation of his principal theorems in his posthumous *Carnets* (1949). What actually appears in the crucial entry, however, is a statement of the goal toward which the work of his later phrase had been tending. "For some time I have not spoken of a logic other than our own, nor used the term 'prelogical,' and have given up speaking of the law of participation. . . . There is not a primitive mentality distinguishable from the other by two characteristics . . . (mystical and prelogical). There is a mystical mentality which is more marked and more easily observable among 'primitive peoples' than in our societies, but it is present in every human mind."[30] He thus reaffirms at the end of his life that the emotionality coloring to some degree the mental life of all human beings is particularly apparent in the "collective representations" of "primitive" peoples. His language is perhaps more cautious, but his position is substantively the same he takes in his first and most influential contribution to the field in the heady years before the *first* World War.

Lévy-Bruhl's specific theorizing about "myth" appears only in the final chapter of *Les fonctions mentales,* "The Transition to the Higher Mental Types." This location indicates general agreement with Durkheim's view of myth as a late, secondary form of "collective representation." But in the matter of "Higher Mental Types," too, Lévy-Bruhl proceeds to transform Durkheim's intellectualist position. He conjures up a stage of group unity *prior* to that which produces "collective representations": "At this stage . . . rather than speak of collective representations, it would be wiser to call them collective mental states of extreme emotional intensity in which representation is as yet undifferentiated from the movements and actions which make the communion toward which it tends a reality to the group. Their participation in it is so effectually lived that it is not yet properly imagined" (362). This is Lévy-Bruhl's emotivist description of what might be called first-stage, or primordial collective representation. In the second, the proper stage of "Higher Mental Types," "in proportion as the individual consciousness of each member of the group tends to declare itself, the feeling of a mystic symbiosis . . . becomes less intimate and direct and less constant. . . . In a word, participation tends to become ideological" (365–366). The term "ideological" here designates self-conscious tenets of belief in contrast to what is felt or acted out unselfconsciously. Since this fall into self-consciousness is the ultimate tendency of all collective representation, it follows *a fortiori* that it's the tendency of the late type designated as "myth." Myth, in fact, is the type assigned the particular role of evoking, and even aspiring to restore, the earlier, unselfconscious unity. After observing that "where the participation of the group . . . is actually lived . . . myths are poor in number and of poor quality," Lévy-Bruhl asks rhetorically, "Can myths then likewise be the products of primitive mentality which appear when that mentality is endeavoring to realize a participation no longer felt?" (368–369).

La mythologie primitive, published a quarter of a century later, reflects the extent to which Lévy-Bruhl continued to respond to current ethnological fieldwork and theory. He now maintains that myths mediate between "a world of invisible and supernatural powers" and "the one of sense experience" by supplying the narrative coherence that brings two "worlds" into relation (Lévy-Bruhl 1935, 81). For this reason, Lévy-Bruhl (unlike anyone else discussed in this chapter) now insists on the importance of both oral storytelling *per se* and its social contexts. "From the emotional point of view, the mere listening to myth is to them something quite different than what it is to us. . . . This element alone gives myth and legend their value and social importance and, I might almost add, their power" (369–370). This insight also leads him to stress the contrary—that myths torn from their contexts by outsiders will prove unintelligible or misleading. He joins specifically the twentieth-century repudiation of "nature myths" as especially likely to be "artificial," "highly elaborated," and risky to interpret (372). The most reliable kind, on the contrary, are the sort Malinowski had by this time labeled "charter myths," stories that "most directly express the sense of the social group's relationship, whether it be with its legendary members and those no longer living, or with the groups that surround it." In *La mythologie primitive* he has developed, too, a more concrete, strikingly Freudian version of his early insistence that modern Westerners are by no means free of emotional responses to the storytelling embodied in the "primitive" religious representations known as myths: "As soon as they catch our ear, this constraint [rationality] is suspended, this violence calls a truce. In an instant, at a single bound, the repressed [*refoulées*] tendencies recover the ground lost. When we hear these tales, we abandon voluptuously our rational posture. . . . This relaxation, all the while it lasts, soothes us in our more profound depths. . . . It is more than recreation. It's a release of tension [*détente*]. The enjoyment it procures us goes far beyond simple entertainment" (318). On this view, rationality comes to us only with "unnatural" effort and under a strain that demands emotional compensation.

Lévy-Bruhl's concinnity with Freud about the appeal of traditional tale is one more instance of the countless ways in which the two new disciplines of anthropology and depth psychology converge to help shape the larger affective turn in the new century's construction of "myth." As the first deliberate emotivist theorizing, *Les fonctions mentales,* which was widely read, made a stout contribution to this construction. But it was also widely misunderstood, so badly, in fact, that it's hard not to see poetic justice at work avenging Lévy-Bruhl's misreading of Durkheim. A surprising number of critics have mistaken it as badly as Malinowski, who thought it claimed "that primitive man has no sober moods at all, that he is hopelessly and completely immersed in a mystical frame of mind."[31] But this is no more inaccurate than those who have taken Lévy-Bruhl to task for the contrary fault of not recognizing adequately that modern persons are just as illogical as "primitive" ones.[32] Durkheim's own criticisms, as one would expect, are much more informed. He *understands* Lévy-Bruhl, but he rejects the notion of a separate logic indifferent to the law of non-contradiction, insists that Lévy-Bruhl's "participations" are merely the logic of "primitive" science, and objects to any claim for a continuity between primordial and contemporary thought that is not explained by development in reasoning power.[33] In short, he can see nothing at all in the claim that there must be an emotive element in collective representations.[34]

Both of the extremes of criticism mentioned above are also motivated in varying degrees by the suspicion, or conviction, that Lévy-Bruhl's contrast between "primitive" and modern thought is ethnocentric and racist. Certainly Lévy-Bruhl, a distinguished advocate for liberal causes, entertained no such conscious design. On the contrary, he understood his work as making a relativistic case that the thinking of so-called "primitive" peoples is *not* inferior, but simply *other.*[35] As he saw it, his emphasis on the study of comparative structure was an escape from the condescension inherent in nineteenth-century intellectualist theories with their uniformitarian yardstick. The disagreement here turns on a problematic with which we've become much more familiar since the rise of "identity politics." One set of thinkers wishes to "essentialize" a perceived difference in order to distinguish and celebrate an oppressed group, while an opposed set argues that no such "essential" difference exists and to pretend it does reinforces stereotypes and thus plays into the hands of the victimized group's actual enemies. Lévy-Bruhl's political intentions as an "essentialist" have been more widely appreciated in recent decades, as has been also his foreshadowings of cognitive and symbolic anthropology and even of the structuralisms of both Dumézil and Lévi-Strauss.[36]

JANE HARRISON'S *THEMIS* AND CAMBRIDGE RITUALISM

The shift in fashion from cognitive to emotive folkloristic theories of myth culminates in the work of the "Cambridge Ritualists."[37] As scholars in what would now be referred to as "classical studies," they bring to bear upon ancient Greek culture the new English anthropology and French sociology. But their thinking is also deeply colored by the vitalistic philosophies of Nietzsche and Bergson. This aspect of their work leaves them stranded high and dry off the main channel of developments in modern anthropology, while within their own field their scholarly methods and conclusions are strongly impugned from the start by more conventional philology and eventually discredited in considerable detail.[38] But the Ritualists, like Frazer, bulk large in the early twentieth-century construction of myth. First, their popularizing of rites of initiation and sacrifice and their connections of myth with ritual do blaze the way for three later versions of myth-and-ritual theorizing.[39] Second, the very "vitalist" extremism of affective theory that diminishes their impact upon mainline anthropology augments their attraction for the modernist poets (Yeats, Pound, Eliot) and novelists (Lawrence, Joyce) who popularize the notion that "myth" enables modern rapport with the "primitive" within the individual psyche. Whereas the artists have to read Frazer against the grain to derive this notion from him, they acquire it straightforwardly from the Ritualists. Third, the Ritualists offer an "anthropological" rationale for the neo-romantic idea that literature descends from religion by way of myth. By thus appearing to discover the transformative route "from ritual to romance," they inaugurate the literary "myth criticism" that, taken together with the success of the artists mentioned above, legitimates the revival of romantic conceptions of "myth" in midcentury literary culture.

The appearance of the Ritualists is an outcome in classical studies of several of the trends we have encountered. Perhaps the broadest is the "othering of Antiquity," the growing awareness throughout the nineteenth century of the continuity of so-called "classical" civilizations with their prehistoric pasts and thus with cultural institutions very different from those fondly imagined during the early modern period to be more or less like our own. This awareness was considerably abetted by the great widening of the base of knowledge about Greek antiquities that followed the discoveries of Troy, of the Mycenaean ruins and the remains of Minoan civilization. Jane Harrison, Frazer's contemporary at Cambridge, and first and foremost a student of Greek art and archaeology, graduated from Newnham College, as she herself liked to put it, in the year of Schliemann's discovery of Troy, 1879. The third *sine qua non* of the Ritualists' emergence is the demonstration of the anthropological establishment from Tylor to Frazer that the continuity of human cultures inheres especially in the conservative nature of ritual. The essence of ritualism, the presumption that in "primitive" religion the action of ritual is primary and its rationalization in myth secondary, is in the air by 1890. H. S. Versnel reminds us that Jane Harrison subscribes to it explicitly in her introduction to *Mythology and Monuments of Ancient Athens,* published in the same year as *The Golden Bough* and only a year after *The Religion of the Semites.*[40] By 1903 the Ritualist group is in place, held in the gravitational field of Harrison's authority, energy, and friendship, and from then until approximately the outbreak of World War I their many-faceted writings contribute to a demonstration of the ritual origins, if not of Greek culture as a whole, at least of an impressive range of its institutions.

Harrison's *Themis: A Study of the Social Origins of Greek Religion,* published like the related masterworks of Freud and Durkheim in an *annus mirabilis* of modern mythography, 1912, is the central expression of the group. Although the conception and execution of the whole is Harrison's, the work is a collaboration, the chief features of which are expressed thus on the title-page: "With an Excursus on the Ritual Forms Preserved in Greek Tragedy by Gilbert Murray and a Chapter on the Origin of the Olympic Games by F. M. Cornford" (Harrison 1977). In her preface to the second edition (1926), Harrison describes herself as "a disciple . . . of Nietzsche" in the matter of "the intoxication of Dionysos the daimon" (viii), and in the text she sums up her central distinction between the rationalized Olympian deities and the instinctual vegetation deities of the seasonal rituals by assimilating it with Nietzsche's between Apollo and Dionysus. In the introduction to her original edition, however, she credited a more recent enthusiasm, "first and foremost," for inspiring her insight into the distinction between the Olympians and the "mystery-gods." She tells us that she read *L'évolution créatrice* with great excitement in the year of its publication (1907) and "saw in a word that Dionysos, with every other mystery-god, was an instinctive attempt to express what Professor Bergson calls *durée,* that life which is one, indivisible and yet ceaselessly changing" (xii). The switch of allegiance between editions matters little; the two philosophers contribute comparably in the shaping of her vitalism.

Considering these sources of inspiration, the second part of what she calls her "double debt" to France *is* surprising. It is owing

> to a thinker whose temperament, manner and method are markedly differ-
> ent, and whose philosophy is, I believe, in France accounted alien to profes-
> sor Bergson, Professor Émile Durkheim. . . . In the light of [Durkheim's
> preliminary essays on religion and collective representations], I saw why
> Dionysos, the mystery-god, who is the expression and representation of *durée,*
> is, alone among Greek divinities, constantly attended by a thiasos [a chorus
> of worshipers]. . . . The mystery-god arises out of those instincts . . . which
> attend and express life; but these . . . in so far as they are religious, are at the
> outset rather of a group than of individual consciousness. (xiii)

Harrison is obviously another who supposes that her exaltation of the emotional unity of ancient religion is sanctioned by Durkheim.[41] She appears quite oblivious in this passage of *why* the philosophies of Durkheim and Bergson are "accounted as alien" in that odd country, France. She ignores the slight logical difficulty that they happen to involve some deeply contradictory epistemological presuppositions. What counts for her is a Nietzschean vision of a whole *thiasos* rapt in an ecstasy of seamless rapport with the cosmos.

The strength of Harrison's debt to Frazer is manifest in her taking *The Golden Bough* as a model for the design of her argument. As Frazer raises his huge structure by the Archimedean lever of the rite in the grove of Nemi, she employs a similar strategy to organize both *Prolegomena to the Study of the Greek Religion* (1903) and *Themis,* though she characteristically finds her lever in both cases not in a curious textual "survival," but in an exhumed artifact.[42] In *Prolegomena* a clay seal discovered at Knossos reveals the Minotaur as the king of Crete in a bull mask and thus unlocks the ritual nature of Minoan society. In *Themis,* another Cretan find, a stele carved with a ritual hymn celebrating the birth of Zeus, exposes, when all its cryptic sections are unpacked, nothing less than "the social origins of Greek religion."[43]

Harrison promptly establishes that the hymn carved on the stele is the mythic elaboration of a "primitive" rite of initiation. The group of Kouretes who sing and dance the "Hymn" are "the initiated young men of a matrilinear group. The Daimon they invoke is, not the Father of Gods and men, but the Greatest Kouros" (xiv), a personification of the worshipers themselves. The "Hymn" carved on the stele does celebrate the birth of Zeus, but the name of the god is detachable from the rite itself, which is much older. This conception of the gradual concretizing of the deity in the person of the chosen representative of the *thiasos* is plainly a version of Nietzsche's evolution of Dionysus from his satyr-chorus. "Theatrically speaking [the members of the *thiasos*] become an audience, religiously, the worshippers of a god" (46).

After a massive set of digressions (chapters 3 to 6), which introduce anthropological topics—initiation rites, magic, taboo, totemism, and sacrifice, for example—in a manner also recognizably imitated from Frazer, the remainder of *Themis* is devoted to similar readings of major social and cultural conventions or institutions whose anomalies suggest that they are "survivals" of "primitive" rites. In chapter 6 Harrison argues that Aristotle was right to suggest that tragedy arose from the dithyramb, because dithyramb is a form of ecstatic Dionysian lyric connected, as *mythos,* with the ritual slaying of a sacrificial bull. In chapter 7 Cornford demonstrates that the Olympic games arose from similar rites. Their ritual origin explains both Pindar's religious attitude in his victory odes and why the winner was often worshiped after death ("He had once been an incarnate god" [221]). This insight supplies the key in turn to the cults of heroes. Harrison devotes her next chapter to showing that the early heroes of Athens, Cecrops, and Erectheus, and the somewhat later heroes of Attica, Ion, and Theseus, each in turn wore the mask and absorbed the ritual and the life-history (the myth) of the *"Eniautos-Daimon,"* the fertility god of the year. Harrison maintains that the heroes of Homeric saga were originally such beings also and that, as a consequence, when the Athenian playwrights made Homer their chief source of plots, the archaic fertility religion was actually determining both the form and the content of the drama, the former directly, the latter indirectly. This assertion introduces Gilbert Murray's "Excursus," a concise case for the ritual origins of Agon, Pathos, Messenger, Threnos, and Theophany in each surviving member of the corpus of Athenian tragedies. The three collaborators' strategic understanding is obviously that Murray and Cornford focus tersely and technically in areas of traditional classical scholarship, thus documenting Harrison's argument while leaving to her the presentation of the visionary sweep.

The scope of this vision becomes fully apparent only in the last three chapters. Harrison commences by asking in chapter 9, "From Daimon to Olympian," why certain Greek deities, notably Herakles and Aesclepius, never became full-fledged Olympians. Her answer is that their worshipers, regarding them primarily as saviors and healers, could never rid them of their functions as cyclic fertility gods. Most of the chapter concerns a successful candidate, Apollo, though even in his case Harrison is not interested in his career but in his origin as *kouros*. She analyzes in detail the archaeology, legends, and three major enneateric festivals of Delphi to show that Apollo's original role at the shrine was strictly analogous to Dionysus's (which explains why they alternately share it). The two gods are "Kourai and Year-Gods caught and in part crystallized at different stages of development" (443). Crystallization is one of Harrison's central metaphors for expressing the difference between the old year-gods and the new Olympic deities, which is the subject of her next chapter, "The Olympians." These gods shed their totemic form, insist on immortality, and withdraw from humankind, refusing the functions of the *daimon.* "Instead of being himself a sacrament [a god of this kind] demands a sacrifice" (467).

Harrison's argument culminates in her final chapter on Themis herself. She introduces into evidence in chapter 9 the famous opening speech of *The Eumenides,* which becomes to the last part of her long essay what the "Hymn of the Kouretes" is to the first part. The Pythia, standing at the doors of the temple at Delphi, makes her morning prayer to the succession of gods who have occupied the seat of prophecy—Gaia, Themis, Phoebe, and finally Phoebus—that is to say, the goddesses of earth, social custom, and the moon, before the god of the sun. In our day any respectable school-edition of *The Oresteia* comments on the anthropological significance of this sequence, which represents, like the plot of *The Eumenides* as a whole, an evolution from earth goddesses to sky gods, pre-Olympians to Olympians, a society matrilineal in structure and behavior to one heavily patriarchal. But we owe the general acceptance of this interpretation in considerable part to the argument Harrison makes in *Themis.* The goddess herself, she affirms, was considered by Aeschylus to be a personification of Gaia, "the oracular power of Earth" (480), understood "in the old sense of prophecy, utterance, ordinance, not in the later sense of a forecast of the future" (482). Themis is the incarnation of social conventions, of customs that hold sway by common consent. "She is the force that brings and binds men together, she is the 'herd instinct,' the collective conscience, the social sanction" (485).[44] Henri Bergson reminds us in *his* venture into "primitive" religion, *Les deux sources de la morale et de la religion* (where he probably follows Harrison), that "Themis, goddess of human justice, is the mother of the Seasons (*Horai*) and of *Dike* who represents the physical law as well as the moral law" (Bergson 1977, 124). She represents, that is, the ultimate naturalization of human morality. When Harrison identifies her with Durkheim's *"conscience collective"* (group awareness), she deliberately promotes her as the very personification of religion that originates in society's worship of its own cohesion.

It follows from this account of the argument of *Themis* that Harrison agrees with the general consensus in both French sociology and English anthropology; high mythology is a late, secondary abstraction as compared to ritual activity. But this conclusion does not do justice to Harrison's full conception of "myth" in *Themis*. Although she does regard myth as secondary in her *Prolegomena*, arising only *out* of rite, she graduates in *Themis* to describing it as "the spoken correlative of the acted rite" (328). "Ritual," she says in her initial formulation, "is the utterance of an emotion, a thing felt, in *action*, myth in words or thoughts. They arise *pari passu*. The myth is not at first *aetiological*, it does not arise to give a reason; it is representative, another form of utterance, of expression" (16). Myth and rite, then, are contemporaneous and complementary modes of emotive expression. Myth never *originates* as cognition; "it does not arise to give a reason," even though, as Harrison goes on to allow, it may later be interpreted as "aetiological" when its companion rite is no longer understood. This later theory reveals, as Versnel notes, a shift of allegiance from Frazer to Durkheim, that is, from a conception of "myth" as invariably rationalization of rite, to a view of it as an "elementary" emotive mode as "primitive" as gesture itself. The new allegiance appears in Harrison's choice of an illustration of what she means by "the spoken correlative of the acted rite"; she rejects the model of late Mediterranean antiquity in favor of the Durkheimian field of evidence: "In the Grizzly Bear Dance of the North American Indians [actually, the Dakota Sioux] the performers shuffle and shamble about like a bear in a cave waking from his winter sleep. That is the action, the *droumenon*. They also at the same time chant the words: 'I begin to grow restless in the spring, / I take my robe, / My robe is sacred, / I wander in the summer.' These are the *legomena*, the things uttered by the mouth, the *myths*. As man is a speaking as well as a motor animal, any complete human ceremony usually combines both elements" (328–329). But the chant that accompanies the Dakota shuffle is a far cry from the act of imagination that redesigns the incarnated and sacrificial year-god as an immortal Olympian demanding sacrifice.

The nature of *Themis* as an account of the evolution, or devolution, of ancient Greek religion lures Harrison into entertaining both conceptions of "myth," depending on whether she is considering the beginning or end of the process. The shift from Frazer to Durkheim is further obscured by her reluctance to abandon belief in what she calls "the comparatively permanent element of the ritual and the shifting character of the myth" (16). She still valorizes the conservative strength of motoric gesture over verbal formulation. Rituals tend to survive their myths and to require replacements, like changes of spark plugs in an internal combustion engine. Hence the widespread impression that Harrison, in spite of her proclamation of a "separate but equal" status for myth and rite, maintains the primacy, even the priority, of ritual. The principal effect of her shift toward the more "elementary" conception of myth, however, is to render more conspicuous the fundamentally emotive nature of her theory. She hijacks *both* the would-be rationalists, Frazer and Durkheim, for the new emotivism.

Considered strictly in terms of the continuity of anthropological or folkloristic theories of myth, ending the chapter with the Cambridge Ritualists may strike the reader as puzzlingly arbitrary. But there are some good reasons for doing so even internal to the history of anthropology. First, the chronological point we've reached, roughly the beginning of the World War years, is the watershed between the dominance of what Malinowski was to call "armchair" theory, on one hand, and the institutionalizing of professional fieldwork on the other. Second, this period of time, in anthropology and ethnology as in so many other disciplines, appears to separate the hegemony of developmental theories that dwell on issues of origin from that of broadly structural theories that foreground function. But my principal reason for concluding here is admittedly external to the history of folkloristic theories. As the result of a lag of the kind so familiar in cultural and intellectual history, it happens that affective and developmental theories of "primitive" religion and myth become immensely influential in the new field of depth psychology and in the modernist movement in the arts just when the discipline of anthropology itself is refocusing. These two movements seize upon some of the most unguardedly transcendentalist implications of the previous half-century of ethnological investigation with an imaginativeness that creates major channels for the transmission of neo-romantic thinking about myth into the later twentieth century. I pursue these developments in the next three chapters before returning to the construction of "myth" in later anthropology, which is quite another story.

[5]

The Role of Depth-Psychology
in the Construction of Myth

This chapter concerns what Eugen Bleuler, the Swiss psychiatrist, usefully christened early in the century as *tiefenpsychologie,* an umbrella term for the range of psychologies of the unconscious developed by Freud and Jung and their followers. These have been so consistently associated with "myth" since early in the twentieth century that few, I imagine, need convincing of their importance in constructions of the concept. Geoffrey Kirk voices the general impression when he identifies one of the "three major developments in the modern study of myth" as "Freud's discovery of the unconscious and its relation to myth and dreams" (Kirk 1973, 42). Freud is not, strictly speaking, the discoverer of either the "unconscious" or "its relation to myth and dreams" any more than Columbus is the discoverer of the Americas, where some eighty million people were already living. Notions of both "the unconscious" and of its relation to dreams, if not to myth, are current in the latter part of the nineteenth century (Ellenberger 1970). They are products of the general turn toward affective explanations of mind and behavior, combined with a growing post-Darwinian awareness that the circumvention of rationality sought by the romantics in transcendental intuition must be looked for from below, in the obscure regions of "instinct." Kirk is nonetheless right to single out Freud, because the new depth psychology is crucial in *validating* these trends. It provides, or claims to provide, the "scientific" hypotheses that can explain the workings of this circumvention from below.

I am uncertain whether depth-psychological accounts of myth are sufficiently distinctive to require inclusion in the small band of the most fundamental kinds. Insofar as depth psychologies offer clinical support to the idea that mythopoeia is a universal feature of the human mind, they can be regarded as "scientific" confirmations of the grand romantic revaluation of fantasizing and storytelling. But insofar as such psychologies deny any form of transcendence, as Freud's does, they cannot be properly classified as romantic. I will maintain, however, that C. G. Jung's "analytic psychology," in which myth plays a much more prominent part, does smuggle back into the twentieth century a version of romantic transcendence. In fact, I will argue that, although Freud's conception of myth is not itself romantic, his sponsorship of certain key notions, especially of "the hero," of what he called "fixed symbolism" and of the mental inheritance of acquired characteristics, lends far more aid and comfort to the heretical Jung than is generally realized by cold warriors on either side. In order to bring out more clearly the extent to which Freud's thinking about these matters affected some of his stronger followers and was in turn affected by them, I will pursue an approximate chronological sequence while alternating between the development of Freud's thinking and that of his associates, especially Jung.

"THE COMMON CONTENT OF DREAMS AND MYTHS"

Freud launches in *The Interpretation of Dreams* both his general and his specific connection of myth with the unconscious. First, his analysis of the general dynamic of dreams—the interaction between "primary" and "secondary" or unconscious and conscious processes—supplemented by his specific analysis of the mechanisms of "the dream-work"—"condensation," "displacement," signification by tropes—underwrites with unprecedented clinical authority the romantic claim for the mind as "a poetry-making organ" (Trilling 1976, 52).[1] Freud extends his heuristic model of dream in the following years to various forms of waking behavior: to "parapraxes" ("Freudian slips") in *The Psychopathology of Everyday Life* (1901) and to jokes in *Jokes and Their Relation to the Unconscious* (1905). It might be already possible for an astute sympathizer to deduce from this sequence that Freud would explain the origin, function, and true subject matter of any form of imaginative narrative, including, therefore, myth, in terms of a dynamic analogous to, if not the same as, that of dream. Triggered by some everyday occasion, unconscious wishes, repressed since childhood, get expressed in disguised, distorted fashion by means of the same mechanisms that account for the dream-work.

Freud does also introduce in *The Interpretation of Dreams* certain hints of the specific connection of myth with the unconscious. These are clustered in the section of chapter 5, headed "Typical Dreams." Here Freud cites both literary representations of dreams and the direct expression of Oedipal wishes in various modern literary works, from Shakespeare's *Hamlet* to Anderson's "Emperor's New Clothes." He actually lays down the general principle that "the connections between our typical dreams and fairy tales and other kinds of creative writing are neither few nor accidental" (Freud 1965a, 279). In two different discussions of the story of Kronos's devouring of his children, he even appeals directly to Greek myth, assumed to be on a par with other genres of narrative (290, 657). But the most memorable, eventually famous, hint in the work is the discussion of Sophocles' *Oedipus Rex,* perhaps because it illustrates so succinctly Freud's "Freudian" point about the incestual basis of its universal appeal.

In 1908, however, in "Der Dichter und Phantisieren," Freud extends his model again, this time to encompass the vast and protean form of waking fantasy known in English as "daydreaming," a mode that includes, as his title suggests, the productions of the storyteller.[2] This brief essay is well known in twentieth-century aesthetics; Freud's account of daydreaming as neurotic but also as the source of the creative writer's power to captivate has been widely recognized as his most considerable theoretical statement about the psychic roots of literature. Our business here, however, is with three sentences near the end of the essay. Acknowledging that he has concentrated upon the psychology of modern inventors of "original" stories, Freud turns briefly to those who relay traditional tale. "In so far as the material is already at hand . . . it is derived from the popular treasure-house of myths, legends and fairy-tales. . . . It is extremely probable that myths, for example, are distorted vestiges of the wishful phantasies of whole nations—the *secular dreams* of young humanity" (Freud 1989, 439). While the first part of these remarks still refers to modern adaptations of traditional material, Freud reveals in his last sentence his crucial assumption about how the material itself was produced. The suppressed connection between the two parts expresses the same assumption that governs Freud's seminal pages about the appeal of Hamlet and Oedipus—the modern artist who joins this body of story plugs into the power source of age-old ("secular") dreams. Freud never suggests that modern persons are capable of creating new myths; he presumably agrees with rationalists like Comte and Tylor that humanity has outgrown the genre, but he obviously assumes that we have not outgrown the genre's appeal. The phrase "distorted vestiges" indicates that anonymous, communal story, too, must be decoded as displaced libidinal desire. But this assumption depends, in turn, upon the remarkable new one visible at this juncture—that a strict homology obtains between the fantasizing of individuals and that of whole nations over millennia. Freud's consciousness here of the need to distinguish between the products of individual authorial fantasizing and the anonymous products of oral tradition reflect the fact that by 1908 he is no longer working alone in this area. His characterization of myths as "distorted vestiges of the wishful phantasies of whole nations" epitomizes the direction given to his own thinking by the interests of the first two in a trio of brilliant disciples who emerged in 1906 and 1907—Otto Rank, Karl Abraham, and Carl Jung.

For several years, it seems, the one place in Europe where Freud's work had made visible headway was the Burghölzli Mental Hospital in Zürich where Carl Jung, Max Eitingon, Franz Riklin, and Karl Abraham were among Eugen Bleuler's staff members. Perhaps because of their avant-garde work with schizophrenics, this group were particularly interested in the narrative and imagistic dimensions of Freud's discoveries, and they were among the first to take up the potential analogies between dream and myth. By the end of 1907 both Jung and Abraham had made their pilgrimages to Vienna, the latter apparently with his idea for his *Traum und Mythus: Eine Studie Zur Völkerpsychologie* already in mind (Abraham and Freud 1965, 34). In 1908 Freud published both this essay and Ricklin's essay on fairytales, long trumpeted by Jung, in his new journal, *Schriften Zur Angewandten Seelenkunde (Papers in Applied Psychology)*.[3]

Abraham testifies in his essay to the crucial importance for his own thinking of the pages in *Interpretation of Dreams* that suggest "the common content of certain dreams and myths" (Abraham 1955, 159).[4] This acknowledgment becomes the universal tribute among Freud's followers interested in myth, and it indicates the circularity of influence; if they urged him on during these years, his pages initially inspired them. Abraham's argument is strictly Freudian; he aspires to demonstrate the "common content" by showing that myth is, like dream, disguised wish-fulfillment, encoded in condensation, displacement, representable symbols, and secondary elaboration. His plan is crisp in conception, but its execution is muffled; he spends too much time explaining and defending Freud's still novel theory of dreams and not enough on his own analyses of the mechanisms of the dream-work in the Hindu, Greek, and Hebrew myths of his choice.

Abraham's essay displays very clearly, however, several of the crucial assumptions that Freud adopts in "The Creative Writer and Day-Dreaming." The first of these is the homology of origin and function between "myth" and dream. And this assumption is closely connected to another with a large future in depth psychology—the persuasion that the psychic development of the individual repeats the development of the race. This notion, increasingly widespread throughout the nineteenth century, seems to begin in the transcendentalist biologism of Lamarck, whose fourth "law" of organisms, first defined in 1815, states that "all which has been acquired . . . in the organization of individuals during the course of their life is conserved by generation and transmitted to new individuals" (Leaf 1979, 98). The embryological experiments of von Baer and others in the 1840s appeared to confirm this idea in a specific form that inspired Ernst Haeckel to formulate in 1866 his earliest version of the so-called "biogenetic law," "ontogeny is the short and rapid recapitulation of phylogeny" (Sulloway 1979, 199).[5] This law need not entail inheritance of acquired characteristics, but it was generally interpreted as doing so. Darwin, for example, accepts it thus in *The Origin of Species* as one of the factors supplemental to natural selection. Herbert Spencer takes the next step as early as 1852, asserting that past experiences of the race modify not only the body but its thoughts and emotions.[6] In *First Principles* this most esteemed and popular of philosophers in England in the latter part of the century declares, "The terms *a priori* truth' and 'necessary truth,' as used in this work, are to be interpreted . . . as implying cognitions that have been rendered organic by immense accumulation of experiences, received partly by the individual, but mainly by all the ancestral individuals whose nervous system he inherits" (Burrow 1966, 211). Between 1895 and 1910 the pioneers of modern genetics discover transmission by gene and discredit the notion of inheritance of acquired characteristics even in its relatively probable physical sense. Nevertheless, the doctrine in its extreme mentalistic sense soldiers on to become one of the more widely held *idées reçues* of the early twentieth century, in no small part because of its persistence in depth psychology in general, and in its explanations of myth in particular.

"Modern science," Abraham asserts, "regards as a fundamental principle of biogenetics the fact that the development of the individual recapitulates the evolution of the species," and he is equally confident that "a corresponding process takes place in the psychic sphere where philogenetic [*sic*] development is likewise recapitulated" (207). Myth, according to Abraham, plays a very special part in certifying this latter development. With absolutely no indication of awareness that he is constructing a circular argument, Abraham adduces the survival of myths as "the most important proof" of the extension of the biogenetic law to mental functions. The survival proves the law; the law explains the survival. Freud was doubtless predisposed to accept these assumptions for the same reason that Abraham was, namely, their sponsorship by such prestigious advocates of positivistic materialism as Comte, Spencer, and Haeckel. It's Abraham on myth and dream, however, who first calls Freud's attention to their potential usefulness in theorizing the universality of the Oedipus complex.

According to Ernest Jones, Otto Rank showed up on Freud's doorstep in 1906 with the manuscript copy of *Der Kunstler*, nothing less than a psychoanalytic study of creativity extrapolated from hints in Freud's earlier writings (Jones 1953, vol. 2, 8). Rank turned next to "myth," and early in 1909 his *Myth of the Birth of the Hero: An Essay in the Psychological Interpretation of Myth* appeared in Freud's *Schriften*. Rank commences by reminding us of the striking similarities among the heroic sagas of ancient peoples. These resemblances can be explained, of course, only by "universal . . . traits of the human psyche" (Rank 1964, 8). Psychological conceptions of such "universal traits" were as common at the turn of the century in German mythography as in English, but Rank ignores Bastian's *"Elementargedenken"* and Wundt's *"Völkerpsychologie"* to point to the specific example of Freud's treatment of Oedipus in *The Interpretation of Dreams*. He, too, insists that "the manifestation of the intimate relationship between dream and myth . . . justifies the interpretation of this myth as a dream of the masses of the people" (9), and he refers us for confirmation neither to Abraham nor to Freud but to his own *Der Kunstler*. The uniform functioning of myth, artistic fantasizing, daydreaming, and certain neurotic mental processes authorizes us to assume that we can explain the recurrent patterns of heroic saga by appeal to the laws of individual psychodynamics. After conducting us through the parallel cycles from Sargon to Lohengrin, Rank attempts his psychoanalytical generalizations about the common plot. The hero is a high-born child, abandoned by or cut off from his parents for various reasons, often involving the father's rejection. He is rescued by humble folk or animals and lives in obscurity until he grows up to reclaim his rightful place by some spectacular exertion. The psychological key lies in Freud's discoveries about "the family romance of neurotics" (69). Rank introduces into his text at this point Freud's now well-known but then unpublished essay on this topic, with its thesis that needy prepubertal children often imagine their "real" parent or parents to be far grander personages than the ones they have actually been stuck with.[7] Analogously, Rank argues, "the true hero of romance is the ego. . . . Myths are . . . created by adults, by means of retrograde childhood fantasies." As a contribution to a psychoanalytic theory of myth, it's questionable if Rank does any more than echo Freud's speculations in "The Creative Writer and Day-Dreaming." What is original, however, is his articulation of a Freudian hero, his recognition that Freud's account of the libidinal development of boys in the first part of life appears to have been projected over and over in the hero myths of the ancient Near East. Between the two of them, Rank and Freud introduce in this long essay a new psychological explanation of the genesis of "the hero" out of the wish-fulfillment fantasies of ordinary persons. This explanation constitutes in turn the potential universalizing of the heroic as a psychological adventure; every man his own myth.

Apart from its psychoanalytic basis, Rank's work is methodologically primitive; the possibilities of diffusion among neighboring peoples are too easily shunted aside in favor of independent, individual invention, and Rank also seems blissfully unaware of any need to consider on what generic basis his heterogeneous group of stories may be defined as "myth." But Freud valued the essay highly. Besides its general confirmation of the relevance of the biogenetic law to psychoanalysis and its specific confirmation of Abraham's equation of dream and myth, it clinched, for Freud, a conviction that remains from this point on consistent in his thinking. This is the belief expressed in his own contribution to the essay—that in neurotic regression the mind reverts to myth; the individual relives, as it were, a phylogenetic childhood. When Freud finally attends to myth on the theoretical level in "The Creative Writer and Day-Dreaming," then, he probably owes much about his explicit attention to the genre to what he has learned through participation in the work of his two new disciples. It takes the impact of the third of these disciples, however, to push Freud into a full-scale recognition of the importance of phylogenetic fantasy in the cultural formation of the Oedipal situation.

SYMBOLS OF TRANSFORMATION

In October of 1909 Jung announced his enlistment in the company of Abraham and Rank, writing to Freud that "mythology has got me in its grip" (McGuire 1974, 251–252). Freud was delighted, replying, "We must conquer the whole field of mythology. Thus far we have only two pioneers" (255). It is easy for us with the advantage of hindsight to perceive that he should have been worried rather than delighted. Jung had come to psychiatry by a very different route than Freud. What corresponds to Freud's post-Darwinian background in biology is Jung's enthusiasm for Goethe, the romantic poets, Schopenhauer, and Nietzsche. What corresponds to the importance of "Anna O." in Freud's career is, as Jung himself pointed out, his observation of the mediumistic trances, fantasies, and jargons of his young cousin, Hélène Preiswerk. These were the subject of his doctoral dissertation of 1902, "On the Psychology and Pathology of So-Called Occult Phenomena." Even his early enthusiasm for *The Interpretation of Dreams*, probably the principal factor in Freud's currency at the Burghölzli, is intimately connected with Jung's studies of word-association tests and analyses of the fantasies of schizophrenics. Whereas Freud, given his background in positivistically oriented biology, is predisposed to view fantasizing as a symptom of neurosis, Jung is primed to view it in terms of romantic expressivity. It is no accident that Jung, once launched on his research, was soon telling Freud about his reading in "the 4 volumes of old Creuzer" (McGuire 1974, 258), and preaching him a mini-sermon on the need "to revivify among intellectuals a feeling for symbol and myth" (294).

The first part of the resulting text, *Wandlungen und Symbole der Libido,* was published in the Society's *Jahrbuch* in 1911 and the second, in spite of Freud's now open misgivings, in 1912.[8] Like *The Golden Bough, Symbols of Transformation* organizes encyclopedic information upon the armature of an explanatory pretext. "The whole thing" Jung tells us, "is really only an extended commentary on a practical analysis of the prodromal stages of schizophrenia" (xxv). According to his own testimony, he did not know what to make of his obsessive studies in mythology until he happened upon "the fantasy material of an unknown young American woman, pseudonymously known as Frank Miller . . . published by my respected and fatherly friend [his dissertation director] the late Théodore Flournoy" (xxvii). Then, he confesses in his autobiography, these fantasies "operated like a catalyst upon the stored-up and disorderly ideas within me" (Jung 1961, 163). Jung resorts to the same allusion as Frazer does in order to characterize the resulting structure: "The symptoms of the case form the Ariadne thread to guide us through the labyrinth of symbolistic parallels" (xxv). A labyrinth it is: the "amplifications," which Jung describes as "absolutely essential if we wish to establish the meaning of the archetypal context," stand to the direct evidence (the four Miller fantasies) in a ratio of 30 to 1. This feature alone would guarantee that the work differs from any study of Freud's. In 1910, after he had begun work on his own manuscript, Jung recommended that Freud analyze Daniel Paul Schreber's *Memoirs of My Nervous Illness* (1903). Many years later, in the revised *Symbols,* Jung expresses his dissatisfaction with the result—Freud's handling of Schreber's fantasies in his essay of 1911, "Psychoanalytical Notes upon an Autobiographical Account of a Case of Paranoia," generally known as "The Psychotic Dr. Schreber." Jung proceeds to suggest in his own text a number of ways in which Schreber's fantasies resemble Miller's and are amenable to the same method of analysis.[9] Since these notations appear only in the late revision, they suggest that Jung had come to understand, *ex post facto,* that his disappointment with Freud's too narrow conception of the place of fantasy in psychic life was an unconscious motivation in the production of *Symbols.* In its elaborate contextualizing of the written fantasies of a stranger, *Symbols* is Jung's exemplary, "improved" Schreber case.

To appreciate Jung's understanding of the nature and function of fantasizing, it's important to review several of his crucial conceptual innovations in *Symbols,* beginning with his revised "libido." In spite of his support of psychoanalysis, Jung had never really accepted Freud's sexual determinism. Whereas for Freud "libido" is specifically humankind's sexual drive, Jung redefines it as "psychic energy in the widest sense" (64). Freud's conception of libido follows from his Darwinian biologism, while Jung's stems from his romantic developmentalism. Jung repeatedly compares *his* "libido" to Schopenhauer's "Will" as "a ceaseless forward movement, an unending will for life" (438) that underlies all human representations *(vorstellungen).* But Schopenhauer's Will is utterly indifferent to the desperate representations that humankind invents for consolation, whereas Jung's "libido" is ultimately benign, suspiciously like the universal process envisaged by various romantics, or by Goethe in *Faust,* for example. Libido, Jung says, "is the unconscious creative force which wraps itself in images" (222). In Schopenhauer the "images" or representations are saving lies we are obliged to invent for ourselves; in Jung they are saving truths communicated by the universal dynamism. Jung's American translator, Beatrice Hinkle, is closer to the mark than Jung himself when she compares his "libido," not to Schopenhauer's Will, but to Bergson's *élan vital.* But the essential point, in either case, is that all symbols ultimately signify this process itself and "can be reduced to a common denominator—the libido and its properties" (97). As a consequence, there is no "literal" level or floor of specifically sexual causality beneath the signifiers of our fantasizing. "A phallic symbol does not denote the sexual organ, but the libido, and however clearly it appears as such, it does not mean itself but is always a symbol of the libido" (222). Sex is merely an important source of signifiers, not the libidinal signified.

It follows that the Oedipus complex, if taken as a universal causal explanation, is a Whiteheadian "fallacy of misplaced concreteness." Jung does not deny the existence of Oedipal fantasies, but he insists that they are the retrospective invention of the adult psyche. Under certain neurotic conditions they are "bound to arise, because when the regressing libido is introverted . . . it always reactivates the parental imagoes and thus apparently reestablishes the infantile relationship" (204). But this relation can't be reestablished on the basis of the original presexual infancy in which Jung believes because "the libido is an adult libido which is already bound to sexuality and inevitably imparts an incompatible, incestuous character into the reactivated relationship to the parents." These Oedipal fantasies are no less real and dangerous for arising after the fact, that is, during adult regression. In sketching the result of their resolution, Jung anticipates Freud's theory of culture in *Totem and Taboo.* "Because the incest taboo opposes the libido and blocks the path to regression, it is possible for the libido to be canalized into the mother analogies thrown up by the unconscious. In that way the libido becomes progressive again, and even attains a level of consciousness higher than before" (213). Culture is the result of something like Freudian sublimation, but this result seems determined by an inherent unconscious wisdom rather than by guilt.

These considerations bring us to Jung's next major innovation, his conception of fantasizing as a teleological process. Phenomena like the Oedipus complex, far from being adequate causal explanations of culture, themselves demand explanation in terms of the apparent *directedness* of the libido. "The incest prohibition acts as an obstacle and makes creative fantasy inventive, . . . gradually opens up possible avenues for the self-realization of libido" (224). Thus the construction of this prohibition is already an act of culture that reveals the libido directing its own self-transcendence. Jung points out that even in the most "primitive tribe . . . we find that creative fantasy is continually engaged in producing analogies . . . in order to free libido from sheer instinctuality" (227). Wherever we look for the origins of culture, we find this immense process of fantasizing always already there. The existence of this benign teleological process is Jung's foundational article of belief. He does not argue for it or pretend to explain it; he merely affirms that "there are no 'purposeless' psychic processes" (58), that there is, on the contrary, "a secret purposiveness bound up with the supposedly devious path of the libido" and that this "transformation of libido moves in the same direction as . . . the cultural modification, conversion or displacement of natural drives" (58). The standard Freudian objection to this view of "libido" is to complain that it is so extended as to be virtually meaningless, and that it is, above all, "mystical." Certainly when Jung speaks of it, he does often sound like a religious visionary: "A process of transformation is going on in the unconsciousness whose dynamism, whose contents and whose subject are themselves unknown but become visible indirectly to the conscious mind by stimulating the imaginative material at its disposal, clothing themselves in it like the dancers who clothe themselves in the skins of animals or the priests in the skin of their human victims" (430). Jung's simile suggests not only that the individual consciousness is the site of an ongoing rite of sacrifice but also that this ritual dance expresses experience of very remote origin in the history of the race. We cannot know consciously what prompts the impulse to sacrifice or who or what the dancers are. What we do know is that, since the process of acculturation requires such sacrifice of libido, it is crucial for us to attend to what *is* observable—those skins. The skins are themselves a metaphor that expresses with melodramatic force the importance for Jung of "symbol" and "myth," the two large modes of archetypal representability through which the ongoing stream of Will communicates.

These two modes must eventually be considered in detail. It is enough for now to attend to Jung's clear recognition in *Symbols of Transformation* of what constitutes the essence of his philosophic and clinical break with Freud: "Whence has fantasy acquired its bad reputation? Above all from the circumstance that it cannot be taken literally. . . . If it is understood *semiotically,* as Freud understands it, it is interesting from the scientific point of view; but if it is understood *hermeneutically,* as an authentic symbol, it acts as a signpost, providing the clues we need in order to carry on our lives in harmony with ourselves" (Jung 1972, 291). Both psychologists avoid the mistake of taking fantasy literally, but Freud's reading halts at the "semiotic" because it regards the encoded structure of fantasy as determined by past psychic events, whereas Jung's reading is "hermeneutical" because it calls for the tentative interpretation of an ongoing process whose signifiers refer to the fantasist's present and future condition. Freudian psychology instructs us that the fantasist needs the analyst, Jungian that the analyst needs the fantasist.

"ONE STORY ONLY": JUNG'S PLOT OF LIBIDINAL DEVELOPMENT

Before we leave our focus on the Oedipal rebellion of *Symbols of Transformation* for later stages of intertwined and complementary developments in the depth psychologies of Freud and Jung, one major topic remains to be considered. This is

Jung's influential revision of Freud's schema of libidinal development, especially as it is represented narratively in his and Rank's account of the Freudian hero. Freud's paradigm, brilliantly set forth in *Three Essays on Sexuality* (1905), is the central floor-beam of psychoanalysis. The growing person passes through the polymorphous perversity of infancy, the formation of the Oedipus complex in early childhood with its concomitant risks of perversion through premature fixation, into the latency period and thence into resolution of the Oedipus complex in adolescence, with its attendant risks of correspondingly severe, *nachträglich* neurosis. It seems unlikely that without Freud's construct, and Rank's extrapolation of part of it onto world mythology in *The Myth of the Birth of the Hero,* Jung would have imagined so clearly in his first major work a rival plot of libidinal development that simultaneously organized his researches in "myth."

The nature of Jung's rewriting follows from the nature of his disagreement with Freud about libido itself. If, rather than being a congeries of animal urges whose repression is the work of civilization, libido is a benign, dynamic process transforming lower instincts into higher, then it makes sense that its crucial psychodynamics begin where Freud's leave off, not with the vicissitudes of childhood sexuality, but with the transformation of youth into adulthood. This may be why Jung selects for his exemplary case the prodromal schizophrenia of a young adult. Jung's adventure of the libido is recognizably a version of Freud's adolescent resolution of the Oedipus complex, but one in which the adolescent's sexual relation with his or her parents is itself signifier rather than signified. Stated in as rigorously non-figurative a manner as possible, the child must enter an introspective quest for his or her own identity, which involves breaking from both parents, but especially the mother, and discovering the inner strength that enables adult responsibility. Jung's report on "Frank Miller" is negative; her sanity is at risk because even at the age of twenty-four (in the fourth fantasy) she is still at home, childishly dependent on her parents, yet indulging in narcissistic "masculine" fantasies of exalted achievement long after she ought to have accepted her destiny as a woman to fall in love, marry, and bear children.

But a non-figurative summary of this sort is hardly recognizable as "Jungian." His universal crisis of libido never manifests itself abstractly; it always works through the richly symbolic flow of traditional "myth" and "symbol" that he was later to regard as the manifestation of "archetypes." Jung pursues through "Miller's" fantasies and their self-identified cultural sources the paradigm of a quest romance. The youthful hero of the cycles celebrated by Rank breaks away from his childhood environment, embarks upon a dangerous journey in quest of a treasure guarded by a dragon or giant, and returns triumphantly to the social world with his authenticating prize.[10] The better to express that this quest is an interior journey, Jung borrows from his favorite anthropological source, the late-romantic Africanist and cultural diffusionist, Leo Frobenius, the concept of the "night sea journey" of world-wide sun-gods. According to Frobenius, this journey is typically conceived in African mythologies as taking place inside the body of a devouring or "Terrible" Mother. Jung takes this mythologem to signify on the sexual (or Freudian) level the child's ambivalence about breaking with his source of security, and on the "properly psychological" level his longing to remain unconscious. "This longing can easily turn into a consuming passion which threatens all that has been won. The mother then appears on the one hand as the supreme goal, and on the other as the most frightful danger—the Terrible Mother" (235–236). Jung is careful here to preserve the distinction required by his difference from Freud about the nature of libido. "Regression leads back only apparently to the mother; in reality she is the gateway into the unconscious, into the 'realm of the Mothers.' . . . Regression, if left undisturbed does not stop short at the "mother" but goes back . . . to the prenatal realm of the 'Eternal Feminine,' to the immemorial world of archetypal possibilities" (330). As the phrases from *Faust* indicate, Jung himself follows Frobenius deep into the prenatal realm of German romanticism when he personifies the universal process as feminine. We could scarcely hope for a better distinction between the naturalistic literalism of Freud's account of libidinal development and Jung's assumption that sexual fantasy is a set of signifiers displacing the true ground of meaning, the mind's own inadvertent processes of transformation.

The act of introversion that produces this regression is necessary for psychic growth. The first test of the hero (in world story) is to take this plunge. The second test is to triumph in the undersea or underground battle with the Mother, generally in the guise of a devouring monster or dragon guarding the tree of life or a hoard of treasure. The monsters signify fear of incest, but since "incest" itself is not to be taken literally but rather as "the urge to get back to childhood" (235), only the failure of the hero to differentiate himself by slaying the blocking agent would be truly "incestuous." Since "the mother corresponds to the collective unconscious, and the son to consciousness" (259), the symbolic role of the father in this struggle is secondary. He is "the representative of the spirit, whose function is to oppose pure instinctuality. That is his archetypal role, which falls to him regardless of his personal qualities; hence he is very often an object of neurotic fears for the son" (261). It might seem that as the "representative of the spirit" the father ought logically to be the son's ally. But he stands for the Law, the social *status quo,* the way things have traditionally been done. He does insist on the son's becoming a responsible grown-up, but only on society's terms. In short, "the danger comes from both parents: from the father, because he apparently makes regression impossible, and from the mother, because she absorbs the regressing libido and keeps it to herself, so that he who sought rebirth finds only death" (331).

The third stage in the monomyth is the triumphant return of the hero to the social world. This is the normal "Oedipal" resolution projected in terms of world mythology. "All over the earth, in the most various forms, each with a different time-coloring, the savior-hero appears as a fruit of the entry of the libido into the maternal depths of the unconscious" (345). He brings back from his "night sea journey" the treasure of the hoard. This thesaurus, which Jung refers to in traditional biblical diction as "treasure laid up in Heaven," "the pearl of great price," and so forth, is the insight conferred by confrontation with the archetypes evoked and crystallized in the act of regression. The fabulous triumph of the hero of myth and tale represents the achievement in the quotidian world both of numberless individuals' acquisitions of identity and all those acts of civilization that are the reward of internal conquest. It is easy to recognize in this Jungian movement from separation through confrontation to reintegration the old romantic paradigms—Blake's dialectic of innocence, experience, and higher innocence, or Hegel's of unselfconsciousness, alienated consciousness, and consciousness at home with itself. Jung's "archetypal plot" is the great conduit feeding this stream of romantic thought into the hanging gardens of mid-twentieth-century mythographers like Northrop Frye, Robert Graves, and Joseph Campbell.

In his later work Jung subjects this pattern to a very important qualification. In the original *Transformations,* "answering" Rank and Freud, he focuses wholly upon the hero of the first half of life. Even the archetypal imagery of the return with the treasure is presented as the achievement of the young hero who has triumphed over the lure of the maternal abyss. In Jung's revision of 1952, however, although he lets his earlier treatment stand, presumably for historical reasons, he adds at this juncture a long note pointing out that what is appropriate to the first half of life is not to the second. The young hero, having established his conscious identity, tends rigidly to reject its contrary even when his sun of life declines toward its horizon. "The mind shies away, but life wants to flow down into the depths" (357). The heroic acceptance that is the proper response to this latter condition belongs to a later phase in the archetypal life of the hero, the phase of the redeemer-figures of various world religions, who conquer the Mother most brilliantly and gain the greatest treasures for the race by acknowledging that they must at last succumb to her. "The hero suspends himself in the branches of the maternal tree. . . . We can say that he unites himself with the mother in death and at the same time negates the act of union. . . . The sacrifice is the very reverse of regression—it is a successful canalization of libido into the symbolic equivalent of the mother, and hence a spiritualization of it" (263). As part of his articulation of the heroism and the heroes appropriate to the second half of life, Jung assigns a more sublime version of the motif of the return with the treasure to this second sort of triumph over the Mother. The romantic love-death that now concludes the Jungian plot bears a striking resemblance to the equally romantic biology of the death-instinct at which Freud had arrived some thirty years earlier in *Beyond the Pleasure Principle.*

TOTEM AND TABOO: "PHYLOGENETIC FANTASY"

Freud's direct contribution to a psychoanalytic theory of myth ends with his brief suggestion in "The Creative Writer and Day-Dreaming." Myth, like other forms of narrative fantasizing, originates in, and functions to express, long-repressed wish. Its subject matter is the generically appropriate coded form of that wish. But two of Freud's most important *indirect* contributions to depth psychology's construction of myth remain to be discussed. The first of these is Freud's consistent reliance, from *Totem and Taboo* forward, upon the inheritance of acquired mental characteristics as brought to his attention by Abraham. It becomes a staple of his thinking for the rest of his career, but only a part of that reliance calls for attention here. This is the line of speculation, from *Totem and Taboo* (1912–1913) through *The Ego and the Id*

(1923), which appears to corroborate the assumption of Jung and others that access to archaic mental representations is part of our biological inheritance.

Totem and Taboo is in considerable part the product of the ferment among Freud and certain of adherents that we have been following. *The Freud/Jung Letters* provides, in particular, a good deal of evidence that *Totem and Taboo* was inspired and shaped by the progress of Jung's *Transformations*. When Jung assures Freud early in his research that his reading is opening up "rich lodes . . . for the phylogenetic basis of the theory of neurosis" (258), Freud understands him to be planning a study that he himself had desiderated, a work that would explore the analogies between age-old "myth" and the fantasies of neurotics. Even as late as September of 1911, when Freud offers as a talk at the Third Psychoanalytic Congress his postscript to his analysis of Schreber's *Memoirs,* he assumes that Jung's expressed dissatisfaction with its treatment of Schreber's symbolism has been prompted merely because it did not deal sufficiently with such analogues. Freud expresses the hope that his belated acknowledgement of the presence of analogues to "myth" in Schreber's fantasies will "serve to show that Jung had excellent grounds for his assertion that the mythopoeic forces of mankind are not extinct, but that to this very day they give rise in the neuroses to the same psychological products as in the remotest past ages" (Freud 1963, 185). Thus far, Freud's comments seem intended to placate Jung, but he then concludes with a flourish that advertises a work in progress. It is as if he were now, like Jung, engaged in producing the work that he had in vain urged the other man to write. "The time will soon be ripe . . . to complete what has hitherto been only an individual and ontogenetic application by the addition of its anthropological and phylogenetically conceived counterpart. 'In dreams and in neuroses,' so our principle has run, 'we once more come upon the *child* . . . and we come upon the *savage,* too . . . upon the *primitive* man'" (186).

Totem and Taboo is subtitled "Some Points of Agreement between the Mental Lives of Savages and Neurotics." But even though the analogy between the thinking of "primitive" humankind and modern neurotics may be the broadest structural principle in the work as originally conceived, Freud actually develops a number of related parallels; between, for example, the thinking of "primitives" and modern children, between Comte's three ages of thought—the animistic (or mythological), religious, and scientific—and the stages of normal libidinal development, and between social institutions and neuroses. ("It might be maintained that a case of hysteria is a caricature of a work of art, that an obsessional neurosis is a caricature of religion and that a paranoiac delusion is a caricature of a philosophical system" [73].) As long as the exploration of Oedipal wishes is confined to the neurotic patient in the context of analysis, no etiology is called for beyond the childhood of the individual, but as soon as those wishes are projected as agents in the formation of cultural institutions, the question of how they are transmitted cries out for explanation. Freud acknowledges his own choice with his usual directness near the end of *Totem and Taboo:* "I have taken as the basis of my whole position *the existence of a collective mind* [my italics], in which mental processes occur just as they do in the minds of an individual. In particular, I have supposed that the sense of guilt for an action has persisted for many thousands of years and has remained operative in generations who can have had no knowledge of that action" (157–158). The only feasible explanation, he insists, is "inheritance of psychical dispositions."

Freud's allusion to a "sense of guilt" that has "persisted for many thousands of years," refers to the boldest of this family of phylogenetic hypotheses in *Totem and Taboo*. By the time Freud read the completed *Transformations* in the summer of 1912, when he himself had only published the first half of his book, he found himself confronted with a work much different from what he had stubbornly imagined it would be. Far from confining himself to agreement with the master about the neurotic's regression to mythological fantasies, Jung proposes a grand psychological theory of the origins of culture in a spiritualized, unmistakably non-sexual libido. Freud rises to Jung's challenge by preparing as a counterblast in the second half of *his* work in progress his own etiological myth, his sacred story of cultural origins. While agreeing with Jung that civilization arises from the sublimation of instinct, he opposes to Jung's generalized "symbol"-producing dynamism, a specific origin in acts of parricide, invention of the incest taboo, and totemic communion. Where Jung appeals to romantic poetry and philosophy, Freud turns to recent anthropology as he understands it. He imagines humans living originally in small hordes, ruled by a despotic male who appropriates all the females. This system ends in a rebellion by the sons, who kill the father and devour him. The new social system, a totemic brother-clan, is based upon guilt. The brothers renounce the women on whose account they killed their father and institute exogamy, based, of course, upon the incest taboo. They also create a totemic religion in which the animal representing the primal father is worshiped as an ancestor. In keeping with the sons' ambivalence toward their deed, however, once a year at a ceremonial meal the totem animal is torn to pieces and devoured.

Freud affirms on the basis of this tissue of conjecture that "the beginnings of religion, morals, society and art converge in the Oedipus complex" (Freud 1950, 156). Most readers of *Totem and Taboo* probably find it difficult to take as anything but a particularly farfetched "just-so" story this very specific extrapolation of the Oedipus complex into a monolithic explanation of the origins of culture. This was the general (though by no means universal) reaction among anthropologists at the time. Much of the psychoanalytic community itself has regarded the story with embarrassment, particularly during the heyday of ego psychology, when even some of Freud's more sober metapsychological speculations were the object of the sort of squirming generally associated with adolescents over their parents' behavior. How seriously did Freud take his story? In the late *Moses and Monotheism,* after acknowledging the widespread rejection of it among anthropologists, he insists, "To this day I hold firmly to this construction" (131). The word "construction" implies, however, a certain recognition of the "just-so" quality of the specific plot, even as he insists on its truth. Like a modern theologian confronting the account of Adam and Eve in *Genesis,* Freud seems willing to take his story as fable, but not to reject its symbolic validity. He remains convinced that human culture developed through the agency of *some* such Oedipal dynamic.

The importance of *Totem and Taboo* as an indirect contribution to constructions of myth in depth psychology lies, however, not in Freud's invented myth, *à la* Plato, but in the forceful surfacing there of his psychic Lamarckianism and its powerful role in his subsequent thought.[11] During the decade of what is sometimes (rightly) called his "romantic biology" (roughly between 1911 and 1923), we can see the new impetus of this speculation at work in three interrelated aspects of Freud's theorizing: (1) direct elaboration of the sort of etiology opened up by *Totem and Taboo,* (2) renovation of his theory of instincts, and (3) development of his so-called second metapsychological concept of the structure and function of the mind. The first of this triad can be described quite briefly. During the war years Freud carries on with Sandor Ferenczi an extravagant speculation about the phylogenetic experiences that might account for the structures not only of neuroses in particular but of the development of libido in general.[12] Both Freud's new work during these years and his revised editions of his two classics, *The Interpretation of Dreams* (1914, 1918) and *Three Essays on Sexuality* (1915), bear the pervasive stamp of this obsession.

Second, Freud's absorption in the concept of psychic biogenesis leads him during these years into a sustained reexamination of the one likely vehicle of such transmission, namely, instinct. He describes instinct in 1915 as a "borderland concept between the mental and the physical," since it entails both a demand made from within the organism and a *"mental representative"* (my italics) of the organic stimuli (Freud 1963a, 87). He consistently respects in his subsequent work this paradoxical, amphibious nature of instinct. In what is probably the densest of his late work, he admits ironically that "the theory of the instincts is so to say our mythology," meaning, I take it, that because the biologist or psychologist cannot do without some theory of instinct, which nevertheless remains ineluctably obscure, the theorist must be resigned to producing what Nietzsche, too, would call "mythology" (Freud 1965b, 84). Certainly Freud mythologizes instinct, beginning in his first metapsychological paper, "Formulations Regarding Two Principles of Mental Functioning" (1911), when he posits, on the evident analogy of his "primary" and "secondary" processes of mind, two opposing sets of instincts, those of the libido, concerned with blind gratification, and those of the ego, concerned with self-preservation. Freud tells us in his retrospective account in *Beyond the Pleasure Principle* (1919) that this confident dualism threatened to turn into a monistic nightmare when he realized (as he records in "On Narcissism: An Introduction" [1915]) that narcissism is by its very nature the cathecting of the ego itself with libido. If the two supposedly watertight compartments actually leak into each other to form a single solution, then either Freud's desexualized libido can't be distinguished from Jung's or else "everything is sex," as the opponents of psychoanalysis have been maintaining all along. According to Freud's account, he remained trapped in this dilemma for several years, until his discovery of the "death instinct" (grounded in the repetition assumed by the "biogenetic law") enabled him to set up a new antagonism of mighty opposites, the life-force, Eros, against what others, though not he, took to calling Thanatos. By attaching to these instincts names that recall the quasi-mythological cosmic principles of pre-Socratic philosophy, Freud manages to remind us simultaneously, as in his etiological tale in *Totem and Taboo,* that he mythologizes ill-understood forces, but that these forces are nonetheless the genuine shapers of human culture by virtue of their phylogenetic contents.[13]

Third, Freud's combined focus during these years on psychical biogenetic explanation and on theory of instinct feeds into his second metapsychological sketch of the mind as presented in *The Ego and the Id* (1923). It's possible to observe Freud's first step toward integrating these three interests in one burst of illumination that occurs toward the end of his long "Wolf-Man" case study (written during 1914–1915, though not published until 1918). Having puzzled over the ambiguities of whether the Wolf-Man as a small child actually came upon "the primal scene" or only imagined it, Freud finally decides that in either case the boy's "remodeling" of it according to the Oedipal pattern shows that there was some mysterious anticipatory mechanism at work. "We can form no conception of what this may have consisted in; we have nothing at our disposal but a single analogy—and it is an excellent one—of the far-reaching instinctive knowledge of animals" (Freud 1971, 261). He leaps from this hypothesis to the next, that "this instinctive factor would then be the nucleus of the unconscious," a proposition that generates his great paper "The Unconscious," written directly after the Wolf-Man study. This identification of the nucleus of the unconscious itself as an instinctual acquisition of Oedipal guilt enables, in turn, Freud's articulation in *The Ego and the Id* of his revised metapsychology, that is, his account of the economic, dynamic, and topographical relations among the superego (or "ego ideal"), the ego, and the unconscious, now redescribed as the id. As Freud chillingly summarizes these relationships, "The ego ideal is therefore the heir of the Oedipus complex, and thus it is also the expression of the most powerful impulses and most important libidinal vicissitudes of the id. By setting up this ego ideal the ego has mastered the Oedipus complex and at the same time placed itself in subjection to the id" (Freud 1962, 36). Instinct shaped by phylogenesis holds sway even in the most exalted reaches of mind.

Like the consideration of "the hero," the first of Freud's indirect contributions to the impact of depth psychology on the construction of myth, this brief sketch of his second, more complex one, the theorizing of the psychoanalytic consequences of biogenetics, exhibits the extent to which his thinking, especially during the years of his "romantic biology," works in certain significant respects more in tandem with Jung's than in opposition. It is apparent, for example, that Freud equates psychic biogenesis with a collective unconscious. Both Freud and Ferenczi agree about the existence of such an unconscious, and Freud even speaks, as we've seen, of a "collective mind" and states explicitly during the teens that he has no quarrel with Jung's formulation of it. Furthermore, Freud's mythologized account of Eros, the renunciation and sublimation of instinct that produces civilization, resembles Jung's notion of the power that creates civilization by transforming lower instincts into higher ones. It is as if, having evaded Jung's "monism" by the discovery of the "death instinct," Freud felt free to permit his "libido" to approximate Jung's without fear of coalescence. In this spirit, for example, he speaks in *The Ego and the Id* of a store of "displaceable and neutral energy" in both superego and ego as "desexualized Eros" (Freud 1962, 44–45). Freud's Eros, to be sure, does not work alone in the creation of civilization; it achieves its aim only in Empedoclean struggle with "the death instinct." But how different is this process from the lure of the Mother in the second half of life over which the Jungian hero triumphs by securing the treasure only at the cost of death?

"FIXED SYMBOLISM" AND "ARCHETYPE"

Before any final reckoning with the combined Freudian and Jungian impact, however, there still remains to be considered Freud's third, and truncated, indirect contribution and its remarkable Jungian extension. This is the issue of recurrent patterns in the symbolism of dreams and fantasies and their relation to traditional symbolism of all sorts. The standard nature of this symbolism had certainly not struck Freud as particularly significant when he first wrote *The Interpretation of Dreams,* even though dream interpretation bears down consistently upon a small set of underlying wishes and therefore contains *in ovo* a predictable symbolism. This blind spot was perhaps a result of his therapeutic orientation; symbolism initially acquired significance for him only in the larger context of the individual analysis, still a basic rule of psychoanalytic practice. Whatever the explanation, there's considerable evidence that Freud became seriously interested in this topic, as in the instances of the two preceding "indirect" contributions—the hero and biogenetic transmission—when the seriousness of its import was pressed upon him by his early followers. Ellenberger cites in *The Discovery of the Unconscious* "the influence of Abraham, Ferenczi, Rank and Stekel" (493), to which we should add Jung. By 1909 Freud himself is telling the Vienna Psychoanalytic Society, in connection with a projected second editon of *The Interpretation of Dreams,* that the major defect of the original, along with insufficient attention to the role of sexuality, is that "far too little importance has been ascribed to the fixed symbolism of dreams" (Sulloway 1979, 305). In one of his notes on a draft of Jung's *Transformations* in the following year he admits to Jung, "I didn't go deeply enough into symbolism in my dream-book. Stekel is now filling in the gaps in his papers" (McGuire 1974, 333). Wilhelm Stekel's *Speech of Dreams* appeared in 1911. Although both Freud and Jung express reservations about Stekel's tendency to make Freudian dream-analysis sound like the automatic decoding in popular manuals, the book is an important contribution to the psychoanalytic recognition of the phenomenon. Freud acknowledges this in the preface to the third edition of *The Interpretation of Dreams* (1911): "my own experience, as well as the works of Wilhelm Stekel and others, has since taught me to form a truer estimate of the extent and importance of symbolism in dreams (or rather in unconscious thinking)" (Freud 1965a, xxvii). Freud's testimony to the importance of such symbolism culminates in the tenth lecture, "Symbols in Dreams," of *Introductory Lectures in Psychoanalysis* (1915–1917). In the process of laying before the general public an epitome of what psychoanalysis has thus far learned about this symbolism, Freud out-Stekels Stekel; he presents a brilliant but inevitably reductive catalogue that is probably more responsible than anything written by others for the popular stereotype of the Freudian analysis of dreams.

The final parenthetical phrase in the passage quoted above, "(or rather in unconscious thinking)," is especially significant. It recognizes the relation between the symbolism of dream-work and other forms of fantasizing, thereby connecting the issue of the "fixed symbolism" with the analogous recurrences of plot and image that Freud's colleagues were discovering in traditional story. When Freud finally carried out for the fourth edition of *The Interpretation of Dreams* the serious overhaul he had been desiderating for several years, his two major alterations were, first, hugely increasing the amount of material on "fixed symbolism" and assigning it its own section in chapter 6, and, second, appending at the end of that chapter two essays by Otto Rank, "Dreams and Creative Writing" and "Dreams and Myth."[14] These two moves acknowledge between them that the recurrent symbols of dream and the reiterated plots and images of both modern fantasy and traditional story are all of a piece. But Freud, in the face of this remarkable and increasingly evident fact, does not indulge in any theoretical speculation about the universal prevalence of what he calls, in his revealingly stiff and literal phrase, "fixed symbolism." He insists on the inheritance of acquired psychic characteristics, on the *vehicle* of mythic transmission, and is even willing to mythologize our ultimate instincts. But, although he affirms that instincts are accompanied by "the mental representative" of organic stimuli, he does not, after all, imagine any *specific* contents of the unconscious, apart from our phylogenetic experience of the Oedipal situation, that are actually carried by this vehicle.

Freud projects a vehicle empty of all but the Oedipal fantasy; Jung, in contrast, deduces the very existence of the vehicle from the abundance of the recurrent cargo of myth and symbol that *something* delivers ceaselessly to the doors of our perception. As a consequence he posits, from the original version of *Transformations* onward, a "collective unconscious" structured in "archetypes" that manifest themselves through the mediation of culturally specific myths and symbols. Jung's concept of a "collective unconscious" is not as original as he seems to assume. His lifelong insistence that for Freud "the unconscious is of an exclusively personal nature" mistakes for a difference in kind what is only a difference in degree (Jung 1959a, 3). This error has disseminated a popular misconception, obscuring the openness of early depth psychology in general to the idea. Jung's actual originality consists in his hypotheses about this mode of unconsciousness, which "is not a personal acquisition but is inborn," with "contents and modes of behavior that are more or less the same everywhere and for all individuals." By "contents" he refers to "archetypes" and by "modes of behavior" to the way these "archetypes" manifest themselves to consciousness. Since "we can . . . speak of an unconscious only in so far as we are able to demonstrate its contents," we only know the "collective unconscious" as the putative source of archetypes. To make any qualification of it is inevitably to speak of these archetypes, which alone permit us to infer its existence.

When the definition of "collective unconscious" is thus rendered transparent, the burden of the problematic is merely shifted onto the definition of "archetype." And on this topic Jung, never famed as a systematic presenter of his ideas, deploys a gallant but desperate range of sometimes inconsistent terminology. When he first introduces the term in "Instinct and the Unconscious" (1919), he defines "archetypes" as *"a priori* inborn forms of intuition," invoking the Platonic sense of "archetype" in general and (as his *"a priori"* and "intuition" suggest) Kant's "archetype" in particular. Jung's "archetypes" are first Kant's with the emotion restored—by way of Kant's "instinct," defined in his *Anthropologie* as "inner necessity" (Jung 1969, 133).[15] But Jung later exhibits an eclectic willingness to equate them with disparate ethnological concepts: with Durkheim and Lévy-Bruhl's *"représentations collectives,"* with Hubert and Mauss's "categories of the imagination," with Bastian's *"Elementargedenken"* (Jung 1959b, 42–43). On the rare occasions when he attempts a genetic explanation, he sounds very much like Freud: "their origin can only be explained by assuming them to be the deposits of the constantly repeated experience of humanity" (Jung 1972, 69).[16] No sooner does he put forth the hypothesis, however, than he feels obliged to testify that archetypes seem to dictate further experience: "They behave empirically like agents that tend toward the repetition of these same experiences" (70). Twenty years younger than Freud, after all, Jung most typically reacts to this chicken-and-egg ambiguity about origins by abandoning Lamarck for agnosticism, origin for structure. In the revised *Symbols,* for example, he characterizes the archetypal images as "belonging to the stock of inherited *possibilities* of representation" (my italics). As he puts it succinctly in *Two Essays on Analytical Psychology,* "it is not a question of inherited ideas, but of inherited thought-patterns" (138). Though Jung distinguishes between "instinct" and "archetype" in many contexts and even sometimes treats them as contraries, he also entertains the possibility that the archetypes *are* some evolution of instinct, "the unconscious images of the instincts themselves, in other words . . . *patterns of instinctual behavior"* (Jung 1959a, 44). In *Symbols* he neatly combines the instinctual and structural explanations by calling the archetypes "the sum total of inborn forms peculiar to the instincts" (408). This late formula may imply a metaphysics like Bergson's, an *élan vital* in which instinct is itself a primordial form of intelligence.

Jung's terminological struggle over "archetype" is characteristic. A reader can only attempt a normative synthesis abstracted from the varying diction in dozens of contexts. I concur with what is now the finest of such efforts, Robert Segal's recent essay, "Jung on Mythology," that Jung most consistently intends us to understand archetypes as structural possibilities for representations accessible to consciousness, not, as has often been assumed, the representations themselves (Segal 1999, 92–95). If, however, to declare that the collective unconscious is knowable only as archetypes throws the burden of explanation on the concept of "archetype," then to declare the archetypes knowable only as "symbol" and "myth" transfers the epistemological burden to these latter terms. We therefore need to consider how first "symbol" and then "myth" function as the actual representations, the "transformers" between the unconscious and the conscious.

Jung derives his conception of "symbol" unadulterated from the romantics, especially Creuzer. The provenance is blatant, for example, in the numerous characterizations of the term that stud his revised *Symbols of Transformation.* The images in fantasy "are not to be understood semiotically, as *signs* for definite things, but as *symbols.* A symbol is an indefinite expression with many meanings, pointing to something not easily defined and therefore not fully known" (124). He echoes the romantic's diacritical distinction between "symbol" and "allegory": *"Symbols* are not allegories and not signs: they are images of contents which for the most part transcend consciousness" (77). Even this association of "symbol" with the unconscious is anticipated in nineteenth-century romanticism (by Carlyle, for example), though Jung offers a more definite psychodynamics. His "symbols" are amphibious creatures. "Their manifest forms are moulded by the ideas acquired by the conscious mind," but what prevents them from being grasped semiotically as mere signs is that they are "always grounded in the unconscious archetype" (232). They are thus, by definition, mediators between the "unconscious archetype" and the conscious mind. "The symbols act as *transformers,* their function being to convert libido from a 'lower' into a 'higher' form." This last remark explains the double significance of Jung's revised title, *Symbole der Wandlungen* (*Symbols of Transformation*), which means not only "symbols of the process of transformation," but also "symbols that transform." The grammatical structure of his earlier title, *Wandlungen und Symbole der Libido,* "transformations and symbols of libido," suggests that he did not recognize quite clearly in 1911–1912 that the "symbols" *are* the "transformers."

In fact, as with most of Jung's key terms, the reader encounters numerous inconsistencies and lapses from the normative in Jung's sense of the relation between "symbol" and "archetype." Whenever Jung slips from his theoretically rigorous agnosticism about the nature of the archetypes, for example, he tends to speak of them as images. It's symptomatic that his original designation for "archetype" was *"Urbild,"* primordial picture or image. Nor is it very surprising that many of his readers have made the mistake of identifying "archetype" and "symbol," when one of Jung's favorite substitutes for "symbol" is the stunningly ambiguous phrase "archetypal representation." This phrase is exact in itself, if taken correctly, but it can be easily misread as signifying "a representation that is an archetype." Even in the relatively well-thought-out language of the revised *Symbols of Transformation,* Jung is still capable of setting in apposition "the primordial images, the archetypes" (293). And the yucca moth he adduces as an instance in "Instinct and the Unconscious" "must carry within it an image . . . of the situation that 'triggers off' its instinct" (Jung 1969, 137). In other words, the structured instinct, alias archetype, *is* a specific image! A detailed list of such departures from the norm could run for pages, even without including the many invitations in the master's writings to identify his personified representations, his familiar Halloween cast of characters—anima, shadow, *puer aeternus,* Terrible Mother, and the rest—as archetypes rather than as symbols. Most of these confusing vestiges of Jung's struggle to theorize "symbol" do fall into line, however, if one adheres to Segal's clear and well-judged set of displacements: collective unconscious-archetype-symbol.

The most striking aspect of Jung's treatment of myth is how highly he honors it as the coadjutor of symbol. This exaltation is a bit of a logical surprise because Jung clearly valorizes image over narrative; while symbol is the absolutely necessary "transformer" between the unconscious and consciousness, myth is merely a contingent one. Even though the archetypal contents of the collective unconsciousness are rich in mythologems, to the extent that myths are consciously composed, even in "primitive societies," they do not, according to Jung, convey archetypal material, nor are imagistic forms of this material confined only to narrative expression. Jung's high valuation follows logically, however, from his adoption of the romantic consensus. His normative conception of myth and its relation to symbol follows Creuzer's eye to ear, image to narrative, distinction; symbol is to myth as instantaneous visual pattern is to temporally discursive narrative. In the normative view this means that Jung regards myth as a carrier of symbol. In "On the Relation of Analytic Psychology to Poetry," for instance, the essay that occupies the niche in his work that "The Creative Writer and Day-Dreaming" does in Freud's, Jung opposes to Freud's art as wish-fulfillment his own conception of art as conjuration of the symbol (here referred to as "archetypal image"): "The creative process . . . consists in the unconscious activation of an archetypal image, and in elaborating and shaping this image into finished work." "The moment . . . when this mythological situation reappears is always characterized by a peculiar emotional intensity" (Jung 1966, 82). The phrase "mythological situation," refers in context to the local conditions of narrative that trigger an outbreak of the thrilling imagistic moment. Myth could be said to contain and carry symbols as a stream coming off a glacier carries chunks of ice bobbing in its current. The archetypes would be the icepack, the glacier itself, perpetually concealed in mist, but a presence inferable from the stream and its cargo.

As in the cases of archetype and symbol, however, the abstraction of a normative overview of Jung's concept of myth can create a sense of his consistency as a theorist that is no one's experience in reading him. Problems abound. Jung sometimes conflates myth with archetype just as he does symbol. In "On the Relation of Analytic Psychology to Poetry," for example, shortly after he speaks of the "mythological situation" mentioned above, he calls it an "archetypal situation." Again, as in the case of symbol, he inherits by adopting Creuzer's view the whole problematic that exercised his predecessor. The normative concept of myth requires, for instance, that symbols be distributed serendipitously within a narrative frame; yet Jung sometimes contradicts this (as in the account of the work of art in "On the Relation of Analytic Psychology to Poetry" quoted above) by speaking as if an entire narrative could constitute a single symbol. As the glacial run-off is frozen in winter? That is, as if a temporal narrative could be sublated into an instantaneous image. But Jung's wholesale romanticism involves him in larger, more consequential difficulties. When he flourishes the word "myth" he generally has in mind sacred narrative produced in "primitive" societies, of which a considerable amount has been embedded in the collective unconscious. But Jung's uncritical romanticism leads him into simultaneously envisioning myth as Schelling does, as the virtual equivalent of imagination. In this very diffuse sense, myth becomes a mode of apprehending the world as in the theories of Lucien Lévy-Bruhl and Ernst Cassirer. But these writers hold that "mythic thinking," while a component of all human minds, predominates only in archaic or "primitive" thought, whereas Jung promotes the notion of a deliberately cultivated mythic sensibility invaluable for the mental health of the modern person. Joseph Campbell and comparable New Age nebulosities are only a step away.

Whether or not depth psychology's view of myth is *sui generis,* it is certainly distinctive. As Segal points out, relatively few theories of myth provide explicit answers to the three major questions that can be asked about myth: what is its origin, function, and subject matter (Segal 1999, 2–3, 67). But the theories of both

Freud and Jung are clear about all three. They are in agreement, above all, that the proper subject matter of myth is the symbolic expression of internal psychological processes. They also agree about its archaic origin and phylogenetic transmission, though Freud focuses solely on transmission of the Oedipal material while Jung holds that it involves an indefinite number of archetypes. They disagree about origin, however, insofar as they disagree about function. For Freud, myth, like other forms of fantasizing, expresses repressed wishes in disguised form, whereas for Jung the primary function of myth is to serve as one of the vehicles by which the collective unconscious communicates with the consciousness.[17] Freud's specific theory is obviously much narrower than Jung's and might even be considered insignificant in isolation. But it does not stand in isolation. First, as an aspect of Freud's general revelation of the clinical relevance of fantasy, it is part of a necessary propaedeutic to Jung. Second, Freud's major indirect contributions to the construction of myth, all collaborative—his work on the concept of the hero, psychic phylogenesis, and "fixed symbolism"—promote the currency of these topics well into the midcentury, not least because they travel in the same direction, unintentionally perhaps, but not accidentally, as Jung's bolder hypotheses.

The philosophical differences between the pair are as profound as they are well known. Freud's tragic vision of inherited Oedipal guilt and the contest between Eros and the death instinct remains grounded in his positivistic biologism whereas Jung's comedic vision of the symbols of libidinal transformation soars unimpeded toward the stratosphere of process philosophy. From the perspective of the depth-psychological construction of "myth," however, these differences matter less than their joint establishment, together with their colleagues, and with successors mentioned in later chapters, of a view of myth as the unconscious biogenetic heritage of every human being. They thus appear to confirm in the realm of psychology that coexistence of the archaic with the modern mind so widely hypothesized in affective terms by contemporaries in other fields.

[6]

The Modernist Contribution
to the Construction of Myth

This chapter is an examination of the important mediating role of modernist literary art in the twentieth-century construction of "myth." The artists' contribution is not so much innovation in theory as it is the rich embodiment of a set of assumptions, the success of which inspires a later revival of theorizing. The arts of the early century famously express the growing agreement, examined in the two previous chapters, about the structural rapport of the modern mind with the "primitive." This response is far from confined to literary expression. One need only recall instances like the evocation by Stravinsky and Diaghilev in *The Rite of Spring* of an archaic moment in the oldest of the arts, or of Gauguin's attempts to recuperate among Breton peasants and Marquesas Islanders the visual correlatives of a sense of the sacred lost to modernity.[1] My restriction to the discussion of literary manifestations is purely practical, as is its further limitation to the handful of writers in English most inescapable in discussions of this topic. The outburst of literary experimentation generally labeled "modernist," whose recourse to "myth" is one of its best known features, was also an international movement; much of the kind of case made here with reference principally to W. B. Yeats, T. S. Eliot, D. H. Lawrence, and James Joyce could be made by a study of Mann, Kafka, Hesse, and Broch, or of Cavafy, Kazantzakis, and Seferis.

This modernist literary contribution to "myth" stands in complicated relation to its romantic or transcendentalist predecessor. We've seen that by the 1880s transcendentalist myth has become ossified and sentimentalized. While certain prescient artists (like George Eliot in *Daniel Deronda*) express an uneasy sense that myth may be a radical clue to "the buried life," they lack the conceptual context that would encourage them to pursue such suspicions. Among the generation of high modernists, however, the literary construction of "myth" rebounds with an intensity stimulated by the new matrix of affective theory in anthropology and depth psychology. The first three of our four modernist examples—Yeats, Eliot, and Lawrence—agree in their conviction that the distance can be annihilated, that in myth we experience the racial past immediately. In reply to the melancholy historicism of their Victorian predecessors, they develop concrete phenomenological accounts of transactions that occur in a special space, comparable to Bergson's "intensive manifold," outside of clock-time and history. These writers espouse implicitly the Virgilian line that Freud adopts explicitly as the epigraph of *The Interpretation of Dreams, "Flectere si nequeo superos, Acheronta movebo"* ("If I cannot soften the high gods, I will stir up the depths of hell"). If connections with the past and with timeless truth are interdicted from above, they can be recuperated from below. These writers often present themselves as in revolt against nineteenth-century romanticism and their success in challenging the canons of "realism," the brilliance of their innovations in technique, and even their embrace of the new anthropology and psychology, appear to ratify their assertions of a radical break. In the matter of myth, however, as in much else, their manifest differences from their predecessors mask latent continuities.

The modernists' reassertions of transcendentalist assumptions about myth are particularly evident at precisely those points where they have to misunderstand the new psychology or anthropology in order to make it work for them. Their persistent misconstrual of *The Golden Bough,* for example, is a recurrent motif in the first part of this chapter. They ignore its Whiggish view of mankind's evolution from magic and religion into the light of science; they read it as a demonstration of the permanent and intimate structural relation between the "savage" mind and the civilized. The ambiguities in Frazer's text that permit this reading could scarcely account by themselves for such consistent indifference to the author's intentions. The pervasive misreading is an effect of the way that the homogenizing of geographical and historical differences in Frazer's "comparative method" plays into the inherited assumption that myth communicates permanent truth. In his critique of the MoMA's "Primitivism in Modern Art" exhibition of 1984, James Clifford identifies as the principal assumption shared by the organizers of the show and the modernist artists themselves "the capacity of art to transcend its cultural and historical context" (Clifford 1988, 195). This persuasion of the universalizing power of art smoothes the way in turn for the widespread belief, systematized by Hegel, that modern Western art sublates the art of earlier and non-Western cultures in a superior, totalizing synthesis.[2] This is a conviction widespread, too, among the visual artists' literary contemporaries.

After presenting the rather remarkable accord on these matters among three such strongly distinctive artists as Yeats, Lawrence, and Eliot, I turn to James Joyce for a revealing contrast. Joyce is as much as anyone at the center of the modernist resort to myth, but he differs from the others in two respects. First, he regards myth in *Ulysses* not as a means of evading secular time and history, but as a structural mode of literary allusion. In a chirographic culture like ours, "work *on* myth," as distinguished from the "work *of* myth" in traditional cultures, must inevitably be a self-conscious form of literary allusion rather than a reliving of "sacred time."[3] Joyce's recognition of the self-consciousness of modern mythopoeia opens a gap between himself and the renewed transcendentalism of the post-Frazerian group. And so, too, does his second difference from the others. In certain respects in *Ulysses*, and completely in *Finnegans Wake*, he undercuts the signifying reliability of myth just as he does the stability of all other forms of verbal and narrative construction. Where the others are most in earnest, he is ironic and playful. In comparison to them he flattens, secularizes, and demystifies the concept of "myth." If the modernist contribution to the construction of "myth" is to be seen as a coherent chapter in the genealogy of the concept, it helps to view it in relation to what succeeds it as well as to its antecedents. In my conclusion, I prolong the contrast between Joyce and the other writers discussed in order to make the point that, while the "Frazerian" syndrome common to the first three produces the midcentury flourishing of a like-minded myth criticism and theory, Joyce's treatments of myth provide models for a postmodernist practice that helps to set the modernist achievement in historical perspective.

W. B. YEATS: THE EGO'S SALVATION IN MYTH

Yeats's relation to myth offers an especially instructive starting point because in the course of his career it goes through a crucial change that reflects the more general break between Yeats the late Victorian romantic and Yeats the modernist. In the first quarter-century of his career he acts out intensely, almost as if it were a piece of Freudian *nachträglichheit*, the romantic program of constructing a national culture around a newly refurbished indigenous mythology. In the second quarter, however, he repeats a process of internalization remarkably similar to the earlier romantics' withdrawals from public rejection of *their* utopian politics. He identifies what he perceives as the tragedy of his own life with the tragic pattern of dying gods in vegetation myths and invents a spatializing metahistorical system that rationalizes the identification.

Yeats's role in the revival of Irish mythology extends, of course, across his entire career, but it does belong in a special way to the activities of its first half. In the early part of this period, perhaps because of his start as a collector of folktales, his relevant lyrics center especially upon the Tuatha Dé Danaan, whom he identified with the fairies of oral tradition, the Sidhe. In the later part of the period, as he came to articulate more directly his hopes for a national culture unified by the ancient stories, he turned increasingly to a more heroic treatment of the Ulster and Fenian cycles. This more objectified treatment is related to his turn to drama and culminates in his narrative poems and mythological plays of the first decade of the new century. But Yeats's impact upon this revival is not attributable solely to his distinction as poet and dramatist. One must take into account his prose fiction, essays, reviews, introductions, and other journalism during those whirlwind years; his part in founding the National Library Society (1892) and the Abbey Theatre (1898); and his encouragement of various collaborators, especially, with reference to mythology, of Augusta Gregory's *Cuchulain of Muirthemne* (1902) and *Gods and Fighting Men* (1904).

Whatever the exact nature of the complex crisis he passed through in the years between 1903 and 1917, it seems safe to say that it was caused in part by the pain of failing in this quixotic campaign to provide his country with a new religion. Looking back from the far shore of his personal divide, he tells us in "The Trembling of the Veil" (1922) that his goal during the 1890s had been to extract out of the occult tradition a "philosophy" that would "set before Irishmen for special manual an Irish literature which, though made by many minds, would seem the work of a single mind, and turn our places of beauty or legendary association into holy symbols" (Yeats 1965, 170). From his new perspective, he sardonically dubs this program out of Friedrich Schlegel "nation-wide multiform reverie" (176) and judges flatly that "this dream of my early manhood that a modern nation can return to unity of Culture, is false" (196). In a similar act of judgment, Yeats gathers in 1925, under the ironic title *Mythologies,* his principal prose writings of the 1890s together with *Per Amica Silentia Lunae* (1916), where he works out his scheme of self and anti-self. The effect of this gesture is to relativize and subjectivize the meaning of "mythology." Instead of signifying the impersonal "work of a single mind" around which a culture coheres, it now signifies a series of fragmented cast-off masks of belief that sustained their wearer only until he wore them out. This new relativizing of "mythology" assumes the epistemologically radical notion that human meaning is constantly under construction and that the invention of private, individual mythologies must be a continual process.[4] Even as Yeats criticizes his early faith in "nation-wide multiform reverie," he is already committed to a private mythology of reverie that is a much more radical consequence of his youthful romanticism.

The most important conceptual component of this new internalization of myth is Yeats's application to himself of the anthropological notion, popularized by Frazer, of the "dying god." Yeats comes to see his own life, or, in principle, the life of any modern person, as an acting out of the tragic pattern of sacrifice symbolized by the annual death of the god in ancient fertility religions. Yeats did not need Frazer to teach him that myth represents the recurrence of universal experience; both of them learned it from nineteenth-century romanticism. It is one thing, however, to assume vaguely that traditional story expresses universal experience, and quite another to assume that modern persons relive this experience, that is, that the myth lives in them, that they *live* the myth. Even in his earlier phase Yeats differs from the best Victorian retellers of archaic tale in his stronger sense of the immediacy of myth. But the moment when he abandons entirely the perspectivism of the older writers and identifies with the "dying god" marks an irruption into the twentieth century of a radical conception of myth as a living presence.[5] It also initiates the exemplary "strong" reading of Frazer. In choosing to celebrate the *Bough*'s subliminal message—the permanent presence of the archaic within each human consciousness—Yeats establishes what will turn out to be the canonical modernist hermeneutics of their new scripture.

Yeats actually reads Frazer through Nietzschean spectacles. Nietzsche made a profound initial impression on him in 1902–1903, and it is Nietzsche's paradoxical celebration of "tragic joy" in the face of "eternal recurrence" that enables Yeats's application of Frazer's evidence to contemporary persons. "Eternal recurrence" names the condition of Frazerian myth, and "tragic joy" characterizes the condition of our participation in it. This participation in life as a ritual can even be unwitting, for "All men are dancers and their tread / Goes to the barbarous clangor of a gong" (Yeats 1956, 206). The ending of "No Second Troy" is so moving precisely because the speaker's growing understanding of the hate-filled termagant about whom he's so bitter, culminates in his recognition of who she really is: "Was there another Troy for her to burn?" (89). Maud Gonne is transfigured by her role in a way she herself would not recognize. In "Her Vision in the Wood," however, Yeats uniquely dramatizes the moment of tragic induction into the eternal recurrence of the myth.[6] A woman "too old for a man's love" (269) recognizes what her role has been. She sees in her vision a procession of "stately women" carrying a wounded man on a litter and singing "of the beast that gave the fatal wound." The wounded "thing" on the litter, "all blood and mire, that beast-torn wreck," turns and fixes an eye on her and she passes out with a shriek, realizing that "they had brought no fabulous symbol there / But my heart's victim and its torturer" (270). These last six words identify the myth of Adonis with the mutually suffered love affair. As Yeats remarks in "The Trembling of the Veil," "we begin to live when we have conceived life as tragedy" (128). True tragic heroism requires *anagnorisis* and willed participation in the dance.

To envision oneself as playing a role in an archetypal drama or cosmic dance obviously implies, however, surrender to the determination of mysterious, impersonal forces beyond the self. Yeats's most conspicuous symbol for this surrender is the mask, an image with two broad significations, one figurative, one literal. In the generally earlier and figurative sense it signifies the willed construction of the antithetical self. In the generally later literal sense, it is the impersonal vizard of the performer in a classical Greek or Japanese play that signifies the desired identification, in the performance of the rite, of the wearer with the deity. These two senses are not contraries; they fuse in Yeats's plays for masks; indeed, he seems to find in these dramas his most nearly perfect expression of life as ritual in which men and women dance or act fated roles. But the later and more literal sense of mask emphasizes the participation of the wearer in patterns much greater than his or her personal existence. In correspondence with this shift, Yeats's conception of tragedy in this late stage of his career seems to edge away from Nietzsche's, with its element of willful joy, toward Schopenhauer's emphasis upon the condition of willlessness in the contemplation of the sublime. "Tragedy," Yeats proclaims in his *Autobiography*, redefining Nietzsche's *frölichkeit*, "has not joy, as we understand the word, but ecstasy, which is from the contemplation of things vaster than the individual and imperfectly seen, perhaps, by those that still live. The masks of tragedy contain neither character nor personal energy. . . . Before the mind can look out of their eyes the active will perishes, hence their sorrowful calm" (Yeats 1965, 319). Yeats here associates this paradoxical ecstasy with an "eternal recurrence" become metahistorical in scope, and some of the famous formulations of it in *Last Poems* celebrate just such contemplation of the end of entire civilizations. In "The Gyres," "Hector is dead and there's a light in Troy: / We that look on but laugh in tragic joy" (Yeats 1956, 291). In "Lapis Lazuli" the eyes of the three Chinamen seated in their halfway house on the mountain, staring out "on all the tragic scene," "their eyes / Their ancient glittering eyes, are gay" (293).

This shift toward emphasis on the impersonal and public aspects of tragedy occurs in the years after Yeats shapes a suitable theodicy out of his wife's sessions of automatic writing. In the introduction he wrote for the revised edition of the result, *A Vision,* Yeats offers his own concise summary of the origins and principal content of the work:

> The unknown writer took his theme at first from my just published *Per Amica Silentia Lunae.* I had made a distinction between the perfection that is from a man's combat with himself and that which is from a combat with circumstance, and upon this simple distinction he built up an elaborate classification of men according to their more or less complete expression of one type or the other. He supported his classification by a series of geometrical symbols and put these symbols in an order that answered the question in my essay as to whether some prophet could not prick upon the calendar the birth of a Napoleon or a Christ. (Yeats 1966, 8–9)

Yeats had developed in *Per Amica* the figurative sense of "mask," the willed construction of an antithetical self. In building upon this conception, Mrs. Yeats and her spirit collaborators proved themselves remarkable adepts in the hidden sources of his creativity, for that work embodies a crucial breakthrough—the poet's connection of his trivial and otherwise pointless subjectivity with the timeless roles played out by the avatars of the dying god.[7] He there dramatizes his turn from what he calls *"Anima hominis,"* the soul of man, the limited subjectivity that has gone as far is it can in extrapolating out of its quarrel with itself its antithetical masks, to what he calls the *"Anima Mundi,"* the soul of the world, the great spiritual reservoir from which the inadvertent timeless images come. In *A Vision* the "unknown writer" who preempted Mrs. Yeats's pen taps this reservoir to do three things: to create an ethical taxonomy in which a highly limited number of human qualities recur endlessly, to adduce the geometric figures that symbolize this recurrence in spatial form, and to invent a correspondingly spatialized theory of *historical* recurrence.

The brilliant artistic achievements subsequently based in part on *A Vision* confer upon it a prestige otherwise unimaginable and make it one of modernism's most influential centers for the dissemination of renovated transcendentalist notions of "mythic" or cyclical time. In the revised version of the work, Yeats tells us that "when the automatic script began neither I nor my wife knew . . . that any man had tried to explain history philosophically" (261). When a translation of Oswald Spengler's *Decline of the West* was published a few months after the first edition of *A Vision,* Yeats "found there a correspondence too great for coincidence." He then discovered "Spengler's main source in Vico" and learned, apparently by reading Croce, "that half the revolutionary thoughts of Europe [he mentions Marx and Sorel] are a perversion of Vico's philosophy." The "correspondence too great for coincidence" between himself and Spengler would lead anyone thinking of concrete historical contingency to suspect a common cultural derivation. Yeats might well have recognized at this point his place in the modern tradition of stadial meta-histories constructed as circular or spiral patterns by romantic historicism. For Yeats, however, the "coincidence" confirms the objective existence of both the *Anima Mundi*—the timeless storehouse of images that transcends concrete historical context—and the cyclical periods that impose their oscillating pattern upon the apparent temporal flow.[8]

This belief in a cyclical historical process that can be known only by tapping a timeless storehouse of images strikingly resembles the contemporaneous gnosticism of Jung's theory of libidinal development, except that Jung's vision is comic because he believes the process behind the images is benign, whereas Yeats's is tragic because he holds this process to be indifferent to consciousness. Yeats himself indicates that *A Vision* constitutes his theodicy when he remarks at the end of his introduction that his "periods" "have helped me to hold in a single thought reality and justice" (25) But "reality" is eternal recurrence, which demands godlike heroism, "tragic joy" in the face of suffering and evil, and we are asked to believe that this "reality" is transmuted into "justice" merely by accession to a spatialized historical periodicity. This is an appalling conception of "justice," a theodicy at once both godless and inhuman. Nietzschean eternal recurrence was invented, after all, to combat the Judeo-Christian scheme of a providential history, and Yeats's cycles swing remorse-lessly between the poles of phase 1 and phase 15, both of which are alien to human existence. Furthermore, as Harold Bloom points out in his particularly insightful critique of *A Vision*, this system, "the darkest of bondages to the idols of determinism," underwrites the cruelty celebrated in the late poetry (Bloom 1970, 436).[9] What is most disturbing in these late poems is the tone, not of joy, or even of gaiety, but of glee in which their speakers, secure in their own enlightenment, express indifference toward the actual suffering of others and exalt the violence that wipes out whole civilizations. Perhaps in the 1870s Nietzsche's acceptance of eternal recurrence could sound like heroic individualism. By the 1930s, however, Yeats seems to have melded Nietzsche and Frazer into a vision of myth as the naming of dark forces before which humanity can only bow down.

D. H. LAWRENCE:
HUMANITY'S TRUE RELATION TO THE COSMOS

D. H. Lawrence shares with Yeats a set of familiar convictions: that prehistoric cultures possessed an esoteric wisdom (curiously resembling philosophies of post-Nietzschean vitalism) now lost; that broken and obscured fragments of this wisdom survive in folk traditions among certain ancient and non-Western peoples; that these fragments emit in "symbol" and "image" direct affective appeals circumventing mere cognition; that modern people can and must reconnect with this perennial religion. During the last fifteen years of his short life, Lawrence expressed various combinations of these notions in a number of "anatomies" (roughly comparable to Yeats's *Vision*) that he produced concurrently with his fiction. It may useful to consider these anatomies before proceeding to the subtler representations of "myth" in the formal fiction.

The first two, *Psychoanalysis and the Unconscious* and its prompt sequel, *Fantasia of the Unconscious,* published separately in 1923, register Lawrence's encounter with Freud rather than with Frazer. We know from his letters that he studied Frazer, both *The Golden Bough* and *Totemism and Exogamy,* in the autumn of 1915. But Lawrence's manner of misreading Frazer produces a significant difference from Yeats's and indicates why his more important encounter would be with Freud. He tells his correspondent, Bertrand Russell at the time, that "now I am convinced of what I believed when I was about twenty—that there is another seat of consciousness than the brain and the nervous system; there is blood-consciousness which exists in us independently of the ordinary mental consciousness" (Lawrence 1962, vol. 1, 393–394). Lawrence's comparable enthusiasm for Frazer's universalized evidence blinds him as it does Yeats to Frazer's framework of evolutionary rationalism, but Lawrence misreads the text in terms of psychology and biology rather than ritual. Frazer convinces him that he must look for a biological explanation of the "blood-image," a position not far removed from Freud's Lamarckian "phylogenetic fantasy" of these same years. But Lawrence's conception of "blood-consciousness" foreshadows his critique of Freud in the two psychoanalytic anatomies. Lawrence dismisses the Freudian concepts of the unconscious, repression, and the Oedipus complex as mere mental constructs; they are not, for him, sufficiently naturalistic. He understands by the "unconscious" something like Heidegger's "Being," something "by its very nature unanalyzable, undefinable, inconceivable . . . it can only be experienced" (Lawrence 1973, 15). The "unconscious" is an ineffable ground upon which the centers of consciousness flower, and Lawrence notoriously corrects Freud by concentrating upon the four seats or centers of consciousness within the physical body. This amateurish bricolage presents, of course, a misreading of Freud considerably more startling than the misconstrual of Frazer, but it does capture Lawrence's intense combination of naturalistic vitalism with an intuitionist psychology.

He also produced a later pair of anatomies especially germane to his conception of myth, *Etruscan Places* and *Apocalypse.* Where the earlier pair concern the psychodynamics of mythopoeia in the living, the later duo engage the historical evidence that this mythopoeic power has long been the permanent possession of the race. In a curious passage near the beginning of *Fantasia* Lawrence affirms that "the great pagan world which preceded our own era once had a vast and perhaps perfect science of its own, a science in terms of life. . . . taught esoterically in all countries of the globe" (54–55). This worldwide system naturally included Atlantis, since it prevailed before the melting of the polar ice cap created our present oceans. Some of the survivors degenerated into "cave men" of the Stone Ages; some "wandered savage in Africa"; some, like "South Sea Islanders," "retained their marvellous beauty and life-perfection"; and some, like "Druids or Etruscans or Chaldeans or Amerindians . . . refused to forget, but taught the old wisdom only in its half-forgotten, symbolic forms . . . remembered as ritual gesture and myth-story." This history explains why "the great myths all relate to one another" and why "the intense potency of symbols is part at least memory." It explains, conveniently enough, both Frazerian diffusionism and Freudian inheritance of racial memory. Lawrence portrays himself as the archaeologist who must "proceed by intuition" in his effort "to stammer out the first terms of a forgotten knowledge" (56).

Hence, *Etruscan Places* is an attempt to read the tomb paintings of the ancient people as an expression of oneness with the vital universe, and *Apocalypse* is a comparable effort to discern the original communication of this same rapport concealed beneath the Judeo-Christian palimpsest of the Book of Revelation. The Etruscan wall paintings reveal directly a "phallic" as opposed to a "mental" consciousness (10), a "free-breasted naturalness and spontaneity" (12), "a sense of living things surging from their own centre to their own surface" (68).[10] Compared to these wall paintings the proper decipherment of a deeply acculturated text like Revelation is heavy going. But armed with his own hermeneutical principle, which might be called in imitation of Augustine's "principle of charity," the "principle of vitality," Lawrence works backward through the layers of Judeo-Christian obfuscation motivated by Nietzschean *ressentiment,* responding always with intuitive rapport to the "flashes" (3) of "the great images" (27). What he bares at last is summed up in one of the best known purple passages outside his novels: "We ought to dance with rapture that we should be alive and in the flesh, and part of the living, incarnate cosmos. I am part of the sun as my eye is part of me. . . . There is nothing of me that is alone and absolute except my mind, and we shall find that the mind has no existence by itself, it is only the glitter of the sun on the surface of the waters" (126). As in *The Birth of Tragedy,* only the Apollonian mind, that filmy epiphenomenon of individuation, prevents us from merging ecstatically with the All. This belief the whole world once lived.

Lawrence's concurrent fiction celebrates this "pagan" naturalism in a series of lessening displacements. I borrow the concept of "displacement" employed in this sense from Northrop Frye, for whom it signifies the way the mythic basis of literature is increasingly obscured as literature descends the historical scale toward realistic and ironic modes of representation. Lawrence's fiction proceeds (on a mini-scale) in the opposite direction; it grows out of Victorian social realism and gradually, in certain texts, in particular *The Rainbow, The Plumed Serpent,* and *The Man Who Died,* expresses with increasing directness a central fable about humankind's true relation to the cosmos.

The Rainbow, perhaps precisely because it is so richly anchored in social realism, is Lawrence's most brilliant representation of the plight of modern consciousness cut off from all but private, asocial "flashes" of rapport with the cosmos. The three generations of the Brangwen family upon whom the narrative is centered have privileged access to this sort of rapport, yet even within the family it must be locked in individual consciousnesses; none of them shares the knowledge the reader is granted, that certain experiences of ritual impulse and symbolic imagery have been repeated generation after generation. Corporately, the Brangwens refigure Genesis, as Lawrence himself does Revelation, so that each text expresses the natural religion of cosmic unity. The reader follows through the novel complexes of private, yet corporate associations with the Creation, the irruption of the Sons of God, the Flood, and the Rainbow itself.

Ursula Brangwen's grandfather, Tom, and her parents, Anna and Will, are represented, for example, as experiencing moments of rapport with the cosmos, mediated through sex, that they represent to themselves as the presence of angelic powers. When the fourteen-year-old Ursula begins to brood over the strange passage in Genesis 6 that tells of the "sons of God" mating with the fair "daughters of men," she commences to repeat a version of the family experience.[11] The narrator tells us that "she moved about in the essential days," a fine naming of the necessary, "intensive" time of myth as opposed to contingent, historical clock-time (Lawrence 1981, 276). This assertion is elaborated in the characteristic Lawrentian manner: "She lived a dual life, one where the facts of daily life encompasses everything . . . and the other wherein the facts of daily life were superseded by the eternal truth. . . . The fact that a man was a man . . . did not exclude that he was also one of the unhistoried, unaccountable Sons of God" (276–277). These last epithets, "unhistoried" and "unaccountable," characterize precisely the modernist refuge in the permanent truth of myth. Most of the narrative of *The Rainbow*, and its semi-sequel, *Women in Love*, works out the relentless social constructions of personal ego and gender roles that subvert the possibility of actually living by this private sexual apocalypse. Ursula herself attains it on only one occasion (in *Women in Love*). But Lawrence dramatizes its reality and validity with an insistence as strong as that which Victorian intuitionists (Dickens, Browning, or Thackeray, for example) reserve for more orthodox religious assertions of moments that transcend the secular social world.

In *The Plumed Serpent*, however, Lawrence takes the bold experimental step of imagining the introduction of his perennial religion into the social world. Even so, this step is hedged about with typical qualifications. First, he focalizes much of the story through heroine Kate Leslie's resistant intelligence. Second, he surrounds Don Ramon's preachments with a critical heteroglossia as blunt as what it resists is extreme. Don Ramon's family think him mad; the local innkeeper voices a persistent suspicion of readers when he calls the religion of Quetzalcoatl "another dodge for national socialism," and so forth (Lawrence 1959, 299). Third, Lawrence locates the movement so explicitly in the revolutionary Mexico of 1923 that the ultimate result is to exacerbate our consciousness of its non-historicity, its status as a conscious fable.

Both the metaphysics behind the religion of Quetzalcoatl and its relation to the universal archaic religion repeat the poetry of the contemporaneous anatomies. The metaphysics is Lawrence's familiar vitalism. He expresses his own abiding consciousness of the dark ground upon which the phenomena of existence gleam when Don Ramon makes Quetzalcoatl say in his first hymn that he has been sleeping "in the cave which is called Dark Eye / Behind the sun" (129). (This figure also takes advantage of the nice coincidence that Lawrence's favorite figure of the "dark sun" appears in the actual creation myths of a number of Mezoamerican societies.) Kate Leslie voices the general mythopoeic application when she thinks,

"Gods should be iridescent, like the rainbow in the storm . . . storms sway in heaven, and the god-stuff sways high and angry over our heads. Gods die with the men who have conceived them. But the god-stuff roars eternally, like the sea" (61). Once again Lawrence succeeds here in housing within novelistic discourse the language of romantic poetry, in this case specifically Hölderlin's. The romantics seem to roar eternally like the sea, too, in Don Ramon's insistence that he wants the revival of culturally organic, indigenous paganisms: "I wish the Teutonic world would once more think in terms of Thor and Wotan, and the tree Igdrasil. And I wish the Druidic world would see . . . that they themselves are the Tuatha Dé Danaan, alive but submerged. And a new Hermes should come back to the Mediterranean, and a new Ashtaroth to Tunis . . . and the oldest of dragons to China" (273). Passages like these combine Yeats's youthful program with Lawrence's own Sons of God ("the old giants") and the gnostic knowledge of the "submerged" world before the Flood.

Lawrence's most original contribution to this romantic primitivism in *The Plumed Serpent,* however, is to imagine the poetry set into political action. Both Don Ramon and Kate view the religion of Quetzalcoatl as especially appropriate to Mexico because there is something "serpent-like" about both the land and its people. Since the novel is centrally concerned with the necessity of uniting Quetzal with Coatl, the serpent of earth with the bird of the sky, Cipriano with Kate, the "undeveloped" yet "vital" blood of the indigene with the overdeveloped "spirit" of the white European, the racism involved is of that ambivalent, self-loathing kind characteristic of Western primitivism. It is at its deepest in Lawrence's association of the exotic other with extra-rational violence. This proto-fascistic, *Blut und Boden* aspect of the new religion of Quetzalcoatl is most repellently represented by the lovingly detailed ritual in which Cipriano executes three prisoners. Lawrence clearly intends this scene to shock the liberal sensibility, as he demonstrates in dramatizing Kate's reaction to it, but he is also shocked himself by where his artistic imagination has carried him. His prophetic role compels him to acknowledge honestly that the sleep of reason of the despised secular West will produce monsters. His exploration of the social consequences of a religion of "blood-consciousness" at least expresses a tormented ambivalence missing from Yeats's lyric exultations.

This ambivalence may constitute Lawrence's virtual admission of the necessarily fabular quality of the conversion experience he wishes to narrativize. *The Man Who Died* reverts to an expert plucking of this private, personal experience free from all the complexities of social realism. The narrative core is by this time familiar: a man who has experienced the death of his ego and rebirth into selfless wonder encounters a woman who has gone through an analogous discipline while seeking just such a man, and in their sexual union they discover the perfection of their relation to the cosmos. The brilliant fabular gesture of *The Man Who Died* is to imagine this man as Jesus, the woman as a priestess of Isis, and their union as a conscious reenactment of the myth of Osiris.

Jesus escapes from his tomb and convalesces in a spring sun that teaches him to reject (in predictably Nietzschean terms) the concealed egotism, the condescending pity for the masses, and the hatred of the physical world that stamped his former sensibility. He learns instead to identify with "the short, sharp wave of life" (Lawrence 1953, 171). The "priestess of Isis," also unnamed in the story, is the daughter of a patrician Roman family who has built at her own expense a little temple near her mother's villa on the coast of Lebanon. This is a yearning vocation; the temple is dedicated to "Isis in Search." She is "looking for the fragments of the dead Osiris. . . . She must gather him together and fold her arms round this re-assembled body till it became warm again, and roused to life, and could embrace her, and could fecundate her womb" (188). When "the man who died" appears on the scene, the priestess, acting on her intuition, asks him in a dazed way if he is Osiris, to which he is inspired to respond, "Yes, if thou wilt heal me" (197). His grievous wounds make him a convincing Osiris, and after the priestess has anointed and embraced them, his sexual vigor awakens and he notoriously exclaims, "I am risen!" Lawrence knows he is on the brink of bathos here, but risks it for the epigrammatic force of this quintessential naturalization of the Resurrection. In what follows, the narrator focuses not upon the act of intercourse as such, but upon the two participants' isolated but analogous responses as they separate. "The woman of the pure search" thinks, "I am full of the risen Osiris" (208), and "the man who died" thinks, "How plastic it is, how full of curves and folds like an invisible rose of dark-petalled openness that shows where the dew touches its darkness! . . . How it leans around me and I am part of it, the great rose of Space." These complementary fullnesses, the one introjected, the other projected upon the cosmos, are their rewards for a perfectly unegoistical, sacramental completion of what the cosmos required of them. Their separation at the end of their springtime idyll, when the priestess announces herself "big with Osiris," is part of the ever-recurrent mythic event. "The man who died" must leave to save his life, but he promises his partner that "when the nightingale calls again from your valley-bed, I shall come again, sure as Spring" (210).

Lawrence is not original among modernists in rewriting the life of Jesus, or even in representing him as surviving his crucifixion to enjoy, in Gide's phrase, *"les nourritures terrestres."*[12] But he is original in positioning his Jesus so distinctively in the perspective of the new comparative mythology. In a notorious passage added to the second edition of *The Golden Bough,* Frazer attributes the success of Christianity to the mistake of the authorities in unwittingly enabling the martyred troublemaker, Jesus of Nazareth, to be assimilated to the age-old pagan religion: "A chain of causes . . . determined that the part of the dying god in the annual play should be thrust upon Jesus of Nazareth" (Frazer 1966, vol. 9, 421–422). After Lawrence, both Yeats in *The Resurrection* (1931) and Robert Graves in *King Jesus* (1946) explicitly place Jesus in this Frazerian role. But these later fictions, like Frazer's, require a Jesus who dies on the cross in order to qualify as eternal scapegoat. Lawrence's solution expresses more deeply his own and his fellow modernists' assumptions about the timeless quality of myth. He splits the God-Man, the construction of whose two natures has been the labor of two millennia of theologians, back into his contrary extremes and confers on him a second chance at life as simultaneously an ordinary mortal who must be content with the fruits of the earth *and* as the embodiment of the eternally recurrent Osiris.

T. S. ELIOT: "THE MYTHICAL METHOD"

Eliot asserts as boldly as Yeats and Lawrence the buried connections between modern humanity and "primitive" myth and ritual. He differs from the others, however, in confining his embrace of "myth" to only a certain, quite sharply defined segment of his career. This is the cultural moment in which he thinks he recognizes a great exemplar in James Joyce's *Ulysses*. He appears to misread Joyce, but reveals in the process, as usual, a good deal about his own crucial assumptions. The heart of this misreading is perhaps the best known and, unfortunately, for many years, the most influential of responses to *Ulysses*—Eliot's review of it in *Dial*. The key pontifications there pertain only slightly to Joyce's *Ulysses*, but they have everything to do with the poem Eliot himself had published the previous year, *The Waste Land*.

The famous passage begins with Eliot's claim that "in using the myth [the plot of *The Odyssey*] in manipulating a continuous parallel between contemporaneity and antiquity," Joyce is an Einstein of narrative art who has created a new scientific paradigm, a "method," of such technical brilliance that "others must pursue [it] after him" (Eliot 1923, 483). We are quickly apprised of the reason why others *must* follow Joyce's lead; his method is a means of "controlling," of "ordering" the "immense panorama of futility and anarchy which *is* [my italics] contemporary history." The fear of social change, the disgust and despair expressed here do not consort very well with what we know of Joyce and *his* work, but they do conform with emotions that dominate *The Waste Land*. In fact, Joyce's method, which is now baptized as itself "the mythical method," is also declared to be, not (as common sense might automatically rewrite it) a means by which the artist might impose control on his *work*, but rather by which the work might impose control on the "anarchy" and "futility" of his *world*. "The mythical method" is "a step toward making the modern world possible for art," as if the artist could not comes to grips with this world until he succeeded in imposing upon it a pattern out of the remote past, a grid of "myth." In semiological terms, Joyce's running invocations of *The Odyssey* are merely a structural device for redoubling allusiveness; Virgil's *Aeneid* and Kazantzakis's *Odyssey: A Modern Sequel* do the same. But, as Eliot sees it, "the mythical method" is something like the artist's apprehension of his chaotic world through the frame of a traditional sacred narrative so as to fix upon it by means of his artistic "form" a public "order" that isn't otherwise there. When Eliot initially refers to the entire *Odyssey* as a "myth," it's easy to take this as a mere negligence, but when he tells his readers that the "mythic method" has been made possible only very recently by the concurrence of "psychology . . . ethnology and *The Golden Bough*," we realize that he actually does subscribe to a new and extreme version of the high romantic notion. He understands myth as produced by a permanent stratum of the human mind, essentially one and the same thing whether given utterance by a preliterate shaman, by Homer or by Joyce when he pays tribute to its contrast with the sordidness of modernity.

At the moment of *The Waste Land*, several years before his personal conversion, the only actual religious vision Eliot seems to have in mind is the same retrospective linking of contemporary life with the perennial "dying god" of seasonal fertility ritual that we find in Yeats and Lawrence. In the review, Eliot ranks *The Golden Bough* on a par with psychology and ethnology in general as enablers of "the mythical method," but in the prefatory note to *The Waste Land* the thinker "who has influenced our generation profoundly" occupies the stage alone (Eliot 1962, 50). If Eliot differs at all from the others in his mistaking of Frazer, it is only in being more aware of the latter's ambiguity and therefore of his own options. In a 1921 review of *The Rite of Spring,* Eliot (though praising Stravinsky's music) complains that the ballet's primitivism does not connect in any significant fashion with the present, and he contrasts it in this respect with the way "*The Golden Bough* can be read . . . as a collection of entertaining myths, or as the revelation of that vanished mind of which our is a continuation."[13] Eliot perceives the *Bough* as presenting a religious *choice:* if read on Frazer's own positivistic premises, the work, however fascinating, is only part of the modern "dead anatomy of culture"; if read on Eliot's premises, it establishes a salvific escape from this pointlessness. Frazer is co-opted just as Yeats, the pioneer of "the mythic method," and Joyce, its Einstein, are.

The most startling feature of Eliot's conception of myth surfaces when he pontificates in the review that "instead of narrative method, we may now use mythical method." This notion that myth can *replace* narrative is clearly a revival of one of the most questionable aspects of the problematic of "myth" developed by the romantics—the impulse to consider an entire narrative as somehow constituting a single, non-linear, spatialized "symbol." If Eliot's either/or division between "narrative" and "mythical" method is taken seriously, it produces absurd aporiae even within his paragraph. It follows, for instance, both that *The Odyssey* and *Ulysses* are not narratives because they are "mythical," and that "the mythical method" cannot possibly present a "continuous parallel" with some other work because if it is not a narrative it possesses no linear, syntagmatic dimension. We're faced once more with assertions that make little sense with reference to Joyce's fiction, but illuminate and are illuminated by Eliot's effort at a double suspension of narrative in *The Waste Land.*

By double suspension I mean that Eliot first represents the many narrative elements in the poem as contained within the witnessing consciousness of "Tiresias" and then leaves these episodes unresolved, creating the effect of their being apprehended more or less instantaneously within this super-consciousness. Tiresias is obtruded on the reader without warning when, just after the account of the assignation between the typist and the house-clerk's agent, a voice announces, "And I Tiresias have foresuffered all / Enacted on this same divan or bed" (44). Without the poem's notes this would merely be puzzling; with them it is astonishing as well. For what reader, left to his or her own devices, would ever have imagined, as the note claims, that Tiresias is "the most important personage in the poem, uniting all the rest" and that "what Tiresias sees, in fact, is the substance of the poem" (52)? Since Tiresias appears nowhere else, these assertions make sense only if we take him as the quondam first-person narrator's designation of himself. But why does he mask himself as Tiresias? The passage from Ovid about Tiresias that Eliot cites in his notes as "of great anthropological interest" (52) reveals that Eliot identifies the seer with the chthonic wisdom of the fertility cults celebrated by Yeats and Lawrence. But Tiresias is also, according to *The Odyssey,* the only mortal who (in the highly relevant translation of Ezra Pound) "even dead, yet hath his mind entire" (Pound 1995, 236)![14] Eliot associates him closely with the Cumaean Sybil of the poem's epigraph as a prophet burdened with excessive and scandalous knowledge who wishes to die but cannot.[15] To claim that this persona or mask of the poet unites "all the rest" and that what he "*sees* . . . is the substance of the poem" is to express an intention to conjure up a consciousness that suspends in contemplation the entire history of Western culture. Tiresias is a figure, in fact, for going one better than "manipulating a continuous parallel between contemporaneity and antiquity"; he personifies the "superorganic" "mind of Europe." He contains in the tragic awareness of co-presence everything from the perennial archaic wisdom to the cultural amnesia of the degraded present beneath which it lies buried.

"What Tiresias *sees*" is a cultural palimpsest suspended in infinite arrest, and it is this condition that makes him so yearn to die. On one hand, the poem does in fact introduce many narrative situations, or impulsions, including the central quest alluding to the "Fisher King" motif of medieval romance.[16] On the other, none of these situations can be resolved dramatically because each is held in the immediate manifold of consciousness of Tiresias.[17] This consciousness is very rich in objective awareness of its world, but it occupies only an instant of clock-time, a single moment during which the yearning Tiresias quests for an absent center. The Derridean "supplementarity" of the poem's notes teaches us that Tiresias will never catch up with his own presence as the missing "Hanged God" of the Tarot deck. Meanwhile (if that expression is allowable), his consciousness expands in the elaboration of potentially infinite cultural "parallels" of the sort desiderated in the review-essay—parallels without convergence or closure.[18] *The Waste Land,* crowded with consciousness as it is, goes nowhere because, while there is every quest, every journey to be aware of, there is nowhere to go.

The Waste Land, not Joyce's *Ulysses,* is the true subject of Eliot's review, and only the poem enables one, in turn, to grasp concretely what he meant by his bold contrast between "mythical" and "narrative" method. If Eliot's "mythical method" could break through into apotheosis, it would transgress not only the sequential nature of narrative, but even the syntagmatic aspect of language itself; it would perfect that "spatial form" that Robert Frank identified a half-century ago as one of the tendencies (as distinguished from fully realized achievements) of modernist narrative. In actuality, even Eliot's practice in *The Waste Land,* gallant as it is as a try at burking narrative, is a falling-off from the hyperbolic doctrine proclaimed in the review-manifesto, and Eliot himself never attempted again to wield the "mythical method" in so radical a fashion. But the prestige of his two examples, of theory and practice respectively, probably did more even than the work of Yeats and Lawrence to encourage midcentury literary theorists to imagine "myth" as an entity existing in an intensive, extra-historical dimension, accessible to all and recuperable in modern art. The review, moreover, foists these notions upon James Joyce.

JAMES JOYCE:
MYTH AS ALLUSION, ALLUSION AS PLAY

Joyce's actual treatment of "myth" is remarkably different from Eliot's account of it. Rather than confirming the views of the other modernists, it subverts them. But there are features of his treatment of myth in *Ulysses* that go some way toward explaining how readers as acute as Pound and Eliot were misled. First, there is the fact of the appeal to the "continuous parallel" epitomized in calling a novel about a day in the life of a Dublin ad salesman *Ulysses*. Second, Joyce does seem to manifest the same totalizing ambition as the others insofar as his Odyssean parallels imply generalizations about an unchanging human nature. Third, the *narrative* (pace Eliot) is so structured that it may seem at first blush to converge, especially in terms of its principal "mythic" patterns—Oedipal triangle, Christian Trinity, Homeric *nostos*—upon significant thematic closure. These aspects of the work help to explain why the earlier reception-history of *Ulysses* is the story of its assimilation, particularly via "archetypal" or "myth" criticism, into the project of modernist myth sketched by Eliot in his manifesto-review. But a look from outside this ideology discovers a Joyce whose practice is much more parodic.

Joyce seems to recognize implicitly that when he reconceives *The Odyssey* in contemporary terms, he is actually transposing what is itself a highly sophisticated, slightly older, immensely influential poem in his own chirographic tradition, and that the result must be a piece of extended literary allusion rather than anthropological fantasy. The resonance thus achieved is a matter of wit; it depends, not upon tapping mysteriously into a well of primal wisdom, but upon the reader's familiarity with Homer's story and consequent recognition of the running set of comparisons and contrasts. Perhaps nothing suggests so well the purely *structural* nature of this recourse as the notorious one-page table of correspondences, first circulated by the author himself, between the sections of the novel and episodes in *The Odyssey,* location of action, time of day, dominant body part, color, art, and symbol and narrative technique. The Odyssean parallels *are not different in kind* from the other sets of correspondences in the way they stiffen for the writer the texture of his episodes and disseminate for the reader the networks of symbol and allusion. As the other sets are local structural rules, arbitrary in the sense that they might well have been arranged otherwise, so is the set of Odyssean parallels. Joyce's conformation with Homer is minimal, scarcely consisting of more than beginning with Telemachus, switching to Ulysses, and concluding with the meetings of father and son, husband and wife on Ithaca. Within that framework Joyce transposes, emphasizes, deemphasizes, and transmutes episodes with a freedom that makes a hash of the structure and significance of Homer's plot. If Joyce had actually maintained a "continuous parallel" with Homer as Eliot asserts, Bloom, for example, would have seen Gerty McDowell early in the morning at the bathhouse, encountered "the Citizen" before visiting the newspaper office, entered the whorehouse in pursuit of Stephen before attending Paddy Dignam's funeral, and so forth. Indeed, Joyce's selection and disposition of what he chooses to count as "episodes" in Homer resembles the "mythemes," "codes," and "functions" into which narrative elements are scissored in the structuralist grammars of Lévi-Strauss, Propp, and Barthes. Joyce's rearranged *découpages* make it clear that Homer's plots and themes interest him only insofar as they can be fitted as counterpoint to a privileged narrative that dictates their placement.

Joyce achieves by this method a set of intertextual comparisons and contrasts between archaic Greece and modern Ireland that mutually illuminate and undermine one another. Eliot reads *Ulysses* as if Joyce's intention were his—to denigrate modern squalor by juxtaposition with glamorous antiquity. The Rorschach quality of the text, combined with Eliot's authority, has encouraged dedicated scorners of the present to echo and enlarge upon this one-sided view, but for every sense in which juxtaposition belittles Joyce's modern characters or settings, one can find a contrary sense in which it aggrandizes them. Stephen Dedalus, brooding as he walks over the garbage on the beach, is pathetically confused, defensive, and vulnerable compared to the newly awakened Telemachus inspired by Athena. But his efforts, as he encounters the shape-shifter, Proteus, to grasp the signs and forms of things display both an interiority in the character and a profundity in the sense of what "Proteus" represents that are far more moving than the mere unresponsive listening to Menelaus's tale that Homer depicts as the lot of Telemachus. The same ambivalence of significance applies to Leopold Bloom as *polumetis Odysseus* and to the adulterous Molly foregrounded against the West's archetype of faithfulness. Molly's "soliloquy" raises into consciousness the mundane considerations in a woman's daily life that Homer ignores in his idealized portrait. Joyce obliges us to read *The Odyssey* in the spirit in which Lévi-Strauss maintains that all versions of a myth, Freud's of Oedipus, for instance, are of equal status in considering its structure. And what is true of characterization is true of event. Bloom's descent to the dead (no Tiresias for him as for Pound and Eliot), his encounters with Nausicaa and Circe, his joining with Telemachus, and his homecoming do not, in any simple sense, merely convey the impoverishment of the modern world; they convey simultaneously that cumulative *Erinnerung* that Hegel saw as the history of consciousness. At the very least Eliot gets the proportions wrong in his review; Homer is of minor assistance to Joyce in ordering contemporary "futility," but this "futility" enables Joyce to set Homer in a profoundly different perspective.

While Joyce's totalizing ambitions in *Ulysses,* then, may drive him toward the essentializing of experience expressed in his adoption of the Homeric correspondences, his representation of what is "universal" in that experience is, compared to the other modernists, secularized, demystified, and flat. For the others, modern reversion to archaic experience enables participation in a religious vision. For Joyce, there is no such privileged access, no reason to think that humankind once possessed a gnostic wisdom lost today. Joyce's essentializing of experience is perhaps most overt in the "Ithaca" chapter, where the speaker of the "impersonal catechism" (as Joyce himself labeled his narrative technique) increasingly generalizes Bloom's consciousness well beyond anything "realistically" appropriate. When Bloom, for example, notices upon getting into his bed physical traces of Molly's adultery, the narrator asks, "If he had smiled why would he have smiled?" The answer comes back: "To reflect that each one who enters imagines himself to be the first to enter whereas he is always the last term of a preceding series even if the first term of a succeeding one, each imagining himself to be first, last, only and alone, whereas he is neither first nor last nor only nor alone in a series originating in and repeated to infinity" (Joyce 1967, 863). As a version of Nietzschean eternal recurrence this statement is not inconsistent with an essentialist view of human nature, but it *is* inconsistent with a hierarchical valorizing of priority. For Joyce "myth" is a species of literary allusion that can recuperate belatedness with respect to tradition by turning it into critical recontextualization; it is not, as for Yeats, Lawrence, and Eliot, a vehicle for willfully transcending this belatedness by a return to sacred origins.[19]

The reception-history of *Finnegans Wake* affords a heightened version of the fate of *Ulysses*. On one hand, the *Wake* would seem to establish overtly the discrediting of origins, the demystifying of myth implied by *Ulysses*. On the other, it quite arguably contributed even more than *Ulysses* to the midcentury enthusiasm for myth and the academic industry of myth-criticism. As in the case of the earlier work, Joyce himself is partly responsible. The *Wake's* remarkable ambiguities of reference and meaning are shot through with encyclopedic allusions to world myth and religion and enclosed in a cyclic structure that hints at a totalizing design even more ambitious than in *Ulysses*. The work does present an irresistible opportunity to commentators obsessed with organic unity, stimulated by the authority of Eliot on Joyce's "mythical method," and encouraged by depth psychology to search out a consistent and universal symbolism. In their pioneering *Skeleton Key to Finnegans Wake* (1944), Joseph Campbell and Henry Morton Robinson present the work as a "mighty allegory of the fall and resurrection of mankind," which takes advantage of recent discoveries of the "essential homogeneity" of world mythology to construct "a titanic fusion of all mythologies" (Campbell and Robinson 1977, 361–362). This "fusion" transcends "every limitation of individual, national, racial" difference to dramatize universal "Man the Hero, triumphant over the snares of life and the sting of death." Campbell's case is particularly revealing of the connection between the modernist resuscitation of romantic myth and its popularizing by midcentury theorists. His work on *Finnegans Wake* led directly to *The Hero with a Thousand Faces* (1949) and his subsequent career as the promoter of a "monomyth" according to which the universal pattern of myth is indeed that "allegory of the fall and resurrection of mankind" that he projected upon Joyce (Campbell 1977, 362). The treatment of the *Wake* represented by *A Skeleton Key* reads Joyce's "farced epistol to the hibruws," not as a water pistol of absurdity squirted at the highbrows, but as a First Epistle to the Hebrews, a scriptural supplement solemnly advocating much the same eternal gospel we have seen advanced by other modernists (Joyce 1988, 228.33–34).

In the past twenty-five years, however, poststructuralist commentary has proven remarkably successful at refreshing our sense of what is surreal and disruptive in *Finnegans Wake:* its shifting evasions of the individual subjectivity traditionally signified by "character," its recursive emergences and submergences of narrative impulsions, its employment of these impulsions principally to express Oedipal dynamics in the Earwicker family, its constant parodic defacements of the rhetorical constructions that think us in daily life, its paranomastic, rebus-like linguistic play that approximates so nearly the duplicity of meaning in dreams and slips of the tongue.[20] In the light of this broadly poststructuralist reading, it is easier to see what Joyce does with, and to, myth.

First, myth follows the fate of narrative in general. It is robbed, not of import, but of closure, determinate meaning, and authority. The letter accusing HCE of sexual misbehavior in Phoenix Park has often been taken in recent times as an "allegory of reading" and may serve here as a paradigm of the text's narrative impulsions. Of uncertain origin, the letter seems always already in circulation, though recently unearthed again; no one clearly possesses a copy, yet its contents are widely known. Though HCE and ALP are so anxious about its potential for scandal, its Heideggerian surfacings conceal the truth even as they purport to reveal it, and it is never quite delivered but fades from the dream with its issues unresolved.[21] This letter, like the later one "selfpenned to one's other, that neverperfect everplanned" (489.33–34), is indeed a structural model of the dozens of storytelling initiatives in the text, including, of course, whatever "mythic" material floats into view.

Second, myth is deprived, much more systematically than in *Ulysses,* of hierarchical status. Mythical elements are not privileged over "burst loveletters, telltale stories . . . alphybettyformed verbage . . . quashed quotatoes, messes of mottage" (183.11–23) and the rest of the food for thought. Whatever tales turn up, however ancient or recent, inhere in the mind of the dreamer in an egalitarian community of rumor, outside or beneath the critical consciousness that might assign them stable cultural significance. Far from being a "titanic fusion of all mythologies," *Finnegans Wake* is a Pandoran *con*fusion of whatever bits of myth happened to get caught in this particular night's collision between the dreamer's unconscious and his cultural preconsciousness. Myth is just another mode of what Heidegger calls the *gerede,* the chatter or gossip of the race.

In one of the myriad of self-reflexive passages in which the author seems to be teaching us to read his text, HCE, beginning to wake from his Wake, asks, "You mean to see we have been hadding a sound night's sleep? . . . of all the stranger things that ever not even in the hundrund and badst pageans of unthowsent and wonst nice or in eddas and oddes bokes of tomb, dyke and hollow to be have happened! The untireties of livesliving being the one substance of a streamsbecoming. Totalled in toldteld and teldtold in tittle-tell tattle" (597.1–9). HCE may be astonished that "his" dream-state has produced more strange and foreign matter than the hundred worst pageant-pages of world story and scripture, but he nevertheless manages to sum up his experience with Chaplinesque *sang-froid:* the untiring entireties of the process of living were the one substrate-substance of the dream's Liffeylike flow of becoming. But is this insight the recognition of a Bergsonian intensive manifold or an anticipation of chaos-theory? And HCE's ambiguities only grow more amusingly competent as he turns from the dream's ontological status to its mode of communication. On one hand, the dream is a *gestalt, "totalled* [my italics] in toldteld"; on the other, its narration is a scandal, "teldtold in tittle-tell tattle." Insofar as the author flirts with a total toldteld he lends aid and encouragement to the Campbelletristic synthesizers. But what sort of scripture is teldtold in tittletattle? Where Joyce's modernist readers see a massive "key to all mythologies," his postmodernist ones see pastiche and parody.

AFTERMATH: MODERNIST THEORY, POSTMODERNIST PRACTICE[22]

The rich *practice* of the modernist moment represented here only by Yeats, Lawrence, Eliot, and Joyce helps to fuel, in a number of fields, a midcentury outburst of neo-romantic *theorizing*. But, paradoxically, while myth flourishes thus in theory it withers in practice; its serious advocacy along lines exemplified in this chapter virtually perishes with the major modernists themselves. Poets and novelists continue, of course, to deploy in all sorts of ways what passes for myth, but less and less often with any commitment to the notion of the modernists considered above that it affords a viable escape from existential situation in history. To take the easier case of the novel, serious practitioners who invoke myth might be divided into those complicit with it and those critical of it.[23] Both types could be said to be modeled on Joyce's practice; the "complicit" on *Ulysses,* the "critical" on *Finnegans Wake.* John Updike, for example, in *The Centaur* and John Barth in *Giles Goat-Boy* toy wittily and self-consciously with a "mythic" dimension in their plots and/or characters that they are prepared neither to take altogether seriously nor to disown.[24] In comparison to this complicity, novelists like Samuel Beckett and Alain Robbe-Grillet, perhaps precisely because they are closer to the major phase of modernist fiction and reacting directly against it, are directly critical of myth. Robbe-Grillet's *Erasers,* for instance, echoes teasingly the plot of *Oedipus Rex,* but only to mock it as a piece of cultural baggage literally of no consequence. Similarly, Beckett's Molloy emits bursts of a wild mythopoeia, which he neither invites nor understands, as if they manifest exactly the same combination of phenomenological indisputability and epistemological incomprehensibility as the rest of his experience. Meanwhile, Beckett dares his reader to treat these allegorical ruins of meaning as if they signify the same aspirations toward depth and coherence expressed in high modernist invocations of myth. Both complicit and critical stances suggest that withdrawal of trust in "master narratives" that Francois Lyotard points to as a crucial distinction between modernism and postmodernism. The shift in the fate of thematized "myth" in twentieth-century fiction is a small instance that might support the likelihood of some such large closure. In any case, this shift sets off in relief those gestures toward transcendence that distinguish the modernist contribution to the midcentury construction of "myth."

[7]

Neo-Romantic Theories of the Midcentury 1: Myth as Mode of Thought and Language

The construction of "myth" grows exponentially in diversity and popularity through the middle decades of the twentieth century before peaking, as it now appears, in the late sixties or early seventies. The next two chapters follow only one of the increasingly entangled skeins of this general expansion. This is the rise of neo-romantic or neo-transcendental theories nourished by developments we've been considering in the three previous chapters, specifically by "ritualist" anthropology, depth psychology (especially of the Jungian variety), and the thematizing by influential literary artists of the role of myth in modern life. These thinkers share, most generally, a persuasion that the recent discoveries in ethnology and depth psychology provide crucial new evidence for the existence and nature of a universal power of mythopoeia that has always enabled humans to transcend in some fashion their existential and historical plights. But the group also share several conditions that make it difficult to present their theories in a significant chronological sequence. They flourish in a relatively narrow time frame (centered in the forties and fifties) and exhibit both a good deal of awareness of, responses to, and even borrowings from one another and, at the same time, quite distinct intellectual and disciplinary orientations. I have grouped them under two very broad rubrics: in chapter 7 those who focus especially on the linguistic, epistemological, and aesthetic implications of a universal mythopoeic faculty, and in chapter 8 those concerned primarily with what might be called its ethical implications, its role in everyday modern life.

ERNST CASSIRER:
MYTH AS SYMBOLIC THOUGHT

Cassirer is yet another instance of a thinker lured, like Durkheim and Lévy-Bruhl, into the investigation of "primitive" religion and myth by the prospect that the new troves of empirical evidence being amassed by ethnologists offer the key to the evolution of human thought. He was, like Lévy-Bruhl, a philosopher of broadly neo-Kantian persuasion, caught up in the turn-of-the-century effort to reconcile emotivist and intellectualist epistemologies, yet also deeply influenced by Hegelian history of consciousness. He comes upon the importance of myth by discovering in his early work on the history and philosophy of science that "there is scarcely any realm of 'objective spirit' which cannot be shown to have entered at one time into this fusion, this concrete unity, with myth."[1] In fact, "the history of philosophy as a scientific discipline may be regarded as a single continuous effort to effect a separation and liberation from myth" (xiii).

Here Cassirer makes his distinctive foundational move by introducing the concept of "symbolic form." All thinking is one or another kind of formal mediation between humankind and brute "reality." In *The Myth of the State,* Cassirer remarks that "what distinguishes [most human responses] from animal reactions is their symbolic character" (Cassirer 1979, 45). In *An Essay on Man* he asserts, in reply to Rousseau's view that humankind did ill in exceeding the boundaries of organic life, that "there is no remedy against this reversal . . . no longer can man confront reality immediately; he cannot see it, as it were, face to face. . . . He has so enveloped himself in linguistic forms, in artistic images, in mythical symbols . . . that he cannot see or know anything except by the interposition of this artificial medium. . . . Instead of defining man as an *animal rationale,* we should define him as an *animal symbolicum*" (Cassirer 1966, 25). As this passage makes clear, in the phrase "symbolic form" the word "form" refers to the work produced by symbolic thinking. Taken as a totality, this work is nothing less than the whole of human culture. The word "symbolic," however, is not so perspicuous. Cassirer employs it consciously, not in its romantic sense, referring to a sign that enables participation in transcendence, but in the sense derived ultimately from Leibniz and widespread in modern semiotics, signifying merely a functional designator within a semiotic system. But, as we will shortly see, what Cassirer means by "symbol" actually encompasses an affective dimension that inevitably plunges his theory into the familiar problematic of the romantic symbol.

Much of Cassirer's career after the inception of *The Philosophy of Symbolic Forms* was devoted to what he called in *An Essay on Man* "the phenomenology of human culture" (52), that is, discrimination of the distinctive modes of symbolic form. In the big work itself and in *An Essay on Man,* he distinguishes six: religion and myth (discussed together), language, art, history and science. The posthumously published *The Myth of the State* still offers six, but poetry achieves independence from art (by which Cassirer always seems to understand *visual* art), and history fades from the scene. Since all symbolizing has in common "the task of objectification," differences in the number of modes will depend upon how many independent sorts of objectifications are identifiable (Cassirer 1979, 45).[2] Cassirer declares in this same passage that "linguistic symbolism leads to an objectification of sense impressions; mythical symbolism leads to an objectification of feelings." In the same sense, science objectifies analytical thinking, art an intensified sensuous apprehension of reality, history the past perceived as meaningful.

Cassirer's neo-Kantian categorizing of "mythical thought" betrays the same unresolved tensions between emotion and rationality that we find in the thinking of Durkheim and Lévy-Bruhl.[3] Cassirer is well aware of these tensions but believes he resolves them satisfactorily in a manner analogous to Kant's in his third *Critique*. On one hand, "mythical thought" is a major mode of cultural objectification. Cassirer recognizes as the great merit of Schelling's *Philosophy of Mythology* that, in spite of its deductive, non-empirical categorizing, it holds myth to consist in "autonomous configurations of the human spirit which one must understand from within by knowing the way in which they take on meaning and form" (4). But what myth objectifies are *"feelings."* Like aesthetic judgments in Kant, "mythical thought" displays "purposiveness without purpose"; it attempts to bring under the rule of law responses that do not compel logical assent. The three principal divisions of *Mythical Thought* themselves represent this Kantian antinomy and its proposed resolution: myth is "A Form of Thought," "A Form of Intuition," and "A Life Form." Myth is a "form of thought" simply by virtue of being a mode of symbolism. At the same time as being a form of thought, myth is "a form of intuition," in the Kantian sense of "intuition"; the concept of "myth" would be empty if not shaped by apprehensions of the sensuous manifold, the categories of which are given by the structure of the mind. Each mythmaker constructs, as it were, his own phenomenology. But myth is also simultaneously "a life form"; it objectifies a deeply felt subjective sense of the unity of all life, a sense that stands as the contrary of scientific analysis. To follow Cassirer's argument, however, we need to take a closer look at *Mythical Thought*.

Cassirer opens his examination of myth as a form of thought with his distinction between science and myth. Scientific thought is based on "a progressive analysis of the elements of experience," whereas mythic thought "lives entirely in the presence of its object—by the intensity with which it seizes and takes possession of consciousness in specific moments" (34–35). "Above all [myth] lacks any dividing line between mere 'representation' and 'real' perception, between wish and fulfillment, between image and thing" (36). Cassirer thus seconds Freud in identifying myth with fantasy, and he quickly goes on to reinforce another of the fundamental tenets of the new anti-intellectual theories, that myth as narrative is a secondary elaboration of a deed done, a ritual enacted. "The part of myth which belongs to the world of theoretical narrative must be understood as a mediate interpretation of the part which resides immediately in the activity of man and in his feelings and will" (39). Narrative, then, is only a "part" of myth, and a second-rate part at that, a mere "mediate interpretation" of a prior movement of "feeling and will" that can somehow be "myth" while yet in a condition that precedes mental script or story. We encounter once again this fundamental stumbling block of romantic speculation.

Cassirer then proceeds to show, in the same vein, that mythical thinking is "distinguished from a purely theoretical worldview as much by its *concept of causality* as by its *concept of the object*" (43). Mythical thought reduces causality to Humean association, or contiguity, and is finally disqualified as analysis by its unwillingness to subordinate parts to wholes. In this latter claim Cassirer seems to impute directly to mythical thought one of the most important features of the romantic "symbol," the efficacy of the "concrete universal." Mythical thought, furthermore, "clings to bodies" (59); it cannot rise, that is, to a self-conscious view of its conceptualizations as pure function. "Whatever things it may seize upon undergo a characteristic concretion; they grow together" (63). Some of Cassirer's most effective pages follow this assertion, illustrating under the Kantian rubrics of quantity, quality, and similarity how mythic thinking binds "particulars together in the unity of an image, a mythical figure" (69).

In the conclusion of this demonstration that mythical thought is thoroughly "illogical" and governed by emotion, Cassirer himself raises the question of whether it isn't "a false rationalization of myth to attempt to understand it through its *form of thought.*" "Does myth," he asks, "not signify a unity of intuition . . . preceding and underlying all the explanations contributed by *discursive thought?*" (69). The word "intuition" is wielded here in its Bergsonian sense, which is more or less its sense in common speech. But before Cassirer gets down to this vitalistic "unity of intuition" in his third part, he devotes his second to "Myth as a Form of Intuition," in the Kantian sense of "intuition" as the immediacy with which the mind grasps the sensuous manifold. The result is deliberately paradoxical. Having demonstrated in his first part that mythic *thought* is thoroughly a matter of "illogical" intuition, he now proceeds to display mythical *intuition* as a species of systematic thought. He constructs upon the basis of Robertson's and Durkheim's distinction between the sacred and the profane, a case for Codrington's Melanesian *mana* as the most basic of religious concepts, and he then develops out of these assumptions a "specific morphology of myth" (82), a phenomenology of his own according to Kantian categories like space, time, and number.

Cassirer's third part, "Myth as a Life Form," is yet another conjectural version of the evolution of religion, which thus displays the continuity of his ambitions with those of Tylor and Spencer, Durkheim, and Lévy-Bruhl. For Cassirer, however, religious *thought* can evolve only in tandem with religious *feeling.* Even the "form of intuition" that yields the morphology developed in the second part "does not yet designate the ultimate stratum from which [myth] arises and from which new life continuously pours into it. For nowhere in myth do we find a passive contemplation of things; here all contemplation starts from an attitude, an act of the feeling and will" (69). A "world of forms" configured by myth "becomes intelligible to us only if behind it we can feel the dynamic of the life feeling from which it grew." Cassirer traces this growth of the symbolic forms of religion in three concurrent but logically distinguishable strands. His first chapter treats the gradual separation of subject from object; the second the rise of what he calls "a still more fundamental contrast" (175), that between self and community; and the third the slow interiorizing of cult, especially in the concepts of sacrifice and prayer.

The third part is subtitled "Discovery and Determination of the Subjective in the Mythical Consciousness," and he obviously yokes his affective anthropology to a Hegelian history of religious consciousness. He seems to revert to the romantics themselves in his conception of the world as (in Keats's phrase) "a vale of soul-making" in which ego evolves only in dialectic response to the not-I. "Primitive thinking," he maintains, "is actually characterized by the peculiarly fluid and fugitive character of its intuition and concept of personal existence" (159). But a decisive turn occurs "when the soul ceases to be considered as a mere vehicle or cause of vital phenomena and is taken rather as the subject of ethical consciousness" (166). He traces an analogous development in his subsequent chapter on the differentiation of self from the community. In its first section he focuses upon the phenomenon of totemism as both a system of intellectual classification and an emotive expression of the oneness of all life, but in its second section he reverses perspective in keeping with his dialectical principle and reconstructs humankind's increasingly differentiated sense of self as projected in its evolving conceptions of deity. Following Hegel, as he confesses, Cassirer stresses here his notion that in proportion as humanity acquires technological power over nature it must lose immediacy in increasingly sophisticated systems of mediation, that is to say, in symbols. Insofar as this general fate applies to mythology, he affirms in a striking echo of Schelling that "the mythical gods signify nothing other than the successive self-revelations of the mythical consciousness" (217). Cassirer carries this dialectic to its synthetic conclusion in his third and last chapter, "Cult and Sacrifice": "Each new form of prayer and sacrifice opens up a new meaning of the divine and a new relation between them. . . . the religious consciousness *creates* this gulf in order to close it; it progressively intensifies the opposition between God and man in order to find in this opposition the means by which to surpass it" (230).

As an optimistic history of the evolution of religious consciousness, this third part of *Mythical Thought* is reminiscent of the theology of Paul Tillich, the other significant thinker of the twentieth century strongly influenced by Schelling's *Philosophy of Mythology.* And Cassirer follows up his triadic exposition with a brief concluding section that makes it clear that this dialectic within mythic consciousness between constructed objectivizations and growth in self-conscious critique culminates in a proper Hegelian act of historical self-recognition. Just as, in the first volume of *The Philosophy of Symbolic Forms,* language evolves dialectically through "mimetic," "analogic," and "symbolic" stages into its self-conscious recognition that it is a functional tool, so "it is only in the history of modern philosophical idealism that the new view of the [religious] 'symbol' . . . achieves its full intellectual form" (258). As Cassirer represents it this "form" is still semiotic, not "miraculous," entirely immanent in cultural constructs, not participatory in transcendence. His phenomenological method thus permits him to finesse the whole issue of belief, but, as we will see in the next chapter, this same method in the hands of Rudolph Otto and Mircea Eliade is capable of being manipulated to a contrary conclusion.

Mythical Thought, we're now in a position to see, displays two contrary movements. On one hand it progresses through a broadly diachronic account of the cultural development of religious ideas, toward their self-conscious recognition as symbolic tools. But it discovers with increasing explicitness, on the other hand, the original affective core of this symbolic mode. Behind "mythical thought" lie its intuitive categories of representation, and behind these a driving sense of the unity of all life. "Primitive religion," Cassirer says in *An Essay on Man,* "is perhaps the strongest and most energetic affirmation of life that we find in human culture" (84). No matter how dialectically refined religion and myth become, they express intrinsically this Bergsonian *feeling* of the energy and oneness of life.

But Cassirer does not establish his *via media* between affective and cognitive theories without paying a price in conceptual ambiguity and downright *aporiae.* These stem particularly from the genetic or evolutionary obsession he shares with his predecessors, the lure of explaining how the heavily emotive ratiocination of "primitive" humanity evolved into the logical scientific thought of the modern West. Cassirer is adamant that all the other modes of symbolic thought originally "resided in the immediate and undifferentiated unity of mythic consciousness" (xv). The difficult questions, then are how, whether, and to what degree they have escaped that matrix. The status of language is especially crucial—and especially ambiguous. Cassirer observes in *An Essay on Man* that "wherever we find man we find him in possession of the faculty of speech and under the influence of the myth-making function" (109). This is tantamount to an admission that, so far as anthropological evidence goes, the claim that language, too, resided originally only inside the matrix of myth is purely hypothetical; modern inquirers first meet the two as distinct entities whose relations are unclear. Nor is Cassirer's distinction between them on the basis of what they objectivize of any serious help. Myth is said to objectivize "feeling" whereas language objectivizes "sense impressions," but the semantics and psychology of these terms are too unanalyzed to be persuasive. This weakness, combined with Cassirer's acceptance of the coeval entrance of the two modes into history, leaves open the possibility that language may be inherently *in*distinguishable from mythical thought, as a certain romantic line from Vico, through Herder and Humboldt to French *symbolisme,* had maintained. Cassirer's emphasis on the profound connections between the two modes, in conjunction with his ambiguity about how they are to be distinguished, transmits the problematic, alive but unwell, to the theorists of myth as "constitutive" of all our thinking discussed in chapter 13.

If language does not entirely escape mythical thought, *a fortiori* the other symbolic modes do not. This might appear logically to include even the mode called "science," but Cassirer's conception of science presents special difficulties that require its being set aside for the moment. The other modes are all emotive and hence have escaped the matrix of mythical thought only to a certain degree. Religion, poetry, art, and history detach themselves from mythical thought, not by rejecting it, but by becoming self-conscious in their employment of it. Religion, for example, makes the break when "in its use of sensuous images and signs it recognizes them as such—as means of expression which, although they reveal a determinate meaning, must necessarily remain inadequate to it, which 'point' to this meaning but never wholly exhaust it" (239). Art, in contrast to religion, remains concrete like myth itself but defines its difference by refusing to its mythological constructions the ultimate commitment of belief. Cassirer takes his cue from Kant's position that "aesthetic contemplation is entirely indifferent to the existence or nonexistence of its object," whereas in mythical thought proper "there is always implied an act of belief" (Cassirer 1979, 75). "The symbolism of art must be understood in an immanent, not in a transcendent sense." Yet art remains for Cassirer more directly even than religion in touch with their common mythic source. "The poet and the maker of myth," we're told in *An Essay on Man*, "are endowed with the same fundamental power" (153). In modern art, then, the ultimate self-consciousness about our symbol-making propensities fuses with the most complete openness to their primal energy. These are familiar romantic assumptions, but Cassirer's message that mythical thought is enmeshed in the *symbolic form* of the artist's work constitutes an important mediation between nineteenth-century romanticism and mid-twentieth-century literary theorists of a New Critical bent.

Consideration of symbolic modes like religion and art that patently preserve elements of their origin brings us up sharply against the most conspicuous aporia, or at least unresolved ambiguity, in Cassirer's work. Is mythical thought, in all the other modes descended from it, an atavism destined to be superseded by science? Is scientific thought different in kind or only in degree? The conclusions may appear foregone on the strength of what we have reviewed so far, but these questions are not merely rhetorical. There are certainly moments when Cassirer appears to envision an absolute difference and the ultimate elimination of the affective modes. He tells us, after all, that science is the objectification of analytic reasoning rather than, as the other modes are, of the "oceanic" *Lebensgefülle*. And he is capable throughout his work of judgments like the one in *An Essay on Man* in which he declares that the mythical conceptions of time, space, and number out of which modern physics grew comprised "a false and erroneous form of symbolic thought that first paved the way to a new and true symbolism" (49). Cassirer seems unwilling to abandon either position, and passes on, in his philosophy of symbolic forms, the set of antinomies characteristic of the older thinkers of his generation—Freud, Durkheim, Frazer, Lévy-Bruhl. Consciousness in general *is* evolving from the hegemony of pre-scientific into that of scientific thought, but at present mythic thinking survives in varying degrees, quite possibly in *all* the modes of symbolic thought.

This genial, humanistic view of mythical thought pervades Cassirer's work right through the publication of *An Essay on Man* in 1944, but it is far from his final legacy. Even as *Essay* was in press Cassirer was busy producing the very different assessment of mythical thought published, after his sudden death in 1945, as *The Myth of the State*.[4] The equanimity with which thinkers of the early twentieth century contemplate the survival of myth in the modern mind depends upon an assumption at least as old as Vico. The once explosive force that generated the stupendous rudiments of culture has been safely harnessed in the "civilized" West and confined to producing the most charming and consoling features of our otherwise pragmatic existences. But *The Myth of the State* is the passionate palinode of a refugee from Hitler's Germany. It should be classed with the rueful second thoughts of Marcel Mauss (quoted in chapter 4) about the unintended effect of Durkheim's picture of "primitive" religious unity. Some of the vehemence with which Cassirer reverses his assessment of the role of myth in his posthumous essay expresses not only his shock, but some need to compensate for his previous miscalculations.[5]

In *The Myth of the State* he seizes upon Malinowski's pragmatic theory of myth and Durkheim's sociology of religion as proof that the function of myth is to secure the social cohesion that will swallow issues of individual belief in the group's affirmation of life and defiance of death. This being its business, mythical thought in "primitive" communities is totalitarian. Cassirer now views this kind of consciousness as manifesting its imperious nature so consistently even throughout the history of Western political thought that he calls the central section of his work "The Struggle against Myth in the History of Political Theory." (The argument repeats his earlier pattern of describing the struggle of the other symbolic modes to separate from mythical thought.) In his final section Cassirer pursues this intensifying duel through the romantic reaction to enlightenment that produces the concept of organic community and the xenophobic nationalism underlying German National Socialism. Cassirer brilliantly and bravely (given the hysterical climate in which he was writing) defends various nineteenth-century thinkers against the popular charge of advocating fascism. He demonstrates not only that none imagined such an outcome but also that none could have accepted it consistently with his own principles. The upshot of Cassirer's comprehensive exoneration is to create a disconnect between fascism's intellectual origins and the actual emergence of National Socialism. But this gap is not an oversight; it expresses accurately Cassirer's actual sense of astonishment and dismay. No more to him than to Mauss does any *rational* explanation appear adequate. In his concluding pages he slips increasingly into this sort of rhetoric: "In all critical moments in man's social life, the rational forces that resist the rise of the old mythical conceptions are no longer sure of themselves. In these moments the time for myth has come again. For myth has not really been banished or subjugated. It is always there, lurking in the dark, waiting for its hour and opportunity" (280). Myth has now become a monster lurking in timeless dark. The power Cassirer had formerly supposed only vestigial waits perpetually for its opportunity to break through the constraints that harness it for useful social work: "Our science, our poetry, our art, our religion are only the upper layer of a much older stratum that reaches down to a great depth. We must always be prepared for violent concussions that may shake our cultural world and our social order to its very foundations" (297).

Cassirer's final bequest would certainly seem to settle where he stands on the question of whether myth is *passé* or permanent. Even "science" appears in the list of those modes of symbolic thought now restricted (in the same figure that appealed to Frazer and Freud) to the fragile "upper layer" of "a much older stratum." But Cassirer declines in *The Myth of the State*, too, to confront major inconsistencies. What is the relation of his new theory to his old? Can the existence of the timeless monster of group-think be reconciled with enlightened progress of thought in the symbolic forms, science in particular? In any case, his final version of mythical thought as potential totalitarian ideology is a severe warning against any version, including his own earlier one, that flirts too easily with romantic affectivity.

URBAN AND WHEELWRIGHT: FROM SYMBOLIC FORM TO SEMANTIC USAGE

By envisioning language and myth as symbolic modes, Cassirer contributes notably both to the century's "linguistic turn" and to its hypostatizing of "myth." But Cassirer's conception of the duo as co-equal and independent entities, reigning over separate realms of objectivization, also inhibits examination of the intimate connections between them that he himself recognizes as manifest from the earliest cultural stages of which we have knowledge. Indeed, he is inclined, in spite of his awareness that "myth and language are . . . twin brothers," to attribute logical and evolutionary priority to myth because it objectivizes the very feeling of life as a unity (Cassirer 1966, 110). Even language, he tells us in *An Essay on Man,* develops in this matrix and is understood by humanity to have a sacred, magical function before the discovery that its true function is semantic. This is why his chapter "Myth and Religion" in *Essay* precedes the chapter "Language." If this preference now seems a bit fantastic, it is not only that its expressionist premise is suspect but also that the "linguistic turn" has gone so much further in the intervening half-century that it is difficult for us not to assume that the mode of language must underlie and pervade all the rest.

In fact, even between the thirties and the fifties, the period of Cassirer's greatest influence, his speculations inspired a number of strong admirers to attempt their own accounts of relations among the expressive symbolic modes not only of myth and language but also of poetry as well.[6] The American philosopher Wilbur Urban, reacting especially against what he regards as the shallowness and naiveté of the linguistic theories of logical positivism, and therefore against the split between "emotional and propositional language" that infects Cassirer, too, advances in *Language and Reality* (1939) a scheme of symbolic modes based on a reconciling semantics.[7] According to him, language has always three aspects; conceptual, emotive, and intuitive. He adds to the standard dichotomy, then, a third epistemological condition—to knowledge by description and knowledge by acquaintance, knowledge by interpretation. (This latter concept seems akin both to C. S. Peirce's semiotic "interpretant" and the "hermeneutical" insight of the phenomenologists.) Value-judgments are therefore constituent in all language and in all symbolism. Like Cassirer, Urban understands "symbol" fundamentally in its scientific rather than its romantic sense, but he does hold that the intuitive element in our apprehension of it entails judgments of value. A symbol (1) stands for something that can be expressed by interpretation, (2) refers by "analogical" predication both "to the original object and to the object for which it now stands," and (3) contains both truth and fiction (Urban 1939, 423). "A symbol must stand for something, otherwise it would not be a symbol. . . . It cannot stand for anything in a wholly unambiguous way. If it did it would not be symbol" (424). "Truth" itself he defines as "adequate expression," determinable only by interpretation and verifiable by "authentication" (624). Truth, in this sense certainly a truth of coherence rather than of correspondence, is immanent in all discourse, which aspires toward a universe in which "'existence,' 'intelligibility,' and 'value' are inseparable" (675).

It follows that all four of the symbolic modes Urban distinguishes—poetry, religion, metaphysics, and science—are on one hand permeated by analogical thinking and on the other revelatory of reality. His characterizations of these modes do suggest an implicit continuum; "poetry" is defined in its broadest romantic sense as "an aspect of all language that is *alive*" (457), whereas "science" does its best to exclude "the qualities and values of things" (565). Hence, "the opposite of 'poetry' . . . is not prose but science" (565). Urban thus avoids Cassirer's positivistically infected ambiguities about the status of "science"; it plainly differs from the other modes only in degree, not in kind.

Urban adopts Cassirer's specific difference between poetry and religion; the intentional object of poetry is purely immanent, whereas that of religion is transcendent. In characterizing religion he relies even more heavily than Cassirer on Rudolph Otto's account of "a sense of the numinous . . . the *mysterium tremendum*, the wholly other, the Holy or Sacred" (577). At this point we come across Urban's conception of "myth" as a generic product of religious emotion. Humankind expresses its experience of the sacred in two generic modes, lyric and dramatic. The lyric is direct address, song, or prayer, whereas the dramatic mode is myth. "Dramatic language is not . . . primarily the language of emotion . . . but rather of will and action. The myth is the fundamental form, but the entire mode may be described more accurately as the historical element in religion" (574). Whereas Cassirer merely accepts the "myth-and-ritual" demotion of myth to a secondary rationalization of action, Urban's view of "will and action" as themselves secondary, generic elaborations of the original religious emotion induces him to *identify* myth and ritual. In describing them as parts of a broader "historical element in religion" he appears to mean all that religion as an institution does to pass on in narrative form the emotion of the original encounter with the *mysterium tremendum*.

Urban's treatment of myth is most significant, however, in displaying so clearly the rise of what turns out to be in the twentieth century a significant split between "myth" in the relatively narrow generic sense and "the mythical" as the fictive aspect of all our mental constructions. Urban generally presents "myth" as the narrative dramatization of religious emotion from which religion proper (as in Cassirer) separates itself by recognizing self-critically the deficiencies of analogical predication. Elsewhere, however, Urban admits the broad conception of "myth" as the necessary element of analogical thinking in all language and in the construction of all symbolic forms. "We could speak equally well of the myths of science . . . for the dramatic and anthropomorphic way of rendering the events of nature is, from the mathematical-logical point of view, mythical in this technical sense" (574). "Living knowledge," he declares at this point, meaning all knowledge that retains its valuing function, "is always mythical in character." A metaphysics that harmonizes value and "reality" comes very close to proposing "myth" or "the mythical" as what Wallace Stevens calls "the supreme fiction." In this respect, *Language and Reality* is, like Cassirer's twinning of language and myth, a harbinger of the fourth and last of my major classifications of "myth" in chapter 13.

With Philip Wheelwright we reach a theorist prepared to take what he himself calls "the semantic approach to myth" (Wheelwright 1965, 154). The word "approach" is the appropriate one, however. Compared to the phenomenologists and the advocates of symbolic form, Wheelwright is committed to the New Critical principle that the impact of literary expression must be accounted for by criteria as nearly as possible internal to the work itself. But he is so deeply influenced by both the former schools that his "semantic approach" scarcely gets any closer to this autotelic ideal than a gallant and instructive attempt to tame a number of the key concepts entangled in the problematic of "myth" from its beginnings. Like Urban, Wheelwright resists the positivist semantics (represented for him especially by Ogden and Richards's *Meaning of Meaning* [1923]) that divides language into the emotive and the referential. He argues persuasively on semantic grounds alone, as the philosophers of symbolic form do not, that referential and emotive language are not contraries, but independent variables, capable in fact of combining in the sort of language he calls "expressive." Having established this accord, however, he, too, identifies a fundamental terminological rift—between "expressive" language and "literal" or "scientific," which is "referential, but non-emotive" (Wheelwright 1954, 49).[8] On one side stands what he calls "steno-language," the language of science, logic, denotation, but also of dead metaphor, cliché, in short, as the name suggests, of any stereotypical usage. On the other side is "'depth language,' as exemplified in religion, in poetry and in myth" (3–4). This last clause should set off alarms, of course, because if these three fields share a common "depth language" the fact bodes ill for distinguishing among their referents. The blurring of these fields as they approach the limits of the expressible turns out indeed to be a prominent feature of Wheelwright's theory, but it is best approached by an examination of his attempts to stake out the truth-claims of "depth language."

Wheelwright's account of the qualia of this "depth language overlaps at points Susanne Langer's synthesis of Cassirer and Freud. It also becomes entangled in a considerable amount of circular definition. "Depth language" is characterized by (1) iconic signification (that is, by signs that, "although they may point beyond themselves, have a largely self-intentive reference as well" [60]), (2) plurisignation (plural references), (3) soft focus (approximately, connotation), (4) contextualism (significance conferred by context), (5) paralogical dimensionality (reference to experience not susceptible to rational categorizing), (6) assertorial tone (rhetoric based on assertions that can't be demonstrated logically), (7) paradox, and (8) significant mystery ("the truth or falsity . . . transcends to some degree any possible set of propositions which might stand in the relation of ground . . . to consequent" [73]). Of these marks, (1) repeats the definition of depth language, (4) seems true *to some degree* of the syntagmatic aspect of all language use, and (5), (6), and (8) merely affirm that language that speaks of what can't be said in steno-language is depth language. This leaves (2), (3), and (7), plurisignation, soft focus, and paradox, the three qualities most often identified as marks of "poetic" language in New Critical theory and in Langer's Cassirer-Freud amalgam as well. In spite of the mighty effort, Wheelwright's most meaningful attributions are those already widely recognized, while those peculiarly his own resemble the tautologies typical of acts of faith, whether religious or secular.

Wheelwright next takes a step backward toward the philosophers of symbolic form. He says that "depth-meanings" are distinguished from "steno-meanings" by "the greater vivacity of imagination that goes into their making" (76) and then proceeds to identify "four ways of imagination." These are: (1) the confrontative (I-Thou relations), (2) the distancing (as in Edward Bullough's concept of "psychical distance," his phenomenological elaboration of the Kantian notion that aesthetic judgments involve a special act of disinterested contemplation), (3) the archetypal, and (4) the metaphorical. Since these are modes of imagination, they must in some fashion precede embodiment in "tensional" language. They must be something like the philosophers' category of myth as a symbolic form. And in fact, in his later work, Wheelwright not only appears to add both "myth" and "symbol" to this class of ways-of-imagining, but even seems to give qualified assent to Cassirer's idea that myth is a symbolic mode.

Before turning to Wheelwright on myth, however, we would do well to look more closely at what he means by the "archetypal" and "metaphorical" as modes of imagination. Like many twentieth-century theorists of metaphor, he wants to define it very broadly and to emphasize its dynamic, metamorphic function. In *The Burning Fountain* metaphor is "fusing or recontextualizing old ideas in such a way as to generate new ones" (123). In *Metaphor and Reality* (1962), however, it is said to combine "epiphor," an Aristotelian term here signifying "outreach and extension of meaning through comparison," with Max Müller's analogical neologism "diaphor," signifying for Wheelwright "the creation of new meaning through juxtaposition and synthesis" (Wheelwright 1962, 72). We are handed a clue to his reason for separating the act of "recontextualizing" into two parts when he remarks later in the same chapter that "the role of epiphor is to hint significance, the role of diaphor is to create presence" (91). "Epiphor" is still on the horizontal plane of fallen aspiration, whereas, the theological diction suggests, "diaphor" is a miraculous act of creation. In the revised *Burning Fountain* of 1968, Wheelwright has it both ways, on one hand withdrawing into a strictly semantic explanation of metaphor as an "energy-tension" between simile and plurisignation, but maintaining, on the other, his claim that it creates presence. The reader of Wheelwright soon discovers, however, that, ambiguous as his eventual position may be about the ontological status of metaphor, it is at least better grounded in actual semantics than his accounts of "symbol" and "archetype" tend to be.

In *The Burning Fountain* Wheelwright distinguishes "archetype" from "metaphor" as "grasping the particular idea and the transient image in relation to something more universal and enduring" (123). This "grasping" sounds remarkably like the "concrete universal" function of the romantic symbol, and in *Metaphor and Reality* Wheelwright acknowledges this grand tradition of discourse and his location within it. "Symbol" is "distinguished from metaphor by its greater stability and permanence" (98), and "archetype" is reduced to the ranks as a mere subset. These moves may well be the result of Wheelwright's having read in the interim Northrop Frye's *Anatomy of Criticism,* but they enable him, in any case, to take into account the split history of the concept "symbol" and hence to project this particular mode of imagination along a continuum that includes all referential language. He now distinguishes two kinds of symbol—the "steno-symbols" of mathematics and highly stipulative denotation, and the "depth" symbols of poetry—and five degrees of the latter, depending upon their level of "stability and permanence." These range from the presiding image of a single poem, symbols of private, personal significance, and symbols that allude to a literary tradition to "those which have a significant life for members of a community" and, finally, to archetype, now defined as "symbols that have an identical or similar meaning for mankind generally, or at least for a large part of it" (110).

It is very apparent, in surveying this list, that Wheelwright's criterion for deciding the degree of "permanence and stability" is *width* of social recognition. Yet the list purports to identify degrees of *"depth."* The crucial enthymeme here is that the "depth" of poetic symbolism can be judged by the *extent* of its dissemination or reception. This assumption, so fallacious at first blush, is itself based upon the romantic doctrine that what is most common in human thought and feeling must somehow be the most profound and true and therefore source of the greatest creativity. Hence, "archetype," for Wheelwright the most socially broad of symbols, is also the deepest. But the great problem for the theorist of this kind of symbol is to explain how it yields up its depths. Wheelwright, like his immediate model here, Northrop Frye, rejects explicitly Jung's genetic explanation of "archetype." For Wheelwright and Frye the "collective unconscious" is, as Frye puts it, an "unnecessary hypothesis"; social ubiquity speaks for itself (Frye 1957, 112). The mere fact of ubiquity does not explain, however, what prevents the archetype, if it is based solely on the principle that "forty million Frenchmen can't be wrong," from being the most banal, the most "steno," of all "stenotypical" language. Wheelwright's one attempt at a truly semantic explanation, in *The Burning Fountain,* proposes that "in many of the most heightened passages of poetic utterance the effect comes from a combination of the metaphoric and archetypal modes of envisagement" (149). He appears to mean that in such "heightened passages" the new seeing induced by metaphor refreshes the banal archetype, while the archetype simultaneously universalizes the metaphor. The two "modes of envisagement" thus empower each other, metaphor as a whole performing the ontological function of "creating pres-ence" that "diaphor" is earlier said to perform within metaphor itself. Apart from this vivifying interaction, however, Wheelwright has still failed to establish an "archetype" that is not either as "miraculous" as Jung's, or as shallow as the flattest of "stenotypes."

Wheelwright's struggle with "myth" is nearly as complicated as the semantics of the familiar related terms. Nevertheless, a general pattern of development does emerge. In the original *Burning Fountain* he seems distracted between the "narrow" sense of "myth" as a narrative genre of archaic or exotic societies and Cassirer's view of it as a mode of thinking. In the fifteen years between the two versions of *Fountain,* he brings the competing versions into accord by developing his conception of the "mythoid" state of mind.

In the original *Burning Fountain* he criticizes Cassirer and Langer for their "one-sided" conception of myth as "a kind of primitive epistemic" (159). Even in that text, however, and even on the same page, he makes a major concession to Cassirer's view when he allows that "genuine myth is a matter of perspective first, invention second." He concedes much the same when he suggests in his essay of the following year, "The Semantic Approach to Myth," that myth may be classified as "primary" (a mode of "envisagement" like Cassirer's mode of thought), "romantic" (in the sense of being "a deliberately contrived story," that is, a romance), and/or "consummatory" (a self-consciously modern imitation) (155–156). There is an undeveloped hint of an historical schema here, but the more important point is the acceptance of Cassirer's version as "primary." Near the conclusion of this same essay, Wheelwright sketches the first version of his reconciling theory by proposing that "primitive myths may be regarded as the early expression of man's storytelling urge so far as it is still conditioned by such proto-linguistic tendencies as diaphoric ambiguity and the several kind of sentential polarity" (167). "Diaphoric ambiguity" refers to that mutual support of "archetype" and the "creative" aspect of metaphor we have already encountered in connection with the theory of "archetype." "Sentential polarity" signifies the tendency of the "expressive" sentence "to involve simultaneously . . . affirmation and questioning, demanding . . . and acceptance, commitment and stylization" (163). (This last term means recognizing that the symbols to which you commit yourself are only symbols.) Wheelwright adumbrates here with his "storytelling urge . . . conditioned by proto-linguistic tendencies" a hypothesis rather like Urban's view that myth results from the impulse to rationalize prior emotive forms of imagining by expressing them as narrative. Wheelwright's proposal is closely related, too, to Jung's conception of myth as a narrative distinguished by the presence within it of symbols.

Up to this point Wheelwright's theory offers a purely secular explanation of the origin, history, and function of myth, but in *Metaphor and Reality* and the revised *Burning Fountain* he resorts to the phenomenological verity that for most humans "myth" has pointed to a "reality" beyond itself. Speculating now as freely as Cassirer himself about the state of mind of "primitive" humanity, he describes their world as "presential." "By this I mean something fairly close to what Rudolph Otto has called 'the numinous' . . . which the primitive myth-maker, the man of religious sensitivity and the developed poetic consciousness all have in common" (135). Wheelwright now takes for granted the working within myth of the epiphoric and diaphoric functions of metaphor. The former appears "wherever man sees through the immediate to some lurking, perhaps some 'higher' reality" (135) and the latter where "the semantic movement is from an outward shape . . . to a latent meaning" (137). These dual operations are now said to belong to "a stage of awareness before the explicit formulation of a myth, which strongly disposes the persons who share it to formulate and rationalize various experiences in descriptive and narrative accounts. That early stage of mythic growth may be called a *mythoid,* or a mythoidal situation" (136). We are plainly told here that this "mythoid" stage both precedes description and narrative and yet "disposes" the experiencer to "formulate" those sorts of discursive rationalization. Wheelwright concludes the chapter that contains these hypotheses, "On the Verge of Myth," by finding also in the "mythoid" state what he now calls "tendencies of personification," a version of the "way of imagination" called in *The Burning Fountain* "confrontative" (creating "I-Thou" relations). With this addition, the "mythoid" now includes three of his four original "ways of imagination"—the "metaphorical," "archetypal," and confrontative"—and the fourth one, "distancing," is presumably excluded by definition because it applies to the conscious creation of a work of art. Myth, then, begins in a Cassirer-like epistemic, a "mythoid" disposition characterized by activity of the "ways of imagination" that provokes the production of the actual narratives. This conception of mythmaking as a two-phase *process* resolves for Wheelwright the split between myth as mode of thought and myth as narrative and constitutes the heart of his "semantic study" of the topic.

It seems that Wheelwright might well have developed his full conception of the two-phase creation of myth without recourse to "the numinous." But the fact is that he does appeal to it in his later work as the name for the kind of experience that precipitates or provokes myth as a response. His formulations of the relation of "myth" to "the numinous" do raise an important question: Does he hold that "myth" actually puts us in touch, in the romantic sense, with an objective "reality" of a transcendent or even supernatural character? Or does he merely represent with phenomenological neutrality what he considers the nature of the mythmaking process to be like for those who experience it? Hazard Adams makes a strong argument that the former is the case, that Wheelwright's "depth language" does claim transcendental sanction, that his notion of "symbol" is, in Adams's stipulative sense, "miraculous," and that he should be classed with Mircea Eliade as a "sentimental archaizer" (Adams 1983, 252–262). I am not so sure. It's true that much in Wheelwright invites Adams's assessment. He does sound like an "archaizer," for example, when he spends a significant part of a chapter in *Metaphor and Reality* making the kind of case for Max Müller's notion of "radical metaphor" (the ancient roots of a language preserve metaphors of unusual power and wisdom) that seems to appeal recurrently to those who believe in some form of a Vico-like First Age. In *The Burning Fountain* he does claim that poetry, myth, and religion are one in affirming a reality beyond the threshold of words. He also attempts to demonstrate (in a move interestingly related to Urban's) that the capability of expressive language for meaningful assertions of belief justifies us in adding to the "correspondence" and "coherence" theories of truth a third, the "intuitive." "The existential structure of human life," he proclaims in the revised *Fountain,* is radically, irreducibly *"liminal"* (18–19). Talk like this does sound theological. And yet Wheelwright, like Urban, is careful not to speak of what (to say nothing of who) might be the object of this liminal experience, and each of the observations cited may be read in a more neutrally phenomenological vein. The dictum about life's existential structure being radically liminal, for instance, may be taken as an enthusiastic seconding of Eliade's claim that humanity is "naturally" and indefeasibly religious, but it need not be read so positively; it can be understood with strict literalness to mean that humans have everywhere and in all times experienced the teasing sense of encountering a threshold of mystery that they cannot cross. And if he speaks in *The Burning Fountain* of expressive language as able to ground acquiescence in belief, he also speaks of it in "The Semantic Approach to Myth" as capable of simultaneous "stylization." We meet in Wheelwright and Urban theorists who find the language of religious phenomenology congenial for thinking about myth but make an effort, unlike Otto and Eliade, to remain noncommittal about the ontological status of what is conjured up. Perhaps we should think of Urban and Wheelwright as "liminal" theorists. On one hand, they do attempt to accommodate the religious dimension of mythmaking. But in leaving open, on the other, the possibility that even the most ambitious and intense of humanity's mythologized experiences may be only self-projection, they anticipate the more radically "constructive" theories discussed in chapter 13.

NORTHROP FRYE'S "ARCHETYPAL" CRITICISM: MYTH AS UNION OF RITE AND DREAM

Northrop Frye does not propound a new theory of myth, but his *Anatomy of Criticism* (1957) is a very significant attempt to construct a systematic theory of both literature and of literary criticism based on concepts of "archetype" and "myth."[9] Frye defines "myth" technically as being, in the "archetypal" stage of symbolism, "the union of ritual and dream in a form of verbal communication" (Frye 1957, 106). To put it provisionally, the *narrative* element in myth is an expressive analogue of the way our experience of natural cycles is expressed in archaic ritual, and the *thematic* element in myth is a comparable analogue of the dynamic of libidinal desire and fear ("dream") most basic to our emotional lives. Frye claims, then, that literature arises out of a combination of the sort of ritualized experience of nature celebrated by Frazer and the kind of experience of psychological vicissitudes identified by Freud.

Apart from its grounding in Frazerian anthropology and Freudian psycho-analysis, Frye's theory of literature is an impressive synthesis of two centuries of romantic speculation about the relation of "myth" to "literature." Vico postulated the existence of an original mythopoeic age, its characteristic qualities of expressive thought and language, and a verbal art that descends, in both senses of the word, from this primal source. The romantics impose the crucial qualification that in genuine "literature," the modern artist accedes in some degree to the original power of "myth." In spite of the romantics' intuitions, however, critical systematization of their thinking waits upon the stimulus of the neo-romantic strains in ritualist anthropology and in depth psychology and their acting out in modernist poets and novelists. Unlike the numerous creative artists and theorists who fail to recognize the romantic provenance of their ideas and consequently pay a price in terms of coherence and consistency, Frye owes much of his success to his acute grasp of the tradition in which he works. As he acknowledges in his prefatory statement, he has developed from an earlier study of Blake a set of "principles of literary symbolism" whose universal applicability to the study of literature he now aspires to demonstrate. He offers in his "Polemical Introduction" a different and more general explanation of his work when he says it investigates "the possibility of a synoptic view of the scope, theory, principles and techniques of literary criticism." Frye finds no contradiction between these two ambitions, however, since, as *Anatomy* is designed to show, other sorts of literary criticism can cohere in a unified enterprise only if they are subsumed under the sort that he draws from Blake, Shelley, and other romantic theorists and that he calls "archetypal." To understand what he means by "archetypal" criticism, however, it is necessary to follow the argument in the first two of the four essays that comprise his text.

Frye commences in his first essay with what he calls "historical" criticism, and he characterizes the principles that shape it as a "theory of modes." He defines "mode" as "a conventional power of action assumed about the chief characters in fictional literature, or the corresponding attitude assumed by the poet toward his audience in thematic literature" (366). "Such modes," he adds, "tend to succeed one another in historical sequence." There are two kinds of "modes," then, which Frye will employ heuristically to distinguish literature in historical sequence—the "fictional," referring to characters in fiction interposed between author and audience, and the "thematic," referring to an unmediated relation between the audience and an author. And since literature, for Frye as for Freud and Jung, is the artful projection of fantasy, it is bound to be primarily about "His Majesty the Ego," or else his thinly veiled substitute, "the Hero." Frye distinguishes in the "fictional mode" a sequence of five historical periods distinguished by the degree of "the hero's power of action" (33). If it's superior in kind to others and to the environment, the hero is divine and the story a myth. If he is superior in degree to others and the environment, he is the hero of a romance, but if superior only to other men and not to his environment, he's a leader of some sort in a story in the high mimetic mode of epic or tragedy. If the hero is not superior either to persons or milieu he's "one of us" (34) in a story in the low mimetic mode, and if inferior to ourselves "belongs to the ironic mode" (34). Having descended his pentatonic scale of heroism, Frye makes his primary concession to actual history. He proposes a highly generalized parallel between these five phases of the hero's relation to society and stages in the course of (Western) history: "We see that European fiction during the past fifteen centuries has steadily moved its center of gravity down the list" (34). Myth's "center of gravity" lies in prehistory, romance's in later oral culture up through the Middle Ages, the high mimetic's in the Renaissance, the low mimetic's in the eighteenth and nineteenth centuries, the ironic's in the twentieth.

Frye then proceeds to distinguish between "tragic" fictional modes, "in which the hero becomes isolated from his society," and "comic" fictional modes in which "he is incorporated into it" (35). (Notice again here that the difference between tragedy and comedy, two of the broadest of generic moods, depends upon the individual's relations with society.) The tragic fictional mode of "myth" is about dying gods, of "romance" about fading heroes, of "high mimetic" about the fall of a leader, of "low mimetic" about one of us pathetically defeated, and of "ironic" about a scapegoat victimized. The comic fictional mode of myth is about a hero welcomed into the society of the gods, of romance about a pastoral escape, of high mimetic about a triumph over society, of low mimetic about social success, and of ironic about the enjoyment of a scapegoat's purging. In the second half of the essay, Frye describes a similar declension of the "thematic" mode, where the social relation between writer and society isn't mediated through characters but obtains directly. In the "thematic" mode the distinction that corresponds to the split between "comic" and "tragic" in the "fictional" mode is that between authors who speak only as private individuals and those who adopt the role of social spokesperson. The private persons tend to produce "episodic" forms of writing and the spokespersons "encylopaedic" ones. Both kinds of direct authorial roles decline in heroic status as they descend the historical stages of Western culture, just as in the case of the characters in the "fictional" mode.

Insofar as this first essay purports to locate literary history within a "synoptic" view of the whole critical endeavor, it is a satire upon literary historians' pretensions. Not only is Frye's loose fit of heroic attitude to historical stage as close as he ever comes to concrete history, but he actually undercuts any possibility of genuine contingency by introducing a hint of Viconian *ricorso*. There are signs in the present "ironic" era of a return to myth; "our fives modes evidently go round in a circle" (42). This proposal hypostatizes the five-mode sequence and produces a cyclical metahistory reminiscent not only of Vico, but of Schlegel, Schelling, Nietzsche, and Spengler.[10] Even setting aside the issue of a *ricorso,* the five descending modes, as Angus Fletcher pointed out many years ago, constitute a kind of Hegelian metahistory of "the evolution of the idea of a hero" (Fletcher 1966, 46). This evolution is paradoxical; as we become increasingly conscious of our social and political situation and correspondingly free to think what we will about it, we grow proportionally aware of our helplessness and bondage. When Frye later envisions literature as apocalyptic in its disinterestedness, he can sound as if he were imagining it primarily as the instrument of radical social change. But the structure of his metahistorical schema appears to entail a repetition of the historical fate of the romantics' visionary aspirations—demoralized withdrawal from political commitment into a quest for purely private, internalized enlightenment. And if the ironic awareness of bondage that encourages such withdrawal into private salvation can be succeeded only by a return to "myth," isn't Frye, in spite of his greater sophistication, contemplating with equanimity the same kind of flight from "meaningless" modernity actively preached by Mircea Eliade or Joseph Campbell?

The likelihood that this may be so is increased by Frye's innovative and influential employment in this first essay of the concept of "displacement." In the book's glossary, the term is dryly defined as "the adaptation of myth and metaphor to canons of morality or plausibility" (365). In each descending historical stage beyond that of "myth" itself, the archetypes embodied in myth and in metaphor will be read according to a hermeneutic prescribed implicitly by that era's prevailing social and literary norms. By importing from Freud the term "displacement" to designate this phenomenon, Frye calls attention to the resemblance between the way the dream-work substitutes progressively censored symbols for its deepest emotional contents and the way the changing historical modes impose progressively rationalized interpretations on their deepest mythical contents. This transferred concept of "displacement" offers an elegant, systematic explanation of a problem that haunts the romantic construction of "myth" from Vico onward—what to make of the alleged decline in humanity's imaginative power from an original mythopoeic age. Vico is sufficiently a product of Enlightenment to express ambivalence about this original state and humanity's decline from it, but he does not doubt the fact of either thing. He describes with still-unequaled eloquence what becomes thoroughly unambivalent dogma among nostalgic romanticists from Schiller onward. In the most important formulation before Frye's own, Jacob Grimm, as we've seen, throws the weight of his authority behind a theory of generic degeneration from myth to tale, thus disseminating the assumption not only among folklorists but, through them, among cultural anthropologists as well. Embryonic fragments of similar metahistorical schemata emerge subsequently in many theorists of neo-romantic orientation, including Eliade, Wheelwright, and Neumann. It is Frye's achievement to have incorporated this set of hypotheses within the larger structure of a coherent theory. Precisely because he has managed this so plausibly, however, with such an appearance of neutrality, it is important to attend to his genealogy, which scarcely differs in this matter from Eliade's or Campbell's. Frye would presumably defend beginning his historical sequence of modes with "myth" on the grounds that human storytelling actually does begin there. But this is itself an unwarranted assumption. Even granting for the moment that we are justified in distinguishing an oral genre called "myth" from ordinary "tale," the consensus of opinion in modern anthropology is that we cannot now recover the information necessary to determine for certain that either genre originally preceded the other. As we will see later, what ethnological evidence we do have actually favors, at least in structural terms, the precedence of tale. The point here, however, is that Frye's claim that literary history commences in "myth" is not a neutral statement of fact; it is a *parti pris,* whose ideological significance becomes more clear upon inspection of the second essay in *Anatomy.*

This second essay, "Ethical Criticism: Theory of Symbols," is the theoretical heart of Frye's system. Here he works out the functions of those terms in which he tells us he was "entangled" after his work on Blake: "'symbol,' 'myth,' 'ritual' and 'archetype'" (vii). He presents us with five phases of "symbol," which turn out rather ominously to correspond, in inverse order, to the five historical modes of literature. Frye's procedure in accounting for each phase of "symbol" is to characterize it as a type of meaning, explain how it communicates, isolate the typical structure of its use of metaphor, and relate it to its appropriate historical mode. Thus, the first phase of "symbol" is the "literal," the phase of centripetal patterning, which communicates only ambiguously since it refers inward to itself. Metaphor in this phase is simple juxtaposition, which might be represented abstractly as A : B, the terms to be compared simply presented side by side. This phase of "symbol" is characteristic of the most recent historical mode, the ironic literature of our own day. The second phase of "symbol" is the "descriptive." Here meaning is communicated in hypothetical verbal structures that aspire to imitate "reality" "as if." The dominant form of metaphor is the simile, A is (like) B. This phase is characteristic of the low mimetic historical mode, of the nineteenth-century "realist" novel, for example. The third phase, centered in the "high mimetic" mode typified by Renaissance literature, communicates in the "imitative image." As poetry lies for Aristotle midway between the concreteness of what happens, which is history, and the contemplation of what ought to happen, which is philosophy, so, in this phase, literature typically depends on the image, which is halfway between the concreteness of the specific example and the abstraction of the precept that the example illustrates. The typical employment of metaphor is in an "analogy of proportion": A is as B. The fourth phase of "symbol," the "archetypal," consorts with the historical mode of "romance." The unit of meaning of the "archetype" is the "recurrent, associative cluster," and this is communicated by "myth," a genre that joins ritual with dream and mythos (patterns of experience expressed as plot) with dianoia (patterns of desire expressed as theme). The dominant form of metaphor in this fourth phase of "symbol" is the "concrete universal." Frye does not offer a paradigm of this sort of metaphor, but since this is the "romantic symbol," in which each particular instance participates in the nature of its general class, perhaps it may be represented as a < A. The fifth and last phase, companion of the historical mode of "myth" itself, is the "analogical," in which each monad of meaning stands for all and communicates the union of total ritual (social action) with total dream (private desire). Metaphor in this phase tends to assert the potential identity of one thing with another; A is B.

The first thing we must return to in reflecting upon this "theory of symbols" is the relation of the five phases of "symbol" to the five historical modes. Frye maintains only that these pairings are "typical." But this claim is itself immense, since it assumes that the hermeneutic by which myth is "displaced" in successive historical modes is determined by (or varies together with?) the era's implicit understanding of the trope of metaphor. We are encouraged to imagine at work a law of the transformation of metaphor that might be thought of as the specific linguistic vehicle of "displacement." (In his definition of "displacement" Frye speaks of "the adaptation of myth and metaphor.") The suspicion that myth and metaphor must be closely related runs throughout the history of our topic, but Frye is unique in asserting a strict homology of function and then refusing to argue the case. On one hand, he implies that the "displacement" of narrative and tropology in a particular historical mode will mirror one another; on the other, he merely sets them side by side, like the structure of metaphor itself in the ironic mode.

When *Anatomy* first appeared Frye was thoroughly suspect to New Critics and always labeled a "myth" or "archetypal" critic. Now that both approaches to literature have fallen out of fashion, he is often lumped together with his antagonists by virtue of their mutual neo-Kantian premises. Frye himself is, as usual, well aware of the neo-Kantian and even New Critical premises of his first three phases of "symbol." They underlie both the normal dialectical appearance of the first, "literal" or self-referential, phase together with the second, "descriptive," one to produce "hypothetical" meaning, and also the tendency of the third phase, the "formal," to produce what might now be called "allegories of reading." But Frye sets up these first three phases of "symbol" only to discount their sort of "ethical" criticism, just as he implicitly discounts "historical" criticism in the first essay. These phases enable literature to communicate to the private sensibility. But this limitation permits merely the pointless accumulation of discrete works, and the piling up of endless commentary about them without any progress in knowledge of the whole. Furthermore, the treatment of literature as merely "hypothetical" or "as if" is a miserable failure as "ethical" criticism. Only the fourth, the "archetypal," phase of "symbol" permits cumulative, socially meaningful thinking about literature. This is the core of Frye's argument. While he allows each major critical theory its place in the grand synopticon, the study is a tendentious plea for the necessary hegemony of "archetypal" or "myth" criticism.

This hegemonic claim stands or falls on the strength of Frye's explanation of how "symbol" communicates in its fourth, "archetypal," phase. Frye commences by reiterating a version of his distinction in the first essay between the "fictional" and the "thematic," *mythos* and *dianoia,* to use his Greek terms for them, or, as he calls them here, "narrative" and "meaning." To these polarities he adds another set that he dubs "recurrence" and "desire." The "exemplary events" of narrative tend to recur, and the "precepts" of meaning tend to express "wish-thinking" (104). "These elements of recurrence and desire," he observes, "come into the foreground in archetypal criticism." Frye's conception of "archetype" is very broad; he defines it in the glossary as "a symbol . . . which recurs often enough to be recognizable in one's literary experience as a whole" (365). Broad as the definition is, however, all archetypes fall under the aegis of either anthropology or psychology, that is, of either "ritual" or "dream." "The narrative aspect of literature is a recurrent act of symbolic communication: in other words, a ritual. Narrative is studied by the archetypal critic as ritual or imitation of human action as a whole . . . Similarly . . . the significant content is the conflict of desire and reality which has for its basis the work of dream. Ritual and dream, therefore, are the narrative and the significant content respectively of literature in its archetypal aspect" (104–105). Frye thus combines in a unified theory ritualist anthropology with depth psychology, Frazer with Freud.

Having identified the two broadest cultural foundations of "archetype," Frye identifies in the next paragraph the natural sources from which he believes they arose. The poem in this phase "imitates nature" as a recurrent cyclical process and "the nightly waking to a titanic self" that we experience internally. Frye's conviction that symbolic thinking rests upon a biological basis resembles Langer's and stems from a comparable expressive aesthetic. Most fundamentally, recurrence in literature expresses our experience of natural cycles just as (Frazerian) rituals proper do, and the special recurrence of desire expresses the relation between our experience of the external natural cycles and our psychodynamics. Far from being locked in self-referentiality and unprogressive reiteration, literature thus communicates what is most common and enduring in human experience. It is this universal expressiveness, not its historically situated particularities, that confers upon literature its social significance.

It is important to notice in this connection a certain tension between the external natural cycles and our internal experience of desire. For Frye as for Freud and Jung this desire, or "libido," is the motive force of culture; it pulls against mere cyclical repetition in a "dialectic" that alternates between our worst fears and our greatest hopes but always sets before us the goals of human work. Hence, literature, considered archetypally, combines recurrence with desire, the structure of ritual with the dynamic of dream, to articulate not merely our past experience but our utopian goals. Frye's conception of the origins of culture patently owes a great deal to Freud's version of civilization and its discontents. In the actual structure of our archetypes we can read the cumulative expression of our struggle as a species to construct culture out of nature.

Here we reach Frye's second definition of "myth," this time as "the union of ritual and dream in a form of verbal communication" (106). Bearing in mind that in the fourth, "archetypal," phase of "symbol" this unit of communication, "myth," consists not only of an element of *dianoia* or theme but also of an element of *mythos* or narrative plot, we can appreciate how the integration of the two "gives meaning to ritual and narrative to dream" (107). Frye goes on to say that myth is, in fact, "the identification of ritual and dream." Given this definition of myth, we can deduce Frye's position on the anthropological disputes about the relation of myth to ritual; ritual can be meaningful to human beings only to the extent that they mythicize it. In a similar vein, his implicit position on the relation of "mythical thought" to actual "myths," so troublesome to Cassirer and Wheelwright, is that each requires the other; "mythical thought" without narrative is analogous to dream without ritual outlet, and "myth as story" without the thematizing of "mythical thought" could never take shape.

There is one sense, though, in which this second definition of "myth" as "the union of ritual and dream" clashes conspicuously with the first, folkloristic definition of myth as a historical genre in the "Theory of Modes." Frye's second definition is crucial to his entire argument. The conception of myth in the fourth phase of symbol as "union of ritual and dream" enables him to celebrate the social value of the knowledge accumulable by archetypal criticism. If "civilization . . . is the process of making a total human form out of nature" (105), the function of literature is to express "a vision of the goal of work and the forms of desire" (106). This claim for the social value of literature as utopian vision is the familiar romantic one voiced, for example, by Shelley and Matthew Arnold, and it is logically the capstone of Frye's plea for archetypal reading. But it is not sufficient for Frye. He proceeds to adduce a fifth phase of "symbol," the "anagogic," which would unite "total ritual, or unlimited social action, with total dream, or unlimited human thought" (120) inside "the mind of an infinite man who builds his cities out of the Milky Way" (119). In this mental state the entire accumulation of literature (as always for Frye "hypothetical verbal construct") would be "existing in its own universe, no longer a commentary on life or reality, but containing life and reality in a system of verbal relationships" (122). To be fair to Frye, he presents this "still center of the order of words" (117), however logically hypothesized, as a condition of which humanity has attained only a few discontinuous glimpses. Nor is this "center" religious in any sectarian theological sense as carelessly alleged by some of Frye's more impatient critics. Frye takes pains to explain in Kantian terms why the disinterested state of literary imagination has nothing to say about religious belief and could never rest content under the compulsion of theological prescription (125–128). The most that he can be convicted of along these lines is imagining a liminal experience that (like the comparable ones of Urban and Wheelwright) does not exclude the possibility of a given visionary assigning to it a culture-bound theological interpretation. Though Frye borrows the term from medieval theory of allegory, his "anagogic" phase of symbol is secular, not sectarian, a version of the romantic "apocalypse" (as Frye himself terms it) of Novalis, Shelley, and Blake. Its most serious weakness repeats theirs. Whereas the poet (or critic as poet) dreams of the transformation of society, what he enacts and truly celebrates is a moment of private illumination that demands as its first precondition withdrawal from the world. It is only the isolated, disinterested savant in his crisis of "ironic" Hegelian recognition, "all Heaven blazing into the head," as Yeats puts it, who glimpses humanity's cumulative archetypes. Although Frye's version is more subtle and complex, we find ourselves once more in the presence of the antinomy so apparent in Graves, Eliade, and Campbell—an enlightenment alleged to be universally available happens also, somehow, to be accessible only to the gnostic hero. It is very understandable why, in the face of this withdrawal, combined as it is with Frye's neo-Kantian insistence on the "hypothetical" nature of literary constructs, his claim for the hegemony of archetypal criticism on the strength of its social relevance has struck historically oriented critics, especially on the Left, as particularly outrageous.

Let us return at this point to the crux of the two differing conceptions of myth, which Frye acknowledges but treats (on page 106) as only an apparent or superficial difference. The "folkloristic" version presumes a popular, anonymous genre, widely, if not universally, accessible, whose contents are of special significance, often sacred, within a given community. In contrast, the union in the "anagogic" phase of "total social ritual, or unlimited social action, with total dream, or unlimited individual thought" (120), must therefore logically be, though Frye does not say so, "total myth." This is no bad name for the "apocalyptic" vision of the poet-experiencer or self-conscious practitioner of "archetypal" criticism who attempts to "fit poems into the body of poetry as a whole." But "total myth" is a term that can also mark usefully the historical gulf between romantic visionary experience and the conventional acceptance in a traditional society of the mythology into which one is born. When Frye couples his historical mode of "myth" with that of the "anagogic" phase of symbolism, he engages in serious sleight of hand. It is highly doubtful that the visionary's belief in his apocalyptic can be equated with collective representations in traditional communities. Furthermore, since literature is always for Frye a "hypothetical verbal construct," it would seem that the visionary's commitment to this totality must be, at most, a paradoxical and ironic "willed suspension of disbelief," rather like Wallace Stevens's "belief" in "the supreme fiction."

Frye's substitution of "total myth" for traditional belief in the shift from historical mode to anagogic phase of symbol is probably not a conscious shell game but genuine blindness to the disjunction between these two conceptions. The consequences of Frye's failure to distinguish them adequately can be exemplified by asking what he has in mind when he suggests that our "ironic" historical mode appears to be circling back to the initial mode of "myth." Does he contemplate a reversion to some condition of unified sensibility in which humanity could rest once again in uncritical belief? Or does he imagine the recycling as a Hegelian spiral, in which case we will carry into this return the *erinnerung* of our post-romantic self-consciousness? Frye sows ambiguity wherever he touches on the problem. When he describes the function of metaphor in the "anagogic" phase as asserting identity (A is B, in violation of the law of non-contradiction), he is most probably thinking of Blakean "apocalypse," but his paradigm suggests with equal plausibility Lévy-Bruhl's account of the "law of participation" in "primitive" thought.[11] Frye would presumably take both these modern constructions, in utterly unhistorical fashion, as merely alternative accounts of a mythopoeic power always and everywhere the same. But that position entails cave-Blakes in the caverns of Lascaux. In the end, Frye's effort to integrate his "total myth" as vehicle of romantic transcendence within his vision of socially responsible criticism is counterproductive. It exposes how historically bound the romantic version of myth actually is, and it even undermines the validity of his fourth-phase claim for myth as the union of ritual and dream.

The last two-thirds of *Anatomy* sketches a system of studying literature as a whole organized around its most salient archetypes. This part of the text is thus relatively practical criticism. While it has proven by far the most useful and influential part of the book among students of literature, it isn't of comparable theoretical relevance for Frye's construction of "myth." The third and largest essay is titled "Archetypal Criticism: Theory of Myths," but this means only that archetypal criticism organizes literature by patterns of "myth," just as historical criticism does by "mode," and ethical by "symbol." These patterns are, most broadly, either thematic ones that express libidinal fantasy and are classified by image, or narrative ones that express our experience of natural recurrence and are classified by type of plot. This practical analysis thus affirms the naturalistic origins of expressive literature in ritual and dream. The fourth and last essay, "Rhetorical Criticism: Theory of Genres," is designed "to show how conventional archetypes get embodied in conventional genres" (293). It assumes that the principal genres are each based upon a type of rhythmic recurrence and hence derived, like the archetypal moods of plot, from experience of the cycles of the natural world. The job of the archetypal critic, as Frye exemplifies it in the last part of *Anatomy* and in most of his later writing, remains always to counter the processes of social and historical differentiation, to take views that recover, from the disjunctive and bewildering complexities of particular cultural products, our most universal patterns of expressive response to natural periodicities and libidinal dynamics.

Anatomy of Criticism is certainly the high-water mark of midcentury claims for "literature" as "myth." In its scope, synthesizing ambition, and (mostly) coherent theoretical articulation of two centuries of romantic assumptions, Frye's effort deserves to stand at the end of this chapter as a bookend worthy of the one on the opposite side of the shelf, by which it was in fact greatly influenced, Cassirer's *Philosophy of Symbolic Forms.*

[8]

Neo-Romantic Theories of the Midcentury II: Myth and Ritual in Quotidian Western Life

The midcentury revival of transcendentalism includes ambitious attempts to theorize what the modernist artists sampled in chapter 6 maintain in practice—the active presence of myth (and ritual) in the daily life of the ordinary person. These efforts focus accordingly less on the aesthetic, linguistic, and epistemological features of the alleged mythopoeic faculty than on what might broadly be called its ethical consequences. Until the middle decades of the twentieth century the construction of myth is the concern of relatively isolated intellectuals. At this point, however, it becomes the business of talented popularizers—Mircea Eliade, Erich Neumann, Robert Graves, Joseph Campbell—who disseminate to large middle-class audiences versions that promise what amounts to gnostic enlightenment. For the first time myth becomes the conceptual property of millions of people searching for spiritual guidance. It is difficult not to regard this outcome with a certain amount of irony. Here we encounter the ostensible triumph of the very religious appeal that produced "myth" in the first place; yet this flood of recycled romanticism issues from theorists who seem startlingly oblivious of their intellectual origins. The theorists' confidence in their interpretation and deployment of evidence from the new social sciences of ethnology and depth psychology seems to mask, even from themselves, the provenance of their ideas.

The domesticators of transcendentalist myth grouped in this chapter are also united in their elaboration of that shadowy personage, "the Hero." As Northrop Frye recognizes in his schema of historical genres, the democratizing and psychologizing of the hero extends over the history of "Western" literature. It can be said to be already apparent in Homer's move from Achilles to Odysseus, present in Dante's *Commedia,* conspicuous in the Early Modern heroic romances of Italy and England, and so forth. But the most significant turn of the screw in this evolution of the hero is the romantic "internalization of quest romance" exemplified in chapter 2 by Novalis, Blake, and the other poets who exalt the power of the mind to create its own salvific mythopoeia. We first find a self-conscious historicizing of the concept in the "displaced" avatars of the hero in Carlyle's *Heroes and Hero-Worship,* which begins with the hero as divinity and concludes with him as "man of letters" in the modern world. E. B. Tylor inaugurates the hero's career in anthropology; he seizes specifically upon the similarities in worldwide "hero myths" to make his characteristic case for the comparative method, which "makes it possible to trace in mythology the operation of imaginative processes recurring with the evident regularity of mental law" (Tylor 1958, 282).[1] It seems doubtful, however, that there is any sustained folkloristic analysis of the hero-tales capable of defining any "mental law" of their "imaginative processes" before Raglan's *Hero* (1936) (Segal 1990, vii–viii).[2] The great advance that enables the midcentury domestication stems, rather, from depth psychology. Freud's speculations about the fantasies of "his majesty the Ego" in "The Creative Writer and Daydreaming" (1908), Rank's *Myth of the Birth of the Hero* in the following year, and, above all, Jung's *Psychology of the Unconscious* (1912) (eventually *Symbols of Transformation*) inaugurate the ultimate democratizing and psychologizing of the notion of "the hero" by affirming the universality of this type of fantasy and its role in libidinal development. Three of the four major theorists examined in this chapter—Eliade, Neumann, and Campbell—build explicitly on Jung, and may in fact fail to recognize their romantic heritage partly because it is mediated to them through Jung's version.

These midcentury *theories* are also conspicuously related to the preceding representations of comparable *experience* by modernist artists, as exemplified in chapter 6. In some cases there is genuine influence, as between Yeats and Graves, Joyce and Campbell. But even where no influence can be demonstrated, these later, explanatory modes plainly issue from the same conviction of the indwelling presence of myth in daily life that the artists testify to in their more "presentational" modes.

"RELIGIOUS PHENOMENOLOGY" AND MIRCEA ELIADE'S MYTH AS ALTERNATIVE TO THE MODERN WORLD

Mircea Eliade addresses the concept of myth from the perspective of what may be called the phenomenological study of religion. The actual phrase "phenomenology of religion" seems to have been intended by its inventor, Chantepie de la Saussaye, to signify the systematic attempt to get at the essence of religion through comparative description of its exhibited phenomena.[3] But the impact of Edmund Husserl's *Logical Investigations* (1900) and *Ideas for a Pure Phenomenology* (1913) altered decisively the twentieth-century conception of how any such analysis ought to be attempted. Husserl impressed on his successors above all the importance of analyzing afresh the phenomena of ordinary experience, and the need, in the face of this very difficult feat, to develop a strenuously scrupulous method of blocking out or "suspending" habitual presuppositions. In his immensely popular and influential work of 1917, *The Idea of the Holy,* the Lutheran theologian Rudolph Otto honors the first of Husserl's goals while flouting the second.[4] By careful attention to experience of the sacred, or "holy," he produces some brilliant characterizations of the qualia of this "irrational" element in religion. But the work displays an extremely uncritical projection as universal of religious and philosophical beliefs peculiar to their time and place.

Its fame rests upon the broadly "phenomenological" descriptions in its early chapters. Otto promotes use of the abstract noun "the numinous" to designate what he admits is a "category of value" and a "state of mind" (Otto 1978, 7). In this "state" we experience the holy as "the *mysterium tremendum*" (12). The adjective signifies feelings that range from bliss to horror, but are marked in general by a sense of "awefulness," "overpowering majesty," and "'urgency' or 'energy' in the numinous object" (23). The noun *mysterium* communicates our sense of being in the presence of the "Uncanny," the "Wholly Other" (26). But the *mysterium tremendum* is not merely daunting; it is also "fascinating"; if it "bewilders and confounds," it also "captivates and transports" (30), and this paradoxical tension is of the essence of the experience, which is beyond reason, including the rationality of ethics. It is some measure of the success of the work that even so brief an account will sound familiar to most readers; terms like "the numinous" and "the Wholly Other" have simply become part of the standard vocabulary of twentieth-century theology.

Otto's book might be described positively as an attempt in the wake of Dilthey's "idiopathic" or (in a later, anthropological, vocabulary) "etic" concept of *"verstehen"*—sympathetic insight—to develop a neo-Kantian hermeneutics of religion. But Otto begins with a direct incursion in the fashion of the romantic Idealists across the line drawn by Kant between pure reason's ignorance of the noumena and its knowledge of phenomena. Otto actually designates "the holy" in several contexts in his later chapters as "an *a priori* category," by which he seems to mean, not one of Kant's categories of understanding, which would be a bold claim, but something even more startling, a fourth faculty of mind on a par with reason, understanding and judgment, a faculty Kant would have had to address, if he had only known of its existence, in a fourth *Critique.* This familiar romantic anxiety to reclaim for a mere phenomenon its own metaphysics is an essential source of the work's appeal for Eliade.

But so, too, is Otto's insistence that the object of an experience so intense must exist objectively outside the individual's apprehension. He chides William James for listing in *Varieties of Religious Experience* the "feeling of objective presence" as if this were just another phenomenon; for Otto, "the latter presupposes the former" (10–11 n.). This is as much as to say that if (in the Husserlian sense) you intend "the holy" as an object of consciousness, it must exist independently of your intention. This presumption generates a mode of argument that Eliade will also adopt, in which phenomenological *description* metamorphoses without argument into a celebration of the objective reality of the experience described. Thus, for example, Otto's neologism, "the numinous," hypostatizes a subjective apprehension in a manner so insistent as to persuade the reader that "the numinous" is an external thing that *causes* the internal awareness of it.

Finally, Otto passes on to Eliade the temptation to construct both an essential human nature and a universal experience of "myth," based upon a highly parochial and hierarchical conception of each. Otto is as frank as Hegel about his conviction that religion culminates in contemporary German Lutheranism. In spite of his dislike of William James's "empiricist and pragmatist standpoint" (11), he resembles no one so much in understanding religion as virtually synonymous with the highly interiorized, private, and culturally Protestant business of bourgeois self-fashioning, scarcely imaginable before or outside of early modern Europe. Otto appeals for support to the new ethnologies of "primitive" societies, and occasionally remembers to pay lip-service to the historicist recognition that humankind has not always and everywhere conceived of "the holy" in the same way. But the unmistakable gravamen of his discourse as a whole is that the species has indeed experienced the same unqualified "numinous" as awe-inspiring "Wholly Other" with which modern Lutheran theologians are presumed to be familiar.

Eliade finds in Otto, then, a model of phenomenological analysis that, far from attempting the methodical exclusion of pre-judgment that Husserl calls for, actually makes such prejudiced activity the heart of his enterprise. Like Otto himself, Eliade tends to avoid referring to his approach as "phenomenology of religion." When he locates himself in a scholarly tradition he typically invokes, not phenomenology, but a branch of knowledge he calls History of Religion, a study inaugurated formally, according to him, by Max Müller. Eliade has on occasion defined this field's proper practitioners so exclusively, however, that they might seem to consist only of himself, his quondam mentor, Raffaele Pettazzoni, and Gerardus Van Der Leeuw. And sometimes, as in the old joke, he wonders about the two of them. We owe to Van Der Leeuw, after all, a canonical *Phänomenologie der Religion* (1933) that strives to observe Husserl's strictures about method. Eliade is inclined to see himself as perhaps the only pure "historian of religion," because even Van Der Leeuw and Pettazzoni may be too close to the traditional concerns of comparative religion. When Eliade characterizes himself as a "historian" he has in mind a highly personal, Otto-like version of the role. The "historian" is responsible for penetrating by sympathetic intuition the inner religious experience of a given group, however exotic, and then for connecting this particular historical experience with that which all human beings apprehend in common. Given this definition of "historian," it is understandable that Eliade sees no irony at all in his career as a historian who denies historicism, who affirms instead universal participation in an ahistorical reality everywhere and always the same, who even, as we will see in the case of his conception of "myth," celebrates the power of the human mind to escape from the contingencies of history.

Eliade pays tribute to the formative influence of Otto by beginning *The Sacred and the Profane: The Nature of Religion* (1956, 1957) with an account of the theologian's eye-opening originality of approach in *The Holy*. Eliade declares his intent to go beyond Otto by presenting "the phenomenon of the sacred in all its complexity and not only in so far as it is irrational," but his conception of the rationality of the sacred is based upon declaring "the holy" or "the sacred" to be an autonomous and inalienable faculty of the mind (Eliade 1957, 10).[6] "The 'sacred,'" as Eliade puts it in the preface to *A History of Religious Ideas* (1976–1978), "is an element in the structure of consciousness and not a stage in the history of consciousness" (Eliade 1978, xiii). In the introduction to *The Sacred and the Profane* he expresses his rapport with Otto on this matter by introducing what becomes his favorite designation for humanity, *"homo religiosus."* By thus labeling the species on the analogy of *homo sapiens, homo faber,* and so forth, he signifies as succinctly and unarguably as possible his conviction that a religious response to existence is of the essence of human nature.

As the "Sacred and the Profane" of Eliade's title indicates, he seizes upon the familiar Smith-Durkheim distinction between the broadest of psychological dispositions with respect to religious feeling and transforms it into a metaphysical divide. Hence he will speak of "the coexistence of contradictory essences: sacred and profane" as a "dialectic of hierophanies" (Eliade 1963, 29). On the strength of this belief, Eliade constructs a defense of transcendentalism as truculent as any we possess. Without being familiar with Schelling's term, he holds the religious faculty of apprehending the sacred to be "tautegorical," understandable only from within in its own realm of experience. Any attempt to understand religion in terms of something else, he disparages as "reductive," although he doesn't hesitate to "reduce" ruthlessly other interpretations judged from the infallible vantage of his own "creative hermeneutics" (Eliade 1969, 62).[7] This latter phrase signifies his extrapolation of his metaphysical distinction into a metahistorical theory, a committed reading of the religious record of humanity that will edify his secularized, profane contemporaries by demonstrating their unprecedented and disastrous separation from the perennial sacred wisdom of their kind.

This program obviously has its positive and negative sides. On the positive side, the preponderance of Eliade's work as a "historian of religion" consists in the collection, comparison, and more or less systematic analysis of the religious symbolism of humanity. Eliade is remarkably complacent about what he means by "symbolism"; he is innocent of those struggles with the inherited terms—"image," "symbol," "archetype"—that so exercise the thinkers considered in the previous chapter. Eliade merely echoes Jung's and therefore the romantics' formulas with the air of a man reinventing the umbrella: "A symbol speaks to the whole human being and not only to the intelligence" (Eliade 1957, 129). "It is through symbols that the world becomes transparent, is able to show the transcendent." "By understanding the symbol ['premodern' man] succeeds in living the universal." He projects a comparable naiveté or indifference about contemporary critiques of "the comparative method," which is always in danger of simply assuming the universality it aspires to prove. But, epistemological and comparative issues aside, Eliade presents us, of course, with a major instance of those large-scale, systematic decodings of networks of "symbolism"—those of Frye, Bachelard, Neumann, and Ricoeur, for instance—that mark the midcentury after the dissemination of depth psychology.

The negative side of Eliade's program is a critique of what he perceives as the irreligion of modernity. Believing as he does in the indefeasibility of humanity's religious faculty for apprehending "the sacred," Eliade is at something of a loss to explain its currently obscured condition. He seems most often to regard this as arrogant sin against the light on the part of modern unbelievers. He speaks revealingly of his contemporary *"homo religiosus"* as *choosing,* on the contrary, to live in the sacred in order "not to let himself be paralyzed by the never-ceasing relativity of subjective experiences" (Eliade 1957, 28). The truth of transcendence is so patent and transparent that only deliberate perversity of will can explain the wholesale modern defection from it. The work of the proper historian of religion must also be, then, to exercise a hermeneutic capable of unmasking the stubborn survival deep within modern life of those traces of the sacred officially denied. Eliade thus co-opts the strategy of Marx's and Freud's "hermeneutics of suspicion" to expose the blindnesses of a culture in which, as he perceives it, belief in transcendence, not its contrary, is repressed.[8]

Eliade's particular conception of myth is deeply embedded in these larger views of religion as a whole. He does not speculate specifically about its *origin,* but it follows from his theory of religion that myth originates as a narrative expression of the hunger of *homo religiosus* for the sacred. (Perhaps because he is himself the author of novels, Eliade does recognize, with a firmness that we've seen can't be taken for granted in the transcendentalist tradition, that myth indicates deployed narrative.) He further achieves a certain amount of precision about the nature of this narrative because he is in accord with Van Der Leeuw and Pettazzoni about the *function* of myth. The Dutch scholar defines myth as "a spoken word possessing decisive power in its repetition" and as "the reiterated presentation of some event replete with power" (Van Der Leeuw 1986, 413–414).[9] Pettazzoni declares "it is precisely the tales of beginnings, the cosmogonies, theogonies, and legends of superhuman beings who brought things into existence and founded institutions, which are myths" (Pettazzoni 1984, 101). "Myth," Eliade remarks, "is always an account of a 'creation'; it relates how something was produced, began to be. Myth tells of that which really happened, which manifested itself completely" (Eliade 1975, 6). All three writers characterize myth, then, according to its cosmogonic mode in which its function is to shape the beliefs and values around which a society coheres. This particular kind of exclusion has tempted religionists across the whole history of the construction of myth. It exposes a biased "Western" presumption that the sacred must always be expressed with high seriousness. By the usual folkloristic standards this is a very narrow definition of sacred story. It excludes, for example, a high proportion of the ludic ritual and bawdy comic narrative regarded as sacred in many Amerindian societies. Of the hundreds of pages of sacred stories collected in Franz Boas's *Tsimshian Mythology,* for instance, all but two or three would have to be excluded as irrelevant. It isn't sufficient to say that for History of Religions the *subject matter* of myth is "the sacred"; it is a bowdlerized, sentimentalized version of what counts as "sacred."

Perhaps no other twentieth-century mythographer reverts quite so ingenuously as Eliade to the stage of Schiller's *"Wie ganz anders, anders war es da!"* At the same time, Eliade is equally unmatched (with the possible exception of Joseph

Campbell) in his obliviousness to the romantic sources of his ideas. Instances of this unconsciousness stud his texts. It is manifested most formally perhaps in his encyclopedia article on "Mythology in the Nineteenth and Twentieth Centuries," which commences with Max Müller. Eliade might well be fixated on Müller, whom he regards as the founder of History of Religion and a kindred spirit in identifying the subject matter of myth as the sacred. But it is difficult to understand how Eliade could be so oblivious of the centrality of this latter idea in romantic thought as to attibute its origin to a fumbling epigone like Müller. The student of Eliade's thought is frequently reminded of Santayana's dictum about those who do not remember history.

Eliade's best known contribution to the phenomenology of the sacred is probably his insistence that when humans experience it through ritual or myth, they enter the timelessness of the original event. Eliade's brinksmanship about Platonism often inclines him to speak as if the original occasion celebrated in a myth possesses a grade of ontological reality greater than that of its subsequent rehearsals, but in other contexts his denial of temporal sequence in the experience of the sacred is so radical that it abrogates any gap. *"Sacred time is reversible . . . it is a primordial mythical time made present. . . .* the participants in the festival meet in it the first appearance of sacred time, as it appeared *ab origine, in illo tempore"* (Eliade 1957, 68–70). Eliade is especially fond of the latter phrase as a means of signifying the utter difference between human or "profane" time and "sacred time," which is not time in our secular sense at all but *"that* time," a condition of eternity that tongue-tied humankind can only point at with a demonstrative pronoun and an attribution of temporality. The participant also apprehends a "sacred space," which is not homogeneous and amorphous like the space of modern physics, but significantly structured, "homologizable to a founding of the world" (Eliade 1957, 20). It is because of this experience, which seems to organize and orient a world, that cosmogonic creation myths dwell upon such structuring.

Eliade follows, in these attempts to characterize the experience of the sacred according to temporal and spatial categories, the neo-Kantian tradition that affected Durkheim, Lévy-Bruhl, Otto, and his fellow historians of religion, but his conception of the "exemplary" aspect of myth is very much his own. His constricted identification of myth with its cosmogonic type makes it easy for him to insist that "the foremost function of myth is to reveal the exemplary models for all human rites and all significant human activities" (Eliade 1975, 8). It is an ethnological commonplace that a culture's creation myth, if elaborate, expresses (and is alleged by its believers to prescribe) much of its worldview and ritual behavior. But Eliade turns this familiar idea too into fodder for his metahistory by transforming an observable social fact into a transcendent metaphysical principle. The verbal key to his distortion is his fondness for referring to the cosmogonic models in the myths as "paradigms." This is Plato's term for his Forms, and here again Eliade's account of the relation of exotic cultures to their creation myths does often suggest, unguardedly perhaps, a Platonic mimesis by humankind of ontologically superior models. Eliade's position presumes in any case divine dictation inscribed either in the language of the myth or in the perspicuous Book of Nature. Hazard Adams remarks that "Eliade's own myth is that of a titanic archetypal figure who reads nature silently without the mediation of language" (Adams 1983, 252). This could be a description of one of Vico's *giganti,* but it aptly hits off the unfallen *homo religiosus,* of whom Eliade says, "the world stands displayed in such a manner that, in contemplating it, religious man discovers the many modalities of the sacred and hence of being" (Eliade 1957, 116).

A brief sketch of the specific metahistorical scheme is in order here. The first chapter that "religious man" reads is the sky, in which he finds displayed a single supreme being, a masculine sky-god with all the qualities of Otto's "holy." Hence, the one school of twentieth-century ethnology that truly captures Eliade's imagination is Wilhelm Schmidt's. Eliade follows Schmidt even in the adoption of the *kulturkreis* theories of German neo-romantic anthropologists like Leo Frobenius and his student Adolphe Jensen, who derive from Ratzel's cultural geography the distinction between "planter" cultures (with vegetation myths and mother-earth goddesses) and "hunter" cultures (with animal myths and father-sky gods). Later fieldworkers tended in general to find that Schmidt's original male sky gods seemed to play little part in the religious life of the "most primitive" peoples. Eliade's positive spin on this negative evidence develops thus: "Celestially structured supreme beings tend to disappear from the practice of religion, from cult; they depart from among men, withdraw to the sky, and become remote, inactive gods (*dei otiosi*)" (Eliade 1957, 121–122). As Eliade rather dazedly observes about his own interpretation, "It is remarkable that the man of the archaic societies, who is generally so careful not to forget the acts of the Supernatural Beings as the myths record them for him, should have forgotten the Creator God [*sic*] transformed into a *deus otiosus*" (Eliade 1975, 98). It is more than "remarkable," however; it is downright contradictory, given the alleged transparency of the Book of Nature to the *homo religiosus.* This paradox at the heart of Eliade's vision acknowledges implicitly, like every myth of the fall, that humanity is always already fallen. But Eliade's commitment requires a rationalization. Mankind (it's men Eliade has in mind) transfers its allegiance to modes of the sacred nearer home: "Other religious forces came into play—sexuality, fertility, the mythology of woman and of the earth and so on" (Eliade 1957, 126). Man "gave himself up to vital hierophanies and turned from the sacrality that transcended his immediate and daily needs" (Eliade 1957, 128). He "fell" foolishly, that is, into matriarchal vegetation religions that exalt womanhood and materiality (if these are for Eliade two distinct things). He was then on the slippery slope at the bottom of which modernity awaited.

When Eliade surveys the floor of this latter abyss from his station within it, he virtually recapitulates the religious reaction we associate with romanticism. Finding the intellect darkened, our ability to read the Book of Nature puzzlingly occluded, he excavates the ruins of that abstract fallen giant, the human race, seeking whatever springs of mythic affectivity may still indicate life. He valorizes Tylorian "survivals" in reverse. Where the rationalists trace the dwindling remnants of archaic religious practices as a Whiggish history of humankind's escape from superstition, Eliade reads this same evidence as the sole meaningful traces of genuine religion, trivialized by modernity but still witnessing stubbornly to humanity's true nature. He turns in particular to two twentieth-century sources of hope. The first of these is the aspiration of modernist art to reestablish communication with the archaic and to "revolt against historical time" (Eliade 1975, 192). Eliade speculates that the novel as a genre, while it "does not have access to the primordial time of myths," nevertheless creates in its construction of imaginary time analogous escapes from "historical and personal time" (192). This is a species of romantic aesthetic theory we have witnessed inhabiting the work of various modernist writers, but it takes on a keener ideological edge in Eliade's treatises. While literature does not attain the "primordial" time of "the sacred," it evinces, as Eliade puts it in *The Sacred and the Profane*, "at once thirst for the sacred and nostalgia for being" (94).

The second great source of hope is Jungian psychology. Eliade surely cannot subscribe to Jung's promethean, self-validating pragmatism, but he rejoices in Jung's evidence of "the subconscious survival in modern man of a mythology that is ever abundant and, in our view, of a spiritual authenticity superior to his 'conscious' living" (Eliade 1969, 16).[10] Eliade (unknowingly) follows Schelling in conceiving of this "eclipsed" condition of self-proclaimed "nonreligious" man as a second fall within the first one, a fall from "divided consciousness" into the "unconscious," so that "the possibility of reintegrating a religious vision of life lies at a great depth" (Eliade 1957, 213). Even in such cases, however, man "remains the prisoner of his own archetypal intuitions, formed at the moment when he first perceived his position in the cosmos" (Eliade 1963, 434). Thus, even the "phylogenetic fantasy" of the depth psychologists is co-opted for religious ends. Eliade's appeals to modernist fiction and Jungian psychology for support of his fanciful metahistory of religion enters him in that curious midcentury Ponzi scheme in which a neo-romantic theorist within one discipline builds his case on claimants in other fields without recognizing that they, too, are circulating the same overextended transcendentalist capital.

ERICH NEUMANN: MYTH AS THE HISTORY OF JUNGIAN LIBIDINAL DEVELOPMENT

Neumann's *Origins and History of Consciousness* appeared originally in the third of the *anni mirabili* of our topic, 1949, with a remarkable imprimatur from Jung himself. Upon the foundation of *his* discoveries, Jung asserts, Neumann "has succeeded in constructing a unique history of the evolution of consciousness, and at the same time in representing the body of myths as the phenomenology of this same evolution. In this way he arrives at conclusions and insights which are among the most important ever to be reached in this field. . . . The author has placed the concepts of analytical psychology . . . on a firm evolutionary basis" (Neumann 1954, xiv). Jung's description of the work is as accurate as it is approbative; this is a clear-eyed endorsement. It's especially revealing, therefore, that he repeats the piece of circular reasoning at the core of Neumann's argument. The sole evidence that consciousness evolves as Neumann claims consists in his interpretation of "the body of myths," while the interpretation of this "body" is based upon his prior assumptions about how consciousness evolves. Neumann tells us directly what these convictions are and where they come from. His project "links up with that fundamental early work of Jung's, *The Psychology of the Unconscious*" (xvii).[11]

As Jung observes in somewhat different language, Neumann's chief originality consists in projecting the Jungian scheme of libidinal development onto the denatured and homogenized corpus of world mythology. Neumann combines with the Jungian psychology a Hegelian history of consciousness and thus reads world mythology as the stadial growth of archetypal symbolizing that culminates in the self-consciousness of analytical psychology itself. Neumann's historiography resembles Hegel's in its deficiencies also. He repeats the Eurocentrism of Hegel's *Philosophy of History*, purporting on one hand to be describing a universal evolution of consciousness while asserting on the other that only in "Western culture" has "the canon of stadial development embodied in mythological projections become a model for the development of the individual human being" (xix). He indulges continually, too, in a pair of the trickiest of Hegelian practices; he plays fast and loose with the distinction between individual experience and the history of the species and between his schematic generalizations of stages and their applicability to concrete historical circumstances.

Origins is not only a throwback to Hegel; it comprises a showcase of the cultural assumptions of later nineteenth-century romanticism. Neumann's flamboyant and eclectic discourse presses even some of the most far-fetched of these speculations to that point of unintended caricature that makes them especially visible. His unquestioning acceptance of the inheritance of acquired mental characteristics affords an example. His fundamental project—the mapping of Jung's pattern of individual archetypal development onto the psychological development of the species—depends utterly upon the validity of applying the "biogenetic law" in reverse, that is, upon assuming that the phylogeny of the mythological archetypes can be reconstructed retrospectively from present ontogenetic development. Neumann strangely mocks Freud's reliance upon the inheritance of acquired characteristics while accepting without analysis Jung's equally problematic versions of the same doctrine. Neumann cites with approval and everywhere assumes, for example, Jung's sometime claim that "the archetypes . . . of the collective unconscious [are] 'the deposit of ancestral experience'" (24). But Neumann himself is not at all interested in the problem of how this experience can possibly be transmitted. He merely hypostatizes the "psyche" as "a numinous world of transpersonal happenings" (xxiv). Whereas Jung at least acknowledges the difficulties and occasionally brings forward a more plausible hypothesis of a broadly structural sort, Neumann simply waves away the problem as inconvenient to his constructing upon this unexamined foundation his grand history of consciousness.

In the first part of his work Neumann sets out to demonstrate how fully world mythology confirms Jung's identification in his brilliant first book of the heroism of every consciousness as it struggles to escape the primordial unconscious. He dockets "the body of myths" under three Jungian rubrics, "The Creation Myth," "The Hero Myth," and "The Transformation Myth." The Creation Myth is itself subdivided into three stages, "The Uroboros," "The Great Mother," and "The Separation of the World Parents: The Principle of Opposites." For Neumann the *uroboros,* the world-serpent with its tail (or its tale) in its mouth, the ancient symbol of eternity or endless repetition, is the archetype of "the time before the birth of the ego, the time of unconscious envelopment, of swimming in the ocean of the unborn" (12). Even when "Man's" consciousness begins to stir sporadically, he still "for the most part unconscious . . . swims about in his instincts like an animal" (15). Neumann melds here the two presumably literal states of thalassic and amniotic natation, universal and individual, with the third, figurative one of sporadically conscious humankind swimming about "in its instincts." These fusions are characteristic of Neumann's thinking whether at the micro-level of the sentence or the macro-level of his conceptual schema. The embryo is now enjoying a state that he will ever afterward perceive as paradisal. He (it is always *he* in Neumann) also experiences it as union with "the Great and Good Mother" (15), into whom he desires to return in "uroboric incest" (17). Unlike social incest, the uroboric type is the passive desire to dissolve again "in the ocean of pleasure—a *Liebestod*" (17). "The uroboros reigns on as the great whirling wheel of life, where everything not yet individual is submerged in the union of opposites, passing away and willing to pass away" (16). This "non-differentiated state of union between opposites" (18) will be recognized as an echo of Jung's metaphysics, most obviously derived from Schopenhauer. Although Neumann specifically denies that the uroboric state was ever a historical stage, the logic of his appeal to the biogenetic law requires that this once have been the case. He assumes this implicitly when (in a typical instance of contradiction) he remarks "even today we can see from primitives that . . . the desire to remain unconscious is a fundamental human trait" (16). "Primitives" are closer to the early state of the race as children are to its repetition in individuals. Assuming this hoary analogy, Neumann finds it natural to borrow from Lévy-Bruhl a term to express the coziness of the unborn: "One's own being and the surrounding world—in this case, the mother's body—exist in a *participation mystique,* never more to be attained in any other environmental relationship" (33). In short, Neumann's "uroboric" fantasy on the emotional life of the embryo exceeds even Ferenczi's as the ultimate biogenetic version of that *topos* of "dissociation of sensibility" invented by the early romantics.

The second stage of the Creation Myth is dominated by myths of "the Great Mother." "The world experienced by the waking ego of humanity is the world of J. J. Bachofen's matriarchate with its goddesses of motherhood and destiny" (39). It would be inconvenient for Neumann to recognize any anthropology more recent or more informed by investigation than Bachofen's; the evidence would spoil his posited symmetry between racial and individual development. As the newborn's primary relation is with his mother, so must that of males in general must have been to "the matriarchate." Neumann, following Jung into the mists of one of the most pervasive of nineteenth-century cultural clichés, identifies consciousness with masculinity ("consciousness has a masculine character" [42]) and unconsciousness with femininity. As the individual child's maturation consists in gradually conscious detachment from the pull of his unconscious relation with his mother, so this historical stage is the tale of the struggles of the "masculine" ego for independence. This is a world of "primitive dread" (41). "The maternal *uroboros* overshadows it like a dark and tragic fate" (45). Neumann concurs, however, with the sometime Freudian anthropologist Géza Róheim that ego-anxiety is the source of culture. Out of the dread of the female unconsciousness the daylight consciousness of the male constructs "culture, religion, art and science . . . to overcome this fear by giving it concrete expression" (41). The only original aspect of this fantasia is the fervor with which Neumann dwells on the stages of the male escape from female engulfment.[12] He incorporates Frazer's fertility gods in the next substage, "the figure of the son-lover," by remarking, for example, that "the young men whom the mother selects for her lovers may impregnate her, they may even be fertility gods, but the fact remains that they are only phallic consorts of the Great Mother, drones serving the queen bee, who are killed off as soon as they have performed their duty of fecundation" (48).

This evolution leads to the third major substage of the Creation Myth, "The Separation of the World Parents." Here Neumann attempts to fit to his pattern the tales, disseminated worldwide, that describe creation as the separation of the earth and sky by their rebellious children. He allegorizes this immense range of tales, abstracted even more forcibly than usual from their cultural settings, as signifying the achievement of self-consciousness, with its concomitant guilt over the detachment of the ego from primal unity. This is the Jungian equivalent to Freud's fable in *Totem and Taboo*. Though Neumann makes a stab at including both "World Parents" in his phenomenology of alienation, his equation of consciousness with masculinity constrains him (just as it does Jung in *Symbols of Transformation*) to represent the revolt as being primarily against the Great Mother. Neumann passes this off with his usual graceful jugglery, but the element of revolt against male sky gods as well as female earth gods, so much more consonant with Freudian theory, drops out of focus, even though it is dominant in mythologies such as the Greek and the Polynesian.

The second of the three major categories into which Neumann shoehorns world mythology is "The Hero Myth." He distinguishes three subdivisions, "The Birth of the Hero," "The Slaying of the Father," and "The Slaying of the Mother," all three, in a sense, expansions of "The Separation of the World Parents." But "developments which, at that stage, could only be represented in cosmic symbols now enter the phase of humanization and personality formation" (131). That is to say, now that Neumann's evolutionary schema has caught up with Jung's stages in *Symbols of Transformation*, he is ready to focus his allegory on the growth of the individual ego rather than on the development of corporate humanity. The hero is the "twice-born," he who is inducted into the life of the spirit, that is, into culture itself, by initiation into the male secret societies whose *raison d'être* is to transcend in the spiritual bonding of masculine totemism the biologically natural units of matriarchy. These ideas blend Harrison and Jung, Bachofen, and Briffault. Again, what is distinctive is the scope of the sexism. "All human culture, and not Western civilization alone, is masculine in character" (143).

Neumann of course prides himself on his Jungian (and romantic) exaltation of "the feminine" and seems oblivious of the actual attitudes he expresses toward women, which range from patronizing containment to open fear. When he reaches his next subset, "The Slaying of the Mother," he announces his intention of correcting Jung's early version of "the dragon fight." Jung, he says, was still so much under the influence of Freud that he made the mistake of viewing the temptation of the hero to revert to the Mother as "the regression of an already developed masculinity" (157). He ought to have distinguished between "the feminine element in the androgynous son-lover," an immature phase of development, and the hero's "active incest, the deliberate, conscious exposing of himself to the dangerous influence of the female" (156). Only this latter type of incest ("incest" presumably because every woman is Mother) is the properly fecundating return to the unconscious that is the source of creativity. The male visitor is there to pick up something he needs, while carefully controlling the experience. By thus correcting Jung's notion that this act of introversion is "regression," Neumann sentimentalizes Jung's psychology of creativity in a manner strikingly analogous to the way in which the Freudian ego-psychologists sentimentalize Freud's conception of the unconscious. For Freud and Jung creative breakthroughs do involve just that "archaic and regressive phenomenon . . . relapse into a primitive mode of functioning" (207), that their embarrassed followers try to rationalize as well within conscious control. Where Jung describes a merging with or incorporation of the *anima,* Neumann advocates a sanitized sampling of it. He preserves the Jungian identification of the unconscious as feminine but expresses everywhere that "fear of the female" that he swears is universal in the other half of the human race. When *his* hero descends into the depths to do battle with the mother-dragon, he goes armed with the blinding, apotropaic shield of the higher, masculine "spirituality." Neumann downplays correspondingly "The Slaying of the Father." Whereas for Jung both parents are equally dangerous to the young hero, for Neumann "compared with the uniform frightfulness of the mother dragon, the father dragon is a culturally stratified structure. . . . she is nature, he is culture" (189).

After "The Hero Myth" comes the third major rubric, "The Transformation Myth." Neumann thus adapts as the name for his third category of world myth Jung's term for the psychic gain induced under pressure from the archetypes. He considers the title appropriate because he holds that myths of this type allegorize self-reflexively acts of psychic empowerment. As in the case of Hegel's phenomenology of the spirit, they refer to the very movements of mind that have now revealed themselves to their enlightened proponent, that is, to the principles of analytic psychology. Neumann carries Jung, as usual, one step further. Jung cites the myths of the freeing of the captive maiden and the winning of the treasure as the prime examples of stories that celebrate the transformative process itself. But Neumann maintains that these myths express the implicit recognition by "early man" of the significance and even the specific concepts of analytic psychology, the "primary reality of psychic dominants, archetypes, primordial images, instincts and patterns of behavior" (210). Analytic psychology in the caverns of Lascaux.

This claim is based in what might be called Neumann's philosophy of the image. His psychological determinism impels him to out-Lamarck even the privately indulged speculations of Freud and Ferenczi. He asserts that the nervous system itself is "an organic product of the unconscious" (296) and that the unconscious, having constructed an organ for itself, proceeded to build the mind as we know it. The ego is only "a sense organ which perceives the world and the unconscious by means of images" (294). These images are what Neumann understands Jung to mean by "archetypes," the pictorial form in which instincts manifest themselves to consciousness. The harnessing of these "numinous" signals from the benign universal Process not only benefits the individual psyche; it is also the source of humanity's total cultural achievement. "The reality of all culture, our own included, consists in realizing these images which lie dormant in the psyche" (210). A writer who claims that the invention of dairy-farming and pottery, mathematics and music, are all the result of realized "images" is clearly in the late stages of that *imagitis panglossialis* that took so fearsome a toll during the midcentury and for which there is still no known cure.

The second half of *The Origins and History of Consciousness* takes up "the archetypal stages of conscious development—as known from mythological projection—with a view to understanding their psychological significance for the formation and development of the personality" (266). Insofar as it does focus on this task, it is not directly relevant to the conceptualizing of "myth." But the very recapitulation that Neumann postulates between phylogenetic and ontogenetic experience guarantees indirect relevance. The second half of the work, freed of the pressure of fitting world mythology to the procrustean bed of Jungian libidinal development, clarifies in particular some of Neumann's affiliations with and appropriations of other parts of the neo-romantic canon that seems to be cohering in the midcentury.

The most significant of these relationships is his co-opting of religious phenomenology. In Neumann's scheme of things, the history of the evolution of religious consciousness is a special case of the evolution of all culture from awareness of the archetypes. He adopts the notion, popular among affectively minded social theorists, that "the group psyche" preceded development of individual awareness. He cites approvingly "Tardes' formula that 'the social, like the hypnotic, state is only a form of dreaming'" (270) and to characterize this state he borrows from Lévy-Bruhl the term "participation mystique." "A mythological apperception of the world and an archetypal, instinctive mode of reaction are accordingly characteristic of the dawn man" (274). This condition produces "hypostatization of a group soul, a collective consciousness" of a highly religious nature and "a primitive monotheism . . . for it is just here that we find the uroboros projected as a totality figure" (282).

Neumann explains in similar fashion "the age of the great mythologies" (304) after the Magna Mater has succeeded the uroboros as "the fragmentation—splitting up or splitting off—of archetypes and complexes" (320). "The unbearable white radiance of primordial light is broken up by the prism of consciousness into a multicolored rainbow of images and symbols" (323). The believer responds to the manifestation of the Process/Deity in the archetype and promptly refracts it in whatever wavelengths of cultural interpretation are available to him. The results may be expressed equivocally as either religious or psychological. In Neumann's obligatory third stage of mythmaking, "secondary personalization," this ambiguity is interiorized. He defines "secondary personalization" as "a persistent tendency in man to take primary and transpersonal contents as personal" (336). Neumann's account of this personalization makes it clear that he reduces religion, in the end, to psychological explanation. In his metaphors religion is the vehicle, psychology the tenor. Even if humankind invents its gods according to culture-bound hermeneutics, it discovers them in encounter with the Process that manifests itself through archetypes. Analytic psychology is Neumann's religion; yet he does affirm the existence of a "transpersonal" Reality revealed, not in discreditable words, but in "numinous" images, not in history, but in eternally recurrent oracles, and in doing so he increases the amenability of Jungian psychology to traditional religious interpretation.

Neumann also sketches in the latter part of the work some of the narrative consequences of the course of "secondary personalization." In the third stage of mythmaking the gods arrive, he says, "with their earthly counterparts, the *mana* heroes, who possess an archetypal rather than an historical character. Hence the dragon-slaying hero . . . is the archetypal exemplar . . . of all historical heroes" (337). At first "the earliest historiographers always tried to bring the individual hero into line with the archetype of the primordial hero and thus produced a kind of mythologized historiography. An example of this is "the Christianization of the Jesus figure, where all the mythical traits peculiar to the hero and redeemer figure were sketched in afterwards" (337 n.). This particular "mythologizing process is the exact opposite of secondary personalization," but Neumann maintains that in the long run personalization guarantees that "the center of gravity of the hero figure is displaced towards the human activity of the ego." Its advance "can be observed in literature," for instance, "where mythological motifs turn into fairy tales and finally into the earliest romances" (338). He cites as a good example of this "descent" the way in which the Egyptian myth of Osiris (which he examines at length in *Origins* as the consummate symbol of psychic self-transformation) "changes into the Story of the Two Brothers . . . and finally dwindles to a 'family' novel in which the immemorial drama has taken on personalistic features." This descent of the archetypal model toward increasingly "realistic" heroes does not entail for Neumann, however, any sense of loss; secondary personalization means that the archetypal heroism projected externally by archaic humanity is now to be encountered and repossessed within the psyche. Neumann's version of this "displacement" strikingly resembles Frye's and is almost certainly his complementary rejoinder to the ritualist version of it in Lord Raglan's *Hero*.

AVATARS OF THE HERO: RAGLAN, GRAVES, CAMPBELL

Lord Raglan makes out "the Hero" through the spectacles of Ritualist anthropology rather than depth psychology and thus has little to say directly about myth. But the impact of his work upon mythographic theorizing is considerable. *The Hero* commences with a sustained attack on the reliability of traditional narrative as history. "All traditional narrative," Raglan proclaims, "originates in ritual" (Raglan

1975, 41). He is similarly absolute about "myth," which is always "a narrative linked with a rite" (117). He marshals in support the names of Frazer and all the principal luminaries of both ritualist schools. He is in particularly close accord with the later group who consider myth to be derivative from rituals of divine kingship, and he quotes with approval S. H. Hooke's summary of the general plot of such ritual-myths. "'This pattern consisted of a dramatic ritual representing the death and resurrection of the king who was also the god. . . . It comprised a sacred combat, in which was enacted the victory of the god over his enemies, a triumphant procession . . . an enthronement . . . and a sacred marriage'" (150). At this point, Raglan takes his original leap. He maintains that we can find these god-kings' stories "displaced" in the tales of legendary heroes—Achilles and Ajax, Moses and Samson, Cuchulainn and King Arthur.

"The god," Raglan explains, "is the hero as he appears in ritual, and the hero is the god as he appears in myth" (203). This epigrammatic summary of the understanding that prevailed in the kingship rites may appear merely to assert the identification of god and hero, but it contains that romantic principle of decline initially articulated in the work of the Grimms and subsequently widely disseminated among folklorists and ethnologists. *Narrative* is by definition a secondary rationalization of the primary deed of ritual. It isn't surprising, therefore, that some of the stories accompanying rites later become detached, degenerate into "saga," "a form of novel based chiefly upon myth" (129), and eventually into "folk-tale," which does not originate among "the people" as secular story but only winds up there as the ultimate debasement of aristocratic religion. Meanwhile, as a story descends the scale of genres, it presents increasingly "displaced" analogues of the plot and characters of the sacred original. Thus, for example, "romance is . . . myth in disguise" (216). This theory should suggest immediately Northrop Frye, but we have also encountered embryonic versions of it in Wheelwright and Neumann, all three testifying to the widespread impact of *The Hero*. Raglan's influence in literary circles is broader still because his work promotes the corollary that every narrative will reflect to some degree its origin in ritual, of which it remains an analogue. If all narrative descends from myth and myth is always connected to rite, then narrative must still remain to some degree what it once supremely was, an analogue of ritual. More specifically, the thesis that dominates the last third of *The Hero*, that "traditional narrative, in all its forms is based . . . upon dramatic ritual or ritual drama" (278), links the Cambridge Ritualists and the Divine Kingship school with midcentury American analysts of drama as ritual like Francis Fergusson and C. L. Barber, and it constitutes an important element in New Critical theories of literature.

Raglan does not subscribe explicitly to the domestication of the hero. His account of the devolution from god to hero deals only with a remote, oral past, and, on top of this, he scorns depth psychology, the one theoretical development most responsible for encouraging the direct connection.[13] (It would be natural to suppose that he was inspired by Rank's *Myth of the Birth of the Hero,* but apparently he never read his psychoanalytic predecessor.) Nevertheless, Raglan does stimulate the trend toward domestication. As Northrop Frye teaches us in his "historical theory of modes," any given conception of "the hero" will express the fantasy of its particular historical era. The famous section of *The Hero* in which Raglan discriminates twenty-two features of the archetypal biography and checks against this list the careers of twenty-two traditional heroes, reveals how well his conception of "the hero" dovetails with the clinical picture sketched by the depth psychologists. The first twelve features of the life match impressively the features distinguished by Rank in *The Myth of the Birth of the Hero*.[14] Rank, of course, is interested in the Oedipal patterns in the life of the *youthful* hero and, like Jung in *Symbols of Transformation,* says little about the hero's later trajectory. For the hero in old age Raglan's model is the story of Oedipus as represented in Sophocles' two dramas. The king reigns until he loses the favor of the gods and/or his subjects, is driven from the throne, and meets a mysterious death, often upon the top of a hill. His children don' t succeed him, and his body isn't buried; nevertheless, he is worshiped at one or more shrines. This late pattern is quite as amenable to depth psychology as the early one, and subsequent midcentury theorists have by and large found Raglan's work highly complementary to the psychologists' account of the hero.

Raglan also adumbrates in *The Hero* a further step in the psychological domestication of "myth," a step usually credited to Joseph Campbell in *The Hero with a Thousand Faces.* Raglan argues that the consistency with which the heroic life pattern centers upon the great liminal moments—birth, initiation, marriage, death—demonstrates its descent from early "rites of passage." Rites of this sort have been understood at least since Arnold van Gennep's pioneering *Les Rites de Passage* (1908), to have accompanied most members of early societies in all parts of the world through life's major transitions. By arguing that the life-pattern of "the Hero" evolves from such generally experienced rites, Raglan inevitably implies that this pattern of fantasy projects the actual experience of immemorial generations of ordinary people. Given Raglan's scholarly orientation and his distrust of depth psychology, it isn't surprising that he doesn't himself extrapolate the relevance of so universal a pattern onto the lives of modern persons, but the clue is there.

Robert Graves shares with Raglan a broadly ritualist orientation. While Raglan is closest, however, to the scholarly antiquarians of the Divine Kingship school, Graves belongs to the livelier branch represented by the writings of Jessie Weston and Margaret Murray. Like them, he extrapolates from the assumptions of Frazer and Harrison the disguised survival throughout Christian Europe and into the present of a pagan fertility religion that celebrates a supreme mother-goddess. Graves's *White Goddess* (1948) is probably second only to Weston's *From Ritual to Romance* in lodging this notion in the popular imagination. Graves promptly confronts the reader of his foreword with the argument in all its vulnerability: "My thesis is that the language of poetic myth anciently current in the Mediteranean and Northern Europe was a magical language bound up with popular religious ceremonies in honor of the Moon-goddess, or Muse, some of them dating from the Old Stone Age, and that this remains the language of true poetry" (Graves 1966, 9). This magical language was nearly obliterated along with the religion it expressed as "patrilinear" invaders from Asia spread across Europe, but both survived through the Middle Ages "in the poetic colleges of Ireland and Wales, and in the witchcovens of Western Europe." Three intertwined assumptions of this argument seem particularly relevant here: (1) the worship of a mother goddess lies behind Mediterranean, Germanic, and Celtic mythology; (2) survivals of "poetic myth," reveal, if properly understood, traces of this religion; (3) the "grammar and vocabulary" of this "magical language" are still interpretable by a few *cognoscenti* who understand the hermeneutical practice of "iconotrophy."

Graves quite plainly conceives of *The White Goddess* as an improved, properly generalized *Golden Bough*. The goddess is a fertility deity, the product of a putative "matriarchal" stage of Paleolithic culture. She is associated above all with the three principal phases of the moon—new, full, and waning—analogous with the three phases of woman: maiden, nymph, and crone. The male worshiper (with whom Graves is exclusively concerned) experiences these trinal aspects as the three phases of his destiny with respect both to the goddess herself and to the mortal women who are her avatars. He is in turn child, hero-lover, and doomed mortal trapped in the inexorable rotation of her immortal seasons. We are in the grip of yet another post-romantic, male construction of experience itself as female, and represented as a mysterious woman, generally (as in Keats, Pater, Rossetti, Rider Haggard, and so forth) an immortal being whose relation to her mortal lovers is sadomasochistic. Graves's special contribution to this nineteenth-century *topos* has been to promote it from literary fantasy to anthropological verity.

But Graves's assertions about the active presence of this religion in the lives of contemporary men and women, which resemble those of Yeats discussed in chapter 6, forbid us from relegating it to the remote past. To the extent that Graves holds encounter with the goddess or her earthly representatives to be the fate, or potential fate, of men even today, he, too, participates in that domestication of "myth" that consists so largely of transmuting an anthropological past into the psychological present. John Vickery points out in his study of Graves that the goddess represents a double identification of the female, not only with nature, but with the unconscious (Vickery 1972, xi). In imagining the ordinary male as a questing hero who experiences the Goddess as maiden, nymph, and crone, Graves echoes, knowingly or not, Freud's personifications of this process at the end of his essay on the death-instinct, "The Three Caskets." As for Jung's presence, his version of the hero's libidinal development could be illustrated by passages from Graves's most famous poem, "To Juan at the Winter Solstice." *The White Goddess* engages Frazer's subject and employs his method in order to elaborate a post-romantic allegory derived from the sexist thematics of Freud and Jung.

The second and third strands of Graves's argument—that evidence of Goddess worship has survived and that this evidence is apparent to anyone who knows how to look for it—comprise another instance of the midcentury reemergence of the romantic symbol as vehicle of mythic insight. Like Harrison and Weston, Graves imitates Frazer in stringing the "curious learning" that supports his argument upon the thread of a purported solution to a scholarly puzzle—how the religion of the goddess managed to survive, encoded in the work of two medieval Welsh poets. Graves's specific hermeneutical principle is the detection and reversal of what he calls "iconotrophy," defined as "a technique of deliberate misrepresentation by which ancient ritual icons are twisted in meaning in order to confirm a profound change of the existent religious system" (219 n.).[15] His iconotrophic-decoding construal of a woodcut of "The Judgment of Paris" may serve as a brief illustration of the method: "Obviously the three Goddesses are, as usual, the three persons of the ancient Triple Goddess, not jealous rivals, and obviously the Love-goddess is giving the apple to the Shepherd . . . not receiving it from him. It is the apple of immortality and he is the young Dionysus" (257).

This example of the method, as well as the etymology of the term, indicates how thoroughly Graves's conception of "iconotrophy" is dominated by visual symbolism. The skill required to decode it is a kind of "poetic thought" that resolves "speech into its *original* images and rhythms" (my italics) and recombines these "on several simultaneous levels of thought into a multiple sense" (223). This is symbolist aesthetics as hermeneutic principle. It's no surprise that the result resembles so closely D. H. Lawrence's *Apocalypse* (discussed in chapter 6) in its recovery of a repressed Paleolithic religion, alleged to survive in distorted, encoded texts, above all in visual images, whose true meaning is accessible, in flashes, to the right sort of poetic intuition. This "language of true poetry" is everywhere the same and communicates across all barriers of time and culture to the initiate who has learned to "think mythically" (409). Graves promises his readers in the subtitle of *The White Goddess* a "historical grammar of poetic myth," but this is pretentious hyperbole. "Poetic myth" that conveys fleeting imagistic insights into an alleged Stone Age religion is not susceptible to being analyzed as a grammar, even a metaphorical one. Graves's argument is a string of idiosyncratic beads of insight, and the failure of its aspirations stands revealed when he remarks that the results of iconotrophic decoding are "mythographic statements . . . perfectly reasonable to the few poets who can still think and talk in poetic shorthand" (223). The systematic "grammar" is now reduced to a "poets' . . . shorthand," helpless to close the gap between these fortunate few and *hoi polloi. The White Goddess* is essential reading for anyone seeking to understand Graves; it is his *ars poetica,* even his *apologia pro vita sua.* But it asserts the reality of every man's potentially heroic experience of the goddess when the only hero in sight is the author, celebrating his gnostic salvation.

Joseph Campbell is closest to Graves in his background in literary romanticism, and to Neumann in both his broadly Jungian orientation and his ambition to abstract from the culture-bound and historically situated mythologies of the world a unified-field theory. The comparison with Neumann is particularly inevitable since Neumann's *Origins* and Campbell's *Hero with a Thousand Faces* both appeared in 1949, as a kind of two-pronged Jungian *blitzkrieg,* the former focused on world mythology as expressive of the heroism appropriate to the first half of life, and the latter of the heroism appropriate to the second half. Campbell's totalizing ambition first appears, only slightly displaced, in *A Skeleton Key to Finnegans Wake* (1944), where the goal and its alleged attainment, as suggested in chapter 6, are projected upon James Joyce.[16] Within five years Campbell produced in *Hero* what he describes as both "an elementary comparative study of the universal forms" of myth and a prolegomena to a full synthesis of world mythology (Campbell 1973, 39). This latter he published as *The Masks of God,* in four volumes, between 1959 and 1968.

Although some of Campbell's later writings occasionally introduce changes of mind and new inconsistencies, *Hero* and *Masks* carry the major weight of his theorizing.

The division of *Hero* into "The Adventures of the Hero" and "The Cosmogonic Cycle" is broadly expressive of the same "biogenetic analogy" that determines Neumann's bipartite division into mythological and psychological stages in the evolution of consciousness. But this broad resemblance houses within it major philosophical disparities. Neumann hews to the Jungian tenet that, since the highest object of knowledge is the very process of analytic psychology, the representations of the archetypes ultimately symbolize transformation itself. This is why he begins with mythological stages of consciousness and concludes in the second half in a parallel history of psychological evolution. Campbell, in contrast, intends "a comparative, not genetic, study" focused entirely on "the hero" (39). Hence he devotes the first part of his work to the morphology of the hero's "adventure" in *both* mythological and psychological terms, and reserves the second half for an account of the hero's spiritual biography, centered on his religious enlightenment and on the subsequent benefits he returns to confer on his society. Whereas Neumann's work moves toward the culmination of consciousness in analytic psychology, Campbell's proceeds, in his own words, "from psychology to metaphysics" (255). He might better have said "to epistemology." His metaphysics, such as it is, is very close to Jung's—Schopenhauer's will sentimentalized as beneficient—the most significant difference being that Campbell understands that he does entertain metaphysical presuppositions whereas Jung blindly denies it. What Campbell actually dwells on in his second half, departing radically in this respect from Jung and Neumann, is what the hero can know about this universal process and how he knows it.[17] For Jung, and even for Neumann, myth is merely an important tool in the study of the archetypes, which constitute in turn the most valuable form of evidence salvaged from the unconscious in the conduct of an individual therapy. Though the archetypes are manifestations of a benign universal process, we do not, cannot, and need not know anything more about the nature of this process. For Campbell, on the contrary, "myths" are the necessary and entirely self-sufficient pathway to direct knowledge of the universal will. Neither the unconscious nor therapy enters the picture; the "goal of myth" is a conscious gnostic wisdom that effects "a reconciliation of the individual consciousness with the universal will" through a "realization of the true relationship of the passing phenomena of time to the imperishable life that lives and dies in all" (238). The hero is he who comes to *know* the universal will, and Campbell's "cosmogonic cycle" is the record of this individual life-story "repeating itself world without end" (261) in the fables and scriptures of corporate humanity.

Invoking without irony Joyce's mocking term from *Finnegans Wake,* Campbell summarizes thus his own "monomyth": "A hero ventures forth from the world of common day into a region of supernatural wonder: fabulous forces are there encountered and a decisive victory is won: the hero comes back from this mysterious adventure with the power to bestow boons on his fellow man" (30). This tripartite pattern of "Departure," "Initiation," and "Return" derives most specifically from Jung's account of youthful libidinal development. But it is also inspired, as Campbell notes, by van Gennep's systematic classification of "primitive" "rites of passage," according to the major stages of life. Campbell views these rites in Jungian terms as designed to help members of small, traditional societies over life's "difficult thresholds of transformation" (10). By thus connecting the Jungian story of the archetypal quest with very generally experienced "rites of passage," Campbell makes an explicit move toward the domestication of "the hero" that remains only potential in his predecessors. Whereas "the Hero" of Rank and Raglan is the larger-than-life protagonist of legend, Campbell's is, in theory at least, the ordinary human being who has known how to take advantage of universally available enlightenment. The eventual reduction of his missionary zeal to the notion that heroic transformation of the self through myth is no further away than your corner bookstore is nicely travestied in the title of his *Myths to Live By* (1972).

   The Hero with a Thousand Faces has provoked from the start serious scholarly objections that only increase in volume and intensity in response to Campbell's later work. Apart from the central gnostic claim, he has been most generally criticized, perhaps, for the scissors-and-paste ransacking of the world's archives of sacred story that is his version of the Frazerian comparative method. Campbell, too, habitually prescinds from cultural contexts and levels generic distinctions between everything from folktale to sacred scriptures. And in one respect he outdoes Frazer. He seldom sticks with a particular story long enough to demonstrate the soundness of his reading of it; instead he trims relentlessly whatever tidbits he plucks from their original contexts until they fit his universal allegory. Equally exasperating is the continual inconsistency of his key concepts, including "hero" and "myth." But the one inconsistency that calls for particular notice before we leave *The Hero with a Thousand Faces* is that same central contradiction about the availability of heroism so evident in Graves. On one hand, Campbell sells "myth" as the universal panacea. On the other, he represents "the hero" as being, in the more conventional sense, a remarkable exception. "The hero" breaks through the limitations of the ego to a moment in which, like Nietzsche's Zarathustra recognizing and accepting the eternal return of the same, he identifies with the universal will. He also comprehends that his newly acquired wisdom casts him as the only hope of renewal for the culture in which he lives. Campbell categorizes according to a Carlylean taxonomy the historical roles, the "transformations of the hero"—Warrior, Lover, Ruler, World Redeemer, Saint—through which this salvific act has been accomplished. None of these capitalized roles appears quite the right fit for the person reading in his aromatherapist's waiting room a newly purchased copy of *Myths to Live By*.

   Campbell presents *Hero* as a kind of *Skeleton Key* to *The Masks of God*. His pretext for homogenizing in the earlier work the "adventure of the hero" and a "cosmogonic cycle" that is "presented with astonishing consistency in the sacred writings of all continents" (39) is that he reserves developmental and cultural distinctions for the sequel in preparation. But *Masks of God* is so constructed that beneath its pose as a disinterested survey of the structure and history of world mythology, it constitutes an enlarged special plea for the romantic gnosticism advocated in *Hero*. The work is built, in fact, upon a complex of rather startlingly regressive cultural presuppositions whose cumulative effect suggests a mind dominated almost exclusively by the stereotypes of late romanticism. The most fundamental of these appear in a series of diacritical contraries—hunter/planter, shaman/priest, male/female, exaltation/submergence of the individual, West/East, Aryan/Semite—in which the left-hand concepts are assimilated to one another and valorized over the comparably associated right-hand terms.

The major distinction by which Campbell organizes his first volume, *Primitive Myth,* is the same division of world cultures into tropical plant-growers and northern-hemisphere hunters favored by Eliade, the distinction pioneered by the cultural geographer Ratzel and prolonged in the German anthropological tradition by Schmidt, Frobenius, and Jensen. Campbell extrapolates this contrast into a version of Bergson's "two sources of morality," the lower conservatism of the masses and the higher innovativeness of independent individuals. He doesn't deny the efficacy of the planters' religion, the ritual sacrifice for fertility beloved of Frazer, for it seems that in this act the "primitive" planter experiences the love-death mystique of Schopenhauer and Wagner, "an effective realization of the immortality of being itself and its play through all things . . . in a stunning crisis of release from the psychology of guilt and mortality" (Campbell 1976, vol. 1, 180–181). But Campbell valorizes by comparison the religion and mythology of the northern hunters, centered upon the psychology of their spiritual leader, the shaman. Whereas the spiritual leader of planter religion is the priest, official representative of the cult, the shaman is the lone individual who "as a consequence of a personal psychological crisis has gained a certain power of his own" (231). We have met this fellow before. In a prime example of circular reasoning, Campbell later decides that "since it has been precisely the shamans that have taken the lead in the formation of mythology and rites throughout the primitive world, the primary problem of our subject would seem to be not historical or ethnological, but psychological" (350). There is no entry for "Durkheim" in the indices of *Masks.*

The second volume, *Oriental Mythology,* attends primarily to the "higher" religions of Egypt, Mesopotamia, India, China, and Japan. Campbell now shifts the burden of his subtext onto three new pairs of contrasting concepts, West/East, Aryan/Semitic, and life-affirming/life-negating. He sketches these dichotomies in his opening chapter, "The Signatures of the Four Great Domains." The first division, between East and West, is straight romantic orientalizing of the sort formulated by Friedrich Schlegel when he recoiled after his conversion to Catholicism from his earlier enthusiasm for the wisdom of India. As Campbell puts the point, the East teaches that "there is nothing to be gained, either for the universe or for man, through individual originality and effort" (Campbell 1976, vols. 2, 3). Though Campbell is fascinated by and approves of much in "Oriental" mythology, his New Shamanism guarantees that in the last analysis he will treat "the East" as Hegel does in *The Philosophy of History.*

But he divides his dichotomy again, to produce his quadripartite "domains." He distinguishes within both East and West between religions that are life-affirming and life-denying. Western religions can be sorted into those of "Levantine" (alias "Semitic") inspiration—Zoroastrianism, Judaism, Christianity, and Islam—that magnify the almightiness of God at the expense of humanity, and those of "Aryan" inspiration like Greek Olympianism that engage in promethean affirmation of humanity. Eastern religions display a comparable difference; whereas the goal of Indian religion has been escape from the phenomenal world, the goal of Chinese and especially of Japanese has been to live in total rapport with it. Campbell offers us a representative image of religious behavior in each of these "domains": "Prometheus, Job, the seated Buddha, eyes closed, and the Wandering Sage, eyes open" (33). As a consequence of this table of values, Campbell reverses the Hegelian direction of march; he starts with the hieratic city-states of Egypt and Mesopotamia and ends with Japan. Even at its best in Zen Buddhism, however, Eastern religion is limited by its refusal of the absolute value of individual experience. It is from this perspective, too, that Campbell now denigrates the "seated Buddha, eyes closed," whose advocacy of "dissolution of the ego" he had previously celebrated in *Hero*. Campbell is still not rejecting this "dissolution" as a good, but, rather, assuming that its only properly earned context would be the culminating acceptance by the assertive, masculine, Western "hero," of the passive, feminine, "Oriental" side of his own nature. Such a moment of mystical breakthrough constitutes, after all, not only the full psychological integration of the hero, but also the reconciliation of all apparent "cosmogonic" contradictions. Belief in this ultimate reconciliation of opposites may account, in fact, for Campbell's seeming indifference to the major inconsistencies and downright antinomies in his own work.

Campbell's "heroic" subtext becomes increasingly apparent in his third and fourth volumes. *Occidental Mythology* celebrates the "humanistic . . . native mythologies of Europe; the Greek, Roman, Celtic and Germanic" (Campbell 1976, vols. 3, 4) as opposed to the anti-humanistic and invasive religions of "Levantine" origin. This distinction between foreign, Semitic religions and indigenous Indo-European or "Aryan" ones betrays with particular directness the extent to which Campbell's metahistorical fancies are dominated by the racist doctrines of the late nineteenth century that grew in particular out of German romanticism and are transmitted to Campbell through a number of his most formative enthusiasms.

The indigenous religions of Europe are not only superior to the "Levantine" in their masculinity but, paradoxically enough, in their femininity, too. For even though the "Aryan" religions replace matriarchy by patriarchy, they are distinguished from their rigid Semitic rivals by their implicit tolerance of the ancient Goddess worship. Borrowing a figure in which Frobenius characterizes the planter mythologies as "the invisible counterplayer in the history of the culture of mankind," Campbell declares the repressed Mother Goddess to be "effective as a counterplayer in the unconscious of civilization as a whole" (70). By thus psychologizing Frobenius's concept Campbell re-creates the standard romantic identification of "woman" with both nature and the unconscious that appears in various modernist artists and in depth psychology. In one of his few sustained comments on any text, he reads *The Odyssey,* including the role of Tiresias, in terms remarkably similar to Ezra Pound's in his *Cantos*. Odysseus's encounters "represent psychological adventures in the mythic realm of the archetypes of the soul, where the male must experience the import of the female" (164). Campbell echoes Jessie Weston, Pound, and

Graves in discovering everywhere, encoded in textual, archaeological, and above all iconographical evidence transparent to those who possess the hermeneutical key, the survival into the early Middle Ages of a secret tradition of true *illuminati* privy to this form of sexual enlightenment.

After its long career underground, this esoteric knowledge of the goddess breaks into the open in the great romances of the high Middle Ages, then disappears until it flourishes again in Wagner and the modernist masterpieces of Joyce and Mann. This is the principal historical burden of the final volume of *Masks, Creative Mythology*. Campbell defines "creative mythology" as "the vision of an adequate individual loyal to his own experience of value" (Campbell 1976, vols. 4, 7). The "adequate" individual is one capable of wresting for himself the timeless enlightenment continually rediscovered by this line of esoteric descent. A certain flavor of Cold War chauvinism creeps into this later conception of the hero, who is expected to exhibit the self-reliance and individualism of your real American and is most likely to be found these days in the land of the free.

After the two-thousand-plus pages of Campbell's treatise on mythology, we are left more uncertain than ever of just what he understands by myth. At the beginning of *Hero* "myth is the secret opening through which the inexhaustible energies of the cosmos pour into human cultural manifestations" (3). Although Campbell does take a stab near the beginning of *Masks* (vol. 1, 30–49) at theorizing the *origin* of myth in "innate releasing mechanisms" and "supernormal sign stimuli," (a kind of *Gestalt* modification of the Jungian archetype), this explanation quickly collapses into the notion of "myth" as an honorific term for any sign that stimulates a sense of special illumination. Near the end of the work (vol. 4, 608–624) Campbell lists the four *functions* of myth as (1) religious (to stir in us the sense of the sacred); (2) cosmological (to provide us with a coherent world-picture); (3) sociological (to validate the social order); (4) psychological (to center and harmonize the individual). But he proceeds to argue (like Wheelwright and Eliade) that the first three functions have collapsed in our day, and he concludes that we must therefore depend for salvation on the fourth.[18] In the end he is so intent upon this personal psychological rescue that he is interested only in the *meaning* of myth for the individual.[19] His shifting employment of the concept in *Masks* merely throws us back upon the paradoxical opening definition in *Hero*. Myth is any sign that induces a gnostic epiphany of romantic panentheism; it is "secret" and yet so universally available that it is responsible for "every human cultural manifestation." It is worth noticing, finally, the ironic historical gap in Campbell's canon of *illuminati*. He projects romantic values backward upon the twelfth-century narratives of Gottfried von Strassbourg and Wolfram von Eschenbach and forward upon the modernist artists while remaining entirely silent about the actual historical intervention of which his sensibility is largely the product. If Campbell ignores his historical rootedness in the romantics, his unrecognized and uncritical magnification of their thinking is the return of the repressed with a vengeance.

[9]

Folkloristic Myth in Social Anthropology I:
Malinowski, Boas, and Their Spheres of Influence

In the four preceding chapters we have observed transcendentalist constructors of myth quick to buttress their theories with the authority of ethnographic evidence. But the decades of sedentary speculation based upon the likes of Frazer and the Cambridge Ritualists are also those of the rise of modern social anthropology, characterized by its own rite of initiation—systematic fieldwork. This activity goes its own way, developing a wealth of observation and hypothesis that seriously challenges, when it does not undermine altogether, the pretensions of much of the theorizing about myth represented in the last three chapters. Anthropological fieldworkers find the sort of storytelling *they* label "myth" to be far too deeply expressive of the interrelated social phenomena of given cultures to permit of its communicating a universal significance that transcends history. Even these observers do not escape unscathed from the consequences of applying to certain indigenous oral narratives the term "myth," with all its romantic freight upon its back. But they profit immensely from the fact that their "myth" denotes actual performances in concrete social contexts.

The following two chapters supply particulars of these very broad assertions. They focus especially upon three central theorists—Bronislaw Malinowski, Franz Boas, and Claude Lévi-Strauss—and to a lesser degree upon some of their predecessors and successors who have contributed to the construction of "myth" in twentieth-century anthropology, especially English and American. This attention excludes a number of distinguished contributors, Continental anthropologists in particular, who seem relatively dispensable here because their assumptions and conclusions reflect by now familiar thinking, especially of transcendentalist varieties. I have in mind, for instance, the quondam Freudian Géza Róheim; Wilhelm Schmidt, organizer and chief theorist of the quest for "high gods" behind "primitive" mythologies; and Leo Frobenius, the inventor of an essentialized black African consciousness. The list might well include Frobenius's student Adolph Jensen, whose work in New Guinea, like that of the French missionary and ethnographer Maurice Leenhardt in New Caledonia, is deeply affected by phenomenology of religion. It should also include Marcel Griaule and his co-workers, whose inductions by the Dogon of Nigeria into their intricate levels of symbolic thought return us to Frobenius's essentializing. The most truly innovative theorizing about myth is the work of the more positivistic and pragmatic investigators in the English and American traditions, the latter including (as I will argue) Claude Lévi-Strauss.

The two ethnographies commonly considered the foundation of modern social anthropology in England, Malinowski's *Argonauts of the Western Pacific* and Radcliffe-Brown's *Andaman Islanders,* appeared in 1922, the year of *Ulysses* and *The Waste Land.* Interesting work has begun to appear in the last ten years exploring the historical and intellectual connections between literary modernism and the new anthropology.[1] Both tend to foreground experimental design and valorize structural analysis, laying themselves open, consequently, to later generations' accusations that they attempt to evade history. The two movements differ sharply, however, in their views of the ethnological evidence about the nature of myth. This divergence may be illustrated in many ways, but one particularly significant expression of it lies in their contrasting responses to Durkheim's work. The literary modernists tend to read *The Elementary Forms of the Religious Life* as they do *The Golden Bough.* They envision a condition of group-think, sharers of an organically unified society celebrating this unity in a holistic, communal state of religious belief and practice. This is how Jane Harrison, T. S. Eliot, and D. H. Lawrence take Durkheim's work on religion, and it is a reading (or misreading) they share with various social thinkers of the early century whose work provides some of the theoretical underpinnings of fascism. Meanwhile, the pioneers of social anthropology are inspired by a different Durkheim, one whose early and late work appears continuous in its advocacy of the interrelatedness of all cultural phenomena and of the need for sociological method that could isolate and analyze the functioning of the variables.[2] As we've seen, Durkheim himself finds little place for myth among the "elementary forms" of religion. Onto this nearly blank slate, Malinowski, Radcliffe-Brown, and others project, in contradistinction to the "savage source within" conjured up by the creative artists, a Durkheimian conception of myth as one of the integral social functions of societies without writing.

W. H. R. Rivers, to take a significant transitional example, publishes in *Folk-Lore* in 1912 an essay with the blunt title, "The Sociological Significance of Myth." The first feature of this essay deserving attention here may be its venue of publication. Along with his new professionalism and his taste for structural rather than genetic explanation, Rivers passes on to ethnological neophytes like the gold-dust twins of 1922 a sense of continuity with nineteenth-century folklorists in the collection of indigenous story. This orientation inclines the new investigators to find among peoples without writing the same romantic classifications of popular storytelling genres—myth, legend, and tale—first discriminated by the Grimms, and then domesticated by the great folklorists of the latter part of the nineteenth century. This ready acceptance of the folklorists' established categories is not at all surprising on the part of investigators obliged to translate terms for concepts so deeply embedded in specific cultural understandings as those for genres of storytelling must inevitably be. But with the fraught term, "myth," its new users import the entire problematic.

Rivers announces early in his essay that its special business is "to discover a general principle which may guide us in the attempt to assign their proper value to myths as evidence of the history of social institutions" (Rivers 1968, 32–33). He defines myth as "a narrative which gives an account of the coming into being of man himself or of any feature of his environment, natural or social" (28). He thus directs students of "social institutions" to the study of cosmogonical and more broadly etiological stories. But he is not sending them there for insight into any structural foundation of the society studied; he is after "the *history* [my italics] of social institutions." The "general principle" that Rivers unveils in his subsequent examination of the Australian Arunta story is that a mythology that conspicuously explains a society's social institutions does so as a means of rationalizing its blending of disparate cultures. This "principle" might henceforward guide a student employing mythology as a tool in studying that historical diffusion of cultures to which Rivers was increasingly committed in the last decade of his short life. In spite of the questionable usefulness of Rivers's specific "principle" in this essay, his general ambition to connect myth properly with social institutions indicates how aware British anthropology was becoming, even before the impact of Durkheim, of the desirability of this connection.

"A HARD-WORKED ACTIVE FORCE": MALINOWSKI'S FUNCTIONAL THEORY OF MYTH

When Rivers classifies myths as narratives that exhibit a cosmogonic or etiological function, he hastens to declare in a footnote that he won't use the word "explain" in his text because it "bears a rationalistic connotation which makes it a very inexact means of expressing the mental attitudes of those among whom myths arise" (28). This negative construction, buried in a note, is a genuine, though very circumspect, declaration of rebellion against intellectualist theories of myth. Its modesty is appropriate, perhaps, to the Rider Haggard of anthropology, but not to its Conrad.[3] Malinowski not only makes myth a more conspicuous object of attention than any anthropologist since Tylor, he presents so bold and persuasive a conception of it as functional, pragmatic, and affective that on this topic the rest of British social anthropology is virtually a series of footnotes to him.

As a consequence of the attention paid in the last fifteen years to Malinowski's Continental antecedents, we can follow some of the connections between the conception of myth that formerly seemed to come out of nowhere in *Argonauts of the Western Pacific* and the larger turn-of-the-century strains of thought that enact the shift from origin to structure and cognitive to affective social theory.[4] The most unexpected of connections, in relation to Malinowski's theory of myth, is his youthful essay on Nietzsche's *Birth of Tragedy.* The view of myth it expresses is pretty much that standard late-romantic identification of myth with Greek tragedy that was peddled in German-style *gymnasia* from Herder's day to World War II. Myth immerses its characters in "a mysterious necessity" and opposes "thought . . . because the events of myth can neither be justified nor explained" (Malinowski 1993, 85–86). It serves a religious purpose: it is "the prototype of countless reproductions" (85) that "turn[s] ordinary matter into something superhumanly radiant" (82) and produces in its audience "an elevation beyond the level of common human emotional oscillations" (85). The young Malinowski reads *The Birth of Tragedy* very much as W. B. Yeats was doing in that same year (1904), and speaks of it in terms that might seem to spring from the pen of Mircea Eliade. It is no wonder that Marxist-influenced thinkers educated in this same tradition, like Georg Lukács, Walter Benjamin in "The Storyteller," or Horkheimer and Adorno in *The Dialectic of Enlightenment,* come to identify myth (as we will see in chapter 12) with the oppressiveness of fascist ideology. Between this essay and Malinowski's later conceptions of myth rests the entire alembic of his initiation into social anthropology. He passes from the Durkheim read through Nietzsche, as he was by modernist artists, to the Durkheim read by sociologists. What survives the transformation, however, is Malinowski's continued conception of myth in terms of the pragmatic, vitalist *Lebensphilosophie* that had come into fashion in his youth.[5] Sigmund Freud, Henri Bergson, William James—all are likely influences.

The other influence on Malinowski's conception of myth that calls for some further attention is that of Wilhelm Wundt, with whom Malinowski studied at Leipzig during the academic year 1909–1910. As Adam Kuper points out, Wundt was important not only to Malinowski, but to Boas and Durkheim as well (Kuper 1983, 11). Wundt shared with Rivers the combination of training in experimental psychology and a deep interest in anthropology. He published in 1912 his most comprehensive work, *Die Elemente der Völkerpsychologie.*[6] Wundt means by these "elements" the "mental products created by a community" (3), a conception obviously related, as Kuper also notes, to Durkheim's "collective representations." His masterwork is another grand synthesis like Frazer's or Lévy-Bruhl's and is built, as its subtitle reveals ("Outlines of a Psychological History of the Development of Mankind"), on the older taste for genetic thinking. This induces Wundt to indulge in explanations of prehistory that are blatantly "just-so stories," but it also encourages empirical common sense about the evolution of the more complex from the simpler elements. It prompts Wundt to reverse the Grimmian doctrine of tale as a degenerate survival of myth. Wundt insists that myth is normally elaborated out of tale, that even sophisticated theogonic myth bears the marks of its origins in its folk-motifs.[7] This is not a line of thought that interests the more synchronically minded Malinowski, but it bears fruit, as we will see, in Boas's demonstration that there is no *structural* difference between the two genres. What Malinowski does carry from Leipzig to London is Wundt's conviction that myth, like all the "elements" of folk psychology, is communal, loaded with affect and, perhaps above all, knowable only through experience of it in its living contexts.

It is thus that the reader first encounters Malinowski on myth in *Argonauts,* not primarily as a theoretician, but as a witness and recorder of the role of myth in the everyday lives of the Trobriand Islanders. A number of recent writers seem to agree that Malinowski's strongest contribution to the shaping of social anthropology may consist in the artfulness with which he represents in his ethnographies the role of the lone, heroic fieldworker who abandons the verandah for the village.[8] In George Stocking's amusing hyperbole, *Argonauts* is an "Euhemerist myth divinizing the European Jason who brings back the Golden Fleece of ethnographic knowledge" (Stocking 1983, 109). What is true of *Argonauts* as a whole is true of its treatment of Trobriand myth. The chapter "In Tewara and Sanaroa—Mythology of the Kula" introduces the stories within the larger context of the (actually only hypothetical) *Kula* voyage that constitutes the dramatic framework of the central part of the text.[9] The effect is as if Malinowski were discovering the stories just as they come up in the Trobrianders' minds during the voyage and, when he introduces his brief theoretical remarks about them, as if his observations arose naturally out of his sharing in the general rapport. The narrative method is thus an attempt to re-create the functionally integrated, existential contexts in which the stories were originally told. We can see through the lens of the major theoretical effort of four years later, "Myth in Primitive Psychology," that, with one possible exception, Malinowski's case for the function of myth in oral societies is already there, in solution, in *Argonauts.* The theoretical essay precipitates these assumptions into explicit formulations.

"Myth in Primitive Psychology" opens with a move that sometimes seems de rigueur among mythographers, a damning summary of "the present state of the science" (Malinowski 1992, 78). It is instructive that Malinowski, in 1926, regards the two "up-to-date theories" (78) deserving of the most extensive critique to be those of the "school of Nature mythology" and the "so-called Historical School" (that is, the historical diffusionism "represented in England by Dr. Rivers" [80]). Malinowski does recognize predecessors on the right track: "Psychologists such as Wundt, sociologists like Durkheim, Hubert, and Mauss, anthropologists like Crawley, classical scholars like Miss Jane Harrison have all understood the intimate association between myth and ritual, between sacred tradition and the norms of social structure" (80). Malinowski's acknowledgment of Frazer here is especially ticklish. All of the writers just mentioned are said to have been "to a greater or lesser extent influenced by the work of Sir James Frazer," and "the great British anthropologist, as well as most of his followers," are admitted to possess "a clear vision of the sociological and ritual importance of myth." Nevertheless, "the facts which I shall present will allow us to clarify and formulate more precisely the main principles of a sociological theory of myth." This careful wording makes it sound as if Malinowski wishes to blur the extent to which Frazer is the implied target of the assault that follows, which is likely enough since the essay was originally delivered as an address in honor of Sir James. In any case, Malinowski's promise to deliver clarified "principles of a sociological theory of myth," a phrase that probably echoes

Rivers deliberately, serves notice that mentors and predecessors, as well as opponents, will be overgone by someone with a fresh basis for his authority.

Malinowski commences his review in a gesture with which it is easy for any student of myth to sympathize; he lists, in addition to the various theories, the formidable array of fields whose practitioners lay special claim to the concept, "so that when at last the poor anthropologist and student of folk-lore comes to the feast, there are hardly any crumbs left for them" (81). Having attained this pitch of mock-pathos, he then proceeds to wheel in a whole new dinner for the starving anthropologists and folklorists with his invitation to his auditors to "step outside the closed study of the theorist into the open air of the anthropological field" and "listen to the stories" the natives tell while we are "sharing their meals around their fires." This reversion to the narrative mode of *Argonauts* sets in perspective the entire range of the previously rehearsed notions of myth; regardless of their differences from each other, they are lumped into the single category of theories too baselessly speculative about the uses of story in an oral culture. In the contention over theories of myth the fieldworker has the singular advantage of having "the myth-maker at his elbow" amid "a host of *authentic* commentators" (my italics) and a "live context" from which "there is as much to be learned about the myth as in the narrative itself" (81).

We can enhance our sense of the very significant, but condensed, final phrases in this passage by departing briefly from "Myth in Primitive Psychology" to examine a more expansive, autobiographical section in a later essay (Malinowski 1992, 131–172). Malinowski there tells his audience that he only gradually learned in Melanesia that when he was eagerly "writing down any story that was told to me," he was missing aspects of the social situation "quite as important as the text itself" (139). What he presents as fresh discoveries are nowadays, of course, the merest truisms about methodical collection. But they represent for Malinowski the steps in a conversion experience. He goes on to confess that "I missed not only the context of situation but very often the context of further elaborations and commentaries. . . . After telling me some important and sacred story, the narrator would often continue into what seemed to me entirely irrelevant verbosities" (139–140). He recalls the example of how, after the first time he was told "the myth about the brother and sister incest," he cut short the narrator, who was rambling on into apparently irrelevant bragging. "It was only later that I realized that . . . my informant, in a characteristically boastful manner, was simply stating how the myth acts as a warrant for the correct performance of the magic; how it gives a right of ownership and control to the natives of the community where the magic originated. . . . He was, in short, giving me the sociological function of myth" (140). This is the blinding light on the road to Damascus that Malinowski has in mind when he speaks in "Myth in Primitive Psychology" of the "live context" from which "there is as much to be learned about the myth as in the narrative itself."

From this grounding of ethnographic authority in lived experience, Malinowski constructs a theory of myth as itself an expression of lived experience. It exists in its community, he asserts, not merely as "a story told but a reality lived" (81). "Studied alive, myth . . . is not symbolic [as the "school of Nature-mythology" held] . . . not an explanation in satisfaction of a science interest [as Tylor, Frazer, and others, especially in England, held], but a narrative resurrection of a primeval reality" (82). This wonderfully compact phrase captures Malinowski's sense that the story is the medium through which the believing community conjures up and dwells again in the presence of the supernatural beings who founded it. By calling the "reality" "primeval" he signifies the common notion in such societies that these origins and originators belong to a condition of the world prior to the one of everyday familiarity. Narratives of this sort are "told in satisfaction of deep religious wants, moral cravings, social submissions, assertions, even practical requirements. Myth fulfills in primitive culture an indispensable function: it expresses, enhances, and codifies belief; it safeguards and enforces morality; it vouches for the efficiency of ritual and contains practical rules for the guidance of man. Myth is thus a vital ingredient of human civilization; it is not an idle tale, but a hard-worked active force . . . a pragmatic charter of primitive faith and moral wisdom" (82).

This often-quoted passage is the nub of Malinowski's theory, but, precisely because it is so packed, it calls for some opening up. Forms of the key words by which the theory is generally characterized are all here—"vital," "function," "charter," "pragmatic"—but these are plainly not synonyms no matter how intricately they are knotted together. Malinowski speaks of myth as fulfilling a single large "function," for instance, but immediately breaks this down into three subordinate functions according to what he usually understands as the three modalities of religion: belief, morality, and ritual practice. With respect to belief, myth is expressive, intensive, and canonizing, whereas, with respect to morality, it is custodial and coercive, and to ritual, authorizing and prescriptive. It is said to be a "vital ingredient of human civilization," which means, then, as Malinowski makes clear in other contexts, that *religion* is such an ingredient. (Malinowski denies being a believer himself in any specific religion, but he holds that human societies cannot, or will not, cohere without some form of it.[10]) The epitomizing phrase "a hard-worked, active force" is quite vague in itself, but the context shows that Malinowski opposes it to what he views as myth's relegation by most previous theories to mere otiose speculation whether poetic or scientific.

When he designates myth climactically in this context as a "pragmatic charter" of faith and morality, he means the phrase to cover all cases. Every myth in an oral society "charters" certain functions of the three modalities of religion. But later on in the essay he employs "charter" in a second and more specialized sense that has caused a certain amount of confusion. He declares during his discussion of local myths of origin that such a story "literally contains the legal charter of the community" (93). This section of the essay is the most brilliantly Durkheimian in its demonstration of the fungibility of religion and social structure, and perhaps for that reason the phrase "charter myth" has been widely adopted to designate the type of story that rationalizes a community's possession of its land. In order to avoid confusion, these two senses of "charter," the broad and the narrow, must be carefully distinguished in usage. Since the second, narrower and more specialized sense of a claim for tenure of land is now so well established, it would be wise to avoid misunderstanding by dropping the characterization of Malinowski's whole conception of myth as a "charter theory" in the first and broader sense of the word.

But one striking passage in the paragraph under consideration still calls for comment. The one piece of important theorizing in "Myth in Primitive Psychology" that we do not find in solution in *Argonauts* surfaces here in the assertion that myth is "told in satisfaction of deep religious wants, moral cravings, social submissions." This diction may well convey Malinowski's growing persuasion that myth, like other social institutions, is an expression of biological need. During the twenties and thirties Malinowski's use of the term "functionalism" evolves from a meaning sufficiently close to the broad Durkheimian conception (of co-variable social phenomena) toward a meaning that signifies the biological determinism of these phenomena.[11] Malinowski's religious "cravings" and "submissions" also remind us of his propensity, conspicuous throughout "Myth in Primitive Psychology," for foregrounding the psychology of the individual believer as the basis of any social construction.[12] His emergent insistence in his later career upon both biological determinism and the privileging of individual psychology certainly contributes mightily to Radcliffe-Brown's celebrated and much-analyzed denial that he himself was, or ever had been, that creature now so compromised by Malinowski's usage—a functionalist.

Ivan Strenski, the closest student of Malinowski on myth, suggests that the general shift in Malinowski's orientation that provoked Radcliffe-Brown to distance himself from this variety of "functionalism" manifest itself also in Malinowski on myth. Strenski argues that myth in the earlier *Argonauts* is a somewhat jarring *mélange* of German *lebensphilosophie*, Frazer's connection of myth with rite, and Durkheim's brand of functionalism, whereas myth in the essay of 1926 is already the fully pragmatic reflector of biological determinism (Strenski 1987, 50–55, 60–66). I am not sure, however, that biological need isn't already implicit in the treatment of myth in *Argonauts,* and that "Myth in Primitive Psychology" is not just as eclectic as its predecessor. For vitalist philosophies—as the instances of Nietzsche, James, Bergson, and Freud all suggest—far from excluding biological need, tend to take it for granted. Malinowski's mature pragmatic position can well be viewed as the consistent working out of his youthful vitalism. As for the continued presence of Frazer and Durkheim in the essay, Malinowski appears untroubled by their coexistence within his pragmatic theory of myth for much the same reason that he argued in his public debate with Radcliffe-Brown in 1938. Malinowski holds out there for distinct levels of usage in the definition of "function," levels that would include both Radcliffe-Brown's more rigorous Durkheimian notion of social co-variables and his own biologism.[13] This genial inclusiveness may help to explain why Malinowski's vivid evocation of myth in the essay as a "hardworked . . . force" continues to dominate social anthropology for a generation in spite of the debatable reconcilability of its vitalistic individualism with the privileging of impersonal systemic analysis.

After the *locus classicus* of his initial characterization of myth, Malinowski reverts in earnest to the narrative method of *Argonauts*. He conjures up the setting in which folktales are told, the leisure of the village fireside on a rainy November evening when the gardens are just sprouting and the sailing season still lies ahead. His characterization of this genre, *kukwanebu* or what he calls indifferently either "fairy tale" or "folk-tale," leads in turn to his presentation of two further genres, *libwogwo* or "historical accounts . . . legends . . . and hearsay tales" (85) and *liliu* or "myths" (86). The folktale, *kukwanebu,* is an entertaining fiction, "a seasonal performance and an act of sociability" (86), whereas *libwogwo* can be told anytime and are regarded as true human history. *Liliu* are also without seasonal restrictions and received as true. When it comes to identifying their distinctive qualia, however, Malinowski's change of mind between *Argonauts* and "Myth in Primitive Psychology" marks one of the major fault-lines in modern efforts to apply Grimm's trinity of genres to indigenous classifications. When he first introduces in *Argonauts* the subject of *"lili'u"* (so spelled, presumably to indicate a glottal stop that has unaccountably disappeared four years later), he classifies them as a mere subset of *libwogwo,* true stories. Yet the Trobrianders do, he admits, "distinguish definitely between myth and historic account," even though "this distinction is difficult to formulate" (Malinowski 1968, 74). The following pages demonstrate why it is difficult. On one hand, Malinowski discovers the useful formal rule that "in the mythical world . . . people were endowed with powers such as present men and their historical ancestors do not possess" (76). On the other hand, however, he is obliged to recognize (as on page 79, for example) that some stories classed by his informants as myths, that is, *liliu,* are set on the "present"-world side of this great division. Although a formal distinction on the basis of the principal characters' possession of supernatural powers may be generally workable, Malinowski can fall back in the last analysis only upon the authoritative designations of his informants: "Tradition, from which the store of tales is received, hands them on labeled as *lili'u,* and the definition of a *lili'u* is that it is a story transmitted with such a label" (74). This unsatisfactory foreclosure suggests that even though the islanders make a clear-cut distinction on the formal level between myth and legend, the ethnographer cannot come up with an unexceptionable rule for how they do it. In the essay of 1926, however, Malinowski focuses, with a different result, not upon formal criteria but on functional ones. Where *kukwanebu* are "told for amusement" and *libwogwo* "to make a serious statement and satisfy a social ambition," *liliu* "are regarded, not merely as true, but as venerable and sacred. . . . the *myth* comes into play when rite, ceremony, or a social or moral rule demands justification, warrant of antiquity, reality and sanctity" (86). *Liliu* are defined, then, partly, like *libwogwo,* by two formal considerations—truth and prescriptive gravity of content—but partly, also, by psychological response, by a certain awe attendant upon belief in matters of such cultural moment. This last condition could be identified only by observing how myth *functions* in Trobriand society.

As is the case with Malinowski's attention to myth in general, his applications of the romantic trio of oral genres have had a great impact, for better and for worse. On the negative side, they have encouraged the perpetuation, along with the terms themselves, of some of their more dubious Grimmian baggage. This includes the assumption that myth precedes tale as the sacred precedes the secular, and its corollary, that tale is a Tylorian "survival," consisting of the degenerated shards of myth. Malinowski himself did not subscribe to any such thing; if he had been sufficiently interested in the developmental history of the genres to pay attention to this issue, it seems likely that he would have followed his teacher, Wundt, in assuming that myth is built up out of ideologically elaborated tale. This is the position implicit in his discovery that the Trobrianders distinguished *liliu* from the other genres not primarily because it presents differences in plot, characters, or setting, but because it grounds matters essential to cultural cohesion. By so strikingly identifying *liliu* with Western "myth," however, and juxtaposing it sharply with Grimm's other two genres, Malinowski creates the impression that distinctions among the three genres are more clear-cut than he himself is able to demonstrate. He thus leaves ajar yet another tempting door for those transcendentalist theorists like Eliade anxious to assemble ethnological "proof" of the existence of a universal genre, and he encourages among social anthropologists themselves a tendency toward uncritical appropriation of these generic terms. This tendency has only begun to be reversed within the last generation by closer attention to the properties of oral storytelling.[14] On the positive side, however, Malinowski's specific attention to the forms of Trobriand story does teach memorably the important lesson that the concept of "myth," applied to the narratives of an oral culture, necessarily entails the existence of a generic contract whose complex significance can scarcely be detached from its context.

This embeddedness might be said to be the subject of the two-thirds of "Myth in Primitive Psychology" remaining to be examined after the criticisms, definitions, and generic distinctions of the introductory section. Malinowski's subsequent section-headings display his abiding conviction that myth is always in the service of a specific business and therefore best apprehended, not in general, but under the rubric of some functional typology. Even the central treatment of myth in *Argonauts* is labeled "The Mythology of the Kula," as if each major cultural institution could be expected to have its own. In comparable fashion, the subsequent sections of "Myth in Primitive Psychology" are titled "Myths of Origin," "Myths of Death and of the Recurrent Cycle of Life," and "Myths of Magic." Each of these categories imposes a somewhat different view of the function of myth. Myths of origin supply a community's "charter" (91) and reconcile fictively the "logically irreconcilable facts" (94) of historical disruption and "sociological strain" (100). Myths of death and the recurrent cycle of life screen from the islanders "the vast emotional void gaping beyond them" (109). Myths of magic bridge "the gaps and inadequacies in highly important activities not yet mastered by man" (110). These ascribed functions fall obviously into two groups that reflect neatly Malinowski's larger split between collective social and individual psychological explanation. But he never attempts any more formal taxonomy. It is left to a reader to decide, for instance, what relations obtain among the mixed mythology of institutions like the *kula* or, later, the coral gardens on one hand, and the three presumably major types presented in the essay on the other. One gets the impression that these categories are makeshift, the products of a rather nominalistic sensibility; Malinowski is not so much interested in docketing as in re-creating the ways in which this most "hard-worked" of genres is actually employed. For there is, in the last analysis, something uniquely personal about Malinowski's enthusiasm for myth. A striking proportion of his best known formulations of the advantages of the fieldworker over the "armchair" theorist appear in "Myth in Primitive Psychology," as if nothing had so impressed these advantages on his mind as his immersion in living story. To be sure, he went to Melanesia imbued with Rivers's rule that story is one of the great keys to cultural insight, but his dramatic account in "The Foundations of Faith and Morals" of what I have called his "conversion" expresses the force with which his *experience* of this embedded storytelling actually struck him. His re-creations of Trobriand mythology not only shed a great burst of light upon the concrete functions of such story, but also model for the ethnologist a remarkable standard of sympathetic insight.

BRITISH MYTH AFTER MALINOWSKI

"The Malinowskian preoccupation with myth is not much in evidence during this period." Thus the historian of "the modern British school" sums up in a single understatement the fate of myth during the hegemony of structural-functionalism (Kuper 1983, 139). Though Malinowski succeeds in voicing the movement's most eloquent registration of the nature and function of myth, few of his younger colleagues display anything like his interest in attending to it. This relative silence may be explained in part by the preemptive effect of Malinowski's account, in part by others' lack of comparable rapport with indigenous story. But it is probably the result, above all, of a conception of the function of myth more thoroughly Durkheimian, that is, more strictly sociological, than the one colored by Malinowski's strains of biological determinism and psychological individualism.

That is the case with the treatment of myth in the other breakthrough ethnography of 1922, A. R. Radcliffe-Brown's *Andaman Islanders*. Radcliffe-Brown can't be accused of neglecting story in this early work; like Malinowski, he shares Rivers's respect for it as an avenue into oral culture. About one-quarter of the primary text of *The Andaman Islanders* is occupied with recording and interpreting "myths and legends." Besides its sheer attention to story, Radcliffe-Brown's ethnography so closely resembles Malinowski's in its general conception of myth as an affective mode of expressing and reinforcing social values that it is easy to see how the two writers could be taken initially as working in tandem. Nevertheless, a closer look discloses a set of potential rifts between them. First, Radcliffe-Brown exhibits none of Malinowski's sensitivity to genre. He makes no distinction at all between "myth" and "legend," employing the terms interchangeably, and he never mentions the category of "tale." Nor does he anywhere offer a formal definition of "myth"/"legend." Andamanese story appears, in consequence, as an undifferentiated phenomenon: issues of performers' intentions; audiences' understandings; reception as religious truth or as secular entertainment; and differences in plot, characters, setting, circumstances of telling and so forth do not arise. This treatment of story as monolithic and unproblematic may be a result of the second potential rift between the two ethnographers. If Radcliffe-Brown's consciousness of the contractual aspects of storytelling is much cruder than Malinowski's, his conception of what motivates

it is a good deal more philosophically developed. By 1922 he was a more programmatic Durkheimian, a believer in collective representations and in the intermeshed
functioning of all cultural phenomena toward the goal of perpetuating society
itself. Furthermore, he had worked out in argument with his mentor, Rivers, in
the years just before the First World War, a determinedly synchronic, perhaps even
proto-structuralist, conception of systematic ethnography.[15] And he had developed
out of the social psychologies of William McDougall (1908) and Alexander Shand
(1914) a consistent theory of social cohesion as a product of conditioning in "sentiment." Thus primed, he is much more inclined than Malinowski to make of his
ethnological material a schematic theoretical demonstration. Yet a third incipient
difference develops out of the second. The psychologies of McDougall and Shand are
contributions to that general shift of focus onto the irrational elements in human
behavior that is so striking a feature of turn-of-the-century social and psychological
thinking. Most such theories, in emphasizing distinctions among what people *say*
their motives are, what they privately *think* they are, and what they *appear* to others
to be, presume either implicitly or explicitly the operation of unconscious factors.
As the very type of this sort of assumption one might recall Freud's boast that
psychoanalysis delivers to human pretensions a third blow as devastating as those of
Copernicus and Darwin—that we are not masters in our own house of mind. The
affective theories of both Malinowski and Radcliffe-Brown assume that it is the
business of the ethnologist to detect the true motives for myth, which are concealed
from its makers. Though they do not differ in kind about this, they do differ in
degree. Malinowski's valorizing of individual psychology permits the practitioners
of myth some degree of potential awareness, whereas Radcliffe-Brown's insistence
on a unique and totalizing collective motive precludes virtually any possibility
of individual comprehension. In this matter as in some others, Radcliffe-Brown's
arrogation to the anthropologist of a level of insight and metacommentary beyond
the reach of the storyteller foreshadows the structural theory of Claude Lévi-
Strauss.

Radcliffe-Brown defines "sentiment" as "an organized system of emotional
tendencies centered about some object" (Radcliffe-Brown 1964, 234). "A society
depends for its existence on the presence in the minds of its members of a certain
system of sentiments by which the conduct of the individual is regulated in
conformity with the needs of the society" (234). As a consequence, "every feature of
the social system itself and every event or object that in any way affects the well-
being or the cohesion of the society becomes an object of this system of sentiments"
(234). Since these sentiments "are not innate but are developed in the individual
by the action of society upon him," the function of both "ceremonies" (rituals) and
"legends" (myths) is to maintain them "at the requisite degree of intensity . . . and
to transmit [them] from one generation to another" (234). Radcliffe-Brown even
attempts to explain, at this level of abstraction, why "story has ever been a popular
medium by which to appeal to sentiment of all kinds" (394). His nineteenth-century
humanistic answer—that the exercise of the imagination is fundamental to the
development of both the individual ego and its social relations—is less interesting
than the fact that he feels constrained to rope even the phenomenon of storytelling

within the confines of his utilitarian determinism. The storytellers are, of course, unconscious of such impersonal, collective motivation. It is a rule of Radcliffe-Brown's ethnographic method that "the native" must always be asked for his explanation, and his text is consequently littered with the formulaic "If the native is asked . . ." If asked, he is precluded by definition from making a satisfactory answer, for "he is not himself capable of thinking about his own sentiments" (324), and is, *a fortiori,* unaware of his relentless shaping by the superorganic goal. Since Radcliffe-Brown's procedure in the text is first to assemble and order the stories (in chapter 4) and then systematically to "interpret" each group in sequence (in chapter 6), commencing with the "native" explanation, the reader repeatedly experiences this discrepancy at its maximum, sometimes trembling on the brink of the comic, between the concrete, puzzled replies of the islanders and the abstruse, but lucid, and utterly foregone solution of the ethnographer.

Although his early work does pay an attention to story comparable to Rivers's or Malinowski's, Radcliffe-Brown's treatment of it suggests that he sees it as far less transparent, and therefore less trustworthy and even less valuable, than the romantic premises of post-Grimmian folkore have encouraged his colleagues to assume. And it is his distrust and diminishment of story, not Malinowski's enthusiasm and empathy, that are prescient of the course of British social anthropology. The principal targets of ethnographic research become, instead, kinship relations and political organization. Not only is there no important theory of myth after Malinowski, but the most effective and original work that appears on the topic is nearly all negative, undermining or qualifying Malinowski's exuberance, as the following cases will illustrate.

Myth might, for instance, be suspected of falling victim to the wider neglect of religion during this time, but the work of Edward Evans-Pritchard provides a distinguished example of how thoroughly even the study of "primitive" religion can be conducted along Durkheimian lines with only minimal attention to storytelling. A reader confined to Evans-Pritchard's ethnologies, and willing to take him at his word, might well conclude superficially that central Africa is nearly devoid of sacred story. He declares explicitly that the two principal groups he sojourned among, the Azande and the Nuer, are highly impoverished in this respect (Evans-Pritchard 1937, 195; 1956, v). A closer look at his texts, however, uncovers a more complicated, ambiguous picture. General denials are contradicted by a steady seepage of information that suggests abundant traditions of sacred narrative lurking on the edges of the anthropologist's horizon, discounted for various reasons.[16] One of these reasons, I suspect, is that Evans-Pritchard's standard for what counts as "myth" is more in tune with the formal cosmogonical sacred story demanded by transcendentalists like Eliade than it is with the more relaxed standards typical of the folkloristic tradition. Another reason is basically political. Evans-Pritchard's conviction that cognition functions alike throughout our species and his persistent effort to "undarken Africa," as Clifford Geertz puts it (Geertz 1988, 70), may have biased him against a conceptual tool so closely associated with attempts to essentialize an African "other." For the deeper reasons, however, we might turn for an answer to Mary Douglas, Evans-Pritchard's former student and a particularly fine expositor of his work. Douglas's witty essay "What If the Dogon . . ." befriends us especially here because it confronts directly the question of why British fieldwork becomes generally inimical to myth.

Douglas commences by asking her (originally French) audience to perform the thought experiment of imagining what would have happened if the Dogon had been studied by Evans-Pritchard and the Nuer by Marcel Griaule and his associates. She suggests amusingly that the results would have been reversed according to national differences in personal and professional orientation. Evans-Pritchard would have stolidly reported the Dogon as notably lacking in mythology while Griaule would have discovered among the Nuer a rich and sophisticated symbolic world, worthy of Parisian intellectuals nursed on Surrealism. *One* of Douglas's purposes in introducing this complex game, however, is to persuade her audience that Evans-Pritchard (and English anthropology in general) is every bit as interested as the French in the mental functioning of the groups studied. "All our professed interest in politics and kinship is an interest in the machinery that casts shadows on the wall . . . in trying to discover the social determinants of cosmology" (Douglas 1975, 131). In fact, between exploring, as the French do, "cosmology," the shadows on the wall of Plato's cave, and examining the machinery that throws the shadows, there can be, she implies, little question about which ought to take logical and epistemological precedence.

In her subsequent monograph on Evans-Pritchard, Douglas aligns him still more explicitly with the contemporary fashion in English common language philosophy. In his quest for how to "sociologize theories of the mind that hitherto had no grounding in social theory," he "extraordinarily anticipate[s] the intentions of everyday language philosophers by his recognition of the need to interpret speech fully in its context of functioning social relations and especially, of course, in social accounting" (Douglas 1981, 12, 4). One might as well expect a treatise on myth from Gilbert Ryle. Douglas's two contributions—connecting Evans-Pritchard with the English language philosophers on concepts and the accountability of agents, and contrasting him with the *Missions Griaule* on the evidential value of cosmological symbolism—frame Evans-Pritchard as the exemplary case of what happens to myth in British social anthropology after Malinowski.[17]

Perhaps the most significant post-Malinowskian contribution to the structural-functionalist conception of myth is the pejorative demonstration, particularly by Raymond Firth and Edmund Leach, of what Firth calls in an essay thus titled "the plasticity of myth" (Firth 1984). The phrase refers to the availability of sacred narrative for purposes of current legitimation. The idea stems from various formulations of it in Malinowski's "Myth in Primitive Psychology," such as "myth . . . cannot be sober, dispassionate history, since it is always made *ad hoc* to fulfill a certain sociological function, to glorify a certain group, or to justify an anomalous status" (Malinowski 1992, 108). This line of thought subverts the conception of myth as the timeless product of an organic community swayed in unison by its collective representations. The radical potential in these remarks was perhaps not evident at first, since Malinowski confines himself to generalities and does not press, presumably for lack of diachronic evidence, the implied "plasticity" of his "myths of origin." But his former student, Raymond Firth, discovered an abundance of such evidence during his return visit to Tikopia in 1952, after an absence of twenty-three years, and pursued its implications in a number of publications during the sixties.[18] In "The Plasticity of Myth" he focuses on two concrete examples, the second and more significant of which involves the elaboration of "contemporary myths" (215) about the fate of a sacred stone. In the interim between Firth's visits, the Christian faction on the island had several times stolen the stone, hidden it, or put it to blasphemous uses, but each time the stone reappeared miraculously in its shrine. According to Firth, this version of events was widely accepted even among Christians. The result was a social compromise; the Christian harassment did succeed in bringing to an end a particular rite associated with the shrine, but the pagans were able to compensate by establishing a new myth about the power of their deity. The significance of Firth's concrete examples is more conspicuously theorized, however, in "Oral Tradition in Relation to Social Status." He there insists explicitly that oral tradition not only reflects and reinforces the status quo but also "perpetuate[s] relations of disunity" (Firth 1968, 173). And he pursues an interesting corollary. "The series of competing tales" (176), which might be expected to be most discordant about recent conditions and events, actually display more agreement with them, and less about the remote past where "ultimate origins and former prestige . . . can be treated as quite independent of the recent structure" (176). The tales, in short, are "largely a projection of the present into the past" (181). For this reason, Firth insists on the "arbitrary nature of any attempt to distinguish clearly myth, legend and history in the field material" (182). In his headnote to "The Plasticity of Myth" Alan Dundes indicates that he regards Firth's "contemporary myths" as legend, but Firth is at pains to show there that these narratives fulfill all the folklorists' usual criteria for myth except the temporal one that is precisely what his evidence calls into question as a valid criterion. The stories appear to be *young* myths, and anyone who is disturbed by that concept should ask him- or herself why.

Firth acknowledges in "Oral Tradition in Relation to Social Status" and elsewhere the influence of Edmund Leach's *Political Systems of Highland Burma* (1954), to which he also supplied a foreword. *Political Systems* is the one work that Adam Kuper recognizes as an exception to his generalization about the lack of attention to myth after Malinowski. Leach's study is iconoclastic and provocative on a number of subjects, myth among them. He holds that "while conceptual models of society are necessarily models of equilibrium systems, real societies can never be in equilibrium. The discrepancy is related to the fact that when social structures are expressed in cultural form, the representation is imprecise compared with that given by the exact categories which the scientist, *qua* scientist would like to employ. . . . These inconsistencies in the logic of ritual expression are always necessary for the proper functioning of any social system" (Leach 1964, 4). For Leach, who finds Durkheim's "absolute dichotomy between the sacred and the profane untenable" (12), myth is simply another mode of such ritual expression of social structure, not in Harrison's or Durkheim's or Malinowski's sense that myth and rite are "conceptually separate entities" (13) that complement one another, but in the more rigorously functional and materialist sense that as behavior they "say" the same thing. It follows then that "in the case of Kachin mythology there can be no possibility of eliminating the contradictions and inconsistencies. They are fundamental. . . . the contradictions are more significant than the uniformities" (265). The narration of a myth "is a ritual act . . . which justifies the particular attitude adopted by the teller at the moment of telling" (277). Pressing this line of thought to its radical conclusion, Leach declares expressly that Malinowski and Firth are mistaken to view the local tensions and oppositions expressed by myth as being balanced within a larger social equilibrium. "What I am suggesting is exactly the opposite to this. Myth and ritual is a language of . . . argument, not a chorus of harmony" (278). As Leach observes, "a proper assimilation of this point of view requires . . . a fundamental change in the current anthropological concept of social structure" (278). Pending the advent of that particular revolution, Leach's case for "Myth as a Justification for Faction and Social Change" (the title of his chapter) can at least be taken as a brilliant investigation of the negative problematic implicit in Malinowski's recognition of myth as charter.

A brief glance at Jack Goody's *Myth of the Bagre* may serve as coda to this consideration of the construction of myth after Malinowski. Coming from a very different direction than Leach, Goody arrives at a comparably severe critique of the exalted view of myth as story that establishes cultural coherence. He discovers to his surprise that the supernatural agencies that figure in the grand cosmological myth of the Bagre secret society among the LoDagaa of Northern Ghana also turn up in folktales told chiefly by children, but not in the "everyday religion" (Goody 1972, 30). "In other words, the powers to whom the LoDagaa appeal in sacrifice, prayer and oath are not those with which either myth or folk-tales are concerned. This fact suggests that we need to rethink radically the role of myth in relation to cosmology and to culture" (31). Goody himself concludes that "myth . . . does not have the central role in human cultures that Malinowski, Lévi-Strauss, and others have assigned, but is in many ways peripheral, changing, the sort of thing mankind can take or leave" (33). He ends his introduction by speculating that those "writers and anthropologists" (33) who have found myth the heart of human cultures have done so, in part at least, as "a reflex of the greater fragmentation of beliefs in industrial society" (33). It is ironic to witness the accusation that myth expresses religious nostalgia turned inward upon the very tradition of social anthropology that indirectly empowered the insight to begin with, and to reflect that, as Goody stands to this tradition, it stands to the neo-transcendentalist theories outside the discipline.

AMERICAN "MYTHOLOGICAL WORLDS": BOAS TO LÉVI-STRAUSS

Presenting Franz Boas as an important theorist of myth may appear a dubious enterprise. His distaste for premature speculation was legendary. In "more than 10,000 pages on the Northwest Coast alone," as Marvin Harris notes, he presents his primary material mostly "'without commentary, without the bare information that would be needed to render it intelligible to the reader'" (Harris 1968, 261).[19] But Boas earns his post of honor by virtue of extracting, from the immense attention he paid and taught others to pay to indigenous oral story, certain significant conclusions, both negative and positive, about the nature of myth. First, he recognizes that myth is not a fixed genre, above historical contingency, but a shifting mosaic of fragments subject to social pressures. Second, he demonstrates that its tellers do not distinguish it from folktale by the criteria of its sacredness or its preponderance of deities as characters but only by its setting in an age before the present separation of humans from other animals. Third, he concludes that tale must logically precede myth, even though it is impossible to establish such precedence historically. And on the negative side, Boas refutes two of the most enduring of nineteenth-century romantic ideas about myth—that it embodies symbolic responses to natural phenomena and that folktale is the degenerate "survival" of original sacred myth.

Boas matches Malinowski as a missionary for the importance of narrative in small oral societies. Like Malinowski, he sets forth the central significance of story in his own ethnography and promotes its cause by virtue of his institutional position as a founding father of modern anthropology in *his* adopted country. While Boas does not attain Malinowski's level of notoriety as a theoretician, he surpasses him in imbuing two generations of his students with his own confidence in the value of the collection and close study of myth and tale. Boas's attention to oral narrative is only one aspect of his interest in "primitive" culture, and "culture" itself vies for his attention throughout his career with "race" and "language," as he himself acknowledged by titling his selected essays *Race, Language and Culture.* George Stocking points out the symbolic significance of Boas's publishing in 1911 "his most important work" in each of these three areas; *Changes in the Bodily Form of Descendants of Immigrants, Handbook of American Indian Languages,* and *The Mind of Primitive Man* (Boas 1989, v–vi). In spite of this range of competing interests, however, indigenous story can be justly said to be the primary focus of Boas's ethnology. Stocking attributes this bent to the influence of the great German folklorist and ethnologist Adolph Bastian, with whom Boas worked for a year and a half after his maiden research expedition to Baffin Island in 1883–1884. "Following Bastian, he felt that folktale and myth were the most characteristic expression of the *Völkergedanken*" (86).

It may be, however, that Boas had already discovered his affinity for oral tradition during his actual sojourn among the "Eskimo." He left Europe intending to study migration patterns but returned fascinated with Inuit culture and possessed of a large collection of folklore (Boas 1989, 53). We can't know for sure, since he left no personal account comparable to Malinowski's, but the pattern was set in any case by the time he migrated to the United States in 1885. According to Stocking, Boas first went "to the Northwest Coast in 1886 with the idea that mythology—like language and physical characteristics—might be a 'useful tool for differentiating and judging the relationships of tribes,' and from the beginning he spent much of his time collecting myths" (85). After his work came to the attention of Tylor, he made five fieldtrips between 1888 and 1894 under the auspices of the committee set up by the British Association to study the Northwest tribes of Canada. These expeditions apparently featured the collection of myth to the point that both Tylor and Boas's American supervisor, Horatio Hale, questioned the emphasis, thereby eliciting from Boas the defense that nothing revealed customs and character like story, particularly since these records eliminated the subjective distortions of the European observer. As Stocking proceeds to point out, this *apologia* implies a deeper, unspoken reason, the wish to preserve for posterity at least this record of cultures that were rapidly disappearing. (The decade of the 1890s was the actual nadir of the survival of Native Americans in the United States and Canada.) This ultimate personal motive was in fortunate accord with the great "salvage" project of the American Bureau of Ethnology, launched in 1879. Boas's *chef d'oeuvre, Tsimshian Mythology,* was published as part (an enormous part) of the Thirty-First Annual Report of the Bureau to the Secretary of the Smithsonian Institute (Boas 1916). By 1916 Boas's important work on indigenous narrative was virtually over; it lay in the quarter of a century stretching back to 1891. But his power to implement his visionary program of mapping indigenous languages and mythologies had been increased exponentially by his appointment at Columbia in 1896. Robert Lowie, Alfred Kroeber, Alexander Goldenweiser, Edward Sapir, Paul Radin, Ruth Benedict: even so brief a list of a few of his students particularly relevant to this study will serve to make the point.

Boas's most fundamental theoretical discovery—that mythologies are cobbled out of preexistent fragments of story—is a direct result of the diffusionist interest with which he began. The idea that cultural innovations spread primarily by contact would produce in the early years of the new century several schools committed to geographically sweeping monotheories of prehistoric cultural contact. Boas is certainly predisposed to diffusionist work by his new, neo-Kantian preference, after his Baffin Island experience, for tracking instead of the physical migrations of peoples the dissemination of their cultural constructions. At the same time, however, any potential anticipation of the doctrinaire schools of diffusionism is checked by stubborn allegiance to the positivistic fact-gathering of his early scientific training; this anchors his studies in the details of the slow changes in visual design, language, and traditional narrative among neighboring Northwest peoples The thousand-plus pages of *Tsimshian Mythology,* for example, include not only three hundred and forty-some pages of Tsimshian narrative, but a comparative study of its relation to its neighbors' storytelling that is nearly as long. When Boas applies to Northwest storytelling his idiosyncratic "historical" method, the result is a picture of the dissemination of tale and the elements of tale remarkable in its fluidity and complexity, range, and probable reach into antiquity. A study of any one mythology, that of the Kwakiutl, for instance, discloses a pattern of "borrowings" that moves out in concentric circles of lessening density through neighboring peoples into the distribution of tales across North and South America on one side and far into eastern Asia on the other. And the complexities of distribution are immensely complicated by the length of the process. Boas remarks in "The Mythologies of the Indians" (1905) that a "general resemblance in style in most American mythologies which sets them off fairly sharp [*sic*] from those of other continents" must be "an effect of dissemination and acculturation that have been going on for thousands of years, now in one direction, now in another" (Boas 1989, 147). And yet, compared to the state of European folklore, the amalgam of story the ethnologist encounters in the Americas is further jumbled by extreme cultural contrasts so that "the make-up of the stories exhibits much wider divergence" (Boas 1982, 402). In America, in contrast to Europe, "the complex stories are new . . . there is little cohesion between [*sic*] the component elements . . . the really old parts of tales are the incidents and a few simple plots" (403). In his most sustained theoretical essay, "Mythology and Folk-tales of the North American Indians" (1914), Boas accepts Wundt's distinction between "mythical concepts and tales" (Boas 1982, 476), a recurrent theme in the problematic of myth ever since Creuzer. This concession does allow for a more conservative element in tales that undergo ideological elaboration, but insofar as concepts remain embodied in narrative they are subject to the rule that "constant diffusion of the elements of stories . . . must have been the essential characteristic of the history of folk-tales" (484). It is this conviction that underlies Boas's most memorable formulation of the condition of Amerindian mythologies: "It would seem that mythological worlds have been built up, only to be shattered again, and that new worlds were built from their fragments" (424).

The principal casualty of this folkloristic, genre-centered conception of myth is the favorite nineteenth-century notion of myth as a response, cognitive or affective, to natural phenomena. Both Boas and Malinowski, influenced more by the later social thinkers rather than by the earlier poets, understand this notion as a cognitive theory and both repudiate it on the strength of their experience of actual indigenous storytelling. Whereas Malinowski rejects it on the psychological grounds that it is too rationalized and abstract a conception of the workings of human belief, Boas rejects it on the formal grounds that the instability of tale precludes *any* definitive attempt to explain myth by origin. In a 1933 review of a book on Kwakiutl religion based, according to Boas, on the assumptions that "every mythology must be systematic" and that the researcher can restore "the original meaning," he thunders, "every non-historical explanation of myths which seeks to establish a systematic symbolism suffers from the same error in logic," that is, failure to deal with the diachronic evidence that "mythologies are not stable" (Boas 1982, 447–449). (If he sounds here startlingly like Firth and Leach, that is because he is in fact, as we shall see later, in strikingly close agreement with structural-functionalism about the manipulation of myth for social legitimation.) Like everyone of his generation Boas had cut his teeth on the doctrine of myth as a response to "Nature," and occasional lapses and waverings indicate that he gave it up only gradually. Nevertheless, each of his major treatments of indigenous storytelling, commencing with the earliest in 1891, contains unambiguous recognitions that the fundamental hypothesis of nature-myth must be mistaken. In "The Mythologies of the Indians" (1905), for example, he says, "if it is true that there has been extended borrowing, even in the most sacred myths, then they cannot be simply a rationalistic attempt to explain nature [and] our first efforts at explanation must therefore be directed toward an interpretation of the reasons leading to borrowing and to the modification of mythological material by assimilation" (Boas 1974, 147). Boas never attained this systematic interpretation of the borrowing and modification of mythological material—his visionary challenge was to be taken up only by Claude Lévi-Strauss—but he shares with Malinowski, by virtue of his negative critique, the distinction of discrediting, for the later twentieth century, the theory first popularized by the likes of Schiller and Wordsworth.

Boas often alternates the terms "myth" and "tale" as if they were virtual synonyms, or, worse, as if they sometimes were and sometimes weren't. This wavering practice reflects his actual uncertainties about the precision of the conventional distinction. Out of this struggle he shapes his second major theoretical contribution, the definition of myth still observed to this day by most Americanists. Myth is any tale set in the age before the separation of humans from other animals. This is a clear and precise definition, but is apt to confuse at first anyone raised on the conventional myth/legend/tale hierarchy derived from Jacob Grimm. Though Grimm's triple distinctions and his degenerationism were disputed by some schismatic folklorists during the nineteenth century, by the early twentieth the triad was beginning to harden into dogma. Frazer employs it, for example, and Malinowski "discovers" that it must be hard-wired in humankind since his Trobriand Islanders know all about it. We can get a good sense of its recent status, as well as a closer look at the specifications of the terms, by examining the folklorist William Bascom's orthodox formulation of 1965, "The Forms of Folklore: Prose Narratives."

Bascom's object was to secure more precise consensus among folklorists, but his essay has been widely recognized outside his field, too, and is still often accepted as definitive. Writing after the revolution effected by British and American fieldwork, Bascom takes it for granted that the three genres are neither degenerative in Grimm's sense nor universally found among oral societies; he presents them merely as "analytical concepts which can be meaningfully applied cross-culturally" by the folklorist in the field (Bascom 1984, 10). Nevertheless, his characterizations of these genres still perpetuate the romantic, semi-theological hierarchy. In a convenient synoptic table (9), Bascom distinguishes among the three genres first by the primary categories of Belief and Time, and then by the subsidiary ones of Place, Attitude, and Principal Characters. Myth is believed in as fact; is set in the remote past, in an other or earlier world; is regarded as sacred; and displays principally non-human characters. Legend is also believed as fact, but is set in the relatively recent past, in the present world; is regarded either as sacred or secular; and exhibits principally human characters. Folktale is considered as fiction; is set in any time, in any place; is regarded as secular; and presents us with both human and non-human characters.[20]

This is the point at which Boas must be reinserted into the picture. He looms both behind and in Bascom's text as a large but very uneasy presence. Bascom assumes the soundness of the tripartite division of genres, but his synopses actually point to a more radical, Boasian conclusion, which Bascom is aware of and tries to finesse. If, contemplating Bascom's table of distinctions, we set aside for the moment the intermediate genre, legend, and focus on the dominant polarity between myth and folktale, we see that the two genres are not consistently distinguishable by any formal, literary norms. No criterion of form or content precludes a folktale from being a myth. If a folktale happens to be set in the remote past when the world was different, as many are, the Grimmian formal distinctions are otiose. The only consistent criteria left are the two psychological ones, Belief and Attitude.[21] It follows that the final arbiter of whether a narrative is myth or folktale must be the "native informant" because only he or she can testify to the presence of the appropriate subjective response. Boas's early recognition and complete acceptance of this limitation results in the methodological principle exemplified in the opening sentence of his "Comparative Study of Tsimshian Mythology": "The present collection contains a series of tales all of which are considered by the Tsimshian as myths, and I have used the term in this sense" (565). It is especially on the strength of Boas's example and teaching that this reliance upon indigenous classification (where equivalent native terms appear to exist) has become the rule, particularly among Americanists. The Boasians are not, it should be clear, asserting the complete identity of the two classes of narrative; Boas himself points out repeatedly that in many obvious cases the Grimm-Bascom criteria work well enough. He merely denies that the distinction is without excluded middle; a Venn diagram would display an overlap. His ultimate resort to the testimony of the cultural insider reflects his experience in the field that he could not always rely on the either/or of the Western formal distinction in order to know whether what he heard should be classed as myth or tale.

Bascom clearly perceives Boas as a major threat; he devotes an entire troubled page to an effort to explain away Boas's position that "it is impossible to draw a sharp line between myths and folk tales" (Boas 1984, 13).[22] Bascom supposes that Boas refers only to the inadequacy of the theories of his day, and that his reservations would have vanished if he had only considered the two genres "together" (as Bascom is doing) "under the rubric of prose narratives" (14). This is in fact what Boas does, but he arrives at the more radical conclusion, implicit in Bascom's own table, that instances of the two genres sometimes reveal no formal difference. Bascom further misinterprets the central passage from "Mythology and Folk-tales of the North American Indians" in which Boas lays out his view of the generally operative distinction between myth and folktale: "In the mind of the American native there exists almost always a clear distinction between two classes of tales. One group relates incidents which happened at a time when the world had not yet assumed its present form, when mankind was not yet in possession of all the arts and customs that belong to our period. The other group contains tales of our modern period. In other words, tales of the first group are considered as myths; those of the other as history" (Boas 1982, 454–455). Perhaps misled by the somewhat unusual force here of "history," Bascom reads this passage as being about the distinction between myth and *legend* and then proceeds to puzzle over Boas's lack of clarity about the status of folktale. But Boas's distinction is between myth and *tale*. If there is any doubt, it may be dispelled by the comparable passage in the introduction to "Comparative Study of Tsimshian Mythology," to which Bascom does not refer: "The Tsimshian distinguish clearly between two types of stories—the myth (*ada'ox*) and the tale (*ma'lesk*). The latter is entirely *historical* [my italics] in character, although from our point of view it may contain supernatural elements. The incidents narrated in the former are believed to have happened during the time when animals appeared in the form of human beings" (565). Boas plainly has in mind in these remarks an ontological gap between what he sometimes calls "the mythological age" and "the modern period." In stark contrast to the former, the latter includes the entire course of "fallen" human experience in the flow of contingent events that we call "time." The terms "history" and "historical" in these contexts refer to this latter existential condition, not to any veridical establishment of *"was eigentlich gewesen ist."* If a story is set in the earlier condition of the world, the Tsimshian classify it as *ada'ox,* "myth," and if in its current condition as *ma'lesk,* "tale." What is most surprising about Bascom's misreading is his notion that Boas would be thinking at such a juncture of "legend." Boas cares nothing about this intermediate concept and seldom even mentions it, probably because he finds everywhere among the groups he studies the same kind of *two-term* distinction between myth and tale that he attributes to the Tsimshian. Bascom's purely Grimmian intrusion of "legend" obscures for him and for his readers the dynamic central to the workings of indigenous narrative as Boas actually perceived and reported it.

Last, but far from least, Bascom departs from his elder's model in declaring under his rubric of "Attitude" that myth is received as "sacred." The rest of Bascom's descriptive definition of myth owes much to Boas, and is in every other respect consonant with his; myths are "narratives which, in the society in which they are told, are considered to be truthful accounts of what happened in the remote past" (9). Bascom even qualifies his characterization of their reception as "sacred": "they are *usually* sacred, and they are *often* [my italics] associated with theology and ritual." Boas, however, emphasizes positively in numerous contexts that myth is not necessarily received as sacred at all. He admonishes us to remember that "in the mind of the Indian it is not the religious, ritualistic or explanatory character of a tale that makes it a myth, but the fact that it pertains to a period when the world was different from what it is now" (Boas 1916, 565). This warning decrees that the setting is primary, and the attribution of sacredness secondary. The religious or sacred feel of a story does not induce the Tsimshian to class it as a myth; first comes the recognition by temporal setting that the story is or is not a myth, then, secondarily, whatever religious sentiments it may be appropriate to attach to that fact. This is a relatively radical proposition. Bascom's generalization that myth is usually received as sacred is much more traditional, and all the more understandable if one recalls that he is attempting to characterize world mythology, not merely Amerindian. For that matter, there is plenty of evidence that most American societies have regarded their myths as "sacred" in some sense of this phenomenologically difficult term, even if in many cases—of scabrous joking or farce, for example—the grounds for the attribution elude "European" conceptions of sacredness. A further case could be made, too, for the possibility that Native Americans are, or were, so conditioned to respond with religious awe to stories set in the mythological age that even if the perception of sacredness is not a *sufficient* cause of their receiving a story as myth, it is a *necessary* one. But, however Boas's claim for the primacy of temporal setting is to be assessed, acceptance of it entails the sometime formal identity of myth and tale, and demolishes essentializing distinctions among the hierarchical and degenerationist troika of genres bequeathed to us by Grimm.

In fact, Boas's third major contribution to the problematic of these genres reverses Grimm's degenerationism outright by showing that myth results from the ideological elaboration of folktale and that the homelier (less *unheimlich*) genre has the better claim to developmental precedence. To get this argument in clear perspective, though, we must first face what might look like a serious inconsistency. In keeping with his deep distrust of *a priori* theories, Boas asserts in a few contexts that the ten-thousand-year-old buildup and shattering of "mythological worlds" has created a situation in which "the contents of folk-tales and myths are largely the same . . . the data show a continual flow of material from mythology to folk-tale and *vice-versa,* and . . . neither group can claim priority" (Boas 1982, 405). He never backs down from this position that the state of the evidence precludes *historical* proof of either genre's priority. But he does depart from this seemingly even-handed treatment of both sides by emphasizing in many contexts the *logical* case for the priority of folktale. This case is grounded in Boas's first and fundamental theoretical contribution, his Wundt-like persuasion that more complex stories are constructed out of the simpler elements of folk-tradition, "adopted ready made and . . . adapted and changed according to the genius of the people who borrowed [them]" (Boas 1974, 96). Boas recognizes that under the pressure of religious and social beliefs such elements have often been molded into systematic mythologies, and he confronts in a number of contexts the question of how this can result from unsystematic, even unconscious, borrowing. His answer is that such mythological systems are always conscious, secondary elaborations. After making his characteristic point in a review, for example, that "the material of every mythology does not by any means represent an old system, but has been assembled from many sources," he continues: "If in spite of this fact a system should exist, it would have arisen out of the reorganization of all the native and foreign material into a new unity" (Boas 1982, 447). Where such reorganization occurs, Boas looks especially for individual agents, a religious reformer or group of reformers. "The priest or chief as poet or thinker takes hold of the folk-traditions and of isolated rituals and elaborates them in dramatic and poetic form" (482).

In spite of this emphasis upon the invention of creative individuals, Boas agrees essentially with Durkheim and British structural-functionalism about the social pressures behind such systematizing. Indeed, his account of how the clans of the Bella Coola produce out of hostile rivalry "the most contradictory myths in regard to important events in the world's history" (153) would seem to corroborate Leach's view of myth as the site of contestation rather than of Malinowskian compromise-formations. Boas most typically views the systematizers as engaged in producing ideological rationalizations of the status quo: "The more important the tale becomes on account of its association with the privileges and rituals of certain sections of the tribe . . . the more have the keepers of the ritual brooded over it in all its aspects. . . . This accounts for the relation between the occurrence of complex rituals in charge of a priestly class or of chiefs, and of long myths which have an esoteric significance" (482). Boas anticipates not only Foucauldian but feminist critique in his sardonic view of esoteric myth as the typical product of a caste of initiated males who are dissatisfied with the exoteric traditions of folktale available to everyone, including women and children.

Boas generally attacks degenerationism, too, by contrasting the logical priority of the folktale elements with the ideological elaboration that produces myth. He points out, first, how suspicious it is that where mythology has been elaborately mystified, "the exoteric mythology seldom agrees with the esoteric system" (448). (The discrepancy Goody finds among the LoDaaga of Ghana perfectly illustrates this point.) Because "the materials for the systematic composition are the disconnected folk-tales," it is "from a psychological point of view . . . therefore not justifiable to consider the exoteric tales, as is so often done, degenerate fragments of the esoteric teaching" (483). Not only is there a constant dialogue between outside tale and inside myth that modifies both, but there can be no serious question about priority: "The theory of degeneration is not supported by any facts; and I fail entirely to see how the peculiar form of American systematic mythology can be explained, except as a result of the artistic elaboration of the disconnected folk-tales" (483). Because myth as we encounter it in living oral societies is elaborated out of tale and demonstrably unable to transcend its origins, it is in theory junior to its much-patronized sibling, even though historical proof of this priority will always remain unattainable. Only when we grasp this last facet of Boas's testimony are we in a position to appreciate fully the force of his epigram: "It would seem that mythological worlds have been built up, only to be shattered again, and that new worlds were built from the fragments."

While Boas's extended investigation of folkloristic genres has never enjoyed the same resonance as Malinowski's unveiling of a new theory, it is a comparable achievement in mythography. It builds upon a solid base of empirical experience a formidable refutation both of the romantic degenerationism current in Boas's day and the glorification of esoteric "primitive" mythologies by later twentieth-century neo-transcendentalists. That this critique, entirely in place by 1914, should have been so thoroughly ignored by the latter even into the midcentury is further indication of their fixation upon outmoded work more conformable with their purposes. It would also be difficult to overestimate the value internal to anthropology itself of Malinowski's and Boas's combined emphasis upon story in relation to the modern institution of fieldwork. The problematic of indigenous narrative forms confronts every outside observer willy nilly, and there are serious interpretive issues implicated in every response to it. Boas, like Malinowski, not only understood this, as it would seem any field-collector must, but committed a considerable portion of his career to the struggle to measure his inherited terms against his actual experience. In consequence, his analyses of the formation of myth both provide invaluable evidence of the internal dynamic of the genres and corroborate the extent to which myth is constructed as social legitimation. Finally, Boas's work inspires, to a degree still inadequately recognized, the ambitions of the third major anthropological theorist of "myth" in the twentieth century, Claude Lévi-Strauss. Suffice it to say here that Lévi-Strauss finds a way to carry out Boas's grand diffusionist conception of pursuing through the mythologies of the Americas the "reasons leading to borrowing and . . . modification of mythological material" (Boas 1974, 147). It's true that he conducts this pursuit by means of a theory of which it is hard to imagine Boas approving, but his methods as well as his goal are nevertheless built in fundamental ways upon a number of Boasian insights. These include assumptions that (1) the real "reasons" for mythological transformations may be as little known to the storyteller as "the grammatical system of his language" (Boas 1982, 447); (2) all variants of a story should be included in its analysis; (3) the whole complex of a culture's symbol systems, including its art and ritual, may be transpositions of its myths and *vice versa;* and (4) myths undergo generic transformations at cultural borders. In fact, Lévi-Strauss's pursuit of these lines of thought helps to clarify in retrospect the nature and scope of Boas's aspirations.

MYTH BETWEEN BOAS AND LÉVI-STRAUSS

During the forty years between Boas's major work on myth and Lévi-Strauss's initial venture, the situation in the United States resembles that in England after Malinowski; there is little innovation in folkloristic theorizing of myth. Unlike what occurs in Britain, however, where Malinowski's interest in individual psychology evokes no major response, a number of Boas's students and others affected by him attempt serious psychological interpretations of traditional oral story.

This psychologizing trend develops with his blessing. In a late (1936) defense of his consistency he describes thus what many had and have seen as a break in his interests: "In my early teaching . . . I stressed the necessity of the study of acculturation . . . and dissemination. When I thought that these *historical* methods were firmly established I began to stress, about 1910, the problems of cultural dynamics, of integration of culture and of the interactions between individual and society" (Boas 1974, 311).[23] Lowie and Kroeber may be taken as typical of the older generation of Boas's students, producing, on one hand, their excellent, untheorized collections of tribal "mythologies" and, on the other, theoretical essays on "primitive religion" in which, as in Durkheim, the concept of myth scarcely figures. By 1924, however, Sapir, Radin, Benedict, and Mead were reading and discussing Jung's *Psychological Types* (1919) and Sapir and Benedict, at least, were pursuing Koffka's *Gestalt* psychology as well (Stocking 1992, 298). This cross-disciplinary study suggests a new determination, if not desperation, to get beyond Boas's reluctance to theorize.

Marvin Harris maintains in *The Rise of Anthropological Theory* that Boas's turn to psychology and eventually to "culture and personality" is the result of his increasing pessimism about the discoverability of law-like regularities in cultural phenomena (Harris 1968, 277–282, especially 280). Paul Radin, in many respects the closest follower of Boas's methods among his younger students, appears to support Harris's conjecture when he affirms in the conclusion to his early *The Method and Theory of Ethnology* that only "a psychoanalyst like Jung is on the correct trail" toward the student of culture's ultimate ambition, a "satisfactory knowledge of what constitutes human nature" (Radin 1965, 267). In his two most important efforts, Radin remains faithful to the Master's method of exploring in detail cycles of story and their diffusion through neighboring cultures, while managing at the same time to discover in them a Jungian pattern of psychological development through time that confers upon his inquiry the kind of genuine historical dimension he complains is lacking in Boas's own. The first of these works is the speculative sketch in *The World of Primitive Man* of the history of libidinal development implicit in the Winnebago hero cycles, and the second is the detailed analysis of this development of one such cycle in Radin's masterpiece, *The Trickster*.[24]

In the earlier work, Radin hypothesizes that the four Winnebago hero cycles can be disposed along a developmental continuum. Trickster represents the lowest, "primordial" stage of both physical and psychic individuation, and Hare, whose story is set in the world as we know it today, manifests the stage of imperfect libidinal development indicated by Hare's ambivalence about human beings. Red Horn shows the same well-differentiated libido signified by the Olympian deities' displays of morally good and bad behavior, and the Twins exhibit the truly integrated development characteristic of humankind's mastery of the earth in the Age of Prometheus. In *The Trickster,* Radin focuses his analysis upon the first of these cycles, though he includes as supplements for comparative purposes summaries of the Hare cycle and the Assiniboine and Tlingit Trickster cycles. In his brilliantly detailed analysis and subsequent comparative analyses, Radin finds in this first cycle a compressed version of the development of all four. He argues that in the Winnebago Trickster tales, someone with "consummate literary ability" has remodeled this most ancient of story-cycles, with its typically Boasian "composite nature" into "an aboriginal literary masterpiece" (Radin 1972, 146). It dramatizes "the evolution of a Trickster from an undefined being to one with the physiognomy of man, from a being psychically undeveloped and a prey to his instincts, to an individual who is at least conscious of what he does and who attempts to become socialized" (136).[25] This ambitious hypothesis is persuasive in context because it is so precisely and carefully supported by detailed Boasian study of the cycle and its analogues in neighboring mythologies.

The best representative of the turn toward Freud is probably Clyde Kluckhohn's stodgy but mollifying synthesis, "Myth and Rituals: A General Theory," first published in 1941. Kluckhohn is perhaps more interested in ritual than in myth, but he tries to be evenhanded in this matter as in all else. Though he allows for the sometime independence of myth and rite, he plumps for their generally "intricate mutual interdependence" (Kluckhohn 1968, 147). He declares that Malinowski has "brilliantly" set myth on a proper basis in "Myth in Primitive Psychology" and established there "the fallacy of all unilateral explanations" (145). Some myths do explain natural phenomena, some accompany rituals, some express "the culturally disallowed but unconsciously wanted," and some "stand apart" as "symbolic representations of the dominant configurations [principles that structure implicit patterns] of the particular culture" (145–146).[26] Then, after expressing his gratitude to "the French sociologists" and British structural-functionalists for teaching us that myth and ritual are "symbolic processes for dealing with the same type of situation in the same affective mode" (149), Kluckhohn makes his defining American move: "If Malinowski and Radcliffe-Brown (and their followers) turned the searchlight of their interpretations as illuminatingly upon specific human animals and their impulses as upon cultural and social abstractions, it might be possible to take their work as providing a fairly complete and adequate general theory of myth and ritual" (148). For actually acknowledging the impulses of these specific animals, however, "psychoanalytic interpretation . . . seems preferable" (149). The French and British establish that "myths are adaptive from the point of view of society" (155), that is, conducive to its biological survival, but the question remains what the individual gets out of them that has enabled them for so long "to prevail at the expense of more rational responses" (155). Kluckhohn's concise answer is that "myth and rituals provide a cultural storehouse of adjustive responses" (159–160). Myth and ritual are particularly conservative modes of symbolic expression precisely because "they deal with those sectors of experience which do not seem amenable to rational control and hence where human beings can least tolerate insecurity" (158). Taking a cue from behavioral psychology, Kluckhohn argues that humans can be motivated either by current needs or anticipated ones and that myth and ritual "are reinforced because they reduce the anticipation of disaster" (159). The forms this anticipation or "anxiety" takes differ with the culture. Among Kluckhohn's Navaho (who serve as his source of illustrative examples throughout) the "type anxiety" is about health, and "every ceremonial still carried out today" (160) is a curing ritual.

Kluckhohn's characterization of myth as being a storehouse of "adjustive" responses, and his identification of the "anticipation of disaster" with "anxiety," particularly "neurotic" anxiety, inevitably suggest the neo-Freudian ego-psychology in fashion at the time he wrote. The connection is confirmed when he remarks, "Of the ten 'mechanisms of defence' which Anna Freud suggests that the ego has available, their myths and rituals afford the Navaho with institutionalized means of employing at least four" (160). These are said to be reaction-formation, introjection, projection, and sublimation. As Kluckhohn goes on to remark, "these 'mechanisms of ego defence' will come into context only if we answer the question 'adjustive with respect to what?'" He spends his last few pages answering that question (very movingly) with respect to the Navaho. The components of their "anxiety" range from "'threats' which may be understood in terms of the 'reality principle'" (160), such as the marginality of their survival in the environment and their high incidence of organic disease, to isolation, intense interpersonal and intra-familial hostilities bred from it, and the pressure of the encompassing white society. Insofar as recourse to myth as a mode of ego-defense "reaffirms" under these conditions "the solidarity of the Navaho sentiment system" (163), myth's restoration of the individual to the traditional ways of his community is adaptive as well as adjustive.

In the course of a century rich with complex interchanges between two of its most striking new disciplines, this psychological modification of the Boasian critique of myth constitutes a definite movement, though a small and slightly desperate one. While remaining rooted in their field experiences of myth in its folkloristic sense, Radin and Kluckhohn appear to wish to supplement Boas's conception of its *subject matter* (tales of the world as it was) with explanations of its *origin* (in mental need) and *functions* (in maturation and adaptation). In these attributions they are virtually at one with psychologists coming to social anthropology from the opposite direction. The real tribute to the originality of Boas's contributions to establishing the subject matter of myth in the folkloristic sense is the extent to which American cultural anthropologists, folklorists, and their fellow travelers continue to employ them, and thus continue to honor the concept of "myth" in a degree that has sometimes struck English social anthropologists after Malinowski as chimerical. Meanwhile, however, substantive innovation after the American master is, if anything, even less in evidence than after the English one. When a strong new theory does arise at midcentury, it comes as a genuine intellectual surprise.

[10]

Folkloristic Myth in Social Anthropology II:
From Lévi-Strauss to
Withdrawal from Grand Theory

The first two-thirds of this chapter takes up the grandest of grand theories, while the last third tracks the more recent subsidence from such totalizing aspirations. Claude Lévi-Strauss is unique both in dedicating the majority of his career to the study of myth and in moving the topic from its modest, ancillary role in ethnological inquiry to center stage in a discourse that has attracted since the mid-fifties broad interest even outside his own discipline. His work on myth has often, and rightly, been viewed as an idiosyncratic mix of French sociology with structural linguistics and Americanist anthropology. But, of these three, the last and least examined has the best claim to temporal priority.[1] Lévi-Strauss tells us in his memoir, *Tristes Tropiques* (1955), that his initial attraction to anthropology in the early thirties was to the Boasian tradition, represented in particular by Lowie's *Primitive Society*. That he actually became an Americanist, however, was a serendipitous result of an appointment to teach sociology at the University of Sao Paolo, with the understanding that he would have the opportunity do fieldwork among the indigenous peoples of the Brazilian interior. His subsequent expeditions of 1935 and 1937–1938 launched his anthropological career and a more general accident of history guaranteed that he would remain during his most formative decade oriented especially toward the study of Amerindian cultures. The Nazi occupation of France and a postwar appointment as cultural attaché determined his sojourn in New York between 1941 and 1947, thus ensuring personal contact with his sponsor, Lowie, with Boas himself, and with the American establishment in general. What this meant for the direction of his interests is encapsulated in his moving account of discovering in Manhattan in 1941 a secondhand bookstore specializing in government documents where one could pick up the classic reports of the American Bureau of Ethnography. "It was as though the American Indian cultures had suddenly come alive" (Lévi-Strauss 1976, 50). As he goes on to remark, this was only a few months before he was invited to Washington by this same Bureau and asked to contribute to its current major project, the seven-volume *Handbook of South American Indians.*

Lévi-Strauss's articles for *Handbook,* which might be considered as the visible sign of his acceptance by the Americanist establishment, appeared in the third volume in 1948 and 1950, thus bracketing neatly the startlingly different appearance in 1949 of *Les structures élémentaires de la parenté.* Lévi-Strauss has consistently claimed that his interest in "structure," as manifested, for example, in the work of Granet, Dumézil, and Benveniste, was merely confirmed by his intercourse with Roman Jakobson during the years in New York (see, e.g., Lévi-Strauss 1991, 99). At the same time, however, he acknowledges the importance of Jacobson's linguistic messianism, and it is certainly possible to specify his debts to structural linguistics (Leitch 1983, 16). He has also paid tribute to Jacobson's specific role in encouraging his younger colleague to undertake in 1943 what turned out to be the *Elementary Structures* (Lévi-Strauss 1991, 43). This work on kinship foreshadows the work on myth both in its bold aspiration to order one of the topics of traditional ethnology that had accumulated the largest and most bewildering mass of seemingly disparate data, and also in its polemical confidence that a method modeled on structural linguistics could cut through the tangles. Lévi-Strauss concurs with the founders of kinship studies in finding at the core of this data the incest taboo. But, rather than essentializing the taboo, he employs a version of Marcel Mauss's conception of general exchange to show that the taboo helps to structure a system of gift-giving in which daughters and sisters are the medium of exchange that cements social relations between men.

Mauss represents the third of the author's commonly alleged realms of intellectual indebtedness—French, that is to say, Durkheimian, sociology. In his 1950 *Introduction to the Work of Marcel Mauss,* Lévi-Strauss turns Mauss into a proto-structuralist who understands that the grasp of "total social fact" requires that empirical observation be subsumed in the discovery of laws analogous to those of linguistics, laws that function, like them, at a level deeper than the subjective awarenesses of the observer or the observed (Lévi-Strauss 1987, passim). Lévi-Strauss's responses to Durkheim himself are a good deal more complicated and ambivalent.[2] But he is unquestionably a descendant in two general senses. The first of these, as he points out in his centennial tribute, is being enabled by Durkheim's work to envision "a systematic typology of beliefs and behaviors" (Lévi-Strauss 1976, 48). The related, second sense is his interest in "primitive thought," especially in the mode of mental construction that Durkheim called *"représentations collectives."* For Lévi-Strauss the concept includes both kinship relations and myth.

Myth may have succeeded kinship as the object of Lévi-Strauss's structural study partly through another piece of serendipity, an appointment to the chair of

"Religions of Nonliterate Peoples" in the *École des Hautes Études* that required his attention to what he came to call "religious representations." But the explanation that consorts best with the kind of ambition on display in *The Elementary Structures* is expressed in the "Overture" to *The Raw and the Cooked*. Here Lévi-Strauss constructs his own variation on Tylor's famous apothegm that appears as epigraph to *The Elementary Structures*. Tylor's "if law is anywhere, it is everywhere" becomes Lévi-Strauss's "if the human mind appears determined even in the realm of mythology, *a fortiori* it must also be determined in all its spheres of activity" (Lévi-Strauss 1969, 10). By 1955, after about five years of research, he was ready to present to the world his account of how the mind is indeed so determined. It is laid out in the well-known and often reprinted talk he first delivered in a symposium on myth at Indiana University, "The Structural Study of Myth." Since this essay does present the core of his structural theory, it deserves examination in detail.

After commencing with the virtually de rigueur account of the chaos in the field of mythography, Lévi-Strauss confronts his audience with the paradox that the wild arbitrariness of content in myths "is belied by the astounding similarity" of these stories worldwide (Lévi-Strauss 1965, 83). He proceeds immediately to argue that a solution to this apparent antinomy can be discovered by thinking of myth as analogous to language. Indeed, myth is the contrary of poetry in being that "part of language where the formula *traduttore, tradittore* reaches its lowest truth-value" (85). The values of myth, in other words, "remain preserved even through the worst translation." This innocuous-sounding remark conceals a stunning implication; the assertion can be true only if some generic quality in myth succeeds in escaping, in transcending, any verbal formulation. The issue Lévi-Strauss confronts here has been part of the problematic of myth since Creuzer. But when he adopts Creuzer's *solution,* we are in the presence of the most radically anti-diachronic, that is, anti-narrative, move since the palmy days of the invention of the "romantic symbol" itself.

By pursuing his linguistic analogy, Lévi-Strauss soon identifies "on the sentence level" the "gross constituent units" (86) of narrative, roughly comparable to the morphemes and phonemes of the linguist, that are in fact responsible for conveying subliminally the presence of myth. Thus Lévi-Strauss's claim that we recognize myth intuitively, a claim that sounds on the face of it as mystical as anything in Creuzer or Jung, is put on a material basis that in fact undercuts any religious phenomenology. To get at these "units," each sentence in a story is reduced on an index card to the shortest possible statement of relation between the subject and the function predicated of it. What this procedure isolates, however, must be the constituent unit of *every* narrative. Lévi-Strauss's way of acknowledging this difficulty is to complain that we still find ourselves in the realm of "non-revertible" time since the numbers of the cards correspond to the unfolding of the informant's speech. "Thus, the specific character of mythological time, which . . . is both revertible and non-revertible, synchronic and diachronic, remains unaccounted for" (87). He produces, consequently, the "hypothesis which constitutes the very core of our argument: the true constituent units of myth are not the isolated relations, but *bundles of such relations* and it is only as bundles that these relations can be put to use and combined so as to produce a meaning." Here we encounter the prime corollary of his initial assumption that something in myth transcends narration. For he is not merely asserting the truism that every narrative (once written down) can be laid out schematically for diachronic inspection. He is maintaining, rather, that myth is distinguished from other genres of narrative by the fact that it commands a different sort of time. The primary feature of "mythological time" is that real "meaning" inheres not at all in the diachronic dimension of performance, but only in a synchronic dimension in which the structural invariants that underlie all performances can be determined by synthetic comparison.

The (faulty) analogies that follow, to the structures of musical scores and playing cards, do not prepare us for the surprise that awaits when we encounter the consequences of this thinking in its first, model application to a myth. The author tells us he picked the central story of the House of Thebes for its familiarity, yet it may well have been also for the guaranteed shock value when he reveals that in the light of synchronic analysis the myth "means" something deeply *un*familiar, namely, that "the overrating of blood relations is to the underrating of blood relations as the attempt to escape autochthony is to the impossibility to succeed in it" (90). It does not matter if no one in the ancient world and no one else since has ever understood the story in this way; the *method* understands it thus, and that must suffice. By subjecting his audience to this excoriation and substitution of meaning in a story familiar to them, Lévi-Strauss brings home the full significance of his dismissal of intentionality and conscious understanding in acts of storytelling. We might be able to assent without much reflection to a claim that the "simple" tales of "primitives" do not mean merely what their tellers think they do. But the chorus of protest and emendation from learned professionals and common readers alike in response to Lévi-Strauss's reading of the Theban cycle indicates how difficult it is to accept this assertion when it concerns a story whose cultural significance we have participated in constructing.[3]

Recognizing this claim—that myth yields to structural analysis a level of signification that eludes its tellers—is crucial to a grasp of Lévi-Strauss's theory. The idea stems from the joining together of his very early acceptance of the Freudian unconscious, with the same modification of Freud epitomized in Lacan's dictum that the unconscious is structured like a language. Both of these ideas then combine with Lévi-Strauss's conviction that the endless and apparently pointless variations of behavior in some of humanity's most universal institutions must be built upon law-like invariants that operate in us unawares. In the case of the Theban stories his structural analysis leads him to conclude that "the myth has to do with the inability, for a culture which holds the belief that mankind is autochthonous . . . to find a satisfactory transition between this theory and the knowledge that human beings are actually born of the union of man and woman" (91–92). The myth, then, serves a pragmatic purpose, as surely as in Malinowski, though this purpose is cognitive rather than affective and unconscious rather than conscious: "although experience contradicts theory, social life verifies cosmology by its similarity of structure" (92). Myth, that is to say, mediates or rationalizes an aporia between nature and culture. This is not only what it does, but also the most general message it conveys, behind the backs, beyond the consciousnesses, of its makers.

Some early readers of Lévi-Strauss were reluctant to believe that he means what he says here, but his later clarifications leave little room for doubt. In the "Overture" to *The Raw and the Cooked,* for example, he begins his most explicit confrontation of this issue mildly enough by allowing that "the possibility cannot be excluded that the speakers who create and transmit myths may become aware of their structure and mode of operation" (Lévi-Strauss 1969, 11). But he proceeds to argue that "this cannot occur as a normal thing" (12) for two reasons. The first is the same as for why even a trained linguist cannot readily analyze her own phonology or grammar in the act of speaking. The second is related but special to myth's status as belief—commitment is not consistent with analytical dissection. This line of reflection culminates in the declaration "We are not, then, claiming to show how men think in myths, but how myths think themselves in men, and unknown to them."[4] This diction evokes the resonance of Heidegger's famous aphorism that language speaks us.

This distinctive conception of myth as subject to laws of thought, but only on a level unknown to its utterers, positions Lévi-Strauss quite uniquely athwart two of the classic ethnological disputes—whether myth is primarily cognitive or affective and whether it is primarily a result of diffusion or of independent invention. In each case he is able to have it both ways. Nothing in the theory, to take the first case, precludes his commonsense recognition that myth is emotionally significant to its circulators. "The Structural Study" belongs to the same year as *Tristes Tropiques,* and the author of the haunting elegy on the fate of the Nambikwara has not turned overnight into an "antihumanist," icily indifferent to what moves people without writing to cherish their stories. What his structural analysis does reject is the traditional Western assumption, "humanist" if one likes, that this subjective, personal level of meaning is the one that uniquely matters. Lévi-Strauss easily concedes the presence of emotive values in myth (and ritual), but he has very little to say about them because they afford no purchase to structural analysis; they merely occasion the unconscious elaboration of the cognitive regularities that do.[5] The theory also makes room for both positions in the dispute between diffusion and independent invention. The claim for the existence of unconscious structural laws might seem to favor independent invention, but Lévi-Strauss takes it for granted that these laws do not operate in a vacuum. He adopts Franz Boas's conception of Amerindian storytelling as a single diffusional field reflecting most basically the original patterns of migration and involving over centuries the continual collapse and reconstruction of the material of myth. People first encounter the stories, then slowly transform them, ostensibly in direct or indirect relation to their communal values, but also, "unknown to themselves," within the constitutive limits of the laws of mythical thought. With respect to theories of independent invention, Lévi-Strauss's differs from psychological explanations like Jung's in being purely a structural, operational set of rules free of determined content. Lévi-Strauss himself has sometimes cited as if it were a badge of honor Paul Ricoeur's early negative characterization of the theory as "Kantianism without a transcendental subject" (Lévi-Strauss 1969, 11). What Ricoeur sees as a logical contradiction—regulative epistemological categories beyond the thinking subject—Lévi-Strauss sees as simply the case.

At this point in "The Structural Study" Lévi-Strauss introduces a very important corollary to his proposition that a myth is defined by its gists of translatable "meaning" rather than by its plot. This is the rule that a myth is present in all its variations, none of which is to be preferred as the true or the original version. This principle is also a logical consequence of the systematic valorizing of synchrony over diachrony. As Lévi-Strauss points out, it obviates "one of the main obstacles to the progress of mythological studies" (92), the quest for origins. The rule applies with singular felicity to anonymous, communally disseminated oral tale. In fact, its appearance in "The Structural Study" coincides with the propagation in the field of classical studies of the Parry-Lord hypothesis that each performance of an oral tale is the creation of a new variant of which none may be considered definitive. Lévi-Strauss's insight has worked its way in tandem with Parry-Lord into a new orthodoxy in our day about the nature of oral narrative.[6]

Lévi-Strauss immediately tops this insight by introducing a further corollary destined, in his own work at least, to outshine its predecessor. It is stated with disarming simplicity: "If a myth is made up of all its variants, structural analysis should take all of them into account" (93). Lévi-Strauss notoriously carries this so far as to insist that modern Western versions must count, that Freud's version of Sophocles' *Oedipus* ought to be, and can be, absorbed within his own structural reading of the Theban cycle. The full significance of this new theorem only begins to unfold, however, when we see where it leads in the second half of "The Structural Study." Lévi-Strauss slips into this half by telling us, again disarmingly, that "in order to check" his new theorem, "an attempt was made in 1953–54 towards an exhaustive analysis of all the known versions of the Zuni origin and emergence myth. . . . A preliminary attempt was made at a comparison of the results with similar myths in other Pueblo tribes. . . . Finally a test was undertaken with Plains mythology" (95). Lévi-Strauss manipulates the reader here by a characteristic rhetorical move. The proposition that structural analysis should include all relevant variants cannot be either confirmed or disconfirmed by any amount of testing, nor does it need to be; the gesture toward scientific method distracts us from recognizing that Lévi-Strauss's actual purpose in running Southwest and Plains mythologies through his new machine is to demonstrate how well the machine works, how effectively his method appears to order a disordered field.

One can almost hear the sigh of relief with which he shifts from ancient Greek to Amerindian mythology. His initial resort to the Theban cycle has its strategic merits; it not only appeals to our familiarity with the story in order to defamiliarize it, but also expresses a comparativist ambition. Like Durkheim and Mauss in "Primitive Classification," or even Frazer in *The Golden Bough,* Lévi-Strauss intends his juxtaposition of mythologies from chirographic and oral cultures to imply the universal applicability of his method. But he pays a steep price for his use of the Greek material, as he partly anticipates in his apologetic introduction of it. His choice of the matter of Thebes obscures the normal working of his analysis in two important respects: first, by the very act of focusing on an "advanced" mythology, and, second, by limiting him to the deduction of an ultimate "meaning" that is structured as a formal analogy rather than as the transformation of a mediating term. But the implications of each of these flaws calls for further examination.

In order to appreciate the risk Lévi-Strauss takes by demonstrating his method upon a story shaped by at least two of the ancient world's most skillful literary artists, it is necessary only to recall his fundamental assumption that the "meaning" of a myth is to be found by reducing a narrative to its armature of "constituent units." I have already suggested that the result is the most anti-narrative theory of myth since the invention of the romantic symbol; let me go a step further and assert that for Lévi-Strauss *pure* myth, could there be such a thing, would transcend discursive recounting altogether and present itself as a visual diagram. In fact, the characteristic diagrams that stud his work partly express this nineteenth-century *symboliste* ideal.[7] It cannot be stressed too emphatically that for him the strongest myths are not the most aesthetically rich or culturally complex, but those that display most cleanly their paradigmatic structure. Indeed, he maintains in contradiction to the usual evolutionary piety that myth actually degenerates as it accumulates complexities deleterious to its structural message.

This conviction determines his pragmatic selection of mythologies for study. A number of critics have objected that by focusing exclusively (after "The Structural Study") upon the mythologies of totemic areas at the expense of classical or Near Eastern or Asian myth, he makes too easy his Rousseauvian demonstration that divisions between nature and culture constitute the great theme of "primitive" thought. These latter mythologies, it is implied, being more sophisticated, would not prove so tractable.[8] This may be a valid objection to the limits of Lévi-Strauss's self-testing, but it overlooks the theoretical principle motivating his choice of sites, a choice as deliberate and as practical as Durkheim's. Both thinkers hold it difficult enough to get down to "the elementary forms" of religion or myth without taking on advanced cultures in which these forms are concealed beneath impeding layers of complexity. Readers of *Mythologiques* can scarcely avoid noticing that, although Lévi-Strauss prefers on principle to trace transformations of myth across contiguous cultures where diffusion may be assumed, his many shuttlings between South and North America leap evasively over a silent center. In *The Raw and the Cooked* he tells us why: "I have deliberately avoided using the myths of the advanced civilizations of Central America and Mexico because, having been reformulated by educated speakers, they call for prolonged syntagmatic analysis before they can be used as paradigms" (177). Having put this methodological rule at risk for limited strategic purposes in the first half of "The Structural Study," he silently reinstates it in the second.

I have also remarked that Lévi-Strauss's treatment of the Theban cycle obscures part of his usual method of analysis when it presents the "meaning" of the cycle as a formal analogy instead of a transformation through mediating terms. The difference between the two confronts us when we compare at the beginning of the second half of the essay the master-chart of the Zuni emergence myth to the earlier chart of the Theban cycle. "The purpose of myth," Lévi-Strauss informs us near the end of his essay, "is to provide a logical model capable of overcoming a contradiction" (105), and he promptly adds parenthetically that this is "an impossible achievement if, as it happens, the contradiction is real." Given the fundamental nature of the problems unconsciously modeled in the storytelling of humanity, the contradictions usually *are* "real," that is, basic antinomies of existence. Certainly this is true of both the Greek and Zuni myths; the one struggles to reconcile cultural belief in autochthony with the natural fact of sexual engendering, and the other attempts nothing less than "discovering a mediation between life and death" (96). When we compare the two charts, however, we see that they represent very different stages in "the overcoming of a contradiction." In the case of the Greek myth Lévi-Strauss presents us only with the relatively abstract final result, a formal analogy between an aspect of kinship and an aspect of religious belief; the overrating of blood relations is to their underrating as the denial of autochthony is to its persistence. The relation between the parts can be expressed by the formula for a formal analogy: a: b:: c: d, or, in this particular case, a: b:: d: c. The distributed variants of the Zuni myth, however, display a series of mediations (which Lévi-Strauss rather questionably calls "dialectical") between two sets of contraries, on both the synchronic and diachronic axes. If one were to express these sets of contraries, employing Lévi-Strauss's labels for them, as a four-term analogy, the result would be: increase: death:: death: permanency [of the species], or, for purposes of comparison, a. b(1):: b(2): c. The difference between this result and the formal analogy expressed in the Greek case is the Janus-like mediating function of the middle term "death," the significance of which shifts with respect to the other term of the comparison. A further glance at the two charts reveals that the Zuni supplies us with a great deal more information than does the Greek about the logical stages by which the culture constructed its model. It follows that the Zuni mode of transformation occurs at a relative micro-level; it requires for its analysis much more detailed information about conventional analogical associations in the culture involved, but it yields correspondingly richer results. This gain in purchase constitutes another important reason, besides the greater strength and clarity of the oppositions in "primitive" myth, why the expert on the analogical thinking of totemistic Amerindian societies prefers to work with their mythologies.

Lévi-Strauss will continue to refer to and employ both of these phases, or levels, of analogical deduction in his later work, but he focuses for the remainder of "The Structural Study" on adducing Southwest and Plains examples of the level of mythical "meaning" constructed by mediation. In the pages immediately following the introduction of the Zuni master-chart he illustrates the flexibility of a field of oppositions set up by mediation. First he shows in more detail that the western Pueblos proceed from the extremes to the middle in a series of narrowing mediations till they reach a poise on the antinomy that hunting provides animal food but only at the cost of life destroyed. Lévi-Strauss points out that it is possible to reverse the procedure, as some central and eastern Pueblos do, starting in the middle with the paradoxical identification of hunting and cultivation and then trying "to derive both life and death from that central notion" (99). Whether negotiated from outside in or inside out, the distributed variants of the synchronic network express the same "meaning" by means of a series of mediations.

This demonstration of the symmetries and reciprocities brought out when all the variants of a myth are ranged schematically presents a model of the method that has since dominated Lévi-Strauss's entire practice. "By using systematically this

kind of structural analysis it becomes possible to organize all the known variants
of a myth as a series forming a kind of permutation group, the two variants placed
at the far-ends being in a symmetrical, though inverted, relationship to each other"
(99). No sooner does Lévi-Strauss announce this general rule than he sets off
exuberantly on a series of discursions intended, he claims, to show us three of the
"basic logical processes which are at the root of mythical thought." But these are
also, and hardly incidentally, calculated to demonstrate the power of his method to
illuminate several of the major puzzles of North American mythology.

The first of these excursions applies the "law" we have already seen in operation, "mythical thought always works from the awareness of oppositions towards
their progressive mediation" (99), to the question of why the Trickster figure is so
often imagined as either coyote or raven. In a variation on the Zuni master-chart,
Lévi-Strauss shows that coyote and raven are assigned this role because as carrion-
eaters (they eat meat but don't kill it) they mediate on an ecological level between
herbivorous and preying animals, a triad that mediates, in turn, the prior triad,
on the cultural level, of agriculture, hunt, and war. Lévi-Strauss adds in the next
paragraph a qualification that is of great significance for the operation of his method.
In this "double process of opposition and correlation" (100), which develops figures
of mediation, "correlations may appear on a transversal axis" (101). He means by
this that analogical thinking, the "logic of sensible properties," may produce out
of a given environment any number of analogues to the way a particular mediator
works. "Coyote is intermediary between herbivorous and carnivorous in the same
way as mist between earth and sky, scalp between war and hunt (scalp is war-crop),
corn smut between wild plants and cultivated plants, garments between 'nature'
and 'culture,' refuse between village and outside, ashes between roof and hearth
(chimney)" (101). Lévi-Strauss is here back on the grounds of Durkheim and Mauss's
Primitive Classification, and he proceeds to suggest in their spirit that this sort of
thinking by association "probably corresponds," even in the modern Western world,
"to a universal way of organizing daily experience." Certainly his own pursuit
of schematic symmetries among variants relies very heavily for evidence on such
"transverse" cultural associations. Their recognition and application demand both a
special facility, which Lévi-Strauss plainly has, and familiarity as deep and complete
as possible with the folkways of the culture concerned. This is the aspect of his
argumentation most often criticized as hard to follow, far-fetched, or arbitrary.

He illustrates the power of his method not only to account for "the ambiguous
character of the trickster" (103), but also to explain "how the same god may be
endowed with contradictory attributes" and to discover the logic in the sequences
of emanations of supernatural and early human beings in the Pueblo and Plains
mythologies. Each of these latter exercises involves the application of a different
"law" of "mythical thought." In the first case the good and bad qualities of the
god appearing alone constitute the polar extremes mediated, in a kind of cosmic
pecking order, by the god's relative behavior in association with other gods. In the
second case the sequence of emanations in the Zuni emergence myth exemplifies
another form of mediation: "some myths seem to devote themselves to the task of
exhausting all the possible solutions to the problem of bridging the gap between

two and *one*" (102). Thus we get the series: messiah > dioscurs > trickster > bisexual being > sibling pair > married couple > grandmother-grandchild > 4 term group > triad.

At this point, Lévi-Strauss tells us that in Cushing's version of the Zuni emergence myth "this dialectic is accompanied by" an interchange between the functions of time and space, and he proceeds to acknowledge that this sort of interchange is paradigmatic for all such operations: "the logic of myth confronts us with a double, reciprocal exchange of functions" (103). Having demonstrated with tantalizing compactness the power of structural analysis simultaneously to discover some of the "laws" of "mythical thought" and to organize several of the chaotic puzzles of North American mythology, Lévi-Strauss introduces the general covering law of such permutation groups of variants. The second half of his essay culminates in his "approximate formulation" of what he will later come to call "the canonical rule" of these groups:

> Every myth (considered as the collection of all its variants) corresponds to a formula of the following type:
> f x (a): f y (b) ≈ f x (b): f a-1 (y)
> where, two terms being given as well as two functions of these terms, it is stated that a relation of equivalence still exists between two situations when terms and relations are inverted, under two conditions: 1. that one term be replaced by its contrary; 2. that an inversion be made between the function and the term value of two elements. (104)

Stated as nearly as manageable in ordinary language, the "rule" says that the "constituent units," or combined subjects and predicates, of a set of variants will be so distributed that two contrary units, the second formed by inverting the subject of the first and then reversing subject and predicate, will be mediated by a third subject about which properties can be predicated that are comparable to those of both contraries.

Like his "transverse" cultural associations, Lévi-Strauss's applications of this "canonical rule" have been lightning rods for criticism. He is sometimes reproached for not observing his own rule, but he has repeatedly insisted on his fidelity to it. Critics may underestimate its tentative and generalized nature; not only do all three of the kinds of mediation exemplified in "The Structural Study" fit under its umbrella, but it is also capable of internal variation, since the two conditions of inversion do not have to appear, as they do in the classical form above, only in the fourth member of the equation.[9] As we shall see, however, the more frequent and more serious charge alleged against the formula focuses upon the conditions of inversion themselves. Lévi-Strauss's formulation of the rule admits of a great deal of ambiguity, in no way mitigated by the latitude he permits himself in practice about what counts as a "contrary" of the first term and what as an "inversion" of function and term. A good deal of what strikes his critics as his sleight-of-hand centers upon the liberties he appears to take in these two kinds of transformation.

"The Structural Study of Myth" may culminate in the "canonical" formula, but it actually concludes with two sets of observations whose anticlimactic function as a coda must not be allowed to obscure their importance. The first of these mounts into a visionary statement of the relation between the single motive for myth and its manifestations in a myriad of overlapping and repetitive tales. Lévi-Strauss begins by raising the question of why oral storytelling is so "addicted" to repetition of sequences. Behaving as if the long tradition of rhetorical and psychological explanations of repetition did not exist, he responds: "If our hypotheses are accepted, the answer is obvious: repetition has for its function to make the structure of the myth apparent" (105). This is an answer that combines the concept of "redundancy" in communication theory with that of the "constituent units" of genuine "message." Lévi-Strauss's "synchro-diachronic" layout of variations shows that "myth exhibits a 'slated' structure which seeps to the surface, if one may say so, through the repetition process." The slates are overlapping, but "not absolutely identical" and "since the purpose of myth is to provide a logical model capable of overcoming a contradiction . . . a theoretically infinite number of slates will be generated." The more existentially or objectively "real" the contradictions, the more massively we might expect generations of storytellers to accumulate the slated increments of their unconscious "solutions." No myth, however, actually generates infinite variations. Lévi-Strauss alters his analogy to convey this point. Like crystal, myth grows "spiral-wise . . . in a continuous process whereas its structure remains discontinuous . . . until the impulse which has originated it is exhausted." In the case of myth, of course, this impulse is "intellectual" and a myth's exhaustion of it signifies a limit at which, for whatever reasons, a people have built new stories out of the ruins of the old. Lévi-Strauss opens in these packed remarks a set of questions inherited from Boas that foreshadow the expansion of this point signified in his later title "How Myths Die."

His second and final set of observations touches, even more briefly, yet another topic that will call for future elaboration. Here he frames his grand vision of the work of myth within the still larger context of one of the dominant themes of his career—the intellectual parity of "primitive" humanity with its "civilized" offshoots. The conclusion of "The Structural Study" ranks with certain chapters of the contemporaneous *Tristes Tropiques* as an eloquent locus of this claim, and it adumbrates the full-scale demonstration in *The Savage Mind* that "the kind of logic which is used by mythical thought is as rigorous as that of modern science" (106).

THE CULTIVATION OF WILD THOUGHT: ELABORATIONS OF THE THEORY

On the model of Whitehead's epigram, the history of Lévi-Strauss's major works over the next thirty-five years could be called a series of footnotes to this essay of 1955. Some of these "footnotes," however (like those to Plato), dwarf their progenitor, and all convey an air of improvisation and discovery. The account of these that follows takes some liberties with chronological order for the sake of thematic clarity. It begins with the two surprising books of 1962, *Le totémisme aujourd'hui* and *La pensée sauvage,* in which the theme of the closing paragraph of

"The Structural Study"—the parity of "primitive" and "civilized" thought—erupts on a much larger scale. Lévi-Strauss may appear to break off his work on myth to pursue this broader topic, but there is a dialectical relation between the two projects. His excogitation of the theory of myth in the essay of 1955 seems to have brought into focus the argument for the parity of "primitive" thought, while the study of the latter illuminates the kind of thinking of which myth is a special product.

Lévi-Strauss establishes on the first page of the preface to *The Savage Mind* the relation of that work to its predecessor, *Totemism Today*. He there describes the latter as "a kind of historical and critical introduction" that explains why "the anthropologists of former times were the prey to an illusion" in their conceptions of totemism (Lévi-Strauss 1966, xi). This first book's function is to clear the way for the exploration in *The Savage Mind* of "totemism's positive side." To understand why Lévi-Strauss finds it so important at this juncture to take on the problematic of totemism, it is only necessary to recall how enmeshed the concept has been since the nineteenth century in ethnological thought about both kinship *and* myth. Thanks to the development of his structural theory, Lévi-Strauss is now primed to take to the great tree of extant cognitive and affective theories about totemism the ax of his discovery that the totemic is nothing more nor less than one level of classification among the taxonomic categories available to "primitive" thinkers.

The basic law of such analogical thought is that the "symbolic operators" of a given "code" or "level" are not only "endowed with a theoretically unlimited extension" within that code, but are also always convertible by metaphor or metonomy into other codes (153). It is this fungibility of codification that Lévi-Strauss signifies in the algebraic notation of his "canonical law." There can be no complete table of codes. In "The Story of Asdiwal," Lévi-Strauss contents himself with identifying four very broad ones: the geographic, techno-economic, sociological, and cosmological. In *Mythologiques*, however, in the course of decoding over eight hundred myths, he discriminates, according to my informal census, an additional fifteen codes, and he finally confesses in *The Story of Lynx* that "at least theoretically their number is limitless, as codes are tools forged to satisfy the needs of the analysis" (Lévi-Strauss 1995, 186). The fact that any given set of symbolic operators is such a volatile matrix of exchange among codes damns all previous single-level hypostatizings of totemism: "All the levels of classification . . . authorize—or even imply—possible recourse to other levels. . . . The mistake which the upholders of totemism made was arbitrarily to isolate one level of classification, namely that constituted by natural species, and to give it the status of an institution" (Lévi-Strauss 1966, 135–136). The kind of charge leveled here against "the upholders of totemism" is a refrain throughout Lévi-Strauss's work. Whether the subject be kinship, totemism, or myth, other theorists characteristically fail, in his judgment, by committing themselves to some reifying version of a mono-code.

Lévi-Strauss's goal in *The Savage Mind* is not merely to put totemism on a proper footing. As the title itself indicates, the book celebrates the power of what is ironically called "savage" thought, a form of taxonomic speculation still tied to the concreteness of physically observable properties. Lévi-Strauss manages to compress this idea with metaphysical wit into his punning title. *"La pensée sauvage"* translates as both "savage thought" and "wild pansy"; this form of cogitation does not abstract from the local wildflowers, it thinks by means of them. Lévi-Strauss insists, as he first suggests in the conclusion of "The Structural Study," that the difference between such a "science of the concrete" and modern science is one only of degree, not of kind, of the objects studied and the level of abstraction involved, not of any leap in human ability to think logically. The "primitive" thinker may be a *"bricoleur,"* building his mental contraptions out of what he finds on hand, but this is the mode of thought that produced the "neolithic revolution,"—horticulture, astronomy, the major art and crafts: civilization. In sum, Lévi-Strauss takes time out in these two books from examining the species of classical topics in ethnology—totemism, kinship, myth—to establish the basis of the genus itself, the nature of "primitive" thought. From this broadest of excursions into theory, he returns, refreshed, to commence his masterwork, the four volumes of *Mythologiques.*

Just before, during, and just after writing the tetralogy, however, Lévi-Strauss produced a number of essays that both clarify certain aspects of his theory and reveal how consciously he understood himself to be working out solutions in his structural terms to various problems set by Franz Boas. Four of these essays in particular deserve notice before we reach *Mythologiques.* The earliest and longest is "The Story of Asdiwal," which is obviously intended to be a more explicit and detailed demonstration of method than the introductory nature and lecture format of "The Structural Study" permitted. "Asdiwal" improves on the latter in two particular respects. First, it dramatizes the kind of close attention to the life-conditions of the generating culture that is the necessary precondition to grasping its metaphorical and metonymical economies of association. The myth concerned is a Tsimshian tale of the adventures of the culture-hero Asdiwal, four different versions of which were published by Boas between 1895 and 1916. The means by which Lévi-Strauss achieves his first improvement is expressed concisely in announcing as his first aim "to isolate and compare the various levels on which the myth evolves: geographic, economic, sociological, and cosmological—each one of these levels . . . being seen as a transformation of an underlying logical structure common to them all" (Lévi-Strauss 1976, 146–147).[10] In "Asdiwal," unlike the Greek and even Pueblo instances, we are generously provided with the cultural information appropriate to grasp these "levels" or codes, and so enabled to follow the processes of reasoning by which Lévi-Strauss constructs the axes of his integrating schemata.[11]

The second improvement consists in his more careful attention to the workings of the chiasmic reversals in the fourth members of sets of variants. In relating the odd-man-out fourth version of the story to its three more normative versions, Lévi-Strauss describes what he characterizes as "a double mechanism of the *weakening of oppositions* accompanied by a *reversal of correlations*" (182). This "weakening of oppositions" means that in the fourth version the binary contraries of "the mythical schema" don't appear as sharply defined to the eye of the structuralist. This account is Lévi-Strauss's best explanation and justification of the "reversal of correlations" that characterizes the fourth member in the canonical formula. His discrimination of a *joint* "weakening" and "reversal" expands the process represented in the formula into a rule of transformation. The fourth member now appears not merely as the closure of one set of variants, but also as the opening of another. In the conclusion of "The Story of Asdiwal" Lévi-Strauss expresses this double movement in social terms: When a mythical schema is transmitted from one population to another, and there exist differences of language, social organization, or way of life that make the myth difficult to communicate, it begins to become impoverished and confused. But one can find a limiting situation in which, instead of being finally obliterated by losing its outlines, the myth is inverted and regains part of its precision (184). Resorting to the same example from optics that Marx and Engels employed to figure "ideology," Lévi-Strauss compares this reversal to the inverted projection of an image transmitted through the pinhole of a *camera obscura.* In this case, the pinpoint represents the moment "when communication is about to vanish." Lévi-Strauss's account of this "law" of the conservation of myth constitutes his solution to a problem identified but left untheorized by Boas—the "weakening" of story at cultural borders. This revision of Boas is only a first example of Lévi-Strauss carrying out by structural means a part of the Boasian program to compel the narratives of the Northwest peoples to yield as much light as possible on the tantalizing puzzles of their historical and cultural interrelationships. Levi-Strauss expresses his imaginative rapport with this goal in his choice of epigraph to "The Structural Study of Myth." He there singles out unerringly the one lapidary remark of Boas that might be said to epitomize his researches into Northwest story: "It would seem that mythological worlds have been built up only to be shattered again, and that new worlds were built from the fragments."[12] Lévi-Strauss says nothing explicit in the essay that connects this grand pronouncement to his own project. But we can see in hindsight that it represents quite wonderfully the entire arc of that trajectory from "The Structural Study" through the volumes of *Mythologiques* and their *sequelae.*

As the instance of "Asdiwal" indicates, Boas's presence in Lévi-Strauss's project is not restricted to general inspiration. The latter's turn in the following year to "Asdiwal's" sibling, "Four Winnebago Myths," indicates how important he considers the Boasian procedure of assembling unjudgmentally all known variants and attempting to connect them. In general organization, this second essay closely resembles "The Story of Asdiwal." The four myths of the title were collected by Paul Radin, the great student of the Winnebago, trained by Boas and in some respects, as I've mentioned, especially true in spirit to his ambitions and methods. Radin, too, collects four variants, intuitively grouping the fourth with the other three, while confessing that his historical, diffusionist explanation of the connection is unsatisfactory. Lévi-Strauss is prepared, of course, to explain it elegantly, as an inverted version of the other three. In the process he identifies explicitly one of his two fundamental criticisms of the Boasian tradition. "Since the publication of Boas' *Tsimshian Mythology,*" he complains, "anthropologists have often simply assumed that a full correlation exists between the myths of a given society and its culture," whereas in fact, "this correspondence is not necessarily an exact reproduction; it can also appear as a logical transformation" (Lévi-Strauss 1976, 203–204). This criticism should be combined with the still more basic one leveled at Boas himself in *The Savage Mind.* There Lévi-Strauss remarks that Boas, having identified the problem to be solved—the laws behind diffusional variation—failed to find the correct route to a solution, which would have been "instead of reducing the story or myth to a mere narrative, to try to discover the scheme of discontinuous oppositions . . . behind the mythical 'discourse'" (Lévi-Strauss 1966, 136). The true successor knows how to abandon narrative for the symmetries of invertible mythemes.

The later theoretically significant essays, "Relations of Symmetry between Rituals and Myths of Neighboring Peoples" and "How Myths Die," are contemporaneous with the completion of *Mythologiques* (1971) and exhibit further aspects of Lévi-Strauss's structuralist transformation of Boas. In the first of these, "Relations of Symmetry," Lévi-Strauss attempts to show that the Mandan and Hidatsa, close neighbors on the upper Missouri, have contrived over the centuries of their settlement to construct mirror inversions of one another's myths and rituals. As he summarizes the matter, "everything transpires as if the Mandan and Hidatsa had succeeded in organizing the differences in their beliefs and practices into a system. One could almost believe that each tribe—aware of the corresponding effort of the other tribe—had made the effort to preserve and cultivate the oppositions and to combine the antagonistic forces in order to form a balanced whole" (Lévi-Strauss 1976, 240). One could *almost* believe that the effort was conscious, but not quite. The important theoretical point, however, is that the dynamic relations within myth are now extended to ritual as well. This is already Lévi-Strauss's unstated practice throughout *Mythologiques,* and he subsequently extends it in *The Way of the Masks* (1988) to the relations between myths and masks of the Northwest Coast. In effect, he comes to hold that the tensions expressed in a culture's storytelling also prevail within its other symbol-systems, so that these form a single, integrated web of symmetrical oppositions.[13] This expansion of the field of symbolic operators secures for Lévi-Strauss yet another dimension of flexibility, one perhaps even comparable to the fungibility of codes and the double inversions of the canonical formula, in its usefulness for discovering significant oppositions. And in this case, too, he has transmuted into structural "law" Boas's under-theorized but highly suggestive juxtapositions of Northwest arts, crafts, rites, and stories.

Like its predecessors, "How Myths Die" takes up a problem identified by Boas—what happens to stories at cultural and linguistic borders—and presents a structural solution. Superficially, the essay appears particularly Boasian, since its author for once discusses narrative genres and employs the traditional terms. A glance at the argument will suffice to indicate, however, the extent to which these terms have suffered a sea change into something that from a Boasian point of view would appear a good deal more strange than rich. To deal concretely with the puzzle of why some myths are reinvigorated at cultural and linguistic borders while some, as the title has it, "die," Lévi-Strauss commences by summarizing a widespread narrative, the story of Lynx and/or Coyote.[14] This story, he alleges, displays its maximum "length and richness of . . . narrative . . . and . . . dramatic intensity of . . . motifs" among the Thompson River Indians (Lévi-Strauss 1976, 259). Among their remote but still Salish-speaking neighbors to the north, the Shuswap, the story exhibits "a diminishing" that affects the quality of both narrative and motifs "as though the plot were collapsing and contracting at the same time" (259). When the weakened story crosses the language barrier into the Athapascan-speaking Chilcotin to the northwest it regains part of its strength through canonical inversion, but when it passes to the Carrier to the north of them it turns into a tragic, romantic tale in which "the initial myth . . . appears as its own metaphor: the monstrous lynx looming up without motivation at the end, and castigating, not so much the hero adorned with all the virtues, as the narrative itself for having forgotten or failed to recognize its original nature and disowning itself as a myth" (265). Crossing another linguistic and cultural threshold to the west, the story is transformed by the Tsimshian "to the order of legendary tradition" (267), thus providing ideological support of the social hierarchy, while the Algonkin-speaking Cree to the east of the Carrier employ it to rationalize a part of their history, intermarriage and active cooperation with whites.

This is indeed a concrete analysis of how myths are transformed generically at cultural and linguistic borders, but it is not hard to imagine Boas's dissatisfaction and even bewilderment. Lévi-Strauss's literary judgments are determined by the conception of myth expounded in the opening pages of "The Structural Study," according to which the criterion of strong oppositions is inimical to the very principle of diachronous narration; it aspires asymptotically instead toward the condition of a purely visual, synchronic diagram. When Lévi-Strauss falls back, therefore, upon terms of conventional literary evaluation like "richness of narrative" and "dramatic intensity" to characterize the proper "myth" among the Thompson River nation, the reader must bear in mind that because he valorizes narrative according to the pointedness and clarity of its mythemic oppositions his axiological remarks virtually reverse what they would customarily signify. The more the bones stick out, the more highly Lévi-Strauss rates the beauty and richness of the story. Thus, when he employs what looks like a Grimmian schema of generic degeneration to characterize the collapse of the "myth" into "legend," "history," and "romantic tale" among the Tsimshian, Cree, and Carrier, he is describing what to anyone else might appear as *increases* in the beauty, detail, and quite possibly significance of the respective accounts.

This unique taxonomic principle for categorizing narratives looms large in Lévi-Strauss's pages and creates some conceptual anomalies that call for further attention. The most important to attend to here is his distinction between myth and tale. Like post-Boasian Americanists in general, he often treats the distinction as questionable or nugatory, but when he does observe it he intends it to signify *the relative, diacritical difference between narratives built on strongly opposed mythemes and those built on weaker ones*. Lévi-Strauss does acknowledge that stronger oppositions are likely to appear in narratives that are ideologically important to the groups that circulate them, but it is strength of the mythemic oppositions and not the social or religious status of the narrative that determines its classification.[15] Whereas Boas, then, distinguishes myth from tale by two psychological criteria, the first necessary and primary (genre based on setting in the former age) and the second contingent and secondary (perception of ideological importance or sacredness), Lévi-Strauss distinguishes by two criteria, the second of which is the same as Boas's second, but the first of which is formal, contingent, and primary (strong mythemic oppositions versus weak ones). Lévi-Strauss's difference entails two significant corollaries. First, the replacement of indigenous belief by the discrimination of mythemic oppositions recoups taxonomic authority for the anthropologist rather than conceding it to the "native informant." Second, no distinction between myth and tale is a necessary one; as the result of a subjective decision based on a relative diacritical difference, each is contingent. Just as Boas will accept any Grimmian folktale as myth if its meets his primary criterion of setting, so Lévi-Strauss will accept any that meets his standard of strong mythemic oppositions.

"How Myths Die," then, proposes an elegant solution to the Boasian problem; at cultural and linguistic borders, myths either revive by regaining their strong mythemic oppositions through inversion, or else they slide into mere tale, lose the coherence of their coded messages, and drift into death as pointless entertainment. As Lévi-Strauss puts the latter potentiality, "the tale offers more possibilities of play, its permutations are comparatively freer, and they progressively acquire a certain arbitrary character. . . . the already very small oppositions indicate a lack of precision *which allows the shift to literary creation*[my italics]" (Lévi-Strauss 1976, 128). Story for story's sake is the polar contrary to the ideal aspiration of myth to escape narrative altogether, and a "shift to literary creation" is the last indignity for noble preliterate narrative, a fate worse than death. Lévi-Strauss concludes his analysis of the memorable story of Cimidyuë in *The Origin of Table Manners* by asking if the reduplicated episodes in which it dribbles away its "last murmur of expiring structure" is not "precisely what constitutes the novel. . . . The novelist drifts at random among these floating fragments [of myth] that the warmth of history has, as it were, melted off from the ice-pack. He collects these scattered elements and re-uses them as they come along . . . dimly aware that they originate from some other structure" (Lévi-Strauss 1973b, 129–131). This condition renders the Western artist a far more pathetic *bricoleur* than any "savage" thinker. The novel in its self-reflexive postmodern phase finally dies like the story of Cimidyuë: "The hero of the novel is the novel itself. . . . It tells its own story, saying not only that it was born from the exhaustion of myth, but also that it is nothing more than an exhausting pursuit of structure" (131). This *jeu d'esprit* may be a bit of Parisian one-upmanship, but, besides being a characteristic *apologia* for "primitive" humanity, it sketches a serious logical consequence of the author's unique theory of generic degeneration.[16]

Up to this point we have been contemplating a series of theoretically significant but self-styled interim reports from the immense ongoing project of research in Lévi-Strauss's laboratory and seminars at the *École des Hautes Études*. Apart from these appetizers, the fruits of this applied research are served up to the public in the four volumes of *Mythologiques* and its supplements, *La potière jalouse* and *L'histoire de Lynx*. In these works the proportion of theorizing to the presentation of results is hugely reversed; the theoretical principles already enunciated unsurprisingly govern the massive production of mythemic analysis. What modest modifications of the general theory do appear in *Mythologiques* and its successors stem directly out of the truly stunning ambition of these volumes—the articulation of networks of transformational sets that are intercontinental in scope. Physical anthropologists have long been persuaded of the relative homogeneity of indigenous populations throughout the Americas, and classifiers and comparers of tale types and their distribution have confirmed this homogeneity in the cultural realm of story. But this latter activity has fallen far short of explaining the teasing hints of connection that seem to lurk beyond historical reclamation.[17] Hence the researches of Boas and those he inspired have had as their implicit goal a unified-field explanation of American mythology.[18] Enter Lévi-Strauss, primed with this ambition and persuaded that synchronic analysis of mythemes can do what attention to the level of plot and motif cannot. He himself describes *Mythologiques* as developing on a double axis of geography and logic. In geographical terms, "*The Raw and the Cooked* . . . is limited to South America, particularly central and eastern Brazil. *From Honey to Ashes* enlarges the field of action, to the south as much as to the north, but still remains in South America. With *The Origin of Table Manners,* the analysis begins with a myth that is still South American, but from further north . . . a kind better illustrated in the myths of North America . . . and the book straddles them both. The final volume, entirely North American, leads the reader further" (Lévi-Strauss and Eribon 1991, 43). Even though the transition between continents occurs only well into *Origin,* the total number of pages is split almost equally between North and South America, and a good deal of both internal and external evidence indicates that the series was designed from the start to dramatize the structural rapports in the mythologies of the two continents.

Lévi-Strauss characterizes his second "axis" as "a matter of logic," by which he means that as the series proceeds the nature of the oppositions he identifies becomes increasingly abstract. In *Honey to Ashes* a "logic of forms" takes over from the "logic of sensible qualities" of *The Raw and the Cooked* and this in turn gives way in *The Origin of Table Manners* to a "logic of propositions" (Lévi-Strauss 1973b, 469). These are not, properly speaking, three different kinds of logic, but only degrees of complexity in the formation of the mythemic oppositions, and all three turn up in South American story before the transition to the North American material that occupies the latter half of *Mythologiques*. In contrast to this hyperbolic rhetoric about logics, Lévi-Strauss gives the reader little formal notice of the truly innovative modification of the "law" of mythic transformation introduced in this latter half, and carried into *The Jealous Potter* and *The Story of Lynx.* This modification is the extension of the search for the opposing members of transformation sets, particularly the inverted fourth, not merely to contiguous cultures but to cultures separated by a hemisphere. Lévi-Strauss sets down very clearly at the beginning of *Origin* the principle that underlies the bold leaps back and forth in the later work among the myths of the Americas: "The mythological universe of a given society, or of a group of societies bound together by geographical and historical ties, always forms a closed system" (1973b, 15). To leap freely, on this basis, between Alaska and Brazil, depends, however, upon assuming the very thing that the resulting transformations purport to prove, "the underlying unity of American mythology" (Lévi-Strauss 1981, 421). This massive begging of the question makes a final demand upon the trust of Lévi-Strauss's readers even as it comprises the most exhilarating and visionary aspect of his reconstruction of Boas's ambitions.

In connection with this concept of a "mythological universe" as forming a "closed system," certain developments in *The Jealous Potter* and *The Story of Lynx* demand attention in their own right. Lévi-Strauss has insisted ever since the "Overture" to *The Raw and the Cooked* that the "closed," global nature of the American system means that in theory any point on it can be reached from any other point. But he also emphasizes that the arbitrary, or semi-arbitrary, point of entry and the resulting spread of the researcher's inquiry will dispose the data in configurations that would be quite different in the case of another inquirer or another point of entrance. The two late studies are practical demonstrations of the significance of such corollaries. They both pursue the investigation of myths and transformations noticed only tangentially in *Mythologiques*. The effect is rather like finding that minor characters in one set of novels have become the principals of another. The "plot" of each book makes surprising intersections with stories and themes from the tetralogy. This increasing cross-hatch of perspectives finally elicits from Lévi-Strauss in *The Story of Lynx* a five-page outburst of theory that may constitute the culmination of what he there calls his "critique of mythological reason" (Lévi-Strauss 1995, 188).[19] While defending the soundness of the concept of binary opposition in general, he acknowledges more directly than ever before that "in the first stages of the research [which he has consistently held all his work to be] the selection and the definition of [both] the axes on which are located the oppositions and . . . the codes to which they are applicable, owe much to the analyst's subjectivity, and thus . . . have an impressionistic character" (186). Still more important, however, is his acknowledgment that this "fluidity of mythical forms" guarantees that "as we progressively deepen analysis, and . . . enlarge its field in time and space," a network will be produced that "comes close to a theoretical state in which each junction would be linked to all others." Hence, as "more resemblances are uncovered . . . they have less and less meaning" (188). Structural analysis of myth thus produces a paradox: whereas the examination of a limited field that sticks close to "ethnographic reality" "overflows with meanings" as it distinguishes differences, the examination of expanded fields makes for decreasing meaning as it rises toward abstraction in the identification of resemblances. At this point Lévi-Strauss saves the appearance of structural analysis of the expanded field by arguing that while limited analysis "matched with a given history and ecological environment" (189) teaches us much about the "inner workings" of particular societies, expanded analysis "reduces mythic thought to its form" (190) and thus "lays bare the mechanism" of the mind's own operations. This rather ambivalent *apologia* is accompanied by a somber warning of the dangers of abstract "general mythology," almost as if Lévi-Strauss were cautioning himself. His "critique of mythological reason" confronts frankly here the most utopian aspect of the revised Boasian program—confidence in mythology's infinite intelligibility—with what may be its ultimate constraints.

Lévi-Strauss's theory has met with criticism proportionate to its notoriety and its large claims. First, and perhaps most devastatingly, there has been general agreement on the unsoundness of his analogies between myth and language. Mythemes do not stand in the same relation to meaning as do phonemes and morphemes; these latter are both more basic units and ones that function in semiological contexts already elaborately conventionalized, whereas mythemes are not only composites, but mean little or nothing till arranged and interpreted by the constructor of the "tertiary code." As Jonathan Culler puts it, "More than anything else it is the lack of data about meaning that vitiates the analogy with linguistics" (Culler 1975, 49). Lévi-Strauss, Culler goes on to remark in an amusing adaption of the anthropologist's own favorite metaphor, "is trying to teach himself and his readers a language of myth, which as yet has no native speakers" (51).[20]

This figure is an effective, if cruel, way of representing the widespread complaint that Lévi-Strauss's analytic deductions almost always involve selections of evidence and decisions about its import that appear arbitrary. Even if much of this appearance is excused on the grounds that he has room only to report the *results* of his painstaking method, we are still left with a disturbing number of crucial points in his procedures that are vulnerable to subjective judgment. I have already called attention to the most controversial: what Lévi-Strauss himself calls above "the selections and definition of the axes" the negotiation of codes, the definition of inversions, the resort in connection with the latter to other symbol-systems and other cultures. The first of these, the definition of the oppositional axes based on selection of relevant cultural associations, is the one most often singled out as far-fetched or unfollowable. Of these nodes of trouble, the laxness of Lévi-Strauss's criteria for what counts as "opposition" (and therefore for mediation and transformation) has understandably come in for special obloquy. Simon Clarke is representative in complaining that Lévi-Strauss fails "to make the fundamental distinctions between the concepts of binary relations, binary oppositions and binary contradictions," with the ultimate result that "a single difference is sufficient to establish an opposition" (Clarke 1977, 759, 761).[21] Lévi-Strauss has himself variously acknowledged these weaknesses, both at the beginning and end of *Mythologiques,* for example, and in the passage from *The Story of Lynx* quoted above, but he tends to excuse them as the insufficiently supported intuitions of a pioneer who can't be expected to be always right.[22] He does not concede, though, that they may be fatal flaws in the method. When the results of such looseness of definition are combined with his increasing insistence that larger transformational patterns can be completed only by appeal to more far-flung elements of a global universe of symbolic forms, the results can appear to the unsympathetic eye as "a true *bricolage* of contrastive elements abstracted from their structural contexts and reduced to a single level of contrasts from which all vestiges of hierarchical structure and segmentary organization have been excluded" (Turner 1977, 140). The ultimate charge against the method, frequently leveled by its anthropological critics in particular, is that it must inevitably produce tautologies, irrefutable because unproveable.[23]

Most of the other important objections to the theory can be generally classed as based on irreconcilable philosophical premises. Even a matter so basic and apparently innocuous as the discrimination of mythemes involves a drawing of battle lines. There are philosophical grounds (in speech act theory, for example) for questioning whether the dissection of a story into its allegedly smallest "constituent units" is not based from the start upon a mistakenly positivistic conception of how narrative signifies. Meanwhile, Lévi-Strauss is simultaneously vulnerable on the other, the idealist, side, as Jacques Derrida demonstrates in his large-scale attack on his "essentialism" in *Of Grammatology*. Another and larger class of philosophical objections might be loosely categorized as "humanist," by which I mean protesting against Lévi-Strauss's apparent displacement of individual consciousness as the site of significance. Nothing characterizes his work on myth so strikingly as its systematic prescinding from the traditional folklorist's interest in what an individual narrative means and does in the context of its telling. This is the fundamental ground on which Boas would be obliged to conclude that his program had been advanced by unacceptable means. If Lévi-Strauss's abstraction from the lived experience of story appeared neutral, critics of it might be more receptive to the patent evidence that the experiential is simply not Lévi-Strauss's business, is not—to invoke his own metaphor—his microscope's level of focus. But, when one finds throughout his work direct expressions of hostility to the valorizing of the self, comparable, say, to the "antihumanism" of Althusser, Lévi-Strauss's choice to avoid the emotive and expressive aspects of story does smack of an ideological position. This consideration carries us into a final and most intractable class of philosophical objections. Lévi-Strauss's theory of myth is the most rigorously cognitive since Tylor's. As a *parti pris* in the dispute that runs the length of anthropological attention to the topic, it must inevitably alienate the emotivists. In the polemical "Finale" of *The Naked Man* Lévi-Strauss himself provides an almost comical instance of the depth of mutual talking past one another. He defends himself against the charge (as brought by Meyer Fortes and Edmund Leach) of neglecting the emotional values of myth in communities without writing, by demonstrating (against T. O. Beidelman and Victor Turner) that *ritual*, too, is a cognitive activity when properly considered. This argument is valuable because it is Lévi-Strauss's fullest and most explicit structural account of ritual, but as a refutation of emotive conceptions of myth it is a *non-sequitur* of the type known on the playground as "and so's your mother."

In spite of the serious charges that can be brought against his theory, Lévi-Strauss's achievement is remarkable on a number of counts. First, he has succeeded to a degree unmatched in modern anthropology in establishing "myth" as an important object of study in its own right. Second, he has developed the most rigorously cognitive conception of it since Tylor's and Spencer's, but a conception free of their Whiggish patronizing of "primitive" thought. Third, however much he may appear to strain the rules of evidence in particular instances, his accumulated testimony has convinced a surprising number of even his most skeptical readers that there may well be unconscious, law-like symmetries at work structuring the seemingly random variations of oral story.[24] Fourth, he has inspired the widespread application of structural methods of analysis not only to recent communities without writing, but also, perhaps especially by virtue of his own "armchair" example, to ancient cultures—Mesopotamian, Hebrew, Greek—whose mythologies are entirely mediated through historical record.[25] These methods stem, like Lévi-Strauss's own, from the general shift in intellectual fashion from origin to structure, and the most successful are serious modifications of his, but it is his inspiration that has established structural analysis as a common tool of contemporary mythography. Fifth and finally, he has breathed new life into what I have called the Boasian program. Most fundamentally, perhaps, he has become, in Dell Hymes's words, "the reviver of serious attention among scholars to the riches of Native American collections" (Hymes 1981, 117). But, as much as Boas would know how to value this achievement, Lévi-Strauss has gone well beyond it. His applications of structural theory to the problematics, as sketched by Boas, of the interrelationships among this "ocean of stories" have revived a glimpse of that teasing goal, "the unity of American mythology."

WITHDRAWAL FROM GRAND THEORY

Lévi-Strauss's career as mythographer stirs almost exactly a century later some curious echoes of Max Müller's. In each case a theorist inspired by the previous generation's discoveries in linguistics applies them by questionable analogy to the study of myth with results that excite wide enthusiasm beyond his discipline. But in each case, too, the apparent *aggiornamento* of the method is tied to a rather outmoded mental theater in which the backward-facing writer does exhaustive battle with his predecessors. By aspiring to settle the problematics of kinship, totemism, and myth, Lévi-Strauss fashions himself as the last of the grand theorists upon these matters. And he is left, like Müller, high and dry by a change of taste in the next generation—in Müller's case, the emergence of Tylorian anthropology; in Lévi-Strauss's, the withdrawal of trust in totalizing theory. Any number of factors might be adduced in explanation of this withdrawal: the virtually contemporaneous rise of cognitive and symbolic anthropology to vie with the "modes of thought" aspect of Lévi-Strauss's structuralism; the rise of Geertzian hermeneutic or "intepretative" anthropology, which has little more use for "myth" as an independent object of attention than Durkheim himself did; the shift of focus from myth to ritual on the part of influential students of religion like Geertz, Mary Douglas, and Victor Turner; the crisis within the discipline over both the nature of representation and the authority of fieldwork; the loss of, and embarrassment about, the "colonial" venues of this fieldwork; the related turn to a "repatriated" ethnography of contemporary Western cultures; the also related growth in awareness that "myth" is, as Johannes Fabian has remarked about "the primitive," "a category, not an object, of Western thought" (Fabian 1983, 82).[26] The "withdrawal" is obviously overdetermined at the level of general explanation. The section that follows focuses concretely upon four sorts of exemplary cases: first, structural studies of myth in the direct wake of Lévi-Strauss; second, studies in symbolic anthropology indirectly affected by him; third, a thrust toward the recombination of myth and history that defines itself partly against him; and fourth, a movement to attend to those aspects of myth as live performance that he himself prescinds from and that are most etiolated by the abstractions of chirographic collection and analysis. Where it seems feasible, I prefer for comparison examples of work in the North and South American fields that will reverberate with his.

Structural studies modeled on Lévi-Strauss's may be ranged along a continuum, from those that attempt to follow most closely the rules represented by the canonical formula to those that merely derive from their exemplar the technique of arraying mythemes in synchronous tables that display parallels. Perhaps the most telling fact about these studies is that none is willing or able to follow blindly the master's recipe; each finds it at least minimally necessary to depart from the tricky "double inversion" that marks the fourth member of the formula. In a relatively recent attempt Mark Mosko points out that even the Marandas, excellent expositors of the formula, who made a serious effort in the early 1970s to apply it in their studies in folklore and oral tradition, found that in practice it often needed modification (Mosko 1991, 129–130).[27] They recognize that Lévi-Strauss's "double inversion" guarantees that the result is non-linear or "helicoidal" rather than linear as in straight analogy, but they find cases where what actually seems to happen is "recuperation" or "reestablished equilibrium" rather than "permutation" (130). For such cases they shift to fx (a): fy (b):: fx (b): fy (ā), where the barred $\bar{a}$ signifies recuperation or "nullification" of the first term. Mosko finds their barred $\bar{a}$ "redundant" and proposes a further simplification that would be "an expression of *bisected* or *recursively* inverted dualism, viz., X′: Y″:: Y′: X″ (130). He argues that this recursively inverted analogy preserves non-linearity, though without the final "gain" and maintains that "it would seem to correspond most closely, if not literally, to Lévi-Strauss's oft-stated assertion that the structure of myth exemplifies the passage or translation of metaphors to metonyms and metonyms to metaphors." The greater part of his essay demonstrates "the revised formula's utility in help-ing to make intelligible non-mythical conceptualizations and practices of a single sociocultural tradition—that of the North Mekeo people of Papua New Guinea" (127). The flattening of the formula enables its extension outside myth to any number of "bodily states and processes . . . constructions of space and time, social classification at a number of levels and political organization" (127).

The next step toward a more generalized structuralism may be represented by Edmund Leach's analyses of biblical themes.[28] Leach's interest in the structure of myth, as we saw in the preceding chapter, antedates his acquaintance with Lévi-Strauss's theory, but following this exposure he does base his biblical essays upon the existence of at least partly unconscious messages encoded by binary opposition in structures that mediate cultural contradictions. Thus, for example, the account of the complicated issues and intrigues in II Samuel and I Kings concerning "the legitimacy of Solomon" mediates between the Israelites' valorizing of endogamy and their actual experience of living among and marrying into a highly mixed population. But Leach has no truck with the ingenuities of Lévi-Strauss's "double inversions," which he has criticized severely during his long and ambivalent career as a commentator on his French colleague's work. Indeed, Leach's biblical pieces might be read as his practical critique of "what is living and what is dead in Claude Lévi-Strauss." His very act of selecting the Bible as object of inquiry expresses both sides of this critique. On one hand, Leach might seem to have discovered the ideal "Lévi-Straussian" text. He appears to assert this good fortune almost parodically when he congratulates himself upon the resemblances between his own synchronic linking of thematic elements in the Old Testament and the traditional ahistorical reading of the Scriptures as a network of prefigurings and correspondences. On the other hand, Leach knows very well that in working on a cultural palimpsest like the Bible, he is rejecting Lévi-Strauss's consistent admonitions (ever since his own abortive attempt on Oedipus) that his methods will work properly only on societies for which there is an adequate ethnology *independent* of the stories themselves. Archaeology and other historical sources may supply bits of such cultural information for ancient societies, but not the richness of ecological and social detail necessary to furnish a sufficient background for a proper structural analysis of the mythology. Leach has repeatedly criticized Lévi-Strauss for sticking to "totemic" societies, and from this point of view his biblical excursions appear as defiant demonstrations of the needlessness of this restriction. Lévi-Strauss has inspired a number of impressive studies of ancient myth by classicists, too—Geoffrey Kirk, for example, and the various luminaries of "the Paris School"—but they are all in the same boat with Leach in regard to sources of evidence and tend, therefore, to confine themselves to some of the more general features of Lévi-Strauss's method.

The second category of withdrawers from grand monotheory consists of practitioners of symbolic anthropology, interested in myth as a mode of cultural symbolism. These tend to be thinkers who owe a considerable general debt to Lévi-Strauss even as they object seriously to the more functionalist aspects of his structuralism. Marshall Sahlins expresses the nature of the debt when he praises as "a decisive step in the development of a cultural theory" Lévi-Strauss's refusal to grant ontological status to "the fateful . . . separation of social morphology from collective representation" and, on the positive side, his "appropriation of the social by the symbolic" (Sahlins 1976, 120).

My first and fullest instance is the work of a philosopher rather than an anthropologist, but one who accepts unreservedly the folkloristic and indeed, Boasian, conception of myth. This is James Liszka's *Semiotic of Myth: A Critical Study of the Symbol.* Liszka departs promptly from Lévi-Strauss by deriving his semiotics from C. S. Peirce. For Peirce every sign is determined by its object, as icon, index, or symbol. Liszka quotes him as declaring a sign to be a symbol when, as in the case of language, "it will be interpreted as denoting the object, in consequence of a habit" (Liszka 1989, 39). This definition implies that all linguistic signs must be triadic; there must be an agency of interpretation, "the interpretant," which mediates between a sign and its object or, in post-Saussurean terms, between the signifier and the signified. A linguistic symbol, then, does include purpose and value; the determination of its object, as Liszka puts it, *"is established within the framework of a speech community"* (32). The Saussurean concept of a merely dyadic sign is fundamentally flawed because it does not allow for this mediation.[29] "Interpretation without system is blind," Liszka declares, paraphrasing Kant, "but system without interpretation is empty" (45). If the latter characterizes Saussurean structuralism, the former characterizes romantic hermeneutics. The wedge of Peirce's "interpretant," Liszka maintains, permits him to open a wide middle ground between these two positions in which to establish his notion of "transvaluation." This latter is, according to him, "the most comprehensive species of interpretant" (71). He defines it as "a rule-like semiosis which revaluates . . . markedness and rank relations of a referent as delimited by the rank and markedness relations of the system of its signans and the teleology of the sign user" (71). Each employment of the system, that is, varies according to the user's purposes and communicates social values in its manipulation of the two technical qualities of "markedness" and "rank." All of this intentionalism is of course heresy by Lévi-Straussian lights, but armed with this "rule-like semiosis," Liszka is prepared to take on myth for himself.

He understands by "myth" simply "the most elementary form of narrative," even asserting, in keeping with his Boas-Lévi-Strauss orientation, that "it serves as the evolutionary ancestor for all the others" (99). Building upon his argument that the "essence of narration" lies in taking "a certain set of culturally meaningful differences and [transvaluing] them by means of a sequence of action," he assesses the structuralist contributions of Lévi-Strauss, Greimas, Bremond, and Propp to the analysis of story. He finds that all four fail (as he says of Greimas) "to make a transition . . . to the valuative function of narration" (111). He does, however, parlay into a theory of two levels of transvaluation Propp's distinction between "agential" and "actantial" functions in story and Lévi-Strauss's conception of the "mytheme" as the smallest unit of myth that links a subject with a function. The actantial level transvalues the agential (what happens to the characters establishes certain values), and the third level, "plot" (in the pre-generic sense signifed by Northrop Frye's four *mythoi,* comedy, romance, tragedy, and irony), transvalues in turn the actantial. Liszka argues that these four broadest of archetypal moods or plots can be reclassified as modes of expressed tension between the violence with which a society affirms its social hierarchy and the contrary violence with which elements in the society wish to transgress that hierarchy. He thus aspires to reconcile the contrary theories of ritual of René Girard and Victor Turner—that the purpose of ritual is to avoid violence, respectively, by *imposing* hierarchy and by *suspending* it.[30] The transvaluing play of myth, the most elementary form of narrative, is capable of expressing sublimated symbolic versions of both social tensions.

Like the theorists of narrative who will be considered in chapters 12 and 13, Liszka responds to the problematic of myth's association with belief by situating it in relation to an antithetical term. "Myth" is for him "that imaginative space in culture which openly transvaluates order" (201). In this Frye-like role it always retains something of the tentative, hypothetical nature of the fictive, and Liszka therefore assigns to the condition of strict belief the labels of "dogma" and "ideology." As his synthesis of Girard and Turner would suggest, Liszka declares that the primary function of myth is to place in a symbolic crisis the values and rules of a given cultural stratum. "In that sense myths are *critical,* for myths walk the line between the cultural value and its antipode. Rather than being part of a cultural stratum, myths lie at the interstices of the strata; they are in that sense liminal and ambivalent. One might even say they are proto-Socratic: myths act as gadflies to the culture, their purpose in life is to disrupt the conventions of the culture, to dismantle complacency" (181). But Liszka immediately adds, "For this reason they are dangerous symbols and must be quickly put to death through incorporation into the culture by means of interpretations which seek to destroy their ambivalence" (181). As this remark shows, he locates "ideology" in the process of reception. In connection with an example from the Kuna in which the performance of a tale is immediately supplemented by an official commentator's moralizing of it, Liszka remarks, "The function of the interpreter is to shortcut any ambivalence here by providing an interpretation which reinforces the dominant rules and values of the culture" (162). Liszka acknowledges that according to Peirce's semiotic, all "determination" is "the process of removing ambivalence" (162). But he maintains that "legitimate discourse allows the possibility of reflection by means of articulating the tensions which frame that ambivalence" (162), whereas "nondialogic" control of the codification, channel of transmission, or interpretation of the story "becomes directed or ideological" (163). Liszka's distinction between "critical" myth and its possibly foreclosed reception seems open to the objection that it is too utopian about the likelihood in small, closed societies of sacred narrative's *not* being hedged about with conventional interpretation. But so goes, at any rate, his claim for the "legitimate discourse" of myth as "gadfly."

In advocating this emotive theory of the origin and function of myth, Liszka departs as widely from Lévi-Strauss as he does in his insistence on myth's significance at the level of communal understanding. It would be hard to imagine a sharper break in principle than his "replacing the notion of transformation with that of transvaluation," a type of analysis that, as he tactfully puts it, "requires a closer tie to the value system of the culture in which the myth operates" and whose permutations "do not form a logical . . . but an axiological set" (213). Nevertheless, Liszka's anthropological imagination is shaped by Lévi-Strauss's work in three significant respects yet unmentioned. The first of these is that when Liszka finally sets his assembled machine to work processing actual myths of the Netsilik and Tlingit of the Northwest coast, the Kuna of the west coast of Panama, and the Bororo of Amazonian Brazil, his analyses are driven by the concept of transformation. They resemble Lévi-Strauss's in character—in their attention to the concrete details that embody mythemic oppositions and in their readiness to bring to bear any scrap of cultural information that may clarify these oppositions. Second, as the range of Liszka's instances suggests, he reveals a particularly keen appreciation of Lévi-Strauss's demonstration in *Mythologiques* of the extent to which the myths of the Americas appear to belong to a single analytic field.

The third Lévi-Straussian perspective is more complex and of considerable theoretical significance for the study of the relation of "myth" to "ideology." In his penultimate chapter, "Myth and Culture among the Bororo: The Pragmatics of Myth," Liszka confronts this relation directly. He notes the long line of social thinkers, descending from Marx on one hand, and Durkheim on the other, who have assumed that myth embodies the ideology of a culture, either in the specific Marxist sense that it is part of the superstructure erected on an economic base or in the broader Durkheimian sense that it is a direct symbolic manifestation of the organization of society. Liszka follows Marshall Sahlins in *Culture and Practical Reason* (himself inspired on this point by Lévi-Strauss) in pointing out that such thinking assumes "a stratum of society which is more real than any other," a stratum that is "nonsymbolic or objective, in the sense that it is the signatum of which everything else is the sign" (167). And just as he perceives Sahlins as objecting that "production is mediated by a cultural semiotic logic" (167), Lizska rejects the "classical" notion of ideology because it rests on "a semantic dualism not tenable from the perspective of Peirce. The meaning of the signatum is found in the process of representation, not in the object represented" (167). It follows that "the so-called infrastructure is as symbolic as is the superstructure" (169). Although there may well be in any given case what Sahlins calls "a privileged institutional locus of the symbolic process" (168), the basic rule is that "one cultural formation may serve as a *transvaluation* of another" (168). Liszka undertakes to show by an examination of Bororo myth, especially in opposition to the well-known "economic" reading of Terence Turner, that "to the extent that the cultural system is symbolic as a whole, so too is the value system" (169). As a representation of his argument, he offers eventually a figure drawn as a Möbius strip with several twists, interlacing in a loose knot. Along the strip, from bottom to top, we read the labels of the "cultural levels," which interact in what Liszka calls "a tangled hierarchy": "ecological," "economic," "household," "communal," "cosmic." There *is* a "hierarchy," with the "ecological" level at the bottom and the "cosmic" at the top, but there is no determinable starting point or single cause-effect sequence; as Liszka puts it, "there is a certain valency but with no clear center of value production" (181).

Liszka's principle of transvaluation is a useful shibboleth for any theory of the origin or function of myth that takes a particular cultural "level" (like the economic) or "code" (like the astronomical) as a literal, unsymbolic base. It is a principle that parallels a significant theoretical movement in symbolic anthropology. It appears consonant, for example, with Roy Wagner's argument in *Symbols That Stand for Themselves* that "the basic frames of culture are formed as large-scale tropes," and with his analysis of the recursive mechanism of "obviation" by which "the essentially paradoxical effect of trope expands from a play on conventional 'points of reference' into an organizer of cultural frames" (Wagner 1986, 129, xi, respectively). This latter process, at least as Wagner exemplifies it at work in the Daribi culture of New Guinea, could be thought of as microanalysis of the large-scale transvaluations considered by Liszka.[31]

Wagner acknowledges in both *The Invention of Culture* (150–153) and *Symbols That Stand for Themselves* (131) the broad impact of Lévi-Strauss upon his theory of symbolic "obviation." In the case of the latter work, he affirms this impact even in the very act of asserting that his conception of the tropological construction of meaning is "the very opposite of structuralism." The work of Marshall Sahlins presents, according to his own testimony as we've seen, a comparable instance of Lévi-Strauss absorbed and transmuted. Sahlins displays the educative impact of Lévi-Strauss most graphically in the fourth chapter of *Culture and Practical Reason,* "La Pensée Bourgeoise: Western Society as Culture," his brilliant "excursion into capitalist economy as a cultural system" (205). His mode of analysis appears to be inspired specifically by "The Individual as Species" chapter of *The Savage Mind,* and his exhibition of the unity of the social with the symbolic in the Western codes of diet and dress proceeds inexorably toward the amusing conclusion that *la pensée bourgeoise* is the cognitive equivalent of *la pensée sauvage.* It would appear to follow that if narrative deployments of the one are structured as myth, so are those of the other.

Sahlins's responses to the structural study of myth move us into the third topic to be considered, the reassertion after Lévi-Strauss of the manifold relations between myth and history. For if Sahlins appears in *Culture and Practical Reason* to wish to salvage Lévi-Strauss for an adequate theory of culture, he appears in his next work, *Historical Metaphors and Mythical Realities,* to aspire to save structural anthropology for historical studies. By carefully setting "the incidents of Cook's life and death at Hawaii" in the context of indigenous myth, rite, politics, and history, he hopes to show that these incidents were for the Hawaiians themselves "in many respects historical metaphors of a mythical reality" (Sahlins 1981, 11). The intrusion of blundering Europeans upon busily interpreting islanders results not merely in the interlopers' incorporation into Hawaiian myth but also in changes in the culture of the incorporators. "The received system did enter into a dialectic with practice. The strong claim of a structuralist understanding does not consist in ignoring that dialectic. Rather, the interaction of system and event is itself susceptible of structural account" (33). Sahlins's detailed demonstration of this interaction supports his ultimate moral: "the dialectics of history . . . are structural throughout" (72).

Sahlins's efforts at seizing the unity of structure and event are far, however, from satisfying the contributors to *Rethinking History and Myth: Indigenous South American Perspectives on the Past* (Hill 1988). In this collection Sahlins and especially Lévi-Strauss figure as whipping boys, latter-day promoters of Hegel's notion that oral societies lie outside history. These depictions serve to construct an "other" to the contributors' determinedly concrete accounts of the complex ways in which a number of Andean and Amazonian societies interweave myth and history. But the price of the contributors' success is a virtually antinomian level of incoherence and inconsistency about what they mean by "myth" and how they distinguish it from "history." Only one of them, Peter Roe, acknowledges that the continuum of narratives intermediate between myth and history has been long identified and denominated in the field of folklore: "The overlap between the two polar types is, in fact, legend" (121). This is right on target, and the label helps to foreground the most distinctive feature of the collection. *Rethinking History and Myth* is not primarily valuable for its theorizing of the two polar concepts; it is, above all, a thesaurus of the inner dynamics of legend-building.

The fourth and perhaps most theoretically important type of particularizing withdrawal is related to the preceding one. The folkloristic conception of myth as a kind of story current in oral cultures implies necessarily that it is communicated by performance. Of course collectors in the field and even readers in their much-patronized armchairs have understood all along that this dimension of tale-telling is badly bleached out when it is reduced to the printed page. But much in the psychodynamics of our chirographic culture nevertheless militates against our grasping clearly the nature and extent of this loss. Only since the 1960s has a sustained effort arisen to realize and minimize the deficiency. This effort is no unified program, but something more like a convergence upon the same large target from different directions by independent, though sometimes overlapping, groups. Perhaps the best way of characterizing the scope of this assault is to distinguish four main columns of attackers.[32]

The group with perhaps the oldest pedigree consists of the discoverers and extenders of the "oral-formulaic" theory of the composition of ancient epic verse. Their pedigree is at least as old as the modern construction of myth itself, since it begins in the eighteenth-century controversies, touched upon in chapter 1, over Homer and the composition of *The Iliad* and *The Odyssey*. The topic enters its contemporary phase in two stages. The first is Milman Parry's research during the 1930s among his illiterate Balkan *guslars,* which led to his discovery of the extent to which they improvised performances with the aid, especially, of formulaic diction. The second stage is the success of Albert Lord's *Singer of Tales* (1960) in organizing, clarifying, and popularizing Parry's results. Though some of its enthusiasts' extreme claims have been rebuked over the last generation, the Parry-Lord hypothesis still provides for many students of narrative their fundamental discovery of the concrete differences between storytelling in an oral tradition and that so easily assumed as universal from a chirographic mind-set.[33]

The second prong of the assault consists of folklorists and anthropologists interested in oral storytelling as performance. Perhaps the most prominent of this group over the years have been Roger Abrahams, Richard Bauman, and Joel Sherzer. These new investigators depart from traditional collectors not so much in kind as in degree. They focus upon the specific performance (including, therefore, both performer and audience) as a social event whose significance inevitably exceeds whatever can be recorded as its text. In *Story, Performance and Event,* Richard Bauman, perhaps the central figure in this group, describes his project thus: "My concern has been to go beyond a conception of oral literature as disembodied superorganic stuff and to view it contextually and ethnographically, in order to discover the individual, social, and cultural factors that give it shape and meaning in the conduct of social life" (Bauman 1986, 2). From a chirographic perspective, as Bauman points out, we have tended traditionally to perceive narratives as "icons of events" (5), whereas a good deal of recent theorizing about narrative in several disciplines suggests "the reverse: Events are abstractions from narrative" (5). "The structure of social roles, relations and interactions; the oral literary text and its meaning; and the structure of the event itself are all emergent in performance" (4). Though Bauman does not pretend in these assertions to speak for anyone but himself, they characterize in general the aspirations of the group.[34]

The third convergent column is related closely enough to the second that essays by members of each have tended to appear in collections edited by members of the other. This third group can be distinguished, however, in at least two ways. First, its members come upon oral narrative from a somewhat different direction—through their more traditionally Boasian ambition to achieve a holistic understanding of Native American societies rather than through studying contemporary storytelling as social action. Second, they are comparatively "literary" in orientation; the group emphasizes a hermeneutics of oral art, explication of the "text's" linguistic and rhetorical subtleties. In *Story, Performance and Event* Bauman aptly distinguishes their work from his own by identifying their central concern as "the poetics of oral literature" (8). At least since the launching of the journal *Alcheringa* in 1970, edited by Jerome Rothenberg and Dennis Tedlock, the efforts of this third movement to recuperate the cultural subtleties of indigenous story have been designated "ethnopoetics," and nothing could better suggest the extent of their common ground with the performance-centered party than Bauman's wish to "appropriate and generalize the term" so as to include the contributions of performance-centered analysis as "an integral part of the ethnopoetic enterprise" (8).

Bauman lists as one of these contributions the performance-centered discovery of "patterning principles . . . obscured by older notions of verbal texts," a discovery that has led the ethnopoeticists, in turn, to "a powerful reconceptualization of . . . the presentation of oral texts in print" (8). The "reconceptualization" to which he refers is their consensus that the dynamics of the speaking voice in the act of storytelling, virtually flattened out of existence by conventional transcription and printing, ought, rather, to be dramatized by every practicable weapon in the typographic arsenal. In effect, this has meant printed pages that look like free verse, experimental prose, or a Menippean mixture of the two. This "reconceptualization" is a prominent feature of the work of both the doyens of the third group, Dennis Tedlock and Dell Hymes, even though they don't agree on their prosodic principles. Hymes, a linguist especially attentive to grammatical niceties, claims to hear a countable "measure" in the transcriptions of indigenous tongues, but his translated lines also coincide relentlessly with grammatical pause. Tedlock's lineation, in keeping with his intuitive hermeneutics, is more supple, a complex orchestration at the least of "pause, intonation, syntax and measure" (Tedlock 1983, 57 n.).[35] Tedlock compares his "scores," as he has sometimes called them, to the "projective verse" of Charles Olson "whose 'measure' . . . is the breath" (130), and his pages do indeed resemble Olson's as well as those of the many contemporary American poets influenced by the latter. Although the specific practices of Tedlock and Hymes have proven controversial, the general "reconceptualization" that inspires them has obviously appealed to a felt need. Many recent translators of Amerindian story have worked out their own versions of it, and the desirability of doing this has fed back through the loop into the transcriptions and renderings of the performance-centered practitioners of the second group as well.[36]

The impact upon anthropological fieldwork of both groups' "voicing" of narrative can be represented by Ellen Basso's two books on the storytelling of the Kalapalo. In her second book, *In Favor of Deceit: A Study of Tricksters in an Amazonian Society*, we find, for example, the characteristic stress on linguistic competence, on translation that communicates the dynamics of performance, and on the social contextualizing of the storytelling. Basso emphasizes especially the importance to the Kalapalo storytellers of dialogical response and she therefore breaks her lines at the point where the narrator paused and she responded, a less subjective criterion than Hymes's or Tedlock's. She also attempts to render the tendency of Kalapalo narrators to express main points more loudly, and "qualifications, elaborations and ornamentation" more softly, by the degree to which she starts lines of the latter sort toward the right margin (Basso 1987, xv). She observes the normative modern practice among folklorists—careful identification of the narrators of her tales (complete with photographs) and, in her case, psychologically acute sketches of their social relations within the community and hints of their dispositions toward the "deceit" that is the subject of their stories. The latter is important because, as the deliberate ambiguity of Basso's subtitle "A Study of Tricksters" implies, Kalapalo tricksters aren't confined to characters in tales; the stories valorize a deeply socialized view of thought and language as illusionary and of deception as a fundamental and delightful human activity. Basso is "above all concerned to show the connections between the content of trickster stories, their tellings, and lives as actually lived" (4). This contextualizing results in a much more subtle, and, to use Basso's word, "elusive" construction of the psychology of the trickster than we find in previous treatments. In similar fashion, Basso corroborates implicitly the indigenous blurring of Western generic distinctions recorded repeatedly by the contributors to *Rethinking History and Myth*. She defines "myths" à la Boas, for example, as "narratives of very ancient times in which the Dawn People . . . figure" (xiii), but later introduces a category of "disgusting Dawn People stories," which she thinks "are considered 'fictive' or even 'made up'" (299). If so, the practice of the Kalapalo contravenes the sole Boasian criterion for distinguishing "myth" from "tale," that is, that stories of the First Age elicit *belief*. In terms of speculation about the nature of myth, then, Basso's work is representative not only of the movement to recuperate story as performance, but of the larger movement to refrain from grand theory in the name of less prescribed, albeit messier, results in the field.

The fourth column in the assault upon chirographic complacency might be said to consist of thinkers who *have* been willing to speculate boldly about the implications of what is now called "orality." Representative scholars and texts here are the anthropologist Jack Goody in *The Domestication of the Savage Mind* (1977) and the literary historians and theorists Walter Ong and Tsvetan Todorov in *Orality and Literacy* (1982) and *The Conquest of America* (1982, trans. 1984). As the allusion to Lévi-Strauss in his title suggests, Goody argues that perceived dichotomies between "primitive" and "Western" or "scientific" "mentalities," like those advanced by Lévy-Bruhl and Lévi-Strauss, can best be explained, and in large measure explained away, by changes in the mode of communication attendant upon the use of writing. Ong reiterates this claim in the course of constructing a much more sweeping set of contrasts—an elaboration of Marshall McLuhan's in *The Gutenberg Galaxy*— between the psychodynamics of communication in oral and chirographic cultures. Todorov, rereading the conquest of Mexico from a semiotic perspective, proposes that the Conquistadors' great advantage over the Aztecs lay in their conception of signs (most acutely manifest in *writing*) as manipulatable, improvisational communication among humans on a terrestial plane. The Aztecs, in contrast, were enmeshed in "a ritual world" that favored "paradigm over syntagm, code over context" and so conceived of signs primarily as communication between humankind and a natural world charged with *mana* (Todorov 1984, 47).

The speculative boldness of these writers has provoked a corresponding reaction. In the first place, all three have been accused of political insensitiveness by writers anxious to deny any alleged differences in mode of thought among human groups. As I observed in chapter 3, however, about comparable criticism of Lévy-Bruhl, the rise of identity politics challenges the complacency of such moralistic judgments. Surely the issue is moot these days as to which approach is more welcome and/or beneficial to oppressed groups struggling for recognition. All three writers have been more substantively challenged, however, for letting their speculative enthusiasm outrun the evidence. Ruth Finnegan, for example, undermines in *Oral Poetry* (1977) McLuhan-Ong (and, for that matter, Parry-Lord) in her detailed "denial of a clear-cut differentiation between oral and written literature," while both Goody and Ong have been criticized by various members of our second and third groups for perpetuating Lord's claim that the dominance of formulaic composition in oral cultures precludes verbatim memorization (Finnegan 1992, 272).[37] Todorov has been castigated not only for the general thesis sketched above, but for various inaccuracies in his supporting evidence (Wright 1992, 7, 76). Thus, the writers gathered under the fourth rubric, those most inclined to speculate on the theoretical implications of oral performance, have been held closely accountable by appeals to the empirical data. But even these boldest projectors offer, in any case, only very tentative gestures toward a view of oral narrative sufficiently radical to produce a new folkloristic theory of myth. The modest empiricism and ever more detailed qualification of the second and third "columns" appears to be the order of the day. The more seriously oral storytelling is investigated along these lines, the more probable it appears that "myth" in its folkloristic sense cannot be distinguished definitively as a genre. Nevertheless, its grand career in the theorizing of Boas, Malinowski, Lévi-Strauss, and others guarantees that in the short run it will continue to be the preferred term to signify the specially privileged narrative products of communities with strong oral traditions.

[11]

No Two-Headed Greeks: The Folkloristic Consensus in Classical Studies

The lessons of modern social and cultural anthropology have been especially taken to heart in the last generation by scholars in the fields of comparative mythology and classical studies. The romantic exaltation of the civilization of ancient Greece, so entangled in the very invention of modern "myth," tended to a vision of Greek culture and mythology as *sui generis,* only minimally related to its neighbors and extremely remote from its own archaic past. But the extrapolation of the folkloristic conception of myth onto the study of ancient civilizations has created widespread recognition of the continuities, horizontal and vertical, of Greek myth with its neighbors and with its own rude beginnings. This revised version of our most familiar and most manipulated trove of traditional story presents a defamiliarizing look that renders it an exemplary case of the heuristic power of the folkloristic or anthropological approach.[1]

GEORGES DUMÉZIL: MYTH AS KEY TO A HISTORICAL SOCIOLOGY

The work of Georges Dumézil might seem a surprisingly early and peripheral starting point, but both Lévi-Strauss and the "Paris School" of classicists have testified to how much it has meant to them. The tag "new comparative mythology" applied to this work by C. Scott Littleton (Littleton 1982) suggests both a continuity with the *old*, as defined initially by Max Müller, and at the same time a distinctive break from it. Dumézil, like Müller, pursues his researches under the aegis of the philological discovery of the "family" of Indo-European languages.[2] Like Müller, too, he begins with Sanskrit studies, focusing upon linguistic analysis of Hindu mythology. And as Müller finds myth a "disease of language" to be explained away by proper textual hermeneutics, Dumézil discovers that Hindu sacred story is structured as a series of fallings-away from an original ideology recuperable only through hermeneutic restoration.

But the appearance of the word "ideology" is the signature for the change of key between the old comparative mythology and the new. Where Müller inherits from romantic idealism the assumption that the non-figurative base of culture is "thought," above all the mental order of a purely monotheistic natural theology, Dumézil follows Durkheim in assuming that this non-figurative base is social structure.[3] He views the pantheon of the ancient Hindus, as represented in the *Vedas*, as itself a symbolic reflection of the division of society into the three "functions," or classes, of priest, warrior, and herdsman or farmer. As Dumézil refines his categories, he comes to hold that in Indo-European mythologies the first function is represented typically by two gods of sovereignty, a contrary pair who divide between them the roles of magical manipulation of the cosmos and the maintenance of the legal and moral order. The second function is represented only by a single god of war and the third again by twins. He sums up thus the situation for the Hindu mythology from which he started: "the first level, the level of sovereignty, is not occupied by a single personage as is the second (Indra). Nor is it like the third, occupied by a pair of two hardly distinguishable twins (the Nasatya), but by two clearly distinguishable gods with different characters. . . . Mitra 'sovereign god of law,' and Varuna 'sovereign god of magic'" (Dumézil 1977, 38–39).

But Dumézil's distinctive contribution to the study of mythology turns upon the extrapolation of his schema of the ancient Hindu pantheon to the various early societies that he presumes on the basis of linguistic evolution to have carried with them throughout their migrations this particular social structure and its inherent ideology. "By 1938," Scott Littleton remarks, "Dumézil came to assert that early Rome, like ancient India and Iran . . . knew a tripartite division of social functions. . . . It is on this Roman-Indo-Iranian equivalence, an equivalence that, in Dumézil's opinion, can be explained only in terms of a common Indo-European heritage, that he has anchored the bulk of his subsequent theories" (Littleton 1982, 60). Once he gains a purchase within a given society's ideological expressions of its social base, Dumézil employs this information heuristically to fill gaps in his picture of the base or superstructure of related societies, and vice versa. The method is so relentlessly sociological that the mythographer or student of comparative religion can easily feel that Dumézil *uses* the phenomena of the superstructure—theology, myth, ritual, epic, history, whatever comes to hand—in order to flesh out once again his schematic disposition of the base. At the very least Dumézil certainly presents the tripartite social structure as what Marshall Sahlins, calls "a privileged institutional locus of the symbolic process" (Sahlins 1976, 211).

Dumézil's work cuts both ways, however. His attempts to establish a sociology of tripartite functions have also produced brilliant hypotheses about the mythologies, in particular, of Rome and the Germanic North. In fact, in proportion as he comes over the course of his long career to take his tripartite functions as proven, he focuses increasingly on what this framework does to explain patterns of storytelling. Dumézil often stresses the importance for his own work of the demonstration by a Swedish follower, Stig Wikander, in 1947, that the five Pandus, the principal heroes of the *Mahabharata,* are humanized versions of the Vedic gods. Inspired by this insight, Dumézil uncovers a principle according to which the pantheon of an archaic age reappears as the heroes of a later one. He generally characterizes this principle as "transposition from myth to epic," "epic" being understood in its broadest etymological sense as *epos,* a genre that encompasses not only epic in the narrow sense, but Livy's *History,* Norse saga, the chronicles of Snorri Sturlesson and Saxo Grammaticus, even aspects of a sacred scripture like the *Zend-Avesta.* Application of this principle of displacement "from myth to epic," from sacred narrative to secular, enables Dumézil to discern new structural significance in various classical and medieval narratives. He finds, for example: the lost mythology of Rome in the historicized legends recounted by Livy; various close links in Snorri's *Edda* with characters and even with the eschatological battle in the *Mahabharata;* the "epic thematization" of gods of the second function in three culturally disparate heroes of romance—Sisupala in the *Mahabharata,* Herakles in Diodorus Siculus's history, and Starkathr in *Saxo.*[4]

Dumézil is certainly interested primarily in reading such "displacements" in reverse; he remarks, for example, that the work of Wikander mentioned above "permits us to know this god [the Vedic Dyaub] better, no longer solely by the direct studying of mythological texts that speak too vaguely of him, but through the magnifying refraction of his epic transposition" (Dumézil 1973, 128). And he makes no secret of his opinion that the diachronic succession of such transpositions in the direction of psychological realism of "character," attribution of motive, and so on, is degenerate. His notion of transposition from myth to epic recalls both Northrop Frye's conception of the historical "displacement" of myth by romance and Claude Lévi-Strauss's rule that a slide into *geste* and *roman* is the consequence of a loss of paradigm. Dumézil actually does assign his revised essay on the romance of Hadingus in Saxo's chronicle the title *"Du mythe au roman"* also employed by Lévi-Strauss.[5] For the proto-structuralist as well as his more theoretically minded disciple, the schematic paradigm in narrative cries out for rescue from its smothering discourse. Dumézil's attention to the structure of the "collective representations" embodied in early texts has made him an inspiration not only to Lévi-Strauss but to the "Paris school" of French classicists as well.

Insofar as Dumézil's central hypothesis applies only to the peoples of the Indo-European migration, however, the master's direct descendants may be condemned to a kind of mop-up operation. The most significant post-Dumézilian publication thus far, Jaan Puhvel's *Comparative Mythology,* is a masterly summation of Dumézil's discoveries but offers surprisingly little advance. The most interesting new hypothesis it presents, based primarily on Puhvel's own work on the legend of Romulus and Remus and Bruce Lincoln's generalization of it, is that behind one twin in each pair of *dioscuri* among the gods of the third function lies a deity sacrificed for ecological abundance (Puhvel 1989, 254–258; Littleton 1982, 284–290). As Littleton has speculated, this possibility may take us down to the bedrock of the evolution of deities of the first and second functions out of the third. If so, it thrusts Dumézilian theory beyond the ken of a historical sociology of religion into that dark backward and abysm of time explored by German anthropology of the *kulturkreis* and by the myth-and-ritual tradition whose modern revival remains to be considered.

THE GROUND OF MYTH RECLAIMED

The "ground" of myth in its folkloristic sense is its utterance as oral story, and the reclamation referred to is the modern recognition, precipitated by the Parry-Lord discoveries, of the implications of oral composition. The most important bearing of Parry-Lord on the study of *myth* resides in the innocent-looking but crucial corollary that oral story lives only in the always different speech acts of its variant retellings. This proposition involves several significant assumptions. The first of these, in terms of logical priority, is simply that a myth is a narrative (not an independent theme or an image as the romantic anti-discursive impulse has ever been to make it). The second is that, as narrative, myth is a type of oral tale that has acquired some degree of special prestige among its disseminators. This acceptance among classicists of myth as ideologically sanctioned oral tale stems indirectly from Boasian anthropology and is transmitted within the discipline particularly effectively by Geoffroy Kirk in *Myth; Its Meaning and Functions in Ancient and Other Cultures* (Kirk 1973). The third implication is that any form In which an oral story reaches us is the result of a historical accident—its particular encounter with chirographic culture—and the fourth is that in its native state it was adrift amid a sea of fellow variants and permutations of themes. The wide sharing of such assumptions among contemporary classicists underlies the rest of their current consensus. As Richard Gordon puts it, "This is the real revolution lying behind current studies, an awareness that a myth is a traditional tale, and that Greek mythology is a shared fund of motifs ordered into a shared repertoire of stories, each of which bears a dense intertextual relation to others in the repertoire. Explaining a myth now means exploring these intertextual relations, and then, where possible, moving out to the realities of the Greek world" (Gordon 1995, 11) Before attending to what Gordon means by "moving out to the realities of the Greek world," we must consider some further implications of viewing myth as a repertoire of traditional tales.

Gordon touches on perhaps the most important of these when he notes later in the same review that "without writing, we could have no knowledge of Greek myth at all; but the uncertainty principle makes us aware that writing itself is implicated in the process of rationalizing Greek myth, which by the Hellenistic period had led to myth's displacement as a source of authority" (11). One of the most stunning results of Parry-Lord (and early work inspired by theirs like Eric Havelock's *Preface to Plato* [1963]) has been to alert us to the nature of the impact of literacy upon oral narrative. Literacy tends, progressively, to freeze traditional tale. We might otherwise be inclined to suppose, for example, that Herodotus exaggerates when he asserts in *The Histories* (253) that the Greeks came to know "the origins and forms" of their gods only with the advent of Homer and Hesiod. But this claim makes perfect sense if we think of the power of these *texts* to create out of an egalitarian welter of competing oral variants authoritative cosmogonies, "titles, offices and functions" as Herodotus says. Homer and Hesiod were probably not perceived as definers of Greek religion when they were composing their hexameters; they *became* such wellheads of orthodoxy by virtue of their ultimate medium.

In his "Teller's Preface" to Marc de Civrieux's *Watunna: An Orinoco Creation Cycle,* David Guss, the work's translator and editor, offers by chance an instructive contemporary analogue. He relays de Civrieux's proud account of how he extracted, over many years and from hundreds of fragmentary pieces let drop by casual informants in the course of daily activities, a coherent mythology of the "Makiritare" (Yekuana) people of the Venezuelan highlands. This he structured in traditional Western fashion as an initial cosmogony that gradually shades into legend. De Civrieux then presented this elegant construction to groups of Yekuana who became his collaborators in fleshing it out with additions and emendations. Allegedly "surprised and delighted. . . . Makiritare came from all over to ask to hear it and each time, large, excited crowds of people would sit down to listen, interrupting every so often to offer their advice or criticism" (De Civrieux 1980, vii). It is easy to understand the (very differently motivated) enthusiasms of both the Yekuana and their Hesiod, but it is a bit saddening, too. This is the very moment in which the floating bits and pieces of an indigenous tradition of oral story are precipitated irretrievably upon a template of chirographic schematism whose sequences no Yekuana was in a position either to invent or to imagine the consequences of inventing. It's not that these consequences would become apparent overnight. The comparable impact upon Greek myth was a process that stretched from Homer and Hesiod to beyond Augustine. Indeed, it is the length, complexity, and richness of the Greek process that has enabled contemporary classicists to make so "thick" a study (in the Geertzian sense) of that particular interface between orality and writing. Nevertheless, in every such case, the handwriting is not only on the wall, it is the wall.

HOMO NECANS: MYTH AND RITUAL REVIVED

Gordon refers to matters well beyond the basic consensus about myth as traditional tale when he says it is assumed these days of the Greek "repertoire of stories" that "each . . . bears a dense intertextual relation to others in the repertoire" so that explaining a myth "now means exploring these intertextual relations, and then, where possible moving out to the realities of the Greek world." He has in mind the work of two movements within classical studies that it is quite possible to distinguish from one another, though both have helped to form our sense of the stories' intertextual densities and each has stimulated in various overlapping ways the productions of the other. The first of these is the revived study of the connections between myth and ritual associated particularly with Walter Burkert, and the second is the study of myth as the key to Greek thought, associated most prominently with Jean-Pierre Vernant, Marcel Detienne, and Pierre Vidal-Naquet.

The revival of interest in the connections between myth and ritual occurred, ironically, just at the point where the first burst of this kind of theorizing in classical studies—the work of Robertson Smith, J. G. Frazer, and Jane Harrison, for example—appeared to be quite generally discredited along with the turn-of-the century vitalist philosophies that nourished them. Although the work of these theorists continued to resonate elsewhere, their influence in classical studies appeared exhausted by the time Joseph Fontenrose excoriated the school in *The Ritual Theory of Myth* (1966), and Geoffrey Kirk underscored its weakness as a "monotheory" in *Myth: Its Meaning and Functions in Ancient and Other Societies* (1973).[6] Yet two of Walter Burkert's important early essays appeared in the very year of Fontenrose's attack, and in 1972 he published his *Homo Necans: The Anthropology of Ancient Greek Sacrificial Ritual and Myth.*

Burkert has succeeded in reviving the problematic of myth and ritual by building his theory upon a base quite different from his predecessors. Where they find support in the voluntaristic psychologies of Tarde and Le Bon and the vitalisms of Nietzsche and Bergson, Burkert derives his authorization from ethological experiment, above all from Konrad Lorenz's sociobiology of aggression, so widely controverted during the sixties. In fact, Burkert's is only one of two theories of ritual that made their strikingly complementary debuts in 1972, both resorting to Lorenz to justify their Hobbesian views of humankind as *homo necans,* the slaughtering animal. The second of these is René Girard's *Violence and the Sacred.* This dark "double" of Burkert is largely outside the purview of the classical consensus, but it is anchored in Greek mythology and does illuminate some of Burkert's intellectual underpinnings.

Violence and the Sacred is a totalizing monotheory of the origins of culture in human sacrifice. However questionable Freud's anthropology may be in *Totem and Taboo,* Girard regards his central intuition as sound—there must have been an original murder. "The mechanism of the surrogate victim" gives rise not only to religion, ritual, and myth but to kinship systems, language, and "symbolic thought" (Girard 1977, 297). Humans have learned to protect their social arrangements against internal aggression by deflecting their inherent violence upon "a 'sacrificeable' victim" (4). This strategy is profoundly conservative. "The purpose of the sacrifice is to restore harmony to the community, to reinforce the social fabric" (8). Girard's elaborate Sartrean hypotheses about the social psychology of the scapegoating need not concern us here. What does, however, is his general claim, and a specific version of it, that because humanity cannot bear to contemplate its violence, the very institutions generated by it are dedicated to a massive cover-up. And since violence is especially "the heart and secret soul of the sacred" (31), religion, rite, and myth are at the core of this conspiracy. Religion is "simply another term for the surrogate victim" (307); ritual masks its origin and purpose by replacing the victim from within by an outsider, even another species, and myths are "the retrospective transfiguration of sacrificial crises, the reinterpretation of these crises in the light of the cultural order which has arisen from them" (64). As Girard remarks sardonically, "the myth is there to prove that we are dealing with a spontaneous process of self-mystification" (83). In the *myth* of Oedipus (as distinguished from Sophocles' dramas), for example, "the fearful transgression of a single individual is substituted for the universal onslaught of reciprocal violence" (77). Since "violence is behind all mythic themes" (244), the inquirer, as the example pithily demonstrates, requires a skeptical hermeneutic that can "gain access to the generative event" (309). As in Lévi-Strauss, though for a very different sort of reason, the actual message of a myth is never perspicuous in its discourse.

The argument of this brilliantly written and suggestive essay is open to very serious objections indeed, but these don't prevent Walter Burkert in his preface to the English edition of *Homo Necans* from crediting the new recognition of "the central role of sacrifice in ancient religion" partly to "the school of Jean-Pierre Vernant and Marcel Detienne" and partly to "*Violence and the Sacred,* which appeared in the same year as *Homo Necans* and may be seen as parallel in intent" (Burkert 1983, xiii). Like Girard, Burkert acknowledges the inspiration of Lorenz's *On Aggression,* and he even echoes Girard's anti-modern animus (though in far less sinister fashion) when he contrasts the attempt of "fashionable psychology . . . to eradicate feelings of guilt from the human psyche" with his own argument that in the ancient world "solidarity was achieved through a sacred crime with due reparation" (xiv). Here, however, Burkert's politics end; the substance of *Homo Necans,* after its theoretical first chapter, is a detailed structural and historical examination, in the light of their sacrificial origins, of the congeries of myths and rites associated with several of the major festivals and shrines of ancient Greece.

Like Blumenberg and Girard, Burkert adopts the Bergson-Gehlen line on culture as what replaces instinct as the mechanism of human survival. But he attends far more explicitly than Girard to the evidence from ethology, physical anthropology, and sociobiology about the part played in the acquisition of culture by ritual. This is understood in the biologist's sense as a pattern of behavior that has lost its original function but "persists in a new function, that of communication" (23). Humanity's biological evolution belongs almost entirely to the Paleolithic era, during which males became specialized as hunters and discovered, by way of their identification with the animals they hunted, the sacrificial killing that is the fundamental experience of the sacred. Out of this experience they constructed the religion that supplements "the psychological mechanisms of imitation and imprinting" in the work of creating societies (35). Burkert's claim for the cultural centrality of ritual sacrifice is virtually as broad as Girard's and may seem at first blush very close to his. But in fact it differs sharply from his in its models of both aggression and sacrifice.[7] Burkert insists that aggression arises out of the hunting pack, not out of the psychological mechanisms of scapegoating, and that the eating of the sacrifice, which Girard ignores, is an integral part of the primal religious experience. In short, he challenges from the perspective of a more rigorous sociobiology precisely those aspects of Girard's explanations of aggression and sacrifice mentioned above as suspiciously "existentialist."

In contrast to Girard, Burkert is also at pains to establish the continuity between religion's Paleolithic origins and its survival in the displaced versions of ancient Greek ritual and its concomitant myth. Applying his central structural principles—that sacrificial ritual embodies "tension between encountering death and affirming life" and that the enduring "external form" of this ritual consists "of preparations, a frightening central moment and restitution" (83)—Burkert conducts us, first through an explanation of funerary rites like the festive meal, funeral games and libations, then through the "sexualization of ritual killing" in phallus cult and maiden-sacrifice, and from thence into the "especially ancient" (83) "rites and myths about the stag and the werewolf" (116) in the Arcadian Lykaia. After tracing analogous complexes of myth and ritual in the festivals of Olympia and Delphi, he pursues a related set of transformations manifested in the linked Athenian New Year's festivals of the Buphonia, Skira, and Arrhephoria, which culminate in the Panathenaia. He follows up by considering the structure of comparable festivals at Argos and Orchomenos, and then takes us through what he calls "the great arc of myth" (212) connecting these rites thematically. He next launches successive new examinations by the same method, first into the Athenian Anthesteria, the great spring festival in honor of Dionysus and then into the Eleusinian mysteries. The effect is a stunning network of Lévi-Straussian transformations spreading out laterally but displaying everywhere beneath their surface the diachronic depths of ritual sacrifice.

Burkert's method of working with myth might seem to imply that he, too, understands it as a simple reflex of ritual. And indeed his sociobiological orientation enables him to propound the temporal priority of ritual in terms much more persuasive than any prior ritualist's: "Ritual is far older in the history of evolution, since it goes back even to animals, whereas myth only became possible with the advent of speech" (31). But this very distinction also enables him to swerve aside from the familiar difficulties into which Girard plows head-on. Since ritual and myth arose so very differently, and the origins of myth must remain unknown because myth "cannot be documented before the era in which writing was invented" (31), Burkert finds it easy to accept the ethnological evidence that they are independent entities that subsequently formed, as he puts it in a later work, *Structure and History in Greek Mythology and Ritual*, "a symbiosis" (Burkert 1982, 57).[8] Burkert is also inclined to this conclusion because he follows Boas, Lévi-Strauss, Dundes, and Kirk in recognizing myth as a special variety of the traditional tale. His account in *Structure and History* of what differentiates it has become the virtual gold standard of the consensus in classical studies. He affirms that "the difference cannot be found at the level of form or structure" (22), and he denies the universal applicability of distinctions according to content. He points out in a particularly devastating refutation of Pettazzoni and Eliade (and of the influential position of the folklorist William Bascom, whom he shows to have been following the "history of religion" claim) that Greek myths, far from being set *in illo tempore*, "are situated in an epoch which the Greeks themselves regarded as historical" (22).[9] He concludes that "the specific character of myth seems to lie neither in the structure nor in the content of a tale, but in the use to which it is put. . . . *Myth is a traditional tale with secondary, partial reference to something of collective importance*" (22–23).

If this definition were not in italics in the original, I would be tempted to add them; this is the soundest definition in print of myth considered primarily in its folkloristic sense. It is particularly significant for its cogent rejection of all attempts to perpetuate, wittingly or unwittingly, the Grimms' romantic hypostasizing of myth and folktale as distinct genres based on differences of structure or content. There are no such consistent differences; there are only differences in the use to which traditional tale is put. Burkert suggests, as an illustration of the proper distinction, that we contrast Ovid, where "myth comes quite close to 'Maerchen,'" with Pindar, "where myth is alive by virtue of immediate reference and relevance to all aspects of genealogy, geography, experience, and evaluation of reality" (24). Whereas Ovid's self-conscious versions echo the stories' long Hellenistic reworkings as literary allusion, the narrative passages in Pindar's odes crackle with the energy of their ideological deployment. Perhaps nothing so distinguishes Burkert's work from Girard's as the specificity and concreteness with which Burkert draws his theoretical speculations from the riches of that ideological sea in which Pindar swims.

THE "PARIS SCHOOL": MYTH AS "COLLECTIVE REPRESENTATION"

In his preface to the English translation of *Homo Necans,* Burkert divides credit for the renewed acceptance of the "central role of sacrifice in ancient religion" between Girard and himself on one hand and "the school of Jean-Pierre Vernant and Marcel Detienne" (xiii) on the other. Burkert is surely right to recognize the Parisians as allies in this broad sense. He is also better justified than one usually is to refer to them as a "school." They have produced, separately and in collaboration, a body of work in which their distinctive differences seem of minor significance compared to the resemblances. At the level of generalization where Burkert and Girard can be said to be united by a sociobiological perspective on sacrifice, the Parisians are united by a cultural studies perspective on the structure of Greek thought between the Mycenaean age and the Hellenistic, a structure that often seems to them most available in the privileged symbolic fields of ritual and myth. While Burkert is accurate in perceiving the Paris School as complementary on the central significance of. ritual sacrifice, the Parisians differ from him in at least two major respects. Sacrifice is for them only one among many interrelated institutions that express a cultural thematics, and the anterior limit of this cultural unity—the Mycenaean civilization—renders nugatory the issue of continuity with the Stone Ages.[10]

As the group themselves tend to see it, their principal intellectual affinities are very much a French affair. They trace their efforts to establish a concrete "historical anthropology," as Vernant likes to call it, back to Durkheim, Mauss, and the circle of *L'Année sociologique.* In the magisterial review already referred to, Richard Gordon characterizes the Parisians' recuperation of the patterns of ancient Greek thought as "a modified version of Durkheimian collective representations." Certainly they do favor those Durkheimian entities, but since they seek structure rather than origin they are free of Durkheim's reasons for confining himself to the "elementary forms" and avoiding the sophistications of myth. In their work myth is as rich and valuable an asset in the study of collective representations as it is a brilliant feature of the culture on which they focus.

As Froma Zeitlin points out in the excellent introduction to her English-language edition of Vernant's collected essays, the School also incorporates "the later shifts in historical method and outlook exemplified by the work of the *Annales* school of historiography" (Vernant 1991, 6). The classicists must have encountered among the *Annalistes* encouraging analogues, if not models, for their own versions of *"mentalités"* and *"la longue durée."* But they have found their principal methodological inspiration, as everyone has acknowledged, among the various national flavors of what we still have to call rather hazily "structuralism." Vernant has paid tribute to his early models, the Sinologist Marcel Granet and the classical historian Louis Gernet. Lévi-Strauss, too, has cited Granet as an important inspiration, and Gernet's significance is underlined by the reprinting of his pioneering "'Value' in Greek Myth," in the important English-language collection of the School's "structuralist essays" edited by Richard Gordon (Gordon 1981). But the two major inspirers of the School's structural methods have obviously been Georges Dumézil and Claude Lévi-Strauss.

Dumézil might seem a surprising candidate here, particularly because his three-class ideology has turned out to be far more difficult to apply to Greek myth and society than to his other Indo-European cultures. But Jean-Pierre Vernant offers in his introduction to Marcel Detienne's *Gardens of Adonis* a particularly illuminating glimpse of the level of generality on which it makes sense to yoke Dumézil with the more obvious Lévi-Strauss. Even before Detienne's demonstration that the ritual and myths connected with the "gardens of Adonis" must be deciphered by means of a "botanical code" of spices, he says, Dumézil and Lévi-Strauss had established the principle that myths are built upon such internal cultural codes. Frazer's famous romantic interpretation assumes that "Adonis" can be understood in isolation from other mythological beings as a "dying god" who represents a natural process, a symbolism universal in world mythology. But "this threefold hypothesis has already been completely demolished by the work of Georges Dumézil and Claude Lévi-Strauss. A god has no more one particular essence than a single detail of a myth is significant on its own. Every god is defined by the network of relations that links him with and opposes him to the other deities included within a particular pantheon; and similarly, a single detail in a myth is only significant by virtue of its place within the ordered system to which the myth itself belongs" (Detienne 1977, iii). Only a structural analysis that finds its categories in a matrix comprised of a culture's network of traditional story *and* of its extra-fictional assumptions can be trusted to recover indigenous significance. To pluck a "myth" free of such a context on the assumption that it communicates universal, transhistorical value is to gaze into a post-Enlightenment mirror and construct an interpretation projected upon that surface. The prevalence of this latter practice since the heyday of romanticism explains why a work like *The Gardens of Adonis* scandalizes our preconceptions of what the traditional tale is about when it discloses a web of Adonic myth and ritual based upon the framework of a "botanical code" opposing myrrh to lettuce. In this it resembles the impact of the Lévi-Strauss who is so plainly Detienne's inspiration. Even *Gardens,* however, which employs Lévi-Strauss's methods exceptionally closely, adopts only his general principle of thematic contrasts, not his subjection of all variants to the inversions of the canonical formula.

Perhaps the most distinguishing mark of the school's broadly "structuralist" studies is the ingenuity with which they bring to bear upon a particular topic a range of cultural phenomena by no means self-evident beforehand and then persuade the reader by the rich and patient accumulation of detail that these phenomena do indeed cohere in the field of focus. The risk in this mode of argument resembles the risk in "cultural studies" arguments in general and "new historical" ones in particular. They tend to be built upon analogies, often quite strained, whose desired coherence depends upon a rather touching faith that within the hypothetical closed field of a given "culture," all significant phenomena *must* somehow be interrelated. But the great gain, when the method is wielded by masters of it like Stephen Greenblatt or the leaders of the Paris School, is access to new sources of ethnographic insight. Claude Lévi-Strauss warns us in *The Story of Lynx,* with respect to his own work, that studies of myth must always come back to "the practices and beliefs of a given society, which are our only source of information on those qualitative relations. This is the reason why we should give up pursuing the structural analysis of the myths of a society for which we lack an ethnographic context or, at any rate, a context that is independent from the information carried by the myths themselves" (189). This warning, as I have already suggested, might seem to apply particularly to the study of ancient societies. But the Paris classicists practice what the anthropologist preaches. Their work is an eye-opening demonstration of the riches to be found in a field as apparently closed as Greek mythology when its structural thematics are set in mutually illuminating relation to their ethnographic contexts.

One example will have to suffice. Since the work of Pierre Vidal-Naquet is not otherwise noticed specifically in this section, let it be his well-known essay "The Black Hunter and the Origin of the Athenian *Ephebeia*" (Vidal-Naquet 1986, 106–128). Vidal-Naquet is primarily interested in offering a new answer to the old puzzle about the origins of the institution, but he makes in the very title of the essay the characteristic move of the School by linking unexpectedly the origins of the *Ephebeia* to the traditional story of the Black Hunter. He commences by recalling the duty of the lightly armed Athenian ephebes to patrol the outer boundaries of the city's cultivated lands. By way of illustrating the liminal citizenship of such youths, Vidal-Naquet cites the "finest evocation" (108) of one, Pindar's representation of Jason in the fourth Pythian ode. He then returns to the world of Athenian ritual, specifically to the etiological myth connected with the autumnal celebration of the Apaturia, "the great festival celebrated by the phratries of the Ionian world" (109). At this celebration the new sixteen-year-old ephebes are inducted by the sacrifice of their long hair into both the phratry and their two years of military service. According to the story, the festival began with a duel in which an Athenian, Melanthos ("the black"), defeated by a ruse ("Who's that beside you?") the Boeotian, Xanthos ("the white"). After reviewing scholarly attempts to relate this etiological myth to the rites of the festival, Vidal-Naquet launches his own solution by noting three peculiar features of the story: it is set in a frontier region, the Athenian is (the normally pejorative) "black," and he wins by a trick that seems to violate the spirit of the hoplite oath that the eighteen-year-olds will swear at their induction into full citizenship. Vidal-Naquet attacks these anomalies by shifting abruptly to a discussion of the Spartan equivalent of the *Ephebeia,* the *Krypteia,* which he demonstrates in a consciously Lévi-Straussian manner to require behavior symmetrically contrary to that expected of the mature hoplite. He proceeds first to point out how pervasively the myths and "rites of passage," especially those of initiation into adulthood, are marked by varieties of a "law of symmetrical inversion" (114). He then turns to detailed examination of the Athenian *Oschophoria.* This is the festival whose etiological myth is Theseus's joyful/sorrowful return from Crete after slaying the Minotaur but forgetting to change his black sail to white, thus provoking his father's suicide—the very death that the traditional black cloak of the ephebe was believed to commemorate. This festival turns out, of course, to be built upon a set of initiatory inversions: male/female, boys' athletic contest/boys processing in drag, dark/light, armed/unarmed.

It is only at this point in the essay that Vidal-Naquet makes the great leap advertised in his title, between the *Ephebeia* and "the theme of the hunt" (117). Although hunting might appear to be clearly an activity of the borderlands, the wild, the "raw" in Lévi-Strauss's sense, and therefore of the ephebe, Vidal-Naquet turns to Plato's *Laws* for a distinction between two kinds of hunting: the adult, heroic, and communal confrontation with the spear as in hoplite warfare, a kind of hunting of which the Calydonian boar hunt is the mythic model, and the single, furtive hunting with a net typical of the adolescent. The model in story for the latter is the Black Hunter, Melanion, whom the chorus of old men refers to in the *Lysistrata.* Melanion appears in their song as "a sort of ephebe *manqué . . .* a version of the widespread myth of the gloomy, solitary hunter who is either a misogynist or tries to insult Artemis, and who, in either case, flouts the social rules" (119). In Greek versions of the story of Atalanta, his female counterpart, it is he who wins her in a footrace, the black against the white, by the ruse of the dropped apples. They are later punished by Cybele—turned into lions incapable of sexual congress, for having intercourse in a shrine sacred to Zeus—violators of sexual convention to the last. Vidal-Naquet concludes, then, by maintaining as his explanation for the anomalies in the etiological myth of the *Apaturia* that because the ephebe was *pre-hoplite,* "in the symbolic enactments that are the rites of passage, he was an anti-hoplite, sometimes a girl, sometimes a cunning hunter, sometimes black" (12). The essay actually ends in a further gesture quite typical of the School, a flare-up of bonus speculation, a moment of self-indulgent high spirits presumably justified by the scholarly restraint of all that has preceded. Vidal-Naquet turns in his final paragraph from Lévi-Strauss to Dumézil, suggesting that the Greek split between ephebe and hoplite may derive from the two-fold aspects of order and disorder characteristic of the warrior's function in Indo-European society. Cuchullain, Publius Horatius, the Spartan "three hundred" of Herodotus, may all display ephebic features. "Young Horatius may thus be distant cousin to the Black Hunter" (122). Even such a *précis* does not convey much sense of the mesh of supporting details that make the argument convincing. But the reliance on analogy, the adducing of evidence that ranges from the anthropology of oral cultures to late Plato, and the manipulation of a three-cornered interplay among social institutions, modes of thought, and the symbolic forms of myth and ritual—all these are typical.

Vidal-Naquet's essay also displays one last quality of the school not so often remarked but certainly a significant feature of much of their work. This is their insistence on the strangeness, the otherness, even the ultimately ungraspable otherness, of ancient Greek culture. If, on one hand, they construct new windows by means of their historical anthropology, on the other they remind us that what we see through them are tantalizing glimpses of a cultural landscape much more unfamiliar than we have traditionally been given to understand. Marcel Detienne sometimes refers to those who have taught us the reassuring view as "the Hellenists." This label signifies in his usage those classicists of the last two centuries whose "humanistic" glorification of the ancient Greeks as the fountainhead of Western civilization has promoted the notion that the Greeks were just like us, only more so. We have thus been led to presume in their case a cultural transparency unlike our expectations about any other ancient people. Louis Gernet fires an early warning shot across the bows of these "Hellenists" when he affirms in the conclusion of his essay "'Value' in Greek Myth" (1948) that there is, in the early conception of "value" that preceded the invention of money, "a core which cannot be reduced to what they call rational thought" (Gernet 1981, 146). The impersonal pronoun is wonderfully ambiguous here; "they" seems to embrace everyone from those patrons of "rational thought," Plato and Aristotle, down to the most recent post-Enlightenment quantifiers of value. Gernet's remark provides a useful clue to the intellectual genealogy of this attitude. It is out of Nietzsche by Heidegger, and it consists in a deep distrust of that post-Socratic tradition of abstract thought now so often referred to pejoratively as "Western metaphysics." The version of it that appears subsequent to Gernet in the work of the School is a more circumspect cousin of Jacques Derrida's critique. The classicists do at least treat the philosophers, Plato in particular, as valuable ethnographic informants, even if they take a special pleasure in catching them testifying against themselves. But the School's most important direct identification with the post-Nietzchean critique, Detienne and Vernant's *Cunning Intelligence in Greek Culture and Society,* does unequivocally attack Platonic rationalism. The authors maintain that the importance of *metis,* the "type of intelligence" and "way of knowing" that involves pragmatic experience and wily improvisation, has eluded students of Greek culture because it was "thrust into the shadows" by its successful enemy, "the concept of Platonic Truth" (Detienne and Vernant 1978, 3–4). "Plato" figures once again as the ambiguous Hermes who conceals as much as he reveals, obscures *because* he illuminates. The Parisians' insistence upon the unfamiliar otherness of the cultural assumptions thus occluded appears as the logical concomitant, the dark side of the moon, to the new perspectives opened by their adventure in "historical anthropology."

Marcel Detienne confronts directly the implications of this elusive cultural otherness for the modern construction of myth in his playful but incisive monograph *The Creation of Mythology.* Detienne signifies by "mythology" in this context not "a body of myths" but, in the older, time-honored sense, "a systematic explanation of myth." His essay is a witty version of Marx's epigram that events of world history not only occur twice, but the first time as tragedy and the second as farce. Detienne establishes a running comparison between the ancient Greeks' own creation of "mythology" in an attempt to rationalize *their mythoi,* and the moderns' far more elaborate attempts to do the job over again. These latter efforts, in Detienne's view, are tinged with the farcical complication of trying to accomplish this re-creation with one eye on the Greek portrait in a distant mirror—a funhouse mirror, as it turns out.

He commences his genealogy, Foucauldian both in structure and attitude, by introducing what he considers to be the first modern "mythologies"—the "anthropological" theories of myth of the latter half of the nineteenth century—as scandalized attempts to explain away the grotesque, obscene, and disgusting aspects of the world's oral storytelling. This whitewashing effort includes not only Müller and Tylor, but the entire movement bent on detaching ancient religion from the source of scandal—Lang, Schmidt, and so forth. Detienne recognizes explicitly that "myth" is reinvented in the eighteenth century, but, because of his emphasis upon the role of the reception-history of "Greece" in the modern construction of myth, his attention to that century and to the part played by romanticism is confined to two remarks. He notes what he regards as the largely contemptuous juxtaposition of Greek with Amerindian myth by Fontenelle and Lafitau, and he observes that the romantics' "Hellenist" glorification of Greek myth is responsible for the efforts of nineteenth and twentieth-century theorizers, beginning with Müller and Tylor, to exempt "the Greeks" from the general imputation of scandal.

Detienne might appear to be headed in the wrong chronological direction in his second chapter. It is taken up with an examination of the literary and anthropological insights into the nature of oral storytelling developed within the last generation. This venture turns out to be no digression, of course; Detienne implies that his sense of these developments determines crucially the difference between *his* view of the Greek construction of "myth" and that of the nineteenth-century theorists. In the third chapter he leaps boldly backward into the heart of his comparison with an account of how the concept expressed by the word *mythos,* originally neutral, slowly took on a negative definition in Herodotus and Thucydides. The fourth chapter, "The Earliest Interpretation—and a Smile," retreats to the sixth century to review the first attack on *mythos,* by the philosopher Xenophanes, and then moves a generation forward to consider the suave, possibly ironic, relaying of *mythoi* by the historian Hecataeus of Miletus, who refuses to distinguish between *mythos* and *logos.* His is "the earliest interpretation" or hermeneutic rendering of myth, and his, too, is the "smile," the ambiguity of his own attitude toward the veracity of what he relates. Detienne sees both of these writers as implicated in the hardening of the distinction between *mythos* and *logos* that results from the distance created by the intrusion of *writing*. The fifth chapter, "The City Defended by Its Mythologists," is perhaps more Derrida than Foucault. It demonstrates how thoroughly Plato, in the very process of enthroning the contrast between *mythos* and *logos*, lie and truth, "which was for so long to obsess the thinking of modern mythologists" (102), undoes his own attack on myth in *The Republic* and elsewhere by his admissions in *The Republic* and in *The Laws* that this very kind of story is a social and political necessity.

Having completed his account of the original, small-scale Greek evolution of a dubious "mythology," Detienne returns us to its bloated and still more dubious modern reenactment. Chapter 6, "Two-Headed Greeks," lands us, rather bewilderingly at first, in the syllabus of the course for colonial administrators given yearly by Marcel Mauss, long-time dean of French anthropology. We quickly find ourselves tossed among some of the chief extravaganzas of hypostatized "myth" in the twentieth century—those of Cassirer, Lévy-Bruhl, and Lévi-Strauss. Detienne is especially concerned to show that even these monotheorists follow their nineteenth-century predecessors in always finding a way to exempt the Greeks from the scandal of oral story. They do this by accepting unquestioningly Plato's fatal distinction and with it the familiar "Hellenist" claim that the Greeks managed to modernize themselves—first pre-Socratic philosophy, then "Western" rationality emerged from their matrix in mythology. In a remark that provides the chapter with its title, Detienne mocks the resulting unresolved antinomies of affective and cognitive explanation: "The Greeks . . . are just like other people, but with a slight difference which is not without significance: they have two heads" (117). The chapter concludes in an argument in much the same tone. Both the rationalistic systematizers and their opposite numbers, the phenomenological asserters of transcendental apperception, still run the risk of "being designated for perpetual residence in that place where the delusions of modern man about mythology redouble the phantoms and fictions produced by the first 'mythologists.'" Detienne's conclusion, "Untraceable Myth," returns to the central importance for this problematic of the concept of orality, but now he dwells upon the trickiness, the paradoxical nature of all modern attempts to pin down oral tradition. "Mythology, comprising *mythos*, is open territory where everything said in different tones of speech is at the mercy of repetition which transmutes it into the memorable, the noteworthy, that which it has selected" (130). Detienne appears to include even genres of storytelling among the features created only in the reception-process of "selection." It's in connection with denying myth "a literary genre or a specific type of tale" (131) that he declares: "mythology, a fish emulsified in the waters of mythology, is an untraceable form" (131–132).

Detienne's nominalism about *mythos* in this text is consistent with the school's Nietzschean animus against the barrier of rationalism (or, in Detienne's sense, "mythology") erected by Plato. Lowell Edmunds points out that for Detienne and Vernant "Plato stands in the same relation to myth as to *metis*, 'cunning intelligence'" (Edmunds 1990, 14). This is a fine insight, but seems, if accepted, to leave Edmunds on shaky ground when he asserts that for Detienne "myth . . . does not exist" (1).[11] Edmunds goes on to show that if one switches from semantic evidence to the evidence of *praxis*, "the Greeks did in fact have a category of discourse or narrative corresponding to 'myth' in the sense of traditional tale" (2). But if we could pin down *polymetis* and protean Detienne outside the dodging and twisting discourse of *The Creation of Mythology,* he might well agree.[12] His skeptical nominalism is not a denial that *oral tradition* exists, nor even that the Greeks signified by *mythos* what a modern folklorist would wish to call "traditional tale." It induces him, instead, to doubt whether the vested interests of categorizers, Greek or modern, permit them to capture under *their* concepts of "myth" the *aletheia,* the Heideggerian "unconcealment," of what actually is there in the *praxis* of oral tradition. Even if it is taken as proved that the Greeks identified a class of traditional tale as *mythos,* Detienne's principal point remains unaffected; modern scholars "run the risk" of delusion if they insist on labeling that elusive quiddity with *our* fraught term, "myth." *The Creation of Myth* is a particularly eloquent warning that the farther away we get from the concrete richness of a particular context of oral story, the more likely we are to be "inventing" "mythology" in the pejorative senses of both words. I suggested in the conclusion of the preceding chapter an ironic possibility. The more intensively oral story is investigated in the field, the more likely it becomes that the folkloristic conception of "myth" that originally inspired the inquiry will be found to be too simplistic a label. *The Creation of Myth* is the work of a classicist whose subtle interrogations of ancient texts have led him toward a similar conclusion.

Detienne's essay is a valuable theoretical foregrounding of the Parisians' assumptions about Greek "myth" and an important study in its own right of the topic that is the subject of this book. In concluding this account of the consensus in classical studies, however, I want to withdraw attention from this *jeu d'esprit* to take a last broad view of an accord that includes not only the new comparativists, ritualists, and members of the Paris School but practitioners of several other approaches as well.[13] This accord builds upon the fundamental agreement that "myth" is traditional narrative with a high degree of ideological saturation, or, as Burkert puts it, "with secondary, partial reference to something of collective importance." In contrast to the "two-headed Greeks" of romantic Hellenism, this accord affirms that ancient Greek story develops consistently with what ethnological investigation shows to be the case elsewhere in the world; it arises in intricate connection with the storytelling of its neighbors, in close association with other cultural institutions such as rites and festivals and embodies the "collective representations" of its perpetuators. It therefore yields its meanings most reliably to anthropological approaches that respect its contexts. These combine structural analysis with painstaking philological, historical, and social detail, postponing the temptation to produce a comprehensive monotheory till that purely hypothetical day when all the individual pieces of the puzzle have fallen into place. The classical consensus about "myth" mirrors the anthropological not only positively in its assumptions and methods but negatively in its distrust of and withdrawal from grand theory.

[12]

Myth and Ideology

"Myth" is one of the small set of words that we are accustomed to employing in contrary senses. The word signifies in everyday parlance either a traditional story commanding special respect or a widely disseminated falsehood. This contradiction appears even more odd if we recollect the highly successful romantic launching of "myth" in the first, positive sense, but notice that it is the second, negative sense that prevails in current speech and writing.[1] This shift of semantic balance is symptomatic of a shift in thinking that it is the business of the present chapter to trace as best it may.

We already have an important clue in hand. The very success of the romantic invention of "myth" as a weapon in what Hegel called "the struggle between Belief and Unbelief" engenders a reaction of comparable intensity, the radical critiques of Marx and Nietzsche. Both are prophets of their century in the traditional double sense—in the perspicuity with which they see what is coming as it comes to meet them, and in the cogency of their denunciations of contemporary refusals to see. Paul Ricoeur, in the process of promoting Freud to the company of his two predecessors, characterized this *troika* as "masters" of the "hermeneutics of suspicion" (Ricoeur 1970, 32–36). This phrase has come into wide use because it does capture the strong unmasking drive shared by the work of all three. But the designation "masters" is equally significant; the trio are "masters" in the sense that the enabling insights of their particular modes of critique, taken separately or in combination, inspire in the new century an abundance of "suspicious" or "critical" successors.

Freud unmistakably deserves to be classed with the other two in terms of his general influence on twentieth-century "suspicion." It could reasonably be argued, in fact, that psychoanalysis has been the most effective, because the most concrete, demonstration of both the need for and the heuristic power of a hermeneutics of suspicion. But Freud's direct role in the development of the "ideological" conception of myth is not of comparable importance to Marx's and Nietzsche's. Psychoanalysis lurks in the background in this chapter, its influence indirect and diffused, whereas so high a proportion of the theory to be examined lies in the domains of the other two "masters" that the chapter is organized accordingly. It commences with an account of the twentieth-century transformation of Marx and Engels' chief contribution to the critique of myth, their concept of ideology. This beginning is diachronically and thematically appropriate since the post-Marxian development of "ideology" is the earliest and most conspicuous integrating feature of the new critiques in general and of their relation to myth in particular. The next section of the chapter takes up the intersection of the theories inspired by Marx and Freud with the principles of the movement loosely referred to as Structuralism. After a brief consideration of the relevance of Lévi-Strauss and Lacan, it examines in particular Louis Althusser's conceptions of ideology and myth and Roland Barthes's semiological version of the latter in his *Mythologies*. Nietzsche comes last, partly because his mode of critique makes its full impact only after its mediation through Heidegger, and partly because its ultimate results prove the most radical. After touching very briefly upon the mediating effect of Heidegger, this section examines first Horkheimer and Adorno's *Dialect of Enlightenment,* a brilliant updating of Hegel's and Nietzsche's history of the conflict of myth and antimyth and a central contribution to the argument for the necessity of critical theory as a permanent critique of myth. It then turns to Jacques Derrida's Nietzschean demonstration in "The White Mythology" of the reliance on metaphor at the heart of several classic texts in Western philosophy. The chapter concludes in a brief set of generalizations prompted by this historical sketch of relations between myth and ideology.

THE DOMAIN OF MARX: MYTH AS IDEOLOGY

The most conspicuous difficulty about any attempt to discuss the relation of "myth" to "ideology" is that the history and definition of this second term are no less complicated and controversial than those of its slightly older sibling. "Ideology" has accumulated in the twentieth century its own rich tradition of interpretation and commentary, made the more urgent by its role in Marxist thought and praxis.[2] Furthermore, volumes have been written about it without mention of the word "myth," just as volumes about myth have managed without "ideology." Each concept encompasses tracts of intellectual life where the other has no portfolio. Nevertheless, Marx himself guaranteed their entanglement within the modern tradition of antithetical critique when he first produced myth's sibling rival by finding "myth" standing on its head and placing it upon its feet as "ideology." For the next forty years "ideology" shares in the general obscurity of Marxism as a system of thought, an obscurity exacerbated in the case of this concept by the fact that its richest con-textualizing, in *The German Ideology,* lay unpublished until 1932. In the late 1880s and the 1890s, however, Marxism ceases to be the affair of radical workingmen's circles, becomes the orthodoxy of burgeoning socialist parties, and begins to exact serious attention even from non-Marxist social thinkers. As this happens, theorists of all flavors begin to pay increasing attention to Marxist doctrine not merely about the economic "base" of society, but about those aspects of its "superstructure" that Marx had seemed to relegate to the realm of ideology.[3] But this sudden and serious interrogation of Marxism as a coherent body of social thought occurs within the immense weather-system of anti-rational, affective theorizing that settles over Europe at the turn of the century, and this atmosphere alters profoundly, among other aspects of Marx's thought, the concept of ideology. In the era of Dilthey's "critique of historical reason," Husserl's phenomenology, and Poincaré's and Mach's epistemological relativizing of the philosophy of science, Marx's accounts of ideology appear increasingly to be built upon a series of naïvely positivistic dichotomies. In the central passage from *The German Ideology* (which fleshes out the more condensed published instances) we find, for example, "consciousness" opposed to "life," and the "ideal" and what humanity has "narrated, thought of, imagined, conceived" opposed to "the material" and "the real."[4] The mordant tone of these contrasts suggests the authors' blithe unawareness of any philosophical difficulties lurking in the unexamined terms. Before Marx's "ideology" passes through the crucible of the century's turn, it is a particular kind of bourgeois lie: deliberate, cognitive, conscious, and personal. By the end of the process (if it can be said to have ended yet), ideology is inadvertent, affective, unconscious, and structural. In this condition, its distinction from "myth" appears more problematic than ever.

This mythward drift of ideology begins within Marxism itself. At least in retrospect, it is incipient in Engels. Intent in their early work on unmasking the capitalist mode of production, he and Marx paid minimal attention to the theory of the superstructure. But Engels found himself increasingly pressed in the years after Marx's death to explain and defend Marxism in relation to anthropology, religion, philosophy—in short, to modes of the superstructure. In a letter to Franz Mehring (1893) he describes ideology as "a process accomplished by the so-called thinker consciously, it is true, but with a false consciousness. The real motive forces impelling him remain unknown to him. . . . As all action is mediated by thought, it appears to him to be ultimately based upon thought" (Tucker 1978, 766). Though Engels may still remain enclosed within a positivist "reflection theory" of the relation of thought to "the real," his appeal to of the concept of "false consciousness" and the acknowledgment that "all action is *mediated* by thought" contribute considerably to the subsequent formation of more subtle versions of "ideology" both inside and outside Marxism. Jorge Larrain makes the important point that the very dichotomy between base and superstructure is a principal source of the widening of "ideology's" meaning. "By itself, the relationship between base and superstructure does not distinguish inverted from non-inverted forms of consciousness. The more ideology is understood within this polarity the more it tends to be substituted for all forms of social consciousness" (Larrain 1979, 76).

We can see this process at work in the '90s in a new generation of Marxist intellectuals, Mehring himself, Labriola, Kautsky, and Plekhanov, for example, who honor the primacy of the economic base but focus upon issues of Marxist aesthetics and philosophy of history that encourage a more affirmative, generalized, and relative sense of ideology. This consensus is "generalized" in substituting a broader for a narrower denotation—in tending to identify the entire contents of the superstructure with the ideological. It is "relative" in its implicit, if not explicit, admission that Marxism, too, must be ideological, and it is "affirmative" (or at least neutral) in accepting ideology as a structural inevitability of thought. This trend even within orthodox Marxist thought is encapsulated in Lenin's own revealing and often-cited remark in *What Is to Be Done?* (1902). "Since there can be no talk of an independent ideology formulated by the working masses themselves in the process of their movement, the *only* choice is—either bourgeois or socialist ideology" (Tucker 1975, 28). This broadening, relativizing, and revalorizing of the concept opens the way, in turn, for a number of later and influential Marxist interventions in its definition, especially the "historicist" theories of Lukács and Gramsci, and Althusser's "structural" equivalent. If this were a full account of the formation of "ideology," these modifications would demand extended discussion. As it is, Althusser comes up briefly later in the chapter, and it must suffice to say here about the theories of Lukács in *History and Class Consciousness* and of Gramsci in *Prison Notebooks* that they are milestones in the progressive diffusion of the concept.[5] When more traditional Marxists and the historians of ideology brand them as "historicist," in the Marxist sense, they mean, roughly, that in conceiving of ideologies as the worldviews of classes in historical development they come uncomfortably close to reintroducing into Marxist theory the Hegelian primacy of consciousness against which Marx reacted in the first place. Perry Anderson has argued influentially that Marxist thinkers in the West (troubled especially by the failure of proletarian revolutions and the abuses of Communist states) have tended to develop theories that temper revolutionary politics by elaborate accommodations with bourgeois society (Anderson 1976, chaps. 3, 4). The specific instance of "ideology" appears to bear out his assertion by evolving toward usages that conflate it with "myth."

When committed Marxists feel justified in thus recalibrating the founder's term of art, it isn't surprising to witness its impious treatment at the hands of thinkers who have no special reason to regard Marx as an oracle. Marxism came forth in the 1890s and 1900s from its relative obscurity among the competing doctrines of radical and revolutionary politics into a glare of attention from a number of the most significant social thinkers of the age. Croce, Durkheim, and Sorel felt its attractions, and Weber and even Pareto acknowledged its power by paying it the compliment of serious attention.[6] Different as these strong theorists are from one another, they can be said to share a general response to Marxism; they co-opt it within their own social schemata, each of which can be coded in Marxist terminology as "idealist," meaning that it denies the cultural primacy of the material, economic "base." Durkheim, for instance, explicitly distinguishes between his thought and "historical materialism" in the conclusion of *The Elementary Forms* on the grounds that "collective consciousness is something more than a mere epiphenomenon of its morphological basis" (Durkheim 1965, 471). And Weber relativizes the material base with comparable *éclat* in his late introduction to *The*

Protestant Ethic and the Spirit of Capitalism when he claims that his study pursues "one side of the causal chain" of "interrelationships between economics and religion" (Weber 1958, 27). It is especially injurious from a Marxist point of view that Durkheim and Weber should agree in finding *religion,* of all things, just as fundamental to social explanation as economics. Neither of their critiques targets "ideology" explicitly but both subvert it by implication. They intimate not only that Marxism must itself be an ideology, but that, judged by its own criterion, it must therefore be a form of religious faith.[7]

In the writings of George Sorel this identification of Marxism as a faith is explicit, and wholly positive. Among our group of turn-of-the-century social theorists, Sorel is particularly useful, not only because he celebrates Marxism's core of messianic zeal but also because he juxtaposes with equal explicitness the two terms "myth" and "ideology" and sets them into dialectical motion with a third term, "Utopia." Sorel's "myth," as he presents it in *Reflections on Violence,* is, appropriately enough, not so much defined as from time to time invoked. In his nearest approach to a definition, he speaks of "a body of images which, *by intuition alone,* and before any considered analyses are made, is capable of evoking as an undivided whole the mass of sentiments which corresponds to the different manifestations of the war undertaken by Socialism against modern society" (Sorel 1950, 140). "The men who are participating in a great social movement," he remarks elsewhere, "always picture their coming action as a battle in which their cause is certain to triumph. These constructions . . . I propose to call myths" (48). The instances he goes on to cite include his present causes, "the syndicalist 'general strike' and Marx's catastrophic revolution" as well as various historical analogues "constructed by primitive Christianity, by the Reformation, by the Revolution and by the followers of Mazzini" (48–49). Myths, then, are always imagistic incitements to revolution, the historically particularized manifestations of "inclinations which recur to the mind with the insistence of instincts" (142). In periods, on the contrary, when "there are no myths accepted by the masses, one may go on talking of revolts indefinitely without ever provoking any revolutionary movement" (57).

As the very principle of revolutionary motivation, Sorel's "myth" is an instantly recognizable avatar of the visionary apocalypses of the high Romantics—of Novalis, Blake, and Shelley. And "a body of images" that evades the intellect while evoking powerful sentiments is clearly a revived form of the romantic "symbol." Comparable resurrections of it are common among the modernist novelists and poets contemporary with Sorel, including those discussed in chapter 6, but they are rare among political thinkers. Sorel's version testifies to the influence of Bergson, whose presence pervades *Reflections.* It is indicated in this same passage by the assertion that the images work by *"intuition."* At the time he published this work (1906) Sorel was regularly attending Bergson's lectures, and he appeals to that philosopher's metaphysics and psychology as the philosophical underpinning of his concept of myth. This association should be sufficient to remind us that Sorel's "myth" is yet another channel, however minor compared to Bergson himself or Freud and Jung, by which the mystique of the romantic symbol, in all its Creuzer-like valorizing of image over discourse, is sluiced into the twentieth century. Sorel's version of it affords us a particularly clear glimpse into the sinister potential of this combination of "myth" and "symbol." For Sorel's "myth" is, above all, kinetic. The images evade intellectual examination by "evoking" a "mass of sentiments" that make their impact as an "undivided whole." This non-discursive, unanalyzable bolus of images inspires violent action, fanatic, triumphalistic, narratable by its subject only as "apocalypse now!" *Reflections on Violence* happens to have been written at a time when Sorel was an apologist for extremism of the Left, but the anti-intellectualism of his "myth" could glamorize with equal aptness extremism of the Right. Sorel's turn toward fascism in his late years is yet another instance of the psychological affinity of extremes that is exemplified endlessly in radical politics of the past two centuries. We know only too well, as Sorel of course did not, where the immediate European future of his "myth" lay.

Sorel's "ideology" is, in comparison, a tame thing. His application of the term sometimes approximates Marx's pejorative sense, except that the labeled group are liberal politicians rather than philosophers and theologians. But Sorel's "ideology" sometimes approximates Lenin's neutral sense, as in his remark (which happens to contradict Lenin's dictum) that "syndicalism creates a real proletarian ideology" (252). Sorel does not define "ideology" in *Reflections* nor employ the term often, but his contextual usages make clear that it denotes for him a settled body of opinion with propositions of its own to defend and rationalize. "Myth" is therefore too specialized in meaning, and too contrary in signification, ever to be a near-synonym. "Ideology," instead, is akin to "Utopia," which signifies for Sorel something quite like what "ideology" did for Napoleon—an abstract scheme of social perfection invented by an impossibly naïve intellectual. Sorel defines it almost entirely in contrast to myth. "A Utopia is, on the contrary, an intellectual product . . . the work of theorists who . . . seek to establish a model to which they can compare existing society. . . . The effect of Utopias has always been to direct men's minds towards reforms which can be brought about by patching up the existing system" (57–58). Nothing in Sorel's vocabulary could so convey his disgust with Utopian thought as his finding it exemplified in that Great Satan of his radical worldview, "liberal political economy." As this example indicates, "Utopia" functions like a particular version of Marx's "ideology"; it is the political opiate analogous to Marx's "religion," another mode of perpetuating the anguish of capitalism by offering a trivial and temporary analgesic. It especially maddens Sorel, as liberalism so often has radicals on the Left, because it lures generous souls into argument instead of action. Sorel has always ringing in his head the words of Marx's last thesis on Feuerbach: " . . . the point, however, is to *change* it." Because it pretends impotently to this very role, the species of ideology that he calls "Utopia" is the dark shadow, the demonic contrary, of what he calls "myth."

Sorel, then, presents us with a puzzle; he is the first to yield explicitly to the new pressure to bring into play the conjoined concepts of "ideology" and "myth," but, far from conflating them, he presents them as opposites. Idiosyncratic as his usage may be, however, his incursion into this problematic teaches a pointed lesson about the volatility of some of its central terms. It will be easier to appreciate what is meant by this volatility if we compare Sorel's "ideology," "Utopia," and "myth" with the way these same three terms are taken up in an influential work of social theory of the next generation, Karl Mannheim's *Ideology and Utopia* (1929). Mannheim is as deeply affected as Lukács by German historicism and especially Dilthey, and in Mannheim's case we should add Lukács himself, with whom he collaborated at the beginning of his career. As an admiring but uncommitted student of Marxism, however, he belongs with the group of earlier thinkers discussed above rather than with Lukács. If Lukács tortuously relativizes "ideology" from within, Mannheim, the outsider, boldly completes the job. Mannheim's opus, furthermore, is the first extended scholarly examination of the concept, and perhaps for both sorts of reasons, has always seemed to provoke a high degree of indignation in the Marxist faithful.[8]

Mannheim not only displays a grasp of the concept's early history that has been only marginally improved from his day to ours, but he also anticipates later students of ideology in attempting a thorough anatomy of its burgeoning denotations. This anatomizing is neither entirely consistent nor adequate; more recent efforts have produced improved versions, but its outlines are clear. Mannheim distinguishes from the start between two senses of the concept: the "particular" and the "total." The two senses share the modern impulse to "unmask" one's opponent, but the "particular" unmasking is restricted to the "psychological level" of individual lie or error, whereas the "total" version "calls into question the opponent's total *Weltanschauung*" (Mannheim 1936, 50). "Corresponding to this difference, the particular conception of ideology operates primarily with a psychology of interests, while the total conception uses a more formal functional analysis, without any reference to motivations" (51). Mannheim instances as precursors Bacon's *idola,* and Machiavelli's and Hume's skepticism about motives, but he attributes the gradual fusion of the two types and the hegemony of the "total" conception over the "particular" especially to Hegel's historicism and Marx's crucial recasting of it in terms of class divisions. At this point, however, Mannheim makes a typical Hegelian move. The subtitle of the augmented English translation of *Ideology and Utopia* is "An Introduction to the Sociology of Knowledge," and this is the key to Mannheim's designs upon "ideology." Though he in no way disparages the historical importance of Marx's shaping of the concept, he introduces a new set of qualifying terms to place in perspective the Marxian application of it. Marx's "total" conception of ideology" (68) is "special" as opposed to "general" because it is applied only to his bourgeois antagonist. In "the general form of the total conception of ideology," on the contrary, the analyst "has the courage to subject not just the adversary's point of view but all points of view, including his own, to the ideological analysis" (68–69). Mannheim maintains that "ideology" had a career far wider than Marxism even in the nineteenth century, that its generalized mode is the next logical stage in its evolution and that "with the emergence of the general formulation . . . the simple theory of ideology develops into the sociology of knowledge. What was once the intellectual armament of a party is transformed into an all-inclusive principle according to which the thought of every group is seen as arising out of its life conditions" (69).

These assertions raise a host of difficulties, but the only criticism of Mannheim required here is that his conception of the general form of total ideology turns out to be in practice surprisingly narrow. It is so unremittingly political that what he calls "the sociology of knowledge" appears, rather, to be the field of study generally known in American universities as "political science" or "government." And, indeed, in the central chapter of *Ideology and Utopia,* titled "The Prospects of Scientific Politics," Mannheim test-drives his new "method of research" by characterizing the ideologies of the principal "ideal types" of nineteenth- and twentieth-century politics. More to our purpose, he then applies the method to a closely related classification of "Utopias." A Utopia resembles an ideology in being a form of political thought "incongruous with the state of reality within which it occurs" (173).[9] The great difference is that "ideologies are the situationally transcendent ideas which never succeed *de facto* in the realization of their projected contents" (175), whereas in Utopias "these wish-images . . . take on a revolutionary function" (174). Ideologues, whether through invincible structural ignorance, bad faith, or "purposeful lie" (176), preserve the *status quo,* but utopians struggle to transform it. Mannheim admits that this easy formal distinction is hard to apply in practical contemporary cases. "Utopian" in common speech signifies "impossible of realization" (rather as "myth" signifies "false belief"), but the judgment as to whether a particular vision *is* impossible to realize may well vary according to ideological bias. Mannheim acknowledges that the only good criterion for distinguishing between the truly utopian and its merely ideological simulacrum is the utterly pragmatic and, sadly, *ex post facto* one of sociopolitical success.

By this point we can begin to see the outlines of a significant antithetical symmetry in the social thought of Sorel and Mannheim.[10] Once we realize that the motivation of Mannheim's distinction between "ideology" and "Utopia" is the need to contrast two principles of social behavior—we might call them the conservative and the radical or the static and the dynamic—we can perceive that Sorel constructs the same kind of contrast, though more extreme in degree, between "ideology" and "myth." Before proceeding further with the implications of the looming symmetry between the two thinkers, however, we must take a quick look at Mannheim on "myth." Although "myth" and its grammatical variants appear many times in *Ideology and Utopia,* it is not for Mannheim what the linguists call a "marked" term, and he shows no interest in defining it. In various contexts it appears to signify "foolish traditional story," in others "fiction invented to manipulate the masses." In most of these contexts it seems to connote an archaic form of narratable lie, a convenient tool, insofar as it survives in the modern world, for reinforcing ideology.[11] Mannheim's treatment of myth, then, contrasts sharply with Sorel's and completes the symmetrical contrast in their respective dispositions of the three concepts, "myth," "ideology," and "Utopia." Each thinker features a relatively unmarked term and two terms that identify the contraries in a struggle between social stasis and dynamism. For Sorel the unmarked term is "ideology," while positive "myth" and negative "Utopia" represent the energies in conflict, whereas for Mannheim "myth" is unmarked while "ideology" and "Utopia" fight it out. For both writers, as suggested above, "ideology" is the middle term that represents conservative stasis. This fact suggests that, in spite of the expansion of the concept at the hands of just such independent outsiders as Sorel and Mannheim, it still preserves the Marxian stamp; it still signifies, even for Mannheim, the stasis of the *status quo,* the hegemonic system. And according to both theorists lukewarm "ideology" attracts to itself at least one of the differentiated concepts. For Sorel, the anti-intellectual man of *ressentiment* and action, this is "Utopia," the everlasting "patchwork" of the liberal and socialist intellectuals; for Mannheim, the scholarly sociologist, it is "myth," the ancient bane of freedom of thought. Of these alignments, Mannheim's clearly represents the mainstream in the developing conflation of myth with ideology. But the juxtaposed antithetical symmetries of the duo adumbrate the presence of a larger problematic under construction. Given the mounting consensus that humankind requires desperately to understand (in Spinozistic terms) its freedom and its bondage, twentieth-century social thinkers, though working often at terminological cross-purposes, increasingly agree on the reality of an underlying struggle between the endless wiles of "false consciousness" and our need to live in the truth about ourselves. And the modern construction of "myth," as much as of "ideology," is caught up in this struggle. This is a topic to which it will be necessary to return in an even wider context in the next chapter, when we consider recent constitutive theories of myth. At this point, however, it is time to admit into consideration of the developing conflation of myth with ideology the structuralist interventions of Lévi-Strauss, Lacan, Althusser, and Barthes.

THE STRUCTURALIST INTERSECTION

The one change in twentieth-century intellectual fashion comparable in pervasiveness to the shift from cognitive to affective theory is the concomitant shift from genetic to structural explanation. The concept of ideology, too, is as much affected by this second trend as by the first. Nor does this shift wait upon the appearance of the movement loosely labeled "Structuralism." Lukács takes the first, and arguably the biggest, step toward the structuralizing of ideology in *History and Class Consciousness* when he fuses in his analysis of "reification" Marx himself on the fetishism of commodities, Simmel on the commodification of culture, and Weber on rationalization.[12] And Mannheim, transferring Lukács's lesson directly to "ideology," conceives of his analysis explicitly in structural terms (Mannheim 1936, 57, 181, 239). The theories characteristic of "Structuralism" proper, however, take their inspiration from Saussurean linguistics. Though varying in the degree to which they conform, even analogically, to their linguistic model, they all seek to isolate the basic structural units of their field of study and to discern the concealed laws that govern these units' behavior.

We have already considered one of the most relevant of such models, Claude Lévi-Strauss's structural theory of myth, which is premised upon the close connection of myth and ideology. The theory presumes the existence, in the tellers of even the most seemingly inconsequential tales, of an unconscious that expresses through encoded networks of mythemes, social and existential concerns of central importance. This unconscious displays, not merely Lacan's "whole structure of language," but, encrypted in the rich levels of analogical thought, the whole structure of collective representations, all of them at least potentially ideological.[13] But even though Lévi-Strauss has consistently cited Freud and Marx (as well as Saussure) as inspirers of his mode of structural analysis, his intersection with their critiques of modern Western society is limited by at least three major disconnections. First and most obviously, he focuses on small totemic societies without writing. His occasional off-the-cuff suggestions about applications of his conception of myth to contemporary politics or literature or history cannot be confirmed by his own rules of analysis and must be taken with a grain of salt. His conception of myth is appropriately understood as confined to its anthropological or folkloristic sense. Second, although his "myth," as the imaginary resolution of real contradictions, is broadly modeled on Marx's conception of the function of ideology, it is, by definition, not consciously "interested" and, indeed, does not even privilege consistently any single code such as the social or economic. Third, Lévi-Strauss's "unconscious" is not Freud's; rather than being a topologically designated function of individual metapsychology, it is the collective expression of a content to which no one but the synthesizing decoder can attain fully intelligible access. For these reasons, it seems that although Lévi-Strauss's "myth" bears a strong family likeness to certain midcentury conceptions of ideology, it is not entirely consonant with any except, perhaps, Louis Althusser's.

Lacan's structuralized recension of Freud is more directly implicated both in the Freudian critique itself and, by way of its influence on Althusser, in the further relativizing and universalizing of the concept of ideology. Two intertwined aspects of Lacan's work are particularly relevant in this context: his assault on the unity of the human subject and his account of the place of this subject in the Symbolic order. Lacan subscribes as vehemently as Horkheimer and Adorno to the Copernican heart of Freud's mode of suspicion, his decentering of the ego. Like the Frankfurters he devotes himself to reasserting, in opposition to the hegemony of American ego psychology, what he regards as genuinely revolutionary about Freud's metapsychology. Unlike the Frankfurters, he brings out Freud's radical implications by reading him through the spectacles of an existentialist phenomenology. What Freud calls "ego" appears as a delusion of unity, while the larger "subject" remains the site of contending narcissistic drives, disunified, "split," tragically incapable of the self-identity assumed by nineteenth-century idealists to be its transcendental birthright. In "The subversion of the subject and the dialectic of desire in the Freudian unconscious," for example, he schematizes in a series of "graphs" the inevitable failure of the "subject," split from the start into its components of "me" and "I" as shaped by "the other" and "the Other," to complete a circuit that would indeed enable it to be a transcendental ego (Lacan 1977, 315). Instead, this "barred subject" is three times sent around the looping relays of a short circuit that frustrates its aspirations. The first of these occurs in the experiential order of the Imaginary, when the child seeing its image in the mirror identifies a delusively unified ego at odds with its experience of itself, a signifier, in short, of the Other. The disunified "subject" is similarly alienated a second time upon entering the order of the

Symbolic, the order of the Law of the Father, the Oedipus complex, and language, when the Other interpellates it as voice but fails to bridge the gap, or complete the circuit, between its disorganized components and the fullness of transcendental meaning. Finally, this "barred subject" comes up against the order of the Real. Its libidinal drive urges it into a conjunction with the "other" that is a concrete version of conjunction with Desire itself. At this limit the crippled "subject" encounters the Phallus, the signifier of lack of the Other, and experiences this *non plus ultra* as castration. Lacan's radicalizing of Freud on the ego is wittily epitomized in his retranslation of Freud's epigram *"Wo es war, soll Ich werden."* This is rendered heroically in the *Standard Edition* as "Where id was there ego shall be" (Freud 1965b, 71) but carefully "misunderstood" by Lacan as "I must come to the place where that [*ça, es, id*] was" (Lacan 1977, 171). To appreciate the pathos of this unfulfillable imperative we need only consider the indirect answer, not unworthy of Beckett's mournful poetry, that Lacan supplies in "the subversion of the subject." To the question "What am 'I'?" he replies, "'I' am in the place from which a voice is heard clamoring 'the universe is a defect in the purity of Non-Being'" (Lacan 1977, 317). As the context makes clear, this "I" has had and can have no other estate.

Considered in relation to our topic, the condition of this "barred subject" in the Symbolic order suggests a universal vulnerability to ideology. In both Imaginary and Symbolic realms the "subject" takes much of what definition he or she does acquire from the gaze and voice of others, but in the Symbolic, the realm of law and language, and therefore of culture itself, these shaping influences become also the collective Other. On one hand we encounter a "subject" yearning to be defined in order to enter the fullness of identity, and on the other a culture that interpellates this "subject" only in language that slides endlessly along the signifying chain without permitting genuine arrival. As provocation for the rise of ideology, this situation combines, as George Bernard Shaw's character says of marriage, the maximum of temptation with the maximum of opportunity, the "subject's" extreme anxiety with the ubiquitous solicitation of illusory messages.

The degree to which Louis Althusser's conception of ideology is based on such Lacanian premises can be gathered from the most concise and elegant of his several formulations; ideology is "the imaginary representation of the subject's relationship to his or her real conditions of existence" (Althusser 1971, 162). The terms "imaginary" and "real" are not to be taken in their ordinary (and remarkably loose) English senses; they refer to the Lacanian orders. In fact, as it is important to recognize, the third of these orders, the Symbolic, appears in this definition also—represented in the word "representation" itself. The "subject" who does such representing is necessarily located within the Symbolic order of culture and language, but squeezed from both sides, so to speak, by the Real and the Imaginary. Of the Real, on one hand, and how it conditions its existence, "the subject" knows nothing; it is by definition the Unconscious. Of the Imaginary, on the other hand, the split and scrambling "subject" might be said to know too much; its fundamental and highly flawed notions of how to get along in life have been formed and still dwell, like its conception of its unified ego, among the illusions and delusions of this realm.[14]

Althusser thus represents ideology as a matter of psychological dynamics that are indirect, normally unconscious, affective, and universal. Ideology is indirect in the sense that it does not simply mirror the economic conditions of existence. Taking as the basis of cultural construction "mode of production," rather than the specifically *economic* mode, Althusser sees ideology as an independent mode with its own laws of production.[15] Perhaps the first of these is that, in accord with the Lacanian conception of encounter with the order of the Real, ideology is normally unconscious ("normally," because the individual can certainly *become* aware of it). It is also affective, a complete way of being in the world. "Ideology," Althusser says in "Marxism and Humanism," "is a matter of the *lived* relation between men and their world. . . . In ideology men do indeed express, not the relation between them and their conditions of existence, but *the way* they live the relation between them and their conditions of existence; this presupposes both a real relation and an *'imaginary'* 'lived' relation" (Althusser 1977, 233). Althusser offers an example that contrives to express at the same time his "antihumanism," his rejection of the bourgeois celebration of the individual as unified self. "The bourgeoisie *lives* in the ideology of *freedom* the relation between it and its conditions of existence: that is, *its* real relation (the law of liberal capitalist economy) but *invested in an imaginary relation* (all men are free, including the free labourers)" (234). Lastly, ideology is universal, "an organic part of every social totality. . . . Human societies secrete ideology as the very element and atmosphere indispensable to their historical respiration and life" (232). Althusser concurs with Mannheim: *"historical materialism cannot conceive that even a communist society could ever do without ideology"* (232).[16] His work is perhaps the supreme example of how twentieth-century structuralism colludes with affectivity, specifically in his case of the psychoanalytic variety, in the relativizing and universalizing of the concept.

But Althusser does not merely extend "ideology" to meet "myth"; he effects the encounter. He employs "myth" and its adjective "mythical" dozens of times in his essays, though never as a "marked" term. This means in practice that he never defines it. His contextual usages, however, can be grouped into three related clusters. He occasionally treats it as an apparent synonym for ideology ("the bourgeoisie has to believe in its own myth" [234]), but more often it appears related as species to genus ("the spontaneous myths of ideology" [148]), and this shades into a set of particulars for which "ideology" is only the group-noun or set-designation ("But what, concretely, is this uncriticized ideology if not simply the 'familiar,' 'well-known,' transparent myths?" [144]). In this third usage "ideology" is to "myth" as "army" is to its "soldiers." It is my impression that Althusser conceives of myth most consistently in the second sense, that is, as a species of narrative that embodies some part of the genus ideology. But the third sense, with its implication that a given ideological complex might consist entirely of its subordinate web of myths, can't be easily dismissed, even though it would entail that all ideology be comprised of myths, whereas all myths would not necessarily be ideological. This conception of the relation of ideology to myth comes closest to fitting the case of Lévi-Strauss. We must not lose sight, however, of the central point, that Althusser comes as near as perhaps makes no difference to conflating the two terms. Furthermore, his most frequent employment of "myth" is in none of the contexts above that might help define it in relation to ideology, but as a term of abuse in phrases like "the myth of the *homo oeconomicus*" (125). This usage is not, of course, inconsistent with any of the three senses in which "myth" is directly associated with ideology, but here we witness, for the first time in our sequence of thinkers, an intellectual wielding the term in the same attenuated sense of "widely propagated lie" that is current in everyday speech.

There is, however, one structuralist critique built frankly upon this popular sense of "myth"—Roland Barthes's *Mythologies*. What Barthes labels "mythologies" is a series of brief *exposés* of the ideology embedded in various aspects of French mass culture. He looks into television wrestling, a guidebook to Spain, soap-powder and detergent ads, the language of judge and prosecution in a sensational murder trial, movie travelogues, a ballyhooed exhibition of photographs, and so forth. Considering these contents, the title might be supposed at first to be merely an easy metaphor, a piece of mock-heroic sarcasm. But the last third of the text consists of a theoretical essay that propounds a double-pronged "semiological" and "ideological" method of analyzing what Barthes persists in calling "myth." In the end, he comes even closer than Althusser to contributing to the conflation of myth with ideology by talking as if "ideology" were something subsisting in practice entirely in its myriad networks of cultural "mythologies."

Barthes's choice of "mythologies" as a title rather than "myths" contributes to the "network" effect by suggesting that each disparate solar system reveals, when the telescope is focused on it, its own assemblage of conglobed myths. This sense of worlds within worlds is closely connected with Barthes's ambitions for the work: "I had just read Saussure and as a result acquired the conviction that by treating 'collective representations' as sign-systems, one might hope to go further than the pious show of unmasking them and account *in detail* for the mystification which transforms petit-bourgeois culture into a universal nature" (Barthes 1983a, 9).[17] His general ambition, then, lies very close to that of Horkheimer and Adorno in their attack on "the culture industry," but Saussure inspires the discovery of a method for getting past the Frankfurters' kind of generalities into the details of how the mechanics of mystification actually work at the linguistic level. Hence Barthes insists on the "necessary conjunction" (9) of the unmasking end with the semiological means: "no denunciation without an appropriate method of detailed analysis, no semiology which cannot, in the last analysis, be acknowledged as *semioclasm*" (9). As for Saussure, Barthes, like Lévi-Strauss and Lacan, extrapolates the linguistic model into shaky territory. Barthes even goes as far in the more systematic successor to *Mythologies, The Elements of Semiology,* as to reverse Saussure explicitly on the relation of linguistics to semiology. For Saussure, linguistics is only a species within the genus of the science of signs, whereas Barthes asserts that linguistics is the genus and semiology only a species, a relation that requires every semiological system to be based on linguistic principles (Barthes 1983b, 11).[18] The result, in *Mythologies,* as in the rest of Barthes's earlier work, is that what purports to be a model of scientific structural analysis produces only, as Jonathan Culler remarks of *Système de la mode* (1967), a "confused, incomplete and unverifiable" account of the code it studies (Culler 1975, 37). Anyone aware of the swift trajectory of Barthes's later career will recall that he soon recognized for himself the impossibility of establishing a scientific semiology. (He demonstrates this in his mockingly "exhaustive" analysis of the "codes" in Balzac's story "Sarrasine," in *S/Z* [1970]).[19] What must count for us in considering *Mythologies* in this context, though, is not the soundness of Barthes's "science" nor his later repudiation of it, but the very effective contribution he made at the time to the increasingly widespread association of myth with ideology.

The first half of the theoretical essay "Myth Today" presents myth as "a second-order semiological system" (114). It is "made of a material which has *already* been worked on so as to make it suitable for communication" (110). That is, it makes use of previously established signs; the combined signifier and signified of the first order of sign becoming the signifier of the second, "as if the myth shifted the formal system of the first signification sideways" (115). This new signifier, being a piece of *"metalanguage"* (115), a second language that comments on the first, is no longer primarily a linguistic phenomenon, but a "global sign," just as likely, for example, to be a picture as a set of words. This new signifier "can be looked at, in myth, from two points of view: as the final term of the linguistic system, or as the first term in the mythical system" (116–117), as either "meaning" in the former case or "form" in the latter. Barthes introduces an example, a *Paris-Match* cover photograph of a black African soldier in French uniform saluting the *tricolore*. Read as final term of the first order linguistic system the "meaning" of the picture is "full" and potentially "self-sufficient" (117): *"a black soldier is giving the French salute"* (116). Read, however, as the first term of the second order mythical system, the "form" of this new signifier is "empty," "drained," "made almost transparent" (118). "When it becomes form, the meaning leaves its contingency behind; it empties itself, it becomes impoverished, history evaporates, only the letter remains" (117). My own figure, not Barthes's, for this phenomenon is the type of optical illusion that appears now one thing, now another, Wittgenstein's "duck-rabbit," for example. Barthes says, "It is this constant game of hide-and-seek between the [full] meaning and the [empty] form which defines myth" (118). When we turn from the duplicitous function of the signifier in this metalinguistic order of myth to the signified, for which Barthes accepts the conventional designation, "concept," we find that the "history which drains out of the form will be wholly absorbed by the concept" (118). In the case of the *Paris-Match* cover, for example, this concept is "French imperiality" (119). This second-order "concept" is composed of vague and confused connotations; its "fundamental character . . . is to be *appropriated"* (119). Or, to view the same matter from the angle of its creators rather than of its consumer-victims, the "concept" is "historical and intentional . . . the motivation which causes the myth to be uttered" (118).

Barthes refers self-consciously in this context to his own invention of "conceptual neologisms" (like "imperiality") (121). The unidentified, dodgy presence of the mythical signified provokes its critic into innovating terms for what will otherwise go designedly unnamed, in order to bring it into focus, force it toward definition. The third term, the sign in which signifier and signified are united,

Barthes calls simply the "signification," and on this metalinguistic level it is, as he puts it, "the myth itself" (121). In the instance of the saluting soldier, this would be something like the "naturalness" of French colonialism for everyone concerned, including the Sudanese recruit himself. Myth does not hide one of its terms behind the other as happens in certain semiological systems; "its function is to distort, not to make disappear" (121). That is, the relation of the "'concept' of a myth to its 'meaning' is essentially a relation of *deformation*" (122). This relation is like a "moving turnstile," like an "alibi" (123). "It is enough that [myth's] signifier has two sides for it always to have an 'elsewhere' at its disposal. The meaning is always there to *present* the form; the form is always there to *outdistance* the meaning. . . . they are never at the same place" (123).

Once Barthes has established the principles of the formal, semiological analysis of myth, he moves gradually into his account of its ideological aspect. This distinction between the two components reflects Barthes's encounter with a familiar, two-fold problematic. The difficulty common to all Marxist theoreticians of ideology is how to demonstrate *their* objectivity in the face of *its* ubiquity, and the difficulty common to all structuralists is how to reconcile synchrony with diachrony, structure with historical situation. Barthes's distinction, relying as it does on the further highly dubious distinction between "form" and "meaning" in the second-order signifier, does not so much resolve these theoretical issues as blur them. Barthes slides from semiology to ideology by shifting aesthetic orientations, that is, dropping autotelic explanation of myth's signifying structure for expressive and pragmatic explanations of its makers' intentions and its audiences' responses. The *producer* of myth focuses on the empty signifier and lets "the concept fill the form . . . without ambiguity"; the "mythologist" (or *critic*) focuses "on a full signifier in which [he] can clearly distinguish the meaning and the form and consequently the distortion"; the *consumer* or "reader of myths" accepts unreflectively the ambiguous signification (128). The first two agents, the producer and the mythologist, are not innocent; the one intends manipulation and the other sees through the intention. But the third, the consumer, who is innocent, takes real harm because the myth "transforms history into nature" (129). "Everything happens as if the picture [of the soldier] naturally conjured up the concept [French imperiality]" (129–130). The consumer knows he is being appealed to, but swallows as merely factual a signification that actually conveys axiological propositions.

At this point Barthes confronts directly what motivates both his theoretical essay, *"Myth Today"* (my italics), and the specific unmaskings of mass culture that comprise the rest of the work. He concedes in passing that other cultures have had their myths, but he is interested only in the sort that pervades ours, for the rather appalling reason that ours is, by virtue of its bourgeois nature, "the privileged field of mythical significations" (137). The bourgeoisie is *the social class that does not want to be named* (138), and this is precisely what makes the task of the "mythologist" (that is, the demythologizer) so crucial. "This flight from the name . . . is not therefore an illusory, accidental, secondary, natural or insignificant phenomenon: it is the bourgeois ideology itself, the process through which the bourgeoisie transforms . . . History into Nature" (141). The "flight from the name" is particularly evident in the bourgeois determination to deny the politics implicit in cultural values.

"To complete the semiological definition of myth in a bourgeois society: *myth is depoliticized speech*" (143). This unprecedented disingenuousness is presumably what renders *bourgeois* myth peculiarly hideous and creates in Roland Barthes the loathing as of a Gnostic clinging to his secret illumination amid a world ruled by the Prince of Darkness. Barthes's sole acknowledgment of the problem of Marxist objectivity is to allow that there *can* be "myth on the Left," but only with two provisos. The first is that "the language of man as a producer" (146) and, therefore, the language of revolution, "cannot be mythical." "The bourgeoisie hides the fact that it is the bourgeoisie and thereby produces myth; revolution announces itself openly as revolution and thereby abolishes myth" (146). Since myth can only distort and deaden, myth on the left, the "myth of Stalin," for example, is un- or anti-revolutionary, a falling away from the visionary ideal. Barthes's conception of the relation of myth to revolution is thus the direct contrary of Sorel's. The second proviso for "myth on the Left" is that it is "inessential" (147); the Left has no ideology of everyday life of its own but can only borrow from its bourgeois antagonist; it has no "fabulizing" power to invent myth for itself because "the Left always defines itself in relation to the oppressed" (148). Whatever the truth-value of these propositions, they reveal Barthes's conception of his role as being like that of the Frankfurters; he is committed to the "permanent critique" of bourgeois society from within. His essays in mythology and his theory of myth are versions of Adorno's "negative dialectics." Barthes's employment of the term "myth" is specialized, as specialized as its polar opposite, Sorel's, but by limiting his range to the structure of the naturalizing obfuscations of bourgeois ideology, Barthes attaches to the demotic "That's just a myth!" a denotation more precise and perhaps more truly close to the bone than anyone else has managed.

THE DOMAIN OF NIETZSCHE: THE STRUGGLE OF MYTH AND ANTIMYTH

Unlike Marx and later Freud, the second of the masters of suspicion did not throw the weight of his authority behind a specific mode of reading comparable to psychoanalysis or to the semiotic outing of ideology. Instead, he develops in his mature philosophy the ultimate hermeneutical antinomy. On one hand, humankind *must* construct its life-enhancing untruths; on the other, untruths that harden into idols have to be assaulted with the hammer of iconoclasm. With some notable exceptions, full recognition of the implications of this antinomy built up only slowly. A cultural history of Nietzsche's reception before World War I would have to focus heavily upon eupeptic versions of his message consonant with *Lebensphilosophie*, with James and Bergson. It took the climate of post-war Europe in general and Heidegger's work in particular to bring out the darkness of Nietzsche's critique. *Being and Time* (1927) takes up where Nietzsche left off, "the destruction of the history of ontology" (Heidegger 1962, 44). "Dasein no longer understands the most elementary conditions which would enable it to go back to the past in a positive manner and make it productively its own" (43). It is too late to guess how recognition of the depth of Nietzsche's critique might have proceeded without *Being and Time*'s originality of style and thought, its fierce phenomenology of existence, its scorn for the extent to which humanity lives for and by the opinion of others, amid the chatter of quotidian distractions, in inauthentic avoidance of its being toward death. That Heidegger saw himself as starting where Nietzsche left off is not explicit in *Being and Time,* but apparent in his later lectures on his predecessor. These lectures, together with Heidegger's other comments on Nietzsche in his later writings construct, along with the powerful tribute of *Being and Time,* a kind of second, mediated Nietzsche, preeminently the master of suspicion.

The most important thinkers who respond to the post-Heideggerian Nietzsche develop certain of his themes into their own strong critiques of modernity. All such critiques, Michel Foucault's, for example, are probably at least indirectly relevant to "myth" as ideological narrative, even when this is not their explicit concern. This is certainly the case with Foucault's Nietzschean principle that "the development of humanity is a series of interpretations," seizures of hermeneutical power whose history it is "the role of genealogy . . . to record" (Foucault 1984, 86). The section that follows concentrates upon two important instances that do focus explicitly upon myth as ideological narrative: Horkheimer and Adorno's *Dialectic of Enlightenment,* which develops Nietzsche's conception of an all-embracing cultural struggle between myth and anti-myth, and Jacques Derrida's "White Mythology," which elaborates Nietzsche's critique of the language of philosophical generalization.

In *Dialectic of Enlightenment* (1944), the work of the Frankfurt School most immediately relevant to our topic, the authors see themselves as engaged in a critique of Enlightenment for which virtually their only predecessors are Hegel and Nietzsche. Hegel constructs the paradigm in *The Phenomenology of Spirit* with his dialectic of "The Struggle of Enlightenment with Belief." But Hegel, according to the Frankfurters, succumbs personally to Belief in the shape of the Absolute, whereas Nietzsche is not only "one of the few after Hegel who recognized the dialectic of enlightenment," but also one of the handful (along with the surprising bedfellows De Sade and Kant) "who mercilessly elicited [its] implications" (Horkheimer and Adorno 1972, 44 and xvi, respectively). Nietzsche exposes the irrational basis of Kant's and Hegel's "Enlightenment" by reconceiving the struggle in affective terms; it is a perpetual duel between the urge to construct life-enhancing lies and the urge to shatter them. When Horkheimer and Adorno choose their terms to characterize this "struggle" that for all four thinkers most broadly defines the history of modernity, they select a pair—"Enlightenment" and "myth"—that locates them in certain respects closer to Hegel and in other respects closer to Nietzsche. "Enlightenment" situates them closer to Kant and Hegel because it implies some ultimate faith, or at least hope, in rationality. "Myth," however, bears the weight of Horkheimer and Adorno's experience of both Nietzsche's nihilism and of the century that Nietzsche predicted but didn't live to see. To appreciate what this means requires a closer look at their "myth."

Although the authors nowhere define the term formally, its meaning gathers definition from its contexts. "Myth" signifies, approximately, any form of oppressive belief or cultural standard that creates a despairing sense of fatality. I have already mentioned, in connection with Malinowski's early interest in Nietzsche, the peculiar prevalence of this notion of myth as fate among German-speakers in the late nineteenth and early twentieth centuries. Adorno shares it with his friend Walter Benjamin, as their correspondence shows, and he certainly shares it with Horkheimer.[20] We encounter a well-known expression of it in Benjamin's "Storyteller," when he contrasts myth with the liberating potential of the fairytale, a genre that "tells us of the earliest arrangements that mankind made to shake off the nightmare which myth had placed upon its chest" (Benjamin 1969, 102). In *Dialectic of Enlightenment* we are told that "myths signify self-repetitive nature, which is the core of the symbolic: a state of being or a process that is presented as eternal. . . . Inexhaustibility, unending renewal and the permanence of the signified are not mere attributes of all symbols, but their essential content" (17). The medium is the message. This pejorative identification of myth with the romantic symbol is a calculated offense; the authors know full well that this identification, made positively and always taken for granted, is standard in the History of Religions tradition, as represented, say, by Eliade, and a commonplace in theological circles since the latter part of the previous century. Their political associations are more clearly on show when they remark a few pages later that "in its figures mythology [expresses] the essence of the *status quo:* cycle, fate and domination of the world reflected as the truth and deprived of hope" (27). Adorno is still more blunt in *Negative Dialectics* in his extended excoriation of Heidegger's effort after his "turn" to celebrate Being and to surprise it through poetry. Adorno accuses him not only of the "mythologization of Being" but of a consequential "attempt to justify the very order that drives men to despair and threatens them with physical extinction" (Adorno 1966, 88–89). Adorno undoubtedly intends his readers to apply this denunciation to Heidegger's quondam embrace of Nazism. But "myth," extended thus, can refer to any cultural institution or hegemonic concept exempted from historical contingency because it is held to be part of an unchanging order of things.

This is the conception Horkheimer and Adorno have in mind when they compress the kernel of their "dialectic of Enlightenment" into two brief theses: "Myth is already enlightenment; and enlightenment reverts to mythology" (xvi). "Myth is already enlightenment" in being a formulation of experience that to some degree distances humanity, for better and for worse, from a state of nature. To illustrate how early and with what complexity this "enlightenment" is embedded in the layers of our cultural constructions, the authors undertake a chapter-length "Excursus" in which they read Odysseus's account of his adventures as an allegory of "the opposition of the surviving individual ego to multifarious fate" (46). While each of the "mythic figures" Odysseus encounters is "a figure of repetition. . . . of compulsion. . . . the self represents rational universality" (58). Thus far Horkheimer and Adorno agree with conventional academic commentators of the generation after Nietzsche, but, since the Frankfurters are reading dialectically, they also discriminate the sinister side of this early celebration of the bourgeois hero. "The wily solitary is already *homo oeconomicus,* for whom all reasonable things are alike: hence *The Odyssey* is already a *Robinsonade.* Both Odysseus and Crusoe make their weakness . . . their social strength. . . . Their impotence in regard to nature already acts as an ideology to advance their social hegemony" (61). Regarded in this light,

Odysseus's triumph over the Cyclops, Polyphemus, for example, manifests a sinister side; it is a victory of bourgeois cunning over an older, "uncivilized" mode of existence. In the episode of the Sirens we see this cunning exercised not only against the exotic singers but also in a casual act of social domination. The adventure in fact affords "a presentient allegory of the dialectic of enlightenment" itself—the aristocratic hero can enjoy the music of the Sirens only because his crews labor at the oars with their ears plugged (34). As these two instances suggest, Homer formalizes in his narrative, by means of his "once upon a time device," what is already a very active "entanglement of prehistory, savagery and culture" (80). And this entanglement reveals even in so early a document of Western history, both parts of the dialectic already at work; myth is enlightenment, but enlightenment, expressed as domination, reverts to myth.

For Horkheimer and Adorno "Enlightenment" generates "myth" from within. This view is implicit in their title. Whereas Hegel's title names his contraries—Enlightenment and Belief, theirs speaks only of a dialectic of Enlightenment, as if to emphasize that the contrary is spun inexorably out of the bowels of the thesis itself. Nor do Horkheimer and Adorno hesitate for a moment to identify the psychology that motivates this fatal reversion. "What men want to learn from nature is how to use it to dominate it and other men" (4). To those two ambitions we should add a third that the Frankfurters early learned from Freud: men also want to learn how to dominate themselves, by repression and sublimation. This triple-headed monster is the same enemy identified by Marcuse in *Eros and Civilization* (1955), the same acknowledged under another name in the title of Horkheimer's *Critique of Instrumental Reason* (1967). It is this perverted use of rationality that has thus far turned each moment of enlightenment into a tyranny of reason, a demonic parody of itself. "The principle of immanence, the explanation of every event as repetition, that the Enlightenment upholds against the mythic imagination, is the principle of myth itself" (12). This principle denies our freedom to think or act otherwise.

Horkheimer and Adorno are pessimistic; the human record is not promising. But they are not determinists; they indict the historical Enlightenment, not the utopian possibility of enlightenment. Their stance is perhaps best captured in their fellow traveler Walter Benjamin's parable of "the angel of history," whose "face is turned toward the past," which the angel perceives as "one single catastrophe" piling up wreckage at his feet. The angel wants "to stay" and repair the damage. "But a storm is blowing from Paradise; it has got caught in his wings with such violence that the angel can no longer close them. This storm irresistibly propels him into the future to which his back is turned. . . . This storm is what we call progress" (Benjamin 1969, 257–258). The angel is of course corporate humanity witnessing history, in Hegel's phrase, as the Last Judgment. Benjamin sets up the reader so that the identification of the storm as "progress" in the final word of the parable comes as a surprise, perhaps a shock. Only then do we realize why the angel opened his wings to the wind in the first place; he did not initially understand that the wind was unmasterable, that it would become so violent it would pervert his wings of desire into demonic sails plunging him backward into a blind future.

It appears that he's being propelled "irresistibly," but he hasn't lost either his knowledge of his utopian goal or his will to struggle. If he could outwrestle the storm wind he would make that "stay" that would become the apocalyptic moment of revolution.

Horkheimer and Adorno don't palliate the Benjaminian possibility that the dialectic of Enlightenment could conclude in the violence of a final myth, the worldwide domination of a wholly instrumental consumer culture, destructive alike of individual subjectivity, social bonds, and the natural environment. But they also express what Ernst Bloch called "hope the principle" when they assert the value of the very kind of "negative dialectics" in which they are engaged. "True revolutionary practice depends on the intransigence of theory in the face of the insensibility with which society allows thought to ossify" (41). It is not inevitable that enlightenment harden into myth so long as it is opposed by critical thinking that keeps it minimally flexible and humane. Myth, as Horkheimer and Adorno conceive it, is procrustean, totalitarian; it is hegemonic identity-thinking that will tolerate no thinking-otherwise. Horkheimer and Adorno seldom employ the term "ideology" in *Dialectic of Enlightenment,* but when they do they seem to have in mind a specifically political application of this broader "myth." Myth, for them, is the genus and ideology the species.

Some twenty years later, Adorno prefers in *Negative Dialectics* to juggle the two terms as if they are virtually interchangeable. "Identity," for example, is said to be "the primal form of ideology," but on the same page failure to admit the non-coincidence of thought with its object, "the thing in itself to its concept," is called "true mythology" (Adorno 1966, 148–149).[21] The proposition that "the myth of total identity is ideological" appears convertible with the proposition "the ideology of total identity is mythical." As the two concepts approach in Adorno's work the point of complete conflation, they also take on their widest signification. The next chapter will consider recent positive theories that hold "myth" to be the proper term to designate all of our cultural constructions. That is the appropriate scale against which to juxtapose the Frankfurters' negative definition.

Given their intellectual descent, it isn't surprising to find that the Frankfurt School shares with the doyens of French structuralism and poststructuralism such broad "family resemblances" as a preference for antithetical critique, and the "anti-humanism" that rejects bourgeois aggrandizement of autonomous subjectivity. More unexpected, however, are specifically shared features like the Frankfurters' closeness to Lacan in undermining the unity of the subject by restoring "tragic" Freud, and to Barthes in developing holistic critical studies of bourgeois culture. Horkheimer and Adorno, particularly the latter, are similarly close to Jacques Derrida in practicing a method of "reading otherwise" that subverts the positive presence of the signified in traditional Western philosophy. Even in *Dialectic of Enlightenment* the authors affirm of their "dialectic" that it "interprets every image as writing. It shows how the admission of its falsity is to be read in the lines of its features" (24). And Adorno in his later text seems to define the very principle of "negative dialectics" when he declares that "totality is to be opposed by convicting it of nonidentity with itself" (147). Derrida's method of "deconstruction" is an extension of this principle (licensed by the Saussurean analogy that inspires his conception of *différance*) into the micro-realm of textuality. While most of Derrida's work pays no more explicit attention to myth than Foucault's, it is, like his, of considerable indirect relevance because of the effect of its critical method upon contemporary attitudes toward claims of transcendence. We can clarify our sense of what this larger, indirect impact may be like by examining the one case in which Derrida does make the connection explicit, his essay "White Mythology: Metaphor in the Text of Philosophy."

Metaphor appears "in the text of philosophy" in two senses, both considered in the essay. In the more restrictive sense, some thinkers, recognizing the imbrication of figurative language even in the most systematic thought, have speculated overtly about the nature of metaphor. Derrida sketches the complicity of such traditional theories of metaphor with the metaphysics they underwrite and are in turn underwritten by. In the less restrictive sense, though, metaphor appears "in the text of philosophy" covertly, unexamined, at the foundation of the most venerable of metaphysical conceptions, and the bulk of "White Mythology" is devoted to demonstrating how ineluctably this co-dependence obtains. In his second section, *"Plus de métaphore,"* which might be rendered contradictorily as "(No) More Metaphor," Derrida plays on the title of Kant's famous essay to propose tartly, "Instead of venturing into the prolegomena to some future metaphorics, let us rather attempt to recognize in principle the condition for the impossibility of such a project" (Derrida 1982, 219).[22] The condition is that "metaphor has been issued from a network of philosophemes which themselves correspond to tropes or to figures. This stratum of 'tutelary' tropes, the layer of 'primary' philosophemes . . . cannot be dominated" (219). At least one metaphor will remain outside the circumscribed field and so "by virtue of what we might entitle . . . tropic supplementarity . . . the taxonomy or history of philosophical metaphors will never make a profit" (219–220). In spite of its anti-dogmatic stance, this essay does in fact set itself up as a "prolegomena to any future metaphorics," just as surely and in the same sense as Kant's does to "any future metaphysics," by adducing the principle that should halt "any future metaphorics" in its tracks. In the central section of the essay "The Ellipsis of the Sun," Derrida supports his case by attending closely to the most foundational of Western theories of metaphor, Aristotle's in the *Rhetoric* and the *Poetics*. By careful textual exegesis of the figurative basis of the relevant concepts, *"metaphora, mimēsis, logos, physis, phōnē, sēmainein, onoma"* (232), he shows that the relation is circular; only resorting to metaphor enables construction of an apparently coherent ontology, while the ontology is necesssary to underwrite the truth-value of metaphor.

This set of reciprocal contingencies, like Escher's two hands drawing each other, awaits the moment of deconstruction, and Derrida tugs on the loose thread that will unravel the web. "Resemblance," he proclaims, in a move that Adorno would approve, "is not an identity" (239). "Identity" would require a fullness or plenitude of "presence" that can be sustained only by an unavailable theological sanction. Aristotle's admission that some analogies have no literal term (the metaphor in the *Poetics,* for example, of the sun "'sowing around a god-created flame'"), stands in aporetic relation to his assumption that "in the truth, language is to be filled, achieved, actualized, to the point of erasing itself, without any possible play" (241). Aristotle's own evidence points instead toward endless room for play, "metaphorization of metaphor, its bottomless overdeterminability" (243). To exemplify how an aporia of this sort becomes embedded in subsequent Western thinking, Derrida pursues it in his last two sections through Aristotle's *Rhetoric* into its avatars in Descartes and in French rhetoricians of the seventeenth and eighteenth centuries. He also focuses his broad topic in these sections by continuing to recur concretely to figures of the sun and its light as metaphors for reason itself. In the title of his fourth section, "The Flowers of Rhetoric: The Heliotrope," the heliotrope is not only the literal sunflower that turns with the sun, but also those figurative "flowers of rhetoric" that do the same, following, after Aristotle, a tropism of tropes in which "the sun represents what is natural in philosophical language" (251). In order to accept this claim literally, Aristotle's successors continue to suppress, as he did, their awareness that the sun is "metaphorical always already" (251). In the end "this metaphor is indispensable to the general system in which the concept of metaphor is inscribed; it is there in order to signify metaphor itself; it is a metaphor of metaphor . . . the self-presence of the idea in its own light" (253).

But this account of "Metaphor in the Text of Philosophy" has thus far ignored the essay's first section, "Exergue," in which Derrida characterizes the concepts of Western metaphysics as "White Mythology." Since an "exergue" is literally the space on a coin reserved for inscription, the word stands figuratively here for an epigraphical preface. Disseminated figures of coinage and economy dominate this section of a richly metaphorical essay on the ineluctability of metaphor in the text of theory. The inspirational presence behind these figures is Nietzsche's aphorism (examined in chapter 3): "truths are illusions of which one has forgotten that they *are* illusions; worn out metaphors which have become powerless to affect the senses . . . coins which have their obverse . . . *effaced* and now are no longer of account as coins but merely as metal." But to help inscribe his exergue Derrida retrieves a more pointed version of Nietzsche's metaphor from a dialogue in Anatole France's *Garden of Epicurus*. One of the speakers, Polyphilos, compares metaphysicians "when they make a language for themselves" (210) to knife-grinders who would "put coins to the grindstone to efface the exergue" and then proclaim that they have freed the coins from all limitations: "they are not worth five shillings any more; they are of inestimable value, and their exchange value is extended indefinitely." Polyphilos concludes his attack with a different metaphor: "The very metaphysicians who think to escape the world of appearances are constrained to live perpetually in allegory. A sorry lot of poets, they dim the colours of the ancient fables, and are themselves but gatherers of fables. They produce white mythology" (213). Derrida confesses that in this last sentence he has altered France's text. The original reads: "Their output is mythology, an anemic mythology." Derrida's stronger version creates a phrase with broader social and political applications. Metaphysics is not only "anemic" or pale mythology; it is also the mythology of the white Eurocentric male: "the white man takes his own mythology . . . for the universal form of that he must still wish to call Reason" (213). And metaphysics is a "white" mythology in yet a third, deprivative sense; its basis in myth, no longer recognized, works covertly.

It is written in invisible ink. "White mythology—metaphysics—has erased within itself the fabulous scene that has produced it, the scene that nevertheless remains active and stirring, inscribed in white ink, an invisible design covered over in the palimpsest" (213). This sequence itself manifests the faded trace of a history; first the mythology of metaphysics is bleached out, then naturalized, then rendered invisible, the more effectively to carry out its "active and stirring" role in the grounding of Western "rationality."

As cryptologist, Derrida works in reverse, treating the invisible writing with just the combination of heat and astringent juice that will make it stand out plainly through the layered commentaries of two millennia. His insistence that the writing thus exposed is "mythology" identifies him as heir to the Nietzsche who asserts that when we create metaphysical abstractions from "a mobile army of metaphors" we "act mythologically." Derrida declares that "metaphor has always been defined as the trope of resemblance," and that this resembling function, in which one sign designates another, authorizes us "to group under this heading [of metaphor] all the so-called *symbolical* or *analogical* figures mentioned by Polyphilos (figure [*sic*], *myth* [my italics], fable, allegory)" (215). If it seems odd to think of "myth" as a subset of the "trope of resemblance," we need to recall that although "resemblance is not an identity," the tropological tradition in Western metaphysics, according to Derrida, pretends that it is. The result of this massive abuse of metaphor is that persons born into our culture inherit a network of assumed "truths" whose origins in and dependence upon figure have been suppressed. It is this *network* that Derrida designates as "mythology." He can be said to understand by "myth," then, that species of the trope of resemblance that has been distorted into predications of identity and elaborated into a system of "invisible" beliefs. This conception of myth as a tropological catachresis resonates interestingly with other linguistic theories, with Max Müller's "disease of language," with Barthes's second-order shift of signifier, and even with Lévi-Strauss's conception of *la pensée sauvage*.

Derrida's confinement of his actual analysis to "white mythology" is an indication of how deeply he is ensconced within the tradition of critique whose practitioners dominate this chapter. Like the comparable work of Nietzsche, Heidegger, Horkheimer, and Adorno, his ranging over the history of Western metaphysics is actually a Foucauldian "genealogy," an investigation molded by a passion to expose the structure of how we think now. Derrida does not mention the word "ideology," yet, if he had substituted in his title "ideology" for "mythology," it is hard to see how his argument would be altered except that the change would probably afford fewer opportunities for wit. His conception of myth as metaphor abused by metaphysics is especially close to Adorno's notion of it as rigidified identity-thinking. So, too, is the *pharmakon* he prescribes for it—a kind of "negative dialectics" dedicated to preventing thought from ossifying. Derrida and the Frankfurters are at one in recognizing that this systematic critique must extend to their own thinking, which is why they strive programmatically to confine themselves to non-dogmatic counter-punching. To clear away transcendental pretensions only in order to make room for their own would be to replace one set of idols with another. Derrida is willing, in "White Mythology," to go so far as to demonstrate by the concreteness and tenacity of his readings the limits of "any future metaphorics," but to go further would be to contribute to the construction of a new mythology, if not to the reinforcement of the old. As it stands, however, Derrida's restriction of his explicit critique of "myth" to the "white mythology," which at first appears rather specialized, carries implications as bold and broad as Nietzsche's own.

THE PROBLEMATIC OF MYTH AS IDEOLOGY

The body of theory we have been examining does not, of course, constitute an adequate *causal* explanation of the currency of "myth" as synonym for "widely repeated lie" or "false belief." To suppose it did would be to privilege intellectual history in the idealist manner. If the OED is to be trusted here, the employment of "myth" in the sense of "false belief" appears only in the mid-1890s, at just about the same time as the Marxian concept of "ideology" comes in for general recognition. My guess is that the joint "arrival" of these related concepts, two generations after Marx and Engels linked them, indicates the rise of widespread suspicion of officially sanctioned social and cultural norms, and the consequent need for terms to articulate the new skepticism. While tracking the permutations of "myth" with "ideology" through the domains of the "masters of suspicion" cannot explain adequately the full social phenomenon, it can serve as an index to the theoretical problems involved. As a means of focusing some concluding generalizations about these problems, it might be useful to consider the findings of a fairly recent theorist of ideology, Terry Eagleton, who undertakes a pithy but direct comparison of ideology with myth. In fact, it is possible to organize the discussion as a series of responses to one revealing and stimulating question with which he leads off.

"Are myths," he asks, "the ideologies of preindustrial societies, or ideologies the myths of industrial ones?" (Eagleton 1991, 188).[23] The query itself indicates that Eagleton agrees with all the theorists examined in the chapter, except Derrida and the later Adorno, that myth and ideology are distinguishable. Derrida never mentions ideology, but it is fair to say, based on his account of "white mythology," that by the standards of the other theorists he identifies the two concepts, as Adorno specifically does in *Negative Dialectics*. Among the others, disagreements arise about the nature of the difference. Mannheim and Sorel agree that ideology signifies a settled body of propositions, but they disagree wildly about the nature of myth, which Sorel regards as kinetic, revolutionary image and Mannheim as the dead hand of custom and oppression. In *Dialectic of Enlightenment* Horkheimer and Adorno agree with Mannheim about myth, and uniquely treat ideology as merely a species of the genus, that is, specifically political myth.

Unsurprisingly, the major difference for some is generic; myth is by definition narrative, while ideology either is not (as with Sorel and Mannheim) or need not be (as with Althusser and Barthes). The latter duo present extremes of latitude, however. For Althusser ideology is the imaginary representation of the subject's relation to the real conditions of his or her existence, which need not involve narrative, but when it does, that narrative is myth, a view that counters the Frankfurters' by making myth the species and ideology the genus. In contrast, Barthes allows no official place for narrative; myths are distorted collective representations and ideology is a network of such representations. Nevertheless, any reader of Barthes can see that elements of narrative slip into many of his "mythologies" in spite of being officially ignored. Eagleton himself is perhaps closest to Althusser in insisting that myths are "typically" narrative whereas ideology is "not invariably" so. We can see a symptomatic difference shaping up here between the theorists of folkloristic myth, who insist that myth is narrative, and the theorists of ideological myth, who are on the whole much more uncertain or even indifferent about the issue of genre. Only Christopher Flood, in *Political Myth: A Theoretical Introduction,* would satisfy the former group by his uncompromising definition of political myth as necessarily narrative, "an ideologically marked account . . . of political events" (42). (Althusser's usage entails this position also, but because he doesn't focus on myth, he fails to make this clear.)

A second look at Eagleton's initial double question will stir to life yet another part of the general problematic. The question seems to imply that we might opt for either concept across the board, decide that ideology prevailed under the guise of myth in preindustrial societies just as in industrial ones, or else the contrary—that myth still prevails in industrial societies under the guise of ideology. What seems immediately obvious is that our theorists would answer in accord with their notions of the two concepts and the relation between them. At the extremes, for example, Horkheimer and Adorno would declare that myth still prevails, while Althusser would reply that ideology always has. Derrida and the later Adorno might reject the choice as a distinction without a difference, while Lévi-Strauss and Barthes might each recuse himself from considering the former the industrial world, the latter the preindustrial. Eagleton himself does not answer the question explicitly, though he may do so implicitly by the very balance of his formulation of it, as if he genuinely thought it might plausibly be argued either way.

But Eagleton's double question harbors yet another important feature of the problematic, which can be raised to visibility by answering with a question of our own. Why does he consider it relevant to distinguish at all between the socially dominant fictions of "preindustrial" and modern societies? One answer is that he seems caught in certain respects between a folkloristic conception of myth and an ideological one. This plight appears in some of the terms (as yet unexamined) of his comparison between myth and ideology. He agrees with the preponderance of the other theorists examined that myths can function ideologically "by naturalizing and universalizing a particular social structure" or supplying "imaginary resolutions to real contradictions," and that "ideological discourses may harness bodies of myth to their purposes." Myth, however, he finds more generally open-ended in its significations, whereas ideology is more pragmatically oriented toward issues of power. Myths "typically" dehistoricize their contents, whereas ideologies "often do" but sometimes don't, and in elevating certain stories to collective "numinous status" myth is "a particular *register* of ideology," since not all "ideological language involves this sort of allure." These distinctions, particularly the last, suggest that while Eagleton sees myth and ideology as playing into each other in all cultures, he has been strongly affected by the assumptions and results of ethnological fieldwork in what he calls "preindustrial" societies. As a consequence, he tends to think of myth folkloristically, as a genre of narrative flourishing in such societies but long extinct, or at least very rare, in modernity. When one thinks of it, the pervasiveness of this opinion sets the folkloristic conception of myth apart from the other three major modes. The romantic mode assumes the capacity for transcendental mythopoeia to be a permanent possession of humanity. The ideological agrees about the permanent possession but adopts a negative stance of suspicion toward its products. The constitutive, whose twentieth-century manifestations are the business of the next chapter, accepts this mythopoeia, true or false, as a constant of consciousness. Only the folkloristic mode can be understood to imply that myth is solely or nearly always a thing of remote times or exotic cultures. Hence the surprise the reader may have felt in turning from the previous three chapters to the first page of present one, where mention of the currency of myth as "widely disseminated lie" suddenly restores the sense of its viability in the modern world.

As a set of final reflections on Eagleton's model effort to discriminate between myth and ideology, it is worth pondering, first, the linking of the terms as a diacritical inevitability. If they signify contraries in Hegel's "struggle between belief and unbelief" or Horkheimer and Adorno's "dialectic of enlightenment," then "myth," the first term in place, required its antagonist, albeit the specific choice of "ideology" is the historical accident of one man's inspiration. Second, the subsequent career of ideology—its relativizing and universalizing, its comparatively neutral elaboration to signify something like what Bourdieu calls the *doxa* of social groups—suggests the likelihood of an analogous fate for its diacritical partner, myth. Just such a development is the subject of the next chapter.

[13]

Myth as Necessary Fiction

Myth has indeed been subject to a process analogous to that undergone by its diacritical partner, ideology. When the romantic inventors of the concept desiderate a new *mythus,* they have in mind a story capable of transforming the social and intellectual disarray of the modern West into a coherent whole. These pioneers spend little time worrying the issue of authenticity, largely because they assume (as Carlyle does, for example, in *Sartor Resartus*) that as long as such shaping myths succeed in sustaining their historical communities, they possess, by definition, "the mandate of Heaven." They are local, temporarily realized manifestations of eternal truths. When the cosmos comes to be perceived as less than benign, however, and our unbefriended species begins to understand itself as the value-creating animal, the significance of "myth" is radicalized; its fictive nature presses into the foreground, and the basis of its perennial authenticity recedes to the vanishing point. "Value-creating animal" is Nietzschean diction. His representations of truth as necessary error and humankind as inveterate makers and breakers of idols are the classic statements of this perceived situation. They mark the bold beginning of a twentieth-century trend toward regarding the foundational assumptions of all cultures as the kind of fictions properly signified as "myth."

    This conception of myth differs from its romantic parent and agrees with its ideological sibling in assuming that such fictions are without transcendental sanction. But it differs from its sibling in viewing neutrally, or even positively, their necessary fictivity. Like the ideological, this conception, which I call the constitutive, gathers force in the turn-of-the-century shift toward affective and structural explanation. Whereas the ideological conception of myth is developed largely by social thinkers, the constitutive is taken up most strikingly by philosophers and poets. The most obvious philosophical strain descends from Nietzsche, through William James's pragmatic "will to believe" to relatively recent social constructivism. Another strain, more aesthetic in cast, descends from Kant, especially from the third *Critique,* through the turn-of-the-century neo-Kantian movement and Croce's aesthetics. We've met a version of it in Frye's *Anatomy,* not merely in his notion that literary expression is "hypothetical," but, more radically, in his suave but startling implication that most of our cultural monuments in history, philosophy, and the human sciences are also instances of the type of prose fiction he calls "anatomy." We might trace a third strain (if it isn't too close to the neo-Kantian) working through Cassirer's idea of myth as one of humanity's fundamental modes of symbolic form. According to Cassirer's admirer, Wilbur Urban, for example, "myth" signifies, in its broad sense, all knowledge that retains its valuing function. Yet a fourth strain, particularly important to the theorists considered in this chapter, derives from existentialist phenomenology, especially in the key established by Heidegger's work after his "turn."

Perhaps the most striking formulations of the constitutive view of myth have been the work of poets. W. B. Yeats is a prime exhibit. As discussed in chapter 6, Yeats's career-long search for a viable mythology culminates in the metahistorical system laid out in *A Vision.* He derives this matter from automatic writings that certain "communicators" "dictated" to his wife, and the many strong poems rooted in them make *A Vision* important reading for students of his later work. But Yeats is elusive about the nature of his belief in these messages. He tells us in his introduction to the revised edition of *A Vision* that the communicators, when asked, said they did not want him to proselytize for their revelations, that they came to bring him "metaphors for poetry," and, later, that he regards the system as "stylistic arrangements of experience" that have helped him "to hold in a single thought reality and justice" (Yeats 1966, 8, 25). The crucial point here isn't the precise degree of Yeats's belief, but his pragmatic commitment to a construction he knows to be objectively dubious. His example was influential during the forties and fifties in establishing in literary circles the notion that possession of some comparable "myth" was the life-blood of great creative work. This assumption, disseminated through American New Criticism especially by Cleanth Brooks specifically in reference to Yeats, represents a modulation toward the subjective of T. S. Eliot's earlier dictum that any sustained production of great poetry is the work of an artist (like Dante) whose society provides him with a coherent conception of the world. Brooks's version implies that for the artist even a homemade myth is far more advantageous than none.

The object of Yeats's search is thematized more starkly in the late poetry of Wallace Stevens as "the supreme fiction." Stevens's concept, as widely influential in literary circles in the fifties through the seventies as Yeats's had been earlier, is, like Yeats's, formulated most pointedly in his prose. "The final belief is to believe in a fiction, which you know to be a fiction, there being nothing else. The exquisite truth is to know that it is a fiction and that you believe it willingly" (Stevens 1957, 163). This is the paradoxical quintessence of the constitutive conception of myth.

In spite of its nineteenth-century origins, this (putative) fourth major conception of "myth" is the last to come into its own. Full-scale theories of myth as foundational fiction begin to appear in the sixties. Of the five investigated in this chapter, the development of the oldest, Paul Ricoeur's, begins with *The Symbolism of Evil* in 1961; Leszek Kolakowski's dates from 1966, though it not published until 1972; Hans Blumenberg's was published in 1979; Eric Gould's in 1981; and Hazard Adams's in 1983. The relative recentness of these theories enables their proposers to confront, absorb, and respond profoundly to the contemporary critique of transcendentalist myth. Many idealist, even outright romantic, treatments of myth continue to appear in print. While some of these acknowledge the existence of the contemporary critique and a few even recognize its seriousness, most are either unwilling or unable to take it to heart. Ability to do just that has been the shibboleth for inclusion here.

It is questionable, however, whether any of the five theorists whose work is scrutinized in this chapter actually attains the ideal proclaimed in Stevens's definition of "the supreme fiction." Each does affirm a version, however tenuous, of what Derrida calls "presence" and may arguably be said, therefore, to fail to break entirely with the transcendentalist tradition. This ambiguity raises the question of whether we really have to do here with a genuine fourth category of "myth," the constitutive, or only with some particularly concessive and attenuated instances of transcendentalism. The answer would seem to depend upon whether or not one thinks these theorists distance themselves adequately from a claim to be underwritten by transcendental authority. My judgment that they do comprise a fourth type (even if they only approach the poets' ideal as a limit) can best be tested by plunging into the theories. These are presented in a sequence both approximately chronological and shaped by a steady movement away from transcendence toward the secularly "constructive."

PAUL RICOEUR'S DEFERRAL OF THE SACRED

Ricoeur is the oldest of the theorists considered here. If his career had for some reason ended with the publication of the work with which he entered the discourse on our topic, *The Symbolism of Evil* (1961), he would have been most appropriately considered among the midcentury neo-romantic theorists. For the concepts of "symbol" and "myth" presented in that work are unmistakably transcendentalist. He himself has several times compared his "Kantian schematism" of the "productive imagination" to the projects of Freud, Bachelard, Frye (whose work he didn't know in 1961), and, especially, Eliade and the other phenomenologists of religion.[1] But Ricoeur had come to *The Symbolism of Evil* by way of the Christian existential phenomenology of Jaspers and Marcel. This orientation, in combination with the altered intellectual climate of France in the 1960s, and his own immense intellectual curiosity and respect for the discourse of his contemporaries, has carried him in a splendidly honest and stubborn course wider and wider of that adequate "schematism" of symbol and myth that seemed so attainable forty years ago.

In a brief sketch of his intellectual history, "From Existentialism to the Philosophy of Language," he himself traces the early stages of his asymptotic quest (Ricoeur 1978, 86–93). He tells us that his previous work on an existential philosophy of the will propelled him into examining the stubbornly *involuntary* nature of the experience of evil and "sin." His discovery that these concepts are always dealt with in "symbolic language" drove him into a hermeneutics of symbol and myth, and both the involuntary and symbolic aspects of the topic led him to Freud. There he found not only Freud's positive contribution to "oneric" symbolism, but also his negative critique of religion, which led him to the discoveries, first, that "there was not only one hermeneutics, but two" and eventually that "Marx and Nietzsche and before them Feuerbach, had to be understood as the fathers of this reductive method" (89). At this point he perceived the hermeneutical analysis of symbolic language "as a battle field traversed by two opposing trends" (89). In his crucial *Freud and Philosophy,* Ricoeur invents for this battle the term he commonly employs thereafter, "the conflict of interpretations," and coins for "reductive" hermeneutics the term that has since come into wide circulation, "the hermeneutics of suspicion."

The subtitle of *Freud* is "An Essay on Interpretation," and Ricoeur develops in it his method of dealing dialectically with this hermeneutics of suspicion. While Marx conceives what is wrong in terms of class struggle, Nietzsche as *ressentiment* and Freud as the semantics of desire, all three have in common the conviction that "illusion is a cultural structure, a dimension of our social intercourse," and they complement one another as unmaskers of the idols of current Western culture (Ricoeur 1978, 214). They expose religion, for example, insofar as it is "a mask of fear [Freud], a mask of domination [Marx], a mask of hate [Nietzsche]" (219). Ricoeur finds these forms of iconoclasm actually liberating because they constitute the antithetic stage in a dialectic set in motion by faith. Since consciousness reveals as well as conceals, "to smash the idols is also to let symbols speak" (219).

We must look somewhat more closely at the religious and philosophical assumptions that underlie this cheerful co-opting of the hermeneutics of suspicion. Upon what grounds does Ricoeur reject so optimistically Heidegger's version of *aletheia* as simultaneous revelation and concealmeant by asserting that when the shells of cultural idolatry are broken through, "symbols" are capable of speaking directly for themselves? First, in semiotic terms, Ricoeur insists even in *The Symbolism of Evil* that Husserlian method entails "a structure of signification which is at once a function of absence and a function of presence," and he makes this position a cornerstone of his subsequent encounters with forms of post-Saussurean structuralism and deconstruction that see signification solely as a function of absence (Ricoeur 1969, 17). The Ricoeurian "symbol" is capable of attaining presence. Second, in terms of philosophical anthropology, Ricoeur sees man as a being alienated from himself ("I do not at first possess what I am") but defined by effort and desire (Ricoeur 1970, 46). We are drawn by a Spinozan *conatus* or effort of will toward the source of knowledge, which we know as the Platonic Eros. "Such effort is a desire since it is never satisfied, but the desire is an effort, since it is an alternative positing of a singular being, and not simply a lack of being" (46). On one hand, Ricoeur shares the existentialist sense that the satisfaction of desire is always deferred; on the other hand, however, he holds that humankind is not barred from legitimate hope; the dynamism of the *conatus* entails a teleology that counterbalances the Freudian and Lacanian archaeology of the desire that is only lack.

What guarantees that signification attains presence, that desire is not debarred as well as deferred, that the teleological dimension of our experience is not simply illusion? These obvious questions carry us into the third and ultimate ground of Ricoeur's confidence in "symbol." In theological terms, Ricoeur's answer is, the existence of the Wholly Other. "I am in accord," he says in *Freud and Philosophy*, "with the way in which Karl Barth poses the theological problem. The origin of faith lies in the solicitation of man by the object of faith" (525). The concept of the Wholly Other suggests a remoteness consonant with infinite deferral. However, in a rather astonishing literalizing of the famous Johannine formula, "and the Word was made flesh" (a kind of resacralizing of its secularization by Joyce in *Portrait* and *Ulysses*), Ricoeur asserts that this Wholly Other incarnates its solicitation of man in language: "As I understand it, man is always sustained by his mythico-poetic core. . . . Is not the Good News the instigation of the *possibility* of man by a creative word" (Ricoeur 1978, 237–238). Insofar as this word addresses humankind, it isn't absolutely Wholly Other; "the kerygma, the glad tidings, is precisely that it addresses itself to me and ceases to be the Wholly Other" (Ricoeur 1970, 525). But the way this word manifests itself does show it to be "Wholly Other than the archê and the telos which I can conceptualize in reflective thought" (525). We know it, that is, as affective formulation. It "annihilates itself in our flesh . . . as logos . . . making itself 'immanent' to human speech" (525). It is discernible not as grasped concept but as apprehended horizon. This Wholly Other, then, as unpossessable, unreachable horizon ahead and behind, creates the hope in our endless effort, while as immanence incarnated in our speech it guarantees that we can know presence and speak of the real.

Since the articulation of this theology, Ricoeur's own effort and desire over the past thirty-odd years has been withdrawn from a direct assault upon the horizons of the sacred and focussed instead upon increasingly painstaking examination of the nature of its linguistic immanence. Dialogue with his antithetical contemporaries has driven him steadily toward critical problems connected with language and narration that require resolution prior to the satisfactory establishment of a phenomenology of symbolism. In order to combat the "excesses of structuralism" on the more level ground of a secular philosophy, Ricoeur has widened his conception of hermeneutics from "the art of deciphering indirect meanings" to the more general analysis of discourse (Ricoeur 1978, 88). And he has turned, for help in doing so, away from his Continental background, to Anglo-American speech-act theory and ordinary language philosophy. Out of this new orientation he has developed his principal contribution to hermeneutics as discourse analysis, the theory that discourse produces a "surplus of meaning," in the disclosure of "a world that constitutes the reference of the text" (Ricoeur 1976, 92). This theory, in turn, seems to have inspired a reexamination of the two central conceptual tools of *The Symbolism of Evil,* "symbol" and "myth." Ricoeur's most relevant works of the 1970s and 1980s, *The Rule of Metaphor* and *Time and Narrative,* redefine these concepts in the light of discourse analysis. Both concepts return in such altered and secularized terms that even a critic as acute as Hazard Adams believes he can reject the early "symbol" while embracing the later "metaphor." Similarly, as insightful a judge as Hayden White of the significance for historiography of Ricoeur's concept of "narrative" expresses only the shadow of a suspicion that it may not be separable in the end from "myth."[2] A view of the arc of Ricoeur's development against the background of his theology reveals, however, a continuity between the two sets of concepts, grounded in Ricoeur's belief that the sacred, no matter how steadily it may appear to recede as horizon, is immanent in language.

The first thing one is struck by in turning directly to Ricoeur's concepts of "symbol" and "myth" in *The Symbolism of Evil* is the extent to which these early formulations redo in the vocabulary of phenomenology the problematic explored by the romantics. To take "symbol" first, we find Ricoeur designating it as a species of sign characterized by a peculiar opacity that is "inexhaustible" (16). Furthermore, this "symbol" does not invent reality, as in a properly constitutive theory, but discovers it. At its lower limit, symbol is "bound" in a sense Ricoeur borrows from Freud, meaning that the mental energy of the symbol is fixed in a material base, yoked, as Ricoeur says, to a non-semantic component that "hesitates on the dividing line between *bios* and *logos*" (Ricoeur 1976, 59). Without myth and ritual "the Sacred would remain unmanifested," but "to speak is founded upon the capacity of the cosmos to signify" and "the revealing grounds the saying, not the reverse" (62–63). This notion of a natural (or semi natural) sign that communicates the sacred seems related to Ricoeur's acknowledged Kantian confidence that a proper "transcendental deduction" is not merely subjective illusion but does, at least as a regulative idea, delineate reality. He is Kantian, too, in accepting what is implied; the possibility of an affective mode of knowing outside the bounds of pure reason. Finally, he follows the romantic distinction between symbol and allegory, the former expressing "analogical meanings which are spontaneously formed and immediately significant," whereas the latter are transparently rationalized: "symbols precede hermeneutics; allegories are already hermeneutic" (16). From this statement it might appear that hermeneutics can only be secondary rationalization of the symbolic mode of knowing, but Ricoeur builds his argument toward the final section of *Evil* in which he affirms that a proper "transcendental deduction" constitutes an interpretation that is not merely allegorical.

To appreciate how this can be, we might begin with two features of Ricoeur's "symbol" that distinguish it from its romantic relatives. First, the symbol is always mediated by language. The romantic symbol need not be verbal at all; it is any moment of perception in which a natural sign reveals the supernatural to "unmediated vision." Against a claim like Coleridge's that the symbol "participates in the nature of that which it renders intelligible," one might set Ricoeur's dictum "participation is rather signified than experienced" (168). This assertion is particularly incisive because it occurs in the context of Ricoeur's argument that even the "intuition of a cosmic whole" claimed for primitive humankind by phenomenologists of religion is in fact not *given,* but simply *aimed at,* that "the man of myths is already an unhappy consciousness" (167). In contrast to Eliade's easy romantic experiencer of primal unity, Ricoeur envisions a "man of myth" who is always already an existentialist. This proposition, by fusing "symbol" with "myth," raises in turn the second difference between Ricoeur's symbol and its romantic predecessor—the Ricoeurian symbol is always mediated by narrative. Creuzer stirred up a storm in 1812 by defining symbol as eidetic, instantaneous, and involuntary, and myth as auditory, temporal, and deliberately narrated. Schelling, on the verge of building his great case for mythology as the cosmogonic unfolding of the sacred, objected that Creuzer thus reduced myth to the secondary function of mere allegory, whereas it is in fact autonomous, or, in his word, "tautegorical." Ricoeur takes up this problematic where Creuzer and Schelling left it, but in order to see what he does with it we must turn directly to his conception of myth.

This conception might seem to situate him rather ambiguously between Creuzer and Schelling. On one hand, he agrees explicitly with Schelling that myth is autonomous; on the other hand, he locates it as a secondary phase of symbol and so teeters rather riskily on the edge of turning myth into allegorical explanation in the manner of Creuzer. Ricoeur, however, claims that symbol may be broken into "primary," "secondary," and "tertiary" components, which he names respectively as "confession," "myth," and "gnosis." The first term, "confession," will not seem so odd if one bears in mind that Ricoeur's project is to analyze "the symbolism of evil," which he divides into the three classes of "defilement," "sin," and "guilt." As the primary phase of symbol, "confession" is that outburst of "analogical meanings . . . spontaneously formed and immediately significant" that we think of as the romantic symbol proper (18). "Myth" is the secondary phase of "symbols developed in the form of narration" (18), and "gnosis," the tertiary phase, is symbol understood in "an abstract language . . . of spontaneous hermeneutics" (9). Particularly because it proceeds from obscure emotional expression toward abstract understanding, the implied temporal succession of these three phases suggests just the kind of relegation of myth to rationalization after the fact that Creuzer posited. But Ricoeur appears to deny this temporal, rationalizing succession in favor of mere "logical" priority by insisting that all three aspects of symbol are englobed within a unitary, expressive signification that precedes any rationalized allegorizing. Even the "hermeneutics" of the third stage of "gnosis" or "speculation" is still "spontaneous." Just as a direct experience of defilement, sin, or guilt "requires the mediation of symbols," so symbols require "the rich world of myths . . . which are the medium" (161). "Speculation is not autonomous," he declares in a different context, "and myths themselves are secondary; but neither is there any immediate consciousness of fault that can do without the secondary and tertiary elaborations. It is the whole circle, made up of confession, myth and speculation, that we must understand" (9). Both its makers' expression of symbolic language and its readers' grasp of it operate within the standard hermeneutical circle that conditions all acquisition of meaning; symbol and myth are alike indispensable because each is virtually untranslatable without the other. Whether or not this balancing act resolves the romantic dispute (and I don't think it does), Ricoeur's conception of the place of myth is original in its insistence that the language of expressive symbol cannot be properly grasped apart from its deployment in the diachronic, syntagmatic dimension of narrative called myth.

Here we begin to see a formidable master-trope of analogy shaping up between incarnated speech and the horizons of desire, on one hand, and symbol and myth on the other. In symbol we experience and express the immanence of the sacred, but in myth we signify the gap between its infinite promise and our finite attainment of it. According to Ricoeur's phenomenology in "The Symbolic Function of Myths," myth adds three things to the "revelatory function of the primary symbols." First, it embraces "mankind as a whole in one ideal history. By means of a time that represents all times, 'man' is manifested as a concrete universal." Second, it sets this archetypal man in "the movement . . . which confers upon this experience an orientation, a character, a tension." Third, it deals with "the discordance between the fundamental reality of man and his present existence, between his ontological status as a being created good . . . and his existential status experienced under the sign of alienation" (162–163). What myth "adds" to symbol is a *plot* that could be summarized as humankind's orientation toward a destiny from which it is at present alienated. Myth arises, then, in order to rationalize the gulf revealed by symbol between signifier and transcendental signified. Ricoeur says, in a remark worthy on the face of it of Lacan or Derrida, that myth "is a narrative precisely because there is no logical transition between . . . ontological status . . . and . . . existential or historical status" (163). The "man of myth" extemporizes (the precise word here) during the ritual occasion a narrative that expresses by virtue of this very act of improvisation his anxiety that "participation is rather signified than experienced." Only one difference separates this view of myth from Derridean deferral, but that difference is crucial—the immanence of the otherwise Wholly Other as it comes to meet us in language. Thanks to this immanence, one hand can wash the other; as myth narrativizes symbol, expatiating it discursively, symbol motivates and valorizes myth. Thus validated, myth is "both the leap and the passage, the cut and the suture" (163).

Ricoeur's most important works may well prove to be *The Rule of Metaphor* and *Time and Narrative*, his patiently detailed, scrupulously situated examinations of metaphor and narrativity. Each of these topics seems to withdraw from such immediate expressions of the sacred as myth and symbol into analysis of their thoroughly secular semantic and narrative preconditions. But both studies do bear at certain points upon the earlier theory of myth. In fact, a case could be made for Ricoeur's "metaphor" as the connecting link between symbol and myth. It is true that he distinguishes "metaphor" from "symbol" in *Interpretation Theory* by pointing out that metaphor "brings to language the implicit semantics of the symbol" (69), whereas the unique feature of symbol is that it derives its archetypal power from the "presemantic" experience to which it is "bound."[3] "Metaphors," Ricoeur says there, "are just the linguistic surface of symbols" (69). But his "tensional" theory of metaphor in *Rule* holds that it is a "transaction between contexts" (Ricoeur 1977, 80) that creates "at once meaning and event" (98). Ricoeur's trenchant critique of post-Saussurean semiotic theories of metaphor, in the light of common language and speech-act analysis, is that by focusing on substitution in the isolated units of *lexis* rather than on the semantic dynamics of the units of sense (like the sentence) that alone confer meaning, these theories miss just this joint innovation of meaning and event. In contrast, metaphor considered as the creation of a new meaning-event not only originates in the presemantic matrix of symbol, but also thrusts toward the next stage of symbol, the temporal redescription called myth.[4]

Ricoeur does not focus upon "myth" in *Time and Narrative* but, like Northrop Frye when *he* considers narrative, upon "mythos," signifying as in Aristotle's *Poetics* "plot" or, better yet, "emplotment." In moving on from a theory of myth to a theory of narrative, Ricoeur proceeds from the particular to the general. Myth is presumably just one sort of emplotment—that which extends and thus contextualizes symbol. Because it is a species of the genus, however, myth, too, is illuminated by Ricoeur's phenomenology of the emplotment of time in Western fiction and history. Ricoeur commences the preface to *Time and Narrative* by declaring that it and *The Rule of Metaphor* "form a pair" because metaphor and narrative produce their "meaning effects" by "the same basic phenomenon of semantic innovation" (Ricoeur 1984–1988, vol. 1, ix). While metaphor does it by "impertinent attribution," "with narrative, the semantic innovation lies in the inventing of another work of synthesis—a plot," which creates "a new congruence in the organization of events" (ix). Ricoeur sees in plots "the privileged means by which we re-configure our confused, unformed, and at the limit mute temporal experience" (xi).[5] Hence, for him "the poetics of narrativity . . . corresponds to the aporetics of temporality" (84). In a vocabulary that he acknowledges owes a good deal to a distinguished predecessor, Frank Kermode's *Sense of an Ending* (1966), Ricoeur proceeds to examine how we impose our fictional concordances upon the discordances of our temporal awareness. In keeping with his general theory of the creation of new meaning in discourse, he theorizes that in narrative *"a prefigured time . . . becomes a refigured time through the mediation of a configured time"* (54). Much as a new metaphor alters our "seeing as" by constructing a transaction between surprising contexts, a narrative, by configuring anew our already prefigured version of the meaning of events, refigures them in fresh alignment. The application of this theory of mythos in general to myth in particular does illuminate the kind of linear restructuring of symbol that Ricoeur takes myth to be. Indeed, his confidence that mythos, like metaphor, not only invents but discovers reality—that it is rooted in "prenarrative" as metaphor is in "presemantic" experience—suggests that "mythos" and "myth" may express something much nearer to identity than Ricoeur's conventional historical separation of them has allowed him to face up to. Even if the two terms *were* identified, however, it should be clear that Ricoeur's would not be a fully constitutive theory of myth because both myth and mythos redescribe a preexistent reality.

Ricoeur's brilliant and meticulous investigations of the nature of metaphor and language ought not to be mistaken, in any case, for an abandonment of belief in the sacred. They are more like an enactment of his recognition that the Wholly Other as horizon exacts increasing deferral. Ricoeur wields Anglo-American common language and discourse analysis in *Time and Narrative* just as he does in *The Rule of Metaphor* to expose the limitations of structuralist and poststructuralist semiotics, but in the end his thorough lack of rapport with these latter theories is a theological disagreement; it stems from his faith in a deity immanent in language. In his respectful critique of Frank Kermode's *Sense of an Ending* Ricoeur opposes to what he sees as Kermode's Nietzschean despair of fiction-making's being anything but self-deception the assertion that "beyond every possible suspicion, we must have confidence in the powerful institution of language. This is a wager that brings its own justification."[6] The first sentence may appear to express a wholly secular confidence, but the reference to the Pascalian "wager" in the second reveals Ricoeur's own history and orientation. His is our finest theory of myth that confronts the century's linguistic turn and yet maintains its roots in the sacred.

LESZEK KOLAKOWSKI: MYTH AS ENDOWMENT WITH VALUE

Kolakowski's early work, *The Presence of Myth,* is approximately contemporary with Ricoeur's *Symbolism of Evil,* and shares with it an initial orientation in Continental phenomenology and post-Heideggerian existentialism.[7] Kolakowski's response to existentialism, however, is primarily to Sartre and Merleau-Ponty rather than to its Christian expositors. He presents a conception of myth that dispenses with theological foundation and takes a large step in the direction of a thorough constitutive theory.

Kolakowski refuses to define "myth" precisely, but he does stipulate that it includes both creation stories in the narrower and more conventional sense and, in a much broader sense, "certain constructions, present (be they hidden or explicit) in our intellectual and affective life, namely those which conditioned and mutable elements of experience allow us to bind teleologically by appeal to unconditioned realities (such as 'being,' 'truth,' and 'value')" (ix). He means by "conditioned and mutable elements of experience" those apprehended by individuals according to their circumstances, which thus constitute particular cultural versions of the "unconditioned realities." Kolakowski apologizes for wrenching the term "myth" from its more or less conventional usages to cover a signification that is indeed very wide. "Myth" labels "a permanently constitutive element of culture" (x), nothing less than the "need" of humanity to avoid, by "acts affirming values," "acceptance of a contingent world" (5). Myth, therefore, is "present in every understanding of the world as endowed with values" (29). Kolakowski's excuse for employing the term in this extended sense is that he could find none more appropriate short of risking a neologism. The existence of this very chapter, however, indicates how little such an apology is necessary and raises, instead, the question of why Kolakowski perceives himself as so isolated. His narrow and broad senses of "myth" are virtually the same as Wilbur Urban's (whose work he probably wouldn't have known) and closely related to the comparable distinction between myth and mythos that turns up in Frye's *Anatomy* and Ricoeur's *Symbolism of Evil* (both likewise beyond his ken).

Belief in myth is not, according to Kolakowski's phenomenological existentialism, a matter of unencumbered choice. He specifically derides the Nietzschean notion of the heroic transvaluator, free at every moment to rewrite the tablets of the law. "The idols of the tribe," he says, "govern in an inescapable manner" (25). We seem, for Kolakowski, to enter the world in a condition of cultural "thrownness" in which "the universe of values is a mythical reality. To the extent that we endow with values the elements of experience, situations, and things, we perceive them as existing in that reality which unconditionally transcends the totality of possible experience." We therefore know this "reality" as "the precondition of all experience," but within experience itself, our experience of history, humanity, culture, "what we actually do know is not [reality] but the *facts* of valuation. . . . value imprisoned in its relativity is a cultural fact" (26). Husserl's project of escaping this phenomenological relativity was doomed to failure. We could escape myth only if we could transcend "the situation of consciousness in the world" (63).

All thought is not mythical, for we do not always "endow with values the elements of experience." Kolakowski does, however, represent all apprehension of the world that is not mythical as the dialectical contrary of that which is. While this strategy enables him to whet his descriptive definition of myth against its opposite, it makes for a somewhat vague sense of the whetstone. Not surprisingly for someone so transparently under the influence of Heidegger, he occasionally speaks of this contrary as the "technological." But he acknowledges in his "Preliminary Distinctions" that this is not an adequate term since scientists, too, "make use of the labors of mythical consciousness" (xi). Kolakowski characterizes his contrary to myth most distinctly when he finds it epitomized in Hume's empiricism: "His tenacious destructive critique has revealed the only world that can emerge from an attempt at a total negation of myth. . . . An antimythical project which is careful to retain its coherence cannot transcend Hume's vision" (64). A reductive empiricism of this sort "produces the instruments of a more efficient manipulation of things, but it does not produce understanding or even information" (65). Its mental universe is the contrary of that in which the mind will "reach for myth when it wishes to name the world in its wholeness" (62).

We might well be suspicious, especially coming fresh from the last chapter, of a Heideggerian argument that presents us with an either/or choice between the bad faith of a "culture of analgesics" (81) and the intuitions of presence that ground mythical thinking. But Kolakowski does not neglect the issue of myth as ideology. Instead, living under a repressive Communist regime, he views it from a perspective that is the political contrary of the thinking represented in chapter 11. He distinguishes two historical kinds of myth in the narrow sense and leaves no doubt about which he respects. On one hand, we find the sort, characteristic of traditional cultures, that attempts "to awaken . . . a *consciousness of indebtedness* towards Being" (95); on the other, we encounter in modernity the contrary sort (precisely Sorel's) that encourages the *"consciousness of a creditor"* and looks to future utopias to redress grievances. This bold contrast obviously expresses a profound social and political conservativism. The first narrow sense of "myth," applies to folkloristic myth a Heideggerian twist that brings it into conformity with Eliade's neo-romantic nostalgia. The second narrow sense transforms Eliade's general hatred of modernity into the specific identification of myth with the aggrieved *ressentiment* of utopian politics. Kolakowski launches at this point into an impressionistic account of what is obviously myth as ideology, but understood as a threat from the Left rather than the Right. He tells us that "all those who warn against the threat of myth" are correct to do so (104). Myth is dangerous in its "tendency to limitless expansion." It may "attempt to take over forcibly almost all areas of culture, and may become encrusted in despotism, terror and mendacity." The individual's search for it, he recognizes, is most often "an attempt to discover a caring authority which easily deals with ultimate questions, equips with stable hierarchies of value, surrounds one with a thicket of signposts, relieves one of liberty, wraps one up again in a cocoon of infancy, and satisfies a lazy need for submission." No doubt the Communist censors who forbade publication in 1966 understood these remarks in the spirit in which they were intended. What isn't clear is whether Kolakowski recognizes that, in the process of moving from positive to negative assessment, he has shifted from referring to myth in the first narrow sense, where it still overlaps with the broad sense of myth as endower of value, to the far more restrictive sense of it as political ideology. The implicit difference might offer a valuable insight into the process by which myth degenerates from general blessing to specific bane, but Kolakowski shows no sign of recognizing here any slip in usage.

The antinomy of myth's simultaneous beneficence and self-aggrandizement drives Kolakowski, finally, upon two ultimate questions. First, "is it possible for a myth to operate in its socially indispensable function without the threat of mythological terror" (104)? He concludes that myth "can be socially fruitful only when it is unceasingly suspect, constantly subject to vigilance which would frustrate its natural tendency to turn into a narcotic" (105). This is a view closely related to Ricoeur's on the permanent role of hermeneutics of suspicion. Kolakowski, however, makes the politically edgier point that we do not know if such critique can be incorporated socially outside a counterculture of individual intellectuals or, as he puts it, without assigning to some "the one-sided dignity of the guardians of myth, while to others the one-sided dignity of its critics" (105). Myth ought, furthermore, he thinks, to help remove our sense of the otherness of the world while simultaneously enabling us "to understand why this is not possible in full." But holding our specifically human reflexivity of consciousness as the creator both of myth and of its critique forces upon us the second ultimate question of the problematic. How can we sustain belief in what we know to be ultimately fictive? As Kolakowski has it, "Is a consciousness possible which acknowledges this genealogy of myth and at the same time is capable of participating in myth" (118)? His answer is a long and intricately qualified "yes." It amounts, as I understand it, to a remotely neo-Kantian claim that our "unceasing attempt to name what is not contingent" (132) belongs to a realm of response to experience which may once have originated in an instrumental function but is now constituted so differently from instrumental reason that in practice it is possible for many of us much of the time to entertain both realms simultaneously without a sense of epistemological crisis. This is not to say that the two orders can be synthesized. What we experience is that "willy-nilly, we have to serve two masters" (134). We are in no position to decide definitively between their rival claims. For us, "they have to coexist, and yet they cannot coexist" (135). This conception of a permanent dialectic of myth and antimyth would seem to place Kolakowski in the line of thinkers from Hegel through Nietzsche to Horkheimer and Adorno who have perceived some version of this struggle as a definitive feature of Western modernity. But this sequence of thinkers entertains increasingly dark views of the risk and the outcome, and tends in proportion to regard the scales as weighed down on the side of "ideology." Kolakowski, in comparison, shares with Ricoeur a hopefulness that prompts them to imagine the scales at least evenly balanced for the possible triumph of "supreme fiction." Kolakowski is confident that the "coexistence, both inevitable and impossible" (135) of myth and its contrary is no cause for alarm because it keeps civilization in working trim. "Cultural momentum always has its source in a conflict of values [compare Ricoeur's "conflict of interpretations"] from which each side attempts, at the expense of the other, to claim exclusivity, but is forced under pressure to restrict its aspirations" (125). But Ricoeur and Kolakowski are both sustained in their hopefulness by religious intimations, Ricoeur of a Wholly Other immanent in language, and Kolakowski of the presence of "unconditioned realities," including, it seems, a positive version of Heidegger's Being. We have yet to contemplate a confident but wholly non-transcendental theory of myth as "supreme fiction."

ERIC GOULD: THE PERMANENCE OF MYTHICITY

Eric Gould's *Mythical Intentions in Modern Literature* (1981) is this animal. Gould follows Ricoeur both in thinking of myth primarily within the tradition of post-Heideggerian phenomenology and in recognizing that this tradition must be confronted with structuralist and post-structuralist semiology. But he departs from Ricoeur in assuming that these two philosophical approaches can be reconciled and that the essence of myth, which he calls "mythicity," can be established as a consequence upon a thoroughly secular basis. He proposes to demonstrate by focusing on the work of three writers—D. H. Lawrence, T. S. Eliot, and James Joyce—the nature of the continuity between myth in traditional societies and in modernist literary texts. Unlike the modernists themselves, however, and the literary critics who have shared their neo-romantic assumptions, he recognizes that the claim to such continuity remains to be established upon adequate theoretical grounds. The heart of his argument consists in an attempt to show that his chosen modernists enjoy just as surely as the storytellers of traditional oral societies access to the permanent expressive feature of narrative that he christens "mythicity." Gould produces in the end a definition of "mythicity" so inclusive that it constitutes, rather than a satisfactory account of the alleged continuity of folkloristic myth with modernist literature, a valuable general theory of necessary cultural fictions.

Gould agrees with the phenomenologists and Freudians in finding the motive for myth in "the anxiety of our finitude" (Eric Gould 1981, 70). Myth is the product of our experiencing *"an ontological gap between event and meaning"* (6), which we try to fill with endless interpretation. He determines, therefore, to "examine myth from the only starting point . . . we can have any confidence in: language itself as a system of signs" (7). From this point of vantage he conducts a very effective critique of "essentialist" theories of the "archetype," like Jung's, Eliade's, or even Frye's, which presume kinds of entities beyond and behind language-events. Gould argues for a purely linguistic conception of "the archetype as concealing nothing" (33) or, rather (in the Heideggerian catachresis that he often uses to dramatize the paradoxical lack involved), the archetype as concealing Nothing. "Mythicity," he suggests, "is the condition of filling the gap with signs in such a way that Being continues to conceal Nothing as a predication for further knowledge" (43). When he turns from direct attention to "archetype" to the related issues of "metaphor" and the existence of the "unconscious," he proposes the application of analogous linguistic criteria. In the case of "metaphor," he argues that in using metaphor we are always aspiring to an unattainable metonym, *"the absent metonomy which lies behind the metaphor,"* or "the rhetorical degree zero of metaphor" (52). "Metonomy," in this formulation, is no longer the humble, hard-working figure of speech, but Gould's own metaphor for the ontological lack itself, the absent center. And the concept of "the unconscious," which Gould does not wish to reject as "the instigation to myth" (87), is saved for linguisticality by elegant resort to Lacan. "For Lacan, quite simply, the unconscious is that discourse which has 'escaped' from the subject, which we produce without knowing why" (74). In terms of Lacanian libidinal development, as Gould puts it, "desire itself is . . . the metonomy in the metaphor of the self" (78). We can't really *explain* our unconscious, suprapersonal desire to fill with signs the gap between meaning and event.

In his next major section Gould turns from what might be called the symbolic or paradigmatic aspect of mythicity—what he terms "archetype"—to its aspect as narrative, "myth as discourse" (88). Unfortunately, in his search for appropriate linguistic models he settles on the theories of Claude Lévi-Strauss and Roland Barthes. These are both projects that require heroic revamping before they are suitable for his use. In the case of Lévi-Strauss, Gould wishes to appropriate Lévi-Strauss's general claim that myth displays a rational structure of transformations. But he naturally feels obliged to dispute at length the anthropologist's notorious denigrations of modern literature. He comparably embraces Barthes's assumption that mythmaking continues unabated into our own day, but dismisses his premise that contemporary myth (including "Literature") is bourgeois ideology. By canceling the particular "pessimism" (124) of each structuralist with what he regards as the other's strength, Gould hopes to salvage a basis for his mythicity. It is a set of rationally coded transformations (Lévi-Strauss), perennial in narrative (Barthes).

But the very honesty of Gould's expositions of the thinking of the two structuralists subverts his efforts to wrest from their contexts only those aspects of their theories that can be co-opted for his own. In each instance the half of the theory that Gould rejects is consistent with and integral to the half he embraces. Lévi-Strauss's attacks on the degeneracy of modern fiction follow from his persuasion that what is structurally significant in myth is strictly conceptual, indeed, diagrammatic. His criticism of the modern novel is not primarily, as Gould appears to assume, that it is "surrealistic" and "discontinuous," but that it is drowned in narrative. For Lévi-Strauss all narrative weakens, and absolute narrative weakens absolutely. Furthermore, the structural significance of myth is apparent only on a level that prescinds from the psychological states of storytellers and their audiences. It seems like wishful thinking to embrace Lévi-Strauss's conception of myth as sets of cognitive transformations while dismissing the logical corollaries that spell out exactly why modern fiction is as far from presenting such transformations as is possible for narrative to get. It is comparably questionable to detach Barthes's view that myth is alive and well and living in Paris from his conception of it as a second-order semiological system, always in bad faith. Its living presence is inextricably bound up with that identity; for Barthes myth has no status as a current phenomenon *except* as bourgeois ideology. Gould apparently calls on these two key witnesses for the defense who turn out to be witnesses for the prosecution because he is unwilling to acknowledge the gulf between their premises and those of his optimistic brand of interpretation theory. This reluctance explains why he criticizes his closest fellow traveler, Ricoeur, for creating a new and unnecessary dichotomy between semiotics and semantics. Ricoeur turns to the "semantics" of speech-act theory and common language analysis precisely because he recognizes how inimical the positivism of structural linguistics is to the possibility of the sort of hermeneutics that he (and Gould) advocate.

Once he has situated his revised "archetypalism" upon what he regards as a proper linguistic basis, Gould proceeds directly into the mythicity of modern literature. He argues that "myth is not so much weakened as dissipated in the modern. . . . *abstracted to a sophistication that only literature can handle*" (134). By saying that modern literature has "abstracted" and sophisticated myth, he means, approximately, that the modern artist, having come to recognize the true essence of mythicity as the construction of mediating signs, creates a self-conscious work that involves the reader in the problematic. "Only literature can handle" myth at this level of abstraction, presumably because it alone offers this interactive opportunity. Gould justifies his selection of three such self-conscious experimentalists as Eliot, Lawrence, and Joyce on the grounds that this trio's recognition of the essence of mythicity and their intentions of involving readers in its enactment are far more significant than any amount of mere cultural allusion.

Gould turns especially to Joyce's work to exemplify this celebration of mythicity; his sequence is capped by his treatment of *Finnegans Wake* as encouraging readers "to be proficient at myth-making ourselves, and to occupy only a world of signifiers" (165). Before Gould proceeds to discuss Eliot and Lawrence, he acknowledges the same broad difference between their work and Joyce's to which I called attention in chapter 6. In Gould's terms, Joyce concentrates self-consciously upon the mythicity inherent in the structuring of signs, whereas Lawrence and Eliot seek "an interpretative medium which aims to rediscover the nature of the mythic and the numinous as the motive for literary experience" (200).

He gains his purchase upon this topic by positing that "the sense of the sacred is created both by the human failure to name and understand experience *and* by the conditions language determines for assigning meaning, . . . the perpetual play in the ontological gap" (175). Granted that this is the case, "in terms of the religious significance of myth, its reference to the ineffable, the real issue is not whether myths perpetuate themselves because they successfully embody the sacred as an objective fact, but whether they offer a lively enough argument to enable us to interpret the numinous—whatever we think that is—in the world of signs" (179). Gould turns at this point, as part of his admirably systematic effort to adhere to linguistic explanation, to a version of Lévi-Strauss's account of the role in myth of its "slated" variations. The intention of myth to offer an interpretation of the numinous in the world of signs informs its structure as a peculiarly effective attempt to close the semiological gap by tautology: "[myths] are so arbitrary, matter-of-fact, and self-contained, and we are not. In effect, what we engage in any myth is a persistent existential crisis and the allegorical neatness of the solution" (183). At the same time as they reiterate their tantalizingly neat solutions, however, myths are paradoxically characterized by their elusive origins and their disseminated suggestiveness: "the power of a myth is expressed not in any literal reference . . . but in the open-ended repetitiveness of the relationships it creates between items" (186). When Gould turns, then, to modernist attempts to affirm or incorporate myth, it is not surprising that he appeals to Jacques Derrida's incipient theology-by-default. "Discourse," as Gould puts it, *"deconstructs transcendence yet perpetuates ontology"* (195). If "myth is a *metaphysics of absence implicit in every sign,"* then, "given the temporal gap between event and meaning, the sacredness of myth and the numinousness of the literary work are potentially one" (198). Granted these premises, Gould makes a good case for Eliot and Lawrence as writing, in their contrasting ways, "allegories of intent." "Allegory," he says, obviously following de Man, "is overdetermination of meaning in the face of language's nihilistic ontology" (211) and therefore "the motive for allegory is the motive for myth" (212). To produce an "allegory of intent," in contrast to de Man's "allegory of reading," is to valorize self-consciously Sisyphean discourse about the "struggle to define an authentic viewpoint on the nature of the sacred, even while the 'language of the tribe' makes full authenticity impossible" (203).

Considered as a whole, Gould's argument is a highly ambitious and sophisticated attempt to ground the romantic identification of "myth" with "literature" in a phenomenological hermeneutics that assimilates adequately the structuralist and post-structuralist critique of both concepts. To accept his claims, however, we must not only dismiss Lévi-Strauss and Barthes but grant Gould's own crucial hypotheses. The first of these is that this handful (and only this handful?) of creative artists has realized the true essence of a diachronically continuous mythicity and the second is that only "literature" permits the proper communication of this insight. Both of these propositions present difficulties. If we assume that "mythicity," in the first one, signifies filling the gap between event and meaning with signs of "the numinous," we're confronted with the evidence that, on one end of the continuum, much traditional story that gets labeled "myth" in the folkloristic sense has little or nothing to do with "the numinous," while, on the other end, Joyce's playful mockery of settled meaning in *Finnegans Wake* doesn't either. It remains unclear, when Gould speaks of "intentions" in modern literature "to acquire the status of myth" (129) (as distinguished from achieved "mythicity"), that this actually refers to anything other than the recurrence of that romantic desire to recuperate an imagined unity of sensibility that is indeed so marked a feature of the work of

Eliot, Lawrence, and others. Gould's second proposition raises a comparable specter. The romantics invented "literature" together with "myth," after all, to signify a class of linguistic usage distinguished by its power to embody poetic insight into transcendental truth and being—a genus of which myth itself is a species. And even though Gould's version of this claim is cast in the terms of an existential phenomenology that makes it much more palatable (an "allegory of intent" is a struggle to arrive, not arrival), the reader still confronts an attempt to universalize conceptions of "literature" as well as of "myth" that come loaded down with the familiar historical baggage.

While Gould's conception of "myth" appears compromised, his conception of mythicity may not be. The reservations registered above depend upon assuming that "mythicity" signifies the filling of the existential gap specifically with signs of "the numinous." But Gould does not always confine himself to this relatively narrow, religious definition of the term. Consider, for instance, his admission that "the intention to go on in the business of making the world transform into further meaning . . . may well be all that we can understand by 'mythic thought'" (180). In this wider sense, what cultural achievement of our species is *not* an attempt to fill with signs the gap between event and meaning? Taken thus, mythicity becomes a general theory of fictions, a status that does secure common ground between traditional and modern thought. When Gould declares in this vein that "literature intends to acquire the status of myth" by "becoming a cultural document . . . offering a genuine attempt to think through a social compromise as an interpretative process" (129), his Lévi-Straussian formulation works appropriately. It is not claiming for "literature" any status that does not apply to every form of narrative in which humans have tried to create such interpretations. Gould's theory of "mythicity" is valuable, even in its vulnerability, because it demonstrates so effectively why anyone promoting the continuity of traditional "myth" with modern literature must come to terms with the linguistic principle of the alleged continuity. But it is particularly valuable, in a wholly positive sense, for its large conception of "mythicity" as motive for the fictions that constitute the entire production of human culture.

HANS BLUMENBERG: WORK ON MYTH

Hans Blumenberg's *Arbeit am Mythos* (1979) was published two years before Eric Gould's *Mythical Intentions* but follows it here because it proposes a striking solution to the romantic claim, revived in so challenging a fashion by Gould, that modern authors produce "myth" as surely as the storytellers of traditional societies.

Blumenberg's massive tome sits at a somewhat awkward angle in relation to much of the work discussed in the last five chapters, like a large boulder partly blocking a mountain path. This distinguished philosopher's venture into mythography appears almost as a by-product, albeit a logical one, of two of his yet more comprehensive and abiding projects—the development of what he calls a "metaphorology" of Western intellectual history and the exploration of what is called in the title of his best known work "the legitimacy of the modern age" (Blumenberg 1983). Witty and brilliant as this *oeuvre* is, it is rooted in that

European, and particularly Germanic, tradition of philosophical anthropology that has so often disdained "positivistic" thought, especially in the social sciences. Blumenberg simply does not address in *Work on Myth* the ideological conception of myth that is the subject of the previous chapter, and his notice of the contribution of modern anthropology is confined to one minor and negative objection to a point of Lévi-Strauss's. He is included here, nevertheless, because he does make a significant contribution toward resolving the problematic established by the romantics of the continuity of modern with traditional "myth."

Blumenberg introduces a useful, indeed, a crucial enabling distinction between the work *of* myth and work *on* myth. This is a distinction, roughly, between myth's function and its fate. Its function, the work *of* myth, was (and still is in more refined fashion) to interpose a merciful veil of explanation between humankind and its dread of the unknown. In *his* etiological myth Blumenberg pictures the human ancestor, driven for the first time from the shrinking rain forest onto the open savanna where, before it takes shelter in caves, it is overwhelmed physically and mentally by the huge horizon. This literalizing of phenomenology's overworked metaphor of "horizon" is typical of Blumenberg's wit, as is his simultaneous employment of the fable to dramatize seriously how the resulting *Angst* would "again and again be rationalized into fear" (Blumenberg 1985, 5). The first step is "substitution of the familiar for the unfamiliar, of explanation for the inexplicable, of names for the unnameable" (5). This "'apotropaic' accomplishment of naming" (13) precipitates the construction of myth; "what has become identifiable by means of a name is raised out of its unfamiliarity by means of metaphor and is made accessible by telling stories" (6).

As a "just-so" story of the origin of both myth and religion, this fable is a tribute to Blumenberg's principal inspirers. First of all, he shares with Freud the age-old notion that *"primus in orbe timor fecit deos."* The word Blumenberg employs to signify the way myth "occupies" or "reoccupies" cultural "positions" is *Besetzung,* Freud's term for the concept rendered in the *Standard Edition* as "cathexis." This non-coincidence encapsulates the degree to which Blumenberg identifies the primal motive for myth with Freud's for religion, that is, the construction of a defense-reaction. Blumenberg's invention of an etiological myth that will inevitably recall Freud's in *Totem and Taboo* seems intended to signal this fundamental agreement. Second, Blumenberg is particularly impressed by Otto's phenomenology of "the holy." The development of myth "seen in terms of the history of religion," he says, "is the confining of a diffusely distributed quality of uncanniness and unmanageability into enclaves limited by strict sanctions" (14). He calls this "confining," this system of cosmic checks and balances, "the archaic division of powers," a separation of "the holy" into contrary qualities that he, like both Freud in "The Antithetical Qualities of Primal Words" and Otto in *The Holy,* appears to have derived from Hermann Usener's *Die Götternamen* (1896). This "division of powers" is the master-concept of *Work on Myth;* Blumenberg finds in this originary "limiting-case" the monad of all later theodicies. He subsequently declares the myth of Prometheus to be "the outstanding figuration" of the "division of powers," and the main business of the latter half of his huge essay is to trace "work on" this single myth through its stunning elaborations in Western culture. Third, as Blumenberg's translator, Robert Wallace, points out, the philosopher follows in his fable Arnold Gehlen's theory that all the "institutions" of culture are "the shared patterns of perception and behavior that man erects to take the place of instincts (with which, in comparison to other animals, he is very poorly equipped) in guiding his actions" (173 n.). Culture replaces instinct as the instrument of survival, and myth is the special cultural institution that relates directly to adjustment to humankind's existential *Angst*. It follows that "the work *of* myth" is not confined to prehistory; it will never be quite done so long as dread of our "thrownness" torments us, which is to say that it will be as endless as it is without beginning.

Without beginning? The phrase appears to contradict Blumenberg's etiological myth. And the validity of this tale is indeed undermined as soon as we turn to his conception of "work *on* myth." The Greek historical record commences with sophisticated *work on* a corpus of inherited story. Herodotus shows that he understands this in his comment on the role of Homer and Hesiod in acquainting the Greeks with their gods, and his recognition exemplifies the universal experience; myth enters history as a body of story whose origins are lost. We can speculate about these origins, but we cannot know them; what we always find is what Herodotus found—work *on* them. In this context Blumenberg views his fable of the cave-Kierkegaard as a "limiting case" and quickly affirms that even the hypothetical stage of "naming" the powers would be already "work on" myth. In fact, "whatever starting point one might choose, work on the reduction of the absolutism of reality [his equivalent of Freud's 'reality principle'] would already have begun" (7). The pure condition of the work *of* myth represented in Blumenberg's "limiting-case" can be conceived as logically prior, like Rousseau's "state of nature," but it is not a condition of which humankind has preserved any experience. The entire shelter of culture is built up from work *on* myth.

Blumenberg defines "myth," this entity that accomplishes its work when it is worked on, as a species of "stories that are distinguished by a high degree of constancy in their narrative core and by an equally pronounced capacity for marginal variation" (34). Blumenberg's definition offers a doubly attractive prospect: it is anchored, like folkloristic myth, in a generic mode of storytelling, and it promises to explain the continuity of this mode across the entire range of human culture, thus deproblematizing the link between the prehistorical and the historical, oral and chirographic culture. Accepting the definition, however, requires that we understand what is meant by "a high degree of constancy in their narrative core" and a "pronounced capacity for marginal variation." These two qualities must be considered one at a time, but, in spite of their apparently contrary centripetal and centrifugal tendencies, the explanation of the "constancy" is also the explanation of the "capacity for marginal variation."

Blumenberg faces anew the puzzle to which Freud and Jung offer their famous, if exasperating, solutions: what *does* explain the persistence, the appeal, of certain perennial stories? Blumenberg's answer is that these tales possess the quality of *Prägnanz*. His translator renders this ordinary word for "precision" or "conciseness" as "pregnance" because, as he explains, it is thus rendered in the translations of

Cassirer's *Philosophy of Symbolic Forms* and in "the literature of Gestalt psychology," the two main influences upon this aspect of Blumenberg's thinking. As Wallace also indicates, we are intended "to connect *Prägnanz* with the verb *prägen* (to stamp or imprint)—which gives us Goethe's *'geprägte Form'*—rather than understanding it as meaning 'pregnancy'" (111 n). The "narrative core" of a myth, then, is a stamped or imprinted precision of form that lasts through all vicissitudes of transmission. To explain how this imprinting works, Blumenberg resorts to a psychobiological version of natural selection. He reminds us of the immensely disproportionate elaboration of culture that predates writing. Any particular tale embodying humankind's apotropaic response to *Angst* will have been sifted through myriads of storytellings over millennia. "The age of oral communication was a phase of direct and continual feedback regarding the success of literary means" (152). The almost unimaginable weight of this reception-history (or reception-prehistory) guarantees a "pregnance" in the surviving stories to which Blumenberg (like Lévi-Strauss) compares pejoratively mere modern *invention*. Hence the continual and continuous appeal of myth.

This ingenious hypothesis bears an evident family resemblance to the Freudian and Jungian explanations. The reader may recall that Jung, at least in certain more soberly scientific moods, even serves up the possibility that his own "archetypes" are a structure of imprinted instincts. Blumenberg lumps Freud and Jung together as believers in the doctrine of "innate ideas," which he rejects on the grounds, common to a wide range of contemporary theorists, that under such an assumption "the capacity for survival that a fictive material possesses becomes a piece of nature and thus something into which further inquiry is impossible" (151). It is far from clear, however, that his own hypothesis escapes the same imputation. Having rejected the Jungian archetype-as-manifestation-of-universal-process, Blumenberg, like Northrop Frye (whose work he doesn't appear to know), falls back upon an environmental explanation that requires the essentializing of universal experience, particularly of nature. He speculates, for example, that "the stability of the narrative kernels" has to do "not so much with preformed and innate models as with the limited multiplicity of those human circumstances, needs and situations that are reflected in mythical configurations" (273). To locate the cause of the stability in certain elementary responses to environment may be to conceive it as "a piece of nature" quite as blatantly as Freud or Jung is accused of doing.

Blumenberg's hypothesis presents as well a second and related difficulty. He believes that he follows Cassirer in envisioning myth as a "symbolic form" but maintains that he succeeds, where Cassirer fails, in crossing the gap between the affective and the cognitive by means of the purifying effect of "pregnance." While *mythos,* he concedes, will never quite be *logos* in the degree that science is, the condition of its having "passed through the agency of reception" and having "been 'optimized' by its mechanism of selection" guarantees that it is "incomparably closer to the kind of acceptance that goes with objectivity than to any affectively tinged experience" of the sort associated with "primitive" religion (168). This claim thoroughly ignores the fact that the myriad personal and social pressures of what is so vaguely called "the agency of reception" will have played their various ideological and necessarily affective roles in persuading audiences what to receive with approbation. The argument in fact appears to require the very sort of Lamarckian assumption employed by Freud in *Totem and Taboo* to explain how the original acts of patricide and incest have come to be inherited by the modern superego. Without some version of the Lamarckian hypothesis, how are a thousand generations of affective response more objectifying than the experience of a single person? It seems moot, in fact, whether Blumenberg's version of the evolution of more rational myth by natural selection—the laundering out of affectivity in the washing-machine of oral reception—is any more probable than Cassirer's Vichian story.

Blumenberg introduces in his discussion of "constancy of the narrative core" a certain type of constancy that may be of crucial importance, although it does not appear as part of his formal definition. This is what he calls "fundamental myth." The phrase appears at first to be a mere question-begging synonym for myth on which accumulating work has conferred special richness and therefore perdurability. But Blumenberg describes "fundamental myth" in terms that reveal the qualities he considers most conducive to survival. Fundamental myth "being radical . . . becomes capable of being total" (175). Blumenberg's contexts make clear that this otherwise undefined "totality" is a positive version of what neo-Marxists intend negatively. A "total" myth attains a degree of comprehensiveness that makes it potentially acceptable as a theodicy. Here we find ourselves over the borders of the realm of belief, and it is questionable whether Blumenberg ever scrambles back again. The "total" myth aspires "to bring myth to an end" (the title of book 2, chapter 4) that is, to compel a belief that would destroy the credibility of its rivals. One wonders if Blumenberg's premises do not demand the conclusion that only "fundamental," totalizing myths could have survived the process of selection. But Blumenberg is so frankly interested only in this kind that he does not even bother to consider the question of the viability of myth that is less than "total." The bulk of *Work on Myth* examines historical Western reinterpretations of myth—Greek, Hebrew, Gnostic, Scholastic, Goethe's, Schelling's, Schopenhauer's, Nietzsche's, Freud's, Cassirer's, Heidegger's—each of which attempts to "bring myth to an end" by declaring its own absolute using up of previous "work on" it. While Blumenberg does, then, recognize myth as originating in generic storytelling, his notion of "work on" the stories that survive into historical times is so exalted that "myth" is transformed from tales told around the campfire or danced out during a village ritual into the ponderous system-building of ambitious philosophers. It would seem to follow, not quite that a new myth could not appear in historical times, but that within the brief time frame of Western culture such an appearance would be merely too incipient to merit attention. Blumenberg is well aware, for example, that Goethe's romantic contemporaries considered his Faust a new mythological character, but Blumenberg subsumes Faust easily under "work on" Promethean theodicy.

But Blumenberg is not nostalgic for total myth. This becomes clear when we turn to the second half of his descriptive definition; myths are stories that display "a high degree of constancy in their narrative core," but they are also stories that exhibit "an equally pronounced capacity for marginal variation." Blumenberg does not mean, as a student of oral literature would, that variation is a universal feature of such storytelling; he means, rather, that myth tends to generate alternative versions of itself in proportion to its pregnance. The freight a myth already carries provokes further "work on" it. A myth like that of Prometheus, so often employed "to bring myth to an end," stimulates a proportionate number of further attempts to co-opt it for the same purpose. Blumenberg pronounces the actual bringing of myth to an end to be as unattainable as its origin. If we are always on *this* side of our *terminus ab quo*, "the absolutism of reality," we are also always on *this* side of that *terminus ad quem*, "the supremacy of the subject." The endlessness of "work on" myth is guaranteed by the nature of the "work of" myth, the rationalizations that domesticate our *Angst.* "Myth has always already passed over into the process of reception, and it remains in that process no matter what violence is applied in order to break its bonds and to establish its final form" (270–271). In fact, violence of this sort is self-defeating: "work aimed at putting an end to myth is again and again accomplished in the form of a metaphor of myth" (629). As Blumenberg puts it in epigrammatic contrast to Schopenhauer's transcendent "Sabbath of willing," "work on myth knows no Sabbath" (633).

The tension between our desire to master our anxiety once and for all and our inability to do so appears historically as what Blumenberg calls "the antithesis of myth and dogma" (216). Whenever a particular version of "work on" myth succeeds in inducing widespread notional assent, it hardens into "dogma." One of the traditional signs of "dogma" is "prohibition of the making of images" (218), and Blumenberg finds this form of repression not only in the religions of the Book, Judaism, Christianity, and Islam, but also in modern "Utopias" of a wide variety, social and religious. On the contrary, "everything that dogma requires, myth exempts people from. It requires no decisions and no conversions, knows no apostates and no repentance. It permits identity even when it is deformed to the point of unrecognizability, indeed even in the effort to bring it to an end" (242). As Blumenberg rather strikingly points out (overlooking New Age popular culture in the United States), "there is no such thing as an 'adherent' of myth" (237). These antithetical terms for flexible hypothesis ("myth") and fixed conviction ("dogma") are Blumenberg's contribution to an aspect of the problematic of "myth" that has come into sharper focus in these two last chapters—namely, the issue of how to evaluate humanity's double-edged power to construct the fictions by which it lives. Granted that we wield this power—as transcendental, ideological, and constitutive theories all do—should the role of myth be regarded as benign or maleficent? Blumenberg leaves no doubt of where he stands, but his diacritical terms are part of a much wider pattern revisited at the end of this chapter.

Blumenberg's finest contribution to the construction of "myth" is his discovery of a relatively demystified rationale for the romantic claim of generic continuity over the course of human storytelling. His first step in this reclamation is to accept implicitly a folkloristic conception of myth as a kind of oral tale that enters history already "worked on" and marked by its twin urges toward constancy and variation. His second move is to explain these urges as the result of the "pregnance" for which this class of tales had been selected over long periods of prehistory. His third is to show in terms of Western intellectual and cultural history that "pregnance" creates a snowball effect; a society is inclined to "work on" what it finds already full of the significance of its *having been* worked on.

The ultimate value of this theory, however, may be that it points the way toward a demystification more stringent than what it achieves. The difficulty seems to lie in a potential aporia between Blumenberg's second step and his third. In the second he invokes the psychological concept of "pregnance," which involves the naturalizing of a psychological process alleged to transform affective response into cognitive. But in his third step Blumenberg demonstrates straightforwardly, on the strength of genuine historical evidence, that the more intensively a tale has been worked into the fabric of a culture, the more likely it is to be worked further. On this showing, "work on" myth in the modern West is a matter of nothing more mysterious than intertextual allusion inspired by the cultural prestige of the stories already most impressively entrenched.[8] Here is a commonsensical *social* explanation that renders otiose the elaboration of psychological machinery. Certain traditional stories strike us as peculiarly meaningful and moving for the good reason that we have been subliminally conditioned, if not actually trained, to experience them thus. Blumenberg teaches us that the romantic revaluation of myth is quintessentially ideological because it invents self-authorizing psychological and metaphysical mystifications that occlude this intertextual convention. Once we perceive it clearly again, it becomes a version of Occam's razor that cuts away not only the Lamarckian mechanisms produced by Freud and especially Jung in response to the concocted "depths" of romantic myth, but even Blumenberg's own "pregnance." As he himself implies in his previously mentioned criticism of Lévi-Strauss, "work on" myth in traditional cultures, had we the means to know, would probably turn out to have accumulated just as in our own. Blumenberg's demonstration of how this intertextuality defines "work on" myth in Western culture serves, whether intended or not, to support two propositions. The first, the folkloristic conception of myth (as defined by Walter Burkert), is that "myth is a traditional tale with secondary, partial reference to something of collective importance." The second is that invocations of such tales in modern texts, however resonant and thrilling, are cultural, if not downright literary allusions, and nothing more mysterious

HAZARD ADAMS'S CONSTRUCTION OF THE LITERARY SYMBOLIC

Whereas Paul Ricoeur attempts to outflank the French critique of transcendental values, Eric Gould to co-opt it, and Hans Blumenberg to rival it in silence, Hazard Adams defies it in the name of a romanticism confident in the possession of its own linguistic philosophy. In *The Philosophy of the Literary Symbolic,* Adams develops his theory by whetting it against the history of the romantic concept of "symbol." I have already cited this work repeatedly; both it and its near-contemporary, Tsvetan Todorov's *Theories of the Symbol,* have been important to me not only as our best historical studies of a concept closely related to "myth," but also as models of how to get at the history of such concepts.[9] In the present context, however, I focus upon the original theory of symbolism—and perforce, of myth—that Adams forges out of his confrontation with the concept's important historical moments.

He is in agreement with Todorov that any sound theory about the nature of the literary symbol must be a linguistic one and yet escape Saussurean positivism. But, unlike Todorov, he works self-consciously in the romantic tradition, which means taking for granted that such a theory must be expressive and must recognize that "the true model of language is trope" (Adams 1983, 5). He sees himself as articulating a theory, incipient in Vico, Herder, and von Humboldt, that language must be constitutive of reality. "A philosophy of literary symbolism . . . would seem to require a theory of the radically creative power of language" (20). "Otherwise," he goes on, in implicit agreement with Todorov, "it relaxes into a theory of universal allegory or signification, in other words a theory of rhetoric only" (20–21). Because his conception of the function of "symbol" is so broad, Adams prefers the German-style noun "symbolic," so that he will not be thought to be referring merely to "a literary symbol in the sense in which the term is used to signify a type of trope" (3). He builds on Vico's insights in reversing classical rhetoric by treating the major tropes as corollaries of "poetic logic" (necessary modes of expression rather like the Kantian categories), in insisting on the identity of the individual with its class in the "imaginative universal," and in promoting the notion of "fiction as a making" (10).

Adams's reading of Blake reinforces his reading of Vico, and vice versa. Because Blake believed that creativity originates in the particular and in an eternal present, he did not, Adams asserts, "intend us to imagine men, at that crucial moment of the invention of language, originally confronting inanimate sensible objects. Rather, he intended the poets by the constitutive power of language—namely metaphor—to have *created* those objects in the way a circumferential power gives life—by anthropomorphizing them" (105). The result of doing this appears to be what Adams means by "myth." Myth is the foundation and the formal expression of all cultural concepts and must therefore be virtually synonymous with the "symbolic" itself. It is what the activity of the symbolic mode produces. Myth, however, is locked in a permanent dialectical struggle with its contrary, "antimyth," which has somehow grown out of it. This latter is a term of equal importance for Adams, who employs it to signify the empiricist epistemology and the normative positivism of the Western scientific worldview to which Blake was opposed. (Adams thus derives from Blake the same conception of "antimyth" that Kolakowski found in Heidegger.) Adams describes it most usefully as "the fictive projection to an 'outside' of something language really retains in itself . . . followed by the fiction that the outside preceded its container" (26). In terms of Blake's own poetic allegorizing (which Adams would call "symbolic"), the power of mythmaking is personified as Los, the eternal re-creator of meaning, perpetually engaged in a struggle with his Spectre, who represents "language converted to 'allegory' or antimyth" (110). Adams identifies Los with "the prolific" of Blake's *Marriage of Heaven and Hell* and his Spectre with "the devourer," that is, the consumer of Los's cultural fictions. "The devourer," the true believer in the scientific worldview, "does not grasp that his antimyth is a created fictive form. He makes it surround and determine him as a fixed 'reality'" (112). As Adams says, this view of the situation makes it sound as if Los were in Hell, since he must always build up myths only to see them again devoured, "and it would be Hell if Los lived only in the externalized time that is antimyth to his myth. Instead, he lives in prolific work, where every moment is imaginatively created" (112). The human mind will always be busy constructing a significant world, in spite of the power of skepticism (its own modern creature) to cast doubt upon its constructions. Adams's dialectic is thus the optimistic contrary to the dark struggle between Enlightenment and myth advanced by Horkheimer and Adorno in *Dialectic of Enlightenment.*

Adams finds in Blake not only a vivid reinforcement of Vico's intuitions about constitutive language, but also a set of what might be called conceptual tools for the grounding of such a language. In adopting Blake's explicit distinction between "the prolific" and "the devourer" and his implicit distinction between "myth" and "antimyth," Adams accepts Blake's endless dialectic of contraries, which differs from Hegel's dialectic, as students of Blake often point out, in not allowing for any synthesizing sublation. Blake seems, rather, to envision the endless strife between contraries as the condition of "mental warfare" in the state of Eden itself. But Adams also adopts, or perhaps adapts, the curious Blakean distinction, found in *The Marriage of Heaven and Hell, Milton,* and *Jerusalem,* between "negations" and "contraries," which is a convenient way of having one's sublation and eating it, too. The distinction enables a thinker to deny that certain apparent contraries are true ones and so to imagine them united in a *tertium quid* that *is.* Adams defines a "negation" as "a situation in which . . . one side is privileged over the other, that is, one side negates the reality or authority of the other, attempting to suppress it" (7). He promptly adds that "this is, in Blake, definitely a historical notion," a remark that may help to clarify what Adams himself means when he singles out "three negations, the contraries of which I shall seek," for these three negations turn out to be "difference/indifference," "subject/object," and "symbol/allegory," all three obvious products of the confusion in romantic and postromantic literary theory that Adams aspires to straighten out. The *true* contraries of these contested "negations" are "secular symbolic" in the case of "symbol/allegory," and "identity" in the cases of "difference/indifference" and "subject/object." Adams's "identity" is difficult to grasp, but appears to signify the kind of unification of paradoxes attained in literary metaphor and named in Vico's identification of class with individual or in Northrop Frye's *archetypal* and/or *anagogic* phases of symbolism. What Adams means by "'secular' symbol" can best be understood from his schematic categorizing of "allegory" and "symbol" that follows hard upon his brilliant sorting out of these concepts among the relevant German and English romantics.

In the end he distinguishes four types of "allegory" and two of "symbol."[10] The first sort of allegory is the "Platonic," which locates reality or the universal in the Form or Idea, treats appearance as a "false copy," and can be represented by Socrates as "guardian angel." The second type, the Religious, locates reality in "truth, silence, nothing, noumena, God"; treats appearance as a veil; centers in theology rather than philosophy; and is represented in its more intellectual form by Thomas Aquinas and in its more mystical form by Hermes Trismegistus. The third sort, the Empirical, locates reality in "general principle, natural law"; treats appearance as "instance, phenomenon, secondary qualities of experience"; centers in science; and can be represented by Blake's Unholy Trinity, "Bacon, Newton, Locke." (This third kind isn't generally thought of as "allegory" except by Blake.) The romantics connected the fourth type, the Substitutive, with classical rhetoric, in which the trope of metaphor conceals beneath its appearance a reality behind or beyond the text. Adams distinguishes three kinds of such concealment: the "codal," in which the secret is deliberately encrypted; the "mythic," in which the code arises accidentally through euhemerizing; and the "oneiric," in which the code is read in terms of modern psychoanalysis. The three "guardian angels" are, respectively, the odd fellowship of Quintilian, Euhemerus, and Freud.

Adams asserts that romantic distinctions between "allegory" and "symbol" arose from determinations to distinguish what was intrinsically "poetic" from the "non-poetic" encroachments of religion, philosophy, and science alike. This position is a constitutive perspective on what is usually understood as expressivist aesthetics. In keeping with his special perspective, Adams distinguishes two types of romantic symbol. Each is distinct from "allegory" in containing mysteriously "in its very nature the being of the thing it stands for" (17), but the first, the "Miraculous," retains something of the theological provenance of the concept "symbol." It assumes that some kind of higher being (what Derrida would call "the transcendental signified") is embodied by "correspondence or ritual identity" (22) in the concrete particular that constitutes the symbol. The "Miraculous" symbol tends, consequently, "to slip back to become a form of 'religious' allegory, and its advocates are particularly subject to charges of self-mystification" (18) of the sort leveled, for example, by Marx, Benjamin, and de Man. The second type, the "Secular," however, assumes the power of the mind in the act of naming to be radically constitutive. Symbolic activity is generated entirely from within the creation of the particular, outward toward cultural reception. This latter type of symbolism is, of course, the constructive power of expression that Adams himself advocates.

Adams represents this "secular symbolic" as the true contrary of the fallacious "negation" created by the literary-historical quarrel between "allegory" and "symbol." Since the "secular symbolic" involves the constant construction of cultural "fictions," he also tracks through the profusion and confusion of romantic theory the closely related concepts of "the constitutive," "myth," and "fiction." He examines in Schlegel and Schelling, for example, the extent to which in their early work "immense claims are made for myth, and myth, symbolism and poetry seem to have been made identical" (66). This is not news in itself, but Adams does illuminate the sources of that tendency to identify an entire narrated "myth" with a single, constitutive "symbol" that characterizes his own position and has made it virtually impossible for anyone confronting "myth" in the transcendentalist tradition of discourse to avoid dealing with "symbol" as well. He similarly illuminates the scattered suggestions in Coleridge of the possibilities of a constitutive language at odds with his "miraculous" symbol, and he stresses the importance of Carlyle's

Sartor Resartus, likewise, in spite of *his* "miraculous" symbol, in suggesting that human culture is a generated symbolic world that undergoes continual aging and rejuvenation.

Adams's gradual extraction of his own theory from its entangled romantic origins exemplifies what he calls his "deliberate combination of historical treatment and polemic" (23). He extends throughout the rest of *The Philosophy of the Literary Symbolic* this method of testing the most significant claims for "the constitutive," "symbol," "myth," and "fiction" against the emerging "secular symbolic." Judged by this standard even the French *symbolistes* remain trapped like the rest of the nineteenth century, and its Freudian and Jungian psychological extensions into the twentieth, in the dominant positivistic dichotomies between poetic fancy and the "really real." Todorov, reconstructing this same history from a semiological orientation, finds no place to go beyond what he, too, agrees is the wasteland of psychology, except for a short hobble on the weak crutch of Saussure. But Adams finds a whole new lease on life for his constitutive theory of language in the successive appearance of the theories of Croce, Cassirer, the later Yeats, and Frye.

Benedetto Croce is important to Adams not only for his crucial reinterpretation of Vico for the twentieth century, but for basing "his whole aesthetic on this Vichean idea . . . that language and poetry are substantially the same thing" (178).[11] Furthermore, Croce adumbrates Ernst Cassirer's *Philosophy of Symbolic Forms,* the next important step forward on the way to an adequate theory of the secular symbol. Cassirer both recognizes the linguistic basis of symbolizing and aspires to delineate the principal forms this fiction-making power has actually assumed in human culture. But Adams expresses his own version of the familiar reservation about Cassirer's ambiguously Comtean metahistory: "the language's progressive development is strictly toward conceptual abstraction" (216). And when Cassirer introduces art as one of his symbolic forms in his *Essay on Man* he leaves a gap between language and art that would require a theory of poetic language to close it. "We sense that the characteristics of myth [in *Mythical Thought*] . . . are analogous to the characteristics of that poetic language to be described in order to complete Cassirer's theory as a theory of literary symbolic . . . it is in this undeveloped analogy that Cassirer's main contribution to literary theory lies" (220). Adams find not advance but backsliding in Susanne Langer's *Philosophy in a New Key* and *Feeling and Form.* "Fundamentally," he pronounces in a now-familiar refrain, "her problem . . . is that her lurking positivistic conception of language insists on pure abstraction as the linguistic model and cannot firmly regard language as in any way *creating* or *containing* the image" (225). In the end Langer fails because she never arrives at the theory of fictions that her analysis seems to require.[12]

Not surprisingly, Adams finds in Northrop Frye the next step past Cassirer in the elaboration of a theory of fictive cultural forms. He interrogates *Anatomy of Criticism* in search of a concept of language as identical with poetry, tautegorical, and creative of symbolic fictions; hence he is interested in showing that Frye's theory of symbols requires that the Blakean circumference of the "anagogic phase" encompass all literary acts, and that Frye's non-psychological "displacement" is always inward, "so that the center of literature is not in some absolute nothingness, ideal silence or mystical beyond . . . [but] . . . in the unique form of each creative literary act" (275). The "sliding scale of kinds of symbolism" (279) that is thus enabled provides the solution for rescuing "allegory" from its romantic denigration. Frye's theory of symbol, he concludes, ought, in spite of Frye's unsatisfactory lapses into theories of imitation, "to require the identity of imagination with linguistic form." It fails to do so because Frye's conception of language is not rigorous or radical enough, vacillating, in Adams's terms, between the mythical and antimythical, constructivism and positivism.

Frye is also very important to Adams as a theorist of fictive cultural forms. "In the conclusion of the *Anatomy,*" he says, "Frye raises questions that verge on a total theory of mythology, a word which in Frye begins to look much like Cassirer's term 'symbolic form'" (276). Though Frye is sometimes too much captured by Cassirer's version of the Comtean metahistorical sequence, his view of the function of myth is essentially "not historical, but dialectical. Myth endlessly provides the forms of culture. . . . Myth, then, is artistic process" (277). These remarks, apart from the issue of their applicability to Frye, display the probable source of Adams's own immensely broad identification of "myth" with the construction of all cultural fictions.

The note of intellectual autobiography is palpable in Adams's siftings of Blake and Frye, but especially apparent in his introduction at this point of the later Yeats, the last of his exemplars. Adams finds in Yeats, particularly in *A Vision,* a twentieth-century corroboration of his Blakean logic of negations and contraries He brilliantly presents *A Vision* as an "anatomy" in Frye's sense, comparable to Carlyle's *Sartor* or to Frye's own *Anatomy* in its necessarily antithetical, ironic elaboration of antimythical myth. "'Antithetical,'" Adams observes, "is an ironic term implying the embattled position of anyone opposing the dominating cultural force" (293). The form of *A Vision,* therefore, supplies a concrete instance of Adams's Blakean conception of "identity" as the "contrary" of the "negations" subject/object and difference/indifference. "The form with which Yeats is concerned is in Yeats' mind 'antinomial' in the very same way that any metaphor is an identity creatively antithetical to difference/indifference. The poet's resolution of the antinomy is to maintain contrariety as the encompassing design of experience itself" (321).[13] Adams quotes Yeats as noting that "philosophers have tried to deny the antinomy and give a complete account of existence either as a unity (as in the case of Spinoza or Hegel) or as a plurality (as in the case of Leibniz) but the antinomy is there and can be represented only by a myth." "Myth, then," according to Adams, "is not a rudimentary form that is surpassed by reflection, but for Yeats the fundamental form of thought, 'antithetical' to its 'devouring' outgrowths" (321).

At this point Adams enters his "Conclusions," in which he constructs his own theory more directly. Even this last section, however, is highly dialectical since Adams proceeds, as he says, "to distinguish a philosophy of the literary symbolic from a variety of structuralist, phenomenological and poststructuralist positions" (325). On one hand, he resembles the phenomenologists in conceiving of language as poetically creative, yet he differs from them in assuming that language is radically constitutive rather than merely hermeneutic. On the other hand, he resembles

E. D. Hirsch, the symbolic logicians, and the structuralists in maintaining that there is no split between poetic language and some other kind. But he differs from them in believing in a "linguistic continuum" that proceeds outward from a mythic core toward the perimeter of the most abstract mathematics and then circles back again—a conception of language as continually regenerated by radical creation. He can therefore criticize Lévi-Strauss, Derrida, and de Man, in spite of the great differences among them, on the same broad grounds that their theories of language are crippled by Saussurean positivism. De Man's "model of language," for example, "is that of symbolic logic" (360), which is why he sees all figurality as deceit, responsible for "epistemological damage." Unlike an outright structuralist like Lévi-Strauss, Derrida and de Man stem in some respects from existential phenomenology, but Adams finds their versions of it far removed from the actual theories of symbolic language in Heidegger, Jaspers, Gadamer, and Ricoeur. Adams sees in this latter group valorizations of the poetic that resemble his own and that would open the way to a secular symbolic if they were not fatally and fundamentally commingled instead with the first, "miraculous" type of symbol. Adams pays Ricoeur, in particular, the compliment of an extended analysis because of the shift in his work that I have discussed above, before concluding that "a theory of literature does not need Ricoeur's symbol. It needs only his metaphor. The 'miraculous' symbol belongs to the antimythical realm of the theological" (387).

The most important elaboration of Adams's theory in this last chapter of polemical differentiation is what he formulates as "The Cyclical Fiction of Cultural Forms" (338). This is a sketch of the circulation of cultural forms produced by the dialectic of myth and antimyth. As the culmination of Adams's theory, it points up dramatically the centrality of his conception of "myth." "The condition of pure myth," he says, "would be the successful taking of everything into one's own imagination" (336). The qualifying adjective "pure" suggests, however, that what we normally call myth is a departure from this apocalyptic state, which results from the admixture of some degree of the pull toward antimyth. "We can declare that the intellectual life feeds on myth . . . and that the proper organization of the liberal arts and sciences is vertical, the fine arts and literature at the foundation, the pure sciences at the top, with the various humanistic disciplines and social sciences in between. Except, of course, that there is always a flow back, with antimyth at the top returning, often as a potentiality for myth" (336). Adams's metaphor in the second sentence is the same employed by Blake and Schlegel in comparable contexts, the falling back into its own cistern of water jetting up from a fountain. The return occurs, of course, because "the antimyth of externality is in the end something that the philosophy of science must recognize as the structure of scientific fictions" (333). Myth in this grand design is apparently synonymous with the "secular symbolic" itself, constitutive of all cultural forms. Adams's theory is thus far the most systematic and detailed account available among those thinkers who view myth as the permanent fiction-making aspect of human thought.

DIACRITICAL SHIFTS IN THE DIALECTIC OF MYTH AND ANTIMYTH

Before we leave Adams, it would pay to consider a difficulty in his "dialectic of myth and antimyth" that thematizes a terminological problem increasingly prominent in the last two chapters. Adams points out that his dialectic, like those of Blake and Yeats, "does not provide for Hegelian synthesis, but for the constantly renewed conflict of Heraclitus" (329). The comparison to Heraclitus suggests that Adams envisions a single dialectic underlying permanently the entire construction of culture. Yet in most contexts, when he refers to "antimyth" he means the materialist and positivist worldview of modern science. To the extent that this is the case, he is primarily concerned, not with a permanent dialectic in human thinking, but with the same historically contextualized struggle that gave rise in the first place to the modern construction of "myth." Adams argues from his symbolic-constructivist point of view that the building up of meaning in myth must logically precede its critique by antimyth. From the perspective of intellectual history, however, this sequence is reversed; antimyth precedes myth; the modern invention of "myth" is a *reaction* to the development of the scientific worldview. From this angle, Adams's myth and antimyth (approximately, "imagination" and "science") appear, not as true contraries, but merely as historically contextualized negations, like the pairs symbol/allegory and subject/object. The reader who recalls that Adams wants to identify myth with the "secular symbolic" itself might be inclined to object that my historical relocation deconstructs his system by rendering its priorities arbitrary—by denying his negation, as he would put it, any genuine contrary. But Adams's "secular symbolic" may still be understood as the true contrary of the historical negation myth/antimyth. The only impediment to doing so is Adams's conflation of a *perennial* grapple between belief and skepticism with the peculiarly *modern* dialectic of myth (imagination) and antimyth (science) first identified by Hegel in the *Phenomenology* as "the struggle between Enlightenment and superstition." This impediment is, in short, a *semantic* problem, occasioned by Adams's employment of the highly contested and historically compromised word "myth" to signify "whatever humankind has constructed to believe in." Nor is Adams alone in his entrapment in "the dialectic . . . of myth and antimyth" (329). He enjoys the company of nearly all the theorists discussed in the preceding chapter and in this one. As we've had abundant occasion to notice, the inquisitors of myth considered in the previous chapter share with its would-be redeemers of this chapter a persuasion that "myth" is the socially significant product of humanity's irrepressible urge to construct meanings. The two parties are at odds only in their moral assessment of this product.

Suppose, however, we try the thought-experiment of prescinding for a moment from the terms of "myth" and "ideology" in which this quarrel has largely been cast, and asking afresh what assumptions join the parties to it. Perhaps these can be fairly described as an implicit agreement that there are conditions under which that immense fiction-making power of the mind foregrounded by romanticism may be a good thing and conditions under which it may not. This faculty is of supreme value while its wielders retain a healthy sense of tentativeness about all its projections, but becomes correspondingly vicious when it inculcates or reinforces rigid orthodoxies. All parties agree, then, on the inevitability (if not the desirability) of large-scale social beliefs, and all acknowledge that the danger of these is mindless conformity. Consistent with such assumptions, most "ideological" and "constructive" theorists of "myth" develop a set of antithetical terms to distinguish between myth's positive and negative potential. But where the esteemers of "myth" tend to employ this term to designate the positive pole of speculative tentativeness, the denigrators tend to reserve it for the negative pole of rigid belief. A brief reprise may help to clarify the point.

Adams's fellow constitutive theorists resemble him in their distinctions between the rigidity of what he calls "antimyth" and the constant inventiveness of "myth." Gould, though he does not pay much attention to the contrary of his myth-as-fiction, does declare "myth" to be "discourse resisting mere ideology" (256), so the latter may fairly be considered his choice as *bête noir*. Kolakowski presents us with *two* contraries to myth as value. The first of these is "anti-myth," employed almost exactly as it is by Adams to designate empiricism and positivism. The second is not named, except as "myth's" own "natural tendency to turn into a narcotic," but both the allusion to Marx and the context refer us unmistakably to political ideology. When we turn, however, to other constitutive valorizers of myth who derive from the phenomenological tradition, such as Ricoeur and Blumenberg, we discover an interesting difference. While they, too, situate myth at the positive pole of subversive tentativeness, they are inclined to select a different set of terms for the negative pole of rigid belief. Ricoeur, for instance, sees the contrary of his fluid "myth-as-narrative-of-symbol" in the hardening of "symbol" into religious "idolatry." Blumenberg unequivocally establishes "myth" at the subversive pole of cultural creation and calls its constricted counterpart "dogma." This difference in terminology suggests that theorists who think of myth primarily as religious orientation will incline to contraries that express ossification particularly in that sphere. Both groups of constitutive theorists are in essential agreement, however, and it may help in understanding why to recall that Adams (who is especially sympathetic with phenomenology) intends his concept of "antimyth" to cover religious as well as scientific dogmatism.[14]

As opposed to the esteemers of "myth," its denigrators tend to use this term to designate the pole of rigid belief and to reserve some contrary one for the pole of fluid hypothesis. When Walter Benjamin celebrates the subversive power of the fairytale by claiming that it "tells us of the earliest arrangements that mankind made to shake off the nightmare which the myth had placed upon its chest," he does not explain what he means by "myth" (Benjamin 1969, 102). The context suggests, however, that it is the weight of immemorial custom, represented ideologically as fate or destiny. Frank Kermode's *Sense of an Ending* offers a particularly interesting instance among the contemners of myth because Kermode is a constitutive theorist who valorizes "fiction" like Gould and Adams. But instead of virtually identifying "myth" with "fiction" as they do, he memorably makes it his term of opprobrium: "if we forget that fictions are fictive we regress to myth" (Kermode 1967, 41). To put this departure in perspective we need only recall that Kermode's conception of fictions, as Ricoeur recognized, is particularly close to the pure Nietzschean paradox, our equal need to make and to break. Hence his identification of "fiction" with the volatile transience of imaginary figments but "myth" with the would-be permanence of ritual repetition.

It is not so easy to bring into this conspectus the denigrators discussed in the previous chapter who do not, in their actual assaults upon myth, offer any contrary term. Barthes and Derrida are the obvious instances. Derrida, does imply, of course, in "White Mythology" as in his *oeuvre* in general, the ineluctable fictivity of all "writing," and Adams is doubtless right to associate his position with Kermode's. Barthes's purely "antithetical" stance suggests that Adams may be correct, too, in asserting that any theory based upon Saussurean linguistics must lack the resources to deal affirmatively with cultural fictivity, let alone myth. The apparent exception of Lévi-Strauss may prove the rule. He presents, to be sure, a theory in which "myth" reigns at the positive pole while "fiction" is relegated to the negative. But the poles themselves do not signify as they do in the rest of the conspectus; indeed, their values are reversed, since positive myth is now a species of rigid scientific classification while fictions are banished into "negative" exile because of their obscuring redundancies and velleities.

The critiques of Cassirer and Horkheimer and Adorno, while they may seem as unsympathetic to "positive" myth as those based upon structural linguistics, in fact stem from Hegel, and participate, however inexplicitly, in his conception of the dialectical "struggle between Enlightenment and superstition." Cassirer presents the anomalous case of a thinker who holds distinguished briefs for both sides. But he maintains these two sides only successively, so that he never presents them *as* a diacritical pairing. Weighing his early conception of "myth" against his later, we might say that he locates "myth" at different times at each pole, signifying at the positive "a mode of symbolic form" and at the negative "an atavistic mode of propaganda." These two unreconciled versions comprise with a vengeance what Adams calls a "negation." While Cassirer can be said to have expressed only diachronically the recognition of Hegel's "struggle," Horkheimer and Adorno present a highly self-conscious intensification of the original. This is summed up in their paradoxical epigram "myth is already enlightenment; and enlightenment reverts to myth." Given their dedication to the "critical thinking" that they identify with "enlightenment," this latter term should surely be stationed at the positive pole, perhaps with a parenthetical "myth" behind it, while the obverse might be done at the other pole. Thus: subversive tentativeness = enlightenment (reverts to myth), < > myth (already enlightenment) = rigid belief. This truly dialectical conception of the relation of the two concepts offers a formulation of a permanent conflict more illuminating than Adams's. At the same time it is grounded more concretely and accurately than any of the other versions considered here in the context of the history that instigates the modern construction of "myth" in the first place.

At the end of the previous chapter I suggested that the rise of "ideology" might be thought of not only as a dialogical but as a "diacritical" development in relation to myth. As significations, according to Saussure, are determined by unmotivated differentiations of phonemes, so "myth" seems to summon forth as an essential condition of its signifying meaningfully the negative differentiator "ideology." And when we come in the present chapter to view the "myth"/"ideology" differentiation itself within the context of the still broader split between tentative hypothesis and dogmatic orthodoxy, we see a comparable "diacritical" elaboration at work on the scale of an incipient theory of fictions. This analogy to linguistics must not be pressed too far, if only because the terms levied to make the antithetical discriminations are anything but unmotivated; they make their entrances, not as arbitrary phonemes, but as emotionally loaded battle cries. The analogy will have served its purpose, however, if it conveys something of the internally generated, family-quarrel intimacy of the semantic struggle, at least as old as Plato, to locate "myth" in relation to "ideology" and to "necessary fiction."

CONCLUDING SUPPLEMENTAL POSTSCRIPT

My heading *is* intended to invoke both Kierkegaard and Derrida; it expresses my sense that this history has no proper conclusion. The reader is now in a position to see what I meant in the introduction by describing this account of where we have got in the construction of "myth" and of how we got there as a series of compromises among three orienting elements—diachronic, taxonomic, and axiological. It hardly seems necessary to say more about the first of these, except to observe that the temporal sequence flows noticeably less smoothly in the latter two-thirds of the narrative. This is a tribute to the surprising scope of myth's vogue in a few decades of the twentieth century, after a relatively gradual two-century rise to prominence. In proportion as the consequent crowding becomes an expository problem, my taxonomic and axiological elements, working in tandem, haul more of the load. The taxonomic categories begin with the given of myth's romantic inventors—that it is a species of narrative whose meaning exceeds rational understanding, conveying transcendent, universal significance directly to individual intuition. Each of the major reconceptions of myth—the ideological, the folkloristic, and the constitutive—stems from this romantic base, and appears roughly within a generation of the others (between Marx and Nietzsche) almost as soon as the romantic version itself is widely assimilated. The taxonomical and chronological pattern might be visualized diagrammatically by imagining an old, climbable beech tree whose branches start close to the ground. The first of these, the ideological, juts out to the viewer's left, nearly as thick as the main trunk, while the second, the folkloristic, takes off to the right only a few feet higher, in balancing massiveness, while the third, the constitutive, departs slightly higher again, at the back of the tree but noticeably less stout. To represent the delay before each of the three limbs flourishes in the twentieth century, one could perhaps visualize each branch presenting massed foliage only far above the ground. But the same must then be done for the romantic trunk itself, which breaks into new profusion high in its long climb.

The classificatory razor that trims my fundamental categories to these particular four is the usual rule of evolutionary taxonomy referred to in the introduction. The reader may judge that I have applied the rule too strictly in treating merely as avatars of the romantic a number of major twentieth century developments—the concepts of "myth" in depth psychology, religious phenomenology, and symbolic form, for example—or that I have not applied it strictly enough in docketing the theorists in this last chapter as constitutive. The reader may also opine that I have not sufficiently justified classifying the "folkloristic" concept of myth as an offshoot of the "romantic." Since my reasons for doing so are scattered among discussions of Grimm in chapter 3, Tylor in chapter 4, and Boas in chapter 9, it may be worth consolidating them briefly here. They amount to a persuasion that the term "myth," with all its infirmities on its head, would never have been imported into folklore and from thence into social anthropology to designate the important stories of traditional societies if the thinking of Tylor and his colleagues on this topic had not been shaped by Max Müller and the romantic folklorists, led by Jacob Grimm. My wish to stress this derivation and its consequences may lead me to understate the Enlightenment strain in folkloristic myth. Perhaps, to revert to the tree analogy, it might be more accurate to describe the folkloristic branch as owing its distinctive appearance to its having been grafted on to the romantic stock. In any case, I can offer here only one brief apology for these or other taxonomic decisions felt to be unsatisfactory. This is the plea, all the more serious for being whimsical, that the "the's" of this world do not like to be classified; they do everything possible to camouflage themselves, elude the net, wriggle off the pin.

My goal has been as much evaluative as historical and descriptive. This axiological element obviously works on two levels—in the assessment of individual theorists and theories, which is methodical and explicit, and in the assessment of the four fundamental categories, which is for the most part more occasional and tentative. On the individual level, I have done my best to describe each theory as fairly as possible. In practice, of course, this utopian goal is undermined as always both by obtuseness and by the impossibility of banishing all judgments of value from perception and description.

But this seems the opportune moment for combining a reprise of the four fundamental types with a more direct acknowledgment of my own opinions about them. My general view of the modern construction of "myth" somewhat resembles Marcel Detienne's when he contemplates its reflection in the funhouse mirror of the ancient Greeks' attempt to capture myth's elusive quiddity. As Plato hypostatized *"mythos"* out of his ambivalent responses to the power of traditional story, several eighteenth- and nineteenth-century generations evolved out of "fable" a narrative genre gleaming with the conveyance of perennial truth. They did this, moreover, largely by projecting "myth" as both a genre of story and a condition of religious rapport possessed in perfection by "the Greeks." Detienne's satirical reduction of this particular fantasy, his "two-headed Greeks," might serve here as the emblem, not merely of romantic Hellenism, but of all constructions of myth as the other of modern Western experience.

The further romantic persuasion that the vehicle of this transcendental rapport is available in the modern world nestles damagingly near the heart of the entire modern construction of the concept. The three fundamental categories that depart from romantic myth are articulated by their radical divigations from this transcendentalism, but none breaks free unscathed. Marx and Engels do achieve a breakthrough of lasting value in constructing the romantic mystification as ideological. As Paul Ricoeur has perceived so clearly, the major modes of the "hermeneutics of suspicion" remain our bulwark, not against religion per se, but against the rigidities of all forms of idolatry. At the same time, however, myth as ideology is limited by its purely antithetical status; it is locked in endless dialectical struggle with its mortal enemy. As proposed in this last chapter, the neutralizing of ideology in the later twentieth century is accompanied by the rise of its specular twin, the constitutive conception of myth. I imagine that my personal attraction to this fourth version is quite transparent. I not only believe there is much to be said for the assumption that all cultural judgments of value are "necessary fictions," but also that "myth," given its history, is a particularly appropriate term to designate this kind of judgment. Yet this constitutive version of the term also exhibits a weakness. While it does appear to *promise* a deployment of "myth" free of its romantic attribution of transcendence, an examination of even its most likely claimants suggests that they are still, in their various ways, sufficiently haunted by the traditional ghosts that they, too, provoke "ideological" critique. Perhaps Plato gets as near the essence of this problematic as anyone ever has when Socrates establishes in *The Republic* not only that the ideal state must be built on necessary fictions but that its fictive status had better be concealed from all but its grievously burdened governors. It is the perennial freshness of this antinomy that renders an account of the semantic family quarrels between and among the advocates of the ideological and constitutive an appropriate halting place for this investigation.

Finally, I view the rise of the folkloristic conception of "myth" as the best thing that has yet befallen the concept during its modern career. This is not because it uniquely escapes ideological projection, but because it is soundly (if ironically) built upon one of the most fundamental of romantic assumptions—that all serious storytelling harbors a valuable record of the world of its practitioners. The relevant corollary—that nothing can inform us about the nature of myth like the practice of traditional storytellers—has enabled the investigation of folkloristic myth to survive its religious definition by romantic folklorists, the limitations of its collectors, its nineteenth-century armchair analysis by theorists of "primitive" religion, its manipulations by various neo-romantic theorists, and the biases of its anthropological interpreters themselves. Yet even this admirably stubborn premise is not to be trusted uncritically if it is based upon the initial fallacy of presuming "myth" to be, not Detienne's "fish emulsified in the waters" of Western mythographical projection, but an observable quiddity as "real" as song or narrative. It may be that current anthropological withdrawal from the latter position will disperse Detienne's apparitional fish ("ay, very like a whale") in the waters that gave rise to it.

Such are my principal axiological commitments, ideological themselves, of course, at least in Habermas's sense of being inevitably "interested." Though I have wanted to be straightforward about these conclusions, I have no wish to proselytize for them any further. All four of the fundamental categories of "myth" are still very much alive in contemporary usage. I find an image of the urge to reform such complex intellectual disagreements in a *New Yorker* cartoon that presents a crowd of commuters rushing for the open doors (in the background) of an uptown "D" train. In the center of the drawing, in the middle of the crowd, which splits to pour around him, stands a man with his back to the doors, facing the oncoming surge (and the viewer), right index finger raised in the air as he cheerfully, if a bit mechanically, intones, "You're all getting on the wrong train!" No glazed commuter is paying the slightest attention. It seems enough to observe the trains, their times, their routes, their passengers, without rushing onto the platform for any dramatic admonitions.

NOTES

1. FROM FABLE TO MYTH

1. For an account of these reservations, see Detienne 1986, chapters 3–5. For relevant discussion in the text, see especially chapter 11.

2. The word "mythology" also shifts during these years. It preserves something of its former meaning as a science of allegorical interpretation in now signifying "the systematic study of myth," but it also acquires a new meaning that focuses entirely on the object; "a collection of related myths." The word is still used in both these senses, often so ambiguously that it hovers between mythology as subject and mythology as object.

3. For a more extensive treatment of this topic, see Engell, 245–271, and specifically 248–253. In this first chapter I am indebted at several points to this succinct yet richly detailed survey.

4. The brief sketch of hostile theories that follows owes a good deal to Manuel 1959 and Feldman and Richardson 1972.

5. For the work's lack of reputation in the eighteenth century, which is still often underestimated, see especially the "Reputation" section of Max Fisch's introduction to *The Autobiography of Giambattista Vico* (Vico 1975).

6. For Vico's intellectual heroes and his sense of his relation to them, see Vico 1975, 137–139, 154–155.

7. Since this edition follows the numbered paragraphing of the text of Fausto Nicolini's standard edition of Vico's works, I have adopted the customary practice of Vico scholarship in citing passages by paragraph rather than page number. It should also be pointed out that Vico radically revised *The New Science* in 1730 and issued a third, definitive edition in 1744. This latter is the text followed by modern editors.

8. "Gentile" because Vico, whether out of policy or piety, follows, as Fontenelle does, the practice of exempting from his speculations the sacred history of the Hebrew people, incontrovertibly true since inspired by God.

9. Although Vico himself unmistakably insists on the centrality of book 2, it has been the last part of the work to be studied seriously. Only during the past twenty years or so has the Vico of "Poetic Wisdom" and of the history of tropes come into clear view. See especially Adams 1983, 7–12; White 1987, 197–217; Verene 1981, chapter 3; and Mali 1992, passim, but especially chapter 3.

10. This last phrase is sometimes translated by Bergin and Fisch as "imaginative class concepts," a phrase I will use instead of "imaginative universals" when it comes up with reference to formal logic.

11. The characterization of the growth of Roman law as "a serious poem" occurs in the title to book 4, section 14, chapter 2, page (not paragraph) 386.

12. Hegel pioneers the confrontation of this problematic in his conception of the "concrete universal." This phrase would be the best name for what Vico and the romantics were after if

it could be detached from its context in the Hegelian idealism, according to which the most abstract is also, paradoxically, the most concrete.

13. Vico's name for the repetition of the pattern is *ricorso,* balancing the *corso* (as in the title of book 4, "The Course the Nations Run"). Bergin and Fisch understandably render *ricorso* as "recourse," but this works in English only if one bears in mind that it is meant here in the sense of a "rerunning" or "recurrence."

14. For an eloquent (but I think mistaken) argument that Vico did unequivocally believe that myth could be "rehabilitated" in the modern world see Mali 1992, especially chapter 3.

15. Compare James Engell's observation that "the rise of modern mythology and the rise of systematic literary history go hand in hand" (Engell 1981, 255).

16. Burton Feldman points out (Feldman and Richardson, 145) that as early as 1704 John Dennis not only promotes the concept of "the sublime" but even asserts religion as the foundation of the most exalted verse and offers as examples the prophets, Job, and The Song of Songs, along with the modern example of *Paradise Lost.*

17. William Collins's "Ode on the Popular Superstitions of the Highlands of Scotland," for example, already lays down in 1749 an uncanny agenda for the production of an "Ossian."

18. For a brilliant account of how close Gray comes, however, to dealing with "the transcendental basis of all experience" (48), see Marshall Brown 1991, 42–48.

19. The concept has a rich romantic history that Eliot took care to suppress; his most obvious source is Wordsworth's "Preface" to *Lyrical Ballads.* For Schiller's essay, see Schiller 1962a, 694–780.

20. I follow Schiller's revised version of 1800, which is shorter but more pointed. The two are printed successively in Schiller 1962b, 163–173.

21. There is a body of older comment on Wordsworth's knowledge of German literature in general and of his echoes of "Die Götter Grieschenlands" in particular. See Bush 1936, 61, n.17.

2. THE INVENTION OF MYTH

1. Blake would object to his narratives being termed either "fable" or "allegory"; in his own terminology they are "Visions" (see Blake 1965, 544). He objects to both of the old terms because he connects them with their traditional significations—respectively, idle tale and moralized interpretation. His choice of "Vision" is closely related to the use of the word among a number of his contemporary English romantics. In sticking to "allegory" and "fable," I express a deflationary view of this article of romantic ideology, which is discussed later in the chapter.

2. Dating these poems is a complicated business. Basically, Blake worked on *The Four Zoas* from about 1795 to about 1807, on *Milton* from 1804 to about 1810, and on *Jerusalem* from 1804 to about 1820. For the relevant textual notes see Blake 1965, 727–728, 730, 737–738.

3. I am indebted to Harold Bloom's commentary on this passage (Blake 1965, 865).

4. Lacoue-Labarthe and Nancy 1988 identify "Ludovico" as Schelling and the other participants as the Schlegel brothers, Tieck, Novalis, Caroline Michäelis, and Dorothea Mendelssohn-Veit. There is a long tradition of dispute about whom some of the pseudonymous characters are intended to represent. Some are surely composites, but the internal evidence for Ludovico as Schelling is very strong.

5. For an excellent study of the vogue of this idea during the romantic period, see Thorslev 1984.

6. This fragment, first published in 1917, is preserved in Hegel's handwriting, but was first attributed to Schelling, then partly to Hölderlin, and has been more recently claimed for Hegel. The disagreement dramatizes the extent to which this trio of schoolmates, like the Jena group a little later, collaborated during their earlier years in working out a number of the crucial concepts of the romantic ideology. For the quoted passage see Hölderlin 1988, 155–156. The editor, Thomas Pfau, summarizes very succinctly the principal claims about the authorship of the text, 182.

7. The Jena lectures were published posthumously as *The Philosophy of Art* but were widely known in their original form. For Schlegel's recommendation, see Todorov, 1982. The quotation of Todorov that follows is from this same page. My discussion of "symbol" and "allegory" in relation to "myth" owes much both to Todorov, 147–221, and to Adams, 29–45 and 46–98.

8. Kant identifies the other mode of the intuitive as the schematic. In the Jena lectures Schelling actually makes, accordingly, a three-term distinction among "schematic," "allegorical," and "symbolic," but the concept of the "schematic" need not detain us in pursuing the connection of these terms to "myth." It is well discussed by Todorov, 207–209, and Adams, 66.

9. Beach (261, n.38) demonstrates that the customary claim for Schelling's priority in using the term is mistaken. He also points out, however, that Schelling believed himself to be employing it differently than Coleridge, indeed in K. P. Moritz's original sense.

10. For further definition, see Adams 1983, 12–23. The Coleridge definition I proceed to cite is excellently discussed in this same text, 70–82.

11. Schelling pays tribute to K. P. Moritz in this same section for first recognizing in his *Götterlehre* the "poetical absoluteness" (49) of mythology, that is to say, its "symbolic" character. Moritz himself did not have the word, though he revealingly contrasts the "allegorical" with the "mythological."

12. Cited by Hayner 1967, 87.

13. For Boehme's effect upon Schelling and the general course of Schelling's later development see Copleston 1965, 158–182; Feldman and Richardson, 315–319; Robert F. Brown 1977, 251–261; Marshall Brown 1979, 129–179; and Beach, 65–91.

14. Lovejoy cites the source as *Denkmal der Schrift von der göttlichen Dingen*. In his influential discussion of Schelling, Lovejoy maintains that his primary importance in the history of philosophy is his inauguration of modern process theologies. See 317–326, especially 325.

15. For this and the two following passages from Schelling's *Einleitung* to *Die Philosophie der Mythologie,* I adopt Burton Feldman's translation (Feldman and Richardson 1972, 325–327).

16. This reading of Schlegel has been affected by Paul de Man's discussion of Schlegel's irony in "The Rhetoric of Temporality," discussed below. But he makes the mercurial and sanguine Schlegel sound like the most depressed of Left Bank absinthe-drinkers. For an excellent corrective, by which I have also been influenced, see Peter Thorslev's connection of Schlegel's irony with the dialectics of organicism (Thorslev 159) and Marshall Brown's connection of it with utopian optimism (Brown 1979, 100). Brown refutes specifically de Man's claim that Schlegel denies reconciliation between the ideal and the real.

17. For further passages see Benjamin 1971, 159–182.

18. For a good discussion of relations between "allegory" and "irony," see Marshall Brown 1979, 99–104.

19. I have been particularly influenced in making these distinctions by two representatives of the trend to examine romantic ideology from the outside rather than to accept it entirely on its own terms. The first is Rajan 1980 and the second is McGann 1983. Rajan, from what might be called broadly an existentialist perspective, distinguishes three phases of romanticism—sublimation, self-consuming artifacts, and Apollonian-Dionysiac struggle. McGann, from what might be labeled a socialist perspective, also distinguishes three—primary vision, self-criticism, and nihilism. My categories parallel McGann's, of which the second and third correspond approximately to Rajan's first two.

20. For an influential older statement of this view, see Bush 1936, 56–61.

21. For a more positive reading of the poem, see Bloom 1959, 65–90. He holds that the speaker recovers in the fifth stanza the "I-Thou" relation with the Spirit that he loses in the fourth.

3. THE STRUGGLE BETWEEN MYTH
AND "SUSPICION"

1. Baillie, the translator of the text I have used, has often been criticized for rendering *Geist* as "Mind"; I call it "Spirit," as in the title itself.

2. For a good demonstration of the centrality of these assumptions to the *Phenomenology*, see Abrams 1971, 225–237.

3. The charge that Hegel produced an "abstract and sentimental" scheme that encouraged later readers of the romantics to take the wish for the deed is argued eloquently in McGann 1983. The quoted phrase is from page 47.

4. Hegel, to be sure, denies that the Absolute is "abstract" in the ordinary sense of the word; he holds that it subsumes the particulars directly within the concept; this is what he means by his "concrete universal."

5. This very brief account of Hegel's impact upon the construction of "myth" may help to suggest why his philosophy has seemed so susceptible to radical and conservative political reading alike. It was D. F. Strauss, describing the situation in theology, who first applied the Revolutionary designations to him by speaking of Left and Right Hegelians. For an excellent account of how and why so much of the action on the Hegelian Left was in theology, see Massey 1983.

6. The letter is quoted in full in Horton Harris 1973, 59–63.

7. I have profited especially here from Frei 1974, especially chapters 12 and 13.

8. Harris cites and discusses this passage, 55.

9. This particular error in logic is rather bizarrely repeated a century later in the "demythologizing" of Rudolph Bultmann, who compounds the mistake of supposing his own thinking free of *vorstellungen* by equating it with the metaphysics of early Heidegger, which he supposes to be similarly free and therefore the perfect expression of scientific materialism!

10. According to Eugene Kamenka in *The Philosophy of Ludwig Feuerbach*, 167 n., this modern sense of the English "projection" actually originates in Marian Evans's translation. She employs it for Hegelian terms that might be rendered "reification" and "alienation," thus cleverly expressing Feuerbach's point that the believer in the supernatural does indeed *reify* that which *alienates* her from her genuine life within.

11. This very brief account of Feuerbach sticks to the essentials of his mediation between Strauss and Marx and Engels; it obviously doesn't do justice to the sophistication of his theologizing nor to the development of his thinking after *The Essence of Christianity*. For a work that does, see Harvey 1995.

12. Any consideration of the importance of Marx's early work must take into account its delayed availability. Engels published the "Theses on Feuerbach" only in 1881. The bulk of the early writings was not edited and published until 1931, and the *Foundations of the Critique of Political Economy* (the *"Grundrisse"*) only between 1939 and 1941.

13. The immediate source for my thumbnail history of the term is Lichtheim 1967, but the story has been often rehearsed since Mannheim 1929. In connection with Marx's development of the concept and its subsequent history, I have benefited particularly from Seliger 1977, Larrain 1979, Geuss 1981, and Eagleton 1991. For extended treatment of the concept after Marx, and some attention to its problematics, see chapter 12.

14. Marx is the forgetful one here. His "comic" premise about contemporary history is an extrapolation, though a delightful one, from Hegel's remarks in the *Phenomenology* about Athenian comedy as social demythologizing. See the section titled "The Spiritual Work of Art," 721–749, in Baillie's translation, and especially 745–748.

15. For a full examination of Carlyle's unsystematic syncretism, see the standard study of his sources, Harrold 1934. Harrold's findings are summarized in the introductions and notes to his excellent edition of *Sartor Resartus* (Carlyle 1937). My subsequent quotations of *Sartor* are taken from this edition and cited by page number in my text.

16. Carlyle's clothes metaphor skirts (as he himself might say) an important philosophical difficulty. As Hazard Adams puts it in his discussion of Carlyle on "symbol," "while we think of

clothes as covering us, we must also imagine ourselves as our clothes." Are clothes constitutive of what we are or disguises of a naked inner essence, a transcendental ego outside of and prior to dress and even language?

17. The narrator of *Sartor* concludes thus his account of Teufelsdröckh's relations with Napoleon: "At last indignantly dismissed . . . [he was] almost thrown out of doors as an 'Ideologist.' 'He himself,' says the professor, 'was among the completest Ideologists, at least Ideopraxists; in the Idea (in der Idee) he lived, moved and fought'" (178).

18. Grimm, however, reserves the category of "tale" for "fairytale" (*märchen*) and classifies "folktale" as "legend," whereas the twentieth-century consensus treats "fairytale" as only a subspecies of "folktale."

19. The most thorough and consistently relevant study of Wagner's sources in English is the long chapter "The Text and the Sources" in Cooke 1979.

20. In his version, *The Story of Sigurd the Volsung* (1876), William Morris also constructs a theodicy that centers upon *Ragnarök,* "the twilight of the gods," which is an extremely marginal concept in the medieval sources. The coincidence—and it can be shown to be coincidence—indicates the spread of the assumption that a properly culture-informing "myth" will follow a pattern of organic rise and fall.

21. This essay would be of little use to a modern student of Greek religious symbolism. Ruskin's free associations belong, rather, to the great series of private mythologies developed by a wide range of post-romantic artists. Ruskin's mythopoeia is the subject of Raymond Fitch's *Poison Sky* (1982) and is brilliantly treated at various points in Paul Sawyer's *Ruskin's Poetic Argument* (1985). Ruskin's evolving experience of contemporary mythography and of Greek myth in particular is elaborately studied in Dinah Birch's *Ruskin's Myths* (1988). All three works have chapters on "The Queen of the Air."

22. These patterns have been spelled out by Duncan 1968, Swann 1973–1974, Knoepflmacher 1975, and Beer 1975. A version of this last also appears in Beer's *Darwin's Plots* (1983).

23. For Freud's reading in English novels, see, for example, Ernest Jones 1953–1957, volume I, 174.

24. In his influential study Gilles Deleuze (1983) maintains that Nietzsche has no use for "the romantic contraries" of the dialectic. This holds good for the contraries of the Hegelian dialectic that Deleuze appears to have in mind, but Nietzsche everywhere assumes the more truly "romantic contraries" of the Blakean sort that consume each other in tragic recurrence, without sublation.

4. MYTH AS AN ASPECT OF "PRIMITIVE" RELIGION

1. By "expansion of the temporal scale" I mean that by the 1860s the work of Lamarck on the development of invertebrates (1815–1822), of Lyell on geological strata and their fossilized remains (1830), of Boucher de Perthes on the existence of human remains in the Pliocene epoch (1839–1859), of Darwin on the origin of species (1859), the discoveries in the Neanderthal (1857) and in Brixham Cave (1858), and so forth, compel at least a ten-fold expansion of the traditional six thousand years alloted to human history by biblical literalists, an expansion that continues, of course, across the whole of the twentieth century. For a richly detailed and qualified account of the multiple contexts in which sociocultural evolutionism developed in England, see Stocking 1987.

2. Besides Stocking 1987, see Said 1978, Fabian 1983, Kuper 1988, and McGrane 1989.

3. There are excellent discussions of Müller's career in Dorson 1968 and Sharpe 1975. I am indebted to both.

4. "Aryan" inevitably conjures up for us Nazi ideology. Its appearance in this early work of Müller's is almost certainly a reflection of the racist-tinged chauvinism of German romantic philologists like Jacob Grimm, but Müller later in life ridiculed "Aryan" as a racial category and insisted on the independence of linguistic and racial classifications. See Stocking 1987, 59.

5. See Lévi-Strauss 1981, 44. See also, for similar comments about both Müller and Freud, Lévi-Strauss 1988a, 186–187.

6. Inspired presumably by Lamarck, Comte asserts that the *individual* passes through these states, too. This assumption has had quite a career in the allegedly positivistic theories of myth of Herbert Spencer and the doyens of depth psychology.

7. See Comte 1875. Comte presents his general theory of the three states in lesson 51 and then, focusing on the "theological" state, outlines fetishism, polytheism, and monotheism, respectively, in successive lessons 52–54. With reference to the continuity of this scheme across Comte's career, his editor remarks in the headnote to lesson 51 that it "is only a restatement, scarcely modified, of the *Opuscule* of 1822" (202).

8. For a good brief account of Tylor's approval of Müller and his followers' difficulties with this, see Dorson 1968, 187–191.

9. In discussing the relation of Müller's theories of language and myth to the evolutionists, I am indebted to Stocking 1987, 304–308, and to Schrempp 1984.

10. The diction in this version of Spencer's definition of "superorganicism" suggests his peculiar combination of the romantic organicism of Schelling and Lamarck with the positive, material science embodied in the laws of thermodynamics enunciated by Helmholtz in 1847 (conservation of energy) and Kelvin in 1852 (entropy). For a good account of Spencer in relation to other thinkers, see Burrow 1966.

11. Spencer insisted on his complete independence from both Comte and Tylor, and claimed priority for his theory of "primitive" religion over Tylor's. For a good summary of this acrimonious tangle, see Service 1985, 159–160,

12. For an excellent account of Spencer's attack, see Stocking 1987.

13. For the currency of Tylor's theory and a comparison to Smith's, see Beidelman 1974, 53.

14. Perhaps the most influential of these separately published parts is *Adonis, Attis, Osiris* (1906). It was itself in its third edition when it appeared in 1914 as part IV of *The Golden Bough*. Frazer also added in 1936 a thirteenth volume, *Aftermath: A Supplement to* The Golden Bough. Previous accounts of Frazer's shaping of the work are superseded by Robert Frazer 1990b and by the relevant contexts in Ackerman 1987.

15. The most elaborate of such attempts is still the third chapter of Vickery 1973.

16. The pioneers in explaining Frazer in literary terms are Northrop Frye, who makes the radical suggestion (in Frye 1957) that *The Golden Bough* "may yet prove to be really a work of literary criticism" (109), and Stanley Edgar Hyman, whose essay on Frazer (in Hyman 1959) treats the work as a cultural document and analyzes its literary effects. The doubleness of Frazer's message is also recognized and described very clearly by Lionel Trilling (in Trilling 1968). Only recently, however, has Frazer's rhetoric been examined critically. See especially Marc Manganaro (1992) and, in *Modernist Anthropology* (1990), his editorial introduction and the essays by Vickery, Roth, and Strathern. Recognition of the modernists artists' misprision is equally recent, but an important topic throughout Robert Frazer (1990a). I have found especially valuable in this collection Connor's essay (61–79), which attempts, along quite different lines than my own, to deal with the discrepancies between Frazer's overt cognitive orientation and his emotivist subtext.

17. I am indebted here and in the following remarks about Mannhardt to Robert Ackerman's lucid pages (Ackerman 1987, 81–82) about early anthropological influences.

18. For Hume's "laws" as the paradigm, see Robert Frazer 1990b, 19–21.

19. For instances of readers who homed in on the unified case for a perennial religion, some of whom mistook Frazer's point to be that this was the *true* religion, see the discussions of Jane Harrison later in this chapter; of W. B. Yeats, D. H. Lawrence, T. S. Eliot, and Ezra Pound in chapter 6; of Northrop Frye in chapter 7; and of Robert Graves and Joseph Campbell in chapter 8. Frazer, of course, took for granted, *at least on the conscious level,* that all religion was outmoded. In the preface to his own one-volume redaction of *The Golden Bough* (James Frazer 1922), Frazer declares that he concentrated on worship of the vegetative cycle only because this was most relevant to explaining the rite at Nemi, not because he believed it the most significant feature in the evolution of religion. "I hope that after this explicit disclaimer I shall no longer be

taxed with embracing a system of mythology which I look upon as not merely false but as preposterous and absurd" (vii). But the mere existence of this embarrassed repudiation confirms the very reception history of the *Bough* by 1922 that I will recur to in the instances of the writers listed above.

20. For a good treatment of this elegiac mood in Frazer and an argument that he conveys it to various modernist writers, see Vickery 1990, 51–68.

21. See Ackerman 1991, 5; 1987, 231–233; and 1973, 115–134.

22. See Ackerman 1987, 224–235, and Robert A. Jones 1984, 39.

23. This is a considerably modified version of a comparable list in Strenski 1987, 133. The chapter in which it appears contains an excellent discussion of Durkheim and his collaborators on "myth."

24. I am particularly indebted to Service 1985, 133–151, and Kuper 1988, 82–122, for guidance through the tangled bank of theorizing about totemism. Durkheim (1965, 107–110, 195–215) conducts his own masterly review of the state of discourse up to about 1910.

25. Critical professional accounts of Durkheim's work on "primitive" religion from Gold-enweiser on, express reservations not only about his general espousal of totemism but about the validity of Spencer and Gillen's ethnography, the accuracy of Durkheim's understanding of it, and the soundness of his assumption that their findings could be extrapolated to Australian totemism in general. For a partial summary of such criticisms, see Edward Evans-Pritchard 1965, 66–67.

26. This formulation appears in *The Birth of Humility,* Marett's inaugural lecture as E. B. Tylor's successor at Oxford. Marett was another early admirer of Durkheim's who believed that the sociologist's account of "collective representations" entailed an unacknowledged emotive element.

27. In leveling this reproach, Evans-Pritchard echoes a charge made over the years by Van Gennep, for example, and by students of Boas from Goldenweiser and Lowie to Benedict. See for a partial list of such critics, Service 1985, 168–171.

28. Quoted in Lukes 1972, 338–339.

29. Durkheim and Mauss's identification of mythology and taxonomy in "primitive" societies is also a central article of faith with Claude Lévi-Strauss, who makes no secret of his debt to *Primitive Classification* and is largely responsible for its revival in the 1960s. But Lévi-Strauss manages to achieve the purely intellectualist stance to which Durkheim aspired.

30. Lucien Lévy-Bruhl, from *Les Carnets,* cited in Cazeneuve 1972, 87.

31. Bronislaw Malinowski, "Magic, Science and Religion," in *Magic, Science and Religion* (New York: Doubleday, 1954), 25.

32. For an account of some of these critics, see Littleton 1985, xviii–xx.

33. Durkheim's half-dozen references to *Les Functions Mentales* in the second half of *Les formes élémentaires* focus upon the threat of the "prelogical" and suggest that he hasn't had time to digest the work. But when he finally reviews it, together with his own *Les formes élémentaires* in *L'année sociologique* (1913, vol. 12, 33–37) he reiterates this same criticism as well as the first and third ones mentioned above. For an English translation see Durkheim 1994, 169–173.

34. For an extended comparison of Durkheim and Lévy-Bruhl that insists on the rightness of Durkheim's differences from his friend, see Horton 1973, 249–305. Horton makes an indignant list of distinguished sociologists and anthropologists who have subsequently "mistaken" Durkheim's theory as containing emotive elements (272–276). He does not mention that what he views as an incomprehensible blunder appears to infect even Mauss and Hubert.

35. Lévy-Bruhl is the oldest writer of whom I am aware to apologize formally for the inevitably pejorative implications of terms like "primitive." In his late work he puts it in quotation marks. The "inférieure" of his title *Les fonctions mentales dans les sociétés inférieures* should be understood as "lower" (in the technological sense), not "inferior." In fact a more *au courant* title true to Lévy-Bruhl's argument would be "Cognitive Functions in Traditional Societies."

36. For a sketch of these anticipations, see Littleton 1985, xxvii–xlii.

37. Uncertainties about how to label this group have long reflected its unsettled relation to traditional academic disciplines, but a consensus seems to have been developing since the

publication of Robert Ackerman's *Myth and Ritual School* (New York: Garland, 1991). I follow his practice as perhaps the least inaccurate compromise.

38. Classicists generally attribute the coup de grace to Arthur Pickard-Cambridge's 1927 review of the second edition of *Themis* in *Classical Review* and his criticism of Murray in *Dithyramb, Tragedy and Comedy,* published that same year. For a more recent attack by a classicist, aimed particularly at the Ritualists' midcentury descendants, see Fontenrose 1966.

39. The first of these, the one most accurately called "The Myth and Ritual School," is composed of biblical scholars, working in Robertson Smith's field, so to speak, and centered most definably in the two anthologies edited by S. H. Hooke, particularly the late *Myth, Ritual and Kingship* (1958). As H. S. Versnel points out in his valuable historical essay on these three different versions of myth and ritual theory (Versnel 1990), Hooke objects to Frazer's and Harrison's "comparative method" and rejects their developmentalism for a diffusionist approach. Versnel distinguishes a second group as consisting on the one hand of Walter Burkert and on the other of the "Paris School" of French classicists—J.-P. Vernant and others. I prefer (in chapter 11) to associate Burkert with René Girard as thinkers who find ritual human sacrifice at the origins of myth, and to distinguish the French classicists as a third, separate group interested primarily in rites of initiation and eschewing issues of ultimate origin.

40. As this date suggests, Harrison cannot be seen simply as heir to Frazer and Smith. Frazer offered the group friendly encouragement and they made strategic appeals to his authority. But Frazer could not have approved of their emotive presuppositions, nor did he approve of their insistence that myth is always rationalization of rite. In his 1921 edition of "Apollodorus's" *Library,* he explicitly rejects the position of certain unnamed but unmistakable "modern writers." See Ackerman 1987, 234–235.

41. Her supposition may have been reinforced by reading Lévy-Bruhl, whom she often cites.

42. *Themis* pioneers in the juxtaposition of the new ethnology and anthropology with the new archaeology. Harrison relies heavily upon pottery designs, carvings in relief, coins, seals, signet rings, votive and funeral tablets, sarcophagi, altar stones, reconstructed temple layouts, and so forth. There are 152 figures in the work. Nietzsche finds a disciple prepared to carry out his plan "to level the artistic structure of the *Apollinian culture,* as it were, stone by stone, till the foundations on which its rests become visible" (Nietzsche 1967, 41).

43. I am indebted to Hyman 1965 (138) for this comparison of the inspirations of *Prolegomena* and *Themis.*

44. With her treatment of *Themis,* Harrison launches what has become a significant feminist interpretation of the anthropological evidence for the archaic social power of women. She defuses Bachofen's misogyny by assimilating his "matriarchal" stage both with Nietzsche's condition of Dionysian unity with the cosmos and with a cultural state that is wholly peaceful and consensual. Even in archaic societies, "woman is the social centre not the dominant force. So long as force is supreme . . . society is impossible" (494).

5. THE ROLE OF DEPTH-PSYCHOLOGY IN THE CONSTRUCTION OF MYTH

1. Freud himself noted in *The Interpretation of Dreams* (Freud 1965a, 375–376) the resemblances between the dream-work and poetry, and it has often been elaborated since.

2. Strictly speaking, this essay is not Freud's first consideration of daydreaming; in *The Interpretation of Dreams* he recognizes "secondary revision" as a kind of daydream and sketches in Chapter 6 the major points of resemblance between day and night dreaming. But in the essay he focuses on daydream as an important psychic construct in its own right.

3. This journal was intended, according to Freud's statement of editorial policy, to be devoted to the psychological knowledge of the themes of art and literature, cultural and religious history. Freud promises confidently that the works to be published "will soon take on the character of a precise research project," which indicates his new enthusiasm for applying his psychology to other disciplines. (For the quoted phrase, see Freud 1970, vol. 1, 82.)

4. G. S. Kirk properly points out (Kirk 1973, 273) that Freud made a much more explicit connection between "myth" and dream in his *On Dreams,* published in the following year, but the passage in *The Interpretation* is the one his followers single out as inspirational.

5. For a history of this theory, see Gould 1977 and Sulloway 1979. Both point out that by the standards of more informed research the "biogenetic law" is overgeneralized; only the embryonic, not later stages, of growth get recapitulated.

6. For a good account of Spencer's role in disseminating the notion of mental inheritance, see Voget 1975, 170–174.

7. In *Schriften* (Freud 1970, vol. 1) Rank speaks as if he were introducing his own extract from material Freud showed him and Freud's essay is set off by quotation marks. Freud's translators, as if not recognizing what follows as Freud's, drop the quotation marks so that modern editions offer no indication whatsoever of Freud's participation. As editor of *Schriften,* Freud must have collaborated with Rank on the exact manner in which his essay is integrated in the larger one. Both the semi-anonymity and the fact of his participation are significant indications of the importance he attached to the project.

8. Some forty years after its appearance, Jung extensively revised *Wandlungen und Symbole der Libido.* It was republished in 1952 under its now familiar title, *Symbole der Wandlungen.* Jung is right to say in the foreword to the English translation of this new edition, *Symbols of Transformation,* that "despite a number of radical interventions . . . I do not think one could say it has turned into a different book" (Jung 1956, xxv). In the interval Jung had come to understand where the early work wanted to go. He clarifies his theory, especially of the libido, underscores much more pungently his departures from Freud, specifies more clearly the relevance of the Miller fantasies to his theoretical positions, and stresses more explicitly the archetypal "plot," particularly the dangerous regression into the Mother. All of the specific comments about the appearance and nature of the archetypes are added in revision; Jung did not articulate his conception of them until several years after the initial writing. But it should be remembered that even though the earlier version is somewhat less focused, neither Freud nor other readers, including Beatrice Hinkle, who translated it as *Psychology of the Unconscious* (New York: Moffat, Yard & Co., 1916), had any trouble grasping the radical tenor of its argument. Since the revision is more sharply presented, I quote from it wherever possible, citing it by page number in my text and referring to it as *Symbols.* In order not to be misleading, however, about the text that the psychiatric community read for forty years, I refer in certain contexts to the original version, designated as *Transformations.*

9. For Jung's sniping at Freud on Schreber, see Jung 1956, notes on pp. 29, 44, 95, 134, 300, and 382.

10. My apparently inappropriate masculine pronoun here reflects Jung's curious maneuver in the text. Even though he is analyzing a woman's psychodynamics, he manages to cast his monomyth almost entirely in terms of male development.

11. For Freud's unwillingness to give up Lamarckian biology, see especially Grubrich-Simitis 1987, especially 98–102, and Sulloway 1979, chapters 10 and 11.

12. This "phylogenetic fantasy" as Freud called it in one letter to Ferenczi, has been widely known only since Ernest Jones revealed it in 1959, and the extent of Freud's participation in it only since Ilse Grubrich-Simitis's discovery among Ferenczi's papers of a draft of the last among Freud's five missing "metapsychological papers." See Grubrich-Simitis 1987. The one publication resulting from this *folie à deux* is Ferenczi's *Thalassa: A Theory of Genitality* (1924). He argues (with Freud's encouragement) both that each act of coitus recapitulates in its stages the phylogenetic development of the erotic zones and that "the purpose of this whole evolution . . . can be none other than an attempt on the part of the ego . . . to return to the mother's womb" (Ferenczi 1968, 18). This latter opinion conforms with Freud's newly identified "death instinct."

13. By far the best account of the role of these instincts in Freud's later thinking is Ricoeur 1970, 261–338.

14. Rank's essays were printed in the fourth through the seventh editions of *The Interpretation of Dreams,* from 1914 to 1922. After the break between Freud and Rank they were omitted.

15. Jung's first use of the term is noted here by the editors of the *Collected Works*. They also point out that up to this juncture he uses Burchhardt's term "Urbild," "primordial image," which introduces yet another romantic source of the concept. In spite of the editors' denials here, Jung continues to speak sporadically of the archetype as if it were a "primordial image."

16. The essay quoted here, "On the Psychology of the Unconscious," is the revised version (1943) of one of Jung's pioneering essays (1917) on "collective unconscious" and "archetype." So far as I can tell, Jung did not really find formulations for "archetype" that satisfied him until about 1928, and quite possibly not until several years later.

17. As usual, the eclectic Jung is not about to confine himself to a single function. Segal, for example, identifies at least four others: to facilitate receptivity to the unconscious, to assist in the interpretation of dream, to help people feel at home in the world, and to offer models of character to be emulated (Segal 1999, 77–79).

6. THE MODERNIST CONTRIBUTION TO THE CONSTRUCTION OF MYTH

1. The exhibition at the Museum of Modern Art in the winter of 1984–1985, "Primitivism in 20th-Century Art: Affinity of the Tribal and the Modern," dramatized forcefully the impact of Amerindian, African, and Oceanic artifacts upon modernist artists. The controversy over the political correctness of the exhibition established the irresponsibility of identifying uncritically at this point in time with the artists' own primitivism, but did nothing to detract from the ocular proof of how widespread this primitivism had been. For the catalogue, see Rubin 1984. For two critiques of the exhibition, see Clifford 1988, 189–214, and Torgovnick 1990, 119–129.

2. "Totalizing" signifies here, and elsewhere in this chapter, in the sense derived from Marxist and poststructural criticism. In *A Poetics of Postmodernism*, Linda Hutcheon helpfully defines it thus "'to totalize' does not mean just to unify, but rather means to unify with an eye to power and control" (xi).

3. The distinction between "the work *of* myth" and "work *on* myth" is derived from Hans Blumenberg. See Blumenberg 1985. He demonstrates at length what "work on" myth means within Western civilization, but the identification of this "work" with literary allusion is my own. For discussion of Blumenberg on myth and the reasons for identifying "work on" it with allusion, see chapter 13.

4. For the conception of this "constitutive" function of "myth," see Adams 1983, especially 287–324, and the discussion of his theory in chapter 13.

5. The standard treatment of Yeats's indebtedness to Frazer and to the theme identified here is Vickery 1973, 179–232.

6. Both Richard Ellmann in *The Identity of Yeats* (155–157) and John Vickery in *The Literary Impact of the Golden Bough* (223–225) make similar points about the significance of this poem.

7. For a demonstration of the crucial importance of *Per Amica* in Yeats's development see Lipking 1981, 47–62.

8. For a more nuanced treatment of the vexed issue of Yeats's belief in his system, see chapter 13.

9. For Bloom's main discussion of *A Vision* see *Yeats*, 210–291. Bloom rightly stresses the "Gnosticism" of Yeats's system, meaning that humankind's "struggle . . . cannot modify or affect that world. . . . Yeats' divine justice is of the Gnostic sort Kafka shows us in his novels" (246).

10. Lawrence had read Tylor's *Primitive Culture* during his anthropological studies of 1915 and reproduces here, unconsciously or not, Tylor's animism. But even if Tylor were willing to concede animism in a people so culturally advanced, it is easy to imagine his astonishment at a contemporary endorsement of it.

11. Lawrence does not invent Ursula's fantasy out of whole cloth. Byron's unfinished drama, *Heaven and Earth*, seems to have promoted it among young women in the nineteenth century. Shirley, for example, in Charlotte Brontë's novel tries out a version on her friend, Caroline, and "Frank Miller," the pseudonymous young American woman whose written fantasies form

the basis of C. G. Jung's *Symbols of Transformation,* points out herself that Byron's drama is an important source of her fourth fantasy. Lawrence actually read Jung's analysis of the "Miller" fantasies, but only three years after the publication of *The Rainbow.*

12. By the later nineteenth century, in the wake of the *Lives* by Strauss and Renan, and the "quest for the historical Jesus" as Schweitzer called it, fictional revisionings of the Gospels were plentiful. For a useful typology and discussion of versions of Jesus in modern literature, see Ziolkowski 1972. George Moore's *Brook Kerith* (1916), which Lawrence probably knew, precedes him in restoring Jesus to "the fruits of the earth."

13. Cited by Levenson 1984, 195, from *Dial,* LXXII (October 1921), 443.

14. This is the opening line of canto XLVII of *The Cantos of Ezra Pound.* Pound considers Odysseus's descent to the underworld to consult with Tiresias to be the oldest part of Homer, and he virtually allegorizes it as a symbolic representation of the same process of the reconnection of the living with chthonic wisdom, specifically through sexual enlightenment, that we find celebrated in Yeats and Lawrence. Eliot would have known since 1915 Pound's initial statement of this theme and his strikingly similar associations with Tiresias may well stem from Pound's. But the two poets reinforce this theme in one another; Pound's later elaborations (like canto XLVII) doubtless resonate with *The Waste Land,* which, after all, he edited.

15. The reason for Eliot's association of the Cumean Sybil with Tiresias isn't apparent from *The Waste Land* itself. But in the *Baldur the Beautiful* section of *The Golden Bough,* Frazer cites the very passage from Petronius that Eliot uses as epigraph, as an example of "the suspension between heaven and earth attributed to beings who have been endowed with the coveted and burdensome gift of immortality" (Frazer 1966, vol. 10, 99).

16. Eliot tells us that "not only the title, but the plan and a good deal of the incidental symbolism of the poem were suggested by Miss Jessie L. Weston's book on the Grail legend" (50). *From Ritual to Romance,* published in 1920, is a work very much in the wake of Frazer and the Cambridge Ritualists (see Weston 1957). It is a flimsy argument that various aspects of the plots and especially symbolism of the Grail romances are "survivals" in Tylor's sense of the archaic fertility religion. Thanks to the spurious fame the book acquired as a result of Eliot's tribute, it remains in print, in paperback, still a partner with *The Waste Land* itself in spreading the gospel that there is a traceable route "from ritual to romance." The two works promote the notion, later popular among midcentury theorists discussed in chapter 8, that a modern literary production may not merely preserve traces of ritual origin but somehow *be* a ritual by virtue of descent.

17. Since the pioneering chapter "Bradley" in Kenner 1959, a number of students of Eliot have explained his conception of consciousness as deriving from the philosopher who is the subject of his doctoral dissertation. This explanation *does* illuminate in particular the invention of "Tiresias" with his timeless awareness of "the mind of Europe."

18. I am indebted here to Levenson 1984, 193–202, for the pioneering recognition of the radical challenge posed by the contrast of "mythical" to "narrative" method, and for his application of it to what he calls the "contextual development" of *The Waste Land.*

19. For a broader consideration of the differences between the responses to modernity of Eliot and Joyce, see Meisel 1987. As a more specific instance of the two authors' significantly contrary responses to Lévy-Bruhl, see Spurr 1994.

20. For Lacan's and Derrida's actual comments on Joyce, see Berressem 1990, 139–164, and Lernout 1990, 41–83. The most relevant critical work includes Norris 1974; MacCabe 1978, especially chapter 6; and Bishop 1986.

21. For relevant treatments of the letter, see Bishop 1986, 310; Berressem 1990; and Kelley 1987.

22. "Postmodernist" here signifies only the practice with regard to myth of poets and novelists writing since the major modernists closed up shop (roughly in the late forties); it should not be construed as taking a position on whether or not there is a clear general distinction between two literary historical periods called Modernism and Postmodernism.

23. I owe my "complicit" conception of novelistic relation to myth to Hutcheon 1988. Proceeding from the model of architecture, she finds the essence of postmodernism in its simultaneous complicity with and critique of mass culture. The position and writing that I

call "critical," however, on the basis of my more circumscribed definition of postmodernism in relation to myth as denial of transcendence, she specifically classifies, on the basis of her broader criterion—refusal of cultural complicity—as "an extreme of modernist autotelic self-reflexion" (40).

24. For sophisticated contrary arguments that Updike and Barth employ myth wholly seriously, see Vickery 1983, 149–183.

7. NEO-ROMANTIC THEORIES
OF THE MIDCENTURY I

1. Ernst Cassirer, *The Philosophy of Symbolic Forms,* volume 2, *Mythical Thought,* xv. *Die Philosophie der Symbolische Formen* was originally published between 1923 and 1929, but Cassirer's influence in English-speaking countries dates from the publication of *Essay on Man,* written in English, in 1944 and the subsequent appearance of translations of his principal earlier works during the forties and fifties.

2. For a good account of "objectification," see Adams 1983, 202–208. I am indebted throughout my account of Cassirer to Adams's excellent discussion of him in this text.

3. For a strong negative assessment of these unresolved ambiguities, see Bidney 1965, 3–24.

4. The basis for claiming that Cassirer was working on this text concurrently with the publication of *An Essay on Man* is that a part of it was published in the magazine *Fortune* in June of 1944.

5. My position here is more or less the standard one, but for an eloquent counter-argument that Cassirer intended to combat irrationalist notions of myth even in his earlier work, see Strenski 1987, 13–41.

6. The best known of these "adherents" is Susanne Langer, but her reputation as such seems to me badly misjudged. Her *Philosophy in a New Key* exhibits a behavioristic orientation thoroughly at odds with Cassirer's. Her account of the expressive origin of language and its maturation into a pragmatic conceptual tool glides over the central contradictions with nary a hint of cognitive dissonance. She regards myth as a non-discursive, "presentational" form of symbolism, rooted in fantasy rather than religion or ritual, which survives by evolving somehow into the equally non-discursive poetry of national epics. In her self-described "sequel," *Feeling and Form: A Theory of Art,* she is at her best in demonstrating that Freud's canons for the work of fantasy are versions of the same laws Cassirer posits for mythical consciousness. Her doctrine of presentational symbolism, which valorizes "image," "symbol," and "archetype" at the expense of narrative, contributes to that expanded sense of the term "image" that becomes the kudzu of post-fifties literary-critical discourse. See Langer 1980.

7. The quoted phrase is Cassirer's own; see Cassirer 1966, 115.

8. Wheelwright published in 1968 a revised edition of *The Burning Fountain* in which he makes some serious changes in terminology and in the structure of the argument. I follow the earlier text because it presents the basic theory and is the one that was influential during the heyday of literary theorizing about myth. Where the version of '68 helps to clarify a point or, in a few cases where it may represent a substantive change, I refer to it by name in the text.

9. Frye's work has attracted massive critical commentary. The best accounts of it by friendly commentators are Hamilton 1990 and Russell 1998. Most of the critical arguments, pro and con, appear elegantly stated in Krieger 1966. A number of significant critiques of Frye appeared in the early eighties. See especially Frank Lentricchia 1980, 2–26; Frederic Jameson 1981, 71–74; and Eagleton 1981, 90–94. For a recent critique of Frye as a mystifying comparatist in the company of Frazer, Eliot, and Campbell, see Manganaro 1992, 111–150.

10. For persuasive evidence of Spengler's considerable influence on Frye's thinking, see Russell 1998, especially 21–43, 64–66.

11. Marc Manganaro calls attention to the connection with Lévy-Bruhl in the course of a strong argument that Frye in fact valorizes a nostalgic return. See Manganaro 1992, 134–141.

8. NEO-ROMANTIC THEORIES
OF THE MIDCENTURY II

1. Tylor assumes here that tales of heroes are "myth," a conflation he passes on to many a successor, including Raglan. The folklorist Alan Dundes feels called on in his essay "The Hero Pattern and the Life of Jesus" to make the point in connection with Raglan's practice that "if one defines myth in the folkloristic sense of a sacred narrative explaining how the world and man came to be in their present form, then it is abundantly clear that Raglan's hero narratives are *not* myths" (Dundes 1990, 180). By contemporary folkloristic standards, the hero narratives are legends or tales or some mixture thereof.

2. Segal's essay has affected my thinking about some of the theorists discussed in this chapter more generally than specific footnotes will suggest.

3. For a succinct account of the relation of phenomenology of religion to comparative religion, see Sharpe 1986, especially pp. 220–241.

4. Otto's work is not in any way a direct response to Husserl's. Though Husserl praised *The Idea of the Holy,* the book itself does not employ the word "phenomenology" and betrays no sign of acquaintance with Husserl's work.

5. For Eliade's characterization of the school, see Eliade 1957, 216–232, and Eliade 1973, 307–318.

6. Ivan Strenski points out Eliade's derivation from Otto of religion as autonomous faculty of the mind in Strenski 1987, 113–114. Strenski is also valuable on Eliade's relation to phenomenology of religion. See especially 114–118.

7. For the phrase, see Mircea Eliade 1969, 62. For analysis see Strenski 1987, 118–122. For an excellent discussion of Eliade's reductionism and antireductionism, see Allen 1998, chapters 1 and 2. This is currently the fullest and most balanced account of Eliade's work.

8. Douglas Allen (1998, 69) points out a passage in Eliade's memoir, *No Souvenirs,* in which he recognizes specifically his reverse application of these "hermeneutics of suspicion."

9. If Van Der Leeuw's second formulation appears to cover ritual as well as myth, that is because he takes the two as different modal expressions of the same event.

10. Eliade specifically declares in the preface to the English version of *Cosmos and History: The Myth of the Eternal Return* that he understands the word "archetype" in its more traditional philosophical sense, not in Jung's, and that he does not "use" the concept of the "collective unconscious" (see Eliade 1954, viii–ix). But this means that his opportunistic adversions elsewhere to Jung's evidence for the "subconscious survival" of mythology are rather irresponsible.

11. This is the title of the English translation of the unrevised *Symbols of Transformation,* which reminds us that Neumann's work, like another important essay in Jungian libidinal development published in the same year, Joseph Campbell's *Hero with a Thousand Faces,* actually precedes Jung's 1952 revision of his first book. These fresh systematizations of Jung's pattern of libidinal development may even have sharpened his recognition of what he had wrought and so contributed to the revision.

12. The shifts in this section between "male" and "masculine," "female" and "feminine" reflect Neumann's blurring of the distinction between biology and culture.

13. For support of the assertions in this and the following sentence, see Segal 1990, xxxix n. and xxiv respectively.

14. Alan Dundes presents in "The Hero Pattern and the Life of Jesus" a useful tabular juxtaposition of Rank's life-features with Raglan's (and those of an earlier comparativist, von Hahn [1876]). See Dundes 1990, 188–189. Rank and Raglan select many of the same heroes, which makes their agreements about the crucial incidents more impressive but lessens their combined statistical sample. Both studies, too, are far from worldwide in scope, being much too concentrated on the Greek and Near Eastern examples familiar from an education in Western classics and the Bible.

15. Graves quotes here his own definition from the preface to *King Jesus.* This work, published two years before *The White Goddess,* is a sustained exercise in the workings of iconotrophy. It is inspired by Frazer's notorious suggestion in the second edition of *The Golden*

Bough that Christianity flourished only because the authorities made the mistake of executing the troublemaker, Jesus of Nazareth, under conditions that assimilated the meaning of his death to the perennial fertility religion. Graves develops the story as a clash between the symbol-system of patriarchal Judaism, subscribed to by Jesus himself, and that of matriarchal paganism, which ironically co-opts him in spite of his own teachings. Graves's other relevant work is *The Greek Myths* (1955). Although Graves soberly admonishes its readers that "a true science of myth should begin with a study of archaeology, history and comparative religion" (Graves 1955, 22) and warns that "any statement made here about Mediterranean religion or ritual before the appearance of written records is conjectural," his notes systematically apply to the topic the convictions enshrined in *The White Goddess,* thus inducting tens of thousands of unadvised or puzzled readers of his dictionary into the Goddess's mysteries.

16. For a fine analysis of the relation of Campbell's mythographical career to *A Skeleton Key,* see Manganaro 1992, 152–158.

17. For an excellent account of Campbell's relation to Jung, see Segal 1987, 125–135.

18. This notion, common to Eliade, Wheelwright, and Campbell, that the perennial *ordering* wisdom of myth has disappeared in our day, is what leads Hazard Adams to group the three in *Philosophy of the Literary Symbolic* as "sentimental archaizers."

19. For a full and more nuanced account of Campbell's shifting conceptions of "myth," see Segal 1987, 101–124.

9. FOLKLORISTIC MYTH
IN SOCIAL ANTHROPOLOGY I

1. For important examples and guides to further work, see Clifford 1988 and Manganaro 1990.

2. This movement is richly detailed in "The Ethnographer's Magic: Fieldwork in British Anthropology from Tylor to Malinowski," in Stocking 1983, 70–120, since reprinted in Stocking 1992a, 12–59.

3. Malinowski's mot about Rivers as the Rider Haggard of anthropology and himself as its Conrad was originally made privately in a letter to Brenda Seligman that Stocking dates from its manuscript source as "6/21/18" (see Stocking 1983, 101). For a rich characterization of the remark's context, see Clifford 1988, 92–113.

4. I have in mind, in particular, the essays in Ellen 1988, the editors' introduction to Malinowski 1993, and Strenski 1987, 42–50.

5. For discussion of these influences, see especially Strenski 1987, 45–50; Malinowski 1993, 16–26; and Jerschina's essay in Ellen et al. 1988, 128–148.

6. The work was translated into English as *Elements of Folk Psychology.* See Wundt 1916.

7. See especially Wundt 1916, 385–388. Wundt does not consistently view myth as narrative, however; in some contexts he transmits a familiar part of the romantic problematic by referring to myth as a "conception" (393) or "a species of idea" (414).

8. See in particular Clifford 1988, 28–30; Geertz 1988, 73–83; and Stocking 1983, 104–110.

9. For the structure of this hypothetical voyage, see Malinowski 1961, 195–375. "In Tewara and Sanaroa—Mythology of the Kula" is chapter 12.

10. For a statement of this opinion set explicitly in relation to myth, see Malinowski 1992, 170–172.

11. For a careful, subtle account of Malinowski's shift and Radcliffe-Brown's ultimate reaction to it, see Stocking 1984, 156–184, and especially 168–175.

12. Malinowski's language about "deep religious wants" sounds surprisingly akin to Mircea Eliade's hypothesis of an ineradicable religious faculty, and Eliade does conclude the first chapter of his *Myth and Reality* by quoting this extended passage from Malinowski's essay as the best possible statement about the religious nature of "primitive" myth. Ivan Strenski makes the point

(Strenski 1987, 43) that "Eliade takes Malinowski's (naturalistic) functionalism and interprets it ontologically and existentially." Yes, but not without considerable encouragement from language that appears to link religion with biological need.

13. For Malinowski on "function" in the debate, see Stocking 1984, 174.

14. This attention is discussed in the final section of chapter 10. The only writer on Malinowski whom I know to have attended to the constructed nature of his equation of *liliu* with "myth" is Ivan Strenski; see Strenski 1987, 50.

15. The best account of Radcliffe-Brown's development, to which my terse summary is indebted, is now Stocking 1995, 298–366. This magisterial account subsumes the author's earlier publications on Radcliffe-Brown and other British anthropology during the years covered.

16. See, for examples, 1937, 442, and 1956, 6, 80, 84, 168–169, 267–269.

17. There are exceptions. Godfrey Lienhardt's *Divinity and Experience: The Religion of the Dinka,* for example, is an excellent study and finds a rich mythological tradition right in the Nuers' backyard among their traditional enemies, thus, perhaps, supporting Mary Douglas's speculations about Evans-Pritchard's blinkers. See Lienhardt 1961.

18. For Firth's account of this double perspective and his reports on it, see Firth 1967, v–vi.

19. These phrases should not be taken as representing accurately Harris's general assessment of Boas. He takes the assertion about the ten thousand pages from Helen Codere's "Understanding of the Kwakiutl" in W. Goldschmidt, ed., *The Anthropology of Franz Boas* (Memoir 89; American Anthropological Association, 61) and in the second half of the quotation he is quoting Leslie White, *The Ethnology and Ethnography of Franz Boas* (Austin; Bulletin of the Texas Memorial Museum, no. 6, 55).

20. To be fair to Bascom, these tabular categories are carefully qualified in his text by "often" and "usually."

21. In a second synoptic table (11), setting out "procedural steps" for field identification, Bascom introduces two further differences, one literary, one social, that "usually" prevail. In contrast to myth, folktale displays a "conventional" opening ("Once upon a time . . .") and is restricted to being told after dark.

22. The formulation Bascom cites is from Boas 1938, 609. For a close variant, see *Race, Language, and Culture,* 454.

23. George Stocking makes a strong case in a number of contexts for the importance of Boas's contribution to establishing the relativistic and pluralistic sense of "culture" general in modern anthropology in lieu of the more monolithic sense pioneered by Tylor. See especially Stocking 1968, 200–206.

24. See Radin 1953, 310ff., and 1972, throughout.

25. In a special coup, doubtless related to Radin's attendance at Eranos symposia, *The Trickster* comes with appended essays by Jung's classicist collaborator, Karl Kerényi, and a rich one by Jung himself intended respectively to connect this ubiquitous archaic figure to worldwide analogues and to a universal archetype.

26. Kluckhohn's notion of myths that "express the culturally disallowed but unconsciously wanted" appears to refer to Ruth Benedict's identification of this type in her "Introduction to Zuni Mythology." See Benedict 1968, 107–112.

10. FOLKLORISTIC MYTH
IN SOCIAL ANTHROPOLOGY II

1. The initial neglect of Lévi-Strauss's Boasian roots has slowly given way to better history of ideas and of anthropology. See especially Strenski 1987, 133–135; Boas 1974, 19; and Pace 1983, 82–85. Both Boon 1982, 98, 241, 243, and Sahlins 1981, 70, make valuable specific contributions.

2. Although Lévi-Strauss was expected to profess Durkheimian sociology in Sao Paulo, there is good reason to think that he made his peace with it, if at all, only after his return

to France to take up an academic career. See Strenski 1987, especially 136–138, 156–159, and Pace 1983, 144–167. See also for a cogent general account of Lévi-Strauss's ideas, Scholte 1974, 637–716.

3. For specific critiques of Lévi-Strauss on the Theban cycle, see Turner 1977, 103–162; Carroll 1978, 805–814; and Peradotto 1995, 85–101.

4. This translation, slightly different from both the published English versions, sacrifices style in order to get as close as possible to the letter of the original: *"Nous ne prétendons donc pas montrer comment les hommes pensent dans les mythes mais comment les mythes se pensent dans les hommes, et à leur insu" (Le cru et la cuit* [Paris: Plon, 1964], 20). This version differs slightly from the two published English translations. Edmund Leach, who certainly agrees in general that Lévi-Strauss regards the process as unconscious, calls attention to an ambiguity lurking even in this sharp formulation. The phrase *"comment les mythes se pensent dans les hommes"* might be rendered "how myths are thought in men," which, as Leach observes, "would reduce the degree of autonomy implied" (Leach 1974, 53). The suggestion is grammatically possible but rhetorically weaker and less consistent with what Lévi-Strauss affirms in other contexts.

5. For Lévi-Strauss's clearest and most eloquent defense of himself against the charge of dismissing affectivity, see Lévi-Strauss 1981, 638–640, for myth and 667–670 for ritual.

6. For further explanation of this assertion, see the concluding pages of this chapter and "The Ground of Myth Reclaimed" section of chapter 11.

7. For Lévi-Strauss's connections with the French *symboliste* movement, see Boon 1972.

8. See especially the introduction to Leach 1967, ix.

9. For an important assertion that he has "never ceased to be guided by" the canonical formula, see Lévi-Strauss 1973a, 249. For an example of an inversion in the third member rather than the fourth, see Lévi-Strauss 1988a, 156. Throughout this latter work Lévi-Strauss points out explicitly his major applications of the formula.

10. This version of "Asdiwal" includes the considerable postscript, written fifteen years after the original essay.

11. Like his treatment of the Theban cycle, Lévi-Strauss's handling of the "Asdiwal" stories has been severely criticized. See especially Thomas, Kronenfeld, and Kronenfeld 1976, 147–173. Lévi-Strauss has seldom replied to specific critics or even criticisms, but after an attack by Marvin Harris upon the accuracy of his facts about Tsimshian culture in "Asdiwal," he did respond in the same issue of *L'homme* (vol. 16, no. 2, 1976, 23–39) in the essay *"Structuralisme et empiricisme."* (Harris's attack is reprinted in Harris 1979 and the rejoinder in Lévi-Strauss 1985, 121–137.) However experts in Northwest cultures might judge the dispute, Lévi-Strauss marshals in this rejoinder an impressive array of the detailed evidence that his method presupposes but he ordinarily suppresses.

12. Lévi-Strauss cites this statement again in *The Savage Mind* as an early account of "wild thought" as bricolage and then goes on to remark, "Penetrating as this comment is, it nevertheless fails to take into account that in the continual reconstruction from the same materials, it is always earlier ends which are called upon to play the part of means: the signified changes into the signifying and vice versa" (Lévi-Strauss 1966, 21). This refinement upon Boas also plays a role in the determination of the canonical formula.

13. Lévi-Strauss seems to prepare the reader of *Mythologiques* for this expansion of the symbolic field when he warns us in the "Overture" to *The Raw and the Cooked* that "it must not be considered surprising if this work, which is avowedly devoted to mythology . . . frequently refers to ceremonies and rites. . . . I claim the right to make use of any manifestation of the mental or social activities of the communities under consideration, which seems likely to allow me, as the analysis proceeds, to complete or explain the myth" (Lévi-Strauss 1969, 4).

14. Twenty years later Lévi-Strauss analyzes this myth on the full two-continent scale in *L'histoire de Lynx* (1991), translated as *The Story of Lynx.* See Lévi-Strauss 1995.

15. For a particularly clear statement of this criterion, see Lévi-Strauss's "Structure and Form: Reflections on a Work by Vladimir Propp," in Lévi-Strauss 1976, 127–130.

16. Lévi-Strauss's inclusion of Freud's version of Oedipus in "The Structural Study" and his occasional excursions into analysis of mythic elements in modern literature and music suggest a

conception of the survival or revival of myth that appears to stand in unresolved contradiction to the theory of degeneration discussed above. The one scholar I am aware of who has paid serious attention to Lévi-Strauss's theory of genre is Michael McKeon. See McKeon 1987, 4–6. He subjects the degenerative theory to a severe critique for its evasion of history but notes the rudiments in Lévi-Strauss's work of what he regards as a proper historical theory of the transformation of myth into other genres.

17. For Lévi-Strauss's critique of the limitations of the historical, or Finnish, school in general and Stith Thompson's *Star Husband Tale* in particular, see Lévi-Strauss 1973b, 227–273, and also 1981, 61.

18. Ivan Strenski plausibly suggests that in treating "the Americas as one vast diffusional field" Lévi-Strauss is directly following Robert Lowie rather than Boas, since it was the former who was persuaded by one of Lévi-Strauss's future senior colleagues, Paul Rivet, to consider the two Americas as one. See Strenski 1987, 133.

19. For the entire passage, see pages 185–190. Lévi-Strauss also lists on page 188 the principal passages in *Mythologiques* that he regards as contributions to this "critique of mythological reason."

20. I cite Culler's version for its wit, but the same point is made by others. See, for example, David Maybury-Lewis 1970, 163.

21. Again, the complaint about a single difference establishing an opposition repeats an earlier professional judgment, in this case Mary Douglas's (1975, 165). Clarke has published a strong book-length critique of Lévi-Strauss's structuralism. See Clarke 1981.

22. See Lévi-Strauss 1969, 31; 1981, 635; and especially 1995, 186.

23. For eloquent examples, see Douglas 1975, 170–171, and Burridge 1967, 110.

24. For typical examples, see Leach 1974, 96, and Maybury-Lewis 1970, 161–162.

25. I have in mind, for example, work by Geoffrey Kirk and Edmund Leach, noted in the next section of this chapter, and by the so-called "Paris School" of classicists, discussed in chapter 11.

26. For cognitive and symbolic anthropology as rivals of Lévi-Strauss's theorizing about "primitive" thought, see especially Horton 1973. For the distracting crises in the discipline, see especially Marcus and Fischer 1986, Clifford and Marcus 1986, Clifford 1988, and the essays in the first part of Marcus 1992.

27. For the work of the Marandas, see especially, Pierre and Elli Köngäs Maranda 1971.

28. Leach's biblical essays are collected in Leach 1969 and Leach and Aycock 1983.

29. Liszka argues in his second chapter, however, that in the case of Saussure himself (whatever may be true of theorists influenced by him), his concept of "value" is the equivalent of Peirce's "interpretant."

30. Liszka's shift to ritual at this point in his argument presumes the Lévi-Straussian assumption that a society's myths and rituals are homologous in function.

31. Unlike Liszka, however, Wagner does not confine his applications to preliterate tale and appears to hold that the "large-scale tropes" of Western culture are also "essentially like myths" (129). In this respect, he is more akin to the constitutive theorists discussed in chapter 13, and his theory might well have been discussed there.

32. My quadripartite division closely resembles the four-fold distinction among these groups by Richard Bauman (Bauman 1986, 7–10).

33. For a relatively recent review of the state of scholarship on this topic, see Foley 1988, and for continuing work see the journal *Oral Tradition,* which Foley edits.

34. For a good survey of the range, concerns, and achievements of this movement, see Bauman and Briggs 1990.

35. This volume collects the most important of Tedlock's previous pioneering essays. For a comparable collection of Dell Hymes's essays, see Hymes 1981a. For direct controversy between Hymes and Tedlock over prosodic principles, see Hymes 1981a, 337–341, and Tedlock 1983, 56–61, 129. For a spirited critique of both Hymes's and Tedlock's principles, see Mattina 1987, 129–148.

36. For an interesting example of this feedback, see Scherzer 1987, 151–197, which includes

translations of a particular story by both Scherzer and Swann, and Scherzer's brief account (195) of what this cooperation meant to him.

37. For Finnegan's critique of Parry-Lord and McLuhan-Ong see, respectively, 69–87 and 254–260. For the criticism of Goody, see Dennis Tedlock 1983, 235 n., and of Ong, Bauman 1986, 9–10.

11. NO TWO-HEADED GREEKS

1. In speaking of a consensus in classical studies I have in mind the absorption of the work subsequently discussed in (1) the textbook tradition; for example, two fairly recent introductory texts, Harris and Platzner 1995 and Powell 1995, which now contest in the United States the generation-long dominance of Morford and Lenardon 1995; (2) recent scholarly introductions to the field; for example, Dowden 1992, Graf 1993, Buxton 1994; (3) recent general collections of scholarly essays; for example, Bremmer 1987 and Edmunds 1990.

2. Müller's argument confines him, however, to the area between India and Greece, whereas Dumézil's hypothesis applies in principle to the entire Indo-European range, and his disciples aspire to extend it to other linguistic areas.

3. This foundational assumption opens him both to the same objections that have been made to Durkheim and especially to the Sahlins-Liszka critique of any such absolutism of cultural code. Dumézil's "Indo-European" concept is also questionable, both, as Littleton points out (Littleton 1982, 228) with respect to its Sapir-Whorf-like homology between language and world-view and also, particularly since the phenomenon of German National Socialism, with respect to its latent baggage of romantic racism.

4. For the phrase "epic thematization" see Dumézil 1983, 1.

5. Lévi-Strauss, who has often paid tribute to Dumézil's influence, at one time considered titling the last volume of *Mythologiques* "du mythe au roman" and does in fact so title the section of *The Origin of Table Manners* that concludes with his remarks on the resemblance between the degenerate nature of the story of Cimidyuë and that of the modern novel.

6. So general a sketch risks misleading by omission of exceptions and qualifications. For a masterly survey of ritualist theories, including a good assessment of their continuities and differences, see H. S. Versnel 1990. For Walter Burkert's own clear and succinct situating of his own work in relation to this tradition, see Burkert 1982, 35–39.

7. Burkert points out these differences himself in a note to the English translation (Burkert 1983, 35).

8. This work, *Structure and History in Greek Mythology and Ritual,* addresses the nature of myth much more explicitly than *Homo Necans* does.

9. Burkert also points out (23) that the Greek identification of myth with saga undermines the folklorists' post-Grimm distinction of the category "legend" between myth and tale.

10. In his inaugural lecture at the Collège de France, "Greek Religion, Ancient Religions," Vernant stresses this second difference when he remarks that in contradistinction to the Meuli-Burkert connection of sacrificial rites with Paleolithic times, "we wish to apprehend the nature of sacrifice in the meanings, values and functions it implied for the Greeks of the archaic and classical periods" (Vernant 1991, 279).

11. Claude Calame, however, in his essay "Narrating the Foundation of a City: The Symbolic Birth of Cyrene" does actually harden Detienne's argument into the assertion that "what we call myth . . . has no existence in itself, nor does it correspond to any universal cultural reality. In essence, myth is only a concept invented by modern anthropology out of the uncertainties gradually recognized by the Greeks themselves as to the historical reality of certain episodes in their tradition" (Edmunds 1990, 278). Calame speaks narrowly, of course, in asserting that the concept was invented by "modern anthropology."

12. I am indebted to Klein 1986 for the suggestion that the style of *The Creation of Myth* is itself *metic*. This issue of *Diacritics* is largely devoted to pieces by and about Vernant and Detienne.

13. The other approaches I have in mind here are particularly: (1) non-Dumézelian work in comparative mythology like that of Geoffrey Kirk, Walter Burkert, and Robert Mondi on the impact of Near Eastern myth on Greek; (2) Carlo Brillante's reconsideration of the role of myth in historical reconstruction; and (3) Claude Calame's semiotic analyses of foundation myths. See Kirk 1973; Burkert 1992; the essays by Brillante, Mondi, and Calame in Edmunds 1990; and by Calame in Bremer 1987.

12. MYTH AND IDEOLOGY

1. In the course of considering these contradictory senses of "myth," I noted for a week instances of its usage in five periodicals: the *Boston Globe,* the *Sunday New York Times,* the *New Yorker,* the *New York Review of Books,* and the *Times Literary Supplement.* I found eleven attestations, all of them in the second, pejorative sense.

2. Apart from some of the "classic" modifications of the concept after Marx, including those of Lukács, Mannheim, and Althusser discussed in the following pages, I have been affected in particular by the relevant essays in Lichtheim 1967, Williams 1977, Seliger 1977, Geuss 1981, Larrain 1979, and Eagleton 1991. Except for a few pages of Eagleton, work on ideology pays little serious attention to myth. For an excellent book that does attend to the close relations between the two, see Flood 1996, which also summarizes and assesses a body of relevant academic scholarship in social psychology and political science that is otherwise out of my purview.

3. This wording is an attempt to finesse two major disputes within Marxian studies. The first is about how the relation of base to superstructure is to be understood, and the second about whether the relation of ideology to the superstructure should be construed broadly or narrowly; that is, whether all aspects of the superstructure are necessarily ideological or whether some of them need not be. For a clarifying analysis of this second dispute, see Larrain 1979, 50–52. Larrain argues for the narrow interpretation and proposes to distinguish ideology, which, strictly speaking, implies "a particular, distorted kind of consciousness which conceals contradictions" (50), from what he views as the larger category of "idealistic superstructure" (51), which reflects class consciousness but does not necessarily disguise what it is.

4. For quotation and discussion of the passage in question, see chapter 3. Raymond Williams has a good critique of this passage along similar lines. See Williams 1977, 58–59.

5. Gramsci's prison writings date from the mid-1930s but were published only between 1947 and 1949; they affect theorizing about the concept of ideology, therefore, only in a late stage of its transformation. But Lukács's *History and Class Consciousness* (1922), probably the best known work of Marxist theory in the century, is pivotal. Lukács not only improves on Lenin by referring to historical materialism as "the ideology of the proletariat" (Lukács 19/1, 228), but he also employs "ideology" to designate the entire "superstructure" (64) and comes near to using "myth" and "mythology" as synonyms for it. He repeatedly resorts to the latter terms, for example, to denote the same Idealist concepts that provoked Marx to label them "ideology" (see 15–18, for example).

6. The standard general account in English of this reception is still Hughes 1958. See especially chapter 3, "The Critique of Marxism."

7. Durkheim actually conscripts "ideology" for service in *The Rules of Sociological Method* where it signifies, approximately, the preconceptions that inhibit accurate scientific observation. This is a usage analogous to Marx's in its fairly narrow, pejorative application, but, as Jorge Larrain points out, more like some of the Baconian "idols" in implying an innate mental tendency unconnected to social causality. Durkheim does not employ the term in *Elementary Forms,* but for a close and subtle analysis of how the conception of "collective consciousness" entails the addition of an affective dimension to his conception of "ideology," see Larrain 1979, 93–99.

8. For two stern but fair assessments by later writers on the topic, both sympathetic to Marxism, see Larrain 1979, 100–122, and Eagleton 1991, 107–110.

9. It may well seem that Mannheim leaves himself no unrelativized basis for evaluating congruence with reality, but he argues, rather like Lukács, that "realistic" value judgments are

possible from within particular social and political positions, and he characterizes his stance as "relationism" rather than "relativism" (76).

10. Mannheim shows no sign of recognizing any such symmetry with Sorel. He refers to Sorel and to *Reflections on Violence* only in the context of characterizing fascism as an "ideal type" in modern politics. See Mannheim 1936, 119, 121–122. Nevertheless, the symmetry is there, first brought to my attention in Halpern 1961, 129–149.

11. In this sense Mannheim's view of the relation between "ideology" and "myth" is very close to that of Christopher Flood's in *Political Myth* (Flood 1996).

12. This conjunction of "structural" influences in Lukács is widely recognized but stated especially clearly in Held 1980, 22.

13. Lacan's conception of the unconscious as displaying "the whole structure of language" very probably owes a direct debt to Lévi-Strauss, especially to *The Elementary Structures of Kinship* (1949) if not to "The Structural Study of Myth" (1955). Lacan points to the significance of Lévi-Strauss's work as early as "The Function and Field of Speech and Language in Psychoanalysis" (1953), and the essay in which the key assertion about language appears, "The Agency of the Letter in the Unconscious, or Reason Since Freud," dates from 1957. For the early reference see Lacan 1977, 73.

14. I accept an Althusserian reading of Lacan that Terry Eagleton finds too politically pessimistic and based on misunderstandings of Lacan's "subject" and its relation to "Subject" or "the Other." For this critique, which at least suggests some of the difficulties in interpreting Lacan that are repressed in my sketch, see Eagleton 1991, 144–146.

15. Frederic Jameson makes this point particularly well in *The Political Unconscious* (Jameson 1981, 33–36).

16. I have attempted an accurate synthesis, but for the history of Althusser's (relatively minor) inconsistencies, retractions, and reassertions on the subject of ideology, see Larrain 1979, 154–164.

17. The passage quoted and the two subsequent ones are taken from the reprinted preface to the French edition of 1970, published thirteen years after the original edition of 1957, at a significantly later stage in Barthes's career.

18. See for discussion Culler 1983b, 73–74.

19. In *Image, Music, Text* he also affirms, with specific reference to *Mythologies,* that deconstructive fissuring of signs and representations of meaning take precedence over the structural semiology of his early work (Barthes 1971, 166–167).

20. For the relevant correspondence, see Jay 1973, 207–208.

21. For comparable exchanges of the two terms, see also 186, 188, 197–198.

22. Translator Alan Bass's notes are by far the best commentary on this text. Among general commentaries on Derrida, I am especially indebted to Spivak 1976, Descombes 1980, Culler 1983a, and Christopher Norris 1987.

23. Others have broached of course the topic of myth and ideology as analogues in traditional and modern cultures. Christopher Flood, for example, asserts categorically in *Political Myth* that in its range of social functions "the role of myth in ancient or traditional societies has been analogous to the role of ideology in modern societies" (41).

13. MYTH AS NECESSARY FICTION

1. Ricoeur associates these projects only at the very high level of abstraction involved in seeing them all as "Kantian schematisms of the productive imagination" or "transcendental deductions" (the latter being defined in *Evil* as "justifying a concept by showing that it makes possible the construction of a domain of objectivity" [355]). In one place or another in his writing, he carefully distinguishes these thinkers from one another and each from himself. For good accounts of Ricoeur's notion of Kantian schematisms of the productive imagination, see Ricoeur 1984–1988, vol. 1, 68 and vol. 2, 18, 164. For his distinction of himself from Eliade, see Ricoeur 1969, 353, and from Frye, Ricoeur 1984–1988, vol. 2, 164–165.

2. See Adams 1983, 372–389, and White 1987, 169–184.

3. For the relevant explanations, severely compressed here, see Ricoeur 1976, 64–69.

4. For Ricoeur's argument, again outrageously compressed here, see especially *Rule*, 244–245.

5. Ricoeur's conception of the role of *mythos* or narrative in creating personal meaning is a distinguished contribution to what has become an impressive interdisciplinary trend in the 1980s and 1990s. In the central chapters of his subsequent *Oneself as Another* (Ricoeur 1990, trans. 1992), he logically extends the thrust of his inquiry to the role of narrative in the construction of personal identity.

6. For this discussion, see Ricoeur 1984–1988, volume 2, 22–27. The passage quoted is on page 22.

7. See Kolakowski 1989. Kolakowski tells us in the preface to this English translation that the work was written in Poland in 1966 but barred from publication by state censorship and first published in France in 1972.

8. Amid the welter of commentary on the connections between myth and modern literature, it is the special distinction of John J. White's *Mythology in the Modern Novel* that it proposes to confine the term "myth" to particular ancient stories and to treat references to them in modern fiction as "an analogical system of comment that precludes certain essentially Romantic views" (John J. White 1971, 14). As White points out, this sort of modern usage should be regarded as an aspect of "the rhetoric of fiction." His own treatment of it as "prefiguration," that is, as a device for anticipating plot, is a valuable start on such a demystified rhetorical analysis. It deserves far more attention than it has received.

9. Todorov's work was published originally in 1977 and translated by Catherine Porter as *Theories of the Symbol* (Ithaca: Cornell, 1982). Adams's appeared in 1983. The two histories, to the extent that they overlap, corroborate one another strikingly; in their accounts, for example, of the romantics' innovations, in their low estimates of later nineteenth-century originality, in their ultimately negative assessments of the contributions of Freud and Jung, and so forth. The extent of their agreement is particularly impressive when one considers that Todorov comes at the history by way of structuralism and semiotics, and pretty much unaware of Anglo-American discourse about romanticism. Even when Todorov goes on to excoriate Saussure's assumption that all semiology must be modeled on linguistics, and seeks for himself the middle ground of a rhetorical mode of symbolism not founded upon the linguistic sign, he writes as if unaware that he works in a *tradition* of critical efforts to reconcile romanticism and positivism. It is no wonder, then, that he concludes "we do not have a simple alloy. . . . one would have to try one's own hand at a 'theory of the symbol'. . . [which] can be produced only by the construction of a *symbolics of language*'" (292). Enter Adams.

10. Strictly speaking, Adams adds a fifth type of allegory, the "Hegelian," but he omits it from his schema because it is unique to Hegel and not exactly romantic allegory as so defined. Adams points out that Hegel uses the term "symbolic" in a maverick sense that has confused the issue in relation to the romantic main stream. (On this point, too, he and Todorov agree.)

11. Adams addresses in the same chapter with Croce, Hans Vaihinger's theory of fictions in *The Philosophy of "As If,"* first published in 1911 (see Vaihinger 1969). But Adams argues that, contrary to the fashionable use made of Vaihinger by certain literary theorists, notably Frank Kermode in *The Sense of an Ending* (1967), Vaihinger's theory is positivistic and will not support any parallel between scientific fictions and literary ones. Adams finds Kermode's own theory "pragmatic" rather than "positivistic" like Vaihinger's, and he objects on revealing ethical grounds to its view that our fictional constructions involve an element of convenient self-deception. "It is not very far," he remarks, "from Kermode's idea of fiction to Jacques Derrida's recent deconstruction of texts . . . grounded in a theory of fictions *all* of which are shown not to be false but 'undecidable'" (198). Ricoeur, who acknowledges Kermode's influence on the shaping of his central conception of how narrative refigures time, recognizes that the way *The Sense of an Ending* "oscillates between the inescapable suspicion that fictions lie and deceive . . . and the equally invincible conviction that fictions are not simply arbitrary" is actually Nietzschean (Ricoeur 1984–1988, vol. 2, 27). If Kermode's view of fiction were applied to

myth, his theorizing would constitute the most purely Nietzschean instance of the paradox of the "supreme fiction." For his actual conception of myth, however, see the last section of this chapter.

12. At this point in his text, Adams discusses the work of three purveyors of "sentimental archaism": Campbell, Eliade, and Wheelwright. They have in common notions about the ability of modern humanity to get back in touch with archaic wisdom. All three "span a range from 'religious' allegory to 'miraculous' symbolism. None reaches a concept of a secular symbolic, but each raises the problem of the relation of poetry to religion" (244).

13. In my own discussion of *A Vision* in chapter 6, I have doubted that Yeats consistently maintains this tension with respect to belief.

14. While this conspectus is restricted to the ideological and constructivist theorists considered in the last two chapters, the penchant for "diacritical" terms tends to include other recent theorists insofar as they confront myth's social function. As an earnest of its presence among folkloristic thinkers, one might recall Liszka's insistence in *The Semiotics of Myth* that myths are by function *"critical . . .* liminal and ambivalent" (181), thus provoking "ideological" interpretations that attempt to defang them even in the process of reception.

WORKS CITED

Abraham, Hilda C., and Ernst L. Freud. 1965. *A Psychoanalytic Dialogue: The Letters of Sigmund Freud and Karl Abraham*. Translated by Bernard Marsh and Hilda C. Abraham. New York: Basic Books.

Abraham, Karl. 1955. Dreams and Myths. In *Clinical Papers and Essays in Psychoanalysis*. Edited by Hilda C. Abraham. London: Hogarth, 153–209.

Abrams, Meyer H. 1953. *The Mirror and the Lamp*. Oxford: Oxford University Press.

———. 1971. *Natural Supernaturalism*. New York: WW Norton.

Ackerman, Robert. 1973. Frazer on Myth and Ritual. *Journal of the History of Ideas* 34: 115–134.

———. 1987. *J. G. Frazer: His Life and Work*. Cambridge: Cambridge University Press.

———. 1991. *The Myth and Ritual School*. New York: Garland.

Adams, Hazard. 1983. *The Philosophy of the Literary Symbolic*. Tallahassee: University of Florida Press.

Adorno, Theodor W. 1966. *Negative Dialectics*. New York: Continuum.

Allen, Douglas. 1998. *Myth and Religion in Mircea Eliade*. New York: Garland.

Althusser, Louis. 1971. *Lenin and Philosophy*. Translated by Ben Brewster. London: New Left Books.

———. 1977. *For Marx*. Translated by Ben Brewster. London: New Left Books.

Anderson, Perry. 1976. *Some Considerations of Western Marxism*. London: New Left Books.

Bacon, Francis. 1963. Reprint. The Wisdom of the Ancients. In *The Works of Francis Bacon*. Stuttgart: Gunther Holzboog Verlag. Vol. 6, 619–764. Original edition, London, 1857–1874. Edited by James Spedding, Robert Ellis, and Douglas Heath.

———. 2000. *The New Organon*. Translated and edited by Lisa Jardine and Michael Silverthorne. Cambridge: Cambridge University Press.

Barthes, Roland. 1971. *Image, Music, Text*. Translated by Stephen Heath. New York: Hill and Wang.

———. 1974. *S/Z*. Translated by Richard Miller. New York: Hill and Wang.

———. 1983a. Reprint. *Mythologies*. Selected and translated by Annette Lavers. New York: Hill and Wang. Original edition, Paris: Editions du seuil, 1957.

———. 1983b. Reprint. *Elements of Semiology*. Translated by Annette Lavers and Colin Smith. New York: Hill and Wang. Original edition, Paris: Editions du Seuil, 1964.

Bascom, William. 1984. The Forms of Folklore: Prose Narratives. In *Sacred Narrative: Readings in the Theory of Myth*, 5–28. Edited by Alan Dundes. Berkeley: University of California Press. First published in *Journal of American Folklore* 78 (1965), 3–20.

Basso, Ellen. 1987. *In Favor of Deceit: A Study of Tricksters in an Amazonian Society*. Tucson: University of Arizona Press.

Bauman, Richard, and C. L. Briggs. 1986. *Story, Performance and Event: Contextual Studies of Oral Narrative*. Cambridge: Cambridge University Press.

———. 1990. Poetics and Performance as Critical Perspectives on Language and Social Life. In *Annual Review of Anthropology,* vol. 19, 59–88.

Beach, Edward Allen. 1988. *The Potencies of God(s): Schelling's Philosophy of Mythology.* Albany: SUNY Press.

Beer, Gillian. 1975. Myth and the Single Consciousness: *Middlemarch* and *The Lifted Veil.* In *This Particular Web.* Edited by Ian Adam. Toronto: University of Toronto Press, 91–115.

———. 1983. *Evolutionary Narrative in Darwin, George Eliot and Nineteenth-Century Fiction.* London: Routledge and Kegan Paul.

Beidelman, Thomas O. 1974. *W. Robertson Smith and the Sociological Study of Religion.* Chicago: University of Chicago Press.

Benedict, Ruth. 1968. Reprint. Introduction to Zuni Mythology. In Georges, 102–136. First published in *Zuni Mythology.* New York: Columbia University Press, 1935. Vol. 1, xi–xliii.

Benjamin, Walter. 1969. *Illuminations.* Edited by Hannah Arendt. New York: Schocken.

———. 1971. *The Origins of German Tragic Drama.* Translated by John Osborne. London: New Left Books.

Benstock, Sheri. 1985. Nightletters: Women's Writing in the Wake. In *Critical Essays on James Joyce.* Edited by Bernard Benstock. Boston: G. G. Hall and Co.

Bergson, Henri. 1977. Reprint. *The Two Sources of Religion and Morality.* Translated by R. Ashley Audra and Cloudesley Brereton. Notre Dame, Ind.: Notre Dame University Press. Original edition, New York: Henry Holt, 1935.

Berressem, Hanjo. 1990. The Letter! The Litter! The Defilements of the Signifier. In *Finnegans Wake Fifty Years.* Edited by Geert Lernout. Amsterdam: Rodopi, 139–164.

Bidney, David. 1965. Reprint. Myth, Symbolism and Truth. In Sebeok, 3–24. First printed in *Bibliographical and Special Series of the American Folklore Society.* Vol. 5.

Birch, Dinah. 1988. *Ruskin's Myths.* Oxford: The Clarendon Press.

Bishop, John. 1986. *Joyce's Book of the Dark.* Madison: University of Wisconsin Press.

Blake, William. 1965. The Marriage of Heaven and Hell. In *The Prose and Poetry of William Blake.* Edited by David V. Erdman. New York: Doubleday, 33–44.

Bloom, Harold. 1959. *Shelley's Mythmaking.* New Haven: Yale University Press.

———. 1970. *Yeats.* New York: Oxford University Press.

Blumenberg, Hans. 1983. *The Legitimacy of the Modern Age.* Translated by Robert M. Wallace. Cambridge, Mass.: MIT Press. Original edition, Frankfort: Suhrkamp, 1966.

———. 1985. *Work on Myth.* Translated by Robert M. Wallace. Cambridge, Mass.: MIT Press.

Boas, Franz. 1916. Tsimshian Mythology. In *Thirty-First Annual Report of the Bureau of American Ethnology to the Secretary of the Smithsonian Institute.* Washington, D.C.: Government Printing Office, 27–1037.

———. 1938. *General Anthropology: With Contributions by Ruth Benedict et al.* Boston: Heath.

———. 1982. Reprint. *Race, Language and Culture.* Chicago: University of Chicago Press. Original edition, New York: Macmillan, 1940.

———. 1989. Reprint. *A Franz Boas Reader: The Shaping of American Anthropology: 1883–1911.* Chicago: University of Chicago Press. Originally published New York: Basic Books, 1974.

Boon, James A. 1972. *From Symbolism to Structuralism: Lévi-Strauss in a Literary Tradition.* Oxford: Basil Blackwell.

———. 1982. *Other Tribes, Other Scribes: Symbolic Anthropology in the Comparative Study of Cultures, Histories, Religion and Texts.* Cambridge: Cambridge University Press.

Bremmer, J. N., ed. 1987. *Interpretations of Greek Mythology.* London: Croom Helm.

Brillante, Carlo. 1990. History and the Historical Interpretation of Myth. In Edmunds, 91–138.

Brown, Marshall. 1979. *The Shape of German Romanticism.* Ithaca: Cornell University Press.

———. 1991. *Preromanticism.* Palo Alto: Stanford University Press.

Brown, Robert F. 1977. *The Later Philosophy of Schelling: The Influence of Boehme on the Works of 1809–1815.* Lewiston, Pa.: Bucknell University Press.

Burkert, Walter. 1982. Reprint. *Structure and History in Greek Mythology and Ritual.* Berkeley: University of California Press. Original edition, 1979.

————. 1983. *Homo Necans: The Anthropology of Ancient Greek Sacrificial Ritual and Myth.* Translated by Peter Bing. Berkeley: University of California Press.

————. 1992. *The Orientalizing Revolution.* Translated by Margaret E. Pinder and Walter Burkert. Cambridge: Harvard University Press.

Burridge, K. O. L. 1967. Lévi-Strauss and Myth. In Leach, 91–114.

Burrow, J. W. 1966. *Evolution and Society.* London: Cambridge University Press.

Bush, Douglas. 1936. *Mythology and the Romantic Tradition.* Cambridge: Harvard University Press.

Buxton, Richard. 1994. *Imaginary Greece: The Contexts of Mythology.* Cambridge: Cambridge University Press.

Calame, Claude. 1990. Narrating the Foundation of a City: The Symbolic Birth of Cyrene. In *Approaches to Greek Myth.* Edited by Lowell Edmunds. Baltimore: Johns Hopkins University Press, 277–341.

Campbell, Joseph. 1973. Reprint. *The Hero with a Thousand Faces.* Princeton: Princeton University Press. Original edition, 1949.

————. 1976. Reprint. *The Masks of God.* 4 vols. New York: Viking. Original edition, 1959–1968.

Campbell, Joseph, and Henry Morton Robinson. 1977. Reprint. *A Skeleton Key to Finnegans Wake.* New York: Penguin. Original edition, New York: Harcourt Brace Jovanovich, 1944.

Carlyle, Thomas. 1918. *Past and Present.* New York: Scribners.

————. 1937. *Sartor Resartus: The Life and Opinions of Herr Teufelsdröckh.* Edited by Charles Frederick Harrold. New York: Odyssey Press.

————. 1968. *On Heroes and Hero-Worship and the Heroic in History.* London: Oxford University Press, 1968.

Carroll, Michael P. 1978. Lévi-Strauss on the Oedipus Myth: A Reconsideration. In *American Anthropologist* 80, 805–814.

Cassirer, Ernst. 1966. Reprint. *An Essay on Man: An Introduction to a Philosophy of Human Culture.* New Haven. Yale University Press. Original edition, 1944.

————. 1975. Reprint. *Mythical Thought.* Volume 2 of *The Philosophy of Symbolic Forms.* Translated by Ralph Manheim. New Haven: Yale University Press. Original edition, 1955.

————. 1979. Reprint. *The Myth of the State.* New Haven: Yale University Press. Original edition, 1946.

Cazeneuve, Jean. 1972. *Lucien Lévy-Bruhl.* Translated by Peter Riviére. New York: Harper and Row.

Chase, Richard. 1949. *The Quest for Myth.* Baton Rouge: Louisiana State University Press.

Clarke, Simon. 1977. Lévi-Strauss's Structural Analysis of Myth. *Sociological Review* 25: 743–774.

————. 1981. *The Foundations of Structuralism.* Brighton: The Harvester Press Ltd.

Clifford, James, and George E. Marcus, editors. 1986. *Writing Culture: The Poetics and Politics of Ethnography.* Berkeley: University of California Press.

————. 1988. *The Predicament of Culture.* Cambridge: Harvard University Press.

Coleridge, Samuel Taylor. 1907. *Biographia Literaria.* Vol. 1. Edited by J. Shawcross. Oxford: Oxford University Press.

————. 1972. The Statesman's Manual in *Lay Sermons.* Edited by R. J. White. In *Collected Works of Samuel Taylor Coleridge.* No. 6. Princeton: Princeton University Press, 3–52.

Comte, Auguste. 1875. *Physique sociale: cours de philosophie positive.* Vol. 2. Edited by J-P Enthoven. Paris: Hermann.

Connor, Steven. 1990. The Birth of Humility: Frazer and Victorian Mythography. In *Sir James Frazer and the Literary Imagination.* Edited by Robert Frazer. New York: Macmillan, 61–79.

Cooke, Deryck. 1979. *I Saw the World End: A Study of Wagner's Ring.* London: Oxford.

Copleston, Frederick. 1965. *A History of Philosophy.* Vol. 7. *Modern Philosophy.* Part I. Garden City, N.Y.: Image Books.

Creuzer, Friedrich. 1821. *Symbolik und Mythologie der Alter Völker, besonders der Grieschen.* 2nd ed. Leipsig und Darmstadt: Heyer und Leske. Original edition, 1810–1812.

Culler, Jonathan. 1975. *Structuralist Poetics.* Ithaca: Cornell University Press.

———. 1983a. *On Deconstruction: Theory and Criticism after Structuralism.* Ithaca: Cornell University Press.

———. 1983b. *Roland Barthes.* New York: Oxford University Press.

De Crivieux, Marc. 1980. *Watunna: An Orinoco Creation Cycle.* Edited and translated by David Guss. San Francisco: North Point Press.

De Man, Paul. 1983. The Rhetoric of Temporality. In *Blindness and Insight.* Minneapolis: University of Minnesota Press, 187–228. First published in *Interpretation,* edited by Charles Singleton. Baltimore: Johns Hopkins University Press, 1969.

Deleuze, Gilles. 1983. *Nietzsche and Philosophy.* Translated by Hugh Tomlinson. New York: Columbia University Press.

Derrida, Jacques. 1982. White Mythology: Metaphor in the Text of Philosophy. In *Margins of Philosophy.* Translated by Alan Bass. Chicago: University of Chicago Press, 209–271.

Descombes, Vincent. 1980. *Modern French Philosophy.* Translated by L. Scott-Fox and J. M. Harding. Cambridge: Cambridge University Press.

Detienne, Marcel. 1977. *The Gardens of Adonis.* Translated by Janet Lloyd. Atlantic Highlands, N.J.: Humanities Press.

———. 1986. *The Invention of Myth.* Translated by Margaret Cook. Chicago: University of Chicago Press.

Detienne, Marcel, and Jean-Pierre Vernant. 1978. *Cunning Intelligence in Greek Society and Culture.* Translated by Janet Lloyd. Atlantic Highlands, N.J.: Humanities Press.

Dorson, Richard M. 1968. *The British Folklorists: A History.* Chicago: University of Chicago Press.

Doty, William G. 2000. *Mythography: The Study of Myths and Rituals.* 2nd ed. Tuscaloosa: University of Alabama Press.

Douglas, Mary. 1975a. Reprint. The Meaning of Myth. In *Implicit Meanings: Essays in Anthropology.* London: Routledge & Kegan Paul, 153–172. Originally published in Leach, 1967, 49–68.

———. 1975b. What If the Dogon. . . . In *Implicit Meanings: Essays in Anthropology.* London: Routledge and Kegan Paul, 124–141. Originally published in Paris: Cahiers d'Études Africaines, vol. 7, no. 28, 1967.

———. 1981. *Edward Evans-Pritchard.* New York: Penguin Books.

Dowden, Ken. 1992. *The Uses of Greek Mythology.* London: Routledge.

Dumézil, Georges, 1977. Reprint. *Gods of the Ancient Norsemen.* Translated by Einar Haugen et al. Berkeley: University of California Press. Original edition, 1973.

———. 1983. *The Stakes of the Warrior.* Translated by David Weeks and edited by Jaan Puhvel. Berkeley: University of California Press.

Duncan, David P. 1968. *Eliot's Casaubon and Mythology.* In ANQ 6, 125–127.

Dundes, Alan, ed. 1984. *Sacred Narrative: Reading in the Theory of Myth.* Berkeley: University of California Press.

———. 1990. The Hero Pattern in the Life of Jesus. In *In Quest of the Hero.* Princeton: Princeton University Press, 180–223.

Durkheim, Émile. 1899. De la définition des phénomenes religieux. In *L'année Sociologique,* vol. 2, 1–28.

———. 1965. Reprint. *The Elementary Forms of the Religious Life.* Translated by Joseph Swain. New York: The Free Press. Original edition, London: George Allen and Unwin Ltd., 1915.

———. 1982. *The Rules of Sociological Method.* Edited by Stephen Lukes. Translated by W. D. Halls. New York: Free Press.

———. 1994. Review. Lévy-Bruhl—*Les functions mentale dans les sociétés inférieures* et Émile Durkheim—*Les formes élémentaires de la vie religeuse: le système totémique en Australie.* In *Durkheim on Religion.* Edited by William Pickering. Atlanta: Scholars Press, 169–173. Originally published in *L'Année Sociologique,* 1913, vol. 12, 33–37.

Durkheim, Émile, and Marcel Mauss. 1963. *Primitive Classification.* Translated by Rodney Needham. Chicago: University of Chicago Press.

Eagleton, Terry. 1981. *Literary Theory: An Introduction*. Minneapolis: Minnesota University Press.

———. 1991. *Ideology: An Introduction*. London: Verso.

Edmunds, Lowell. 1990. Introduction: The Practice of Greek Mythology. In *Approaches to Greek Myth*. Edited by Lowell Edmunds. Baltimore: Johns Hopkins University Press, 1–20.

Eliade, Mircea. 1954. *Cosmos and History: The Myth of the Eternal Return*. New York: Pantheon.

———. 1957. *The Sacred and the Profane: The Nature of Religion*. Translated by Willard Trask. New York: Harcourt Brace Jovanovich.

———. 1963. *Patterns in Comparative Religion*. Translated by Rosemary Sheed. New York: World Publishing Co.

———. 1969. *The Quest: History and Meaning in Religion*. Chicago: University of Chicago Press.

———. 1973. Mythology in the Nineteenth and Twentieth Centuries. In *Dictionary of the History of Ideas*. Edited by Philip Wiener. New York: Scribners, 307–318.

———. 1975. Reprint. *Myth and Reality*. New York: Harper and Row. Original edition, 1963.

———. 1978. *From the Stone Age to the Eleusinian Mysteries*. Vol. 1 of *A History of Religious Ideas*. Translated by Willard Trask. Chicago: University of Chicago Press.

Eliot, George. 1963. *Essays of George Eliot*. Edited by Thomas Phinney. London: Routledge and Kegan Paul.

———. 1967. *Daniel Deronda*. Edited by Barbara Hardy. Hammondsworth: Penguin.

Eliot, Thomas Stearns. 1923. Review. *Ulysses*, Order and Myth. In *Dial* 85, 480–483.

———. 1962. *The Collected Poems and Plays of T. S. Eliot*. New York: Harcourt, Brace and World.

Ellen, Roy, et al. 1988. *Malinowski between Two Worlds*. Cambridge: Cambridge University Press.

Ellenberger, Henri. 1970. *The Discovery of the Unconscious: The History and Evolution of Dynamic Psychiatry*. New York: Basic Books.

Ellmann, Richard. 1964. *The Identity of Yeats*. Oxford: Oxford University Press.

Engell, James. 1981. The Modern Revival of Myth: Its Eighteenth-Century Origins. In *Allegory, Myth and Symbol*. Harvard English Studies 9. Edited by Morton Bloomfield. Cambridge: Harvard University Press, 245–271.

Evans-Pritchard, Edward Evan. 1937. *Witchcraft, Oracles and Magic among the Azande*. Oxford: The Clarendon Press.

———. 1956. *Nuer Religion*. Oxford: Oxford University Press.

———. 1965. *Theories of Primitive Religion*. Oxford: The Clarendon Press.

Fabian, Johannes. 1983. *Time and the Other: How Anthropology Makes Its Object*. New York: Columbia University Press.

Feldman, Burton, and Robert D. Richardson. 1972. *The Rise of Modern Mythology: 1680–1860*. Bloomington: Indiana University Press.

Ferenczi, Sandor. 1968. Reprint. *Thalassa: A Theory of Genitality*. Translated by Henry Alden Bunker. New York: WW Norton. Original edition, Vienna: Internationaler Psychanalytischer Verlag, 1924.

Feuerbach, Ludwig. 1957. Reprint. *The Essence of Christianity*. Trans. by Marian Evans. New York: Harper and Row. Originally published in London, 1854.

Finnegan, Ruth. 1992. Reprint. *Oral Poetry*. Bloomington: Indiana University Press. Original edition, Cambridge: Cambridge University Press, 1977.

Firth, Raymond. 1967. *The Work of the Gods in Tikopia*. London: The Athlone Press.

———. 1968. Reprint. Oral Tradition in Relation to Social Status. In *Studies in Mythology*. Edited by Robert A. Georges. Homewood, Ill.: The Dorsey Press, 1968, 168–183. Original edition, Wellington, New Zealand: The Polynesian Society, 1961.

———. 1984. Reprint. The Plasticity of Myth: Cases from Tikopia. In *Sacred Narrative: Readings in the Theory of Myth*. Edited by Alan Dundes. Berkeley: University of California Press, 207–216. Originally published in *Ethnologica* 2 (1960), 181–188.

Fitch, Raymond. 1982. *The Poison Sky*. Athens, Ohio: Ohio University Press.

Fletcher, Angus. 1966. Utopian History and the Anatomy of Criticism. In Krieger, 31–73.

Flood, Christoper. 1996. *Political Myth: A Theoretical Introduction.* New York: Garland.

Foley, J. Miles. 1988. *The Theory of Oral Composition: History and Methodology.* Bloomington: Indiana University Press.

Fontenelle, Bernard. 1989. De l'origine des fables. In *Oeuvres Complètes,* vol. 3. Paris: Fayard, 187–202.

Fontenrose, Joseph. 1966. *The Ritual Theory of Myth.* Berkeley: University of California Press.

Foucault, Michel. 1984. Reprint. Nietzsche, Genealogy, History. In *The Foucault Reader.* Edited by Paul Rabinow. Translated by Donald E. Bouchard and Sherry Simon. New York: Pantheon Books, 76–100. Original edition, *Language, Counter-memory, Practice: Selected Essay and Interviews.* Ithaca: Cornell University Press, 1977.

Frazer, James. G. 1922. *The Golden Bough.* New York: Macmillan.

———. 1966. Reprint. *The Golden Bough: A Study in Magic and Religion.* 12 volumes. New York: St. Martin's Press. Original edition, London: Macmillan, 1911–1915.

Frazer, Robert, ed. 1990a. *Sir James Frazer and the Literary Imagination.* New York: Macmillan.

———. 1990b. *The Making of the Golden Bough.* New York: St. Martin's Press.

Frei, Hans. 1974. *The Eclipse of Biblical Narrative.* New Haven: Yale University Press.

Freud, Sigmund. 1950. *Totem and Taboo.* Translated and edited by James Strachey. New York: WW Norton.

———. 1953–1973. *Standard Edition of the Complete Psychological Works of Sigmund Freud.* Edited and translated by James Strachey et al. 24 vols. London: Hogarth Press.

———. 1962. *The Ego and the Id.* Standard Edition, vol. 19. Translated and edited by James Strachey. London: Hogarth Press.

———. 1963a. Instincts and Their Vicissitudes. In *General Psychological Theory: Papers on Metapsychology.* Edited by Philip Rieff. New York: Macmillan, 83–103.

———. 1963b. Psychoanalytic Notes upon an Autobiographical Account of a Case of Paranoia. In *Freud: Three Case Histories.* Edited by Philip Rieff. Translated by James Strachey. New York: Macmillan, 103–186.

———. 1965a. *The Interpretation of Dreams.* Translated by James Strachey. New York: Avon.

———. 1965b. *New Introductory Lectures on Psychoanalysis.* Translated by James Strachey. New York: WW Norton.

———. 1971. From the History of an Infantile Neurosis. In *The Wolf Man.* Edited by Muriel Gardiner. Translated by James Strachey. New York: Basic Books, 153–307.

———. 1987. *Sigmund Freud: A Phylogenetic Fantasy.* Edited by Ilse Grubrich-Simitis. Translated by Axel and Peter T. Hoffer. Cambridge: Harvard University Press.

———. 1989. Creative Writers and Day-Dreaming. Translated by James Strachey. In *The Freud Reader.* Edited by Peter Gay. New York: WW Norton, 436–443.

Freud, Sigmund, ed. 1970. Reprint. *Schriften Zur Angewandten Seelenkunde.* Vol. 1. Liechtenstein: Kraus Reprints. Original edition, Wien: 1907.

Frye, Northrop. 1957. *Anatomy of Criticism.* Princeton: Princeton University Press.

Geertz, Clifford. 1988. *Works and Lives: The Anthropologist As Author.* Palo Alto: Stanford University Press.

Georges, Robert A., ed., 1968. *Studies on Mythology.* Homewood, Ill.: The Dorsey Press.

Gernet, Louis. 1981. Reprint. "Value" in Greek Myth. In *Myth, Religion and Society: Structuralist Essays.* Edited by R. L. Gordon. Cambridge: Cambridge University Press, 111–146. Originally published in *Journal de psychologie* 41 (1948): 415–462.

Geuss, Raymond. 1981. *The Idea of a Critical Theory.* Cambridge: Cambridge University Press.

Girard, René. 1977. *Violence and the Sacred.* Translated by Patrick Gregory. Baltimore: Johns Hopkins University Press.

Goody, Jack. 1972. *The Myth of the Bagre.* Oxford: Oxford University Press.

Gordon, Richard L., ed. 1981. *Myth, Religion and Society: Structuralist Essays by M. Detienne, L. Gernet, J-P Vernant and P. Vidal-Naquet.* Translated by Anon. Cambridge: Cambridge University Press.

———. 1995. *The God Game.* Review of Timothy Gantz, *Early Greek Myth,* Fritz Graf, *Greek Mythology: An Introduction,* and Richard Buxton, *Imaginary Greece.* In TLS, April 15: 11.

Gould, Eric. 1981. *Mythical Intentions in Modern Literature.* Princeton: Princeton University Press.

Gould, Stephen J. 1977. *Ontogeny and Phylogeny.* Cambridge: Harvard University Press.

Graf, Fritz. 1993. *Greek Mythology: An Introduction.* Translated by Thomas Marier. Baltimore: Johns Hopkins University Press.

Graves, Robert. 1966. Reprint. *The White Goddess: A Historical Grammar of Poetic Myth.* New York: Farrar, Strauss and Giroux. Original edition, 1948.

Gray, Thomas. 1935. *Correspondence of Thomas Gray.* Edited by Paget Toynbee and Leonard Whibley. 3 vols. Oxford: Clarendon Press.

Grimm, Jacob. 1883. *Grimm's Teutonic Mythology.* Translated by James Steven Stallybrass. London: George Bell and Sons.

Grubrich-Simitis, Ilse, ed. 1987. *Sigmund Freud: A Phylogenetic Fantasy.* Translated by Peter T. Hoffer. Cambridge: Harvard University Press.

Guss, David. 1990. *To Weave and To Sing: Art, Symbol and Narrative in the South American Rain Forest.* Berkeley: University of California Press.

Halpern, Ben. 1961. "Myth" and Ideology in Modern Usage. In *History and Theory,* vol. 1, no. 2.

Hamilton, A. C. 1990. *Northrop Frye: Anatomy of His Criticism.* Toronto: University of Toronto Press.

Harris, Horton. 1973. *David Friedrich Strauss and His Theology.* Cambridge: Cambridge University Press.

Harris, Marvin. 1968. *The Rise of Anthropological Theory.* New York: Thomas Y. Crowell Co. Inc.

———. 1979. *Cultural Materialism: The Struggle for a Science of Culture.* New York: Random House.

Harris, Stephen L., and Gloria Platzner. 1995. *Classical Mythology.* Mt. View, Calif.: Mayfield.

Harrison, Jane Ellen. 1977. Reprint. *Themis: A Study of the Social Origins of Greek Religion.* London: Merlin Press. Original edition, Cambridge: Cambridge University Press, 1912.

Harrold, Charles Frederick. 1934. *Carlyle and German Thought: 1819–1834.* New Haven: Yale University Press.

Harvey, Van A. 1995. *Feuerbach and the Interpretation of Religion.* Cambridge: Cambridge University Press.

Hayner, Paul C. 1967. *Reason and Existence: Schelling's Philosophy of History.* Leiden: E. J. Brill.

Hegel, Georg Wilhelm Friedrich. 1967. Reprint. *The Phenomenology of Mind.* Translated by J. D. Baillie. New York: Harper and Row. Original edition, London: Macmillan 1910.

Heidegger, Martin. 1962. *Being and Time.* Translated by John Macquarrie and Edward Robinson. New York: Harper and Row.

Held, David. 1980. *Introduction to Critical Theory: Horkheimer to Habermas.* Berkeley: University of California Press.

Herder, Johann Gottfried. 1966. Reprint. *Outlines of a Philosophy of the History of Mankind.* Trans. T. Churchill. New York: Bergman Publishers. Original edition, London: 1800.

Hill, Jonathan D., ed. 1988. *Rethinking History and Myth: Indigenous South American Perspectives on the Past.* Urbana: University of Illinois Press.

Hölderlin, Friedrich. 1980. *Friedrich Hölderlin: Poems and Fragments.* Trans. with preface, introduction, and notes by Michael Hamburger. Cambridge: Cambridge University Press.

———. 1988. *Friedrich Hölderlin: Essays and Letters on Theory.* Translated and edited by Thomas Pfau. Albany: SUNY Press.

Horkheimer, Max, and Theodor W. Adorno. Reprint. 1972. *Dialectic of Enlightenment.* Translated by John Cumming. New York: Continuum. Original edition, *Dialektik der Aufklärung,* New York: Social Studies Association, Inc., 1944.

Horton, Robin. 1973. Lévy-Bruhl, Durkheim and the Scientific Revolution. In *Modes of Thought: Essays on Thinking in Western and Non-Western Societies.* Edited by Robin Horton and Ruth Finnegan. London: Faber and Faber, 249–305.

Hubert, Henri. 1903. Les mythes. In *L'année sociologique,* vol. 6. 243–246, 268–271.

Hughes, H. Stuart. 1958. *Consciousness and Society: The Reorientation of European Social Thought, 1890–1930.* New York: Knopf.

Hutcheon, Linda. 1988. *A Poetics of Postmodernism*. London: Routledge.

Hyman, Stanley Edgar. 1959. *The Tangled Bank*. New York: Grosset and Dunlap.

———. 1965. Reprint. The Ritual View of Myth and the Mythic. In Sebeok, 136–153. Original edition, Bibliographical and Special Series of the American Folklore Society, vol 5.

Hymes, Dell. 1981a. "In Vain I Tried to Tell You." In *Essays in Native American Ethnopoetics*. Philadelphia: University of Pennsylvania Press, 117–159.

———. 1981b. Reading Klackamas Texts. In Kroeber, 117–159.

Jameson, Frederic. 1981. *The Political Unconscious: Narrative as Socially Symbolic Act*. Ithaca: Cornell University Press.

Jay, Martin. 1973. *The Dialectic Imagination: A History of the Frankfort School and the Institute for Social Research, 1923–1950*. Boston: Little Brown and Co.

Jones, Ernest. 1953. *The Life and Work of Sigmund Freud*. Vol. 1. New York: Basic Books.

Jones, Robert Alun. 1984. Robertson Smith and James Frazer on Religion: Two Traditions in British Anthropology. In *Functionalism Historicized: Essays on British Social Anthropology*. Edited by George W. Stocking Jr. Madison: University of Wisconsin Press, 31–58.

———. 1986. *Durkheim: An Introduction*. London: Sage.

Joyce, James. 1967. *Ulysses*. London: The Bodley Head.

———. 1988. *Finnegans Wake*. New York: Penguin.

Jung, C. G. 1916. *The Psychology of the Unconscious*. Translated by Beatrice Hinkle. New York: Moffat, Yard and Co.

———. 1953. *The Collected Works of C. G. Jung*. Edited by William McGuire et al. Translated by R. F. C. Hull. Princeton: Princeton University Press.

———. 1956. *Symbols of Transformation: An Analysis of the Prelude to a Case of Schizophrenia*. *CW*, vol. 5.

———. 1959a. Archetypes of the Collective Unconscious. In *The Archetypes and the Collective Unconscious*. 2nd ed. *CW*, vol. 9, Part I, 3–41.

———. 1959b. The Concept of the Collective Unconscious. In *The Archetypes and the Collective Unconscious*. 2nd ed. *CW*, vol. 9, Part I, 42–53.

———. 1961. *Memories, Dreams, Reflections*. Recorded and edited by Aniela Jaffé. Translated by Richard and Clara Winston. New York: Random House.

———. 1966. On the Relation of Analytical Psychology to Poetry. In *The Spirit in Man, Art and Literature*. *CW*, vol. 15, 65–83.

———. 1969. Instinct and the Unconscious. In *The Structure and Dynamics of the Psyche*. 2nd ed. *CW*, vol. 8, 129–138.

———. 1972. *Two Essays on Analytic Psychology*. *CW*, vol. 7.

Kamenka, Eugene. 1970. *The Philosophy of Ludwig Feuerbach*. London: Routledge and Kegan Paul.

Kant, Immanuel. 1986. *The Critique of Judgment*. Translated by James Creed Meredith. Oxford: The Clarendon Press. Original edition, 1928.

Keats, John. 1966. *The Selected Poetry of Keats*. Edited by Paul de Man. New York: National American Library.

Kelley, Donald R. 1987. In Vico's Wake. In *Vico and Joyce*. Edited by Donald Philip Verene. Albany: SUNY Press, 135–146.

Kenner, Hugh. 1959. *The Invisible Poet: T. S. Eliot*. New York: McDowell and Oblensky.

Kermode, Frank. 1967. *The Sense of an Ending*. Oxford: Oxford University Press.

Kirk, Geoffrey S. 1973. Reprint. *Myth: Its Meaning and Function in Ancient and Other Cultures*. Berkeley: University of California Press. Original edition, Cambridge: Cambridge University Press, 1970.

Klein, Richard. 1986. The Metis of Centaurs. In *Diacritics* 16, no. 2 (Summer): 2–13.

Kluckhohn, Clyde. 1968. Reprint. Myths and Rituals: A General Theory. In Georges, 137–167. Originally published in *Harvard Theological Review* 35, 1942, 45–79.

Knoepflmacher, U. C. 1975. Fantasy and Myth: the New Reality of *Middlemarch*. In *This Particular Web: Essays on Middlemarch*. Edited by Ian Adam. Toronto: University of Toronto Press, 43–72.

Kolakowski, Leszek. 1989. *The Presence of Myth.* Translated by Adam Czerniawski. Chicago: University of Chicago Press.

Krieger, Murray, ed. 1966. *Northrop Frye in Modern Criticism: Selected Papers from the English Institute.* New York: Columbia University Press.

Kroeber, Karl. 1981. *Traditional American Indian Literatures.* Lincoln: University of Nebraska Press.

Kuper, Adam. 1983. *Anthropology and Anthropologists: The Modern British School.* Revised edition. London: Routledge and Kegan Paul.

———. 1988. *The Invention of Primitive Society: Transformations of an Illusion.* London: Routledge.

Lacan, Jacques. 1977. *Écrits: A Selection.* Translated by Alan Sheridan. New York: WW Norton.

Lacoue-Labarthe, Philippe, and Jean-Luc Nancy. 1988. *The Literary Absolute: The Theory of Literature in German Romanticism.* Translated by Philip Barnard and Cheryl Lester. Albany: SUNY Press.

Lang, Andrew. 1969. Reprint. *Magic and Religion.* New York: Greenwood Press. Original edition, London: Longmans, Green and Co., 1901.

Langer, Susanne. 1980. Reprint. *Philosophy in a New Key: A Study in the Symbolism of Reason, Rite and Art.* Cambridge: Harvard University Press. Original edition, 1942.

Larrain, Jorge. 1979. *The Concept of Ideology.* Athens: University of Georgia Press.

Lawrence, David Herbert. 1953. Reprint. *St. Mawr and the Man Who Died.* New York: Vintage. Original edition, New York: Alfred A. Knopf, 1925.

———. 1959. Reprint. *The Plumed Serpent.* New York: Vintage. Original edition, New York: Alfred A. Knopf, 1926.

———. 1962. *The Collected Letters of D. H. Lawrence.* Edited by Harry T. Moore. New York: Viking.

———. 1973. Reprint. *Psychoanalysis and the Unconscious and Fantasia of the Unconscious.* New York: Viking. Original edition, 1923.

———. 1981. Reprint. *The Rainbow.* New York: Penguin. Original edition, London: Methuen and Co., 1915.

Leach, Edmund. 1964. Reprint. *Political Systems of Highland Burma: A Study of Kachin Social Structures.* Boston: Beacon Press. Original edition, 1954.

———. 1969. *Genesis as Myth and Other Essays.* London: Jonathan Cape.

———. 1974. *Claude Lévi-Strauss.* Chicago: University of Chicago Press.

Leach, Edmund, ed. 1967. *The Structural Study of Myth and Totemism.* London: Tavistock Publications Ltd.

Leach, Edmund, and Alan D. Aycock. 1983. *Structuralist Interpretations of Biblical Myth.* Cambridge: Cambridge University Press.

Leaf, Murray J. 1979. *Man, Mind and Science: A History of Anthropology.* New York: Columbia University Press.

Leitch, Vincent. 1983. *Deconstructive Criticism.* New York: Columbia University Press.

Lentricchia, Frank. 1980. *After the New Criticism.* Chicago: University of Chicago Press.

Lernout, Geert. 1990. *The French Joyce.* Ann Arbor: University of Michigan Press.

Levenson, Michael. 1984. *A Genealogy of Modernism.* Cambridge: Cambridge University Press.

Lévi-Strauss, Claude. 1965. Reprint. The Structural Study of Myth. In Sebeok, 81–106. Original edition, *Bibliographical and Special Series of the American Folklore Society,* vol. 5.

———. 1966. *The Savage Mind.* Translated by Anon. Chicago: University of Chicago Press.

———. 1969. *The Raw and the Cooked.* Translated by John and Doreen Weightman. Chicago: University of Chicago Press.

———. 1973a. *From Honey to Ashes.* Translated by John and Doreen Weightman. Chicago: University of Chicago Press.

———. 1973b. *The Origin of Table Manners.* Translated by John and Doreen Weightman. Chicago: University of Chicago Press.

———. 1976. *Structural Anthropology,* vol. 2. Translated by Monique Layton. Chicago: University of Chicago Press.

———. 1981. *The Naked Man.* Translated by John and Doreen Weightman. London: Jonathan Cape Ltd.

———. 1985. *The View from Afar.* Translated by Joachim Neugroschel and Phoebe Hoss. New York: Basic Books.

———. 1987. *Introduction to the Work of Marcel Mauss.* Translated by Felicity Baker. London: Routledge and Kegan Paul.

———. 1988a. *The Jealous Potter.* Translated by Bénédicte Chorier. Chicago: University of Chicago Press.

———. 1988b. *The Way of the Masks.* Translated by Sylvia Modeleski. Seattle: University of Washington Press.

———. 1995. *The Story of Lynx.* Translated by Catherine Tihanyi. Chicago: University of Chicago Press.

Lévi-Strauss, Claude, and Didier Eribon. 1991. *Conversations with Claude Lévi-Strauss.* Translated by Paula Wissing. Chicago: University of Chicago Press.

Lévy-Bruhl, Lucien. 1935. *La mythologie primitive.* Paris: Alcan.

———. 1985. Reprint. *How Natives Think.* Translated by Lillian A. Clare. Princeton: Princeton University Press. Original edition, London: Allen and Unwin, 1926. Original edition, Paris: Alcan, 1910.

Lichtheim, George. 1967. *The Concept of Ideology and Other Essays.* New York: Random House.

Lienhardt, Godfrey. 1961. *Divinity and Experience: The Religion of the Dinka.* Oxford: Oxford University Press.

Lipking, Lawrence. 1981. *The Life of the Poet: Beginning and Ending Poetic Careers.* Chicago: University of Chicago Press.

Liszka, James Jakob. 1989. *The Semiotics of Myth.* Bloomington: Indiana University Press.

Littleton, C. Scott. 1982. *The New Comparative Mythology: An Anthropological Assessment of the Theories of George Dumézil.* Berkeley: University of California Press.

———. 1985. Introduction. Lucien Lévy-Bruhl and the Concept of Cognitive Relativity. In *How Natives Think.* Translated by Lillian Clare. Princeton: Princeton University Press, v–lviii.

Lovejoy, Arthur O. 1936. *The Great Chain of Being.* Baltimore: Johns Hopkins University Press.

Lukacs, Georg. 1971. *History and Class Consciousness: Studies in Marxist Dialectic.* Translated by Rodney Livingstone. Cambridge: MIT Press.

Lukes, Stephen. 1972. *Émile Durkheim: His Life and Work.* New York: Harper and Row.

MacCabe, Colin. 1978. *James Joyce and the Revolution of the Word.* London: Macmillan.

Macpherson, James. 1966. *Fragments of Ancient Poetry.* Edited by John J. Dunn. Edinburgh: Augustan Reprint Society, No. 122. Originally published in Edinburgh for G. Hamilton and J. Balfour, 1760.

Mali, Joseph. 1992. *The Rehabilitation of Myth: Vico's New Science.* Cambridge: Cambridge University Press.

Malinowski, Bronislaw. 1954. Reprint. Magic, Science and Religion. In *Magic, Science and Religion and Other Essays.* Garden City, N.Y.: Doubleday and Co., 17–92. Originally published in *Science, Religion and Reality.* Edited by James Needham, 1925.

———. 1961. Reprint. *Argonauts of the Western Pacific: An Account of Native Enterprise and Adventure in the Archipelagoes of Melanesian New Guinea.* New York: Dutton and Co. Originally published in 1922.

———. 1968. Reprint. In Tewara and Sanaroa: Mythology of the Kula. In Georges, 72–101. Originally published in *Argonauts of the Western Pacific,* 1922, 298–330.

———. 1992. Reprint. Myth in Primitive Psychology. In *Malinowski and the Work of Myth.* Edited by Ivan Strenski. Princeton: Princeton University Press, 79–116. Original edition, New York: WW Norton, 1926.

———. 1993. *The Early Writings of Bronislav Malinowski.* Edited by Robert J. Thornton and Peter Skalnik. Cambridge: Cambridge University Press.

Manganaro, Marc, ed. 1990. *Modernist Anthropology: From Fieldwork to Text.* Princeton: Princeton University Press.

———. 1992. *Myth, Rhetoric and the Voice of Authority.* New Haven: Yale University Press.

Mannheim, Karl. 1936. *Ideology and Utopia: An Introduction to the Sociology of Knowledge.* Trans. by Louis Wirth and Edward A. Shils. London: Routledge and Kegan Paul Ltd.

Manuel, Frank. 1959. *The Eighteenth Century Confronts the Gods.* Cambridge: Harvard University Press.

Maranda, Pierre, and Elli Köngäs Maranda, eds. 1971. *Structural Models in Folklore.* The Hague: Mouton.

Marcus, George E., ed. 1992. *Rereading Cultural Anthropology.* Durham, N.C.: Duke University Press.

Marcus, George E., and Michael M. J. Fischer. 1986. *Anthropology as Cultural Critique: An Experimental Moment in the Human Sciences.* Chicago: University of Chicago Press.

Marett, Robert Ranulph. 1910. *The Birth of Humility.* Oxford: Oxford University Press.

Marx, Karl. 1967. *Writings of the Young Marx on Philosophy and Society.* Edited and translated ,by Lloyd D. Easton and Kurt H. Guddat. New York: Doubleday.

———. 1978. *The Marx-Engels Reader.* Edited by Robert C. Tucker. New York: WW Norton.

Massey, Marilyn. 1983. *Christ Unmasked: The Meaning of the Life of Jesus in German Politics.* Chapel Hill: University of North Carolina.

Mattina, Anthony. 1987. North American Indian Mythography: Editing Texts for the Printed Page. In Swann and Krupat, 129–148.

Maybury-Lewis, David. 1970. Reprint. Science or Bricolage? In *Claude Lévi-Strauss: The Anthropologist as Hero.* Edited by F. Nelson Hayes and Tanya Hayes. Cambridge: The MIT Press, 150–163. Originally published in *American Anthropologist* 71, no. 1, 114–121.

Meisel, Perry. 1987. *The Myth of the Modern: A Study of British Literature and Criticism after 1850.* New Haven: Yale University Press.

McGann, Jerome. 1983. *The Romantic Ideology.* Chicago: University of Chicago Press.

McGrane, Bernard. 1989. *Beyond Anthropology: Society and the Other.* New York: Columbia University Press.

McGuire, William, ed. 1974. *The Freud/Jung Letters: The Correspondence between Sigmund Freud and C. G. Jung.* Translated by Ralph Manheim and R. F. C. Hull. Princeton: Princeton University Press.

McKeon, Michael. 1987. *The Origins of the English Novel: 1600–1740.* Baltimore: Johns Hopkins University Press.

Mondi, Robert. 1990. Greek Mythic Thought in the Light of the Near East. In Edmunds, 141–198.

Moore, Harry T., ed. 1962. *The Collected Letters of D. H. Lawrence.* New York: Viking.

Morford, Mark P. O., and Robert J. Lenardon. *Classical Mythology.* 5th ed. White Plains, N.Y.: Longman.

Moritz, K. P. 1792. *Götterlehre oder Mythologische Dichtungen der Alten.* Vienna.

Morris, William. 1904. *The Story of Sigurd the Volsung.* London: Longmans, Green and Co. Originally published 1876.

Mosko, Mark. 1991. The Canonic Formula of Myth and Non-Myth. In *American Ethnologist* 18, no. 1, 126–151.

Müller, F. Max. 1899. *The Science of Language.* Vol. 2. London: Longmans, Green and Co.

———. 1909. Reprint. *Comparative Mythology: An Essay.* Edited by A. Smythe Palmer. London: George Routledge and Sons. Original edition, Oxford: Oxford Essays, 1856.

Neumann, Erich. 1954. *The Origins and History of Consciousness.* Translated by R. F. C. Hull. Princeton: Princeton University Press.

Nietzsche, Friedrich. 1954. *Beyond Good and Evil.* Translated by Helen Zimmern. In *The Philosophy of Nietzsche.* New York: Random House.

———. 1967a. *The Birth of Tragedy and the Case of Wagner.* Translated by Walter Kaufmann. New York: Random House.

———. 1967b. *The Will to Power.* Translated by R. J. Hollingwood and Walter Kaufmann and edited by Walter Kaufmann. New York: Random House.

———. 1976a. On Truth and Lie in the Extra-Moral Sense. In *The Portable Nietzsche.* Edited and translated by Walter Kaufmann. New York: Penguin.

————. 1976b. The Twilight of the Idols. In *The Portable Nietzsche*. Edited and translated by Walter Kaufmann. New York: Penguin.

Norris, Christopher. 1987. *Derrida*. Cambridge: Harvard University Press.

Norris, Margot. 1974. *The Decentered Universe of Finnegans Wake*. Baltimore: Johns Hopkins University Press.

Novalis (Friedrich von Hardenberg). 1964. Klingsohr's Tale. In *Henry von Ofterdingen*. Translated by Palmer Hilty. New York: F. Ungar Pub. Co., 122–147.

Otto, Rudolph. 1978. Reprint. *The Idea of the Holy*. Oxford: Oxford University Press. Original edition, 1923.

Pace, David. 1983. *Claude Lévi-Strauss: The Bearer of Ashes*. London: Routledge and Kegan Paul.

Peacock, Sandra. 1988. *Jane Ellen Harrison: The Mask and the Self*. New Haven: Yale University Press.

Peradotto, John. 1995. Reprint. Oedipus and Erichthonius: Some Observations of Paradigmatic and Syntagmatic Order. In *Oedipus: A Folklore Casebook*. Edited by Lowell Edmunds and Alan Dundes. Madison: University of Wisconsin Press, 179–196. Originally published in *Arethusa* 10, 1977, 85–101.

Pettazzoni, Raffaele. 1984. Reprint. The Truth of Myth. In Dundes, 98–109. Originally published in *Essays on the History of Religions*. Leiden: E. J. Brill, 1954, 11–23.

Pope, Alexander. 1963. An Essay on Criticism. In *The Poems of Alexander Pope*. Edited by John Butt. New Haven: Yale University Press.

Pound, Ezra. 1995. Reprint. *The Cantos of Ezra Pound*. New York: New Directions. Original edition, 1970.

Powell, Barry. 1995. *Classical Myth*. Englewood Cliffs, N.J.: Prentice Hall.

Puhvel, Jaan. 1989. *Comparative Mythology*. Baltimore: Johns Hopkins University Press.

Radcliffe-Brown, A. R. 1964. Reprint. *The Andaman Islanders*. New York: Free Press of Glencoe. Original edition, 1922.

Radin, Paul. 1953. *The World of Primitive Man*. New York: Schuman.

————. 1965. *The Method and Theory of Ethnology*. New York: Basic Books.

————. 1972. Reprint. *The Trickster*. New York: Schocken Books. Original edition, 1956.

Raglan, Lord. 1975. Reprint. *The Hero: A Study in Tradition, Myth and Drama*. New York: Greenwood Press. Original edition, London: Pitman and Sons, 1936.

Rajan, Tillotama. 1980. *Dark Interpreter: The Discourse of Romanticism*. Ithaca: Cornell University Press.

Rank, Otto. 1964. Reprint. The Myth of the Birth of the Hero. In *The Myth of the Birth of the Hero and Other Writings*. Edited by Philip Freund. Translated by F. Robbins and Smith Ely Jellife. New York: Random House, 1–96. Originally published, *Journal of Nervous and Mental Disease*, New York: 1914.

Ricoeur, Paul. 1969. *The Symbolism of Evil*. Translated by Emerson Buchanan. Boston: Beacon Press.

————. 1970. *Freud and Philosophy: An Essay on Interpretation*. Translated by Denis Savage. New Haven: Yale University Press.

————. 1976. *Interpretation Theory: Discourse and the Surplus of Meaning*. Translated by Anon. Fort Worth: The Texas Christian University Press.

————. 1977a. *The Rule of Metaphor*. Translated by Robert Czerny. Toronto: University of Toronto Press.

————. 1977b. *The Philosophy of Paul Ricoeur*. Edited by Charles E. Reagan and David Stewart. Boston: Beacon Press.

————. 1984–1988. *Time and Narrative*. 3 vols. Translated by Kathleen McLaughlin Blamey and David Pellauer. Chicago: University of Chicago Press.

————. 1992. *Oneself as Another*. Translated by Kathleen Blamey. Chicago: University of Chicago Press.

Rivers, W. H. R. 1968. Reprint. The Sociological Significance of Myth. In Georges, 27–45. Originally published in *FolkLore*, vol. 23 (1912).

Roth, Marty. 1990. Sir James Frazer's The Golden Bough: A Reading Lesson. In Manganaro, 69–79.

Rubin, William, ed. *"Primitivism" in Modern Art: Affinity of the Tribal and the Modern.* New York: Museum of Modern Art, 1984, 2 vols.

Ruskin, John. 1905. *The Works of John Ruskin.* Vol. 19. Edited by E. T. Cook and Alexander Wedderburn. London: George Allen.

Russell, Ford. 1998. *Northrop Frye on Myth: An Introduction.* New York: Garland.

Sahlins, Marshall. 1976. *Culture and Practical Reason.* Chicago: University of Chicago Press.

———. 1981. *Historical Metaphors and Mythical Realities: Structure in the Early History of the Sandwich Island Kingdom.* Ann Arbor: University of Michigan Press.

Said, Edward. 1978. *Orientalism.* New York: Pantheon.

Sawyer, Paul. 1985. *Ruskin's Poetic Argument: The Design of the Major Works.* Ithaca: Cornell University Press.

Schelling, Friedrich. 1957. Reprint. *Philosophie der Mythologie.* Erster Band. Darmstadt: Wissenschaftliche Buchgesellschaft. Original edition, 1856.

———. 1972. Introduction to *The Philosophy of Mythology,* Lecture IX. Translated by Burton Feldman. In Feldman and Richardson. Bloomington: Indiana University Press, 325–327.

———. 1976. *Treatise on "The Deities of Samothrace."* Translated by Robert F. Brown. Missoula, Mont. Scholars Press.

———. 1978. *System of Transcendentalism.* Translated by Peter Heath. Charlottesville: University of Virginia Press.

———. 1989. *The Philosophy of Art.* Translated by Douglas W. Stott. Minneapolis: University of Minnesota Press.

Scherzer, Joel. 1987. Strategies in Text and Context: The Hot Pepper Story. In *Recovering the Word: Essays on Native American Literature.* Edited by Brian Swann and Arnold Krupat. Berkeley: University of California Press, 151–197.

Schiller, Friedrich. 1962a. Über naive und sentimentalische dichtung. In *Friedrich Schiller: Sämtliche Werke.* Fünfter band. München: Carl Hanse Verlag, 694–780.

———. 1962b. Der Götter Griechenlands. In *Friedrich Schiller: Sämtliche Werke.* Erster band. München: Carl Hanse Verlag, 163–173.

Schlegel, Friedrich. 1968. *Dialogue on Poetry and Literary Aphorisms.* Trans., introduced, and annotated by Ernst Behler and Roman Struc. University Park, Pa.: Penn State University Press.

Scholte, Bob. 1974. Structural Anthropology of Claude Lévi-Strauss. In *Handbook of Social and Cultural Anthropology.* Edited by J. J. Honigmann. New York: Rand McNally, 637–716.

Schopenhauer, Arthur. 1966. *The World as Will and Representation.* Vol. 1. Translated by E. F. J. Payne. New York: Dover Publications.

Schrempp, Greg. 1984. The Re-education of Friedrich Max Müller: Intellectual Appropriation and Epistemological Antinomy in Mid-Victorian Evolutionary Thought. In *Man,* vol. 18, 90–110.

Sebeok, Thomas A., ed. 1965. Reprint. *Myth: A Symposium.* Bloomington: Indiana University Press. Originally published in *Bibliographical and Special Series of The American Folklore Society,* vol. 5, 1955.

Segal, Robert A. 1987. *Joseph Campbell: An Introduction.* New York: Garland.

———. 1990. Introduction to *In Quest of the Hero.* Princeton: Princeton University Press.

———. 1998. Introduction and Selection of *Jung on Mythology.* Princeton: Princeton University Press.

———. 1999. *Theorizing about Myth.* Amherst: University of Massachusetts Press.

Seliger, Martin. 1977. *The Marxist Concept of Ideology.* Cambridge: Cambridge University Press.

Service, Elman R. 1985. *A Century of Controversy: Ethnological Issues from 1860 to 1960.* New York: Academic Press Inc.

Sharpe, Eric. 1986. *Comparative Religion: A History.* La Salle, Ill.: Open Court Publishing Co. Originally published, London: Duckworth and Co., 1975.

Shelley, Percy Bysshe. 1966. *The Selected Poetry and Prose of Shelley.* Edited by Harold Bloom.

Smith, William Robertson. 1969. Reprint. *Lectures on the Religion of the Semities: The Fundamental Institutions.* New York: KTAV Publishing House Inc. Reprint of 3rd edition of 1927.

Sorel, Georges. 1950. Reprint. *Reflections on Violence.* Translated by T. E. Hulme and J. Ross. Glencoe, Ill.: The Free Press. Original edition, New York: W. B. Heubsch, 1914.

Spencer, Herbert. 1985. Reprint. *The Principles of Sociology.* Vol. 1. New York: Appleton and Co. Original edition, New York: Appleton, 1897, 2 vols.

Spivak, Gayatri. 1976. Introduction to *Of Grammatology,* by Jacques Derrida. Translated by Gayatri Spivak. Baltimore: Johns Hopkins University Press.

Spurr, David. 1994. Myths of Anthropology: Eliot, Joyce, Lévy-Bruhl. In *PMLA* 109, no. 2, March, 266–280.

Starobinski, Jean. 1991. Fable and Mythology in Seventeenth- and Eighteenth-Century Literature and Theoretical Reflection. Trans. David White. In *Mythologies: A Restructured Translation of Dictionnaire des mythologies et des religions des sociétés traditionelle et du monde antique, prepared under the direction of Wendy Doniger.* Chicago: University of Chicago Press, 722–732.

Stevens, Wallace. 1957. *Opus Posthumous.* New York: Alfred Knopf.

Stocking, George. W., Jr. 1968. *Race, Culture and Evolution.* New York: Free Press.

———. 1983. The Ethnographer's Magic: Fieldwork in British Anthropology from Tylor to Malinowski. In *Observers Observed: Essays on Ethnographic Fieldwork.* Edited by George W. Stocking Jr. Madison: University of Wisconsin Press, 70–120.

———. 1984. Radcliffe-Brown and British Social Anthropology. In *Functionalism Historicized: Essays on British Anthropology.* Edited by George W. Stocking Jr. Madison: University of Wisconsin Press.

———. 1987. *Victorian Anthropology.* New York: Free Press.

———. 1992. *The Ethnographer's Magic and Other Essays in the History of Anthropology.* Madison: University of Wisconsin Press.

———. 1995. *After Tylor: British Social Anthropology 1888–1951.* Madison: University of Wisconsin Press.

Strathern, Marilyn. 1990. Out of Context: The Persuasive Fiction of Anthropology. Comments by J. Jarvie, Stephen A. Tyler, and George E. Marcus. In Manganaro, 80–130.

Strauss, David Friedrich. 1970. Reprint. *The Life of Jesus Critically Examined.* Translated from the 4th German edition by Marian Evans. St. Clair Shores, Mich.: Scholarly Press. Original edition, New York: Blanchard, 1860.

Strenski, Ivan. 1987. *Four Theories of Myth in Twentieth-Century Culture.* Iowa City: University of Iowa Press.

Sulloway, Frank. 1979. *Freud: Biologist of the Mind.* New York: Basic Books.

Swann, Brian. 1974. Middlemarch and Myth. In *Nineteenth Century Fiction* 28, 210–214.

Swann, Brian, and Arnold Krupat, eds. 1987. *Recovering the Word: Essays on Native American Literature.* Berkeley: University of California Press.

Tedlock, Dennis. 1983. *The Spoken Word and the Word of Interpretation.* Philadelphia: University of Pennsylvania Press.

Tennyson, Alfred. 1975. Reprint. *Tennyson: Poems and Plays.* London: Oxford University Press. Original edition, 1911.

Thomas, L. L., J. Z. Kronenfeld, and D. B. Kronenfeld. 1976. Asdiwal Crumbles: A Critique of Lévi-Straussian Myth Analysis. In *American Ethnologist* 3, 147–173.

Thorslev, Peter. 1984. *Romantic Contraries: Freedom and Destiny.* New Haven: Yale University Press.

Todorov, Tsvetan. 1982. *Theories of the Symbol.* Translated by Catherine Porter. Ithaca: Cornell University Press.

———. 1984. *The Conquest of America: The Question of the Other.* Translated by Richard Howard. New York: Harper and Row.

Trilling, Lionel. 1968. *Beyond Culture.* New York: Viking.

———. 1976. *The Liberal Imagination: Essays on Literature and Society.* New York: Scribners.

Tucker, Robert C., ed. 1975. *The Lenin Anthology.* New York: WW Norton.

————, ed. 1978. *The Marx-Engels Reader*. New York: WW Norton.

Turner, Terence. 1977. Narrative Structure and Mythopoesis: A Critique and Reformulation of Structural Concepts of Myth, Narrative and Poetics. In *Arethusa* 10, 103–162.

Tylor, Edward Burnett. 1958. Reprint. *The Origins of Culture*. Vol 1. New York: Harper and Row. Original edition, London, 1871.

————. 1974. *Primitive Culture*. Vol. 2. New York: Gordon Press. Original edition, London, 1871.

Urban, Wilbur. 1939. *Language and Reality: The Philosophy of Language and The Principles of Symbolism*. London: Allen and Unwin.

Vaihinger, Hans. 1969. Reprint. *The Philosophy of "As If": As System of the Theoretical, Practical and Religious Fictions of Mankind*. Translated by C. K. Ogden. London: Kegan Paul. Original edition, New York: Harcourt Brace, 1924.

Van Der Leeuw, Gerardus. 1986. Reprint. *Religion in Essence and Manifestation*. Translated by John W. Harvey. Princeton: Princeton University Press. Original edition, London: Allen and Unwin, 1938.

Verene, Donald Philip. 1981. *Vico's Science of Imagination*. Ithaca: Cornell University Press.

Vernant, Jean-Pierre. 1991. *Mortals and Immortals: Collected Essays*. Edited by Froma Zeitlin. Princeton: Princeton University Press.

Versnel, H. S. 1990. What's Sauce for the Goose Is Sauce for the Gander: Myth and Ritual Old and New. In Edmunds, 23–90.

Vickery, John. 1972. *Robert Graves and The White Goddess*. Lincoln: University of Nebraska Press.

————. 1973. *The Literary Impact of* The Golden Bough. Princeton: Princeton University Press.

————. 1983. *Myths and Texts: Strategies of Incorporation and Displacement*. Baton Rouge: Louisiana State University Press.

————. 1990. Frazer and the Elegiac: The Modernist Connection. In Manganaro, 51–68.

Vico, Giambattista. 1975. Reprint. *The Autobiography of Giambattista Vico*. Trans. by Max Fisch and Thomas Bergin. Ithaca: Cornell University Press. Original edition, 1944.

————. 1984. Reprint. *The New Science of Giambattista Vico*. Translated by Thomas G. Bergin and Max Fisch. Ithaca: Cornell University Press. Original edition, 1948.

Vidal-Naquet, Pierre. 1986. *The Black Hunter: Forms of Thought and Forms of Society in the Greek World*. Translated by Andrew Szegedy-Maszak. Baltimore: Johns Hopkins University Press.

Voget, Fred. 1975. *A History of Ethnology*. New York: Holt, Rinehart and Winston.

Wagner, Roy. 1975. *The Invention of Culture*. Chicago: University of Chicago Press.

————. 1986. *Symbols That Stand for Themselves*. Chicago: University of Chicago Press.

Weber, Max. 1958. *The Protestant Ethic and the Spirit of Capitalism*. Translated by Talcott Parsons. New York: Charles Scribner's Sons.

Weston, Jessie L.. 1957. *From Ritual to Romance*. New York: Doubleday.

Wheelwright, Philip. 1954. *The Burning Fountain*. Bloomington. Indiana University Press.

————. 1962. *Metaphor and Reality*. Bloomington: Indiana University Press.

————. 1965. Reprint. The Semantic Approach to Myth. In Sebeok, 154–168. Originally published in Bibliographical and Special Series of the American Folklore Society, vol. 5, 1955.

White, Hayden. 1978. The Tropics of History: The Deep Structure of the New Science. In *Tropics of Discourse: Essays in Cultural Criticism*. Baltimore: Johns Hopkins University Press, 197–217.

————. 1987. *The Content of the Form*. Baltimore: Johns Hopkins University Press.

White, John J. 1971. *Mythology and the Modern Novel*. Princeton: Princeton University Press.

Williams, Raymond. 1977. *Marxism and Literature*. Oxford: Oxford University Press.

Wordsworth, William. 1933. *The Poetical Works of William Wordsworth*. New York: Oxford University Press.

Wright, Ronald. 1992. *Stolen Continents: The "New World" through Indian Eyes*. Boston: Houghton Mifflin Co.

Wundt, Wilhelm. 1916. *Elements of Folk Psychology.* London: Allen and Unwin.

Yeats, William Butler. 1956. *The Collected Poems of W. B. Yeats.* New York: Macmillan.

———. 1965. *The Autobiography of William Butler Yeats.* New York: Macmillan.

———. 1966. *A Vision.* New York: Macmillan.

Ziolkowski, Theodore. 1972. *Fictional Transformations of Jesus.* Princeton: Princeton University Press.

Žižek, Slavoj. 1989. *The Sublime Object of Ideology.* London: Verso.

INDEX

Abraham, Karl, 114–16, 123
Abrahams, Roger, 258
Adams, Hazard, 168, 326–36, 361–62nn10–12
Adorno, Theodor, 279, 293–97, 300, 301, 335
Aeschylus, 109
affective theory, xiii, 87–89, 91, 105–106, 111–13, 191–92, 213
African myth, 214–15
Alcheringa, 259
allegory: of fable, 26–30, 44, 342n1; and meaning, 319; shift away from, 3–15; vs. symbol, 36–37, 43–44, 68, 81–82, 130–31; types of, 328–29
Althusser, Louis, 279, 281, 287–90, 301–302
American Bureau of Ethnology, 219, 251
analogy, 252, 317
Anatomy of Criticism (Frye), xvi–xvii, 62, 165–66, 169–77, 330–31
Andaman Islanders (Radcliffe-Brown), 203, 212–14
anima, the, 190
Anima Mundi, 139–40
animism, 85–86
anthropology: and depth psychology, 105, 111, 174; historical, 270–71, 274; ritualist, xiii, 106–107, 174, 192–94; social, xiii, xiv, 202–61; and the tale, 172; and totemism, 99
anti-fable, 6–8
antimyth, 332–36
Apocalypse (Lawrence), 141–42, 196
Apollonian vs. Dionysian, the, 72–73, 107–111
archetype, 121–23, 128–33, 165–66, 169–77, 187, 191, 318
Argonauts of the Western Pacific (Malinowski), 203–206, 209–11
Aristotle, 1, 11, 103, 108, 312
artist, modern: and affective theory, 111; as *bricoleur,* 246; literary, 134–53; myth-making power of, 19–24, 41–42, 45–47, 160; and Ritualists, 106
"Aryan" mythology, 80–83, 93, 200, 345n4

Bacon, Francis, 3–4, 7
"Bard, The" (Gray), 19
Barth, John, 153
Barthes, Roland, 82, 278, 290–93, 301–302, 317–19, 335
Bascom, William, 220, 222
Basso, Ellen, 259–60
Bastian, Adolph, 93, 117, 218
Bauman, Richard, 258–59
Beckett, Samuel, 153
Being and Time (Heidegger), 74, 293–95
Benedict, Ruth, 219
Benjamin, Walter, 43–44, 205, 295–97, 334
Beowulf, 17
Bergson, Henri, 109–10, 119, 130, 282
Beyond Good and Evil (Nietzsche), 75
Bible, the, 16, 43, 51–53, 252–53
biogenesis, 115–16, 123–27, 187–88
Birth of Tragedy Out of the Spirit of Music, The (Nietzsche), 71–75
"Black Hunter and the Origin of the Athenian *Ephebeia,* The" (Vidal-Naquet), 272–74
Blake, William, 7, 8, 11, 26–31, 38, 39, 60, 123, 327–30, 342n1
Blumenberg, Hans, 320–26
Boas, Franz: influence of, 219, 225–29, 242–46, 250–51; precursors of, 86, 205–206, 221, 226–27; work of, 217–25
Boehme, Jacob, 40
Bonaparte, Louis, 57
British structural-functionalism, 203, 212–17, 224, 227–28
Brooks, Cleanth, 305
Bulfinch, 68, 81
Bultmann, Rudolph, xvii
Burkert, Walter, 267–70
Burning Fountain, The (Wheelright), 165–69

Cambridge Ritualists, 71, 97, 106–11, 193
Campbell, Joseph, xvii; influences on, 74, 123, 132, 194, 196–97, 199; and James Joyce,

151, 196; and modernity, 171–72; as romantic, xii, 196, 201; works of, 196–201

Carlyle, Thomas: as Idealist, 59–62; influence of, 65, 329–30; and symbol, 37, 344–45nn16–17

Cassirer, Ernest, xvii, 9, 83, 87–88, 155–62, 166, 177, 305, 323–24, 330, 335

Chanson de Roland, 17

charter myths, 104–105

Christianity, 145–53

Cimidyuë, 246–48

classical studies, xiv, 262–77

cognitive failure, 78–83

Coleridge, Samuel Taylor, 36–37, 60

collective representations, 98–106

collective unconscious, 127–33

commodity, 58–59

comparative method, 91–97, 198–99, 262–63

Comparative Mythology (Müller), 79–83

Comparative Mythology (Puhvel), 264–65

"Comparative Study of Tsimshian Mythology" (Boas), 222–23

Comte, Auguste, 78, 80, 83–88, 94, 101–102

constitutive theory, xi–xiii, xv, 305–306, 334–37

construction, xi, xvi

Contribution to the Critique of Political Economy (Marx/Engels), 57

Cornford, Francis, 100, 107

Cours de philosophie positive (Compte), 83–84

creation accounts, 80–81, 183–86, 188–92

Creation of Mythology, The (Detienne), 275–277

"Creative Writer and Daydreaming, The" (Freud), 115, 117, 123

Creuzer, Friedrich, 40, 59, 62–63, 81, 82, 118, 130, 132, 232, 310

Critique of Judgement (Kant), 33–36

Croce, Benedetto, 11, 330

Culture and Practical Reason (Sahlins), 255–57

Cunning Intelligence in Greek Culture and Society (Detienne/Vernant), 274–76

Daniel Deronda (Eliot), 68, 70–71

Darwinism, 80–81, 115, 118

Das Kapital (Marx), 58–59

Das Volk, 16

De Man, Paul, 44

"De quelques formes primitives de classification: contribution à l'étude des représentations collectives" (Durkheim/Mauss), 98, 100

Decline of the West (Spengler), 139–40

deconstruction, 74–75, 307–308

degeneration theory, 7–8, 63, 210–11, 218, 224–26

Deities of Samothrace, The (Schelling), 40

depth psychology, xiii, 105, 111–33, 174, 194

Der Ring des Nibelungs (Wagner), 65–67

Derrida, Jacques, 250, 279, 294–302, 332, 335

Detienne, Marcel, 270–72, 274–77, 337

Deutsche Mythologie (Grimm), 62–63

Deutsche Sagen (Grimm), 62

Dialectic of Enlightenment (Adorno/Horkheimer), 279, 293–97, 301

Dialogue on Poetry (Schlegel), 30–33

Die Deutsche Heldensagen (Grimm), 62

Die Elemente der Völkerpsychologie (Wundt), 205–206

"Die Götter Grieschenlands" (Schiller), 21

Die Götternamen (Usener), 321

displacement, 142, 171–72

Doty, William, xv

Douglas, Mary, 214–15, 251

dreams, 112–15, 128–29, 175–77

Dumézil, Georges, 262–65, 271, 358n3

Durkheim, Émile: influence of, 107–108, 110–11, 203–204, 231, 347nn25,29; and Lévy-Bruhl, 101–106; and Mauss, 98, 100; precursors of, 78, 90–91, 97, 205, 281–82; on religion, 97–100

dying god, 137–38, 147–48, 271

Eagleton, Terry, 301–303

Eddas, the, 17, 66, 264

Eighteenth Brumaire of Louis Bonaparte (Marx/Engels), 57

elementardenken (fundamental ideas), 93, 116

Elementary Forms of the Religious Life: The Totemic System in Australia (Durkheim), 97–100, 203–204

Elementary Structures of Kinship (Lévi-Strauss), 231–32

Eliade, Mircea: xvii, 158, 168, 176; influences on, 179–81, 354–55n12; and modernity, 171–72; as romantic, xii, 182, 186, 314–15; work of, 181–86

Eliot, George, 56, 67–71, 79

Eliot, T. S., xiii, 134–36, 146–50, 203, 316–20, 351nn14–18

emotive theories, 78, 99–111, 255

Engels, Friedrich, xii–xiii, 55–59

Enlightenment, 6–8, 77–78

epic, the, 39–40, 264

Essay on Man (Cassirer), 155

Essence of Christianity, The (Feuerbach), 53–56

essentialization, 105–106, 150–51, 203, 214–15

ethnology, 78, 154–55, 172, 202–61

Etruscan Places (Lawrence), 141–42

euhemerism, 7–8, 11, 97

Eumenides, The (Aeschylus), 109

Evans-Pritchard, E. E., 90, 214–15

Excursion, The (Wordsworth), 45, 67

"Excursus" (Murray), 109

exoteric vs. esoteric systems, 224–25

fable: allegory and, 25–31; as mediated allusion, 5–6; vs. myth, 1–24, 30–31; as term, 2–3; "vine of," 15–19, 33

fairytale, 62–63

"Fall of Hyperion, The" (Keats), 47–48

false consciousness, 49, 51–54

Fantasia of the Unconscious (Lawrence), 141

fantasizing, 119–20, 133, 170
fascism, 205
Ferenczi, Sandor, 126, 127, 349n12
fetish, the, 58–59, 75, 83–85, 286
Feuerbach, Ludwig, 53–56
Fichte, Johann, 34
fictional, the, 163, 170–71, 176, 260, 304–36, 331–35
Fingal: An Ancient Epic ("Ossian"), 18
Finnegan, Ruth, 261
Finnegans Wake (Joyce), 136, 151–53, 318, 319
First Age, 9–14, 168
Firth, Raymond, 215–17, 220
folkloristic theory: appearance of, 49; Boas and, 220–26; disciplines influenced by, xiv, 225–26; Durkheim and, 100; Frye and, 175–76; Grimm and, 62–63; and religion, 77–111, 183–86; and romantic theory, xi, xv; and social anthropology, 202–61
Fontenelle, Bernard, 5–9
"Forms of Folklore, The: Prose Narratives" (Bascom), 220
Four Zoas, The (Blake), 26–31
Fragments of Ancient Poetry Collected in the Highlands of Scotland and Translated from the Gaelic or Erse Language (Macpherson), 17–19
Frankfurt school, 287, 290, 293–97, 300
Frazer, James: influence of, 96–97, 106–108, 110–11, 136–45, 193, 195, 198–99, 206–209, 346–47nn16,19, 353–54n15; precursors of, 51, 71, 78, 93–94; and Smith, 91; works of, 91–93
Freud, Sigmund, xvii; and biological inheritance, 115–16, 118, 123–27, 349n12; influence of, 141, 233–34, 267, 287–88, 307–308, 320–26, 329; and Jung, 114–15, 117–33, 190; precursors of, 71, 91, 105; and romanticism, xii, xiii, 117; on the unconscious, 112–15, 126–27, 348nn1–3
Freud and Philosophy (Ricoeur), 307–309
Frobenius, Leo, 121–22, 185, 199, 203
From Honey to Ashes (Lévi-Strauss), 246–47
From Ritual to Romance (Weston), 194
Frye, Northrop, xvi–xvii, 62, 123, 142, 165–66, 169–77, 193–94, 330–31
functional theory, 204–17

Gardens of Adonis (Detienne), 271–72
Geertz, Clifford, 251
Genesis, 40
German Ideology, The (Marx), 56–57, 279–80
"Germania" (Hölderlin), 23–24
Gernet, Louis, 274
Girard, René, 254, 267–70
God, 40–41
god-kings, 193–94
Goddess, the, 194–96, 200–201
Goethe, J. W. van, 34–36
Golden Bough, The (Frazer), 91–97, 107, 110, 118, 145–47

Goldenweiser, Alexander, 219
Goody, Jack, 217, 260
Gordon, Richard, 265–66, 270–71
Gould, Eric, 316–20
Granet, Marcel, 271
Graves, Robert, 74, 123, 194–96, 353–54n15
Gray, Thomas, 19
Greeks: drama of, 66–67, 193; history of, 267, 272–74; myths of, 1–2, 4, 16, 20–23, 37, 42–46, 72–73, 81, 106–11, 233–37, 265–67, 273–77, 337–38
Griaule, Marcel, 203, 215
Grimm, Jakob: influence of, 80, 82, 210–11, 221–24; and romanticism, xiii, 49; on myth, 62–63
Grimm, Wilhelm, 49, 62–63
"group psyche," 191–92
Guss, David, 266

Haeckel, Ernst, 115
Hale, Horatio, 219
Handbook of South American Indians (American Bureau of Ethnology), 231
Harrison, Jane: influences on, 71, 107–108, 203, 348n40; work of, 106–11, 348nn41–44
Hawthorne, Nathaniel, 68, 81
Hegel, G. W. F., 41, 49–53, 55, 123, 294–96, 333, 335, 344nn3–5
Heidegger, Martin, 74, 293–95, 313–14
Heidelberg group, 63
Heinrich von Ofterdingen (Novalis), 28–31
Herder, J. G., 30–31, 38, 67
hero, the: Campbell on, 151, 176, 196–201; Carlyle on, 59–62; Freud on, 113, 121; Frye on, 170–71, 176; Harrison on, 108–109; Jung on, 120–23; and neo-romanticism, 178–79, 187–94; Rank on, 116–17, 121; Tennyson on, 64–67
Hero, The (Raglan), 179, 192–94
Hero with a Thousand Faces, The (Campbell), 194, 196–98, 201
Herodotus, 267
Heroes, Hero-Worship and the Heroic in History (Carlyle), 61–62, 179
Hesiod, 1–2, 4
Heyne, C. G., 30–31
Historical Metaphors and Mythical Realities (Sahlins), 257
history: and anthropology, 257; as epic, 39–40; escape from, 96, 148; and legend, 62–63; and literacy, 265–67; of literature, 169–77; Marx on, 57–58; *meta-*, 10, 14–15, 37–38, 83–85, 94–95, 140, 184–85; and oral tradition, 11; philology and, 79–83; recycled, 14–15; of romantic concepts, 326–36, 336–37
History and Class Consciousness (Lukács), 281, 284, 286–87
Hitler, 160–61
Hölderlin, Friedrich, 19–20, 22–24, 26

Homer, 1–2, 4, 11, 16, 108–109, 149–50, 258
*Homo Necans: The Anthropology of Ancient Greek Sac-
    rificial Ritual and Myth* (Burkert), 267–70
Horkheimer, Max, 279, 293–97, 301, 335
"How Myths Die" (Lévi-Strauss), 242–46
Husserl, Edmund, 179–81, 280
Hymes, Dell, 259
"Hyperion" (Keats), 47–48

Idea of the Holy, The (Otto), 180–82
idealism, 56–62, 79
ideological theory, xi–xiii, xv, 49–76, 278–86,
    301–303, 305, 336–37, 362n14
Idéologues, 56–57
ideology: and comparative mythology, 263;
    as diacritical, 335–36; fascist, 205; and
    language, 254–56; Marx and, 278–86,
    359nn2–7; myth as, 55–59, 301–303,
    314–15, 335–36; romanticism as, 42–48;
    structuralism and, 286–93
Ideology and Utopia (Mannheim), 284–86
Idylls of the King (Tennyson), 64–65
image, 43, 190–92
imaginative universal, 10–11
*In Favor of Deceit: A study of Tricksters in Amazonain
    Society* (Basso), 259–60
individual, the: and meaning, 201; reworking of
    myth by, 224–25
Indo-European, the, 63, 80, 263–64, 358n3
Interpretation of Dreams, The (Freud), 113–17, 126,
    128–29
Introduction to the Work of Marcel Mauss (Lévi-
    Strauss), 231
irony, 13–14, 33, 44, 136

Jakobson, Roman, 231
James, William, 180–81
Jealous Potter, The (Lévi-Strauss), 246–47
Jensen, Adolphe, 185, 199
Jerusalem (Blake), 26–30
Jesus Christ, 51–54
Joyce, James, xiii, 134–36, 149–53, 316–20
Jung, Carl, xvii; and collective unconscious,
    127–33, 349n8, 350nn15–17; and Frazer,
    96; on hero, 120–23; influence of, 123,
    182, 186–92, 196–97, 201, 226–29, 234,
    322–23, 326; as romantic, xii, xiii, 113, 117,
    122, 130–32; on symbols, 117–20
"Jung on Mythology" (Segal), 130

Kalevala, the, 17
Kant, Immanuel: on archetype, 129–30;
    Durkheim on, 97–98; and the transcenden-
    tal, 33–36
Keats, John, 47–48
Kermode, Frank, 312–13, 334–35
Kinder-und Hausmärchen (Grimm), 62
kinship, 233, 237, 251
Kirk, Geoffrey, 269
Kluckhohn, Clyde, 227–29

Kolakowski, Leszek, 313–16, 334
Kroeber, Alfred, 219, 226

La mythologie primitive (Lévy-Bruhl), 103–105
Lacan, Jacques, 279, 287–88, 317, 360n13
Laing, Malcolm, 18
Lamarckian biology, 115–16, 190–91, 324,
    345n1
Langer, Susanne, 164, 330, 352n6
language: "depth" and, 164–67; figurative,
    12–14; magical, 194–95; meta-, 291–93;
    and mythical thought, 159–60; neo-roman-
    ticism and, 153–77; philology and, 79–83;
    positivist view of, 86; semantics and,
    163–69, 318; structure of, 233–35; and
    symbol, 75, 161–63, 307–313
Language and Reality (Urban), 162–63
Lawrence, D. H., xiii, 134–36, 140–45, 194, 203,
    316–20, 350–51n11
Leach, Edmund, 215–17, 220, 252–53, 356n4
*Lectures on the Religion of the Semites: The Funda-
    mental Institutions* (Smith), 89–91
legend, 62–63, 203, 222, 257
Les fonctions mentales dans les sociétés inférieures
    (Lévy-Bruhl), 101–105
Letters on the Aesthetic Education of Man (Schiller),
    33–36
Lévi-Strauss, Claude, xvii; and Boas, 242–46,
    250–51; "canonical law" of, 239–44,
    251–53; ideas of, 230–51, 356n11–13;
    and ideology, 286–87; precursors of, 82,
    220–21, 225–26, 233–34, 238, 251, 255–56,
    356–57n16; responses to, 87, 239–40,
    248–61, 271–72, 317–20
Lévy-Bruhl, Lucien, 78, 101–106, 191, 347n35
libidinal development, 118–23, 125, 174–75,
    186–92, 317
Life of Jesus (Strauss), 51–53
liminal experience, 168–69, 175–76
linguistic theory, 82–83, 86, 155–69, 253–56,
    307–313, 318, 332
Liszka, James, 253–56
literature, 25–26, 42, 134–53, 169–77, 316–20
Locke, John, 14
Longinus, 16
Lord, Albert, xvii, 258, 265–66
Lorenz, Konrad, 267–68
Lowie, Robert, 219, 226, 230–31
Lukács, Georg, 281, 284, 359n5
Luke, 52

Mabinogion, the, 17
Macpherson, James, 17–19
magic, 94, 194–95
Mahabharata, the, 264
Malinowski, Bronislaw: on charter myths,
    104–105; influence of, 161, 202–205, 212,
    354–55n12; precursors of, 86, 99, 203–209;
    works of, 203–12
Mallet, Paul Henri, 17–18

Man Who Died, The (Lawrence), 142, 144–45
Manganaro, Marc, 95
Manifesto of the Communist Party (Marx/Engels), 57
Mannhardt, Wilhelm, 93–94
Mannheim, Karl, 284–86, 301
Marx, Karl: and Feuerbach, 53–56; and Hegel, 49–53, 55; and ideology, 278–86, 359nn2–7; and Lévi-Strauss, 255–56; works of, 55–59
masculine vs. feminine, 188–92, 194–95, 200–201
Masks of God, The (Campbell), 196–201
Mauss, Marcel, 98, 100, 160–61, 238, 276
McDougall, William, 213
McLuhan, Marshall, 260–61
meaning: data on, 249; and deformation, 292; vs. event, 316–20; for individual, 201; translatable, 235–40
Memoirs of My Nervous Illness (Schreber), 118, 124
metahistorical theory, 10, 14–15, 37–38, 83–85, 94–95, 140, 184–85
metaphor, 13–14, 165–69, 172–73, 252, 298–301, 311–13
Metaphor and Reality (Wheelright), 165–69
metonym, 252, 317
Mezoamerican myth, 143–44
Middlemarch (Eliot), 68–69, 79
Milton (Blake), 26–30
mode: symbolic, 162–63, 168–69; theory of, 170–71, 175–77
modernity: belatedness of, 31; epistemological crisis of, 97–98, history and, 14–15, 171–72; legitimation of, xvii, 3, 25; literature of, 134–53; and religion, 53–76, 89; withdrawal from, 171–72, 179–86, 314–15
monomyth, 151, 197–98
Monuments (Mallet), 17–18
Morte D'Arthur, Le (Malory), 64
Müller, F. Max: influence of, 85–86, 88, 168, 251; works of, 78–83
Murray, Gilbert, 100, 107
Murray, Margaret, 194
mysterium tremendum, 180–81
myth: as adjustive response, 228–29; as cognitive failure, 78–83; and criticism, 169–77; as extra-historical, 148; as false consciousness, 49, 51–54; as fiction, 163, 176, 304–36; function of, 204–17; as gossip, 152; as ideology, 55–59, 301–303, 335–36; and "Literature," 25–26, 42; as mode of thought, 87–88, 161–62; motives for, 213–14; as personal salvation, 67–71; as rationalization, 88–91; vs. religion, 87; vs. ritual, 90–91; vs. science, 333–36; as semiological system, 291–93; as story, 59–67, 265–67; and symbol, 34–37, 43–44, 306–13, 326–36; vs. tale, 220–26; as term, 2–4, 59–61; and value, 313–16; variants of, 235–51; work on, 320–26

myth and ritual school, 71, 74, 78, 89–91
"Myth and Rituals: A General Theory" (Kluckhohn), 227–29
"Myth in Primitive Psychology" (Malinowski), 206–12, 215–17
Myth of the Bagre (Goody), 217
Myth of the Birth of the Hero: An Essay on the Psychological Interpretation of Myth (Rank), 116–17, 121, 193–94
Myth of the State (Cassirer), 155, 160–61
mythemes, 248–49
Mythical Intentions in Modern Literature (Gould), 316–20
Mythical Thought (Cassirer), 156–61
Mythography: The Study of Myths and Rituals (Doty), xv
mythoi (plots), 1–2, 66, 73–74, 275–77, 312
mythoid, 167–68
Mythologies (Barthes), 278, 290–93
Mythologies (Yeats), 137
Mythologiques (Lévi-Strauss), xvii, 242–44, 246–49
mythology: and art, 84–85; "creative," 201; as interpretative, 2; as spiral pattern, 37–38; as term, 2, 341n2; as unstable, 220–25; as view of nature, 20–24, 28, 67–68, 82, 86, 104–105, 206–208, 218, 220–26
Mythology (Bulfinch), 68
Mythology and Monuments of Ancient Athens (Harrison), 107
"Mythology in the Nineteenth and Twentieth Centuries" (Eliade), 184
mythopoeic, the: Age of, 81–82, 169, 171–72; and allegory, 26; Greek mode of, 45–46; physical world and, 75; power of, 54; and race, 141–45; renewal of, 65; value of, 59

Napoleon, 56–57
narrative, 156, 167, 174, 192–94, 232–33, 309–13
National Socialism (Nazism), 160–61, 230, 295
Native American myth, 16–17, 143–44, 217–46, 255, 258–61
nature theory, 20–24, 28, 67–68, 82, 86, 104–105, 206–208, 218, 220–26
Negative Dialectics (Adorno), 295, 301
neo-Kantianism, 156–61, 173–74, 180–81, 184–85, 219, 306, 309, 315
Neoplatonism, 3, 68, 75–76, 82, 184–85
neo-romanticism, xiii–xiv, 99, 111, 153–201, 306
Neumann, Erich, 186–92, 196–97
"new comparative mythology," 262–65
New Criticism, xvi–xvii, 164, 173, 193, 305
"new mythology," 42
New Organon (Bacon), 4
New Science of Giambattista Vico (Vico), 3, 8–15
New Yorker, The, 338–39
Nibelungenlied, the, 17, 66–67
Nietzsche, Friedrich: and constitutive theory,

xii–xiii; and ideology, 293–301; influence of, 74, 138–40, 274, 278–79; works of, 71–76
night sea journey, 121–23
non-contradiction, law of, 103, 105
Norse myth, 61–62, 66–67
Novalis, 28–31, 38
numinous, the, 167–68

"Ode to the West Wind" (Shelley), 46–47
Odyssey, The, 146–47, 149–51, 200–201, 295–96
Oedipal complex, 113–14, 116, 119–25, 133, 151–52, 288
Oedipus Rex (Sophocles), 114
Of Grammatology (Derrida), 250
"Oldest System-Program of German Mythology," 33
Olson, Charles, 259
Olympians vs. mystery gods, 107–11
"On Naïve and Sentimental Poetry" (Schiller), 20
"On the Origin of Fables" (Fontenelle), 5–9
On the Origins of German Tragic Drama (Benjamin), 43–44
"On the Psychology and Pathology of So-Called Occult Phenomena" (Jung), 117
"On the Relation of Analytic Psychology to Poetry" (Jung), 132
"On the Wisdom of the Ancients" (Bacon), 4
Ong, Walter, 260–61
oral tradition: and culture, 218–26; and *Das Volk,* 16; genres in, 210–11; history and, 11, 257; and literacy, 265–67, 275–77; performance in, xvii, 258–61; sacred story in, xiii; and social structure, 216–17; written versions of, 17–19
"Oral Tradition in Relation to Social Status" (Firth), 216–17
Orality and Literacy (Ong/Todorov), 260–61
Origin of Table Manners, The (Cimidyuë), 246–48
Origins and History of Consciousness (Neumann), 186–92, 196–97
"Ossian." *See* Macpherson, James
Otto, Rudolph, 158, 167, 169, 180–82

Paris School, 262–63, 270–77, 348n39
Parry, Milman, 258, 265–66
Peirce, C. S., 253–56
Performance and Event (Bauman), 258–59
personification, 86, 97, 110
Pettazzoni, Raffaele, 181
phenomenology, religious, xiii, 50–52, 168–69, 179–86, 191
Phenomenology of the Spirit (Hegel), 50–52, 294–96
philology, 79–83
Philosophie der Offenbarung (Schelling), 41
Philosophy and Religion lectures (Schelling), 39–40

Philosophy of History (Hegel), 41
Philosophy of Mythology (Schelling), 39–41, 79, 156, 158
Philosophy of Symbolic Forms (Cassirer), xvii, 83, 87–88, 155, 177, 323–24, 330
Philosophy of the Literary Symbolic, The (Adams), 326–36
planter vs. hunter cultures, 185, 199
"Plasticity of Myth, The" (Firth), 215–16
Plato, 1–2, 75–76, 184–85, 273–76, 337–38
Plumed Serpent, The (Lawrence), 142–44
Poems of Ossian (Macpherson), 17–19
Poetics (Aristotle), 1, 312
poetry: epic, 16, 26; modernist, 96–97, 106, 305–306; oral, 258–61; romantic, 17–24, 36, 38, 44–48; as symbolic mode, 162–63, 168–69; vs. theory, 42
Political Systems of Highland Burma (Leach), 216–17
Pope, Alexander, 16
popular mythography, 68–69, 74, 81
positivism, 86, 97–98, 162
postmodernism, 136, 153, 351n22
poststructuralism, 74–75, 151–53, 279–302
Prägnanz (pregnance), 322–26
"prelogical," the, 102–103
Presence of Myth, The (Kolakowski), 313–16
"primitive," the: and anthropology, xiii; and childhood, 124–25; and modern anxiety, 97–98; and orality, 260–61; as *other,* 77, 105–106; and race, 144–45; and religion, 77–111, 347nn25,29,35; and semantics, 167–69; and shamanism, 199
Primitive Culture (Tylor), 83, 85–87, 90–91
Primitive Society (Lowie), 230–31
"Primitivism in Modern Art" (MoMA), 135
Principles of Sociology (Spencer), 88, 90–91
Prolegomena (Wolf), 16
Prolegomena to the Study of the Greek Religion (Harrison), 108, 110
psychoanalysis, 113–17, 141, 227–28, 287–88, 329
Psychoanalysis of the Unconscious (Lawrence), 141
Psychological Types (Jung), 226
psychology: analytic, 113, 190–92; depth, xiii, 105, 111–33, 174, 194; *Gestalt,* 226; intuitionist, 141; and romanticism, 19–20; social, 213
Puhvel, Jaan, 264–65

"Queen of the Air, The" (Ruskin), 67–68
Quest for Myth, The (Chase), xiii

race: and the mythopoeic, 141–45; and romanticism, 199–200, 358n3; shared consciousness and, 120
Race, Language and Culture (Boas), 218
Radcliffe-Brown, A. R., 203, 209, 212–14
Radin, Paul, 219, 226–29
Raglan, Lord, 179, 192–94

Rainbow, The (Lawrence), 142–43

Rank, Otto, 114–17, 121, 193–94

Raw and the Cooked, The (Lévi-Strauss), 232, 247–48

Reflections on Violence (Sorel), 282–86, 293

"Relations of Symmetry between Rituals and Myths of Neighboring Peoples" (Lévi-Strauss), 244

religion: Eastern, 82–83, 199–200; of fertility, 108–109, 147–48, 353–54n15; history of, 179–86; and magic, 94; and modernism, 53–76, 89; "natural," 7, 21–22, 28; and Nietzsche, 72–75; nostalgia for, 19–24; origins of, 97–100; "primitive," 77–111; and symbolic form, 155, 159, 161–62; theology and, xvi

Republic, The (Plato), 1–2, 337–38

Rethinking History and Myth: Indigenous South American Perspectives on the Past (Sahlins), 257

"Rhetoric of Temporality, The" (De Man), 44

Ribot, Théodule, 101–102

Ricoeur, Paul, 234, 306–13, 315, 332, 360n1, 361n5

Riklin, Franz, 114–15

Rise of Modern Mythology, The (Feldman and Richardson), xii

Rite of Spring (Stravinsky), 134, 147

rites of passage, 194, 198

ritual: and anthropology, xvi, 106–11; and dream, 175–77; modern search for, 89–91; and narrative, 192–94; and social structure, 216–17; and time, 184–85; and tragedy, 71–76; and violence, 254–55

Rivers, W. H. R., 203–204

Robbe-Grillet, Alain, 153

Robinson, Henry Morton, 151

Róheim, Géza, 189, 203

Roman mythology, 263–65

romantic theory, 81–82, 336–37

romanticism: and allegory, 3, 43–44; in classical studies, 266–70; critiqued, 42–48; and gnosticism, 197–99; and Hegel, 49–52; and modernist literature, 134–36; and nature theory, 82, 86; racism of, 200, 358n3; second-wave, 78; stages of, 19–20; and symbol, 34–37; and Vico, 11–15

Rothenberg, Jerome, 259

Rule of Metaphor, The (Ricoeur), 309–13

Ruskin, John, 67–68, 345n21

sacred, the, 181–86, 306–13

Sacred and the Profane, The: The Nature of Religion (Eliade), 181–86

Sacred Books of the East series, 82–83

sacrifice concept, 91, 120, 157

Sahlins, Marshall, 255–57

Sapir, Edward, 219, 226

Sartor Resartus (Carlyle), 37, 59–61, 329–30

Saussurean linguistics, 82, 286–90, 332, 335–36, 361n9

Savage Mind, The (Lévi-Strauss), 240–42, 256

"savagery," 96–97, 240–42

Saxo, 264

Schelling, Friedrich: and Creuzer, 40; and Hegel, 50–52; influence of, 156, 158, 186, 310; and Müller, 79; and "new mythology," 42; and the transcendental, 31–42

Schiller, Friedrich: and Herder, 31–33; and Kant, 33–36; and nostalgia, 19–24, 26

Schlegel, Friedrich, 137; and mythic consciousness, 30–33, 42; and symbol, 35

Schmidt, Wilhelm, 185, 199, 203

Schopenhauer, Arthur, 66–67, 72–73, 188, 197

Schreber, Daniel Paul, 118, 124

Schriften Zur Angewandten Seelenkunde (Papers in Applied Psychology), 115

Science of Language (Müller), 79, 81–82

scientific worldview, 333–36

Segal, Robert, 130, 132–33

"Semantic Approach to Myth, The" (Wheelright), 167–69

semantics, 163–69, 318

Semiotic of Myth: A Critical Study of the Symbol (Liszka), 253–56

semiotics, 253–56, 307–308, 318

Sense of an Ending (Kermode), 312–13, 334–35

shamanism, 199

Shand, Alexander, 213

Shelley, Percy Bysshe, 46–47

Sherzer, Joel, 258

signifier and signified, 253–56, 291–93, 307–308, 311

similarity, law of, 93–94

Singer of Tales (Lord), xvii, 258

Skeleton Key to Finnegans Wake (Campbell/Robinson), 151, 196

Smith, Robertson, 78, 88–91

"Sociological Significance of Myth" (Rivers), 203–204

sociology, 88–91, 203–217, 227–28, 230, 262–65

Socrates, 1–2

Sophocles, 114

Sorel, George, 282–86, 293, 301

Spencer, Herbert, 70, 78, 80, 115–16

Spengler, Oswald, 139–40

Statesman's Manual, The (Coleridge), 36–37

Stevens, Wallace, 305–306

story: absurd, 4–5; at borders, 244–45; and dream, 113–14, 128–29; and fable, 2–3; function of, 208–12; genres of, 62–63, 204, 210–11, 218–26; myth as, 59–67, 265–67; sacred, 183–86

"Story of Asdiwal, The" (Lévi-Strauss), 242–44, 356n11

"Story of Lynx, The" (Lévi-Strauss), 246–49

"Storyteller, The" (Benjamin), 205, 295–97

storytelling: genres of, 204, 218–26; intentionality in, 233–55; and modern author, 17; as performance, 258–61; and pregnance, 325–26

Strauss, D. F., 51–53
Stravinsky, Igor, 134
"Structural Study of Myth, The" (Lévi-Strauss), 232–41
structuralism, 230–51, 271–77, 279, 297–98, 301–302, 317–20, 332
suspicion, hermeneutics of, 49–76, 307–308, 315–16, 318, 338
symbol: and archetype, 130–33; as concrete manifestation, 60–61, 157; fixed, 113; as imaginative universal, 10–11; and language, 75, 253–56; and literature, xvi, 162–63, 168–69, 172–73, 326–36; Ricoeur on, 307–313; and romantic aesthetic, 34–37, 43–44; and transformation, 117–20, 124–25, 131
symbolic form, 9, 155, 160–64, 305, 326–36
Symbolic order of culture, 288–90
Symbolik und Mythologie der Alter Völker (Creuzer), 40, 43–44, 59
Symbolism of Evil, The (Ricoeur), 306–307, 309
Symbols of Transformation (Jung), 118–20, 131–33, 189
Symbols That Stand for Themselves (Wagner), 256
System of Transcendental Idealism (Schelling), 31–42, 42

Tain Bo Culaigne, the, 17
tale, xvi, 62–63, 204, 210–11, 218–26, 265–67
"Talk on Mythology" (Schlegel), 30–33, 37–38
tautegorical, the, 9–10, 36–37, 41–42, 182
taxonomy, evolutionary, xi–xii, 336–39
Tedlock, Dennis, 259
"Teller's Preface" (Guss), 266
Temora: An Epic Poem ("Ossian"), 18
Tennyson, Alfred, 15, 64–65, 68
Teutonic myth, 63, 66–67
Theban cycle, 233–37
Themis: A Study of the Social Origins of Greek Religion (Harrison), 107–11
Three Essays on Sexuality (Freud), 121, 126
Tillich, Paul, 158
"Timbuctoo" (Tennyson), 15
Time and Narrative (Ricoeur), 309–13
Todorov, Tsvetan, 260–61, 326–27, 330, 361n9
Totem and Taboo (Freud), 91, 119, 123–27, 320, 324
totemism, 91, 99–100, 102–103, 241–42
Totemism Today (Lévi-Strauss), 240–42
tragic, the, 43–44, 71–75, 138–39, 170–71
transcendental, the, 31–42, 59–62, 178–79
Transformation (Jung), 124–25
Trickster, The (Radin), 225–29
trickster figure, 225, 238–39

tropes, major, 13–14
Troy, discovery of, 106
Tsimshian Mythology (Boas), 219–20
Tuatha Dé Danaan, the, 136
Turner, Victor, 251, 254
Twice-Told Tales (Hawthorne), 68
"two-religion" advocates, 6–8, 12
Tylor, E. B.: influence of, 87–88, 90–91, 93–94, 218–19; works of, 78, 80, 83, 85–87

Ulysses (Joyce), 149–51
unconscious, the, 112–15, 126–33, 188–92, 233–34
Urban, Wilbur, 162–63, 168–69, 313
Usener, Hermann, 321
Utopia, 283–86

value, endowment with, 313–16
Van Der Leeuw, Gerardus, 181, 183
variants, distribution of, 235–51
Vedas, the, 80–81, 263–64
Vernant, Jean-Pierre, 270–71
Vico Giambattista, 3, 8–15, 38, 83, 140, 159, 160, 169, 171–72, 327–28
Vidal-Naquet, Pierre, 272–74
Violence and the Sacred (Girard), 267–70
Vision, A (Yeats), 139–40, 305, 331
vitalistic philosophies, 119, 130, 267
Volsungasaga, the, 66

Wagner, Richard, 65–68
Wagner, Roy, 256
Waste Land, The (Eliot), 146–50
Weston, Jesse, 194, 200–201
"What If the Dogon . . ." (Douglas), 214–15
Wheelright, Philip, xvii, 163–69, 352n8
White Goddess, The (Graves), 194–96, 353–54n15
"White Mythology, The" (Derrida), 279, 294–301, 335
Wholly Other, the, 180–81, 308, 312–13, 316
Wikander, Stig, 264
Will, the, 66–67, 72–73, 118–19, 197
Wolf, F. A., 16
Wordsworth, William, 19–24, 26, 45–47, 67, 82
Work on Myth (Blumenberg), 320–26
"World Is Too Much with Us, The" (Wordsworth), 22
World of Primitive Man, The (Boas), 226–27
Wundt, Wilhelm, 205–206, 220

Yeats, W. B., 134–40, 305, 331

Zionism, 70
Zuni myth, 236–39

ANDREW VON HENDY is Associate Professor of English at Boston College and author of articles on late medieval, early modern, and nineteenth-century English poetry, drama, and fiction; on Northrop Frye's mythography; and on conceptions of myth among modernist poets and novelists of the early twentieth century.